The SAGE Handbook of
Evolutionary Psychology

Foundations of Evolutionary Psychology

Edited by
Todd K. Shackelford

Los Angeles | London | New Delhi | Singapore | Washington DC | Melbourne

Los Angeles | London | New Delhi
Singapore | Washington DC | Melbourne

SAGE Publications Ltd
1 Oliver's Yard
55 City Road
London EC1Y 1SP

SAGE Publications Inc.
2455 Teller Road
Thousand Oaks, California 91320

SAGE Publications India Pvt Ltd
B 1/I 1 Mohan Cooperative Industrial Area
Mathura Road
New Delhi 110 044

SAGE Publications Asia-Pacific Pte Ltd
3 Church Street
#10-04 Samsung Hub
Singapore 049483

Editor: Donna Goddard
Editorial Assistant: Umeeka Raichura
Production Editor: Prachi Arora
Copyeditor: Sunrise Setting Limited
Proofreader: Christine Bitten
Indexer: Cathryn Pritchard
Marketing Manager: Camille Richmond
Cover Design: Naomi Robinson
Typeset by Cenveo Publisher Services
Printed in the UK

At SAGE we take sustainability seriously.
Most of our products are printed in the
UK using responsibly sourced papers
and boards. When we print overseas we
ensure sustainable papers are used as
measured by the PREPS grading system.
We undertake an annual audit to monitor
our sustainability.

Library of Congress Control Number: 2020947008

British Library Cataloguing in Publication data

A catalogue record for this book is available from the British Library

978-1-5264-8914-2

Contents

List of Figures and Tables

FIGURES

TABLES

Notes on the Editor and Contributors

THE EDITOR

Todd K. Shackelford received his PhD in Evolutionary Psychology in 1997 from the University of Texas at Austin. Since 2010 he has been Professor and Chair of the Department of Psychology at Oakland University in Rochester, Michigan, where he is Co-Director of the Evolutionary Psychology Lab. In 2016 he was appointed Distinguished Professor by the Oakland University Board of Trustees. He led the founding of new PhD and MS programs, which launched in 2012. Shackelford has published around 300 journal articles and his work has been cited over 22,000 times. Much of Shackelford's research addresses sexual conflict between men and women, with a special focus on men's physical, emotional and sexual violence against their intimate partners. Since 2006 Shackelford has served as Editor-in-Chief of the journal *Evolutionary Psychology*, and in 2014 founded the journal *Evolutionary Psychological Science* as Editor-in-Chief.

THE CONTRIBUTORS

Laith Al-Shawaf is an Assistant Professor of Psychology at the University of Colorado. His research (with collaborators) has been featured in outlets such as the *BBC*, *Washington Post*, *The Atlantic*, *Psychology Today*, *Slate*, *World Economic Forum*, and *Time*, and his essays for general audiences have appeared in *Areo* and *PopMatters*. He has taught and conducted research internationally, been a Visiting Fellow at the Institute for Advanced Study in Berlin, and is an academic adviser at Ideas Beyond Borders. In 2019, the Association for Psychological Science (APS) named him a Rising Star.

Menelaos Apostolou is currently an Associate Professor at the University of Nicosia, Cyprus. He was born in Athens, Greece, and completed his postgraduate and graduate studies in the UK. He has published several peer-reviewed papers, books and book chapters in the area of evolutionary psychology.

C. Ruth Archer, University of Ulm, Germany, is an evolutionary biologist principally interested in understanding the evolution of life histories and how they are shaped by sexual selection and sexual conflict.

Alfredo Ardila received his degree in Psychology at the National University of Colombia in 1969 and a doctoral degree in Neuropsychology in 1976 from Moscow State University, where he worked with A. R. Luria. His main research areas are brain organization of language, bilingualism, cross-cultural psychology, and evolution of human cognition. He has been Professor in a number of countries, including Colombia, Mexico, Spain, Ecuador, Paraguay, Peru, Russia, Serbia, Italy, Bolivia, Chile, Venezuela and the United States. He has published over 400 journal papers and he is author or co-author of about 40 books in cognitive neurosciences and related areas. He has been president of several professional associations and is Editor of the journal *Neuropsicología, Neuropsiquiatría y Neurociencias*. Currently, he is Professor at the Psycholinguistics and Intercultural Communication program at the I. M. Sechenov First Moscow State Medical University in Moscow, and Distinguished Professor at the Albizu University, Miami, Florida.

Nicole Barbaro earned her PhD in Psychology with a specialization in evolution and human development from Oakland University, Rochester, Michigan. She is currently a Research Scientist at WGU Labs, an education innovation hub striving to advance ingenuity in the higher education space. In addition to her work at WGU Labs, she serves as the Communications Officer for the Human Behavior and Evolution Society. Nicole has published more than 40 scholarly articles in leading psychology journals on topics of evolution, development, romantic relationships, and aggression.

Laura Betzig has studied differential reproduction for decades. She's looked at the cross-cultural record, done fieldwork in the Caroline Islands in the western Pacific Ocean, and read ancient, medieval and modern history. Betzig has published over a hundred articles, with three books. Her fourth book, *The Badge of Lost Innocence: A History of the West* should be out this year or next.

Gary L. Brase received his PhD from the University of California, Santa Barbara in 1997 and subsequently worked in Florida, England, and Missouri before arriving in Kansas. He has been at Kansas State University since 2007 where he is a Professor in the Department of Psychological Sciences and Director of the department's Graduate Program. He studies complex human decision making using social, cognitive and evolutionary theories. His research includes work on topics such as medical decisions, relationship and fertility decision making, personality and mating decisions, and reasoning about social rules. He also has done applied research on consumer decision making in areas such as cybersecurity and sustainable behaviours, and has published over 75 journal and book chapters and given over 100 research presentations.

Darren Burke is a Biological/Evolutionary Psychologist in the School of Psychology at the University of Newcastle, Australia. He completed a BSc, majoring in both Psychology and Biology, and a PhD at the University of Sydney, Australia. His research encompasses elements of evolutionary psychology, comparative cognition, behavioural ecology and human ethology. Fundamentally, he is interested in both *how* cognitive/perceptual/neural mechanisms work and *why* they might work that way, from an evolutionary perspective, and so studies them in both humans and non-humans. The ultimate aim of this research is to integrate mechanism and function in a way that makes it clear that either kind of understanding alone is necessarily incomplete.

David M. Buss is a Professor of Psychology at the University of Texas at Austin. Buss previously taught at Harvard University and the University of Michigan. He is considered the world's leading scientific expert on strategies of human mating and one of the founders of the field of evolutionary psychology. His books include *The Evolution of Desire: Strategies of Human Mating*; *Evolutionary Psychology: The New Science of the Mind*; *The Dangerous Passion: Why Jealousy is as Necessary as Love and Sex*; *The Murderer Next Door: Why the Mind is Designed to Kill*; and *Why Women Have Sex* (with Cindy Meston). Buss has more than

300 scientific publications. In 2019, he was listed as one of the 50 most influential living psychologists in the world.

Gerald Carter is an Assistant Professor at The Ohio State University and studies reciprocal cooperation in vampire bats. His work has focused on how female vampire bats form and maintain long-term cooperative relationships that involve reciprocal food sharing and social grooming. He earned a BSc from Cornell University, Ithaca, New York, an MSc from the University of Western Ontario, Canada and his PhD from the University of Maryland. He was also a Smithsonian Fellow at The Smithsonian Tropical Research Institute and a Humboldt Fellow at the Max Planck Institute of Animal Behavior, Department of Collective Behaviour.

Tracey Chapman is a Professor of Evolutionary Genetics at the School of Biological Sciences, University of East Anglia, UK. She is interested in understanding mechanisms of reproduction, sexual competition and sexual conflict, using novel experimental approaches, mainly in the fruitfly. She also has an applied research programme to translate messages from evolutionary biology into new routes for pest control. She gained her PhD from the University of Edinburgh and then worked as a Post-Doctoral Research Associate and Royal Society University Research Fellow at University College London.

Mu-Hsun Chen is a graduate student at The Ohio State University studying reciprocal cooperation.

Alastair P. C. Davies gained his PhD in Evolutionary Psychology under Todd K. Shackelford. His empirical research has most prominently concerned mate poaching. Alastair and his colleagues formulated a novel definition of mate poaching that, unlike the seminal definition formulated by Schmitt and Buss, made explicit that for an attraction to be considered a poach, individuals must be aware at the time that the individual with whom they have sexual relations is already in an exclusive relationship with someone else. As a result, the literature on poaching contains studies based on both definitions. Alastair and his colleagues have, therefore, investigated whether this has led to findings in the literature on poaching being unreliable. They have also investigated sex differences in the motivations for poaching and the effectiveness of poaching across different relationship contexts.

Tara DeLecce completed her bachelor's degree at Penn State University, Altoona, and then went on to complete her Master's degree at Brunel University, London in evolutionary psychology. From there, she went on to Wayne State University and earned her doctorate in cognitive, developmental, and social psychology. She is now a postdoctoral researcher working with Dr. Todd Shackelford, and specializes in sexual conflict, infidelity, and human sperm competition. At this point in her career, she has authored over a dozen journal articles, book chapters and encyclopedia articles, and she also is currently working on an edited volume, *The Oxford Handbook of Infidelity*.

Jared Edge is a doctoral student at Oakland University, Rochester, Michigan, who has interests in studying asexuality and relationship investment as well as causal reasoning in birds.

Aurelio José Figueredo is a Professor of Psychology, Family Studies and Human Development at the University of Arizona and serves as Director of the Ethology and Evolutionary Psychology (EEP) Lab, which engages in cross-disciplinary research integrating the studies of comparative psychology, ethology, sociobiology, and behavioral ecology, genetics, and development. He is Book Review Editor of *Evolutionary Behavioral Sciences*, the first ever APA-affiliated evolutionary journal, and has served as Editor-in-Chief of the *Human Ethology Bulletin* as well as Associate Editor for *Evolutionary Behavioral Sciences*, *Journal of Social, Evolutionary, and Cultural Psychology* and *Evolutionary Psychology*. His major area of research interest is the evolutionary psychology and behavioral development of life history strategy, cognitive ability, sex, and violence in human and nonhuman animals, and the quantitative ethology and social development of insects, birds and primates.

Carey J. Fitzgerald earned his PhD in Applied Experimental Psychology from Central Michigan University in 2011. He is currently an Assistant Professor of Applied Psychology at the Oregon Institute of Technology. Dr. Fitzgerald's research focuses on the evolutionary influences of prosocial behavior in humans.

Mark V. Flinn is a bio-medical anthropologist. He had the good fortune to be mentored by Richard D. Alexander, Napoleon A. Chagnon, and William D. Hamilton from a young age. His research, including a 31-year longitudinal field project in Bwa Mawego, Dominica, examines hormonal responses and health outcomes to social interactions, with focus on the special nature of human family relationships. He received his PhD from Northwestern University and Postdoctoral training at the University of Michigan. He is a professor at Baylor University and a fellow of the AAAS, HBA, and APS.

Emily K. Fowler is a Senior Research Associate at the School of Biological Sciences, University of East Anglia (UEA), UK. She received her PhD in prokaryote genetics from the UEA in 2015. She is interested in the study of reproductive plasticity in the context of changing social-sexual environments, sex-specific molecular responses to mating, and the regulation and expression of seminal fluid components. She works with the model organism *Drosophila melanogaster*.

Jessica Hehman received her BS in Psychology from Northern Kentucky University and her PhD in Developmental and Evolutionary Psychology from University of California, Santa Barbara. She joined the faculty at the University of Redlands, California as a Professor of Psychology in 2009. Her primary research interests are intergenerational interactions, including the investigation of the consequences (as well as mitigating factors) of exposure to ageism. Other research interests have included sibling conflict and the effect of father absence on casual sexual behaviour in young adults and across the life span. Jessica is currently an Associate Editor at *Evolutionary Behavioral Sciences*.

Steven C. Hertler is a licensed examining psychologist with a research programme centring on personality, which uses behavioural genetics, evolutionary biology and behavioural ecology to alternatively explain classic character types. His writings, such as *Life History Evolution: A Biological Meta-Theory for the Social Sciences*, centre on comparative psychology, cross-cultural psychology, biome distribution, and climate as it affects evolved behaviour and human nature. Additional publications deal with what might be called 'biohistory', in that early and late modern group competition, war and demography are studied from a biocultural perspective.

David J. Hosken, University of Exeter, Cornwall, UK is an evolutionary biologist primarily interested in evolutionary conflict, and in sexual phenotypes and how they evolve via sexual selection.

Amity Jordan is a Master's student at Oakland University, Rochester, Michigan, who is studying sensory discrimination in the red-bellied piranha. She is interested in primate cognition and welfare.

Daniel J. Kruger earned his PhD in Applied Social Psychology at Loyola University Chicago and completed a National Institute of Mental Health (NIMH) Postdoctoral Fellowship in Psychosocial Epidemiology at the University of Michigan's Institute for Social Research. He applies evolutionary principles to advance the understanding of a wide range of areas in human psychology and behaviour. Much of his work is founded on life history theory, which provides a powerful framework for understanding individual variation. He pursues both basic research to advance theory as well as applied projects that leverage the most powerful theoretical framework in the life sciences to promote human well-being and sustainability.

David M. G. Lewis is a Senior Lecturer in Social Psychology at Murdoch University in Australia. His research at the intersection of cognitive, social, and evolutionary psychology has been published in outlets such as *Proceedings of the National Academy of Sciences* and *American Psychologist*, the flagship journal of the American Psychological Association (APA). His work has been featured by *Time* and *The Washington Post*, and has appeared on *The Today Show*. In 2018, he received the Dr. Sybil Eysenck Award, an award granted to one researcher globally by the *International Society for the Study of Individual Differences* for his "forward-thinking" research.

Tim Marsh is an evolutionary moral psychologist from Sydney, Australia, whose research primarily concerns the role of empathy in modulating sympathetic responses to social transgressions, and the mechanisms involved in managing actual and potential members of coalitions.

Mario Mikulincer is Professor of Psychology at the Interdisciplinary Center (IDC) Herzliya, Israel. Mikulincer joined the faculty of IDC Herzliya in 2007 after serving as the Chair of the Psychology Department at Bar-Ilan University, Ramat Gan, Israel, Chair of the Interdisciplinary Studies Committee of this university, and Dean of Bar-Ilan University's Regional Colleges. He was the founding Dean of the Baruch Ivcher School of Psychology at IDC Herzliya (2007–2014) and served as the IDC Provost (2014–2017). He has published over 400 scholarly articles and book chapters, two authored books (*Human Learned Helplessness: A Coping Perspective*; *Attachment in Adulthood: Structure, Dynamics, and Change*, co-authored with Phillip R. Shaver) and numerous co-edited books. His research deals with attachment theory, terror management theory, emotion regulation, trauma and post-traumatic processes, and coping with stressful events. He was the Chief Editor of *Journal of Social and Personal Relationships* (2010–2015). In 2004, he received the EMET Prize in Social Science for his contribution to psychology.

Justin K. Mogilski received his PhD in Evolutionary Psychology in 2017 from Oakland University, Rochester, Michigan, and is currently Assistant Professor of Psychology at the University of South Carolina Salkehatchie. He has published over two dozen journal articles, book chapters and encyclopedia entries within the field of evolutionary psychology. His research addresses the mechanisms underlying formation, maintenance and dissolution of interpersonal relationships among humans and features several interrelated programmes of research: (1) relationship processes within, and moral condemnation of, consensually nonmonogamous (CNM) romantic relationships, (2) individual differences in predatory interpersonal behaviour, and (3) application of conjoint analysis to research on human mating and romantic decision making. He is an active reviewer for several prominent journals, including *Journal of*

Sexual Medicine, Human Nature and *Personality and Social Psychology Bulletin*, and is on the editorial board of *Archives of Sexual Behavior* and *Frontiers in Psychology*.

Jennifer Mundale is an Associate Professor of Philosophy at the University of Central Florida. Her teaching and research interests fall primarily within philosophy of psychology, philosophy of neuroscience, and their intersections with cognitive science.

Jacob Pappas is a doctoral student at Oakland University, Rochester, Michigan, who is interested in studying morality from an evolutionary and developmental perspective focused on individuals with autism.

Mateo Peñaherrera-Aguirre is a PhD student in the Cognitive and Neural Systems Program at the University of Arizona. As part of the Anxiety Research Group, and the Ethology and Evolutionary Psychology Lab at the University of Arizona, he is currently involved in various projects examining the socioecological correlates of life history, coalitions and alliances, and lethal conflict in human societies.

Lars Penke is Professor of Biological Personality Psychology at the University of Göttingen, Germany. He studied at the University of Bielefeld, Germany and Humboldt University of Berlin, where he received his PhD in 2007, and worked at the University of Edinburgh's Centre for Cognitive Ageing and Cognitive Epidemiology in the UK. His research concerns the biological foundations of psychological differences in humans. This includes the evolutionary genetics, genomics and neurostructural correlates of intelligence and personality, the endocrinology of human social behaviour and social perception, anthropometric correlates of personality, and mate choice, in particular the predictive validity of mate preferences.

Imran Razik is a graduate student at The Ohio State University who is studying reciprocal cooperation.

Audrey Robeson has a Master's degree in experimental psychology and is interested in human animal interactions and animal memory.

Wayne G. Rostant is an evolutionary biologist currently working as a Senior Research Associate in the School of Biological Sciences, University of East Anglia, UK. He received his PhD (Biosciences) from the University of Exeter in 2013 and has worked in the Chapman laboratory at UEA as a Post Doctoral Research Associate since then. He is mainly interested in evolutionary conflict, with a specific current focus on sexual conflict with respect to nutrition, ageing and lifespan. He uses the fruit fly as a model system and applies experimental and modelling approaches to investigate sex differences in life-history, fitness and underlying gene expression when resources and social context are varied.

Catherine Salmon received her BSc in Biology in 1992 and her PhD in Evolutionary Psychology in 1997 from McMaster University, Hamilton, Ontario, Canada. After a number of blissful years as a post-doctoral researcher at Simon Fraser University in Vancouver, Canada, she fled the frozen north to join the faculty at the University of Redlands in southern California where she is currently a Professor in the Psychology department. She is the co-author (with Donald Symons) of *Warrior Lovers: Erotic Fiction, Evolution and Female Sexuality* and *The*

Secret Power of Middle Children (co-authored with Katrin Schumann). Her primary research interests include birth order/parental investment/sibling conflict, reproductive suppression and dieting behaviour, and male and female sexuality, particularly as expressed in pornography and other erotic genres. Currently, she is the Editor-in-Chief of *Evolutionary Behavioral Sciences.*

Phillip R. Shaver is Distinguished Professor of Psychology Emeritus at the University of California, Davis. Shaver joined the faculty of UC Davis in 1992 after serving on the faculties of Columbia University, New York University, University of Denver and State University of New York at Buffalo. He has published over 300 scholarly articles and book chapters, and has co-authored and co-edited numerous books. His research deals with attachment theory, close relationships, human emotions, and personality development. He is a Fellow of the American Psychological Association and the Association for Psychological Science. He has received numerous professional awards, including a Distinguished Career Award and a Legacy Award from the Society for Personality and Social Psychology and an honorary doctorate from the University of Stockholm in Sweden.

Jody A. Thompson earned his PhD in Applied Experimental Psychology from Central Michigan University in 2017. He is currently an Assistant Professor of Psychology at Newberry College in South Carolina. Dr. Thompson's research is largely social psychological, with an emphasis on the evolutionary influences of various social behaviors in humans.

Matthew B. Thompson investigates human perceptual expertise. He is now Senior Lecturer in Cognition at Murdoch University, Australia, following research fellowships at The University of California, The University of Queensland, and Harvard Medical School. He is working to better understand the nature and development of perceptual expertise, and to reduce error in safety-critical decision making in forensics, medicine, and defence.

Jennifer Vonk is a comparative psychologist and Professor at Oakland University, Rochester, Michigan. She has published more than 100 journal articles and book chapters, and is the joint Editor-in-Chief for *Animal Behavior and Cognition.*

Yzar S. Wehbe is a PhD student in psychology at Oakland University, specializing in the psychology of conspiratorial thinking under the mentorship of Todd K. Shackelford. At Brunel University London, she earned a MS in evolutionary psychology, and at the American University of Beirut, she earned a Bachelor's degree in psychology and a minor in philosophy. Ms. Wehbe has worked in international development for the state department as a program evaluator in her home nation of Lebanon, as well as in effective altruism as a researcher with Animal Charity Evaluators.

Michael A. Woodley of Menie, a Fellow with the Center Leo Apostel for Interdisciplinary Studies, Vrije Universiteit Brussels, Belgium, studies evolutionary psychology, indirect genetic effects, behavioral genetics, and life history. His research on intelligence has exposed potential phenotypic declines in general cognitive ability veiled by the Flynn Effect, documented gains in cognitive evolution during the Holocene using ancient human genomes, and described the specialization of cognitive abilities associated with slowing life history speed exemplified in modern civilizations.

PART I

Foundations of Evolutionary Psychology

Sexual Selection: A Brief Introduction

C. Ruth Archer and David J. Hosken

THE PUZZLE OF THE PEACOCK'S TAIL

I remember well time when the thought of the eye made me cold all over, but I have got over this stage of the complaint, & now ... [t]he sight of a feather in a peacock's tail, whenever I gaze at it, makes me sick! (Charles Darwin, 1860, in a letter to Asa Gray)

When Darwin made this famous comment about his disgust at the sight of the peacock's tail, it was not clear how natural selection could produce such extravagant, exaggerated and conspicuous characters, and as a result, traits like the peacock tail appeared to threaten his evolutionary theory. How could traits that seemingly reduce survival evolve? However, Darwin had a solution – sexual selection – which he defined as 'the advantage which certain individuals have over others of the same sex and species solely in respect of reproduction' (Darwin, 1871: 209). So to a first approximation, sexual selection occurs because of variance in mating (fertilization) success and natural

selection is everything else (Arnold, 1983; also see Alonzo and Servedio, 2019). Darwin (1871) also identified the mechanisms of sexual selection: mate competition and mate choice. He recognized that males tend to be the more competitive sex, competing with each other for access to females, and females tend to be choosier, selecting mates from potential sires, while also noting that there will be instances when delineating between natural and sexual selection will be impossible.

Sexual selection was controversial (O'Donald, 1980; Hosken and House, 2011; Prum, 2012). While male–male competition was readily accepted (after all, male fights are easy to observe and male weaponry widespread), the idea that females choose mates was met with tremendous scepticism even by Darwin's close associates, who frequently did not clearly understand what was being proposed (e.g. Huxley, 1938), and some of this confusion unfortunately continues to the present (reviewed in Hosken and House, 2011; and see discussions in Dall et al., 2006;

Lessells et al., 2006; Pizzari et al., 2006). Hence, despite some early important work (e.g. Fisher, 1930) sexual selection was largely neglected for nearly a century after Darwin, and it was not until the 1970s that research on sexual selection and female choice began to flourish (O'Donald, 1980; Bradbury and Andersson, 1987; Parker, 2006). Since then, sexual selection has become a key element of modern evolutionary research and is widely recognized as an important driver of organic evolution. Here, we introduce some key sexual selection theory and the insights this provides, while highlighting knowledge gaps and suggesting how we might fill them. Sexual selection is a vast field and so our presentation has to be somewhat idiosyncratic, but we think most of the important elements have been covered.

WHY ARE FEMALES USUALLY CHOOSIER AND MALES USUALLY MORE COMPETITIVE?

A girl sees a handsome man, & without observing whether his nose or whiskers are the tenth of an inch longer or shorter than in some other man, admires his appearances & says she will marry him. So I suppose with the pea-hen; & the tail has been increased in length merely by on the whole presenting a more gorgeous appearance. (Darwin, 1868, in a letter to Alfred Russel Wallace)

A general pattern across animals is that females tend to be the choosier sex, while males tend to be more competitive for mates (Trivers, 1972; Andersson, 1994; Kokko et al. 2013). Consequently, in many species, conspicuous secondary sexual traits such as weapons are restricted to males or much less developed in females (Bro-Jørgensen, 2007), and males often develop elaborate sexual ornaments used in sexual display, which females frequently lack (Owens and Hartley, 1998; Hosken et al., 2016) (Figure 1.1). But why is it that males usually compete and females usually choose? Darwin (1871: 224) provided the following insight: 'The female has to expend much organic matter in the formation of her ova, whereas the male expends much force in fierce contests with his rivals'. As Fisher noted (1999: 308) in a letter to A. J. Bateman), 'it was obvious … that the

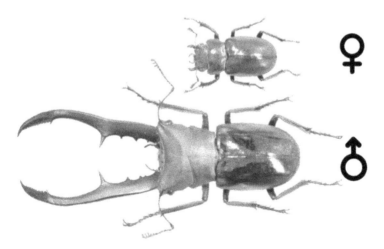

Figure 1.1 Profound sexual dimorphism in a sexually selected trait. The male stag beetle has enormously enlarged jaws compared to the female; these are used in fighting other males (male–male competition). Also note other differences between male and female: head shape, for example, and body size

Source: Redrawn from Gotoh et al. (2016) with permission from the authors.

reproductive capacity of females being more limited than that of males, [meant] it was inevitable that they rather than the other sex should exercise selection and that the males should be more conspicuously modified by sexual selection'. In modern terms, eggs are costlier to produce and in shorter supply than sperm, and hence access to rare eggs determines male fitness. In essence, the laws of supply and demand apply: sperm producers (males) compete for access to rare eggs, which because of their relative scarcity means females can afford to be choosy (female mate choice). This means the variance in male fitness (with respect to phenotype) is frequently greater than the variance in female fitness (for a full discourse see Shuster and Wade, 2003), and sexual selection therefore acts more strongly on males than females, as envisaged by Fisher (1930). And all this means that anisogamy (sex differences in gamete size) ultimately underlies typical sex roles (for further discussion see Parker, 1982; Jennions and Kokko, 2010; Schärer et al., 2012; Kokko et al., 2013).

These ideas were further developed by Trivers (1972) in light of parental investment, defined as 'any investment by the parent in an individual offspring that increases the offspring's chance of surviving (and hence reproductive success) at the cost of the parent's ability to invest in other offspring' (139); this definition includes the costs of producing sperm or eggs, as well as any parental care that follows. Trivers (1972) reasoned that whichever sex makes the greatest parental investment will become a limiting resource for the other sex (the supply and demand point above). As a consequence, the sex that invests less in parental investment will compete for matings, and further, as explained by Queller (1997), (un)certainty of parentage will determine which sex cares more (usually females 'know' they are dams, while males are less certain of paternity). In sum, this logic explains why females tend to choose and males tend to compete, but also explains cases where this general rule does not apply:

female competition and male mate-choice is most common in species where males provide parental care, such as the black-striped pipefish (*Syngnathus abaster*) (Cunha et al., 2017; reviewed in Berglund and Rosenqvist, 2003). Similarly, sex-role reversal occurs in a bush-cricket when food becomes scarce and females compete for nutritional, male-provided, nuptial gifts that are in short supply (Simmons and Bailey, 1990).

It is important to note that although males tend to be less choosy and females less competitive, this *does not* mean there is no male mate choice or female–female competition for males and there are species where both sexes are choosy and competitive (i.e. mutual mate choice; Johnstone et al., 1996). High investment in reproduction can increase male choosiness (Simmons and Bailey, 1990; Kokko and Johnstone, 2002), and so mutual mate choice could be more common in species where both parents rear offspring. However, even in the absence of parental care we might also expect increased male choosiness when reproductive costs are high, as is the case for male bush-crickets that produce large, costly nuptial gifts (e.g. Simmons and Bailey, 1990). As noted above, there are also sex-role reversed species where females are the more competitive sex and males the choosier sex, with pipefish being one clade where this is rather common (Berglund and Rosenqvist, 2003). In these taxa, females tend to be more ornamented and males make their mate choices on these ornaments (Berglund and Rosenqvist, 2001). Nonetheless, from here on we frame our discussion in terms of classical sex roles – females tending to be choosier and males more competitive – as the same broad principles apply regardless of who is choosier or more competitive. However, before we move onto mechanisms of mate choice we need to introduce one more concept, sexual conflict (Parker, 1979; Arnqvist and Rowe, 2005; Kokko and Jennions, 2014; Hosken et al., 2019). This is the evolutionary conflict that occurs between males and females (Parker, 1979) because in nature their fitness interests are never perfectly aligned (Arnqvist and Rowe, 2005; Hosken et al., 2009). Conflict can occur over the outcome of an interaction (e.g. mating) or over the optimal values of traits that both sexes express (e.g. males and females may have different optimal tail lengths) (Arnqvist and Rowe, 2005; Hosken et al., 2019). It is an emergent property of sexual reproduction in systems without perfect genetic monogamy and no other mating opportunities (for a discussion of sexual selection and its relationship to sexual conflict see Kokko and Jennions, 2014), and can lead to selection for all manner of traits that promote the selfish interests of one sex over another (Arnqvist and Rowe, 2005). Now to the mechanisms of sexual selection.

MATE COMPETITION

> A hornless stag or spurless cock would have a poor chance of leaving numerous offspring. Sexual selection, by always allowing the victor to breed, might surely give indomitable courage, length to the spur, and strength to the wing to strike in the spurred leg, in nearly the same manner as does the brutal cock-fighter by the careful selection of his best cocks. (Darwin, 1859: 88)

Male–male competition for matings can be manifest in a number of ways, including competition for territories or specific resources females need, or for the females (or strictly, their ova) themselves (Thornhill and Alcock, 1983). While overt contests between males provide the most striking example of male–male competition, competition can take other forms, including scramble competition and sperm competition (see below), with each potentially favouring different male characteristics (Andersson, 1994). These are not mutually exclusive modes of competition and in some sense the distinctions can be arbitrary. For example, male–male competition in frogs can include both scramble competition and sperm competition (e.g. Byrne et al., 2002).

While much theoretical effort has been expended on exploring the effects of female mate choice on male sexual trait evolution (and we will return to this below), less effort has been spent on the effects of male–male competition on sexual trait exaggeration. This may be in part because it seems obvious – larger weapons or greater courtship effort provides greater access to females directly or indirectly. However, competition more generally has been dissected, particularly using game theory models, which explore different strategies and tactics to identify those that maximize fitness, given other competing strategy/tactic sets. These models include options like whether and how long to compete. Key models include various 'war of attrition' and 'assessment' games, with different models predicated on a range of decision rules and how rivals are assessed (reviewed in Briffa and Sneddon, 2010; and see Kokko, 2013). Two models specifically focussing on classical (pre-copulatory) male mate-competition deserve special attention. First, Parker (1983) assessed outcomes of competition when males differed in their levels of armament. He found that male trait distributions deviated from naturally selected optima, suggesting male–male competition alone can lead to trait exaggeration. Precise outcomes of this model depended on male traits being affected by the environment and the exact function defining the cost of trait elaboration. Second, Grafen (1990) investigated male trait exaggeration when traits signalled a male's competitiveness. His major finding was that trait size should reflect competitive ability, and hence enlarged secondary sexual characters should be honest signals of male quality and treated as such by rivals. The outcomes of these two models are important in showing that male–male competition alone can lead to honest signalling and to the trait exaggeration that Darwin (1871) was trying to explain.

It should also be noted that real-world competitive outcomes can influence subsequent male contest behaviour for significant periods (winner and loser effects, see, e.g. Okada et al., 2019). There may also be a range of strategies employed within a species that are phenotype dependent (Shuster and Wade, 2003). For example, in dung beetles there are large territorial, competitive major morphs that defend females, and smaller less competitive minor morphs that attempt to sneak copulations (Simmons et al., 1999). Because minor morphs have a higher expectation of encountering sperm competition (see below), they tend to invest relatively more in sperm production (Simmons et al., 1999). Similar morphs and strategies can be found in salmon, for example (Gage et al., 1995; also see, e.g. Stiver et al., 2015). Additionally, costs of male–male competition – so important in competition models – have been much documented, and range from significant metabolic expenditure during sexual signalling and fighting, to actual physical injury (e.g. Bailey et al., 1993; Hack, 1997; Bean and Cook, 2001; Briffa and Elwood, 2004).

The two models discussed above focus on overt male contests. This form of competition is the easiest to observe and has selected for large body size, strength, and weaponry, with larger males enjoying a competitive advantage over smaller rivals in many taxa (e.g. Thornhill and Alcock, 1983) (Figure 1.2). For example, larger male yellow dungflies (*Scathophaga stercoraria*) are able to wrestle females away from smaller rivals (Borgia, 1980). Similarly, larger elephant seals win fights to establish beach harems, and because the largest males become more dominant and secure more females (Haley et al., 1994), male–male competition has resulted in males being around three times larger than females (Le Boeuf, 1974). In addition to size, sexual selection has also favoured the evolution of specialized structures specifically for male–male combat (Darwin, 1859, 1871; Thornhill and Alcock, 1983; Andersson, 1994; Berglund et al., 1996). These weapons can take many forms, from horns and antlers, to spines, large teeth, and claws (Emlen, 2008) and can become enormous (Figure 1.1) when sexual selection is more intense (e.g. Bro-Jørgensen, 2007).

Figure 1.2   An example of the sexual dimorphism Darwin was trying to explain with the theory of sexual selection. Shown here are yellow dungflies (*Scathophaga stercoraria*) with the larger male mate-guarding the smaller female while she lays eggs. In this species, larger males have a competitive advantage in fights over females

In the largest bull elk, antlers can reach more than 1 m above their heads and arc back over half the length of their bodies (Emlen, 2014), while the antlers of Irish elk weighed 40 kg and were broader (up to 3.6 m) than the elk were tall (around 2 m). Fighting with these armaments can cause substantial damage – in non-pollinating fig wasps, fights between males involving enlarged mouth parts are often fatal (Bean and Cook, 2001). While overt contests have led to the evolution of striking size dimorphism and impressive weaponry, exaggerated male traits may also function as signals by which males assert their dominance without the need to fight (Grafen, 1990) and serve as ornaments that help females make mating decisions (Berglund et al., 1996).

Another form of male–male competition, scramble competition, is characterized by competitive searching to locate females (Thornhill and Alcock, 1983). Scramble competition often leads to the evolution of traits that help males detect and locate females and then get to them. This can be seen in some praying mantids where scramble competition has favoured the evolution of larger male antennae to rapidly locate females using olfactory cues, while in other mantids it has favoured improved vision (Holwell et al., 2007; and see discussion in Thornhill and Alcock, 1983). Scramble competition can also select for males to emerge earlier in the season than females (protandry). This occurs in some spiders, but getting a head start over their rivals comes at a cost – the evolution of smaller male body size (Danielson-François et al., 2012).

Sperm competition, the competition between the ejaculates of two or more males to fertilize a set of ova (Parker, 1970), is the final form of male competition we discuss here. In internal fertilizers, sperm competition occurs because females usually mate more than once. If this happens in quick succession, or if females store sperm, the ejaculates of different males may co-occur and compete inside a female (NB sperm competition can also occur with external fertilization:

see, e.g. Birkhead and Møller, 1998). This also creates the opportunity for female choice after mating (cryptic female choice – Eberhard, 1996; see discussion below). Thus, sexual selection can continue after mating, leading to a distinction between male–male competition and female choice that occurs before (pre-copulatory) and after (post-copulatory) mating. In some ways, this has been the only major conceptual advance in our understanding of sexual selection *sensu stricto* since Darwin, who despite noting that females can mate with multiple males (polyandry), did not realize the full implications of this. In fact, he suggested polyandry might weaken sexual selection (Darwin, 1871). As post-copulatory sexual selection generally is a 'new' insight, we spend a little more time discussing it, here and below.

As with pre-copulatory male–male competition, sperm competition is a significant element of selection acting on males. It has been the subject of intense theoretical investigation, primarily by Parker (e.g. Parker, 1982, 1990, 1993, 1998; also see, e.g. Cameron et al., 2007; Requena and Alonzo, 2017). When sperm competition operates like a fair raffle and siring success is strictly a function of the proportion of sperm in competition (Parker, 1970), theory predicts selection should favour the production of large ejaculates and greater investment in spermatogenesis (Parker, 1990, 2016). This fundamental prediction has been upheld in comparative and micro-evolutionary studies (e.g. Gage, 1994; Gage et al., 1995; Hosken, 1997; Stockley et al., 1997; Simmons et al., 1999; Hosken and Ward, 2001; Pitnick et al., 2001; reviewed in Pitnick and Hosken, 2010). Additionally, males are able to tailor their ejaculates to perceived sperm competition risk, increasing ejaculate size when apparent risk is high (Gage, 1991; Simmons et al., 1993; Wedell and Cook, 1999; Martin and Hosken, 2002). Sometimes, success in sperm competition is not a fair raffle and, instead, success is weighted in favour of certain ejaculates (Parker, 1990). This can happen if mating order affects the likelihood of fertilization success, as in the sierra dome spider where the first male to mate has a fertilization advantage over subsequent males (Watson, 1991), while in scorpionflies the last male to mate has a fertilization advantage (Thornhill, 1983). These loadings mean that males should also strategically adjust their ejaculate size, fine-tuning how much sperm is transferred depending on a female's mating history (Wedell et al., 2002).

As well as selecting on *how much* sperm males transfer, sperm competition can affect the evolution of sperm themselves if specific sperm attributes increase sperm competitiveness (Snook, 2005). Sperm competition may simply favour large sperm to fill female sperm storage organs to thereby prevent females from storing sperm of rival males (e.g. Pitnick, 1996; Kleven et al., 2009) or fast sperm that win the race to fertilize ova (e.g. Birkhead et al., 1999; Malo et al., 2005; Gomendio and Roldan, 2008; Fitzpatrick et al., 2009; Kleven et al., 2009). The seminal fluid transferred alongside sperm may also be a target for sexual selection to improve sperm competitiveness. We see evidence of this in *Drosophila* ejaculatory proteins transferred during copulation that make females less receptive to remating with rivals (Chapman et al., 1995). Males can also exploit the ejaculates of rival males to lower the cost of non-sperm elements of their own ejaculates (Hodgson and Hosken, 2006; Sirot et al., 2011).

Despite male–male competition being relatively easy to study, it remains unclear if the phenotypes best suited for success in the pre-copulatory arena are also best suited for success in sperm competition (Pitnick and Hosken, 2010). Furthermore, operationally it can be difficult, perhaps impossible, to fully disentangle the effects of sperm competition from cryptic female choice (Pitnick and Hosken, 2010). In some general sense both must operate in conjunction because the female reproductive tract sets the rules by which males compete (Eberhard, 1996).

These are both areas in need of additional exploration. Additionally, we have still only explored a small number of the many ejaculatory proteins males transfer to females during copula (Chapman, 2001) and the precise function of many of the RNAs sperm carry to ova remain unknown, but the possibilities are intriguing (Hosken and Hodgson, 2014).

MATE CHOICE

[I]f man can in a short time give elegant carriage and beauty to his bantams, according to his standard of beauty, I can see no good reason to doubt that female birds, by selecting, during thousands of generations, the most melodious or beautiful males, according to their standard of beauty, might produce a marked effect. (Darwin, 1859: 89)

Despite shaky beginnings, female mate choice is now incontrovertible (Andersson, 1994; Shuster and Wade, 2003; Hunt and Hosken, 2014; Rosenthal, 2017). It has been documented in arthropods, molluscs, fish, reptiles, birds, and mammals (Rosenthal, 2017), and seems to have occurred in extinct taxa such as dinosaurs (Hone et al., 2012). Females make their choices using an array of male characters including colour, song, size, dance, and odour, using an extensive range of sensory modes, and mate choice underpins some of the most extravagant phenotypes, including extended phenotypes, in nature (for an extensive and excellent review of mate choice and its mechanisms see Rosenthal, 2017).

Mate choice can be costly. It requires time and energy (Rowe, 1994) and can expose females to predators (Csada and Neudorf, 1995) and harmful harassment from males. Despite these potential costs, female mate choice is common. So what do females gain by being choosy? This is far less clear than the benefits to males from winning male–male competition. Furthermore, what male traits do females prefer? While these seem like straightforward questions, answers are not always obvious. This may be why so much theoretical work has focussed on the impacts of mate choice on male trait exaggeration. We address these questions below, dividing the benefits of female choice into direct (to female fecundity/longevity) or indirect (to offspring quality) benefits.

Direct Benefits

Direct benefits of choice are those that increase female fecundity or longevity. Benefits include material benefits or resources transferred at mating such as parental care, food gifts (nuptial gifts), or access to territories. Despite direct benefits having been the subject of limited theoretical exploration, one model worth mentioning clearly shows that male sexual trait exaggeration can occur when females are choosing for direct benefits (Price et al., 1993). The model shows that even when the male trait results in female fecundity reductions, trait elaboration will occur if male condition is revealed by the trait (but condition need not be heritable) and also directly benefits the female (e.g. males in good condition provide more care) (Price et al., 1993). Hence direct benefits can lead to the coevolution and exaggeration of trait and preference (Price et al., 1993).

Female choice for direct benefits has been documented in sedge warblers, for example, where preferred males have larger territories (Buchanan and Catchpole, 1997), and scorpionflies, where females prefer males who provide larger nuptial gifts (invertebrate prey) at mating (Thornhill and Alcock, 1983). Ejaculate size can also confer direct benefits, with some females preferring mates that have more sperm to allocate to the current mating, increasing female fecundity (Nakatsuru and Kramer, 1982). Direct benefits are important, and can have a pronounced effect on female fitness, but they are easy to understand and so there is not a huge amount to say about them. Indirect benefits, however, are more complicated, in some ways more controversial, and certainly more interesting.

Indirect Benefits

In the absence of direct benefits, females could still benefit from costly choice by receiving indirect (genetic) benefits that increase the quality of offspring. Some of these genetic benefits are likely to be transient, some are unlikely to lead to male trait exaggeration, and costs of choice are important in determining the outcome of models that explore these benefits, all of which we discuss below. However, at the heart of all indirect benefit models of sexual selection is the lek paradox (Kirkpatrick and Ryan, 1991): how can genetic variation be maintained in traits subjected to a long history of directional selection (as reflected by their exaggerated size), and if there is no genetic variation revealed by sexual traits, why make costly mate choices (for genetic benefits) based on them? In some ways this is a null question because genetic variation abounds in nature and there are many processes to maintain it (e.g. Roff, 2012). But perhaps the most widely accepted explanation for the maintenance of variation in sexually selected traits is genic capture (Rowe and Houle, 1996). Genic capture is a mutation–selection balance argument that effectively suggests all mutations affect exaggerated male traits via effects on condition – the total resource pool available to allocate to competing organismal demands. The argument assumes that most genes influence an individual's overall condition so there is high mutational input to condition, and if exaggerated sexually selected traits are condition dependent, sexual traits will have a high mutational input that balances the selective erosion of genetic variation resulting from mate choice (Rowe and Houle, 1996). Regardless of the veracity of that argument, the Fisher–Lande–Kirkpatrick model has been called the null model of intersexual selection (Prum, 2010) and so we begin there.

The Fisher effect

Much of our understanding of the indirect benefits of female choice, and how this leads to exaggerated male traits, comes from Fisher (1930, 1999). His verbal model went as follows: imagine males varied in some naturally selected fitness component and some element of the phenotype revealed this fitness advantage. Any female paying attention to the phenotype would also enjoy higher fitness and, therefore, the preference for the revealing trait would spread. Thus the trait would enjoy the initial naturally selected advantage and an additional advantage due to female preference (which could persist even if the initial advantage did not), and as preference spreads, it becomes the predominant force acting on the revealing trait. Thus, a trait could be exaggerated beyond the initial naturally selected optima by sexual selection, as long as the benefits of the latter exceeded the cost of the former, and at that point, females only gain fitness benefits via the attractiveness of their sons (Fisher's sons' effect). These fundamental insights (first made in 1930) were largely ignored until formalized by Lande (1981).

The Lande (1981) model mirrors the Fisher argument: it assumes some quantitative variation in male trait size, the trait is subject to natural selection and has some naturally selected optima, there is variation in female preference for the trait but no direct selection on preference, and both preference and trait are heritable. Trait evolutionary trajectories then depend on the balance between natural and sexual selection and the genetic correlation between trait and preference. In Lande's model, because there is no direct selection on female preference, it only evolves via indirect selection due to a genetic correlation between the trait and preference, and this correlation is assumed to build up behaviourally (e.g. females preferring big/small traits mate with males that have big/small traits, so correlations between trait and preference are established). Lande (1981) showed that if natural selection acting on a male trait was relatively weak, accelerating evolution (runaway) between trait and preference was possible as long as the positive genetic correlation between the male trait and female preference was relatively strong, which is why trait-preference correlations are so important in sexual selection (Hosken and Wilson, 2019). Kirkpatrick (1982) effectively found the same results with a different modelling approach. These models were criticized because they did not include costs of preference, which were initially found to collapse outcomes to exclude the potential for massive trait exaggeration (Pomiankowski et al., 1991). More recent work has shown that costs of preference (i.e. direct selection on preference) need not result in this collapse (Hall et al., 2000), refuting a major criticism of the Fisher–Lande–Kirkpatrick model. There have been a range of other models of the Fisher process (e.g. O'Donald, 1980; Iwasa and Pomiankowski, 1995) and together these illustrate that the costs of preference, natural selection on the male trait, genetic variation in both, and their genetic covariances are all important in determining the stability and extent of trait exaggeration. The logic of the Fisher argument is clear and many of its requirements are met in nature (Bakker and Pomiankowski, 1995; Prum, 2010; Greenfield et al., 2014; Prokuda and Roff, 2014; Roff and Fairbairn, 2015; Sharma et al., 2016; also see Hosken and Wilson, 2019), including clear cases of indirect benefits of choice through just the attractiveness of sons (Prokop et al., 2012).

Good genes

It has also been suggested that females could obtain viability benefits for offspring by mating with more attractive males – good genes benefits. Williams (1966) suggested that it is to a 'female's advantage to be able to pick the most fit male available for fathering her brood' and Fisher (1915) suggested that female choice for good genes would initiate what is now called Fisherian sexual selection. Female choice for good genes might feel intuitive, and seem sensible, but the double selective advantage of good genes (through both sexual and natural selection) should mean effects are transitory (Wade, 2014), and there appears to be a contradiction at the heart of the good genes argument.

Fisher's arguments outlined above clearly explain how a good genes process might start and Zahavi (1975) showed how preference for traits reflecting good genes might work: exaggerated traits are costly to produce and only high genetic quality males are able to pay the cost (or reap the reward) of having them. Basically, males are saying: 'Look, even this ridiculous, wasteful trait has not slowed me down, that is how good I am.' Because only the highest quality (genetic quality) males could develop or express such costly traits, the traits are an honest indicator of overall quality (i.e. good genes) (Zahavi, 1975). While this idea was originally criticized and models could not get it to work (reviewed in Bradbury and Andersson, 1987), theory subsequently rescued 'handicap' models of good genes sexual selection (e.g. Iwasa et al., 1991). It should also be noted that there are a number of handicap model types (Iwasa et al., 1991) – revealing handicaps, conditional handicaps, and epistatic handicaps – and it appears that most will generate exaggerated trait and preference (the exception being the epistatic models). Nonetheless, a problem remains: the double selective advantage of natural selection and sexual selection for good genes should soon fix them, leaving no genetic variation on which females could choose (Borgia, 1979; Andersson, 1994), and if there were costs to choice, a non-choosy female would do best. This is the lek paradox arguments above, but seems more problematic given the double selective advantage entailed by good genes.

Hamilton and Zuk (1982) provided a potential solution to this problem that hinged on the ubiquity of parasites. They argued that if the males that are most resistant to parasite infection are those that are better able to invest in sexual display, female preferences

for the most extreme male traits would also be for the healthiest, highest viability males. However, as the parasites that individuals are likely to encounter will keep changing, we should not expect the erosion of genetic variation for overall quality. This then generates another problem: genes that are good in the parental generation are probably not as good in the offspring generation – as good genotype A becomes more common, it is no longer good as it is increasingly targeted by parasites – and the argument effectively becomes a genotype-by-environment model with indirect genetic effects making it hard to see how traits can become exaggerated (for a full discussion see Wade, 2014). There is also equivocal empirical support for the Hamilton–Zuk model (Read, 1987; Martin and Johnsen, 2007; Buczek et al., 2016), questioning its generality. Finally, there seems to be a contradiction between arguments that sexual reproduction helps organisms escape parasites (new genetic variation is good: Hamilton, 1980) and standard good genes ideas (a gene is just good or bad), although perhaps the incongruity can be resolved by considering different temporal scales.

Finally, whether a gene is 'good' also depends on the sex of the organism expressing it. This is due to sexual conflict over optimal trait values, which occurs because the sexes do different things and, hence, the genes to make a good female may not make a good male. This means that males and females may have different optimal values for shared traits – many traits are subjected to sexually antagonistic selection (= intralocus sexual conflict) (Chippindale et al., 2001; Bonduriansky and Chenoweth, 2009). An excellent example of this occurs at the Cyp6-g1 locus of a cytochrome P450 gene in *Drosophila melanogaster*. A transposable element that upregulates this gene makes females super fecund, while at the same time lowering male fitness (McCart et al., 2005; Smith et al., 2011; Rostant et al., 2015, 2017; Hawkes et al., 2016). So, a good gene for females is deleterious for males (at least in the absence of insecticides to which the gene provides resistance). As this example shows, the goodness of genes need not be universal across the sexes, and since large proportions of the genome have sexually antagonistic effects (Mank, 2017), this must weaken good genes (Hosken et al., 2019). Widespread sexually antagonistic genetic variation should, however, make female mate choice for sires carrying genes for good daughters (Seger and Trivers, 1986) more likely.

Good genes versus Fisherian effects

There has been much debate about the relative importance of good genes versus Fisherian effects (Bradbury and Andersson, 1987; Andersson, 1994; Andersson and Simmons, 2006; Hosken and House, 2011; Wade, 2014). Some researchers have even suggested that making a distinction between indirect genetic benefits for enhanced survival and mating success (good genes) and only mating success (the Fisher effect) is arbitrary (Kokko et al., 2002). However, as discussed by Kuijper et al. (2012), there are crucial differences between the two and good reasons to treat the processes as distinct (a view supported by Cameron et al., 2003; Andersson and Simmons, 2006). Most importantly, the Fisher process requires a genetic correlation between trait and preference (Lande, 1981), but this is not necessary for good genes models where preferences can instead evolve via a correlation with heritable genetic quality (Kuijper et al., 2012). Furthermore, Fisher only requires the coevolution of preference and trait, while good gene models of sexual selection also require the inclusion of another heritable parameter – overall viability (Kuijper et al., 2012). As an aside, it is hard to imagine how mate preference could not shift trait values past naturally selected optima by some margin, however small, as long as those optima remain somewhat stable (but see Grafen, 1990). This is frequently where arguments like this finally

settle: how far from equilibrium are populations?

If we do not group good genes and the Fisher process together, does female choice for indirect benefits involve good genes or attractive sons? As noted above, our prejudice is that Fisherian processes should predominate if populations are near fitness peaks and there are issues with the persistence of good genes effects. The Fisherian model has been called the null model of intersexual sexual selection because it should be present (and indeed should be inevitable) if females prefer certain male phenotypes and if phenotype and preference are determined by quantitative genetic variation (and see Bakker and Pomiankowski, 1995; Hosken and Wilson, 2019). That said, statistically significant trait-preference genetic correlations, central to Fisher, are relatively rare (Greenfield et al., 2014). This may just be because investigations to date have been seriously underpowered (Sharma et al., 2016) and the methods we use to detect them may be systematically weakening them (Hosken and Wilson, 2019; also see Roff and Fairbairn, 2015). Recent meta-analyses, however, have found stronger support for the Fisherian process than good genes mate choice, but did detect signals of the latter (Prokop et al., 2012). While it is hard to characterize the nature of indirect benefits females may be enjoying, it is worth attempting. If female choice is for good genes, then sexual selection and natural selection are working in the same direction to promote adaptation and improve fitness to a particular environment. If female choice is just for male attractiveness, then sexual selection and natural selection may be in opposition. That is, female choice would favour traits that reduce overall viability. This means that the nature of female choice has important implications for the net fitness effects of sexual selection, and it should be noted that sexual selection does seem to be an efficient sieve removing deleterious mutations (Agrawal, 2001; Radwan, 2004). This does not necessarily equate with good genes sexual selection, however.

Other drivers of mate choice – sensory bias, genetic compatibility, sexual coercion, mate copying

So far, we have largely restricted discussion of female choice for indirect benefits to either good genes or attractive sons. While these ideas have received the most theoretical and empirical attention, other reasons for mate choice have been proposed. Sensory bias and sensory exploitation models suppose that females have a pre-existing bias to particular stimuli driven by natural selection and males evolving traits that exploit these pre-existing biases are favoured by female choice (West-Eberhard, 1984; Ryan et al., 1990; Endler, 1992; Ryan, 1998). That is, female preferences are honed, at least initially, by natural rather than sexual selection. In one sense, sensory bias must underpin much of sexual selection: signals that are not detectable are not signals after all. Additionally, although Fisher's argument was based on signal senders (males) starting the process, there is no reason why the converse could not be true. Once there is preference and trait the Fisher logic remains, and there is general agreement that such sensory bias could initiate sexual selection, including the Fisher process (Jones and Ratterman, 2009). However, it seems unlikely that sensory bias/exploitation alone drives the evolution of mate choice unless choice become linked to some mate choice benefit (Candolin, 2018), and this is especially true if choice is costly.

Compatibility-based models of indirect benefits propose that females choose mates with genes that complement their own (Trivers, 1972; Mays Jr and Hill, 2004). This can happen when mating between some genotypes are incompatible due to intragenomic conflict, as is the case in insects that harbour particular bacterial parasites which render matings between uninfected females and infected males inviable (Werren et al., 2008). In such cases females may prefer males with which they are compatible (Zeh and Zeh, 2001). There is also evidence of female choice for genetically diverse mates, for example, heterozygotes at major histocompatibility complex (MHC) loci have improved resistance to particular diseases relative to homozygotes and there is evidence that females prefer males with MHC loci that complement their own, increasing heterozygosity at these loci (Wedekind et al., 1995; Mays Jr and Hill, 2004). However, this type of mate choice – effectively where every female prefers a different male – is unlikely to generate exaggerated sexual traits generally and, therefore, cannot explain the patterns Darwin (1871) was trying to explain with his theory of sexual selection.

Females may also be choosing irrationally (Enquist et al., 2002; Taylor et al., 2008). That is, females may be mating with males that are better at coercing them into behaving in ways that increase male fitness to the detriment of females. This may especially be the case in systems where males physically damage females during mating (Arnqvist and Rowe, 2005). Hence, females may not benefit from their choice of mates, and experimental evolution with flies provides evidence for this (e.g. Rice, 1996). This highlights the fact that sexual conflict is inherent in sexual selection (Parker, 1979; Arnqvist and Rowe, 2005; Kokko and Jennions, 2014). As noted by others, males and females may agree on the final destination, but not necessarily how to get there (Hosken et al., 2019). It should also be noted that despite arguments to the contrary, indirect benefits of mate choice are highly unlikely to recoup direct costs (Arnqvist and Rowe, 2005). Finally, mate copying, where females simply copy what other females do (Alonzo, 2008; Rosenthal, 2017), is another mechanism underpinning mate choice and could effectively deliver or produce any of the outcomes described above – from direct benefits to irrational choice.

Cryptic female choice

As noted above, female choice can continue after mating in the form of cryptic female choice (CFC) (Eberhard, 1996) (defined as non-random variation in fertilization success after mating, due to females; Arnqvist, 2014). The benefits of this female choice are as discussed above, but CFC may provide the additional benefit of allowing females to override male interests in instances of forced copulation. Potential mechanisms of CFC are numerous (Eberhard, 1996) and includes ejecting the sperm of non-preferred males from their reproductive tracts, as occurs in feral fowl (Pizzari and Birkhead, 2000). In fact, the widespread evolution of multiple sperm-storage organs may be to facilitate CFC (Ward, 1993; reviewed in Wedell and Hosken, 2010). As noted above, CFC and sperm competition are hard to disentangle, but these processes are clearly important aspects of sexual selection (Parker, 1970; Eberhard, 1996; Simmons, 2001).

MEASURING FEMALE CHOICE

We began this chapter by noting that female choice was controversial, and neglected in the literature (reviewed in O'Donald, 1980; Hosken and House, 2011). Some authors have suggested that research on female choice only began in earnest after the social changes brought about by the 1960s – when views on female promiscuity began to change (Bradbury and Andersson, 1987). However, one reason why female choice remains understudied is that it is hard to measure, so we provide a brief primer here.

Female mate choice can broadly be decomposed into two elements: preference and choosiness (Jennions and Petrie, 1997; Cotton et al., 2006). In general, preference describes how females rank male phenotypes and can be represented by a preference function, which describes the relationship between a male phenotype and female response to it (Kilmer et al., 2017) (Figure 1.3). The shape of these functions illustrates the form of selection females impose on male traits (e.g. directional, disruptive, or stabilizing) and the strength of female preferences (Cotton et al., 2006; Kilmer et al., 2017).

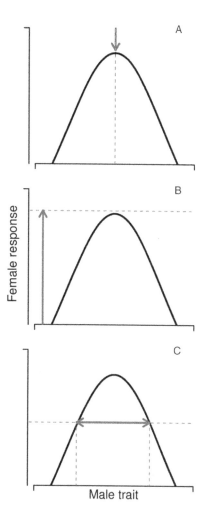

Figure 1.3 An example of female preference functions and what they mean, loosely based on a figure from Rodríguez et al. (2013). Each element shows a female's response (e.g. mate acceptance (realized preference)) to a male trait. The peak in a preference function shows the trait values females most prefer (A). We can also measure the strength of the preference – how much more most attractive males are preferred (B), and the variation around that peak preference that females are willing to accept – a measure of how choosy females are in their choice of mate (C)

We can also use preference functions to assess how fixed in their preferences females are (Figure 1.3). Choosiness describes how much effort a female exerts in mate choice – a choosy female takes longer to mate than a less choosy female or samples more males before making a mating decision (Figure 1.3) (Narraway et al., 2010).

The outcome of choice itself (i.e. whether females accept or reject a particular mate) is perhaps best thought of as realized preference. Thus, any male accepted as a mate by a female need not represent the ideal mate (i.e. the most preferred of all possible males), but rather represents the most preferred male available. Females have imperfect information about the quality of males encountered, incomplete information about the quality of all males, and incomplete information about the likelihood of encountering better males. When deciding whether to mate or not, females have to balance the costs of mating with a less preferred mate, the risks of remaining unmated, and so on. So, characterizing female choice is a considerable challenge and mate sampling (rules employed and numbers and phenotypes of males sampled) can have large effects on outcomes (Roff and Fairbairn, 2014).

SOME REMAINING QUESTIONS

The above discussion provides a brief introduction to core elements of sexual selection, but many unknowns remain, especially around mate choice (see Rosenthal, 2017). For example, female preferences remain poorly understood – what traits do females prefer and why? Are these preferences consistent across female genotypes, and how are they shaped by the abiotic and biotic (e.g. social) environment? Are they open ended or not? What are the molecular mechanisms underpinning female choice? What mate choice rules do females use and how many males do they normally sample? How does cryptic female choice (mechanistically) work,

exactly? How often is female mate choice irrational? Perhaps most importantly, is choice costly and if so, how costly? Costs of preference are a key parameter in many models of sexual selection, so understanding them empirically is important. There is also a lack of data on the prevalence or nature of male mate choice.

Furthermore, the population impacts of sexual selection can depend on whether female choice is for good genes or Fisherian benefits, but our understanding of whether sexual selection is adaptive or not is far from complete. And if sexually antagonistic variation is as common as it appears, how much does that impact the likelihood of mate choice for good genes? Additionally, how strong are trait-preference correlations generally, how strong do we expect them to be and how strong do they need to be to push traits past naturally selected optima? Finally, is the linkage disequilibrium (non-random gene association) that generates trait-preference covariance all due to mate choice?

These are just a few of *our* pet questions. Despite the huge advances in our understanding of sexual selection, there is still much to do.

ACKNOWLEDGEMENTS

We thank the Editor, Todd Shackelford, for inviting us to submit this chapter, helpful comments from an anonymous reviewer, and numerous colleagues for discussion of these topics.

REFERENCES

Agrawal, A. F. 2001. Sexual selection and the maintenance of sexual reproduction. *Nature* 411(6838):692–695.
Alonzo, S. H. 2008. Female mate choice copying affects sexual selection in wild populations of the ocellated wrasse. *Animal Behaviour* 75(5):1715–1723.

Alonzo, S. H., and M. R. Servedio. 2019. Grey zones of sexual selection: why is finding a modern definition so hard? *Proceedings of the Royal Society B* 286(1909):20191325.

Andersson, M. 1994. *Sexual selection*. Princeton University Press, Princeton, NJ.

Andersson, M., and L. W. Simmons. 2006. Sexual selection and mate choice. *Trends in Ecology and Evolution* 21(6):296–302.

Arnold, S. J. 1983. Sexual selection: the interface of theory and empiricism. Pp. 67–107 in *Mate Choice*, ed. Patrick Bateson. Cambridge University Press.

Arnqvist, G. 2014. Cryptic female choice. Pp. 204–220 in *The Evolution of Insect Mating Systems*, eds D. M. Shuker and L. W. Simmons. Oxford University Press.

Arnqvist, G., and L. Rowe. 2005. *Sexual conflict*. Princeton University Press, Princeton, NJ.

Bailey, W. J., P. C. Withers, M. Endersby, and K. Gaull. 1993. The energetic costs of calling in the bushcricket *Requena verticalis* (Orthoptera: Tettigoniidae: Listroscelidinae). *Journal of Experimental Biology* 178:21–37.

Bakker, T. C., and A. Pomiankowski. 1995. The genetic basis of female mate preferences. *Journal of Evolutionary Biology* 8(2):129–171.

Bean, D., and J. M. Cook. 2001. Male mating tactics and lethal combat in the nonpollinating fig wasp *Sycoscapter australis. Animal Behaviour* 62(3):535–542.

Berglund, A., and G. Rosenqvist. 2001. Male pipefish prefer ornamented females. *Animal Behaviour* 61(2):345–350.

Berglund, A., and G. Rosenqvist. 2003. Sex role reversal in pipefish. *Advances in the Study of Behavior* 32:131–167.

Berglund, A., A. Bisazza, and A. Pilastro. 1996. Armaments and ornaments: an evolutionary explanation of traits of dual utility. *Biological Journal of the Linnean Society* 58(4):385–399.

Birkhead, T. R., and A. P. Møller. 1998. *Sperm competition and sexual selection*. Academic Press, London.

Birkhead, T. R., J. G. Martínez, T. Burke, and D. P. Froman. 1999. Sperm mobility determines the outcome of sperm competition in the domestic fowl. *Proceedings of the Royal Society of London B* 266(1430):1759–1764.

Bonduriansky, R., and S. F. Chenoweth. 2009. Intralocus sexual conflict. *Trends in Ecology and Evolution* 24(5):280–288.

Borgia, G. 1979. Sexual selection and the evolution of mating systems. Pp. 19–80 in *Sexual Selection and Reproductive Competition in Insects*, eds M. S. Blum and N. A. Blum. Academic Press, New York.

Borgia, G. 1980. Sexual competition in *Scatophaga stercoraria*: size- and density-related changes in male ability to capture females. *Behaviour* 75(3–4):185–206.

Bradbury, J. W., and M. B. Andersson, eds. 1987. *Sexual selection: testing the alternatives*. John Wiley & Sons Inc.

Briffa, M., and R. W. Elwood. 2004. Use of energy reserves in fighting hermit crabs. *Proceedings of the Royal Society of London B* 271(1537):373–379.

Briffa, M., and L. U. Sneddon. 2010. Contest behavior. Pp. 246–265 in *Evolutionary Behavioral Ecology*, eds D. F. Westneat and C. W. Fox. Oxford University Press.

Bro-Jørgensen, J. 2007. The intensity of sexual selection predicts weapon size in male bovids. *Evolution* 61(6):1316–1326.

Buchanan, K. L., and C. K. Catchpole. 1997. Female choice in the sedge warbler *Acrocephalus schoenobaenus* multiple cues from song and territory quality. *Proceedings of the Royal Society of London B* 264(1381):521–526.

Buczek, M., H. Okarma, A. W. Demiaszkiewicz, and J. Radwan. 2016. MHC, parasites and antler development in red deer: no support for the Hamilton & Zuk hypothesis. *Journal of Evolutionary Biology* 29(3):617–632.

Byrne, P. G., J. D. Roberts, and L. W. Simmons. 2002. Sperm competition selects for increased testes mass in Australian frogs. *Journal of Evolutionary Biology* 15(3):347–355.

Cameron, E., T. Day, and L. Rowe. 2003. Sexual conflict and indirect benefits. *Journal of Evolutionary Biology* 16(5):1055–1060.

Cameron, E., T. Day, and L. Rowe. 2007. Sperm competition and the evolution of ejaculate composition. *The American Naturalist* 169(6):e158–e172.

Candolin, U. 2018. Sexual selection and sexual conflict. Pp. 310–318 in *Encyclopedia of Ecology: Volume One*, 2nd edition, ed. B. Fath. Elsevier.

Chapman, T. 2001. Seminal fluid-mediated fitness traits in *Drosophila. Heredity* 87:511–521.

Chapman, T., L. F. Liddle, J. M. Kalb, M. F. Wolfner, and L. Partridge. 1995. Cost of mating in *Drosophila melanogaster* females is mediated by male accessory gland products. *Nature* 373(6511):241–244.

Chippindale, A. K., J. R. Gibson, and W. R. Rice. 2001. Negative genetic correlation for adult fitness between sexes reveals ontogenetic conflict in *Drosophila*. *Proceedings of the National Academy of Sciences USA* 98(4):1671–1675.

Cotton, S., J. Small, and A. Pomiankowski. 2006. Sexual selection and condition-dependent mate preferences. *Current Biology* 16(17):R755–R765.

Csada, R. D., and D. L. Neudorf. 1995. Effects of predation risk on mate choice in female *Acheta domesticus* crickets. *Ecological Entomology* 20(4):393–395.

Cunha, M. A., A. Berglund, and N. M. Monteiro. 2017. Female ornaments signal own and offspring quality in a sex-role-reversed fish with extreme male parental care. *Marine Ecology* 38(5):e12461.

Dall, S. R., J. M. McNamara, N. Wedell, and D. J. Hosken. 2006. Debating sexual selection and mating strategies. *Science* 312(5774):689.

Danielson-François, A., C. Hou, N. Cole, and I.-M. Tso. 2012. Scramble competition for moulting females as a driving force for extreme male dwarfism in spiders. *Animal Behaviour* 84(4):937–945.

Darwin, C. 1859. *On the origin of species by means of natural selection, or, the preservation of favoured races in the struggle for life*. D. Appleton & Co., New York.

Darwin, C. 1860 (3 April, to Asa Gray). Letter no. 2743. Darwin Correspondence Project, accessed 1.8.2019.

Darwin, C. 1868 (21 March, to Alfred Russel Wallace). Letter no. 6033. Darwin Correspondence Project, accessed 1.8.2019.

Darwin, C. 1871. *The descent of man, and selection in relation to sex*. John Murray, London.

Eberhard, W. G. 1996. *Female control: sexual selection by cryptic female choice*. Princeton University Press, Princeton, NJ.

Emlen, D. J. 2008. The evolution of animal weapons. *Annual Review of Ecology, Evolution, and Systematics* 39:387–413.

Emlen, D. J. 2014. *Animal weapons: the evolution of battle*. Henry Holt and Company, New York.

Endler, J. A. 1992. Signals, signal conditions, and the direction of evolution. *The American Naturalist* 139:S125–S153.

Enquist, M., A. Arak, S. Ghirlanda, and C.-A. Wachtmeister. 2002. Spectacular phenomena and limits to rationality in genetic and cultural evolution. *Philosophical Transactions of the Royal Society of London B* 357(1427):1585–1594.

Fisher, R. A. 1915. The evolution of sexual preference. *Eugenics Review* 7(3):184–192.

Fisher, R. A. 1930. *The genetical theory of natural selection*. Clarendon Press, Oxford.

Fisher, R. A. 1999. *The genetical theory of natural selection: a complete variorum edition*, ed. J. H. Bennett. Oxford University Press.

Fitzpatrick, J. L., R. Montgomerie, J. K. Desjardins, K. A. Stiver, N. Kolm, and S. Balshine. 2009. Female promiscuity promotes the evolution of faster sperm in cichlid fishes. *Proceedings of the National Academy of Sciences USA* 106(4):1128–1132.

Gage, M. J. 1991. Risk of sperm competition directly affects ejaculate size in the Mediterranean fruit fly. *Animal Behaviour* 42(6):1036–1037.

Gage, M. J. 1994. Associations between body size, mating pattern, testis size and sperm lengths across butterflies. *Proceedings of the Royal Society of London B* 258(1353):247–254.

Gage, M. J., P. Stockley, and G. A. Parker. 1995. Effects of alternative male mating strategies on characteristics of sperm production in the Atlantic salmon (*Salmo salar*): theoretical and empirical investigations. *Philosophical Transactions of the Royal Society of London B* 350(1334):391–399.

Gomendio, M., and E. R. Roldan. 2008. Implications of diversity in sperm size and function for sperm competition and fertility. *International Journal of Developmental Biology* 52(5–6):439–447.

Gotoh, H., R. A. Zinna, I. Warren, M. DeNieu, T. Niimi, I. Dworkin, D. J. Emlen, T. Miura, and L. C. Lavine. 2016. Identification and functional analyses of sex determination genes in the sexually dimorphic stag beetle *Cyclommatus metallifer*. *BMC Genomics* 17:250.

Grafen, A. 1990. Biological signals as handi-caps. *Journal of Theoretical Biology* 144(4):517–546.

Greenfield, M. D., S. Alem, D. Limousin, and N. W. Bailey. 2014. The dilemma of Fisherian sexual selection: mate choice for indirect benefits despite rarity and overall weakness of trait-preference genetic correlation. *Evolution* 68(12):3524–3536.

Hack, M. A. 1997. The energetic costs of fighting in the house cricket, *Acheta domesticus L. Behavioral Ecology* 8(1):28–36.

Haley, M. P., C. J. Deutsch, and B. J. Le Boeuf. 1994. Size, dominance and copulatory success in male northern elephant seals, *Mirounga angustirostris. Animal Behaviour* 48(6):1249–1260.

Hall, D. W., M. Kirkpatrick, and B. West. 2000. Runaway sexual selection when female preferences are directly selected. *Evolution* 54(6):1862–1869.

Hamilton, W. D. 1980. Sex versus non-sex versus parasite. Oikos 35(2): 282–290.

Hamilton, W. D., and M. Zuk. 1982. Heritable true fitness and bright birds: a role for parasites? *Science* 218(4570):384–387.

Hawkes, M. F., C. E. Gamble, E. C. R. Turner, M. R. Carey, N. Wedell, and D. J. Hosken. 2016. Intralocus sexual conflict and insecticide resistance. *Proceedings of the Royal Society B* 283(1843):20161429.

Hodgson, D. J., and D. J. Hosken. 2006. Sperm competition promotes the exploitation of rival ejaculates. *Journal of Theoretical Biology* 243(2):230–234.

Holwell, G. I., K. L. Barry, and M. E. Herberstein. 2007. Mate location, antennal morphology, and ecology in two praying mantids (Insecta: Mantodea). *Biological Journal of the Linnean Society* 91(2):307–313.

Hone, D. W., D. Naish, and I. C. Cuthill. 2012. Does mutual sexual selection explain the evolution of head crests in pterosaurs and dinosaurs? *Lethaia* 45(2):139–156.

Hosken, D. J. 1997. Sperm competition in bats. *Proceedings of the Royal Society of London B* 264(1380):385–392.

Hosken, D. J., and D. J. Hodgson. 2014. Why do sperm carry RNA? Relatedness, conflict, and control. *Trends in Ecology and Evolution* 29(8):451–455.

Hosken, D. J., and C. M. House. 2011. Sexual selection. *Current Biology* 21(2): R62–R65.

Hosken, D. J., and P. I. Ward. 2001. Experimental evidence for testis size evolution via sperm competition. *Ecology Letters* 4(1):10–13.

Hosken, D. J., and A. J. Wilson. 2019. The problem of measuring trait-preference correlations without disrupting them. *Behavioral Ecology* 30(6):1518-1521.

Hosken, D. J., S. H. Alonzo, and N. Wedell. 2016. Why aren't signals of female quality more common? *Animal Behaviour* 114:199–201.

Hosken, D. J., C. R. Archer, and J. E. Mank. 2019. Sexual conflict. *Current Biology* 29(11):R451–R455.

Hosken, D. J., P. Stockley, T. Tregenza, and N. Wedell. 2009. Monogamy and the battle of the sexes. *Annual Review of Entomology* 54:361–378.

Hunt, J., and D. J. Hosken, eds. 2014. *Genotype-by-environment interactions and sexual selection.* John Wiley & Sons.

Huxley, J. S. 1938. Darwin's theory of sexual selection and the data subsumed by it, in the light of recent research. *The American Naturalist* 72(742):416–433.

Iwasa, Y., and A. Pomiankowski. 1995. Continual change in mate preferences. *Nature* 377(654):420–422.

Iwasa, Y., A. Pomiankowski, and S. Nee. 1991. The evolution of costly mate preferences II. The 'handicap' principle. *Evolution* 45(6):1431–1442.

Jennions, M. D., and H. Kokko. 2010. Sexual selection. Pp. 343–364 in *Evolutionary Behavioral Ecology*, eds D. F. Westneat and C. W. Fox. Oxford University Press.

Jennions, M. D., and M. Petrie. 1997. Variation in mate choice and mating preferences: a review of causes and consequences. *Biological Reviews* 72(2):283–327.

Johnstone, R. A., J. D. Reynolds, and J. C. Deutsch. 1996. Mutual mate choice and sex differences in choosiness. *Evolution* 50(4):1382–1391.

Jones, A. G., and N. L. Ratterman. 2009. Mate choice and sexual selection: what have we learned since Darwin? *Proceedings of the National Academy of Sciences USA* 106(Suppl 1):10001–10008.

Kilmer, J. T., K. D. Fowler-Finn, D. A. Gray, G. Höbel, D. Rebar, M. S. Reichert, and R. L. Rodríguez. 2017. Describing mate preference functions and other function-valued traits. *Journal of Evolutionary Biology* 30(9): 1658–1673.

Kirkpatrick, M. 1982. Sexual selection and the evolution of female choice. *Evolution* 36(1):1–12.

Kirkpatrick, M., and M. J. Ryan. 1991. The evolution of mating preferences and the paradox of the lek. *Nature* 350(6313):33–38.

Kleven, O., F. Fossøy, T. Laskemoen, R. J. Robertson, G. Rudolfsen, and J. T. Lifjeld. 2009. Comparative evidence for the evolution of sperm swimming speed by sperm competition and female sperm storage duration in passerine birds. *Evolution* 63(9):2466–2473.

Kokko, H. 2013. Dyadic contests: modelling fights between two individuals. Pp. 5–32 in *Animal Contests*, eds I. C. Hardy and M. Briffa. Cambridge University Press.

Kokko, H., and M. D. Jennions. 2014. The relationship between sexual selection and sexual conflict. *Cold Spring Harbor Perspectives in Biology* 6(9):a017517.

Kokko, H., and R. A. Johnstone. 2002. Why is mutual mate choice not the norm? Operational sex ratios, sex roles and the evolution of sexually dimorphic and monomorphic signalling. *Philosophical Transactions of the Royal Society of London B* 357(1419):319–330.

Kokko, H., I. Booksmythe, and M. D. Jennions. 2013. Causality and sex roles: prejudice against patterns? A reply to Ah-King. *Trends in Ecology and Evolution* 28(1):2–4.

Kokko, H., R. Brooks, J. M. McNamara, and A. I. Houston. 2002. The sexual selection continuum. *Proceedings of the Royal Society of London B* 269(1498):1331–1340.

Kuijper, B., I. Pen, and F. J. Weissing. 2012. A guide to sexual selection theory. *Annual Review of Ecology, Evolution, and Systematics* 43:287–311.

Lande, R. 1981. Models of speciation by sexual selection on polygenic traits. *Proceedings of the National Academy of Sciences USA* 78(6):3721–3725.

Le Boeuf, B. J. 1974. Male–male competition and reproductive success in elephant seals. *American Zoologist* 14(1):163–176.

Lessells, C. M., A. T. D. Bennett, T. R. Birkhead, N. Colegrave, S. R. X. Dall, P. Harvey, B. Hatchwell, D. J. Hosken, J. Hunt, A. J. Moore, G. A. Parker, S. Pitnick, T. Pizzari, J. Radwan, M. Ritchie, B. C. Sheldon, D. M. Shuker, L. W. Simmons, P. Stockley, T. Tregenza, and M. Zuk. 2006. Debating sexual selection and mating strategies. *Science* 312(5774): 689–690.

Malo, A. F., J. J. Garde, A. J. Soler, A. J. García, M. Gomendio, and E. R. Roldan. 2005. Male fertility in natural populations of red deer is determined by sperm velocity and the proportion of normal spermatozoa. *Biology of Reproduction* 72(4):822–829.

Mank, J. E. 2017. The transcriptional architecture of phenotypic dimorphism. *Nature Ecology and Evolution* 1:0006.

Martin, C. H., and S. Johnsen. 2007. A field test of the Hamilton–Zuk hypothesis in the Trinidadian guppy (*Poecilia reticulata*). *Behavioral Ecology and Sociobiology* 61(12):1897–1909.

Martin, O. Y., and D. J. Hosken. 2002. Strategic ejaculation in the common dung fly *Sepsis cynipsea*. *Animal Behaviour* 63(3):541–546.

Mays Jr, H. L., and G. E. Hill. 2004. Choosing mates: good genes versus genes that are a good fit. *Trends in Ecology and Evolution* 19(10):554–559.

McCart, C., A. Buckling, and R. Ffrench-Constant. 2005. DDT resistance in flies carries no cost. *Current Biology* 15(15):R587–R589.

Nakatsuru, K., and D. L. Kramer. 1982. Is sperm cheap? Limited male fertility and female choice in the lemon tetra (Pisces, Characidae). *Science* 216(4547):753–755.

Narraway, C., J. Hunt, N. Wedell, and D. J. Hosken. 2010. Genotype-by-environment for female preference. *Journal of Evolutionary Biology* 23(12):2550–2557.

O'Donald, P. 1980. *Genetic models of sexual selection*. Cambridge University Press.

Okada, K., Y. Okada, S. R. Dall, and D. J. Hosken. 2019. Loser-effect duration evolves independently of fighting ability. *Proceedings of the Royal Society of London B* 286(1903): 20190582.

Owens, I. P., and I. R. Hartley. 1998. Sexual dimorphism in birds: why are there so many different forms of dimorphism? *Proceedings of the Royal Society of London B* 265(1394):397–407.

Parker, G. A. 1970. Sperm competition and its evolutionary consequences in the insects. *Biological Reviews* 45(4):525–567.

Parker, G. A. 1979. Sexual selection and sexual conflict. Pp. 123–166 in *Sexual Selection and Reproductive Competition in Insects*, eds M. S. Blum and N. A. Blum. Academic Press, New York.

Parker, G. A. 1982. Why are there so many tiny sperm? Sperm competition and the maintenance of two sexes. *Journal of Theoretical Biology* 96(2):281–294.

Parker, G. A. 1983. Mate quality and mating decisions. Pp. 141–166 in *Mate Choice*, ed. Patrick Bateson. Cambridge University Press.

Parker, G. A. 1990. Sperm competition games: raffles and roles. *Proceedings of the Royal Society of London B* 242(1304):120–126.

Parker, G. A. 1993. Sperm competition games: sperm size and sperm number under adult control. *Proceedings of the Royal Society of London B* 253(1338):245–254.

Parker, G. A. 1998. Sperm competition and the evolution of ejaculates: towards a theory base. Pp. 3–54 in *Sperm Competition and Sexual Selection*. Academic Press, London.

Parker, G. A. 2006. Sexual conflict over mating and fertilization: an overview. *Philosophical Transactions of the Royal Society B* 361(1466):235–259.

Parker, G. A. 2016. The evolution of expenditure on testes. *Journal of Zoology* 298(1):3–19.

Pitnick, S. 1996. Investment in testes and the cost of making long sperm in *Drosophila*. *The American Naturalist* 148(1):57–80.

Pitnick, S., and D. J. Hosken. 2010. Postcopulatory sexual selection. Pp. 379–399 in *Evolutionary Behavioral Ecology*, eds D. F. Westneat and C. W. Fox. Oxford University Press.

Pitnick, S., G. T. Miller, J. Reagan, and B. Holland. 2001. Males' evolutionary responses to experimental removal of sexual selection. *Proceedings of the Royal Society of London B* 268(1471):1071–1080.

Pizzari, T., and T. R. Birkhead. 2000. Female feral fowl eject sperm of subdominant males. *Nature* 405(6788):787–789.

Pizzari, T., T. R. Birkhead, M. W. Blows, R. Brooks, K. L. Buchanan, T. H. Clutton-Brock, P. H. Harvey, D. J. Hosken, M. D. Jennions, H. Kokko, J. S. Kotiaho, C. M. Lessells, C. Macias-García, A. J. Moore, G. A. Parker, L.

Partridge, S. Pitnick, J. Radwan, M. Ritchie, B. C. Sheldon, L. W. Simmons, R. R. Snook, P. Stockley, and M. Zuk. 2006. Debating sexual selection and mating strategies. *Science* 312(5774):690.

Pomiankowski, A., Y. Iwasa, and S. Nee. 1991. The evolution of costly mate preferences I. Fisher and biased mutation. *Evolution* 45(6):1422–1430.

Price, T., D. Schluter, and N. E. Heckman. 1993. Sexual selection when the female directly benefits. *Biological Journal of the Linnean Society* 48(3):187–211.

Prokop, Z. M., Ł. Michalczyk, S. M. Drobniak, M. Herdegen, and J. Radwan. 2012. Meta-analysis suggests choosy females get sexy sons more than 'good genes'. *Evolution* 66(9):2665–2673.

Prokuda, A. Y., and D. A. Roff. 2014. The quantitative genetics of sexually selected traits, preferred traits and preference: a review and analysis of the data. *Journal of Evolutionary Biology* 27(11):2283–2296.

Prum, R. O. 2010. The Lande–Kirkpatrick mechanism is the null model of evolution by intersexual selection: implications for meaning, honesty, and design in intersexual signals. *Evolution* 64(11):3085–3100.

Prum, R. O. 2012. Aesthetic evolution by mate choice: Darwin's *really* dangerous idea. *Philosophical Transactions of the Royal Society of London B* 367(1600):2253–2265.

Queller, D. C. 1997. Why do females care more than males? *Proceedings of the Royal Society of London B* 264(1388):1555–1557.

Radwan, J. 2004. Effectiveness of sexual selection in removing mutations induced with ionizing radiation. *Ecology Letters* 7(12):1149–1154.

Read, A. F. 1987. Comparative evidence supports the Hamilton and Zuk hypothesis on parasites and sexual selection. *Nature* 328(6125):68–70.

Requena, G. S., and S. H. Alonzo. 2017. Sperm competition games when males invest in paternal care. *Proceedings of the Royal Society B* 284(1860):20171266.

Rice, W. R. 1996. Sexually antagonistic male adaptation triggered by experimental arrest of female evolution. *Nature* 381(6579):232–234.

Rodríguez, R. L., A. C. Hallett, J. T. Kilmer, and K. D. Fowler-Finn. 2013. Curves as traits:

genetic and environmental variation in mate preference functions. *Journal of Evolutionary Biology* 26(2):434–442.

Roff, D. A. 2012. *Evolutionary quantitative genetics*. Springer.

Roff, D. A., and D. J. Fairbairn. 2014. The evolution of phenotypes and genetic parameters under preferential mating. *Ecology and Evolution* 4(13):2759–2776.

Roff, D. A., and D. J. Fairbairn. 2015. Bias in the heritability of preference and its potential impact on the evolution of mate choice. *Heredity* 114(4):404–412.

Rosenthal, G. G. 2017. *Mate choice: the evolution of sexual decision making from microbes to humans*. Princeton University Press, Princeton, NJ.

Rostant, W. G., C. Kay, N. Wedell, and D. J. Hosken. 2015. Sexual conflict maintains variation at an insecticide resistance locus. *BMC Biology* 13:34.

Rostant, W. G., J. Bowyer, J. Coupland, J. Facey, D. J. Hosken, and N. Wedell. 2017. Pleiotropic effects of DDT resistance on male size and behaviour. *Behavior Genetics* 47(4):449–458.

Rowe, L. 1994. The costs of mating and mate choice in water striders. *Animal Behaviour* 48(5):1049–1056.

Rowe, L., and D. Houle. 1996. The lek paradox and the capture of genetic variance by condition dependent traits. *Proceedings of the Royal Society B* 263(1375):1415–1421.

Ryan, M. J. 1998. Sexual selection, receiver biases, and the evolution of sex differences. *Science* 281(5385):1999–2003.

Ryan, M. J., J. H. Fox, W. Wilczynski, and A. S. Rand. 1990. Sexual selection for sensory exploitation in the frog *Physalaemus pustulosus*. *Nature* 343(6523):66–67.

Schärer, L., L. Rowe, and G. Arnqvist. 2012. Anisogamy, chance and the evolution of sex roles. *Trends in Ecology and Evolution* 27(5):260–264.

Seger, J., and R. Trivers. 1986. Asymmetry in the evolution of female mating preferences. *Nature* 319(6056):771–773.

Sharma, M. D., A. J. Wilson, and D. J. Hosken. 2016. Fisher's sons' effect in sexual selection: absent, intermittent or just low experimental power? *Journal of Evolutionary Biology* 29(12):2464–2470.

Shuster, S. M., and M. J. Wade. 2003. *Mating systems and strategies*. Princeton University Press, Princeton, NJ.

Simmons, L. W. 2001. *Sperm competition and its evolutionary consequences in the insects*. Princeton University Press, Princeton, NJ.

Simmons, L. W., and W. J. Bailey. 1990. Resource influenced sex roles of zaprochiline tettigoniids (Orthoptera: Tettigoniidae). *Evolution* 44(7):1853–1868.

Simmons, L. W., J. L. Tomkins, and J. Hunt. 1999. Sperm competition games played by dimorphic male beetles. *Proceedings of the Royal Society of London B* 266(1415):145–150.

Simmons, L. W., M. Craig, T. Llorens, M. Schinzig, and D. Hosken. 1993. Bushcricket spermatophores vary in accord with sperm competition and parental investment theory. *Proceedings of the Royal Society of London B* 251(1332):183–186.

Sirot, L. K., M. F. Wolfner, and S. Wigby. 2011. Protein-specific manipulation of ejaculate composition in response to female mating status in *Drosophila melanogaster*. *Proceedings of the National Academy of Sciences USA* 108(24):9922–9926.

Smith, D. T., D. J. Hosken, W. G. Rostant, M. Yeo, R. M. Griffin, A. Bretman, T. A. R. Price, R. H. ffrench-Constant, and N. Wedell. 2011. DDT resistance, epistasis and male fitness in flies. *Journal of Evolutionary Biology* 24(6):1351–1362.

Snook, R. R. 2005. Sperm in competition: not playing by the numbers. *Trends in Ecology and Evolution* 20(1):46–53.

Stiver, K. A., R. M. Harris, J. P. Townsend, H. A. Hoffmann, and S. H. Alonzo. 2015. Neural gene expression profiles and androgen levels underlie alternative reproductive tactics in the ocellated wrasse, *Symphodus ocellatus*. *Ethology* 121(2):152–167.

Stockley, P., M. J. G. Gage, G. A. Parker, and A. P. Møller. 1997. Sperm competition in fishes: the evolution of testis size and ejaculate characteristics. *The American Naturalist* 149(5):933–954.

Taylor M. L., N. Wedell, and D. J. Hosken. 2008. Sexual selection and female fitness in *Drosophila simulans*. *Behavioral Ecology and Sociobiology* 62(5):721–728.

Thornhill, R. 1983. Cryptic female choice and its implications in the scorpionfly *Harpobittacus nigriceps. The American Naturalist* 122(6): 765–788.

Thornhill, R., and J. Alcock. 1983. *The evolution of insect mating systems*. Harvard University Press, Cambridge, MA.

Trivers, R. L. 1972. Parental investment and sexual selection. Pp. 136–179 in *Sexual Selection and the Descent of Man, 1871–1971*, ed. B. G. Campbell. Aldine de Gruyter, New York.

Wade, M. J. 2014. Genotype-by-environment interactions and sexual selection: female choice in a complex world. Pp. 3–18 in *Genotype-by-Environment Interactions and Sexual Selection*, eds J. Hunt and D. J. Hosken. Wiley-Blackwell, Chichester, UK.

Ward, P. I. 1993. Females influence sperm storage and use in the yellow dung fly *Scathophaga stercoraria* (L.). *Behavioral Ecology and Sociobiology* 32(5):313–319.

Watson, P. J. 1991. Multiple paternity and first mate sperm precedence in the sierra dome spider, *Linyphia litigiosa* Keyserling (Linyphiidae). *Animal Behaviour* 41(1):135–148.

Wedekind, C., T. Seebeck, F. Bettens, and A. J. Paepke. 1995. MHC-dependent mate preferences in humans. *Proceedings of the Royal Society of London B* 260(1359): 245–249.

Wedell, N., and P. A. Cook. 1999. Butterflies tailor their ejaculate in response to sperm competition risk and intensity. *Proceedings of the Royal Society of London B* 266(1423): 1033–1039.

Wedell, N., and D. J. Hosken. 2010. The evolution of male and female internal reproductive organs in insects. Pp. 307–331 in *The Evolution of Primary Sexual Characters in Animals*, eds J. L. Leonard and A. Córdoba-Aguilar. Oxford University Press.

Wedell, N., M. J. Gage, and G. A. Parker. 2002. Sperm competition, male prudence and sperm-limited females. *Trends in Ecology and Evolution* 17(7):313–320.

Werren, J. H., L. Baldo, and M. E. Clark. 2008. Wolbachia: master manipulators of invertebrate biology. *Nature Reviews Microbiology* 6(10):741–751.

West-Eberhard, M. J. 1984. Sexual selection, competitive communication and species-specific signals in insects. Pp. 283–324 in *Insect Communication* (Proceedings of the 12th Symposium of the Royal Entomological Society of London), ed. T. Lewis. Academic Press, London.

Williams, G. C. 1966. *Adaptation and natural selection: a critique of some current evolutionary thought*. Princeton University Press, Princeton, NJ.

Zahavi, A. 1975. Mate selection: a selection for a handicap. *Journal of Theoretical Biology* 53(1):205–214.

Zeh, J. A., and D. W. Zeh. 2001. Reproductive mode and the genetic benefits of polyandry. *Animal Behaviour* 61(6):1051–1063.

Inclusive Fitness Theory

INTRODUCTION

When Darwin (1859) proposed his theory of evolution by means of natural selection, he had produced an explanation of how a trait – be it physical or behavioral – could begin as a random mutation within a single organism and, over the course of generations, become a seemingly ubiquitous trait within that organism's entire species. Simply put, a trait that produces stronger benefits to survival and/or reproduction, when compared to a competing trait, will allow its possessor to reproduce more frequently than its fellow species members who do not possess this particular trait. Therefore, any gene that produces a trait which provides greater reproductive benefits than fitness costs (e.g., fewer reproductive opportunities, poorer health, shorter lifespan, etc.) is more likely to be naturally selected than competing alleles that produce traits with fewer reproductive benefits and/or greater fitness cost. Inclusive fitness theory (Hamilton, 1964) takes Darwin's (1859)

explanation one step further by accounting for the natural selection of genes that produce perceptual and behavioral mechanisms that influence other individuals within a species.

Hamilton (1964) proposed inclusive fitness theory as a means of accounting for how and why organisms may engage in social behaviors that are seemingly counterintuitive to their own survival and/or reproduction. It is often described as a theory in evolutionary biology and psychology that provides an explanation for altruistic social behavior within a species. Inclusive fitness theory also provides explanations for several cooperative and non-cooperative mechanisms and behaviors that enhance one's overall inclusive fitness. In the evolutionary literature, the term 'fitness' refers to reproductive fitness (i.e., the probability of reproducing one's genes). An organism may maximize its fitness in a variety of direct and indirect ways. *Direct* ways of improving one's fitness are caused by natural selection (i.e., an organism may have more opportunities to reproduce if it possesses traits that enhance the probability of its survival) and sexual selection (i.e., an organism will have more reproductive opportunities if it possesses characteristics that the opposite sex desires). Inclusive fitness theory (Hamilton, 1964) provides an explanation for the various *indirect* ways of maximizing one's reproductive fitness through using social behaviors to influence other members of one's species.

There are four types of social behavior, each based on whether the actor or the recipient benefits from the action: selfishness, spite, mutual benefit, and altruism. *Selfishness* refers to behaviors that benefit the actor at a cost to the recipient. If neither the actor nor the recipient benefit (and they both incur a cost), the behavior is considered *spiteful*. A behavior is considered *mutualistic* when both the actor and recipient benefit. *Altruism* occurs when the recipient benefits, but the actor incurs a cost (West et al., 2007).

Genes that produce social behaviors (i.e., behaviors which influence others) – even altruistic behaviors – are subject to the same laws of natural selection as any other gene. However, natural selection may not simply favor 'selfish' genes (Dawkins, 1976). Some genes that account for cooperative and altruistic behaviors may have been naturally selected; these include pro-social behaviors such as kin selection (i.e., kin altruism) (Burnstein et al., 1994), and antisocial behaviors such as verbal and physical aggression (Fitzgerald and Ketterer, 2011; Gesselman and Webster, 2012; Webster, 2008; Webster et al., 2012) and jealousy within romantic relationships (Buss et al., 1992). If the genes responsible for producing these particular traits improve survival and reproduction, then they are more likely to be naturally selected and, thus, become more prevalent in future generations. Hamilton created the equation $c < br$ to indicate the conditions under which these genes may be naturally selected. This equation – commonly referred to as *Hamilton's rule* – states that a

gene (for example, a gene responsible for altruistic behavior) may be naturally selected and become prevalent within a species if the gene's reproductive cost (c) is less than the gene's reproductive benefits (b) multiplied by the coefficient of relatedness (r) between the altruist and recipient. Park (2007) illustrated Hamilton's rule in a hypothetical thought experiment that describes the conditions under which an altruistic gene would be naturally selected within a species.

> Imagine ... that a mutant gene emerged in a parent organism making it confer benefits to its offspring, even at costs to itself. Now ... there would have been 50% probability that each of the parent organism's offspring would inherit this particular mutant gene. Therefore, as long as the benefits conferred to the offspring (multiplied by the probability of inheritance) outweighed the costs incurred by the parent (with benefits and costs measured in terms of reproductive success), this mutant gene would have been selected over its alleles. (Park, 2007: 861)

MECHANISMS OF INCLUSIVE FITNESS

Hamilton (1964) stated in his inclusive fitness theory that any gene responsible for cooperative or altruistic social mechanisms/behaviors could have survived natural selection if its possessor were able to reproduce more frequently than those who possess a competing allele. Since Hamilton's (1964) theory was presented, many evolutionary psychologists and biologists have hypothesized various mechanisms and altruistic behaviors that could be the product of particular genes that were naturally selected. These mechanisms and behaviors often focus on kin relations – such as kin recognition and altruism toward kin -- and are therefore usually classified under kin selection theory.

Kin selection refers to the natural selection of genes that are responsible for kin-directed behavior. These kin-directed behaviors may come in the form of (but are not limited to) recognizing factors that identify one's kin

(Hepper, 2005; Park et al., 2008), investing resources and physical care to one's offspring (Trivers, 1972), or engaging in altruistic behaviors to rescue one's kin (Thompson and Fitzgerald, 2017; Fitzgerald et al., 2010; Stewart-Williams, 2007, 2008). Data to support the existence of these mechanisms have been discovered in several non-mammalian and mammalian species – including humans.

Kin Recognition

In order for organisms to be able to engage in altruistic behavior toward their kin, they must be able to recognize their kin from other non-kin members within their species (Hepper, 2005). It is possible that individuals can recognize kin via phenotypic cues: physical details about an individual that may be similar between kin, such as appearance, odor, or vocal sounds (Silk, 2009). Recognizing similar physical details among kin members is known as *phenotype matching*, which has been recorded in many birds and small mammals (Hauber and Sherman, 2001; Holmes, 1986). Evidence suggests that phenotype matching occurs among various primate species, including macaques, chimpanzees, and humans (Boesch et al., 2006; Kazem and Widdig, 2013; Langergraber et al., 2007; Parr and de Waal, 1999; Silk, 2009; Vokey et al., 2004; Widdig, 2007; Wu et al., 1980).

Although phenotype matching may not be the definitive mechanism that primates utilize to identify kin, researchers have also noted that familiarity – caused by the amount of time spent in close proximity (usually during rearing) – may also be used to recognize kin. The evidence indicates that familiarity is the more likely kin recognition mechanism than phenotype matching (Frederickson and Sackett, 1984; Silk, 2009). Familiarity – measured by the amount of time that individuals have spent together – is a reliable predictor of altruistic behaviors between kin. Mandrills display closer affiliation to half-siblings than

non-kin (Charpentier et al., 2007). Baboons are less likely to attempt mating with kin, and even less likely to mate with siblings who are closer in age proximity (Alberts, 1999). This kin recognition, however, seems limited to maternal kin (Silk, 2002). Whether or not non-human primates are able to recognize paternal kin is still a matter of controversy (Widdig, 2007). Primate researchers have argued that non-human primates may be able to recognize maternal kin because of familiarity (Widdig, 2007). Most primate societies are promiscuous, and males often do not remain with their female mate and care for their offspring, thus the offspring are familiar with their mother and maternal siblings because they are together during the rearing period. However, while some researchers have noted a lack of paternal kin recognition among non-human primates (Erhart et al., 1997), other researchers have found data that indicate some non-human primates – including baboons, macaques, and chimpanzees – may recognize paternal kin and behave more prosocially and less aggressively toward them than non-kin (Alberts, 1999; Mackenzie et al., 1985; Smith et al., 2003; Widdig, 2007; Wu et al., 1980).

Phenotype matching and familiarity (measured as length of co-residence) are both widely utilized as kin recognition mechanisms in humans (Alvergne et al., 2009; Bressan et al., 2009; Debruine et al., 2008; Lieberman et al., 2007; Park et al., 2008; Wells, 1987).

Kin Selection

Kin selection theory states that individuals will be more likely to engage in life-threatening altruistic behaviors to rescue close kin (who have a greater probability of possessing the gene responsible for kin selection) over distant kin and non-kin. Similarly, individuals will be more likely to rescue distant kin over non-kin. The probability of inheritance (r) – sometimes referred to as the *coefficient of relatedness* in this context – indicates differences in the probability of the altruist and the recipient sharing copies of the same gene responsible for altruism. Close kin – such as parents, offspring, and siblings – possess $r = .50$ probability of sharing copies of the same 'altruism allele'. Aunts, uncles, nieces, nephews, and half-siblings are denoted by $r = .25$, and cousins are denoted by $r = .125$. Non-kin are denoted by $r = 0$.

Kin selection researchers have reported linear relationships between the likelihood of engaging in life-threatening altruism and (r). As (r) between an altruist and recipient increases, the likelihood of engaging in life-threatening altruism increases as well. This relationship has been extensively studied and supported in human samples. Individuals often give preference to close kin $(r = .50)$ over distant kin $(r = .25$ or $.125)$ and non-kin $(r = 0)$ in resource allocation (Judge and Hrdy, 1992; Lu and Chang, 2016; Neyer and Lang, 2003; Webster, 2003, 2004). In fact, individuals are also less likely to give resources to kin when they are uncertain of their genetic relatedness due to paternity uncertainty (Buss, 1996; Jeon and Buss, 2007; Webster, 2003).

Preferences for close kin have also been reported in polygamous societies in which children co-reside with full-siblings and half-siblings and the culture downplays genetic differences (Jankowiak and Diderich, 2000). When presented with hypothetical life-or-death scenarios, participants consistently indicate a stronger likelihood to rescue close kin over distant kin, and distant kin over non-kin (Bressan et al., 2009; Burnstein et al., 1994; Fitzgerald and Colarelli, 2009; Fitzgerald and Whitaker, 2009; Kruger, 2001; Neyer and Lang, 2003; Stewart-Williams, 2007, 2008). Similarly, individuals are more likely to rescue their romantic partner when they have a biological offspring together than when they only have adopted children or no children together – even when statistically controlling for emotional closeness between the altruist and recipient (Fitzgerald et al., 2010) – indicating that the probability of inheritance may influence altruistic decision-making among kin.

Assessing life-threatening altruism in humans has been criticized for the lack of measuring real-world behavior. However, experimentally assessing humans' responses in actual life-or-death situations would be unethical, if not impossible and/or illegal. Empirical research on life-threatening altruism from a kin selection perspective has relied heavily on self-report methods and the use of written vignettes depicting hypothetical life-or-death situations. As one can imagine, having participants indicate how they would react in a hypothetical scenario may not correlate with how those participants would *actually* react if the life-or-death situation were real. Similarly, individuals may wish to respond in a socially desirable manner, indicating a strong tendency to help their kin, even if they would prefer not to help. Some research has found that individuals report themselves as significantly more altruistic than others – including their spouse – indicating a potential social desirability bias in self-report altruistic decision-making (Fitzgerald et al., 2010). However, in this example, Fitzgerald and colleagues (2010) note that social desirability simply inflated response scores but did not have an influence on the relationship between altruistic intentions and the genetic relatedness between altruist and recipient.

Kin selection has also been well documented in various non-human primate species. For instance, adult female white-faced capuchins give preference to maternal kin during grooming (Perry et al., 2008). Similarly, pigtail macaques prefer to interact with genetically related kin over non-kin (Wu et al., 1980). In the absence of their mother, female vervet monkeys display a preference to care for their siblings over unrelated vervet monkeys (Johnson et al., 1980). Marmosets and tamarins are significantly more aggressive toward unrelated males than siblings (Harrison and Tardif, 1988), and male chimpanzees prefer to form cooperative bonds with maternal brothers over other males (Langergraber et al., 2007). For further evidence of kin selection in non-human primates, see Silk (2009) and Berman (2011) for reviews of the empirical literature.

Kin selection has also been observed in many non-primate mammals, including ground squirrels, meerkats, jackals, and lions (Clutton-Brock et al., 1999; Clutton-Brock, 2002; Moehlman, 1979). Insects in particular have been extensively studied due to their eusocial nature. Army ants and honeybees, for example, engage in altruistic behavior that improves the survival of their overall group even at the cost of their own life (Nowak et al., 2010; Reid et al., 2015; Seeley, 1997). Because of the sacrificial nature of these behaviors, many researchers have attributed insect eusociality to group selection, which is a controversial theory of evolution that argues natural selection can occur at the group level, not just the individual level or genetic level (Nowak, 2006). The majority of the scientific community has rejected group selection theory, arguing that although some cooperative behaviors may seem like they evolved via group selection, they can be accounted for by various inclusive fitness mechanisms (Fitzgerald, 2018).

Aggression

Inclusive fitness theory has accounted for the natural selection of altruistic behaviors; however, recent theoretical and empirical work has suggested that it may account for some aggressive behaviors as well. For example, a mother may instinctively defend her offspring by attacking any threats to its survival. This idea that aggression may be altruistic has been developed as part of the Kinship, Acceptance, and Rejection Model of Altruism and Aggression (KARMAA; Webster, 2008). This relatively new model posits that some forms of aggression may have developed as a means of protecting one's kin and/or the reputation of one's kin. Organisms may respond aggressively to kin-directed threats, which may in turn aid in the kin member's survival and reproduction.

In mammalian species where offspring are altricial and non-mobile, mothers tend to display aggressive territorial behaviors against rival females (Wolff and Peterson, 1998). This territoriality to protect offspring is usually directed against rival females, and territoriality seems to be prevalent in species who engage in infanticide of rival females' offspring. Territoriality has been observed in many carnivorous mammals, including African lions, wild dogs, coyotes, various species of voles, mice, and ground squirrels, as well as solitary primates who deposit their offspring in nests as opposed to carrying their young with them (Wolff and Peterson, 1998; Wrangham, 1987). Therefore, physical aggression may enhance the survival and reproduction of offspring; however, more social primates, such as chimpanzees, do not show territoriality because they do not leave their offspring in a stationary location.

Although humans engage in physical aggression (i.e., violence) and/or verbal aggression (e.g., insults, gossip, etc.) with the intention of harming their target, the aggressive actions may have altruistic motives. However, few studies have been conducted on altruistic aggression in humans. Thus far, research has shown that individuals will respond aggressively to protect their kin and their kin's reputation, and these aggressive responses increase as the genetic relatedness between the participant and the threatened kin member increases (Fitzgerald and Ketterer, 2011; Fitzgerald and Whitaker, 2009; Gesselman and Webster, 2012; Webster et al., 2012).

When observing non-human animals, aggression is often classified as physical attacks against a conspecific. Humans, however, have been known to engage in verbal aggression – denigrating a conspecific's reputation so as to harm his or her chances of social inclusion and reproduction – as well as physical aggression (Bjorkqvist, 1994; Buss and Dedden, 1990). Therefore, humans may engage in a variety of physically and verbally aggressive actions to protect themselves and/

or their kin. Studies have shown that this indeed seems to be the case (Fitzgerald and Ketterer, 2011; Fitzgerald and Whitaker, 2009; Gesselman and Webster, 2012; Webster et al., 2012).

On average, male humans exhibit greater levels of physical aggression than females (Bettencourt and Miller, 1996), and there is some evidence to suggest female humans exhibit greater levels of verbal aggression (Fitzgerald and Ketterer, 2011), though this latter sex difference may not apply to all situations (Bjorkqvist, 1994; Bjorkqvist et al., 1994; Buss and Dedden, 1990). Research into altruistic aggression also reflects these sex differences. Male participants indicated a greater likelihood than female participants of physically retaliating against an individual who insulted their kin (Fitzgerald and Ketterer, 2011; Gesselman and Webster, 2012). Female participants, on the other hand, indicated a greater likelihood than male participants of verbally retaliating against an individual who insulted their kin (i.e., insulting the insulter) (Fitzgerald and Ketterer, 2011; Gesselman and Webster, 2012). These retaliatory responses were stronger when the insulted kin member was a sibling than when the insulted kin member was a cousin. Retaliatory responses were weakest when the insulted target was non-kin (i.e., a friend) (Fitzgerald and Ketterer, 2011). Males are also more likely than females to physically assault someone who is attacking their kin, and participants – both males and females – are more likely to physically assault someone who is attacking their siblings than someone who is attacking their cousins (Fitzgerald and Whitaker, 2009). The data from these studies is derived from self-reported actions to hypothetical scenarios, which brings with it – as discussed earlier – its own limitations. However, the data from human samples thus far seem to generally support Webster's (2008) KARMAA, but further research into human's altruistic aggression is still needed before definitive conclusions can be made.

Suicide

Denys de Catanzaro (1984, 1995) applied inclusive fitness theory to produce an evolutionary theory of suicide. Suicide has often been considered an evolutionary puzzle (Tanaka and Kinney, 2011). There is very little evidence to suggest non-human animals engage in self-destructive behaviors such as suicide (Preti, 2007). However, suicide is regularly witnessed in humans. De Catanzaro (1984, 1995) has argued that individuals may be more likely to commit suicide if they are unable to contribute to their inclusive fitness. If an individual is no longer able to reproduce, but continues to consume a rather large amount of the resources shared with his/her kin (e.g., food, money, time, attention, etc.), that creates a cost that may decrease the probability of his/her kin reproducing (i.e., becomes a 'drain' on the kin member). The individual may then opt to end his/her own life, thus freeing up those resources, and this may improve the chances of his/her kin reproducing. Some scholars have also posited that individuals may commit suicide to reduce the risk of transmitting infection to their kin (Tanaka and Kinney, 2011).

The inclusive fitness theory of suicide is a rather controversial theory. There is evidence to suggest that suicidal ideation is positively correlated to feelings of burdening one's family (de Catanzaro, 1995) and expectations of poor future health (de Catanzaro, 1984). Self-reports in response to hypothetical vignettes involving suicide revealed people were more likely to perceive suicide as morally right when the individual who committed suicide was paralyzed (Sorjonen, 2005). Other studies have found limited support for the inclusive fitness theory of suicide (Driver and Abed, 2004; Syme et al., 2016). Evidence also suggests that suicide rates for childless women are no different from the suicide rates for women with children (Driver and Abed, 2004). Ethnographic data from 53 cultures across six continents, ranging from hunter-gatherer societies to industrialized cultures, indicated feelings of burdensomeness as a major factor among suicide victims. However, there was very little data to show that suicide resulted in improving the lives of the victim's kin. In fact, approximately 40% of the cultures studied displayed evidence that suicide resulted in worse outcomes for the victim's kin (Syme et al., 2016).

MISUNDERSTANDINGS OF INCLUSIVE FITNESS THEORY

Inclusive fitness theory is one of the most widely misunderstood theories in evolutionary psychology (Dawkins, 1979; Park, 2007). One of the most common misunderstandings relates to the *probability of inheritance (r)*. Individuals often mistakenly believe that (*r*) refers to the percentage of total genes shared between two individuals (i.e., the altruist and the recipient). For example, one may incorrectly assume that *r* = .50 indicates that two individuals share 50% of their total genes with each other. This is not the case. The probability of inheritance (*r*) refers to the probability of one individual (e.g., the recipient of an altruistic action) having a copy of the same gene that caused the altruist's behavior to occur (Hamilton, 1964).

CONCLUSION

Inclusive fitness theory (Hamilton, 1964) provides a theoretical framework to account for how various altruistic behaviors could have evolved via natural selection. For over half a decade, inclusive fitness theory has been the source of much debate and misunderstanding (Dawkins, 1979; Park, 2007; West and Gardner, 2013). Inclusive fitness theory accounts for the evolution of genes that promote social behaviors that influence other members of the same species. These social behaviors are often altruistic, but are

not limited to altruism and kin selection. Researchers around the world have found empirical support for the various altruistic and aggressive mechanisms – such as kin recognition, kin selection, reciprocal altruism, parental investment, parent–offspring conflict, and altruistic aggression – that may have survived natural selection because of the reproductive benefits they bestow upon organisms and their kin. Inclusive fitness theory may also help explain some behaviors often thought to be counterintuitive to evolution, such as suicide. While further research into these mechanisms is still needed, many of them seem to be prevalent in various social species ranging in biological complexity from insects to primates. Evolutionary psychologists, biologists, anthropologists, ethologists, primatologists, and entomologists continue to observe these social behaviors to develop a better understanding of inclusive fitness theory.

REFERENCES

Alberts, S. C. (1999). Paternal kin discrimination in wild baboons. *Proceedings of the Royal Society of London, Series B: Biological Sciences*, 266(1427), 1501–1506.

Alvergne, A., Faurie, C., & Raymond, M. (2009). Father–offspring resemblance predicts paternal investment in humans. *Animal Behaviour*, 78(1), 61–69.

Berman, C. M. (2011). Primate kin preferences: Explaining diversity. In T. K. Shackelford & C. Salmon (Eds), *The Oxford handbook of evolutionary family psychology* (pp. 248–278). New York: Oxford University Press.

Bettencourt, B. A., & Miller, N. (1996). Gender differences in aggression as a function of provocation: A meta-analysis. *Psychological Bulletin*, 119(3), 422–447.

Björkqvist, K. (1994). Sex differences in physical, verbal, and indirect aggression: A review of recent research. *Sex Roles*, 30(4), 177–188.

Björkqvist, K., Österman, K., & Lagerspetz, K. M. (1994). Sex differences in covert aggression among adults. *Aggressive Behavior*, 20(1), 27–33.

Boesch, C., Lehmann, J., & Fickenscher, G. (2006). Kin biased investment in wild chimpanzees. *Behaviour*, *143*(8), 931–955.

Bressan, P., Colarelli, S. M., & Cavalieri, M. B. (2009). Biologically costly altruism depends on emotional closeness among step but not half and full siblings. *Evolutionary Psychology*, *7*(1), 118–132.

Burnstein, E., Crandall, C., & Kitayama, S. (1994). Some neo-Darwinian decision rules for altruism: Weighing cues for inclusive fitness as a function of the biological importance of the decision. *Journal of Personality and Social Psychology*, *67*(5), 773–789.

Buss, D. M. (1996). Paternity uncertainty and the complex repertoire of human mating strategies. *American Psychologist*, *51*(2), 161–162.

Buss, D. M. (2015). *Evolutionary psychology: The new science of the mind (5th ed.)*. New York: Taylor & Francis.

Buss, D. M., & Dedden, L. A. (1990). Derogation of competitors. *Journal of Social and Personal Relationships*, *7*(3), 395–422.

Buss, D. M., Larsen, R. J., Westen, D., & Semmelroth, J. (1992). Sex differences in jealousy: Evolution, physiology, and psychology. *Psychological Science*, *3*(4), 251–256.

Charpentier, M. J. E., Peignot, P., Hossaert-McKey, M., & Wickings, E. J. (2007). Kin discrimination in juvenile mandrills, *Mandrillus sphinx*. *Animal Behaviour*, *73*(1), 37–45.

Clutton-Brock, T. H. (2002). Breeding together: Kin selection and mutualism in cooperative vertebrates. *Science*, *296*(5565), 69–72.

Clutton-Brock, T. H., O'Riain, M. J., Brotherton, P. N. M., Gaynor, D., Kansky, R., Griffin, A. S., & Manser, M. (1999). Selfish sentinels in cooperative mammals. *Science*, *284*(5420), 1640–1644.

Darwin, C. (1859). *On the origin of species by means of natural selection*. London: John Murray.

Dawkins, R. (1976). *The selfish gene*. New York: Oxford University Press.

Dawkins, R. (1979). Twelve misunderstandings of kin selection. *Zeitschrift für Tierpsychologie*, *51*(2), 184–200.

de Catanzaro, D. (1984). Suicidal ideation and the residual capacity to promote inclusive fitness: A survey. *Suicide and Life-Threatening Behavior*, *14*(2), 75–87.

de Catanzaro, D. (1995). Reproductive status, family interactions, and suicidal ideation: Surveys of the general public and high-risk groups. *Ethology and Sociobiology*, *16*(5), 385–394.

DeBruine, L. M., Jones, B. C., Little, A. C., & Perrett, D. I. (2008). Social perception of facial resemblance in humans. *Archives of Sexual Behavior*, *37*(1), 64–77.

Driver, K., & Abed, R. T. (2004). Does having offspring reduce the risk of suicide in women? *International Journal of Psychiatry in Clinical Practice*, *8*(1), 25–29.

Erhart, E. M., Coelho Jr, A. M., & Bramblett, C. A. (1997). Kin recognition by paternal half-siblings in captive *Papio cynocephalus*. *American Journal of Primatology*, *43*(2), 147–157.

Fitzgerald, C. J. (2018). Problems with group selection. In T. K. Shackelford & V. A. Weekes-Shackelford (Eds), *Encyclopedia of evolutionary psychological science*. Springer. doi.org/10.1007/978-3-319-16999-6_2127-1

Fitzgerald, C. J., & Colarelli, S. M. (2009). Altruism and reproductive limitations. *Evolutionary Psychology*, *7*(2), 234–252.

Fitzgerald, C. J., & Ketterer, H. L. (2011). Examining verbal and physical retaliation against kinship insults. *Violence and Victims*, *26*(5), 580–592.

Fitzgerald, C. J., Thompson, M. C., & Whitaker, M. B. (2010). Altruism between romantic partners: Biological offspring as a genetic bridge between altruist and recipient. *Evolutionary Psychology*, *8*(3), 462–476.

Fitzgerald, C. J., & Whitaker, M. B. (2009). Sex differences in violent versus non-violent life-threatening altruism. *Evolutionary Psychology*, *7*(3), 467–476.

Fredrickson, W. T., & Sackett, G. P. (1984). Kin preferences in primates (*Macaca nemestrina*): Relatedness or familiarity? *Journal of Comparative Psychology*, *98*(1), 29–34.

Gesselman, A. N., & Webster, G. D. (2012). Inclusive fitness affects both prosocial and antisocial behavior: Target gender and insult domain moderate the link between genetic relatedness and aggression. *Evolutionary Psychology*, *10*(4), 750–761.

Hamilton, W. D. (1964). The genetical evolution of social behaviour: I. *Journal of Theoretical Biology*, *7*(1), 1–16.

Harrison, M. L., & Tardif, S. D. (1988). Kin preference in marmosets and tamarins: *Saguinus oedipus* and *Callithrix jacchus* (Callitrichidae, Primates). *American Journal of Physical Anthropology*, *77*(3), 377–384.

Hauber, M. E., & Sherman, P. W. (2001). Self-referent phenotype matching: Theoretical considerations and empirical evidence. *Trends in Neurosciences*, *24*(10), 609–616.

Hepper, P. G. (2005). *Kin recognition*. Cambridge: Cambridge University Press.

Holmes, W. G. (1986). Kin recognition by phenotype matching in female Belding's ground squirrels. *Animal Behaviour*, *34*(1), 38–47.

Jankowiak, W., & Diderich, M. (2000). Sibling solidarity in a polygamous community in the USA: Unpacking inclusive fitness. *Evolution and Human Behavior*, *21*(2), 125–139.

Jeon, J., & Buss, D. M. (2007). Altruism towards cousins. *Proceedings of the Royal Society of London, Series B: Biological Sciences*, *274*(1614), 1181–1187.

Johnson, C., Koerner, C., Estrin, M., & Duoos, D. (1980). Alloparental care and kinship in captive social groups of vervet monkeys (*Cercopithecus aethiops sabaeus*). *Primates*, *21*(3), 406–415.

Judge, D. S., & Hrdy, S. B. (1992). Allocation of accumulated resources among close kin: Inheritance in Sacramento, California, 1890–1984. *Ethology and Sociobiology*, *13*(5), 495–522.

Kazem, A. J., & Widdig, A. (2013). Visual phenotype matching: Cues to paternity are present in rhesus macaque faces. *PLoS One*, *8*(2), e55846.

Kruger, D. J. (2001). Psychological aspects of adaptations for kin directed altruistic helping behaviors. *Social Behavior and Personality*, *29*(4), 323–330.

Langergraber, K. E., Mitani, J. C., & Vigilant, L. (2007). The limited impact of kinship on cooperation in wild chimpanzees. *Proceedings of the National Academy of Sciences*, *104*(19), 7786–7790.

Lieberman, D., Tooby, J., & Cosmides, L. (2007). The architecture of human kin detection. *Nature*, *445*(7129), 727–731.

Lu, H. J., & Chang, L. (2016). Resource allocation to kin, friends, and strangers by 3- to 6-year-old children. *Journal of Experimental Child Psychology*, *150*, 194–206.

MacKenzie, M. M., McGrew, W. C., & Chamove, A. S. (1985). Social preferences in stump-tailed macaques (*Macaca arcoides*): Effects of companionship, kinship, and rearing. *Developmental Psychobiology*, *18*(2), 115–123.

Moehlman, P. D. (1979). Jackal helpers and pup survival. *Nature*, *277*(5695), 382–383.

Neyer, F. J., & Lang, F. R. (2003). Blood is thicker than water: Kinship orientation across adulthood. *Journal of Personality and Social Psychology*, *84*(2), 310–321.

Nowak, M. A. (2006). Five rules for the evolution of cooperation. *Science*, *314*(5805), 1560–1563.

Nowak, M. A., Tarnita, C. E., & Wilson, E. O. (2010). The evolution of eusociality. *Nature*, *466*(7310), 1057–1062.

Park, J. H. (2007). Persistent misunderstandings of inclusive fitness and kin selection: Their ubiquitous appearance in social psychology textbooks. *Evolutionary Psychology*, *5*(4), 860–873.

Park, J. H., Schaller, M., and Van Vugt, M. (2008). Psychology of human kin recognition: Heuristic cues, erroneous inferences, and their implications. *Review of General Psychology*, *12*(3), 215–235.

Parr, L. A., & de Waal, F. B. M. (1999). Visual kin recognition in chimpanzees. *Nature*, *399*(6737), 647–648.

Perry, S., Manson, J. H., Muniz, L., Gros-Louis, J., & Vigilant, L. (2008). Kin-biased social behaviour in wild adult female white-faced capuchins, *Cebus capucinus*. *Animal Behaviour*, *76*(1), 187–199.

Preti, A. (2007). Suicide among animals: A review of evidence. *Psychological Reports*, *101*(3), 831–848.

Reid, C. R., Lutz, M. J., Powell, S., Kao, A. B., Couzin, I. D., & Garnier, S. (2015). Army ants dynamically adjust living bridges in response to a cost–benefit trade-off. *Proceedings of the National Academy of Sciences*, *112*(49), 15113–15118.

Seeley, T. D. (1997). Honey bee colonies are group-level adaptive units. *The American Naturalist*, *150*(Suppl 1), S22–S41.

Silk, J. B. (2002). Kin selection in primate groups. *International Journal of Primatology*, *23*(4), 849–875.

Silk, J. B. (2009). Nepotistic cooperation in non-human primate groups. *Philosophical*

Transactions of the Royal Society B: Biological Sciences, *364*(1533), 3243–3254.

Smith, K., Alberts, S. C., & Altmann, J. (2003). Wild female baboons bias their social behaviour towards paternal half-sisters. *Proceedings of the Royal Society of London, Series B: Biological Sciences*, *270*, 503–510.

Sorjonen, K. (2005). Attitudes toward suicide as a function of the victim's physical status. *OMEGA –Journal of Death and Dying*, *50*(1), 35–42.

Stewart-Williams, S. (2007). Altruism among kin vs. non-kin: Effects of cost of help and reciprocal exchange. *Evolution and Human Behavior*, *28*(3), 193–198.

Stewart-Williams, S. (2008). Human beings as evolved nepotists: Exceptions to the rule and effects of the cost of help. *Human Nature*, *19*(4), 414–425.

Syme, K. L., Garfield, Z. H., & Hagen, E. H. (2016). Testing the bargaining vs. inclusive fitness models of suicidal behavior against the ethnographic record. *Evolution and Human Behavior*, *37*(3), 179–192.

Tanaka, M., & Kinney, D. K. (2011). An evolutionary hypothesis of suicide: Why it could be biologically adaptive and is so prevalent in certain occupations. *Psychological Reports*, *108*(3), 977–992.

Thompson, J. A., & Fitzgerald, C. J. (2017). Nepotistic preferences in a computerized trolley problem. *Current Research in Social Psychology*, *25*(7), 36–44.

Trivers, R. L. (1972). Parental investment and sexual selection. In B. G. Campbell (Ed.), *Sexual selection and the descent of man, 1871–1971* (pp. 136–179). Chicago, IL: Aldine.

Vokey, J. R., Rendall, D., Tangen, J. M., Parr, L. A., & de Waal, F. B. M. (2004). Visual kin recognition and family resemblance in chimpanzees (*Pan troglodytes*). *Journal of Comparative Psychology*, *118*(2), 194–199.

Webster, G. D. (2003). Prosocial behavior in families: Moderators of resource sharing. *Journal of Experimental Social Psychology*, *39*(6), 644–652.

Webster, G. D. (2004). Human kin investment as a function of genetic relatedness and lineage. *Evolutionary Psychology*, *2*(1), 129–141.

Webster, G. D. (2008). The kinship, acceptance, and rejection model of altruism and aggression (KARMAA): Implications for interpersonal and intergroup aggression. *Group Dynamics: Theory, Research, and Practice*, *12*(1), 27–38.

Webster, G. D., Cottrell, C. A., Schember, T. O., Crysel, L. C., Crosier, B. S., Gesselman, A. N., & Le, B. M. (2012). Two sides of the same coin? Viewing altruism and aggression through the adaptive lens of kinship. *Social and Personality Psychology Compass*, *6*(8), 575–588.

Wells, P. A. (1987). Kin recognition in humans. In D. J. C. Fletcher and C. D. Michener (Eds), *Kin recognition in animals* (pp. 395–416). New York: John Wiley & Sons.

West, S. A., & Gardner, A. (2013). Adaptation and inclusive fitness. *Current Biology*, *23*(13), R577–R584.

West, S. A., Griffin, A. S., & Gardner, A. (2007). Evolutionary explanations for cooperation. *Current Biology*, *17*(16), R661–R672.

Widdig, A. (2007). Paternal kin discrimination: The evidence and likely mechanisms. *Biological Reviews*, *82*(2), 319–334.

Wolff, J. O., & Peterson, J. A. (1998). An offspring-defense hypothesis for territoriality in female mammals. *Ethology Ecology & Evolution*, *10*(3), 227–239.

Wrangham, R. W. (1987). Evolution of social structure. In B. Smuts, D. L. Cheney, R. M. Seyfarth, R. W. Wrangham, & T. T. Struhsaker (Eds), *Primate societies* (pp. 282–296). Chicago, IL: University of Chicago Press.

Wu, H. M. H., Holmes, W. G., Medina, S. R., & Sackett, G. P. (1980). Kin preference in infant *Macaca nemestrina*. *Nature*, *285*(5762), 225–227.

3

Adaptive Problems

Gary L. Brase

INTRODUCTION

Let's start with the scientifically established fact that natural selection is the mechanism by which organisms evolve. As such, evolution by natural selection is a cornerstone of biology (Dobzhansky, 1973). Although certainly true, it is a lofty and abstract statement of principle. How do we proceed from this first principle?

The where, when, and how of the actual evolution of adaptations (i.e., features of an organism shaped by evolution) is something that happens in the realm of *adaptive problems*. In particular, the specifications of what aspects of the environment constitute adaptive problems, the parameters by which those problems are solved via natural selection, and what those specifications mean for the functional structure of an organism (and of the mind, in particular) are fundamental to some of the most important insights in evolutionary psychology. At the same time, an understanding – and often misunderstandings – of these points also lead to some of the most contentious issues regarding evolutionary psychology.

This chapter is divided into three sections. The first gives an overview of what is (and is not) an adaptive problem, along with the implications for psychology. This section will make extensive reference to other chapters within this *Handbook* to help readers see the connections between various ideas. The second section delves deeper into some contentious implications of a psychological perspective informed by adaptive problems, including the modular structure of the human mind, the range and scope of evolved psychological mechanisms, and the very validity of evolutionary psychology as a field. The third section will further the discussion about the nature of adaptive problems and evolutionary psychology by comparing the evolutionary process of solving adaptive problems with the cognitive psychology literature on human problem solving.

WHAT IS AN ADAPTIVE PROBLEM?

From an evolutionary viewpoint, our minds (along with all other aspects of our phenotype) were designed over evolutionary history to solve adaptive problems. This means that there is an evolutionarily designed *functional organization* of the mind. This does not mean that other factors do not also influence our mind's structure and functioning, as will be covered later, but a great deal of our mental processes and phenomenology can be understood with a clear knowledge of the adaptive problems our minds were designed to solve.

There are variations in the definition of what an 'adaptive problem' is, but all the definitions share a number of characteristics. Consider the following examples:

- '[T]he statistically recurrent conditions encountered during hominid evolutionary history constituted a series of adaptive problems.... An adaptive problem can be defined as an evolutionarily recurrent problem whose solution promoted reproduction, however long or indirect the chain of causation by which it did so.' (Cosmides and Tooby, 1994: 87)
- 'Adaptive problems are problems that are specifiable in terms of evolutionary selection pressure – specific, stable, recurring environmental conditions that affect or have affected the reproductive success of individual organisms.' (Atkinson and Wheeler, 2004: 148)
- 'Enduring conditions in the world that create reproductive opportunities or obstacles constitute *adaptive problems*, ... Adaptive problems have two defining characteristics. First, they are conditions or cause-and-effect relationships that were regularly encountered by members of a population or species, and that recurred across sufficiently many generations such that natural selection has enough time to design adaptations in response. Second, they are that subset of enduring relationships that could, in principle, be exploited by some property of an organism to increase its reproduction or the reproduction of its relatives. Alternative designs are retained or discarded by natural selection on the basis of how well they function as solutions to adaptive problems.' (Tooby and Cosmides, 2015)

From these, we can develop a consensus definition for this chapter. Adaptive problems are:

- any aspect of an organism's situation that influences its reproduction, however indirectly (including, for example, survival);
- that situation is recurrent, such that it constitutes a statistically stable and effective influence (i.e., selection pressure);
- there are causal relationships between the situation and the organism's behavior, such that changes in behavior can influence the relationship; and
- there is some heritability of that behavior, leading to probabilistic and differential transfer of genetic material to subsequent generations based on its influences on reproduction.

From this definition it is clear that the concept of adaptive problems is intimately connected with genetics (Barbaro and Penke, Chapter 19, this *Handbook*), the process of natural selection (Betzig, Chapter 4, this *Handbook*) or sexual selection (Archer and Hosken, Chapter 1, this *Handbook*), and that an organism's inclusive fitness (Fitzgerald, Chapter 2, this *Handbook*) is a function of its ability to solve relevant adaptive problems well.

This definition is intentionally broad. It is meant to cover the concept of adaptive problems, whether applied to humans, non-human animals, or plants. It also is meant to work whether one is talking about ancestral environments, in which case the adaptive problems can have built working solutions (adaptations), or current environments which could include new adaptive problems which are as yet unsolved.

A Framework for Organizing Human Adaptive Problems

As one applies the idea of adaptive problems to humans, and in particular to the realm of psychology, a number of further details and implications emerge. These issues have led to some of the most exciting, novel, and contested ideas in evolutionary psychology.

One of these is the functional modularity in structure of the mind. In fact, the issue of modularity, including how it is related to the nature of adaptive problems, requires its own distinct section (see following section). For now it is sufficient to start with the basic idea of modularity. Because the human mind (like all other parts of the human body) evolved to provide solutions to adaptive problems, then those solutions will be specific to the particular problems. This idea is often referred to as domain-specific modularity or *massive modularity*, and is a core tenet of most evolutionary psychology views.

The rest of this section focuses on other ideas needed for a full understanding of adaptive problems and evolutionary psychology. These include the ideas of: (a) multiple levels of understanding for any given adaptive problem, (b) how evidentiary standards should be applied in the larger view afforded by evolutionary psychology, and (c) how adaptations to past environments (i.e., solutions to prior adaptive problems) can create 'mismatches' in modern environments. This section takes each of these topics in turn.

Levels of Understanding: Middle-Level Theories

A corollary of the basic argument for modularity (i.e., specific problems require specific solutions) is that, at the most general and abstract level, the adaptive problem of 'reproduce' is too vague. This is even more true if this 'top level' is elaborated to clarify the problem as being behavior that influences reproduction, however indirectly, which can include survival. This level is similar to other general directives in everyday life: 'be good', 'don't be evil', or 'make good choices'; there is very little in the way of specific guidance in these broad generalities.

To gain explanatory and predictive usefulness, the adaptive problems shaping human (and much of non-human) evolved behaviors are often carved up into classes of problems that relate to parenting, developmental lifestyle trajectories, cooperative relationships with others, and competition with others. These are called 'middle-level' evolutionary theories (Buss, 1995), and they are general classes of adaptive problems which have been long-standing for many species, including humans. As such, this is not an exhaustive list of such problem classes but a good initial organization.

Adaptive problems of parenting

Reproducing is just the first step for many species in successfully passing genes on to future generations. Those offspring – children, when referring to humans, in particular – must survive, become independent, and continue the reproductive cycle. This leads to a suite of middle-level evolutionary theories regarding parenting. Kin directed altruism (Hamilton, 1964) is one middle-level mechanism by which parents devote their efforts to helping their children survive, develop, and be successful.

Parenting efforts, furthermore, are not necessarily distributed evenly across different parents. *Parental investment theory* (Mogilski, Chapter 8, this *Handbook*; Trivers, 1972) uses differences between males and females of most species to understand and predict patterns of differential investment in offspring. For instance, humans follow the more common pattern (shared by all mammals) of females physically committing to more investment in offspring via internal fertilization, gestation, and then lactation. This leads to certain behavioral patterns being more likely, including women being more selective in mate choice, men competing with other men for access to women, and women tending to be more willing to commit further resources to offspring.

Parents and children also can either agree or disagree on the amounts and types of investment, with some of those dynamics mapped out in *parent–offspring conflict theory* (see Apostolou, Chapter 9, this *Handbook*; Trivers, 1974). There is also the possibility, still being evaluated in terms of empirical evidence, that parents may adjust the ratio of male and female offspring based on the amount and variability of opportunities in the environment (i.e., the *Trivers–Willard hypothesis*; see Salmon and Hehman, Chapter 11, this *Handbook*; Trivers and Willard, 1973). Alongside the adaptive problems of parenting there are adaptive problems related to the problems of being a very young offspring, particularly a relatively defenseless and slow developing child. Some of these adaptive problems are addressed in *attachment theory* (Mikulincer and Shaver, Chapter 15, this *Handbook*; Belsky, 1997; Simpson and Rholes, 1998).

Adaptive problems of developmental trajectories

The trajectory of offspring development is another category of adaptive problem: at a middle-level this can be thought of in terms of how much energy to devote to growth, reproduction, and parenting of the next generation. The structure of this adaptive problem is described by *life history theory* (Kruger, Chapter 12, this *Handbook*), which in many ways emerged from the concept of r/K strategies. The idea of r/K strategies (Pianka, 1970) describes how different species can allocate energetic resources differently to successfully pass genes on to a future generation. On the one hand, a species can be 'r-selected', meaning that parents devote resources to producing many offspring with little investment in each of those individuals. Few of these offspring may live to adulthood, but the large number of offspring provides a good chance some will survive. On the other hand, parents in a 'K-selected' species produce few offspring and devote resources to increase the quality and survival likelihood of them. The individual offspring have a higher chance of survival, offsetting their lesser number.

These different strategies were originally descriptions of species-typical characteristics, but they have also been used to describe facultatively adjusted characteristics within a species. The within-species dimension involves generations or individuals who move towards one or the other of these strategies based on environmental circumstances (e.g., abundant versus scarce resources and environmental stability versus instability). Once this idea of differential resource allocation shifts to within-species comparisons of individuals, it is typically referred to as life history theory (Kaplan and Gangestad, 2005; Stearns, 1992), and individuals are described as having 'fast' life history strategies (analogous to r-selected) or 'slow' life history strategies (analogous to K-selected).

Adaptive problems of cooperative relationships

As mentioned previously, kin directed altruism (Hamilton, 1964) is a middle-level theory to explain cooperation between individuals (who are related). Another evolutionary route for cooperative behavior is described by the theory of *reciprocal altruism* (Carter et al., Chapter 10, this *Handbook*; Trivers, 1971). The logic of reciprocal altruism is that two individuals can voluntarily help each other if the helping acts are conditionally exchanged (i.e., reciprocal). This pattern is related to the 'tit-for-tat' strategy in the prisoners' dilemma game, and to the 'gains in trade' idea in economics. As long as the net benefit for each person (the benefit of the received help, minus the cost of the given help) is positive over some period of repeated interactions, reciprocal altruism can evolve and be maintained.

Adaptive problems of competition with others

Cooperative interactions between people can evolve in specified situations (e.g., between kin, or with reciprocation), but outside of those situations the question is about whether other people can be disregarded or not. Often they cannot be ignored, because the others constitute competition for some limited resource or their interests do not align with one's own in some other way. For example, humans have a number of middle-level issues revolving around mate choice. One of these issues is that a particular person you would like to pair with may not share the same feelings. Another issue is that there may be others who are interested in the same potential partner. These are situations of inter-sexual conflict (the former) and intra-sexual conflict (the latter). Competition and conflict can, of course, extend up to larger scales of society and include homicides, warfare, and genocides. It also can extend down to very small levels such as individual tissues and cells (see *sexual conflict theory*, Rostant et al., Chapter 14, this *Handbook*). For example, *sperm competition theory* (DeLecce and Pham, Chapter 13, this *Handbook*) describes the evolved mechanisms by which one male's sperm competes with another male's sperm in order to successfully reproduce with a female. This occurs within the context of two males having relations with the same female within a relatively brief window of time. Given that context, there are physiological processes that evolved to improve one's conception chances, impair the chances of competing sperm, and physically block other sperm (Baker and Bellis, 1995). Additionally, there are also a host of related adaptations involving the psychological and behavioral patterns associated with emotions, thoughts, and actions to gain advantage or forestall such a competition happening in the first place (e.g., Hoier, 2002, Leivers et al., 2014; Shackelford et al., 2002).

Finally, many of the competitive interactions between species can be described as co-evolutionary arms races, often resulting in a dynamic equilibrium. This type of situation is described by the Red Queen hypothesis (Van Valen, 1973; Ridley, 1994). Co-evolutionary races happen across species, such as when plants evolve toxins and thorns as defenses against animals that would eat them, then those animals evolve resistance to those toxins or appendages that evade thorns (and then the plants evolve more toxins, different physical defenses, and the animals evolve further counter-measures, and so on). The dynamic equilibrium is maintained by both actors evolving over time to help attain their antagonistic goals, yet neither species ever attains a definitive advantage that completely overwhelms the other. Similar dynamics can occur between individuals of the same species who are in competition for the same resources (Dawkins and Krebs, 1979), and several aspects of sperm competition appear to be examples of this.

Levels of Understanding: Computational Frameworks

As just illustrated, one method for developing and understanding more specific adaptive problems is to break down the global issue (to reproduce) into more specific classes of problems (e.g., to cooperate, to compete, to parent, and so on). A second method for understanding adaptive problems is to break those middle-level theories of adaptive problems down with more formal frameworks designed to analyze such systems. In many evolutionary psychology approaches, these activities are based on Marr's (1982) computational framework for information processing systems. Marr's computational approach originated in vision science, spread through much of cognitive psychology, and then increasingly has been utilized elsewhere, including in evolutionary psychology.

Marr's framework divides any information processing task into three different levels of analysis: the computational level, the algorithmic level, and the hardware/implementation level (Figure 3.1). The computational level describes the purpose of the information processing system. In other words, what is the problem to be solved and why is it a problem? The algorithmic level describes the relevant inputs into the system, the algorithmic transformations of those inputs, and the resulting outputs. The hardware/implementation level describes the physical instantiation of those algorithms.

Marr's computational framework delivers a number of benefits, much like several other

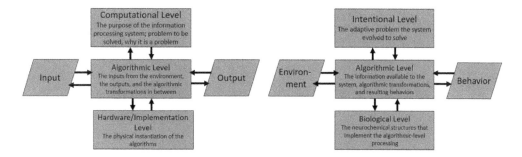

Figure 3.1   Marr's original computational framework (left), and a revision based specifically on evolved biological systems (right; adapted from Cosmides and Tooby, 1995)

systems that have developed levels of analysis to clarify theoretical/conceptual issues, (see Stanovich, 1999, for a summary). For the specific context of biological systems, however, Cosmides and Tooby (1995) point out that there are further constraints on what constitute both possible and plausible computational theories. For example, evolutionary biology can provide a more precise definition of Marr's 'goal' of processing at the computational level: it is a demand to identify the adaptive problem which led to that particular adaptation. Similarly, the hardware/implementation level is the neuroscientific level of the underlying brain circuits. The algorithmic level is most directly connected to cognitive models of the information processing activities. This framework often underlies the use of the term *evolved psychological mechanisms*, in describing adaptations (Lewis et al., Chapter 6, this Handbook).

Another framework that is sometimes used for attaining levels of understanding of an evolved trait is Tinbergen's Four Questions (Tinbergen, 1963). This model comes from ethology, rather than psychology, and has some different advantages and disadvantages relative to Marr's framework (see Brase, 2014 for a discussion of these). The Tinbergen model overlaps in many ways with Marr's framework: the adaptive function and phylogeny questions (ultimate level of analysis) roughly map onto Marr's Computational/ Intentional level of explanation (Figure 3.1),

and the ontogeny and proximate causation questions generally map onto Marr's other two levels (Sherman, 1988; Figure 3.2). The areas of less overlap include Tinbergen's focus on developmental processes (ontogenetically for individuals and phylogenetically for species), and Marr's focus on parsing the proximate factors more finely (distinguishing information processing and physical structures). In principle, though, it is possible to leverage the overlaps and advantages of both models (Brase, 2014).

Evidentiary Standards

Evolutionary psychology, by both its origins and design, is aggressively multidisciplinary. One consequence of this multidisciplinarity is that ideas are often evaluated, not just through the lens of one particular field, but through different lenses of various fields. This evaluation gauntlet can be daunting, but also scientifically rewarding. Why? Because ideas that hold up across different perspectives, methodologies, and standards of evidence are likely to be true. This approach towards evaluating ideas goes by various names, including consilience (Whewell, 1847/1967), abductive inference/inference to the best explanation (Peirce, 1903), and the method of converging operations (Garner, 1954; Garner et al., 1956; see Sternberg et al., 2001, for a summary). In basic terms,

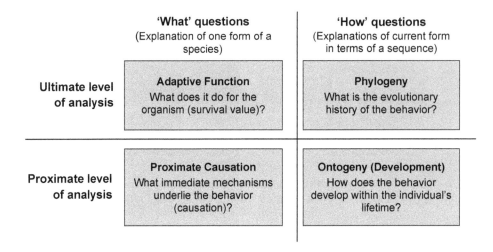

Figure 3.2   Tinbergen's four levels of analysis, as organized by Sherman (1988)

this approach involves the use of multiple, independent, and converging lines of evidence (Brase, 2014).

Schmitt and Pilcher (2004), taking an explicitly evolutionary approach, built a framework of specific guidance about what can constitute the multiple, independent, and converging lines of evidence when studying human adaptations (Figure 3.3). This converging evidence framework includes, at its heart, a hypothesized adaptation. Describing the adaptive problem that led to that adaptation is one of the lines of evidence (Theoretical 'Evidence': the quotation marks

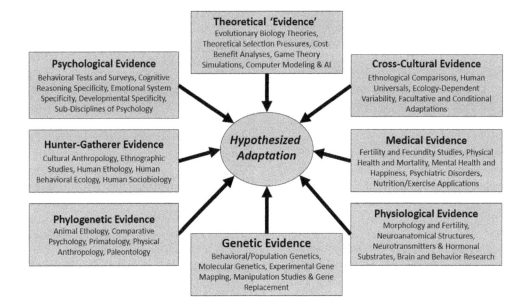

Figure 3.3   Converging evidence framework

Source: Adapted from Schmitt and Pilcher (2004: 645).

indicate that this is more properly the starting point for positing the hypothesized adaptation rather than a subsequently marshaled line of independent evidence).

Many research efforts in the behavioral sciences have used, and continue to use, Tinbergen's, Marr's, or Schmitt and Pilcher's frameworks with varying degrees of utility and success. Each framework has been useful and has enriched the development of scientific knowledge. But each framework also has inherent limitations, which tend to be reflected in the bodies of research produced based on them (see Brase, 2014, for an effort to integrate these frameworks).

To some extent, the field of evolutionary psychology is very well positioned to use interdisciplinary, converging lines of evidence. It is explicitly encouraged, for example, by prominent researchers (e.g., Tooby and Cosmides, 1995:1190–1191). The multidisciplinary nature of evolutionary psychology is also manifested in the range of chapters within this *Handbook*. Evolutionary biology forms the foundation of most chapters in Part 2 of this *Handbook* and can provide what the Schmitt and Pilcher framework calls theoretical lines of evidence: things such as theorized evolutionary selection pressures, cost–benefit analyses, game theory simulations, and computer modeling. Cross-species comparisons (Vonk et al., Chapter 16, this *Handbook*) correspond to phylogenetic lines of evidence: information about either common ancestry or convergent evolution from (non-human) ethology, comparative psychology, primatology, physical anthropology, and paleontology. Cross-cultural methods (Apostolou, Chapter 17, this *Handbook*) clearly map onto cross-cultural (and hunter-gatherer) lines of evidence: the similarities and systematic, ecology-dependent variability across human cultures.

Schmitt and Pilcher's framework contains a line of evidence from psychological research, which includes a wide array of topics and methodologies (e.g., studies of cognitive reasoning, judgment and decision making, memory, attention, language, emotional reactions,

and social behaviors). Also included in this area would be (within cultures) research on sex differences and sex similarities (Davies, Chapter 20, this *Handbook*), and other individual differences (Marsh, Chapter 21, this *Handbook*). Medical and clinical dimensions of evolutionary approaches (Nesse, 2019) can constitute medical lines of evidence, including work on physical health, mental health, and reproductive outcomes. Neuroscientific methods (Mundale, Chapter 18, this *Handbook*) map onto Schmitt and Pilcher's physiological lines of evidence (physical morphology, neuroanatomical structures, neurotransmitters, and hormonal bases). Genetics and behavioral genetics (Barbaro and Penke, Chapter 19, this *Handbook*) research corresponds to genetic lines of evidence, which includes studies of behavioral/population genetics, molecular genetics, experimental gene mapping, gene manipulation, and gene replacement. Finally, developmental research (Sweller, 2020), while not in the original Schmitt and Pilcher (2004) framework, is worth including here because it is prominent as Tinbergen's ontogeny question (and can be considered a friendly addition; Schmitt, personal communication). The developmental line of evidence includes information about clear, sequential progressions of abilities and features across development, in typical environments, and in the absence of developmental disorders.

The EEA: Past as Prologue

Another major concept that connects with the topic of adaptive problems is the relevant timeframe for adaptive problems and the adaptations that evolved to address them. There is, of course, a necessary temporal order that an adaptive problem must first exist in the environment before the evolutionary process can react to it by selecting for an adaptation that addresses that problem. In other words, all adaptations are to past environments (more specifically, to the adaptive problems that existed in the past). The relevant past environment for an adaptation is referred to as the Environment of Evolutionary Adaptedness (EEA: Bowlby, 1969; Crawford, 1998; Hagen and Symons, 2007). Because a very large proportion of this EEA for humans as a species occurred during the Pleistocene era, this is often used as a basic benchmark for the EEA (e.g., Cosmides and Tooby, 1994a: 87). More properly, though, the EEA is not just the Pleistocene era; it may extend further back in time and it may extend forward to the present (e.g., see Tooby and Cosmides, 1990).

The EEA is always (even if implicitly) with reference to a particular adaptation, and the length of each EEA is the entire timeframe in which the selection pressures existed to create and maintain that adaptation. Thus, the EEA for color vision is many millions of year – preceding the successful evolution of adaptations for seeing color, through its development, and continuing to the present day. The EEA for infants digesting lactose would begin somewhere prior to the emergence of mammalian nursing and extend to modern times. In contrast, the EEA for being able to digest lactose into and throughout adulthood would begin with the domestication and availability of milk for adult consumption – probably less than 10,000 years ago.

Because of these long, sometimes open-ended timeframes for an EEA – not to mention the differences across local environments when considering the population of a species within any given timeframe – an EEA is not any one time or place. Instead, an EEA is the statistical composite of all the environments (which provided the relevant selection pressures) that posed a particular adaptive problem for the individuals of a particular species.

Understanding the EEA as a relevant factor in evolution leads to some interesting implications. The adaptations of organisms, including humans, were shaped by long stretches of past environments (i.e., their EEAs). Modern humans, by contrast, live in a radically different environment than in that evolutionary past. We live in world with videoconferencing, jet travel, abundant sugars and fats in our foods, temperature controlled buildings, nuclear weapons, and Beyoncé. Yet our minds are designed for the world of generations past, not the 21st century. The relentlessly historical nature of adaptations, being based on the cumulative EEAs that built them, means that some of those adaptations are not well designed for the modern environment. When an adaptation leads to poorer results in the current environment, this situation is often referred to as a 'mismatch' (e.g., see Hagen, 2005). Evolutionary mismatches have been documented or argued to be factors in domains ranging from food choices (e.g., Logan and Jacka, 2014), to mental disorders (e.g., Silove, 1998), to gambling behaviors (e.g., Spinella, 2003), to media consumption (Davis and McLeod, 2003) and consumer behavior (Hantula, 2003).

Of course, many of these mismatches are not complete disjunctions but rather the result of changes in the modern human environment happening at a pace that outstrips the speed of evolutionary adaptation. Adaptive problems of food choice, sexual behavior, and so on still exist, but the nature and structure of these problems have shifted (sometimes substantially). In this sense, then, the selective pressures posed by those adaptive problems are ongoing – and we are still in the EEA for that adaptive problem – but both the speed of environmental change and the heavy statistical weight of its EEA past lead to changes too small or slow to readily see.

Similarly, there are probably aspects of the modern environment that constitute new adaptive problems, but they are unlikely to have had time for the resulting selection pressures to impact heritable adaptations. They have a brief EEA, relative to many other adaptive problems and their resulting adaptations. And, of course, the more complex the potential adaptation that might result from a modern adaptive problem, the more time it would need in order to evolve.

THE DEVIL IS IN THE MODULARITY DETAILS

The argument for domain-specific modularity (briefly described earlier) is that specific problems usually need specific solutions. This is sometimes explained with a 'Swiss Army knife' analogy: one single blade would be very good for a few tasks (cutting, stabbing), but very poor at doing most other tasks (opening cans, opening wine bottles, sawing, punching small holes, filing nails, removing screws, etc.). Instead, different tools customized for solving each of these different problems are each differentially most effective at tackling those particular tasks. The criteria of what counts as a successful solution to each problem (or doing each task) is what causally determines the shape and other properties of each tool. This is more extensively described, for example, by Cosmides and Tooby (1994a: 89):

> In the first place, the more important the adaptive problem, the more intensely natural selection specializes and improves the performance of the mechanism for solving it. This is because different adaptive problems often require different solutions, and different solutions can, in most cases, be implemented only by different, functionally distinct mechanisms. Speed, reliability, and efficiency can be engineered into specialized mechanisms because there is no need to engineer a compromise between competing task demands. Competing task demands can, however, be handled by separate, specialized systems. This accounts for the pervasive empirical finding that natural selection tends to produce functionally distinct adaptive specializations, such as a heart to pump blood, a liver to detoxify poisons, an immune system to defeat infections. As a rule, when two adaptive problems have solutions that are incompatible or simply different, a single general solution will be inferior to two specialized solutions. In such cases, a jack of all trades is necessarily a master of none, because generality can be achieved only by sacrificing effectiveness. Consequently, domain-specific cognitive mechanisms, with design features that exploit the stable structural features of evolutionarily recurring situations, can be expected to systematically outperform (and hence preclude or replace) more general mechanisms that fail to exploit these features.

You may notice that the second half of this quote shifts to a negative argument: the lack of viability for an alternative possibility of more general systems. Thus, there is both a positive argument for domain-specific modularity and a negative argument about alternatives (domain-general, non-modular/minimally modular systems). This negative argument is based on empirical and theoretical considerations from cognitive science about the feasibility of domain-general systems as mechanisms to solve problems. Most of this work comes from experiences such as building artificial intelligence and computer simulations, along with reverse engineering known mental abilities such as vision and language. The overall conclusion drawn within many of these topics (although not universally, as we will see) is that domain-general, content-independent systems are 'weak': either they cannot solve problems or they reach poor solutions.

Based on this negative argument, evolutionary psychology proponents argue that this domain-general approach is *de facto* unworkable. Based on the positive argument, they argue that the domain-specific modularity approach is the obvious alternative. The idea of adaptive problems leads to the hypothesis of massive modularity being the predominate architecture of human (and other animals') minds. Of all the objections that can and have been raised against evolutionary approaches in psychology, however (e.g., see Hagen, 2005), this topic has been among the longest lasting and most substantive. At the same time, it should be pointed out that this issue exists on a continuum rather than two dichotomous options. The argument is about the *relative amount* of domain specificity.

The history of psychology, and the social sciences generally, created a formidably embedded default position of relative domain generality in terms of the mind's structure and environmentally derived content (e.g., equipotentiality of association assumptions in learning, the 'blank slate' ethos, cultural relativism, and postmodernism). Even as full-throated support of these theoretical paradigms has waned in recent decades, some of the implicit assumptions of a domain-general mental structure continue to be unexamined and adopted by many researchers (for a discussion, see Pinker, 2002). Proposing a massively modular architecture for the human mind, therefore, is nearly antithetical to a strong theoretical tradition in most of western psychology. The idea that the mind is a general-purpose organ for 'thinking' is embedded in the generic nature of research topics such as learning, reasoning, decision making, memory, and social behavior. Reactions to the idea of massive modularity range from disbelief at the very notion, to rejection on principle (e.g., by appealing to 'parsimony'), to rejection based on uncomfortable inferred implications. These reactions are extensively considered and evaluated by Carruthers (2005; 2006a; 2006b; 2006c; 2008a; 2008b), and found to be predominantly based on incorrect understandings of what was being proposed and how the massive modularity thesis has been derived. The following section summarizes much of that evaluation.

The Massive Modularity Controversy

The fundamental question underlying any discussion about the degree of modularity in the mind is: *how can we most accurately characterize the nature of human cognitive architecture*? Even as evolutionary psychology is multidisciplinary, its foundation is in psychology. As such, the massive modularity thesis of evolutionary psychology runs directly against a history of theorizing in psychology that has been minimally modular. Movements such as British empiricism, behaviorism, cultural determinism, and parallel distributed processing have focused on how to get the diversity and complexity of human behaviors with the least possible prior structure (Pinker, 2002) and a correspondingly implied maximum responsibility for the environment. As such, many areas of psychology to this day hold a default ideological position of a sparse architecture filled with domain-general and content-independent modules that handle vast jobs (e.g., semantic memory, attention, reasoning, decision making, helping behavior, aggression, and so on).

Prior to evolutionary psychology, some areas of psychology encountered the idea of modularity in the form of Fodor's *The Modularity of Mind*. Fodor (1983) made a forceful and now widely accepted argument for a particular degree of modularity in human cognitive architecture. Fodor's modularity focused on the input elements (e.g., the various senses) and the output elements (e.g., language and motor movement) of the mind, while retaining the central processes of the mind as continuing to be domain-general and content-independent (i.e., non-modular). This was, at the time, a radical step to propose any type of modular structure, anywhere in the mind. The modularity of mind proposed by Fodor (1983) described characteristics that the modular parts of the mind were posited to have. These included domain specificity, encapsulation, mandatory operation (automaticity), inaccessibility to consciousness, speed, shallow outputs, fixed neural localization, and characteristic breakdown patterns. These suggestions subsequently became somewhat enshrined as necessary properties defining modularity, although this does not appear to have been the original intent (Coltheart, 1999; Barrett and Kurzban, 2006). Later, even Fodor (2000) came to assert that encapsulation, at least, was a necessary property.

Evolutionary psychology, however, comes to the position of modularity via the principle of adaptations that evolved to solve specific adaptive problems (Tooby and Cosmides, 1992), and has largely considered Fodor's properties of modules to be ill-founded. Instead, an evolutionary view of modularity focuses on key properties being formally definable informational inputs and functional specialization (i.e., design features) to produce solutions to evolutionary adaptive problems. Having informational inputs that are constrained by some criteria is important in order to focus the cognitive mechanism on situations that constitute the adaptive problem. ('For example, systems specialized for assessing the numerosity of objects accept only representations previously parsed into distinct objects; systems specialized for speech perception process only transduced representations of sound waves; and systems specialized for making good food choices process only representations relevant to the nutritional value of different potential food items,' Barrett and Kurzban, 2006: 630). Once the information input parameters are satisfied (even if that is done by some means of re-representation or partial distortion), the functionally specialized computational processes of a module allow inferences and other outputs to occur.

Fodor's ideas about modularity were not informed by evolutionary thinking to any meaningful extent, but when evolutionary psychologists raised the idea of modularity in the human mind some people quickly assumed that it referred to Fodorian modularity. They were wrong. Evolutionary modularity quickly went much further than Fodor with the idea of a modular structure of the mind (see Brase, 2003). Evolutionary modularity proposes that functional modularity extends all the way into the parts of the human mind that Fodor reserved as central processing. Furthermore, the rigid characteristics of Fodor's modularity concept were not part of the definition of modularity for evolutionary theorists, notwithstanding attempts by others to impose those characteristics as definitional (Barrett, 2005, 2015; Barrett and Kurzban, 2006).

As the scope and scale of evolutionary massive modularity became clear, it evoked various reactions. One of the reactions against the evolutionary modularity idea was that of simple, personal incredulity at the idea. Appeals to personal disbelief came in different forms. 'Massive Modularity' (Sperber, 1994, 2001)

was coined as a term to express the radical nature of this as a position. For his part, Fodor described the evolutionary psychology position as 'modularity gone mad' (Fodor, 1987: 27; see further discussion on this by Sperber, 1994: 40).

A smattering of biologists, philosophers, and psychologists have attempted to argue against the massive modularity thesis by using similar appeals to personal disbelief. Sometimes this approach is supplemented by vague suggestions of alternatives or by appeals to more domain-general traditions. For example, Lloyd (1999) claims, with little supporting evidence, that domain-general mechanisms could possibly produce adaptive behavior (220) and also suggests vaguely that 'other evolutionary processes – involving chance genetic sampling, various kinds of constraints on variation and development, and phylogenetic history – are ever present, and may even be more powerful than natural selection in the production of a given evolutionary outcome of interest' (223). Such claims are particularly odd given that massively modular structures in organism design are ubiquitous in biology (see West-Eberhard, 1996, 2003).

Similarly, Bolhuis et al. (2011) incorrectly claim that massive modularity is not supported by the neuroscientific evidence, and that 'comparative psychology presents an unassailable case for the existence of domain-general mechanisms' (3, citing themselves and associative learning theories). When Bolhuis et al. (2011) attempt a specific and tractable argument, such as 'there is broad involvement of diverse neural structures in many psychological processes, and there is feedback even to the most basic perceptual processing', their supporting citation is to a textbook (Striedter, 2005). That textbook, though, makes a strong, evidence-based case for extensive modularity (Striedter, 2005: 248–9; see also an array of empirical findings, e.g., Bertolero et al., 2018). All of these (and other) criticisms of massive modularity that are based on an incorrect conflation with Fodor's positions led Carruthers (2008b: 302) to summarize:

> The take-home message is that philosophers of mind need to liberate themselves from the baleful shadow cast by Fodor's (1983), recognizing that there are many more ways of conceiving of, and defending, a massively modular mind than was ever thought of in Fodor's philosophy. And once so liberated, there are many more possibilities for explaining the distinctive properties of human and animal minds, also.

Bolhuis et al. (2011) commit this fallacy of equating evolutionary massive modularity with Fodor's ideas about modularity, then taking Fodor's positions as gospel despite clear indications that this is wrong (e.g., 'Massive modularity is a somewhat idiosyncratic interpretation of Fodor's original concept of modularity': p. 3). As a result, even when Bolhuis and colleagues succeed in showing that evolutionary massive modularity does not satisfy one of Fodor's modularity criteria, their conclusions are non sequiturs. It is analogous to arguing that because a tablet computer does not have pages like a book, it therefore cannot be a thing that people read.

There is perhaps one substantive and important point made out of the critiques of massive modularity as a cognitive architecture. This critique, which becomes more a raising of an important question, is *the grain problem*. The grain problem, in short, is the following: if adaptive problems within specific domains tend to build adaptations that are similarly domain-specific in their proper scope of application, it becomes crucial to clearly define the granularity, or the particular conceptual resolution, of that reference domain. Is the domain 'large' or 'small'? In particular, this chapter earlier discussed how the general goal of reproduction could be broken down into middle-level theories (e.g., parental investment theory, parent–offspring conflict theory, and life history theory). These middle-level evolutionary theories, however, are still a 'coarse-grained' view of adaptive problems, and each of them can be broken down into more specific ('finer-grained')

adaptive problems. Metaphorically, the gain of domains for adaptive problems is like the resolution on a television or camera: very low resolution is vastly better than nothing, but higher resolution allows for better images and understanding. But then what is the 'correct' level, or grain, at which to talk about adaptive problems? And by extension, what is the level (or levels) at which one should talk about adaptations, domain specificity, and other topics? That is the grain problem.

The modularity grain problem was initially pointed out by Sterelny and Griffiths (1999; see also Sterelny, 1995). Sterelny and colleagues decided that the grain problem was insurmountable and that evolutionary psychology was therefore untenable (see discussion of personal incredulity, above). Atkinson and Wheeler (2004; Atkinson et al., 2002; Wheeler and Atkinson, 2001) took a deeper and more balanced approach to the grain problem. Atkinson and Wheeler conclude that 'once the explanatory endeavours of evolutionary psychologists are seen under these lights [i.e., using converging evidence from a number of different levels of organization; see earlier section], the worry that progress in evolutionary psychology is stymied by the grain problem turns out to be unfounded' (2004:163).

A number of prominent evolutionary psychology researchers, meanwhile, continued to clarify their theoretical position. These included ever more clear rejections of the Fodorian criteria for modularity as definitional features, and several different conceptual models to illustrate alternative architectures for a massively modular mind (e.g., Barrett, 2005, Barrett and Kurzban, 2006; Brase, 2003; Cosmides et al., 2010). Fodor's informationally encapsulated criteria for modularity (i.e., the operation of a module is independent of information from any other modules) is perhaps the most clearly rejected by evolutionary models. Barrett (2005) used a metaphor of an 'enzymatic' architecture of massive modularity, in which information is available relatively openly, but admitted into a computational device only when the information had certain criteria properties (i.e., much like the 'lock-and-key' functionality of enzymes). Brase (2003) suggested a similar type of open system based on a signal detection theory model. These systems note that, while it could still be possible to have some modules that are informationally encapsulated within such systems, it is not in any way a definitional – and probably not even a diagnostically useful – property. Another interesting modular structure from an evolutionary viewpoint was proposed by Klein et al. (2002), focusing primarily on human memory. This memory structure includes both domain-specific memory contents (e.g., semantic memories and episodic memories) and domain-specific memory search/retrieval processes (along with learning mechanisms, inference systems, and decision rules). These mechanisms are interconnected based on the information needs of particular adaptive problems they were designed to solve (i.e., regulated but definitely not encapsulated).

FROM HUMAN PROBLEM SOLVING TO ADAPTIVE PROBLEMS SOLVING

The realization in the evolutionary sciences that specific adaptive problems tend to create specific solutions is not unique to that area of science. The relative efficiency and accuracy of specific solutions for specific problems has been rediscovered several times (e.g., as the frame problem in artificial intelligence, as the poverty of the stimuli issue in linguistics, as the problem of referential ambiguity in semantics, as the need for constraints on induction in cognitive developmental psychology, as the situation of stimuli underdetermining interpretations in perception, and as the problem of indeterminacy in philosophy; see Tooby and Cosmides, 1992, for a review). There is a broad principle at work throughout these instances: effective, accurate, and reliable responses to a specific type

of situation is usually best achievable via processes that recognize and take advantage of the situation-specific properties and constraints.

Another parallel case of specific problems driving domain-specific solutions is found in research on *human problem solving* in cognitive psychology. There is a substantial history of psychological research on problem solving as a mental activity, and one of the core insights has been that better problem solving generally comes from more specifically tailored solution methods. In the terminology of the area, more narrowly focused problem solving techniques constitute a computationally stronger method, whereas very general problem solving techniques tend to be computationally weak methods (Simon et al., 1981). The reason for this advantage is that problem solving focused on a narrow set of problems can incorporate more specific information and constraints about the problem to be solved, thus avoiding combinatorial explosion of the possible solution actions. Although there can be some situations in which broadly applicable, computationally weak methods are useful and necessary, these are situations when the problem itself is either unavoidably general or the problem solver understands so little of the problem domain that it is effectively a general problem to them.

Of course, human problem solving and evolved adaptations to solve adaptive problems are not isomorphic situations. Human problem solving is typically done by a single person, with willful intent, over a fairly short and discrete time period. Adaptations are shaped through evolution by natural selection with no foresight or intention, and the process occurs over many generations and centuries. Nevertheless, the parallels between effective human problem solving behaviors and evolutionary solutions to adaptive problems are numerous and interesting. Many of these parallels come from the fact that both contexts involve similar basic properties of defining what constitutes a problem, the process of searching conceptual space for solutions, and the necessary elements for achieving those solutions.

A Brief History of Problem Solving Research

Even the history of research on human problem solving involves some parallels with the emergence of evolutionary psychology. Theoretical visions of human problem solving as an activity began with general processes conducted by general mechanisms, but that has gradually been overtaken by a recognition that the most effective problem solving strategies are more tailored and domain-specific. In particular, an early view of problem solving was based on the gradual associative learning of reproduction (n.b., here 'reproducing' refers to the re-producing of prior behaviors which had led to positive effects; Thorndike, 1898). For example, a cat placed in a 'puzzle box' crate would initially engage in various behaviors before happening upon the one behavior (say, stepping on a paddle) that opens the crate door and allows the cat access to food. Over repeated experiences of being put in the puzzle box and then opening it by stepping on the paddle, the cat gradually comes to the paddle-stepping behavior more quickly. One explanation of this gradual association between the puzzle box, the behavior that opens it, and the food that results, is that there is a very general associative learning mechanism. This general learning mechanism was then presumed to be the source of all learning.

Associative learning as in the above scenario is a valid phenomenon. In particular, the associative learning model of problem solving behavior was (and still is) particularly viable within evolutionarily novel contexts and problem situations. For example, suppose an animal is put into an operant conditioning chamber with a light cue signaling that a lever press will deliver a food reward. It is safe to say that this is an evolutionarily novel context, not recurrently experienced by that animals' ancestors in any inclusive fitness relevant way. As contexts shift in any conceptual direction towards a situation that resembles an EEA adaptive problem, though, the general associative learning model tends to encounter 'problems'. These problems are, in fact, more specific evolved mechanisms designed to solve particular adaptive problems.

If the learning context involves choices between different foods and nausea (and especially if the organism is an omnivore), then the situation is likely to tap into more specific learning and problem solving mechanisms that produce conditioned taste aversion (Garcia and Koelling, 1966). In fact, a variety of learning situations about food selection – a major adaptive problem for omnivores – can tap into specific evolved mechanisms. Rats (a favorite research participant in this area) will taste only a little bit of a novel food to assess its safety. They will taste a novel food which they smelled on the breath of another rat (but not when smelled on another part of a rat or on a dead rat; Bolles, 1970; Domjan, 1983; Rozin and Kalat, 1971). Hungry rats more easily learn to alternate going to different arms of a maze for food rewards, compared to thirsty rats learning to alternate maze arms for water. Petrinovich and Bolles (1954) pointed out that this pattern is consistent with the ecological circumstances in which rats evolved: foraging for food in different places but repeatedly looking for water in the same place.

These are not just phenomena found in rats. Specific evolved solutions have similarly evolved to deal with adaptive problems of food selection in humans and other animals. More broadly there are similarly specialized adaptations designed to effectively deal with adaptive problems ranging from language (Chomsky, 1965), to infant attachment (Bowlby, 1969), to predator avoidance (Öhman et al., 2001; Öhman and Mineka, 2001, 2003).

The domain-general and content-independent approach to problem solving, like the idea of learning as a general process, persisted for quite a while, up to and including the cognitive ideas of the General Problem Solver (GPS) and means–end heuristic (Newell and Simon, 1972). However, as computational models of human problem solving developed they inexorably pushed the field to consider more domain-specific and content-specific approaches. A particularly influential idea within the field of human problem solving was that of problem-space theory (Newell and Simon, 1972). This framework conceptualizes a problem situation as an abstract problem space that encompasses the representation of all the possible states and associated operations relevant to the problem, including the initial starting state and the goal state. A problem space of this sort is often visualized in the form of a decision tree or Venn diagram. The problem solver then 'travels' from the starting state, through the problem space, and ends at the goal state.

It turns out that fully describing a problem space creates a *well-defined* problem: that is, the initial state, the possible operations, and the goal state are all completely specified. Once a problem is well defined, it is easily solved (at least in principle). For example, games such as checkers, chess, football, and baseball are generally well defined. The starting locations of everything and everybody are specified, the permissible (and not permissible) moves are spelled out, and the goal (for 'winning') is clearly understood. A well-defined problem can be optimally solved by a procedure that finds the shortest pathway between the initial and goal states. Such solutions often use algorithmic methods, systematically and exhaustively evaluating all possible states and operations in the problem space. The optimal solution is thus guaranteed to be discovered given unlimited time and computational power (e.g., one can discover any security password by trying all possible combinations). The challenges in these well-defined problem situations are mainly from the sheer size of the problem space (e.g., in chess) and the unpredictability of human actors (e.g., in sports). The computational demands of navigating the problem

space using general methods (e.g., mapping the entire space beforehand) are almost always intractable.

Nearly all real-world problem situations, however, are not well defined; they are *ill defined* to some extent (Simon, 1973). Ill-defined problems have some amount of uncertainty in the initial state, the permissible operations, or the goal state (or some combination of these). Ill-defined problems are usually not easily solved, either in principle or in practice, and even defining what an optimal solution would look like may be impossible.

Dealing with ill-defined problems – nearly all the problems of actual living – requires different approaches than dealing with well-defined problems. Algorithmic methods will not work well for ill-defined problems (even in theory, given unlimited time and computational power), because the problem space is not fully specified. The alternative approach to problem solving is referred to as heuristic methods. Heuristics are strategies, or rules of thumb, that can be applied to a problem and that often help generate a solution. Rather than exploring all of the conceptual problem space, heuristics are designed to identify and attempt the solution paths that are higher probability options based on some prior knowledge of the problem space characteristics (e.g., one can try to discover a security password by guessing what the password-creator would have set it as). Algorithmic methods do not guarantee a solution, and they certainly do not promise optimality, but they can work under limitations of knowledge, time, and computational power.

Ill-defined problems (which, remember, make up nearly all real-world problems) are often dealt with using several complementary solution tactics:

- Solutions to ill-defined problems generally involved domain-specific knowledge and procedures.
- When ill-defined problems are very large or ambiguous (e.g., creating world peace, being happy, don't be evil), they can often be broken down into smaller problems. As the sub-problems get more specific, they often also gain some tractable

properties – becoming less ill structured – and relevant domain-specific knowledge and procedures emerge. This can form a cycle with the first point.

- Because optimality of solutions can be problematic for ill-structured problems (e.g., it is difficult to know you have the best possible solution when the goal state itself is unclear), ill-structures problem solving often aims for *satisficing*. Satisficing is when the objective is to reach an end state that solves the basic problem (often defined as reaching some acceptability threshold), without being concerned about if it is the best possible solution.

Satisficing is ubiquitous in evolved solutions to adaptive problems. An individual does not need to get the most food possible or run as fast as possible; they only need to get enough food to survive and they only need to run fast enough to escape predators (or to catch some prey).

Expertise in Problem Solving

Many of these general conclusions about how human problem solving works come from research on experts in a particular area, usually comparing these experts to beginners in that same area. Expertise is, in a basic sense, superior problem solving ability for some particular domain. For example, some of the early research of this type compared chess masters to amateurs (de Groot, 1965; Chase and Simon, 1973). Other work on expertise and problem solving has utilized people with expertise in physics, computer programming, and radiology (for overviews, see Chi et al., 1982, 1988; Green and Gilhooly, 1992).

So what makes someone an expert? One thing that these studies converge on is that experts have large amounts of domain-specific knowledge, both in terms of information and procedures (n.b., this is a different and independently developed use of 'domain-specific' from the phrase as used in evolutionary psychology). Experts also use the structure of the problem in the environment to inform and

organize all that domain-specific knowledge. For instance, chess masters organize and 'chunk' their chess information in memory in order to simplify (or even enable) the task of addressing the problem of a particular game they are playing.

The semi-convergent use of 'domain-specific' as a term in both evolutionary psychology and the study of expertise in problem solving is interesting. As discussed above, there are some parallels between these two fields that help to make sense of this convergence. In some ways, though, this overlapping terminology can be misleading. Domain specificity in evolutionary psychology has implications for modularity, selection pressures, levels of explanation, and so on. Domain specificity in the study of expertise simply refers to the particular topic in which an expert has built her expertise, and that such expertise does not transfer elsewhere. The 'domains' of expertise have little in the way of constraints; they are simply the topics in which experts exist. Furthermore, the nature of this research is such that the domains of expertise which are typically studied are highly unlikely to be the same as the domains of adaptive problems. The domains for which humans have adaptations to address specific adaptive problems – such as language – will tend to be areas in which pretty much all normally developing people arguably qualify as 'experts'.

Looking at what happens within a domain (be it of expertise or of an evolved adaptation), there are some informative parallels to further point out. Both in the study of human expertise and in evolutionary psychology, there are indications that the domain specificity of solutions to adaptive problems extends to both memory/information systems and to procedural/algorithmic systems. These systems are intertwined (*contra* Fodor), and likely have ongoing interactions while problem solving (e.g., see previous description of Klein et al., 2002).

Information from the environment is extensively structured by the perceiver in order to make it useful for solving particular problems. This is the case for the topical knowledge of experts, and it is also the case throughout the cognitive system: perceptual and memory systems differentially attend to particular bits of information, parse the world in specific ways, and categorize the results as certain concepts. Much of this is so ingrained in our mind's functioning that it can be difficult to not think of the world apart from this structuring (Cosmides and Tooby, 1994b). Using the terminology of expertise, the evolved computational mechanisms of the mind 'chunks' information in ways that are evolutionarily meaningful and will fit into the various adaptations for solving different adaptive problems. Those adaptations, once activated, tend to further impose particular problem representations much like experts applying their developed knowledge representations.

More speculatively, it has been argued in various ways that evolved adaptations sometimes include emotion feedback systems to guide behavior. Actions that tended to solve adaptive problems over evolutionary history will also tend to 'feel right', whereas actions that tended to not solve adaptive problems will 'feel wrong' (e.g., Pinker, 1997). This may be conceptually parallel to the phenomenon noted with experts in which they develop meta-cognitive skills within their expertise domains. These include intuitive senses of things like 'error awareness' and 'time allocation' that alert experts to when things are going well or going astray.

CONCLUSION

There are a number of parallels between the nature of evolved solutions to adaptive problems and the nature of expertise in human problem solving. Implications of these parallels can potentially travel in either direction.

On the one hand, evolutionary insights raise implications for cognitive psychology

of problem solving and expertise. For instance, the pursuit of effective but totally domain-general problem solving (or general expertise) is probably a fool's errand. A system with greater flexibility in solving a wide area of problems is much more likely to come from having a large number of domain-specific problem solving mechanisms (e.g., a lot of experts from different areas, tasked with a common general goal). Furthermore, as societies become more advanced, meaning that the nature of everyday lives is ever more divorced from the EEAs in which our minds evolved, we should expect that there will be more and more topics in which there are experts: people who have developed the non-intuitive knowledge of details and procedures for that topic.

On the other hand, the cognitive psychology of problem solving and expertise can provide insights about evolutionary adaptations to adaptive problems. For instance, one can think of the process of evolution by natural selection, as it builds responses to adaptive problems, as essentially a problem solving process moving through an abstract problem space. There is an initial state (the species as it currently exists), a set of permissible operations (constraints on evolvability), and a goal state (an effective adaptation). It is an ill-defined problem in a number of respects, of course, but the processes are the same at a certain theoretical level (see Barrett, 2015, for a similar discussion of conceptual space and adaptations).

REFERENCES

Atkinson, A. P., & Wheeler, M. (2003). Evolutionary psychology's grain problem and the cognitive neuroscience of reasoning. In K. J. Gilhooly (Series Ed.) & D. E. Over (Vol. Ed.), *Current Issues in Thinking and Reasoning. Evolution and the Psychology of Thinking: The Debate* (pp. 61–99). Hove, UK; New York: Psychology Press.

Atkinson, A. P., & Wheeler, M. (2004). The grain of domains: The evolutionary-psychological case against domain-general cognition. *Mind and Language*, *19*(2), 147–176. doi.org/10.1111/j.1468-0017.2004.00252.x

Baker, R. R., & Bellis, M. A. (1995). *Human Sperm Competition: Copulation, Masturbation, and Infidelity*. London: Chapman & Hall.

Barrett, H. C. (2005). Enzymatic computation and cognitive modularity. *Mind and Language*, *20*(3), 259–287. doi.org/10.1111/j.0268-1064.2005.00285.x

Barrett, H. C. (2015). *The Shape of Thought: How Mental Adaptations Evolve*. Oxford: Oxford University Press.

Barrett, H. C., & Kurzban, R. (2006). Modularity in cognition: Framing the debate. *Psychological Review*, *113*(3), 628–647. doi.org/10.1037/0033-295X.113.3.628

Belsky, J. (1997). Attachment, mating, and parenting: An evolutionary interpretation. *Human Nature*, *8*(4), 361–381. doi.org/10.1007/BF02913039

Bertolero, M. A., Yeo, B. T. T., Bassett, D. S., & D'Esposito, M. (2018). A mechanistic model of connector hubs, modularity and cognition. *Nature Human Behaviour*. doi.org/10.1038/s41562-018-0420-6

Bolhuis, J. J., Brown, G. R., Richardson, R. C., & Laland, K. N. (2011). Darwin in mind: New opportunities for evolutionary psychology. *PLoS Biology 9*(7), e1001109. doi.org/10.1371/journal.pbio.1001109

Bolles, R. C. (1970). Species-specific defense reactions and avoidance learning. *Psychological Review*, *77*(1), 32–48. psycnet.apa.org/doi/10.1037/h0028589

Bowlby, J. (1969). *Attachment and Loss*. New York: Basic Books.

Brase, G. L. (2003). The allocation system: Using signal detection processes to regulate representations in a multi-modular mind. In K. J. Gilhooly (Series Ed.) & D. E. Over (Vol. Ed.), *Current Issues in Thinking and Reasoning. Evolution and the Psychology of Thinking: The Debate* (pp. 11–32). Hove, UK; New York: Psychology Press.

Brase, G. L. (2014). Behavioral science integration: A practical framework of multi-level converging evidence for behavioral science theories. *New Ideas in Psychology*, *33*, 8–20. doi:10.1016/j.newideapsych.2013.11.001

Buss, D. M. (1995). The future of evolutionary psychology. *Psychological Inquiry*, *6*(1), 81–87.

Carruthers, P. (2005). Distinctively human thinking: Modular precursors and components. In P. Carruthers, S. Laurence, & S. Stich (Eds), *The Innate Mind. Vol. 1: Structure and Contents*. Oxford: Oxford University Press.

Carruthers, P. (2006a). The case for massively modular models of mind. In R. Stainton (Ed.), *Contemporary Debates in Cognitive Science*. Oxford: Blackwell.

Carruthers, P. (2006b). *The Architecture of the Mind: Massive Modularity and the Flexibility of Thought*. Oxford: Oxford University Press.

Carruthers, P. (2006c). Simple heuristics meet massive modularity. In P. Carruthers, S. Laurence, and S. Stich (Eds), *The Innate Mind. Vol. 2: Culture and Cognition*. Oxford: Oxford University Press.

Carruthers, P. (2008a). Précis of *The Architecture of the Mind: Massive Modularity and the Flexibility of Thought*. *Mind and Language*, *23*(3), 257–262. doi.org/10.1111/j.1468-0017.2008.00340.x

Carruthers, P. (2008b). On Fodor-fixation, flexibility, and human uniqueness: A reply to Cowie, Machery, and Wilson. *Mind and Language*, *23*(3), 293–303. doi.org/10.1111/j.1468-0017.2008.00344.x

Chase, W. G., and Simon, H. A. (1973). The mind's eye in chess. In W. G. Chase (Ed.), *Visual Information Processing* (pp. 215–281). New York: Academic Press.

Chi, M. T. H., Glaser, R., & Rees, E. (1982). Expertise in problem solving. In R. J. Sternberg (Ed.), *Advances in the Psychology of Human Intelligence, Vol. 1*. Hillsdale, NJ: Lawrence Erlbaum Associates.

Chi, M. T. H., Glaser, R., & Farr, M. J. (1988). *The Nature of Expertise*. Hillsdale, NJ: Lawrence Erlbaum Associates.

Chomsky, N. (1965). *Aspects of the Theory of Syntax*. Cambridge, MA: The MIT Press.

Coltheart, M. (1999). Modularity and cognition. *Trends in Cognitive Sciences*, *3*(3), 115–120. doi.org/10.1016/S1364-6613(99)01289-9

Cosmides, L., & Tooby, J. (1994a). Origins of domain specificity: The evolution of functional organization. In L. A. Hirschfeld & S. A. Gelman (Eds), *Mapping the Mind: Domain Specificity in Cognition and Culture* (pp. 85–116). New York: Cambridge University Press.

Cosmides, L., & Tooby, J. (1994b). Beyond intuition and instinct blindness: Toward an evolutionarily rigorous cognitive science. *Cognition*, *50*(1–3), 41–77.

Cosmides, L., & Tooby, J. (1995). From function to structure: The role of evolutionary biology and computational theories in cognitive neuroscience. In M. S. Gazzaniga (Ed.), *The Cognitive Neurosciences* (pp. 1199–1210). Cambridge, MA: The MIT Press.

Cosmides, L., Barrett, H. C., & Tooby, J. (2010). Adaptive specializations, social exchange, and the evolution of human intelligence. *Proceedings of the National Academy of Sciences*, *107*(Supplement 2), 9007–9014. doi.org/10.1073%2Fpnas.0914623107

Crawford, C. (1998). The theory of evolution in the study of human behavior: An introduction and overview. In C. Crawford & D. L. Krebs (Eds), *Handbook of Evolutionary Psychology: Ideas, Issues, and Applications* (pp. 3–42). Mahwah, NJ: Lawrence Erlbaum Associates.

Dawkins, R., & Krebs, J. R. (1979). Arms races between and within species. *Proceedings of the Royal Society of London B: Biological Sciences*, *205*(1161), 489–511. doi. org/10.1098/rspb.1979.0081

Davis, H., & McLeod, S. L. (2003). Why humans value sensational news: An evolutionary perspective. *Evolution & Human Behavior*, *24*(3), 208–216. doi.org/10.1016/S1090-5138(03)00012-6

de Groot, A. D. (1965). *Thought and Choice in Chess*. The Hague: Mouton.

Dobzhansky, T. (1973). Nothing in biology makes sense except in the light of evolution. *The American Biology Teacher*, *35*(3), 125–129. doi: 10.2307/4444260

Domjan, M. (1983). Biological constraints on instrumental and classical conditioning: Implications for general process theory. In G. H. Bower (Ed.), *The Psychology of Learning and Motivation, Vol. 17* (pp. 215–277). New York: Academic Press.

Fodor, J. A. (1983). *The Modularity of Mind: An Essay on Faculty Psychology*. Cambridge, MA: The MIT Press.

Fodor, J. A. (1987). Modules, frames, fridgeons, sleeping dogs, and the music of the spheres. In J. L. Garfield (Ed.), *Modularity in Knowledge Representation and Natural-Language Understanding* (pp. 25–36). Cambridge, MA: The MIT Press.

Fodor, J. A. (2000). *The Mind Doesn't Work That Way: The Scope and Limits of Computational Psychology*. Cambridge, MA: The MIT Press.

Garcia J., & Koelling, R. A. (1966). Relation of cue to consequence in avoidance learning. *Psychonomic Science*, *4*(1), 123–124.

Garner, W. R. (1954). Context effects and the validity of loudness scales. *Journal of Experimental Psychology*, *48*(3), 218–224.

Garner, W. R., Hake, H. W., & Eriksen, C. W. (1956). Operationism and the concept of perception. *Psychological Review*, *63*(3), 149–159.

Green, A. J. K., & Gilhooly, K. J. (1992). Empirical advances in expertise research. In M. T. Keane & K. J. Gilhooly (Eds), *Advances in the Psychology of Thinking, Vol. 1*. (pp. 45–70). Hemel Hempstead, UK: Harvester Wheatsheaf.

Hagen, E. H. (2005). Controversial issues in evolutionary psychology. In D. M. Buss (Ed.), *The Handbook of Evolutionary Psychology* (pp. 145–173). Hoboken, NJ: John Wiley & Sons.

Hagen, E. H., & Symons, D. (2007). Natural psychology: The environment of evolutionary adaptedness and the structure of cognition. In S. W. Gangestad & J. A. Simpson (Eds), *The Evolution of Mind: Fundamental Questions and Controversies* (pp. 38–44). New York: The Guilford Press.

Hamilton, W. D. (1964). The genetical evolution of social behaviour. I, II. *Journal of Theoretical Biology*, *7*(1), 1–52.

Hantula, D. A. (2003). Guest editorial: Evolutionary psychology and consumption. *Psychology & Marketing*, *20*(9), 757–763. doi.org/10.1002/mar.10095

Kaplan, H. S., & Gangestad, S. W. (2005). Life history theory and evolutionary psychology. In D. M. Buss (Ed.), *The Handbook of Evolutionary Psychology* (pp. 68–95). Hoboken, NJ: John Wiley & Sons. doi. org/10.1002/9780470939376.ch2

Klein, S. B., Cosmides, L., Tooby, J., & Chance, S. (2002). Decisions and the evolution of memory: Multiple systems, multiple functions. *Psychological Review*, *109*(2), 306–329. doi:10.1037/0033-295X. 109.2.306

Leivers, S., Rhodes, G., & Simmons, L. (2014). Sperm competition in humans: Mate guarding behavior negatively correlates with ejaculate quality. *Plos ONE*, *9*(9), e108099. doi:10.1371/journal.pone.0108099

Lloyd, E. A. (1999). Evolutionary psychology: The burdens of proof. *Biology and Philosophy*, *14*(2), 211–233. doi.org/10.1023/A:1006638501739

Logan, A. C., & Jacka, F. N. (2014). Nutritional psychiatry research: An emerging discipline and its intersection with global urbanization, environmental challenges and the evolutionary mismatch. *Journal of Physiological Anthropology*, *33*(1), 22. doi.org/10.1186/1880-6805-33-22

Marr, D. (1982). *Vision: A Computational Investigation into the Human Representation and Processing of Visual Information*. San Francisco: W. H. Freeman.

Nesse, R.M. (2019). *Good Reasons for Bad Feelings: Insights from the Frontier of Evolutionary Psychiatry*. New York: Dutton (Penguin Random House).

Newell, A., & Simon, H. A. (1972). *Human Problem Solving*. Englewood Cliffs, NJ: Prentice-Hall.

Öhman, A., Flykt, A., & Esteves, F. (2001). Emotion drives attention: Detecting the snake in the grass. *Journal of Experimental Psychology: General*, *130*(3), 466–522. doi.org/10.1037/0096-3445.130.3.466

Öhman, A., & Mineka, S. (2001). Fear, phobias, and preparedness: Toward an evolved module of fear and fear learning. *Psychological Review*, *108*(3), 483–522. doi.org/10.1037/0033-295X.108.3.483

Öhman, A., & Mineka, S. (2003). The malicious serpent: Snakes as a prototypical stimulus for an evolved module of fear. *Current Directions in Psychological Science*, *12*(1), 5–9. doi.org/10.1111%2F1467-8721.01211

Peirce, C. S. (1903). Harvard lectures on pragmatism. *Collected Papers, Vol. 5*. Cambridge, MA: Harvard University Press

Petrinovich, L., & Bolles, R. (1954). Deprivation states and behavioral attributes. *Journal of Comparative and Physiological Psychology*, *47*(6), 450–453.

Pianka, E. R. (1970). On r- and K-selection. *The American Naturalist*, *104*(940), 592–597.

Pinker, S. (1997). *How the Mind Works*. New York: W. W. Norton & Co.

Pinker, S. (2002). *The Blank Slate: The Modern Denial of Human Nature*. New York: Viking.

Ridley, M. (1994). *The Red Queen: Sex and the Evolution of Human Nature*. New York: Macmillan.

Rozin, P., & Kalat, J. W. (1971). Specific hungers and poison avoidance as adaptive specializations of learning. *Psychological Review*, *78*(6), 459–486. psycnet.apa.org/doi/10.1037/h0031878

Schmitt, D. P., & Pilcher, J. J. (2004). Evaluating evidence of psychological adaptation: How do we know one when we see one? *Psychological Science*, *15*(10), 643–649.

Shackelford, T. K., LeBlanc, G. J., Weekes-Shackelford, V. A., Bleske-Rechek, A. L., Euler, H. A., & Hoier, S. (2002). Psychological adaptation to human sperm competition. *Evolution & Human Behavior*, *23*(2), 123–138. doi.org/10.1016/S1090-5138(01)00090-3

Sherman, P. W. (1988). The levels of analysis. *Animal Behaviour*, *36*(2), 616–619.

Silove, D. (1998). Is posttraumatic stress disorder an overlearned survival response? An evolutionary-learning hypothesis. *Psychiatry: Interpersonal and Biological Processes*, *61*(2), 181–190. doi.org/10.1080/00332747.1998.11024830

Simon, H. A. (1973). The structure of ill-structured problems. *Artificial Intelligence*, *4*(2), 181–201.

Simon, H. A., Langley, P. W., & Bradshaw, G. L. (1981). Scientific discovery as problem solving. *Synthese*, *47*(1), 1–27.

Simpson, J. A., & Rholes, W. S. (1998). *Attachment Theory and Close Relationships*. New York: The Guilford Press.

Sperber, D. (1994). The modularity of thought and the epidemiology of representations. In L. A. Hirschfeld and S. A. Gelman (Eds), *Mapping the Mind: Domain Specificity in Cognition and Culture* (pp. 39–67). New York: Cambridge University Press.

Sperber, D. (2001). In defense of massive modularity. In E. Dupoux (Ed.), *Language, Brain, and Cognitive Development: Essays in Honor of Jacques Mehler* (pp. 47–57). Cambridge, MA: The MIT Press.

Spinella, M. (2003). Evolutionary mismatch, neural reward circuits, and pathological gambling. *International Journal of Neuroscience*, *113*(4), 503–512. doi.org/10.1080/00207450390162254

Stanovich, K. E. (1999). *Who is Rational? Studies in Individual Differences in Reasoning*. Mahwah, NJ: Lawrence Erlbaum Associates.

Stearns, S. C. (1992). *The Evolution of Life Histories*. Oxford: Oxford University Press.

Sterelny, K. (1995). The adapted mind. *Biology and Philosophy*, *10*(3), 365–380. doi.org/10.1007/BF00852474

Sterelny, K., & Griffiths, P. E. (1999). *Sex and Death: An Introduction to Philosophy of Biology*. Chicago, IL: The University of Chicago Press.

Sternberg, R. J., Grigorenko, E. L., & Kalmar, D. A. (2001). The role of theory in unified psychology. *Journal of Theoretical and Philosophical Psychology*, *21*(2), 99–117.

Striedter, G. F. (2005). *Principles of Brain Evolution*. Sunderland, MA: Sinauer Associates.

Sweller, J. (2020). Evolutionary Educational Psychology. In T. K. Shackelford (Ed), *The Sage Handbook of Evolutionary Psychology: Integration of Evolutionary Psychology with Other Disciplines* (pp. 191–206). London: SAGE.

Thorndike, E. (1898). Some experiments on animal intelligence. *Science*, *7*(181), 818–824.

Tinbergen, N. (1963). On aims and methods in ethology. *Zeitschrift für Tierpsychologie*, *20*(4), 410–433.

Tooby, J., & Cosmides, L. (1990). The past explains the present: Emotional adaptations and the structure of ancestral environments. *Ethology and Sociobiology*, *11*(4–5), 375–424. doi.org/10.1016/0162-3095(90)90017-Z

Tooby, J., & Cosmides, L. (1992). The psychological foundations of culture. In J. H. Barkow, L. Cosmides, & J. Tooby (Eds.), *The Adapted Mind: Evolutionary Psychology and the Generation of Culture* (pp. 19–136). New York: Oxford University Press.

Tooby, J., & Cosmides, L. (1995). Mapping the evolved functional organization of mind and brain. In M. S. Gazzaniga (Ed.), *The Cognitive Neurosciences* (pp. 1185–1197). Cambridge, MA: The MIT Press.

Tooby, J., & Cosmides, L. (2015). The theoretical foundations of evolutionary psychology. In D. M. Buss (Ed.), *The Handbook of Evolutionary Psychology*. Hoboken, NJ: John Wiley&Sons.doi.org/10.1002/9781119125563.evpsych101

Trivers, R. L. (1971). The evolution of reciprocal altruism. *The Quarterly Review of Biology*, *46*(1), 35–57. doi.org/10.1086/406755

Trivers, R. L. (1972). Parental investment and sexual selection. In B. G. Campbell (Ed.), *Sexual Selection and the Descent of Man 1871–1971* (pp. 136–179). Chicago, IL: Aldine.

Trivers, R. L. (1974). Parent–offspring conflict. *American Zoologist*, *14*(1), 249–264.

Trivers, R. L., & Willard, D. E. (1973). Natural selection of parental ability to vary the sex ratio of offspring. *Science*, *179*(4068), 90–92. doi.org/10.1126/science.179.4068.90

Van Valen, L. (1973). A new evolutionary law. *Evolutionary Theory*, *1*, 1–30.

West-Eberhard, M.-J. (1996). Wasp societies as microcosms for the study of development and evolution. In S. Turillazzi & M. J. West-Eberhard (Eds), *Natural History and Evolution of Paper-Wasps* (pp. 290–317). Oxford: Oxford University Press.

West-Eberhard, M.-J. (2003). *Developmental Plasticity and Evolution*. Oxford: Oxford University Press.

Wheeler, M., & Atkinson, A. (2001). Domains, brains, and evolution. In D. M. Walsh (Ed.), *Naturalism, Evolution and Mind (Royal Institute of Philosophy Supplement 49)* (pp. 239–266). Cambridge: Cambridge University Press. doi:10.1017/CBO9780511563843.012

Whewell, W. (1847/1967). *The Philosophy of the Inductive Sciences, founded upon their history, 2nd Edition* (facsimile reprint). New York: Johnson Reprint Corp.

Differential Reproduction

Laura Betzig

INTRODUCTION

Almost 35 years after HMS *Beagle* docked at Falmouth, Darwin published his essay on *The Descent of Man*. Because it was relevant, he attached an essay on *Selection in Relation to Sex*. He noted that, across species, males tend to be better ornamented, and better armed, than females. And that his own species was no exception. From the Australian aborigines he'd watched toss their spears in Sydney, to the native North Americans he'd read about in his study, to the Trojan warriors he'd studied in the Latin Classics, to the South Americans he knew well from Tierra del Fuego, Darwin knew that men everywhere compete for women. And he put their sex differences down, in the most tentative terms, to the amount of effort that mothers and fathers usually devote to their young. 'The female has to expend much organic matter in the formation of her ova, whereas the male expends much force in fierce contests with his rivals,

in wandering about in search of the female, in exerting his voice, pouring out odoriferous secretions, &c' (Darwin, 1874, v.2: 224; with Darwin, 1860, 1/29/1833, 1/12/1836; see also Horace, *Satires* 1.3; Trivers, 1972).

For most of the 200,000 or more years since the evolution of *Homo sapiens*, reproduction has been fairly egalitarian. First south of the Sahara, then across Eurasia about 100,000 years ago, then into Australia around 65,000 years ago, then down through the Americas over the last 20,000 years, most people lived in groups of a few families and had children by one or more mates. Ethnographic, demographic, and genetic evidence suggests that reproductive differentials were small. Some men mated with more than one woman; and some women mated with more than one man. But monogamy was common. Most people had one mate at a time.

Then over the past 10,000 years, we settled down and started to farm. First in the Near East and North Africa around 5000 years ago, then across the Old World in India and China, then in North and South America, civilizations were built. Historical, demographic, and genetic evidence suggest that reproductive differentials shot up. Some men mated with many women. But many men went without.

THE PALEOLITHIC

People evolved in Africa. *H. sapiens* started out on the savannahs of the sub-Sahara, where they lived by hunting and gathering. As far as we now know, for the past 200,000 or more years, most humans across continents were foragers (Lee and Daly, 1999; Kelly, 2013; Richter et al., 2017).

Genetic, demographic, and ethnographic evidence – from the Ju/'hoansi to the Aka to the Hadza across Africa, to the Pumé and Ache in the Americas, to the Meriam of Australia – suggests that most men and women were monogamous. Over the course of a lifetime, some men fathered 10 or more children. But few men fathered none. On every inhabited continent, across Paleolithic time, there were in the order of two breeding women for every one breeding man.

Ethnography

The Hadza live in Africa's Rift Valley, around Lake Eyasi, near the Serengeti. When Ibn Battuta, the Moroccan explorer, sailed down the east coast of Africa in the 1330s, he stopped at the 'Shaykh's palace' in Mogadishu, where a eunuch came out with a plate of areca nuts. But he probably found few hunters and gatherers: the Hadza have remained fairly isolated from their neighbors for thousands of years (Ibn Battuta, *Travels* 1.3; Scheinfeldt et al., 2019). By the time the British zoologist, Nicholas Blurton Jones, and the American anthropologist, Frank Marlowe, came to live with the Hadza in the 1980s and 90s, they found a population of around a thousand.

Like most foragers, they promoted fairness; but some foragers did better than others. 'Hunters get more women,' is how one Hadza summed up (Blurton Jones, 2016: 264, 301). Fewer than 1 in 20 men had two wives at once, and no man had more than two at a time. But men with reputations as better hunters – who brought in more food per hour, and had higher overall food returns – tended to marry more often. They married at younger ages; they married younger women; and they fathered more children. 'Hadza males have greater variance in both births and living children than do females,' at least partly as a result (Marlowe, 2010:167; see also Hawkes and Bliege Bird, 2002; Marlowe, 2003).

As early as the 5th century BC, Herodotus of Halicarnassus wrote about people 'of less than middle height', who lived across 'a waterless and sandy desert'. They either captured their interlopers, or ran off: 'The small men used to abandon their settlements and escape to the hills' (Herodotus: 2.32, 4.43). The American anthropologist, Barry Hewlett visited their remote descendants, the Central African Aka of the Congo Basin, in 1973, and continued to visit them for more than 40 years. Their egalitarianism was stark. Aka men, like Aka women, fed, cleaned, soothed, kissed, carried, and played with their children; Aka women, like Aka men, spent all day, almost every day, tracking and trapping game. But Aka leaders were invariably male. Elephant killers, or *tuma*, were more likely to become leaders, or *kombeti*; and *kombeti* tended to have more wives and to father more children than other men. As Hewlett put it: 'Unlike the Aka women, the men had greater reproductive variability' (Hewlett, 1988, 1991:18).

When Vasco da Gama, the Portuguese explorer, led four ships toward the Cape of Good Hope on his way to India in 1497, he met the Khoisan. Mistaking them for 'men of little spirit, quite incapable of violence', the captain-major and three or four others were wounded by their assegais, or spears (da Gama, *Journal* 11/8/1497, 11/12/1497).

Nearly 500 years later, the Canadian anthropologists, Nancy Howell and Richard Lee, rode into the Kalahari in the 1960s, where they met Khoisan parents who chose husbands for their daughters, and preferred candidates who were good with those spears. Poorer hunters – 14 out of 28 men in the 19- to 28-year-old group – were unmarried; better hunters had wives. But nobody over 40 had never been married, and most men over 50 had been married more than twice. For this group of foragers, who called themselves the 'Real People', or Ju/'hoansi: 'Clearly reproductive success is more unequally distributed among men than it is among women, when whole lifetimes are examined' (Howell, 2000: 269; see also Lee, 1979; Cashdan, 1980; and Wiessner, 2002, 2009, on good hunters).

When Columbus made landfall in the Bahamas in October of 1492, he found natives 'as naked as their mothers bore them'. And in a letter written on the way home, he confided: 'In all these islands, it seems to me that all men are content with one woman, and to their chief or king they give as many as 20' (Columbus, *Diario* 10/11/1492; *Letter* 1493).

Others who lived in the New World would make do without *caciques*. On the Venezuelan savannahs, or *llanos*, south of the Bahamas, Pumé foragers hunt for small game and fish, and gather roots and fruit. The American anthropologist Karen Kramer, with help from the American archaeologist Russell Greaves, has collected censuses and reproductive histories for the Pumé since 1990, and put together a dataset that covers a full 25 years. She's found that most Pumé are serially polygamous. But that roughly 2 in 10 women, and roughly 1 in 10 men, spend time in a polygynous relationship, where more than one woman cohabits with just one man. As a result, once again, reproductive variance among women is lower than reproductive variance among men (e.g., Kramer et al., 2009; Kramer et al., 2017).

Contacted in the 1630s and 40s by the Spanish Jesuit, José de Insaurralde, the Ache of Paraguay got by with little or no hierarchy:

'They don't recognize *caciques*' (Lozano, 1873, v.1: 418). The American anthropologist, Kim Hill, showed up at the Manduvi mission in Paraguay on the first day of 1978. With the anthropologist Ana Magdalena Hurtado, and other collaborators, he'd go on to study the Ache for nearly 30 years. Across the tropical forest highlands south of the Amazon Basin, they collect honey, palm starch, and fruit; but the bulk of their diet comes from meat. And some hunters provide more than others. The households of married men tend to be calorie consumers; single men, usually young men, subsidize everybody else. Some older Ache become serial polygynists; they abandon older wives in order to marry younger women. Other older Ache marry two or more women at a time, with the usual effects on sex differences in reproductive variance. 'It is evident that the variance in cumulative fertility for men is much higher at each age than that observed for women' (Hill and Hurtado, 1996: 45–6, 277–8; Hill and Hurtado, 2009; Hill and Kaplan, 1988).

When James Cook stepped ashore at Botany Bay on his first trip into the Pacific in April of 1770, his assessment of the indigenes was kind. 'They live in a tranquility which is not disturbed by the inequality of condition; the earth and sea of their own accord furnishes them with all things necessary for life' (Cook, *Journals* 5/6/1770, 23/8/1770). But some Australians were more egalitarian than others. When the anthropologists Merton Hart and Arnold Pilling lived on Bathurst and Melville islands in the 1920s and 50s, they agreed that some men had unusually large numbers of women. Hart found that one elder, Turimpi, who was born in the 1830s, had had sons in the prime of life and had collected more than 20 wives. Others of Turimpi's generation had married as many as 22, 25, and 29 women. And the young men hunted for them. 'Tiwi men did very little hunting once they were past about 45, though they hated to admit their hunting days were over. The meat, fish, and game provided for the large household of an old man was obtained by the young' (Hart and Pilling, 1960:17, 34; see also Goodale, 1971).

To the east of Bathurst and Melville Islands, in the 21st century, the spear fishers and turtle hunters of Mer Island are more likely to be monogamous, but the reproductive variance of men remains greater than the reproductive variance of women. Rebecca Bliege Bird, Doug Bird, and Eric Alden Smith, who first studied the Meriam in the 1990s, found that successful hunters become fathers at younger ages, father children by more women, and have above-average age-specific reproductive success (Smith et al., 2003; Smith, 2004; Table 4.1).

Demography

For most contemporary hunter-gatherers, ranges and variances in reproductive success tend to hover in, or around, single digits. At the high end, Ache men report a variance of 15.05, and Pumé men report completed fertilities that range from 4–19. At the low end, among the Ju/'hoansi, men report completed fertilities of 0–12, with a variance of just 8.60.

The figures are similar for forager women. At the low end, Ju/'hoansi women report a range of just 1–9 live births, and the variance for Ache women is just 3.57. At the high end, both Ache and Hadza women report giving birth to 0–12 children, and the variance for the Hadza is 7.70. In these and other forager cultures, the most reproductively successful fathers have more children than the most reproductively successful mothers. But overall, sex differences among hunter-gatherers are consistently small (Betzig, 2012, 2016; Table 4.1; Figure 4.1).

Table 4.1 Range, mean and variance in reproductive success for foragers and farmers

	Male				Female			
	Range	$\bar{X}$	σ^2	N	Range	$\bar{X}$	σ^2	N
Foragers								
Ache (Paraguay)[1]	0–13	6.40	15.05	48	0–12	7.84	3.57	25
Aka (CAR)[2]	0–14	6.34	8.64	29	2–11	6.23	5.20	34
Hadza (Tanzania)[3]	0–16	4.55	14.31	95	0–12	4.58	7.70	93
Ju/'hoansi (Botswana)[4]	0–12	5.14	8.60	32	1–9	4.69	4.87	62
Meriam (Australia)[5]	0–12	3.63	11.69	19	0–11	2.06	6.43	49
Pumé (Argentina)[6]	4–19	7.83	13.25	18	1–11	7.67	5.67	18
Farmers[7]								
Aztec	57D+60S							
Chinese	47S							
Egyptian	53D+50D							
Incan	400D+S							
Indian	101S							
Near East	118S							

CAR = Central African Republic; D = reported daughters; S = reported sons

Notes:

1 Number of live births for men and women aged 50–70 (see Hill and Hurtado, 1996)

2 Number of live births for men and women over age 41 (see Hewlett, 1988)

3 Number of children born to men and women aged 18 and over (see Marlowe, 2010; with Blurton Jones, 2016)

4 Number of children born to men 50 or over and women 45 and over (see Howell, 2000)

5 Number of children born to men and women aged 50 and over (see Smith et al., 2003)

6 Number of children born to men and women 45 and over (Karen Kramer, 2019, personal communication)

7 For historical sources, see main text

Genetics

Genetic evidence is consistent. Across contemporary populations – including the Khoisan – genetic estimates of the breeding sex ratio are consistently biased in favor of women. Autosomal, Y chromosome, and mitochondrial DNA samples from across continents suggest that fewer males than females have contributed genes to descendant generations. For most of our genetic history, the ratio of breeding women to breeding men has been in the order of 2:1. People have been polygynous (Hammer et al., 2008; Lippold et al., 2014).

Other geographically diverse samples of Y chromosome sequences suggest a couple of reproductive bottlenecks over the course of human evolution. One from around 40,000 to 60,000 years ago coincides with *H. sapiens'* move out of Africa into Eurasia by a small number of colonizers. More females than males contributed to that expansion; in that case, the effective breeding population among women was more than twice the effective breeding population among men (Karmin et al., 2015; see also Wilson Sayres et al., 2014). Those ratios increased with the Neolithic.

THE NEOLITHIC AND AFTER

Civilization began in the Near East. Around 10,000 years ago, *H. sapiens* settled down and started to farm. They lived in cities, where they started to keep administrative documents: the writing that became history. As civilizations spread out across the Old and New Worlds, they left records on parchment and papyrus, metal and stone. And they left records in our genes.

Genetic, demographic, and historical evidence – from the Near East to the Nile Delta, from the Indus and Ganges to the Long and Yellow River Valleys, from Mesoamerica to the Andes – suggest that the emperors who built the first empires were polygynous.

Some men collected thousands of women and fathered hundreds of children. Many men – slaves and soldiers and so on – fathered none. At the beginning of Neolithic time, there were in the order of 17 breeding women for every one breeding man.

History

Some of the first histories were written into the Hebrew Bible. They tell the story of how David, the first king of Judah, collected women. The Bible names eight wives: Ahinoam, Abigail, Michal, Maacah, Haggith, Abital, Elgah, and Bathsheba; they bore a named daughter, Tamar, and 19 named sons (2 Samuel 5:13–16; 1 Chronicles 3:1–9, 14:3–7). David lived in an ivory palace, wrapped in myrrh and cassia scented garments, entertained by stringed instruments, and surrounded by virgin companions and ladies of honor (Psalms 45). David's son Solomon took just one wife from Egypt, Pharaoh's daughter, who was given her own palace, but he took 699 others – Moabites, Ammonites, Edomites, Sidonians, Hittites – from all over his empire. And he added 300 concubines on the side (1 Kings 7:8; 11:1–13).

Women across the Near East would be collected as war captives. When the Assyrian emperor, Sennacherib, set siege to Jerusalem in 701 BC, he took Hezekiah's daughters and harem; and when Nebuchadnezzar II of Babylon raided Jerusalem in 597 BC, he took the mother and wives of Judah's king, Jehoiachin (2 Kings 24:15). A decade later, when Zedekiah rebelled, Nebuchadnezzar II came again and took all the wives and all the children of the Judahite king, and burned Jerusalem with fire (Jeremiah 38:23, 52:12).

Other women were brought in as tribute. In the story of Esther, probably about the 5th-century BC Persian king, Xerxes I, this order is issued from the capital at Susa: 'Let beautiful young virgins be sought out for the king.' Esther and other women from all over his empire are basted for six months with oint-ments and six months with spices, then pre-sented to Xerxes. 'And she did not go in to the king again, unless the king delighted in her and she was summoned by name' (Esther 2:2–14).

Across the Sinai Peninsula, over a millen-nium before Solomon, Unis – a 5th-dynasty, 24th-century pharaoh from Old Kingdom Egypt – had these words carved into the walls of his pyramid: 'Unis will urinate and Unis will copulate with his penis; Unis is lord of semen, who takes women from their husbands to the place Unis likes' (*Pyramid Texts*, Unis 222). In the Middle Kingdom, the 12th-dynasty, 20th-century pharaoh, Amenemhet I, left instructions for his son, Senusret, after he was assassinated in his harem: 'Had women ever raised troops? Had rebels ever been nurtured within the house?' (*Teaching of Amenemhet I*, 9). But the best evi-dence from Egypt is New Kingdom evidence. The 18th-dynasty, 14th-century pharaoh, Amenhotep III, supported a Great Wife, Tiye, plus two Syrian princesses, two Babylonian princesses, a princess from Arzawa, and a princess from Mitanni, Gilukhepa, whose entourage included another ('marvels brought to his majesty') 317 women. They carried their hand-bracelets, foot-bracelets, earrings, and toggle-pins (*Marriage with Kirgipa Scarab*; *Amarna Letters*, EA 25).

A couple of millennia later, in the wake of the invasion of Alexander the Great, the first Mauryan emperor, Chandragupta, built an empire that brought the Indus and Ganges together. When Chandragupta's mentor and minister, Kautilya, wrote the *Arthashastra*, or 'Study of Prosperity', he offered emper-ors advice about their harems. No fewer than 80 men and 50 women, in the guise of fathers and mothers, with help from the impe-rial eunuchs, should attend them, and they 'shall not only ascertain purity and impu-rity in the life of the inmates of the harem, but also regulate the affairs as to be condu-cive to the happiness of the king' (Kautilya, *Arthashastra* 1.20–21). Hundreds of years later, Vatsayana's *Kamasutra* advised Gupta

emperors about what to do with the thou-sands of women in their own harems. Every afternoon, after a midday nap, they should be interviewed by the servants of consorts in their fertile season, who should in turn pre-sent the emperor with scented oils stamped with the seal ring of each woman. 'And whichever one among these oils he takes, he announces that the woman who owns it will sleep with him that night' (Vatsayana, *Kamasutra* 1.3, 5.5–6).

The First August Emperor of Qin, who unified China in 221 BC, cracked his long whip and drove the universe before him: 'He scourged the world with his rod.' Elevated walks connected 270 towers and palaces near the capital at Xianyang, and the Emperor filled them with beautiful women taken from the families of 120,000 feudal rulers (Sima Qian, *Shi Ji* 6). These emperors would be polygynous for over 2000 years. The Han dynasty (206 BC to AD 220) reformer, Wang Mang, sent out Palace Grandees Without Specified Appointments and Intermediaries, 45 of each, to inspect the empire and select widely from virtuous young ladies. The Sui dynasty (AD 589–618) emperor, Yang – who built the Grand Canal, and rebuilt the Great Wall – was credited with an incred-ible 100,000 women in his secondary palace at Yangzhou, alone; and the long-lived Tang dynasty (AD 618–907) emperor, Xuanzong, kept palaces with 3000, 8000, or 40,000 women in them. When the Song (AD 960–1279) emperor, Huizong, abdicated in favor of his son, 6000 or 7000 women were let out of the palace, but many stayed. The founder of the Yuan dynasty (AD 1279–1368), Kublai Khan, spent summers in his secondary palace at Xanadu, or Shangdu, where he was enter-tained by the six consorts sent in to him every three nights. Ming (AD 1368–1644) emper-ors supported one Empress, an Empress Dowager and a Grand Empress Dowager, plus various classes of consorts. There were Imperial Honored Consorts, Honored Consorts, Imperial Consorts, and Consorts; there were Ladies of Bright Deportment,

Ladies of Handsome Fairness, Beautiful Ladies, Talented Ladies, Worthy Ladies, Chosen Attendants, and Ladies. Some were teenagers; and there were thousands of them (Ebrey, 2002; McMahon, 2013, 2016).

When the Spanish showed up in the Valley of Mexico in 1519, there was more of the same. Cortés was able to get so many Aztecs to fight against the empire because Motecuhzoma's taxmen had carried off all their daughters and wives—wrote Bernal Díaz del Castillo, who fought with Cortés as a young man (Díaz, Discovery, 60). Motecuhzoma's ancestors fathered sons by so many women, because it fitted the dignity of a ruler—wrote Antonio de Mendoza, the viceroy of New Spain (Codex Mendoza, folio 2). Emperors collected raw cotton and textiles, maize, and other staples as tribute, and "provinces that lacked foodstuffs and clothing paid in maidens"—wrote the Dominican friar, Diego Durán (Durán, History 25). It got so bad that "since the lords and chiefs stole all the women for themselves, an ordinary Indian could scarcely find a woman when he wished to marry"—wrote the Franciscan missionary, Motolinía (Motolinía, History 2.7).

So it went further south. After Cortés' distant cousin, Pizarro, conquered Peru in 1532, many remembered Inca harems. Andean emperors had kept estates all over their empire, and a third part of their revenue was spent on women: "A judge or commissioner named by the Inca was dispatched to each province, and his only responsibility was this matter of collecting girls"—wrote Bernabé Cobo, the Jesuit historian of New Spain (Cobo, History 2.34). Houses of virgins were set up for emperors all over the empire, "and all of them had many children"—wrote another Spanish Jesuit, Pedro Cieza de León (Cieza, Incas 2.10-11). Those girls had to be uninitiated, "and to ensure this, they were set apart at the age of 8"—wrote Garcilaso de la Vega, the son of an Inca noble and a Spanish lord (Garcilaso, Royal Commentaries 4.1). And an emperor would father hundreds of children, "because he had countless wives, all virgins when he took them"—wrote Juan de Betanzos, the Spanish husband of an Inca noblewoman (Betanzos, Narrative 1.23; see too Betzig 2012, 2014).

Demography

In the beginning, the Patriarchs, like Abraham and Jacob, usually counted their women and children in single digits: Jacob, who stood out as Abraham's grandson, had a daughter and 12 sons (Genesis 35:22–26). Judges, like Gideon, Ibzan, and Abdon, usually counted an order of magnitude more: Gideon had 71 sons (Judges 8:30–31). Some kings – like Solomon – kept hundreds of women; others – like Ahab – might have had hundreds of children. Solomon's son, Rehoboam, fathered 28 sons and 60 daughters; Rehoboam's son, Abijah, had 16 daughters and 22 sons (2 Chronicles 11:21, 13:21); and Ahab of Israel had 70 sons in Samaria alone (2 Kings 10:1–7). Contemporary sources from their neighbors corroborate those numbers. In Assyria, Ashurbanipal's clay tablet library kept track of 36 governesses, 145 weavers, 52 maids, and 194 miscellaneous women (Fales and Postgate, 1992: nos. 23–6). There was a House-of-the-Palace-Women in Nebuchadnezzar II's Babylon, with provisioners and overseers of the slave girls, where Belshazzar entertained a thousand with gold and silver vessels from Jerusalem's temple (*Wadi-Brisa Inscription*). When the Persian king, Darius III went to war with Alexander the Great, he took along 200 *propinquorum* (close kin) and 15,000 *cognati* (remoter kin), with the queen mother, the queen, 365 female companions (one for each day of the year) from his harem, his children, their governesses and a herd of eunuchs. His predecessor and possible grandfather, Artaxerxes II, had 115 illegitimate *sons,* besides 3 legitimate ones (Curtius Rufus, 3.3.22–24, 6.6.8; Justin, 10.1.1; see also Betzig, 2005, 2009).

In Egypt, when the 13th-century, 19th-dynasty New Kingdom pharaoh, Ramesses II took a beautiful Hittite bride – the last of his eight or more wives – he added her countless slaves. In tomb KV5 in the Valley of the Kings at Thebes, there were chambers for dozens of their sons. On bas reliefs and ostraca, statues and scarabs from all over his empire, the names of 50 'king's sons' and 'bodily king's sons' and so on – generals, hereditary counts, chiefs of secrets, scribes – survive from his 67-year reign. Other inscriptions are associated with unnamed sons, and there were at least 53 daughters. In his memoirs, Ramesses remembered the day his father gave him a crown: 'He spoke of me, his eyes filled with tears, so great was the love for me within him; he furnished me with a female household and royal apartments surpassing the beautiful females of the palace.' Women came from every corner of his far-flung domains (Fisher, 2001; Weeks, 2006; *Great Abydos Inscription*).

The Mauryan emperor of India, Ashoka, converted to Buddhism in 260 BC and his biography was recorded by the monks and nuns of Sri Lanka. The *Dipavamsa*, or 'Chronicle of the Island', anonymously written in the 3rd or 4th century AD, credits the emperor's father, Bindusara, with over a hundred sons. 'Having killed his hundred brothers, alone continuing his race, Ashoka was anointed king' (*Dipavamsa* 6.22). The *Mahavamsa*, or 'Great Chronicle', written roughly a century later, reports the same. 'A hundred glorious sons and one had Bindusara; Ashoka stood high above them all in valor, splendor, might, and wondrous powers. He, when he had slain his 99 brothers born of different mothers, won the undivided sovereignty over all Jambudvipa,' that is, the human realm (*Mahavamsa*, 5.19).

Chinese dynastic histories offer lists of imperial children: 65 are included for the Northern Song emperor, Huizong. Many emperors kept enormous harems, and could have fathered enormous numbers of children.

When the Yuan dynasty founder, Kublai Khan, spent summers at Xanadu, or Shangdu, Marco Polo, his Venetian friend, counted 25 sons by his concubines, and 22 more sons by the emperor's four wives (Polo, *Travels*, 2.8–9; *Song shi* in Ebrey, 2002).

In the Valley of Mexico, at around the same time, Nezahualcoyotl, the overlord of Texcoco and friend of Motecuhzoma I, had 300 rooms in his palace, with arrangements for his queen's attendants and other servants, where 2000 women, 'reared in seclusion', raised his 57 daughters and 60 sons (Alva Ixtlilxóchitl, *Nezahualcoyotl Acolmitztli*, 4.2). Three generations later, when Motecuhzoma II was entertained by 600 lords and 400 of their sons, he could have been amused by several hundred of their daughters as well (Cortés 1520, see above).

Garcilaso de la Vega and his contemporary, Juan Betanzos, put together numbers for emperors in Inca Peru. In the generations before the conquest, Pachakuti had 300 or 400 children by various women, and other emperors had 300 children, or 250 children, or 200 sons (Garcilaso, *Royal Commentaries* 4, 6.34, 7.26, 8.8, 9.15, 36; Betanzos, *Narrative* 1.23). Guaman Poma de Ayala, another son of Inca nobles, added that access to women was strictly prescribed by law: 'Principal persons' got 50, *hunu kurakas* (heads of 10,000 households) got 30, *waranqa kurakas* (heads of 1000) got 15, *pachaka kurakas* (heads of 100) got eight, *chunka kamayuqs* (heads of 10) got five, and the 'poor Indian' took whatever was left (Guaman Poma de Ayala, *Chronicle* 134).

Genetics

Y chromosome and mitochondrial DNA sequences collected on every inhabited continent suggest a second human population bottleneck in and around the Near East at around 8000 to 4000 years ago – roughly at the start of the Neolithic, roughly at the origin of farming. More or less at the beginning of civilization, more or less as the first words were written, the effective breeding population among women became as high as *17 times* the effective breeding population among men. Polygyny dramatically increased (Karmin et al., 2015; see also Poznik et al., 2016).

Other genetic evidence comes from the Far East. Y chromosome samples suggest an expansion of three East Asian male lineages over the last 6000 years. Those clades represent more than 40% of contemporary Han Chinese. This most important patrilineal expansion in China occurred in the Neolithic, and might be related to the origins of agriculture (Yan et al., 2014). Even more striking evidence suggests a genetic legacy of the Mongol emperors, who ruled China for nearly a century. A Y chromosome star cluster represented in 16 regions across Asia, or 8% of late-20th-century men from the Pacific to the Caspian Sea and in 1/200 of all men worldwide, may have been borne by the male descendants of Genghis Khan. Genghis' grandson, the *taizu*, or Grand Progenitor, who founded the Mongol dynasty in 1271, was Kublai, the Great Khan, of Marco Polo and Coleridge fame (Zerjal et al., 2003; Coleridge, *Kubla Khan*).

THE END OF DIFFERENTIAL REPRODUCTION

Across the Paleolithic, for hundreds of thousands of years, *H. sapiens* was often monogamous. Over the course of a lifetime, most men and women probably mated more than once; and some men mated with more than one woman at a time. Because the extent (number of men mated with more than one woman) and the magnitude (number of women mated with one man) of polygyny may be expected to vary inversely, more men in the Paleolithic were polygynous (Low, 1988; Ross et al., 2018), but polygynous men

had more women in the Neolithic and beyond (Betzig, 2014, 2016).

Darwin prefaced his discussions of elongated beetle mandibles, bower-bird litter, and curved oryx horns in *The Descent of Man, and Selection in Relation to Sex*, with a note on male competition for females: 'This fact is so notorious that it would be superfluous to give instances' (Darwin, 1874, v.2: 323). Over the past several decades, superfluous instances have been adduced. Dominant males have been shown to have higher reproductive success across species (e.g., Clutton-Brock, 1988; Ellis, 1995), across primates (e.g., Alberts, 2012; Dubuc et al., 2014), and across human groups (e.g., Nettle and Pollett, 2008; von Rueden and Jaeggi, 2016). These days, in most human societies, reproductive differentials are small. Reproductive variance among men is remarkably low compared to other mammals (e.g., Hager and Jones, 2009; Ross et al., 2019); and reproductive variance among women can approach reproductive variance among men (e.g., Brown et al., 2009; Borgerhoff Mulder and Ross, 2019).

In early ethnographic reports about hunter-gatherers by traders and travelers, most men were monogamous, but some had a number of wives. Though foragers were often mobile, and kept no more than they could carry, some lived in more sedentary societies, with higher variance in resource access and reproductive success. Demographic evidence from contemporary hunter-gatherer societies suggests that reproductive variance among men is consistently higher than reproductive variance among women. And genetic evidence suggests that for *H. sapiens*, over the long run, the size of the breeding population of women has exceeded the size of the breeding population of men by a ratio of around 2:1.

Reproductive differentials shot up after we settled down. After the Neolithic, historical evidence from the first empires is filled with polygynous emperors who recruited carefully guarded women into their harems and fathered their children. Demographic evidence consistently suggests that emperors supported thousands of women and hundreds of children; genetic evidence backs that up. As the Neolithic began, the effective breeding population among women became up to 17 times the effective breeding population among men.

High reproductive variance persisted in the historical record up to the last few hundred years. In the first Western empires, in Greece and Rome, eunuch-guarded harems were common. Roman emperors, like most emperors, married one wife at a time, but had sexual access to thousands of slaves; and Ottoman emperors, who continued Roman traditions at Istanbul, left records of the hundreds of women who became the mothers of their children. Charlemagne, the 'Father of Europe', and his heirs kept small numbers of wives, but were reprimanded by their bishops for the large numbers of dancers, acrobats,

trollops, and servants at their palaces and estates. Cortés conquered the Aztecs as recently as 1521; and little more than a decade later, Pizarro ended the Inca empire. After the 16th century, on the Indian subcontinent, Mughal emperors hoarded enormous harems; and after the 17th century, Qing emperors scoured their empire for consorts. Leaders of what became the British Empire were reminded again and again by their Houses of Commons to cut the size of their households, and to throw out *femmez de folie, ribauz e ribaudes*, and *meretrices du curia domini Regis*: the whores who followed their courts (Betzig, 1992, 2020; Scheidel, 2009a,b).

Then everything changed. Most of us take monogamy for granted. Our families look more like foragers' than emperors'; we reproduce more like Paleolithic than Neolithic women and men. Reproductive differentials have collapsed. Why is anybody's guess.

ACKNOWLEDGEMENTS

Warm thanks to Polly Wiessner, Barry Hewlett, Nick Blurton Jones, Eric Smith, Kim Hill and Karen Kramer for help with foragers. Franny Berdan and Monique Borgerhoff Mulder kindly provided references on ancient civilizations and reproductive variance in women.

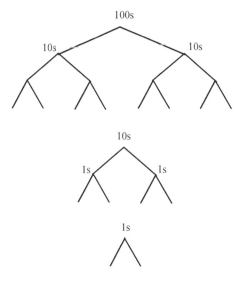

Figure 4.1 Reproductive hierarchies parallel political hierarchies. Powerful men in societies with 1-or-fewer-level hierarchies often have completed fertilities in single digits; powerful men in societies with 2-level hierarchies tend to have completed fertilities in double digits; and powerful men in societies with 3-or-more-level hierarchies have completed fertilities of over 100 (after Betzig, 1986, 1993)

REFERENCES

Alberts, S. C. (2012). Magnitude and sources of variation in male reproductive performance. In *The Evolution of Primate Societies,* edited by J. Mitani, J. Call, P. M. Kappeler, R. A. Palombit & J. B. Silk. Chicago: The University of Chicago Press.

Alva Ixtlilxóchitl, F. de. *Nezahualcóyotl Acolmitztli: Selección de Textos.* México: Estado de México, 1979.

Amarna Letters, translated by W. L. Moran. Baltimore: Johns Hopkins University Press, 2001.

Betanzos, J. de. *Narrative of the Incas,* translated by R. Hamilton & D. Buchanan. Austin: University of Texas Press, 1996.

Betzig, L. L. (1986). *Despotism and Differential Reproduction: A Darwinian View of History.* New York: Aldine de Gruyter.

Betzig, L. L. (1992). Roman polygyny. *Ethology and Sociobiology, 13*(5–6), 309–349.

Betzig, L. L. (1993). Sex, succession, and stratification in the first six civilizations. In *Social Stratification and Socioeconomic Inequality,* edited by L. Ellis. New York: Praeger.

Betzig, L. L. (2005). Politics as sex: The Old Testament case. *Evolutionary Psychology, 3*(1), 326–346.

Betzig, L. L. (2009). Sex and politics in insects, crustaceans, birds, mammals, the Ancient Near East and the Bible. *Scandinavian Journal of the Old Testament, 23*(2), 208–232.

Betzig, L. L. (2012). Means, variances, and ranges in reproductive success: Comparative evidence. *Evolution and Human Behavior, 33*(4), 309–317.

Betzig, L. L. (2014). Eusociality in history. *Human Nature, 25*(1), 80–99.

Betzig, L. L. (2016). Mating systems. In *Encyclopedia of Evolutionary Social Sciences,* edited by T. Shackelford & V. Weekes-Shackelford. Berlin: Springer.

Betzig, L. L. (2020). *The Badge of Lost Innocence: A History of the West,* in prep.

Blurton Jones, N. B. (2016). *Demography and Evolutionary Ecology of Hadza Hunter-Gatherers.* Cambridge: Cambridge University Press.

Borgerhoff Mulder, M. & Ross, C. T. (2019). Unpacking mating success and testing Bateman's principles in a human population. *Proceedings of the Royal Society B: Biological Sciences, 286*(1908), 20191516.

Brown, G. R., Laland, K. N. & Borgerhoff Mulder, M. (2009). Bateman's principles and human sex roles. *Trends in Ecology & Evolution, 24*(6), 297–304.

Cashdan, E. A. (1980). Egalitarianism among hunters and gatherers. *American Anthropologist, 82*(1), 116–120.

Cieza de León, P. *The Incas,* translated by H. de Onis. Norman: University of Oklahoma Press, 1959.

Clutton-Brock, T. H. (1988). *Reproductive Success.* Chicago: University of Chicago Press.

Cobo, B. *History of the Inca Empire,* translated by R. Hamilton. Austin: University of Texas Press, 1979.

Coleridge, S. T. *Kubla Khan,* in *Complete Poems,* edited by W. Keach. London: Penguin, 2004.

Columbus, C. *The Diario of Christopher Columbus's First Voyage to America, 1492–1493,* translated by O. Dunn & J. E. Kelley, Jr. Norman: University of Oklahoma Press, 1989.

Columbus, C. (1493). *Letter, Describing the Results of His First Voyage,* translated in C. Jane & L. A. Vigneras, *The Journal of Christopher Columbus.* London: Anthony Blond; Orion Press, 1960.

Cook, J. (1768–1780). *The Journals of Captain Cook on his Voyages of Discovery,* edited by J. C. Beaglehole. Cambridge: Cambridge University Press for the Hakluyt Society, 1955–1974.

Curtius Rufus, Quintus. *History of Alexander,* translated by J. C. Rolfe. London: Heinemann, 1971.

Darwin, C. R. (1860). *Journal of Researches into the Natural History and Geology of the Countries Visited During the Voyage of the H.M.S. Beagle Round the World, under the Command of Capt. Fitz Roy, R.N.* 2nd edition. London: John Murray.

Darwin, C. R. (1874). *The Descent of Man, and Selection in Relation to Sex,* 2nd edition. London: John Murray.

Díaz del Castillo, B. *The Discovery and Conquest of Mexico, 1517–1521,* translated by A. P. Maudslay. Cambridge, MA: Da Capo Press, 2003.

Dipavamsa, translated by Harold Oldenberg. New Delhi: Asian Educational Services, 1982.

Dubuc, C., Ruiz-Lambides, A. & Widdig, A. (2014). Variance in male lifetime reproductive success and estimation of the degree of polygyny in a primate. *Behavioral Ecology, 25*(4), 878–889.

Durán, D. *History of the Indies of New Spain,* translated by D. Heyden. Norman: University of Oklahoma Press, 1994.

Ebrey, P. B. (2002). *Women and the Family in Chinese History.* London: Routledge.

Ellis, L. (1995). Dominance and reproductive success among nonhuman animals: A cross-species comparison. *Ethology and Sociobiology*, *16(4)*, 257–333.

Fales, F. M. & Postgate, J. N. (1992). *Imperial Administrative Records: Palace and Temple Administration.* Helsinki: University of Helsinki Press.

Fisher, M. (2001). *The Sons of Ramesses II.* Wiesbaden: Harrassowitz.

Garcilaso de la Vega. *Royal Commentaries of the Incas,* translated by H. V. Livermore. Austin: University of Texas Press, 1987.

Gama, V. da. *A Journal of the First Voyage of Vasco da Gama, 1497–1499,* translated by E. G. Ravenstein. London: The Hakluyt Society, 1898.

Goodale, J. C. (1971). *Tiwi Wives: A Study of the Women of Melville Island, North Australia.* Seattle: University of Washington Press.

Great Abydos Inscription, translated in K. A. Kitchen, *Ramesside Inscriptions,* pp. 162–174. Oxford: Blackwell, 1996.

Guaman Poma de Ayala, F. *The First New Chronicle and Good Government: On the History of the World and the Incas up to 1615,* translated and edited by R. Hamilton. Austin: University of Texas Press, 2009.

Hager, R. & Jones, C. B. (2009). *Reproductive Skew in Vertebrates: Proximate and Ultimate Causes.* Cambridge: Cambridge University Press.

Hammer, M. F., Mendez, F. L., Cox, M. P., Woerner, A. E. & Wall, J. D. (2008). Sex-biased evolutionary forces shape genomic patterns of human diversity. *PLoS Genetics*, *4(9)*, e1000202.

Hart, C. W. M. & Pilling, A. R. (1960). *The Tiwi of North Australia.* New York: Holt, Rinehart and Winston.

Hawkes, K. & Bliege Bird, R. (2002). Showing off, handicap signaling, and the evolution of men's work. *Evolutionary Anthropology*, *11(2)*, 58–67.

Herodotus. *Histories,* translated by A. de Sélincourt. Harmondsworth: Penguin, 1996.

Hewlett, B. S. (1988). Sexual selection and paternal investment among Aka pygmies. In *Human Reproductive Behavior: A Darwinian Perspective,* edited by L. Betzig, M. Borgerhoff Mulder & P. Turke. Cambridge: Cambridge University Press.

Hewlett, B. S. (1991). Intimate Fathers: The Nature and Context of Aka Pygmy Paternal Infant Care. Ann Arbor: The University of Michigan Press.

Hill, K. & Hurtado, A. M. (1996). *Ache Life History: The Ecology and Demography of a Foraging People.* Hawthorne, NY: Aldine.

Hill, K. & Hurtado, A. M. (2009). Cooperative breeding in South American hunter-gatherers. *Proceedings of the Royal Society B: Biological Sciences*, *276(1674)*, 3863–3870.

Hill, K. & Kaplan, H. (1988). Tradeoffs in male and female reproductive strategies among the Ache. In *Human Reproductive Behavior: A Darwinian Perspective,* edited by L. Betzig, M. Borgerhoff Mulder & P. Turke. Cambridge: Cambridge University Press.

Horace. *Satires,* translated by H. R. Fairclough. Cambridge, MA: Harvard University Press, 1926.

Howell, N. (2000). *Demography of the Dobe !Kung,* 2nd edition. New York: Aldine de Gruyter.

Ibn Battuta. *Travels in Asia and Africa, 1325–1354*, translated by H. A. R. Gibb. London: Routledge, 1963.

Justin, Marcus Junianus. *Justin, Epitome of the Philippic History of Pompeius Trogus,* translated by J. C. Yardley. Atlanta: Scholars Press, 1996.

Karmin, M. et al. (2015). A recent bottleneck of Y chromosome diversity coincides with a global change in culture. *Genome Research*, *25(4)*, 459–466.

Kautilya. *The Arthashastra,* translated by P. Olivelle. Oxford: Oxford University Press, 2013.

Kelly, R. L. (2013). *The Lifeways of Hunter-Gatherers: The Foraging Spectrum.* Cambridge: Cambridge University Press.

Kramer, K. L., Greaves R. D. & Ellison, P. T. (2009). Early reproductive maturity among Pumé foragers: Implications of a pooled energy model to fast life histories. *American Journal of Human Biology*, *21(4)*, 430–437.

Kramer, K. L., Schacht, R. & Bell, A. (2017). Adult sex ratios and partner scarcity among hunter-gatherers: Implications for dispersal patterns and the evolution of human sociality. *Philosophical Transactions of the Royal Society B: Biological Sciences*, *372(1729)*, 20160316.

Lee, R. B. (1979). *The !Kung San: Men, Women, and Work in a Foraging Society.* Cambridge: Cambridge University Press.

Lee, R. B. & Daly, R. (1999). *The Cambridge Encyclopedia of Hunters and Gatherers*. Cambridge: Cambridge University Press.

Lippold, S., Xu, H., Ko, A., Renaud, G., Butthof, A., Schröder, R. & Stoneking, M. (2014). Human paternal and maternal demographic histories: Insights from high-resolution Y chromosome and mtDNA sequences. *Investigative Genetics*, *5(1)*, 13–30.

Low, B. S. (1988). Measures of polygyny in humans. *Current Anthropology*, *29(1)*, 189–194.

Lozano, P. (1873). *Historia de la Conquista del Paraguay, Rio de La Plata, y Tucuman,* volume 1. Lima: Imprenta Popular.

Mahavamsa, translated by W. Geiger. London: Pali Text Society, 1964.

Marlowe, F. W. (2003). The mating system of foragers in the standard cross-cultural sample. *Cross-Cultural Research*, *37(3)*, 282–306.

Marlowe, F. W. (2010). *The Hadza: Hunter-Gatherers of Tanzania*. Berkeley: University of California Press.

Marriage with Kirgipa Scarab, translated in J. H. Breasted, *Ancient Records of Egypt*. Urbana and Chicago: University of Illinois Press, 2001.

McMahon, K. (2013). *Women Shall Not Rule: Imperial Wives and Concubines in China from Han to Liao*. Lanham, MD: Rowman & Littlefield.

McMahon, K. (2016). *Celestial Women: Imperial Wives and Concubines in China from Song to Qing*. Lanham, MD: Rowman & Littlefield.

Mendoza, A. de. *Codex Mendoza,* edited by F. Berdan & P. Anawalt. Berkeley: University of California Press, 1992.

Motolinía. *History of the Indians of New Spain,* translated and edited by E. Foster. Westport CT: Greenwood Press, 1973.

Nettle, D. & Pollet, T. V. (2008). Natural selection on male wealth in humans. *American Naturalist*, *172(5)*, 658–666.

Polo, M. *The Travels of Marco Polo,* translated by H. Yule & H. Cordier. New York: Dover, 1993.

Poznik, G. D. et al. (2016). Punctuated bursts in human male demography inferred from 1,244 worldwide Y-chromosome sequences. *Nature Genetics*, *48(6)*, 593–601.

Pyramid Texts, translated by J. P. Allen. Leiden: Brill, 1995.

Raghavan, M. et al. (2015). Genomic evidence for the Pleistocene and recent population history of Native Americans. *Science*, *349(6250)*, aab3884.

Richter, D. et al. (2017). The age of the hominin fossils from Jebel Irhoud, Morocco, and the origins of the Middle Stone Age. *Nature*, *546(7657)*, 293–296.

Ross, C. T. et al. (2018). Greater wealth inequality, less polygyny: Rethinking the polygyny threshold model. *Journal of the Royal Society Interface*, *15(144)*, 20180035.

Ross, C. T. et al. (2019). Humans have small sex difference in reproductive skew compared to non-human mammals. *Proceedings of the National Academy of Sciences,* under review.

Scheidel, W. (2009a). Sex and empire: A Darwinian perspective. In W. Scheidel & I. Morris, eds. *The Dynamics of Ancient Empires: State Power from Assyria to Byzantium*. New York: Oxford University Press.

Scheidel, W. (2009b). A peculiar institution? Greco-Roman monogamy in global context. *The History of the Family*, *14(3)*, 280–291.

Scheinfeldt, L. B. et al. (2019). Genomic evidence for shared common ancestry of East African hunting-gathering populations and insights into local adaptation. *Proceedings of the National Academy of Sciences*, *116(10)*, 4166–4175.

Sima Qian. *Shi ji,* translated by B. Watson. New York: Columbia University Press, 1993.

Smith, E. A. (2004). Why do good hunters have higher reproductive success? *Human Nature*, *15(4)*, 343–364.

Smith, E. A., Bliege Bird, R. & Bird, D. W. (2003). The benefits of costly signaling: Meriam turtle hunters and spearfishers. *Behavioral Ecology*, *14(1)*, 116–126.

Song shi. Beijing: Zhonghua Shuju, 1977.

Teaching of Amenemhet I, translated in R. B. Parkinson, *The Tale of Sinuhe and Other Ancient Egyptain Poems, 1940–1640 BC*. Oxford: Clarendon, 1997.

Trivers, R. L. (1972). Parental investment and sexual selection. In *Sexual Selection and the Descent of Man, 1871–1971*, edited by B. G. Campbell. Chicago: Aldine.

Vatsayana. *Kamasutra,* translated by R. Burton. Harmondsworth: Penguin, 1964.

von Rueden, C. R. & Jaeggi, A. V. (2016). Men's status and reproductive success in 33 nonindustrial societies: Effects of subsistence, marriage system, and reproductive strategy. *Proceedings of the National Academy of Sciences*, *113*(*39*), 10824–10829.

Wadi-Brisa Inscription, translated in J. Pritchard, *Ancient Near Eastern Texts Relating to the Old Testament,* 3rd edition. Princeton, NJ: Princeton University Press, 1969.

Weeks, K. R. (2006). *KV5: A Preliminary Report on the Excavation of the Tomb of the Sons of Rameses II in the Valley of the Kings.* New York: American University in Cairo Press.

Wiessner, P. (2002). Hunting, healing, and Hxaro exchange: A long term perspective on !Kung (Ju/'hoansi) large-game hunting. *Evolution and Human Behavior*, *23*(*6*), 1–30.

Wiessner, P. (2009). Parent–offspring conflict in marriage: Implications for social evolution and material culture among the Ju/'hoansi bushmen. In *Pattern and Process in Cultural Evolution*, edited by S. Shennan. Berkeley: University of California Press.

Wilson Sayres, M., Lohmueller, K. & Nielsen, R. (2014). Natural selection reduced diversity on human Y chromosomes. *PLoS Genetics*, *10*(*1*), e1004064.

Yan, S. et al. (2014). Y chromosomes of 40% Chinese descend from three Neolithic super-grandfathers. *PLoS One*, *9*(*8*), e105691.

Zerjal, T. et al. (2003). The genetic legacy of the Mongols. *American Journal of Human Genetics*, *72*(*3*), 717–721.

The Products of Evolution: Conceptual Distinctions, Evidentiary Criteria, and Empirical Examples

Laith Al-Shawaf, David M. G. Lewis,
Nicole Barbaro and Yzar S. Wehbe

Evolution refers to a change in allele frequencies in a population over time. Change in allele frequencies can result from four different forces: mutation, genetic drift, gene flow, and natural selection (e.g., Bergstrom and Dugatkin, 2012; Futuyma and Kirkpatrick, 2017). Mutation is the random change in alleles that constitute the raw material on which selection operates. Genetic drift is the random, chance-driven change in allele frequencies from one generation to the next. Gene flow, sometimes called admixture or migration, is the movement of genes from one population to another. Natural selection is the non-random filtering of randomly mutated genes as a function of differential reproductive success. These four evolutionary forces yield three kinds of products: adaptations, byproducts, and noise. In this chapter, we discuss these three products of evolution.

ADAPTATIONS

An adaptation is a functionally organized biological system that evolved to solve an adaptive problem (Tooby and Cosmides, 1992; Williams, 1966). Adaptations can be morphological, physiological, or psychological. Their most salient feature is that they exhibit functional design (Dennett, 1996; Tooby and Cosmides, 2015; Williams, 1966) – that is, adaptations have a function. For example, the porcupine's quills serve the function of protection, as does the African bombardier beetle's (*Stenaptinus insignis*) ability to project chemical explosions out of its body at potential attackers (Eisner and Aneshansley, 1999). The larvae of the Alcon blue butterfly *(Phengaris alcon)* emit chemical signals designed to manipulate ants into caring for them and feeding them, sometimes to the exclusion of the ants' own offspring (Thomas and Elmes, 1998). The emerald cockroach wasp (*Ampulex compressa*) parasitizes the common household cockroach (*Periplaneta americana*) by injecting it with a precise neurochemical cocktail in two different locations in its brain, turning it into a 'zombie' (Piek et al., 1984). These neurochemical cocktails are specifically designed to rob the cockroach of its ability to *initiate* movement, but *not* actually paralyze it. This is crucial, because the tiny wasp needs to drag the much larger roach to its nest, a feat that would be impossible if the roach were paralyzed. The wasp's solution is to inject the roach with a cocktail that nullifies its willingness to *initiate its own movement,* but does not actually paralyze it – this way, when the wasp begins to drag the roach toward the nest, the roach's legs automatically move in concert, enabling the wasp to drag it. Once it reaches the nest, the wasp lays an egg on the roach's abdomen and buries it alive. When the wasp egg hatches, the larva that emerges eats the roach's internal organs in a precise sequence that keeps the roach alive (and thereby the food fresh) for as long as possible, while also producing another chemical cocktail designed to sanitize the roach and protect itself from pathogenic infection (Herzner et al., 2013). These are examples of adaptations: 'special problem-solving machinery' (Williams, 1985: 1) designed by selection to solve a specific survival- or reproduction-related problem.

Of the four evolutionary forces (selection, mutation, migration, and genetic drift), only selection is capable of producing adaptations. The other three forces can cause evolution – a change in allele frequencies in a population over time – and they can also affect the features of adaptations. But natural selection is the only known causal process capable of crafting an adaptation in the first place; it is the only evolutionary force capable of producing a functional fit between an organism and its environment. In the following sections, we discuss misconceptions about

adaptations, key features of adaptations, and how to test adaptation-based hypotheses.

Misconceptions About Adaptations

Common misconceptions about adaptations include the ideas that (1) adaptations must be present at birth, (2) adaptations are genetically determined, (3) adaptations must be *currently adaptive*, and (4) adaptations cannot have maladaptive effects. We tackle these misconceptions briefly before presenting the key features of adaptations.

Do adaptations need to be present at birth?

A common misconception about evolved adaptations is that they must be present at birth (e.g., see Al-Shawaf et al., 2018b). This is incorrect: selection builds adaptations that emerge at the developmental phase in which they are needed, not ones that are necessarily present at the moment of birth (Al-Shawaf et al., 2018b). Walking and language are two human adaptations that are not present at birth, but emerge later in development. So are beards, breasts, and teeth. Hatchlings of many bird species cannot see or fly, and yet vision and flight are both avian adaptations – they are not present at birth, but they emerge later in development, during the ontogenetic phase in which they are needed (see, e.g., Alcock, 2013; Al-Shawaf et al., 2018b; Williams, 1966).

Are adaptations genetically determined?

Adaptations, like all other features of the body, brain, and mind, are produced by the joint interplay of genes and environment (e.g., Buss, 1995; Dawkins, 1976; Tooby and Cosmides, 1992). There is a tendency to conflate 'evolved' with 'genetically determined', but this conflation is mistaken. Adaptations are sensitive to contextual and environmental input (Al-Shawaf et al., 2019). Evolutionary thinking highlights the central causal role of the environment in the emergence of adaptations. Specifically, environmental pressures drive the evolution of adaptations in the first place, are critical for the normal development of adaptations during an organism's life, and are needed to activate adaptations in the immediate present (e.g., Buss, 1995; Confer et al., 2010; Lewis et al., 2017). Even something as 'basic' as the visual system requires environmental input in order to develop normally (e.g., Wiesel, 1982). Far from adopting a 'genetic determinist' view, an evolutionary approach emphasizes the importance of the environment at every phase of an adaptation's emergence (Al-Shawaf et al., 2019; see also Boyer and Bergstrom, 2011; Tooby and Cosmides, 2015).

Do adaptations need to be currently adaptive?

Whether an organismic feature is an adaptation is distinct from whether it is *currently adaptive*. Adaptations may *not* be currently adaptive for many reasons. These include the fact that selection is subject to time lags, and, for humans, cannot keep up with some of the rapid changes in our environment since the agricultural revolution 12,000 years ago (Dawkins, 1999; Tooby and Cosmides, 1992; but see Cochran and Harpending, 2009 for important exceptions). Adaptations that were beneficial to humans during most of our evolutionary history as hunter-gatherers can be positively harmful in the modern age, leading to outcomes such as obesity, heart disease, and drug addictions (Al-Shawaf and Zreik, 2018; Nesse and Williams, 1994).

Later in this chapter, we discuss evidentiary standards for establishing whether something is an adaptation. For now, we simply note that being *currently adaptive* (i.e., currently linked with reproductive success) is not one of them.

Can adaptations have maladaptive effects?

It may sound surprising, but adaptations can have maladaptive effects for several reasons (Del Giudice, 2018). Below, we discuss

(1) malfunctioning adaptations, (2) evolutionary time lags or mismatches, (3) maladaptive outcomes due to evolutionary conflicts, (4) adaptively biased mechanisms that make maladaptive mistakes as part of their evolved design, and (5) other constraints on natural selection. For more in-depth discussions, see Nesse (2015), Crespi (2000, 2014), and Del Giudice (2018).

Malfunctioning adaptations

Adaptations can malfunction for numerous reasons, ranging from degradation due to pathogens and parasites to environmental circumstances that occur outside the adaptation's normal range of sensitivity. One example of a malfunctioning adaptation is theory of mind in individuals on the autism spectrum. In people with autism, this adaptation for understanding others' thoughts and emotions is impaired (Baron-Cohen, 1996, but see Gernsbacher and Yergeau, 2019). As Nesse has pointed out, when faced with a disorder or disease, the correct question is rarely 'why did this disease evolve?', but rather 'why did selection fashion the body or mind in ways that left us vulnerable to this disease?' (Nesse, 2019).

Maladaptive outcomes due to environmental mismatches

Adaptations can also have maladaptive effects due to environmental mismatches (see Dawkins, 1999; Symons, 1992). Preferences for sugar and calorically dense foods were adaptive during human evolution, when these resources were scarce. However, in modern environments where these resources are available at any time of day and in nearly unlimited quantities, these ancestrally adaptive preferences motivate people to consume unhealthy amounts of sugar and excess calories, leading to maladaptive outcomes such as obesity and Type 2 diabetes (see, e.g., Symons, 1992).

The prevalence of pornography in modern environments captures another evolutionary mismatch. During human evolution, before the advent of pixels on a screen, the retinal projection of a naked and interested conspecific would have represented a real sexual opportunity. Because pixels on a screen were not part of the environment in which humans evolved, our species has not had sufficient evolutionary time to evolve neurocognitive mechanisms that render these virtual simulacra ineffective.

In short, phenomena such as widespread consumption of refined sugar and pornography are maladaptive effects produced by adaptations due to evolutionary mismatch (for more information, see Al-Shawaf and Zreik, 2018; Dawkins, 1999).

Maladaptive outcomes due to evolutionary conflicts, including intragenomic conflict

Different organisms do not have perfectly overlapping fitness interests, so adaptations can produce maladaptive outcomes due to unavoidable conflicts between individuals (Del Giudice, 2018; Trivers, 1974). For example, mother and fetus engage in evolutionarily predictable conflicts during pregnancy because their fitness interests partially diverge (Trivers, 1974). Similarly, conflict within the genome between maternally imprinted and paternally imprinted genes ('intragenomic conflict') can lead to maladaptive outcomes for the developing fetus (Haig, 1993, 1997). Disequilibria in these intragenomic conflicts have been implicated in certain psychological disorders, including autism and schizophrenia (Badcock and Crespi, 2006; Byars et al., 2014; Crespi and Badcock, 2008; Wilkins, 2011).

Maladaptive outcomes due to 'adaptively biased mechanisms' that produce errors as part of their design

Some adaptations even produce errors *as part of their design*. For example, research on error management theory has shown that inferential mechanisms can evolve to be 'adaptively biased' rather than perfectly accurate, as long as the net costs of a mechanism that errs on the side of caution are lower

than the net costs of a maximally accurate mechanism (the latter would make fewer errors, but a larger proportion of them would be in the more costly direction – and selection minimizes net costs, not crude error rate; Haselton and Buss, 2000; Haselton and Nettle, 2006). This logic has led researchers to discover predictable errors in mating cognition (Haselton and Buss, 2000; Henningsen and Henningsen, 2010), environmental navigation (Jackson and Cormack, 2007, 2008), physiological defenses (Nesse, 2001, 2005), auditory perception (Neuhoff, 1998, 2001), and many other domains of psychology (Haselton and Nettle, 2006). These individual errors are often maladaptive, but they are normal and expected outputs of the 'adaptively biased' mechanisms that produce them.

Maladaptive outcomes due to constraints on natural selection

Adaptations do not evolve because they perform perfectly; they evolve because they perform better, on average, than alternative variants extant in the population at the time (Williams, 1966). This means that adaptations are often adaptive, on average, but nonetheless imperfect. Moreover, adaptations are necessarily imperfectly designed because there are constraints on the ability of selection to craft optimally designed mechanisms – and this, too, can lead to maladaptive effects. These constraints include time lags, phylogenetic or historical constraints, lack of genetic variation, unavoidable tradeoffs, environmental accidents, antagonistic pleiotropy, imperfections due to genic-level selection having deleterious effects at the individual level, and tradeoffs between survival and reproduction (see Al-Shawaf and Zreik, 2018; Dawkins, 1999; Nesse and Williams, 1994).

Fuller discussions of these constraints can be found elsewhere (see, e.g., Al-Shawaf and Zreik, 2018; Dawkins, 1999), but here we offer one example of unavoidable tradeoffs. Wild dogs (*Lycaon pictus*) prey upon gazelles (*Gazella thomsoni*) in the African Serengeti. These gazelles could evolve longer legs, enabling them to run faster and escape their predators, but longer leg bones would be more brittle and more likely to break. As a consequence, the gazelles face an unavoidable tradeoff: more robust bones but higher likelihood of being caught by a predator, or longer, more gracile bones that enable faster escape but are more likely to break. The key point is that organisms face unavoidable tradeoffs, and these tradeoffs make it impossible for selection to optimize all the relevant parameters at once. This leads to non-optimal outcomes that are maladaptive on at least one of these parameters. For these and other reasons, natural selection is best conceptualized as a 'meliorizing' force, not an 'optimizing' one (Dawkins, 1999).

Key Features of Adaptations

Adaptations are typically universal at the information-processing level, but may not be universal at the behavioral output level

To think clearly about psychological adaptations, it is essential to distinguish between behavior and the underlying information-processing mechanisms that produce behavior. This distinction is key because most evolutionary approaches suggest that the underlying neurocognitive mechanisms that produce behavior will be universal, but that the behaviors themselves will not necessarily be.

Psychological adaptations can be understood in terms of three components: (1) inputs, which can be external (e.g., ecological, sociocultural) or internal (e.g., body temperature, immune function), (2) algorithms that process those inputs, and (3) outputs (including behavior) produced by those algorithms and decision rules (Lewis et al., Chapter 6, this volume). Evolutionary approaches to psychology typically suggest that the *information-processing structure* of the adaptation will be universal, not the behavior that the adaptation produces (Al-Shawaf and Lewis, 2017; Symons, 1992; Tooby and Cosmides, 1992).

For example, people from different cultures may speak different languages (behavioral output), but appear to be equipped with the same universal evolved language learning abilities (neurocognitive mechanisms). In this way, cross-cultural variation in behavior does not conflict with an evolutionary perspective; rather, it can often be predicted *a priori* on the basis of evolutionary thinking (for example, see Al-Shawaf, 2019; Gangestad and Buss, 1993; Gangestad et al., 2006; Schmitt, 2005). This same distinction between the neurocognitive or information-processing level of analysis and the behavioral output level of analysis also sheds light on how universal psychological adaptations can yield individual differences in behavior (Lewis et al., in press).

Learning is driven by evolved learning adaptations

A commonly held view is that learning and evolution are conflicting explanations for behavior. If something is learned, it's not evolved, and vice versa – at the very least, some things are 'more learned', whereas others are 'more evolved'. This way of thinking is neither accurate nor useful.

Organisms learn by virtue of evolved learning mechanisms instantiated in their brains. Evidence suggests that humans, for example, have evolved learning mechanisms for language, fear of snakes and spiders, and avoiding incest (e.g., Lieberman et al., 2007; LoBue et al., 2010). Humans are not born speaking a language or already fearing snakes – nor are they born feeling disgust at the notion of incest. We must learn these things, but we accomplish this learning by virtue of evolved learning mechanisms designed for these purposes. This is also why different species will learn different things given the same inputs: they are equipped with different evolved learning mechanisms, and what they come away with given any set of inputs depends on the nature of the evolved learning mechanisms instantiated in their brains (e.g., Al-Shawaf et al., 2019). For example, if rats and quail are both exposed to sour blue water and subsequently fall ill, the rats will preferentially avoid sour water in the future, whereas the quail will preferentially avoid blue water (Wilcoxon et al., 1971). Because birds attach greater importance to visual cues, whereas rats attach greater importance to olfactory and gustatory cues, the two species ultimately learned different things despite having been exposed to the same stimulus and the same illness.

Selection is even responsible for *how much learning* is involved in a given outcome (e.g., Alcock, 2013; Frankenhuis and Panchanathan, 2011; Symons, 1979). For example, when a species faces a problem predictably and the problem is invariant, selection minimizes the amount of learning necessary for members of that species to solve that problem. By contrast, when a species faces an unpredictable and changing problem, or one that is complex enough that information acquisition during an individual organism's lifetime is necessary, selection crafts a solution to the problem that requires learning (Symons, 1979). Additionally, animals sample their environments more (i.e., they spend more time learning) when their Bayesian priors are less informative and when environmental cues are moderately informative. When environmental cues are either minimally or very highly informative, organisms derive less benefit from extensive environmental learning (Frankenhuis and Panchanathan, 2011; see also Fenneman and Frankenhuis, 2020).

In sum, evolution and learning are not in explanatory conflict with one another for three reasons: (a) selection crafts evolved learning mechanisms, (b) different species learn different things because they are equipped with different evolved learning mechanisms, and (c) depending on environmental pressures, selection produces psychological solutions that vary in the amount of learning they require. Additionally, the two explanations are not even at the same level of analysis: learning is at the proximate level, whereas

evolution is at the ultimate level (Tinbergen, 1963). To understand how and why organisms learn what they do, we must understand the nature of their evolved learning mechanisms and the selection pressures that crafted them (Lorenz, 1973; Symons, 1979).

Exaptations are a class of adaptations

Many readers are undoubtedly familiar with the term 'exaptations', introduced by Stephen Jay Gould (Gould, 1991; see also Gould and Lewontin, 1979; Gould and Vrba, 1982). Although Gould used the word exaptation in different, sometimes conflicting ways (Buss et al., 1998), an exaptation is a biological feature that either (1) first served one function, or (2) served no function at all, and was later co-opted by natural selection to serve a new function. In other words, an exaptation is a former byproduct (we discuss byproducts later in the chapter) or a former adaptation for X, which, under new selection pressures, acquired a new function and became an adaptation for Y. For example, evidence suggests that feathers may have initially evolved for thermoregulation, and only later acquired the function of flight (Ostrom, 1974, 1979). Another example might be the parental bonding system, which may have later become co-opted for adult pair bonding (Shaver et al., 1988).

Exaptations are sometimes discussed as if they pose a threat to the importance of natural selection or the usefulness of adaptation-based hypotheses. They do not. Exaptations are a normal consequence of the way natural selection works. In fact, most, if not all, adaptations are exaptations: they have gone through many changes in their features and their functions throughout the millennia in arriving at their current state (Darwin, 1859; Dennett, 1996). Since selection is a tinkerer, not an engineer (Jacob, 1977), many adaptations likely had a different function (and different features) at some point in the past, making them exaptations. In Dennett's words, 'every adaptation is one sort of exaptation or the other – this is trivial, since no function is eternal; if you go back far enough, you will find that every adaptation has developed out of predecessor structures each of which either had some other use or no use at all' (Dennett, 1996: 281). In short, exaptations are an important product of the evolutionary process. However, they are a subclass of adaptations, not a mysterious product that falls outside the traditional classification of adaptations, byproducts, and noise.

Hypotheses About Adaptations Are Testable

Psychologists who are not deeply familiar with evolutionary psychology have sometimes alleged that adaptationist hypotheses are inherently untestable. By contrast, this statement is demonstrably false to those who have even a passing familiarity with evolutionary psychology (for discussion, see Al-Shawaf et al., 2018b; Buss et al., 1998; Haig and Durrant, 2000; Ketelaar and Ellis, 2000; Lewis et al., 2017; Sell et al., 2002). What is responsible for the discrepancy between these views?

Adaptationist hypotheses may be informed *by the past, but they yield* predictions *about the present day*

One possible reason for the discrepancy has to do with the historical element implicit in any evolutionary hypothesis. Some writers have correctly noted that (1) we do not have complete knowledge of the conditions present during our ancestral past as hunter-gatherers, (2) evolutionary psychological hypotheses necessarily contain an implicit historical element, and (3) cognition and behavior do not fossilize. Together, these three premises are thought to yield the conclusion that evolutionary psychological hypotheses about adaptations are untestable. But this conclusion does not follow from the premises, for the following reason.

Adaptationist hypotheses are informed by what we know of our past, but *they yield predictions about the present day*. To test them, we do not need to travel to the past, nor do we need to have perfect and complete knowledge of the past – we simply need to test the predictions they yield about how modern humans will behave in the present (Al-Shawaf et al., 2018b). The key point is that while there is a historical component in *generating* adaptation-based hypotheses in the first place, there is no historical component in the *predictions* they yield. And crucially, those predictions can be tested in the immediate present.

In other words, as long as evolutionary hypotheses yield predictions that can be tested in the present, they are eminently testable. However, one might reasonably ask whether we know enough about our ancestral past to generate these hypotheses in the first place.

Do we know enough about our ancestral past to generate hypotheses?

Our knowledge about ancestral humans is limited, but we know with certainty that

> our ancestors, like other Old World primates, nursed; had two sexes; chose mates; had color vision calibrated to the spectral properties of sunlight; lived in a biotic environment with predatory cats, venomous snakes, and spiders; were predated on; bled when wounded; were incapacitated from injuries; were vulnerable to a large variety of parasites and pathogens; and had deleterious recessives rendering them subject to inbreeding depression if they mated with siblings. (Tooby and Cosmides, 2005: 23–4)

Each of these seemingly obvious, quotidian observations can be used to generate novel hypotheses about human psychology and behavior. The observation about deleterious recessives has led to new findings about the psychological mechanisms that govern incest avoidance (Lieberman et al., 2007). The observation about parasites and pathogens has spawned dozens of studies yielding a host of interesting new findings about the link between disgust and food neophobia, mating, pregnancy, and immune function, among others (e.g., Al-Shawaf et al., 2015c; Al-Shawaf et al., 2018a; Curtis et al., 2011; Fessler et al., 2005). The fact about predatory cats, snakes, and spiders has led to numerous hypotheses and findings about our fear mechanisms, including discoveries of biased learning mechanisms geared toward predator avoidance in children (Barrett, 2015; Barrett and Broesh, 2012). Very basic knowledge of features of our ancestral environment, together with a consideration of the cost asymmetries involved in the different kinds of error one can make when facing a decision, has led to novel findings about human visual perception (Jackson and Cormack, 2007), auditory perception (Neuhoff, 1998, 2001), and social cognition (Haselton and Buss, 2000; Haselton and Nettle, 2006) – and there are many more examples. The key point is this: (a) although it is true that our knowledge of ancestral humans is incomplete, we actually know more than many initially realize, (b) mundane and obvious facts, like the (single) fact that we are susceptible to pathogenic infection, can lead to (dozens of) hypotheses, and (c) these hypotheses yield empirical predictions that can be tested in the modern day (Al-Shawaf et al., 2018b; Lewis et al., 2017). Because of this, we can indeed use evolutionary reasoning to generate predictions that can be tested in the present day.

Are adaptationist hypotheses 'just-so stories', evaluated on the basis of plausibility alone?

It has been famously claimed that evolutionary psychological hypotheses about adaptations are evaluated on the basis of plausibility alone (Gould and Lewontin, 1979: 581). The empirical evidence, however, shows that this is false (Alcock, 2001, 2018a; Lewis et al., 2017) and relies on inaccuracies and misrepresentations of how adaptationist hypotheses are evaluated (Alcock, 2018b; Borgia, 1994; Tooby and Cosmides,

1997). Hypotheses about psychological adaptations are never evaluated on the basis of plausibility alone. Rather, they – like all psychological hypotheses – are evaluated based on the cumulative body of the evidence (Al-Shawaf et al., 2015a; Alcock, 2018b; Lewis et al., 2017). Good discussions of this issue already exist in the literature, so rather than repeating those points, we direct the reader to these papers for fuller discussion: Al-Shawaf et al., 2018b; Confer et al., 2010; Ketelaar and Ellis (2000); and Lewis et al. (2017).

Most evolutionary psychologists argue that adaptations are specialized problem-solving machines, and that specific evidentiary criteria are required to invoke adaptation (Williams, 1966, 1985). The central evidentiary criterion is that of *special design* or *improbable utility*: a hypothesized adaptation must appear so well-designed to solve a particular adaptive problem that it is exceedingly unlikely to have arisen by chance (Williams, 1966). The reason this is considered the key evidentiary criterion is that every adaptation hypothesis is, at its core, a probability statement that a collection of parts or features is so well-designed for a particular function that it must have been crafted by selection rather than having emerged as a byproduct of another adaptation or arisen by chance (e.g., Tooby and Cosmides, 1990a, 1992). Consequently, demonstrating adaptation requires evidence of special design or improbable utility (Tooby and Cosmides, 1992; Williams, 1966).

To establish that something is an adaptation, researchers must demonstrate evidence of special design or improbable utility

This reasoning suggests that *special design* is the gold standard for assessing whether or not a feature is an adaptation. The umbrella criterion of special design includes the more specific subcriteria of economy, efficiency, precision, complexity, and reliability. Although these terms were not explicitly defined in their original presentation, we might consider the following acceptable working definitions: economy refers to how economically the mechanism works (e.g., without excessive cost to the organism), efficiency refers to how well the adaptation solves the problem, precision refers to how specifically or precisely matched the mechanism is to the adaptive problem, complexity refers to how many component parts the hypothesized adaptation has, and reliability refers to how predictably the proposed adaptation develops and how predictably it solves the problem in question. Some of these conditions are not individually necessary – for example, some adaptations can be (relatively) simple, so complexity is not a necessary condition. Nonetheless, the more a psychological mechanism meets this set of criteria, the more likely it is to be an adaptation. At present, we know of no formal, quantitative operationalizations of these terms – this may represent a challenging but useful direction for future theoretical work.

Evidence of functional design can come from numerous sources (e.g. cross-species, cross-cultural, experimental), and take numerous forms (e.g., psychological, physiological, behavioral). Psychological and behavioral scientists interested in assessing whether or not a certain feature meets the evidentiary criteria for adaptation can therefore use numerous sources and types of evidence to do so (for more detail on types of evidence, ruling out alternative explanations, and cautionary notes, see Lewis et al., 2017).

What kind of evidence is *not* needed to establish that something is an adaptation?

It may also be useful to consider what is *not* needed to demonstrate adaptation. Three common misconceptions are that researchers must (1) discover the specific genes underlying the trait in question, (2) show that the trait in question is present at birth, and (3) show that the trait is currently adaptive.

These criteria are misplaced for the following reasons.

Misconception 1: Researchers must discover the genes underlying the trait in question. All adaptations have a genetic basis, but this does not mean that it is necessary to pinpoint the specific genes underlying an adaptation in order to show that it is an adaptation (Lewis et al., 2017). Analogously, all adaptations are underlain by brain mechanisms, but nobody argues that we need to identify the specific brain areas or pathways subserving a trait in order to show that that trait is an adaptation. Discovering the specific brain areas involved is necessary if our goal is to develop a complete science of psychology and a comprehensive understanding of the adaptation in question. But if our goal is to demonstrate that something is an adaptation, identifying the specific brain areas involved will not accomplish that goal. Similarly, all adaptations are underlain by genes, and a comprehensive understanding of an adaptation must include knowledge of the genes that underlie it, but it does not follow from this that you must identify which genes are involved in order to show that it is an adaptation in the first place.

Despite this key caveat, molecular genetic evidence can be important in showing that certain alleles have undergone positive selection, thereby pointing to the presence of a possible adaptation (e.g., Barrett and Schluter, 2008; Johnson and Voight, 2018). However, because many genes have multiple different phenotypic effects (pleiotropic effects; e.g., Williams, 1957), this kind of evidence often leaves open the question of *why* these alleles were selected (which phenotypic effect they were selected for). This suggests that molecular genetic evidence can be helpful, but not definitive, in pointing toward the specific function of a hypothesized adaptation.

Identifying the genes underlying a hypothesized adaptation is also important because an understanding of the relevant genetics contributes to the two proximate levels of Tinbergen's 'four questions' (ontogeny and mechanism; Tinbergen, 1963).

For the above reasons, identifying the genes underlying a hypothesized adaptation is important – and is key to a comprehensive understanding of the adaptation in question – but is not necessary to establish *that a feature is an adaptation in the first place*. Only evidence of special design or improbable utility can speak to the issue of whether a feature is an adaptation in the first place (e.g., Lewis et al., 2017; Tooby and Cosmides, 1992; Williams, 1966).

Misconception 2: Researchers must show that the feature in question is present at birth. As we noted above, adaptations often emerge during the ontogenetic phase in which they are needed. 'Presence at birth' is therefore not an appropriate evidentiary criterion for evaluating whether a feature is an adaptation. Accordingly, one does not need to show that a feature is present at birth, or that it develops very early in an organism's life, in order to demonstrate that it is an adaptation. For the same reason, evidence that a trait emerges later in life, or involves learning, does not constitute evidence against the trait being an adaptation (e.g., Al-Shawaf et al., 2018b; Al-Shawaf et al., 2019; Symons, 1979).

Misconception 3: Researchers must show that the feature in question is currently adaptive (currently correlated with fitness). It is commonly thought that adaptations should be currently linked with reproductive success. At first glance, this seems correct. And if it were, then a key method of testing whether or not a feature is an adaptation would be measuring actual reproductive outcomes – such as how many offspring are sired by individuals with and without the trait.

This seems intuitive, but in fact this kind of evidence – evidence of current reproductive success – tells us only about *current adaptiveness*, not about whether a feature is an *adaptation* (Symons, 1990, 1992; Tooby and Cosmides, 1990a). Whether a feature is *currently* adaptive is interesting and important information. However, it does not address the issue of whether that feature is an adaptation because (a) adaptations can be currently maladaptive (e.g., Del Giudice, 2018), (b) non-adaptations can be currently adaptive, and (c) the central question about adaptation is not one of current utility – it is one of

whether the feature's structure exhibits an improbably good fit with the structure of the adaptive problem it purportedly evolved to solve (Symons, 1990, 1992; Tooby and Cosmides, 1990a).

In other words, *adaptation* and *current adaptiveness* can be decoupled in both theory and practice. If researchers want to determine whether something is an adaptation, the best way to do this is to conduct an engineering analysis of its constituent elements to see if they exhibit evidence of special design for solving a particular adaptive problem. Whether they happen to be currently linked with reproductive success is interesting, but not, strictly speaking, relevant to the question of whether the trait is an adaptation. As anthropologist Donald Symons once argued, if you want to demonstrate that vision is an adaptation, the appropriate test is not to check whether people with 20/20 vision have more offspring than people with 19/20 vision – for one thing, many other factors which have nothing to do with vision affect a complex outcome like number of offspring, making it hard to isolate the contributions of vision. Instead, a more theoretically grounded approach would be to analyze the machinery of the visual system to determine whether it fits the statistical structure of the problem it supposedly evolved to solve – whether its component parts exhibit such economy, reliability, efficiency, and complexity that it is exceedingly unlikely to have gotten that way without having been crafted by selection (Symons, 1989).

For these reasons, pinpointing specific genes, presence at birth, and current adaptiveness are not appropriate evidentiary standards for invoking adaptation. Thankfully, a theoretically grounded alternative set of standards exists in the notion of special design or improbable utility (Symons, 1990; Williams, 1966). This set of criteria, along with Williams' (1966) helpful admonition that researchers should not infer the presence of adaptation if the phenomenon in question can be explained by lower-level laws of physics or chemistry, provides a useful set of constraints for researchers wondering when it is appropriate to make claims about adaptation. Interested readers may wish to consult resources that discuss these ideas at greater length, including Williams' classic *Adaptation and Natural Selection* (1966); Tooby and Cosmides' 'The Psychological Foundations of Culture' (1992) and 'The Past Explains the Present' (1990a); Steven Pinker's foreword in the *Handbook of Evolutionary Psychology* (2015[2005]); Donald Symons' 'Adaptiveness and Adaptation' (1990), 'A Critique of Darwinian Anthropology' (1989), and 'On the Use and Misuse of Darwinism in the Study of Human Behavior' (1992); as well as a recent practically oriented guide ('Evolutionary Psychology: A How-To Guide'; Lewis et al., 2017) that discusses how to translate these ideas into a rigorous empirical research program.

BYPRODUCTS

Byproducts, as the name suggests, are concomitants or side effects of adaptations. Unlike adaptations, byproducts did not evolve to solve an adaptive problem and do not have a biological function (e.g., Tooby and Cosmides, 1992). They exist because they are coupled with adaptations, not because they helped solve a problem of survival or reproduction themselves (Williams, 1966). They can arise because of pleiotropy (genes with multiple effects), genetic linkage, as a side effect of developmental mechanisms, or because adaptations can have effects other than their proper evolved functions (Andrews et al., 2002; Barclay and van Vugt, 2015).

For example, reading and writing are byproducts of evolved adaptations for speaking and understanding language. This is likely why humans everywhere learn to speak and understand language with little formal instruction as long as they are exposed to it, whereas tasks such as reading and writing require long hours of formal instruction and sustained effort (Pinker, 1997).

In order to identify a byproduct, one ideally has to identify which adaptation(s) it is a byproduct of, as well as why it is coupled with that adaptation – an issue to which we return later in this section.

Morphological and Physiological Byproducts

The redness of blood, the whiteness of bones, and male nipples are morphological or physiological byproducts. None of these features has a specific function or evolved to solve an adaptive problem. Rather, the redness of blood is a byproduct of the iron in the blood's hemoglobin – the hemoglobin serves an oxygen-carrying function, but the redness itself serves no function and is merely a side effect of the hemoglobin (e.g., Symons, 1995). The whiteness of bones is also a byproduct – their color does not offer any survival or reproductive advantage. Rather, this whiteness is a side effect of the calcium that fortifies them and protects them against breakage (Symons, 1995); in other words, the incorporation of calcium into our endoskeleton is an adaptation, but the color is a byproduct. Male nipples are thought to be developmental byproducts of female nipples, for whom they do serve a function (Symons, 1979). In other words, nipples have a biological function in females, but males may only have them because they are byproducts of a shared developmental pathway with females (Symons, 1979).

Psychological and Behavioral Byproducts

Men have significantly more paraphilias (sexual fetishes) than women (Laws and Marshall, 1990; O'Donohue and Plaud, 1994). Researchers (e.g., Al-Shawaf et al., 2015a) have argued that this higher incidence of fetishism among men is likely a functionless byproduct of (a) males' easier-to-cross thresholds of sexual arousal combined with

(b) biased sexual learning mechanisms. In other words, as in many mammals, human males have lower thresholds for sexual arousal and display a greater eagerness for casual sex than females (e.g., Buss, 2018; Lippa, 2009). Men are also more likely to *learn sexual responses to non-sexual stimuli* – for example, after many pairings of erotic stimuli with non-erotic items such as colored squares or women's boots, some men will exhibit a sexual response to the colored squares or the boots alone (McConaghy, 1974; Rachman and Hodgson, 1968). Male rats and Japanese quail show similar effects of sexual conditioning, and these effects are typically weaker or absent in females (Crawford et al., 1993; Pfaus et al., 2001).

Racial prejudice may be another example of an evolutionary byproduct. Given the continuous nature of human variation and the presumably restricted range of ancestral humans, it is unlikely that our ancestors encountered individuals that belonged to a different 'race' than their own (Kurzban et al., 2001; Lewis et al., 2017). And yet, despite this fact – and the corollary that therefore there could *not* have been selection for categorization along the lines of race – racial prejudice and xenophobia are among humans' most damaging proclivities. Why is this? Kurzban and colleagues (2001) provide a byproduct-based answer to this puzzle. They suggest that racial categorization arises as a byproduct of evolved learning mechanisms. These proposed mechanisms evolved to attend to the local environment for cues that are statistically associated with patterns of cooperation and conflict in order to categorize people by group membership. Adaptations for tracking group membership would have served multiple useful functions for ancestral humans, including facilitating cooperation for tasks such as coalitional hunting, social alliances, and intergroup warfare. Kurzban and colleagues suggest – and provide evidence that – these adaptations for tracking group membership can be 'tricked' into categorizing people along racial lines

even though they did not evolve to respond to race per se (Kurzban et al., 2001). This line of research also suggests that race can be 'erased', meaning you can prevent this kind of 'mistaken' categorization by providing other salient cues for the coalition-tracking mechanisms to use instead (Kurzban et al., 2001; Navarrete et al., 2010). This example of byproduct research highlights the conceptual and practical utility of differentiating adaptations from byproducts.

Another example of byproducts comes from Belyaev and Trut's seminal fox domestication experiment. Over the course of several decades beginning in 1959 and continuing to this day, Belyaev and Trut attempted to domesticate foxes (*Vulpes vulpes*) by artificially selecting for tameness. Despite *only* selecting for tameness, within a few generations, their foxes exhibited several other new traits: floppy ears, piebald coloration, shorter tails and legs, altered head shape, and other new characteristics. These traits emerged as byproducts of selection for tameness – they were not directly selected for, but arose as hormonal and developmental side effects of selection for tameness (Dugatkin and Trut, 2018; Trut, 1999).

A final prominent example of byproduct work centers on why humans believe in supernatural entities. The most widely endorsed position is a byproduct view: humans do not have adaptations for religious belief, but rather are equipped with adaptations that produce belief in gods and invisible entities as an incidental side effect (Atran and Norenzayan, 2004; Boyer, 2001). According to this view, religious and supernatural belief are evolutionary byproducts of adaptations such as agency-detection mechanisms that are biased toward false positives (Atran and Norenzayan, 2004), theory of mind mechanisms (Willard and Norenzayan, 2013), and the parent-child attachment system (Kirkpatrick, 2009). Other researchers disagree, arguing that the human mind is equipped with adaptations specifically designed to produce religious belief (e.g., Alcorta and Sosis, 2005; Bering and

Johnson, 2005). Our purpose here is not to adjudicate between the different hypotheses on this issue, but rather to highlight a prominent empirical program based on byproduct hypotheses, and to emphasize the kinds of evidence a byproduct claim requires. We discuss the latter issue later in this chapter.

Obligate vs. Facultative Byproducts

The *obligate vs. facultative* distinction is frequently applied to adaptations (see Schmitt, 2015). It may be useful to apply the distinction to byproducts as well. Many morphological and physiological byproducts are obligate; that is, they are an unavoidable side effect of the adaptations to which they are coupled. The whiteness of bone, the redness of blood, and the bellybutton are all like this – they are inextricably coupled with their respective adaptations. By contrast, many psychological examples of byproducts are facultative; that is, they are *potential* side effects of the adaptations that produce them, but are not necessarily coupled with their adaptations. Reading, writing, and discriminating along racial lines are like this – they are likely side effects of adaptations that evolved for other purposes, but those adaptations are not guaranteed to produce them.

This distinction has led some to argue that the adaptation-byproduct distinction may not be useful in psychology, or that a different distinction may be required (Park, 2007). These discussions have been useful, but we suggest that the dispute is more terminological than conceptual. For example, based on the above reasoning that morphological byproducts tend to be inextricably coupled with adaptations, but many psychological ones are not, Park (2007) suggests that we should instead conceptualize the issue in terms of *adaptive vs. non-adaptive* effects of adaptations. By this, he means something similar to the distinction in biology between *proper function* and *effect* (the 'proper function' of an adaptation is the

effect it evolved to have, whereas an 'effect' of an adaptation is any other effect it has, even though it did not evolve *because* of that effect). We suggest that in psychology, most byproducts are not inherently coupled with adaptations – they are not guaranteed side effects; they are potential or likely side-effects of adaptations. The adaptation-byproduct distinction can accommodate these psychological byproducts just fine, especially if we conceptualize them as facultative byproducts rather than obligate byproducts. Calling facultative byproducts 'non-adaptive effects' is not quite right because (a) a byproduct can be adaptive or have adaptive effects despite not being an *adaptation* (see below), and (b) an adaptation can have non-adaptive effects – but these non-adaptive effects are not the same as byproducts. We therefore suggest that it would be simpler, and closer to the intended meaning, to borrow the obligate–facultative distinction from adaptations and use it to differentiate between obligate and facultative byproducts whenever the distinction is helpful or illuminating.

Byproducts Can Be Maladaptive

Byproducts did not evolve to solve an adaptive problem, and therefore have no evolved function. They exist merely because they are coupled with adaptations. In the present day, however, byproducts can be adaptive, neutral, or maladaptive. Byproducts have occasionally been defined as having no effect on current fitness (e.g., Buss et al., 1998), but this does not necessarily follow from the fact that they do not have a biological function. Above, we argued that evolutionary thinking requires a firm distinction between adaptation and current adaptiveness. Crucially, this same distinction also applies to byproducts: they should be defined by their history of selection (or lack thereof) and their evolved function (or lack thereof) – not by their current effects on fitness. Consequently, despite not being *adaptations*, byproducts can still be adaptive or maladaptive – they can still have positive or negative effects on fitness.

For example, sickle cell anemia is a maladaptive byproduct of selection for genes that protect against malaria (Allison, 1954). The allele for sickle cell anemia underwent positive selection because it is adaptive when in a heterozygous state – it protects against malaria. However, in a homozygous state this same allele can lead to sickle cell anemia, a potentially fatal disease (Allison, 1954). Tay Sachs disease provides another example. Tay Sachs is an autosomal recessive neurodegenerative disorder, and it is often fatal. The genes for Tay Sachs seem to persist because they protect against Tuberculosis in the heterozygous state. This state of affairs is called heterozygous advantage, and it highlights how selection can produce byproducts that are actively harmful or maladaptive (Allison, 1954; Al-Shawaf and Zreik, 2018; Nesse and Williams, 1994).

Some evidence suggests that there may be psychological analogues in conditions like schizophrenia and bipolar disorder (Del Giudice, 2018). Genes that give rise to schizophrenia or bipolar disorder may be selected due to their beneficial effects in low doses, but if too many of these alleles are present in a single body, they can lead to maladaptive effects that fall outside the normal range of variation for that trait (Del Giudice, 2018; Nesse, 2004). This phenomenon is sometimes known as a cliff-edge effect (Nesse, 2004, 2009; Vercken et al., 2012). There are many other potential causes of schizophrenia, including pathogenic infection, other exacerbating environmental effects, and intragenomic conflict between maternally and paternally imprinted genes (Nesse, 2015). Our point is not to provide a definitive explanation for the etiology of schizophrenia; rather, we wish to highlight the idea that positively selected genes can lead to maladaptive byproducts if those genes (in combination with environmental stressors) give rise to maladaptive levels of a trait that would have been adaptive at lower levels (Nesse,

2004). The broader point is this: even though byproducts did not evolve to solve an adaptive problem, this does not mean that they must have zero effect on fitness – they may indeed be neutral, but they can also be adaptive or maladaptive.

Differentiating Byproducts from Adaptations: Evidentiary Criteria

What kind of evidence is needed to establish that a feature is a byproduct?

The key test of whether a feature is an adaptation or a byproduct centers on whether that feature exhibits evidence of special design (Symons, 1989, 1990; Williams, 1966; see Lewis et al., 2017, for more on how to generate, test, and interpret byproduct hypotheses). Researchers who wish to distinguish between adaptations and byproducts should therefore look for evidence of improbable utility in solving an adaptive problem – something only adaptations will evince. However, a few secondary considerations may be relevant. First, in the case of facultative byproducts like reading, it can be instructive to note how reliably developing the feature is and/or how much formal training is required to acquire it. We noted earlier that spoken language (adaptation) develops more reliably and with less instruction than written language (byproduct). This criterion is only applicable in some cases, however, as obligate byproducts (like bellybuttons) will typically exhibit the same developmental patterns and universality as adaptations. Second, in the case of developmental byproducts such as male nipples, researchers have suggested that the byproduct may appear smaller in size, less complex, more variable, lacking specific features, or vestigial, especially relative to the sex for whom the feature is an adaptation (females; e.g., Puts and Dawood, 2006). In cases like this, it can be valuable to show empirically that there *is* a common genetic or developmental pathway shared by both male and female nipples. A third reasonable consideration in distinguishing between adaptations and byproducts is whether a trait or feature could *possibly* have been selected for in ancestral environments. For example, Kurzban and colleagues (2001) argued on theoretical grounds that it would have been difficult or impossible for racial prejudice to have been selected for in ancestral environments due to the continuous nature of human variation and the limited dispersal of ancestral humans. These kinds of considerations about evolvability constraints can help to differentiate between adaptations and byproducts by providing an *a priori* argument for the (im)plausibility of past selection for a particular trait. We expand on the kind of evidence required to test byproduct claims below.

Byproduct claims require just as much evidence as claims of adaptation – and possibly more

There is a common misconception that if you cannot demonstrate that something is an adaptation, you should automatically infer that it is a byproduct (Alcock, 1998; Buss et al., 1998). This reasoning is tempting, but inappropriate. While it is true that adaptation is a special and onerous concept whose invocation requires that key evidentiary criteria be met, this does not mean that a byproduct is a quick-and-easy null hypothesis for which no evidence is required. Just like claims of adaptation, byproduct claims must meet their own evidentiary standards.

Ideally, to establish that a feature is a byproduct, it is necessary to accomplish three things: (1) identify which adaptations it is supposedly coupled with, (2) articulate why, and provide evidence that, the byproduct accompanies those adaptations, and (3) demonstrate that it does not appear to exhibit evidence of special design for solving an adaptive problem (see Kurzban et al., 2001, for an example of this). This means that establishing that a feature is a byproduct typically requires the same amount of

evidence as establishing that a feature is an adaptation – or possibly more, in the sense that a clear byproduct demonstration requires demonstrating the adaptation that supposedly produces the byproduct *plus* additional pieces of evidence (Andrews et al., 2002; Buss et al., 1998; Goetz and Shackelford, 2006; Tooby and Cosmides, 1992). If studies fail to reveal conclusive evidence for either the byproduct or adaptation hypotheses, it is best not to automatically infer that the feature in question is a byproduct, but rather remain agnostic until further data are available to adjudicate between competing hypotheses.

NOISE

In addition to adaptations and byproducts, evolution also produces noise – sometimes referred to as 'random effects' (e.g., Krasnow and Truxaw, 2017; Tooby and Cosmides, 1992). Noise can be thought of as variation in the structure and function of adaptations or byproducts that was not selected for and did not evolve for any specific reason (Tooby and Cosmides, 1992). It can be genetically or environmentally driven. Examples of noise may include whether one's bellybutton is an 'innie' or an 'outie', whether one's earlobes are attached or unattached, or how noisily one drinks. Here, we delineate two different kinds of noise produced by evolution: selectively neutral noise generated by mutation and subsequently not winnowed out by selection, and deleterious noise maintained by mutation–selection balance.

Types of Noise

Selectively neutral noise

Selectively neutral noise refers to quantitative variation in the minor details of an adaptation or byproduct that has no effect on fitness or is unlinked to the adaptive aspects of design features (Buss et al., 1998; Goetz and Shackelford, 2006). For example, the exact size and shape of one's bellybutton, whether it's an 'innie' or an 'outie', and how fast one's fingernails grow could qualify as selectively neutral noise if they have no effect on fitness and did not evolve to solve an adaptive problem. Neutral noise, then, does not show evidence of special design, did not evolve to solve an adaptive problem, and was not filtered out by selection because it has (or more properly, *had*) no effects on fitness.

Deleterious noise

Some forms of noise do have an impact on fitness. The process of mutation constantly introduces new genetic variants into a population. Although selection works to winnow out the deleterious variants, mutation keeps introducing new variants into the population without cease. Consequently, selection is sometimes unable to completely expunge these deleterious genetic variants before new ones arise (e.g., Bergstrom and Dugatkin, 2012). This process, called mutation–selection balance, is thought to partly explain variation in intelligence (Penke et al., 2007), as well as certain disorders such as familial adenomatous polyposis (Bergstrom and Dugatkin, 2012).

This kind of variation (detrimental heritable variation maintained by mutation–selection balance) does not solve an adaptive problem, does not have a biological function, and does not show evidence of special design. We therefore suggest this qualifies as a form of noise. Although some scholars have characterized noise as necessarily having no effect on fitness (e.g., Shackelford and Liddle, 2014), the same distinction between adaptation and adaptiveness introduced earlier and applied to byproducts can also be applied to noise. According to this view, adaptations, byproducts, and noise should all be defined not by their current effects on fitness, but rather by their history of selection (or lack thereof) and evidence of special design (or lack thereof). This reasoning suggests that deleterious genetic variation maintained by mutation–selection balance should be categorized as noise despite its current effects on fitness[1].

Causes of Noise

Noise can have several causes, including mutation, genetic drift, gene flow (also known as migration), and random environmental effects. In other words, noise arises because of the stochastic elements of evolution (Tooby and Cosmides, 1992).

Mutation can introduce noise into a population, and mutation–selection balance can maintain that noise. As discussed above, if the new alleles are neutral with respect to fitness, they will not be winnowed out by selection, thereby providing a way for noise to remain in the population. If, by contrast, they have negative effects on fitness, selection will cull them – but not necessarily at a rate that ensures they completely disappear from the population (e.g., Bergstrom and Dugatkin, 2012).

Noise can also be produced by genetic drift, which is the random, chance-driven change in allele frequency from one generation to the next (e.g., Futuyma and Kirkpatrick, 2017). By chance alone, some features can become more common in a population than others, even though these features were neither selected for or against (Bergstrom and Dugatkin, 2012). Two important subtypes of drift are founder effects and bottlenecks.

Founder effects occur when some subset of a population – say, one that has a disproportionately high percentage of redheads – founds a new colony for reasons unrelated to being a redhead. In this case, the next generation of the new colony will also have a disproportionate number of redheads, despite no positive selection for red-headedness. In this case, genetic drift has led to a change in allele frequency despite no history of selection on the alleles in question.

Bottlenecks occur when, for example, there is an environmental catastrophe and, by chance, some genetic variants survive better than others, resulting in a post-catastrophe population that exhibits different allele frequencies than the pre-catastrophe population. This is an outcome of chance, not driven by any functional advantage of the alleles that now constitute a greater proportion of the population. For example, imagine that an earthquake causes the death of a large subset of a population, sparing those who happened to be elsewhere at the time. By chance, the group that was elsewhere happens to have an unusually large number of moles on their bodies. If variation in mole prevalence is partly heritable, then the next generation of individuals will have more moles on their bodies than the average individual in the pre-earthquake population – not because the moles were protective against disease or danger, but rather due to the chance effects of who happened to be there when the fatal earthquake struck. This is another process by which genetic drift (in this case, a bottleneck) can lead to noise in a population. These kinds of considerations are important because investigators seeking an adaptive explanation for the increased prevalence of moles in this population will not find one.

Gene flow, sometimes called admixture or migration, can also produce noise. Gene flow refers to the movement or 'flow' of genes from one geographic area to another. For example, if some organisms migrate from one region to another (perhaps in search of mates or food), gene flow has occurred. This kind of migration can lead to noise because the resulting variation between groups may not be adaptively patterned. For example, imagine that relative to those who do not migrate, those who migrate are more likely than average to be double-jointed or have faster-growing nails. This will result in a new population of colonists that has different characteristics than the original population. However, these differences are not produced by adaptation and are not adaptively tied to the ecology of the new location – they are noise. Interpreting these differences as evidence of adaptation would therefore be a mistake.

One caveat here is that it is also possible for gene flow to have an adaptive basis. For example, individuals with higher levels of extraversion and risk-taking may be more likely to migrate than those with lower levels of these traits, in which case the migration is not entirely arbitrary. This may be the case: although the direction of causation is still unclear, studies suggest that nomadic populations have a greater proportion of the 7R allele of the DRD4 gene, which is associated with novelty-seeking (Chen et al., 1999; Eisenberg et al., 2008). Consequently, it is worth keeping in mind that while gene flow can produce evolutionary noise, it is also the case that the patterns of variation produced by gene flow may sometimes reveal an underlying logic that is non-arbitrary.

Finally, noise can be driven by environmental effects such as pathogens, parasites, stochastic developmental effects, and unexpected environmental inputs into evolved mechanisms (e.g., Tooby and Cosmides, 1992). These environmental effects can lead to variation that is not adaptively patterned and does not have a biological function – noise. This does not mean that *all* environmentally-driven variation is noise, however. Much environmentally-driven variation is adaptively patterned, arising from evolved psychological mechanisms responding systematically to environmental inputs. Examples of this kind of environmentally driven, adaptively patterned variation include evoked culture (Gangestad et al., 2006), reactive heritability (Tooby and Cosmides, 1990b; Lukaszewski and Roney, 2011), adaptation to local regional climates and dietary practices (e.g., Fan et al., 2016), and other adaptively patterned individual differences (e.g., Lewis et al., Chapter 6, this volume).

Evidentiary Standards for Invoking Noise

How can researchers distinguish between random noise and adaptively patterned variation produced by adaptations? The primary criterion is again that of special design: evidence that the variation in question seems arranged to solve an adaptive problem, and whose patterning is so improbably useful that it is exceedingly unlikely to have arisen by chance.

For example, the human disgust system produces effects that are remarkably well-suited to solving the adaptive problem of avoiding infection: it is preferentially triggered by more pathogenic items compared to less pathogenic ones (Curtis et al., 2004), releases pro-inflammatory cytokines (Schaller et al., 2010), produces avoidant motor behaviors (Mortensen et al., 2010), leads to decreases in state extraversion and openness to experience (Mortensen et al., 2010), reduces desire for casual sex (Al-Shawaf et al., 2018a), is downregulated in short-term matters (Al-Shawaf et al., 2015b), responds to the odor of sickness in conspecifics (Olsson et al., 2014), might be upregulated during periods of immunosuppression (Fessler et al., 2005), appears to respond more strongly to groups that are likely to carry unfamiliar pathogens (Faulkner et al., 2004; Makhanova et al., 2015; but see van Leeuwen and Petersen, 2018), and is downregulated when caring for one's kin (Case et al., 2006). This pattern conforms to an engineering analysis of what you might expect from a system specifically designed to reduce the likelihood of infection. This pattern is too improbably useful at solving the problem of avoiding infection to be the result of chance. It is therefore unlikely to be noise, but rather the product of an adaptation (Al-Shawaf et al., 2015a; Curtis et al., 2004).

By contrast, consider variation in features such as the length of one's nails, whether one's earlobe is attached or unattached, or how noisily one drinks water. Variation in these features is presumably selectively neutral, and probably was so over long periods of human evolution as well. Additionally, these features are not obviously tied to solving a particular adaptive problem. There is no compelling reason to believe that a systematic

empirical investigation of variation in these traits would uncover adaptive patterning indicative of special design to solve a particular problem. Note that the same lack of adaptive patterning is likely true for *some* of the variation in disgust – even if disgust itself is an evolved adaptation, some proportion of the quantitative variation in the emotion is likely driven by chance and is not characterized by adaptive patterning. Such variation, like variation in earlobe connectedness or how noisily one drinks, is a good candidate for noise.

The key phrase in this analysis is 'good candidate'. These suggestions should be regarded as working hypotheses to be tested, not definite conclusions. As with all questions about adaptations, byproducts, and noise, the above suggestions are empirical questions that can only be settled by testing the patterns of variation in these features and investigating whether they exhibit evidence of special design. Of course, it can be difficult or impossible to answer this question if one doesn't know what adaptive problem to investigate in the first place. For this reason, patterns that initially appear to be noise may later turn out to be the product of an adaptation once a researcher has identified the correct adaptive problem. As is always the case in science, hypotheses and conclusions about noise remain tentative and open to revision (as do hypotheses and conclusions about adaptations and byproducts).

We suggest that noise should be the null hypothesis for researchers testing hypotheses about adaptations – if no special patterning is detected, infer that variation is noise, and only if patterning suggestive of special design is detected, consider the 'special and onerous concept' of adaptation (Williams, 1966: 4). This approach may lead to under-identifying (missing) some adaptations, but of course this can always be overturned by subsequent investigations. Furthermore, because byproduct hypotheses also require that a specific and stringent set of evidentiary criteria be met, noise seems to be the most appropriate choice for a null hypothesis.

CONCLUSION

In sum, the evolutionary process produces three outcomes: adaptations, byproducts, and noise.

Adaptations are morphological, physiological, or psychological mechanisms that evolved to solve an adaptive problem. They are distinguished by evidence of special design – that is, they are patterned in such a way that suggests a tight fit with an adaptive problem. Adaptations do not need to be present at birth, are not genetically determined, and are not in conflict with learning – indeed, learning mechanisms are themselves evolved adaptations.

Adaptations evolved because they served a function, but they do not need to be *currently adaptive*. In fact, they can have *maladaptive* effects for many reasons, including constraints on selection, environmental mismatches, malfunctioning adaptations, interindividual conflict, errors by design, and the on-average nature of selection. Importantly, adaptations are typically universal at the information-processing level, not the behavioral level, so behavioral variation across groups or cultures does not automatically constitute evidence against adaptation. Indeed, evolutionary reasoning often predicts that adaptations will lead to systematically patterned cultural variation in behavior, as is the case with 'evoked culture' (e.g., Al-Shawaf and Lewis, 2017; Gangestad et al., 2006).

By contrast, byproducts exist because they are incidental side effects of adaptations. They did not evolve to solve an adaptive problem and do not have a function. Examples of morphological and physiological byproducts include the whiteness of bones and the redness of blood. Examples of psychological byproducts include reading and writing, discrimination along racial lines, and belief in supernatural beings. Unlike adaptations, byproducts do not evince evidence of special design. Testing byproduct hypotheses requires that one show an apparent lack of special design, identify the adaptations that supposedly lead to the byproduct, and

provide evidence that these adaptations actually do lead to the byproduct as an incidental concomitant.

Noise is variation that is not adaptively patterned, does not appear to solve an adaptive problem, and is not a byproduct. Examples of noise likely include whether one's earlobe is attached or unattached, whether one's bellybutton is an innie or an outie, and possibly other inconsequential variation such as how noisily one drinks water or the number of moles on one's body. Some definitions of noise stipulate that noise must be selectively neutral, but we have argued that noise can have effects on fitness and still qualify as noise as long as it meets the above criteria – especially the criteria of not having evolved to solve an adaptive problem and not showing evidence of special design.

Hypotheses about adaptations, byproducts, and noise are testable (Simpson and Campbell, 2015). One way to proceed is using the top-down method, in which researchers generate *a priori* hypotheses on the basis of theory, use these hypotheses to derive specific predictions, and subsequently test these predictions in empirical studies. Another way to proceed is using the bottom-up method, in which researchers observe an interesting phenomenon, generate a hypothesis to explain it, derive new predictions from that hypothesis, and subsequently test these predictions in empirical studies. The 'just-so' charge (also known as post hoc storytelling) falls flat for hypotheses that were generated *a priori* using the top-down approach. By contrast, hypotheses generated using the bottom-up approach can lapse into just-so storytelling, but – as in all sciences – *only* if the researcher stops halfway through the process and decides to believe the hypothesis he or she just concocted without deriving and testing any new predictions emanating from it (Al-Shawaf et al., 2018b). This can happen, but is relatively rare (for discussions of how to rigorously apply evolutionary thinking to psychological research, see Lewis et al., 2017). By contrast, if the researcher derives novel predictions from the newly concocted hypothesis and conducts empirical tests of these novel predictions, then he or she has proceeded in the normal scientific manner – and the just-so charge falls flat again.

Evolutionary thinking has led to great advances in our understanding of human psychology and behavior over the last 40 years (Al-Shawaf et al., 2018b; Buss, 1995; Confer et al., 2010). The three products of evolution (adaptations, byproducts, and noise) are distinguishable on conceptual and empirical grounds – distinctions that play a key role in explaining known findings and predicting new ones. We hope that this chapter motivates researchers to carefully differentiate these three products of evolution, and contributes in some small way to the light that evolutionary thinking continues to shed on the psychological and behavioral sciences.

ACKNOWLEDGEMENTS

The authors extend their gratitude to John Alcock, Lee Dugatkin, Todd Shackelford, and an anonymous reviewer for helpful suggestions on earlier drafts or portions of the chapter.

Note

1 For the same reason, random variation that contributes positively to fitness – and thus is likely to undergo selection, but currently has no function – should also qualify as (positive) noise.

REFERENCES

Alcock, J. (1998). Unpunctuated equilibrium in the natural history essays of Stephen Jay Gould. *Evolution and Human Behavior*, *19*(5), 321–336.

Alcock, J. (2001). *The triumph of sociobiology*. New York, NY: Oxford University Press.

Alcock, A. (2013). *Animal behavior: An evolutionary approach. Tenth edition*. Sunderland, MA: Sinauer Associates.

Alcock J. (2018a). Just so stories. In T. K. Shackelford & V. A. Weekes-Shackelford (Eds), *Encyclopedia of evolutionary psychological science*. Cham: Springer.

Alcock, J. (2018b). Richard Lewontin and Stephen Jay Gould. In T. K. Shackelford & V. A. Weekes-Shackelford (Eds), *Encyclopedia of evolutionary psychological science*. Cham: Springer.

Alcorta, C. S., & Sosis, R. (2005). Ritual, emotion, and sacred symbols: The evolution of religion as an adaptive complex. *Human Nature*, *16*(4), 323–359.

Allison, A. C. (1954). Protection afforded by sickle-cell trait against subtertian malarial infection. *British Medical Journal*, *1*(4857), 290–294.

Al-Shawaf, L. (2019) https://areomagazine.com/2019/08/20/seven-key-misconceptions-about-evolutionary-psychology/

Al-Shawaf, L., Conroy-Beam, D., Asao, K., & Buss, D. M. (2015a). Human emotions: An evolutionary psychological perspective. *Emotion Review*, 1–14. doi:10.1177/1754073914565518

Al-Shawaf, L., Lewis, D. M., & Buss, D. M. (2015b). Disgust and mating strategy. *Evolution and Human Behavior*, *36*(3), 199–205.

Al-Shawaf, L., Lewis, D. M., Alley, T. R., & Buss, D. M. (2015c). Mating strategy, disgust, and food neophobia. *Appetite*, *85*, 30–35. doi:10.1016/j.appet.2014.10.029

Al-Shawaf, L., & Lewis, D. M. G. (2017). Evolutionary psychology and the emotions. In V. Zeigler-Hill & T. K. Shackelford (Eds), *Encyclopedia of personality and individual differences*. New York: Springer.

Al-Shawaf, L., & Zreik, K. A. (2018). Richard Dawkins on constraints on natural selection. In T. K. Shackelford & V. A. Weekes-Shackelford (Eds), *Encyclopedia of evolutionary psychological science*. New York, NY: Springer.

Al-Shawaf, L., Lewis, D. M. G., Ghossainy, M. E., & Buss, D. M. (2018a). Experimentally inducing disgust reduces desire for short-term mating. *Evolutionary Psychological Science*, *5*(3), 267–275.

Al-Shawaf, L., Zreik, K. A., & Buss, D. M. (2018b). Thirteen misunderstandings about natural selection. In T. K. Shackelford & V. A. Weekes-Shackelford (Eds), *Encyclopedia of*

Evolutionary Psychological Science. New York, NY: Springer.

Al-Shawaf, L., Lewis, D. M., Wehbe, Y. S., & Buss, D. M. (2019). Context, environment, and learning in evolutionary psychology. In T. K. Shackelford & V. A. Weekes-Shackelford (Eds), *Encyclopedia of Evolutionary Psychological Science*. New York, NY: Springer.

Andrews, P. W., Gangestad, S. W., & Matthews, D. (2002). Adaptationism, exaptationism, and evolutionary behavioral science. *Behavioral and Brain Sciences*, *25*(4), 534–547.

Atran, S., & Norenzayan, A. (2004). Religion's evolutionary landscape: Counterintuition, commitment, compassion, communion. *Behavioral and Brain Sciences*, *27*(6), 713–730.

Badcock, C., & Crespi, B. (2006). Imbalanced genomic imprinting in brain development: An evolutionary basis for the aetiology of autism. *Journal of evolutionary biology*, *19*(4), 1007–1032

Bailey, J. M. (2000). How can psychological adaptations be heritable? In G. Bock, J. A. Goode & K. Webb (Eds), *The nature of intelligence* (pp. 171–184). Chichester: J. Wiley & Sons. (Novartis Foundation Symposium 233.)

Barclay, P., & van Vugt, M. (2015). The evolutionary psychology of human prosociality: Adaptations, byproducts, and mistakes. In D. A. Schroeder & W. G. Graziano (Eds), *Oxford Library of Psychology. The Oxford handbook of prosocial behavior* (pp. 37–60). New York, NY: Oxford University Press.

Baron-Cohen, S. (1996). *Mindblindness: An essay on autism and theory of mind*. Cambridge, MA: MIT Press.

Barrett, H. C., & Kurzban, R. (2006). Modularity in cognition: Framing the debate. *Psychological Review*, *113*(3), 628–647.

Barrett, H. C., & Broesch, J. (2012). Prepared social learning about dangerous animals in children. *Evolution and Human Behavior*, *33*(5), 499–508.

Barrett, H. C. (2015). Adaptations to predators and prey. In D. M. Buss (Ed.), *The handbook of evolutionary psychology. Second edition. Volume 1: Foundations* (pp. 246–263). Hoboken, NJ: John Wiley & Sons.

Barrett, R. D., & Schluter, D. (2008). Adaptation from standing genetic variation. *Trends in Ecology & Evolution*, *23*(1), 38–44.

Bergstrom, C. T., & Dugatkin, L. A. (2012). *Evolution*. New York, NY: W.W. Norton & Company.

Bering, J., & Johnson, D. (2005). 'O Lord... You Perceive my Thoughts from Afar': Recursiveness and the evolution of supernatural agency. *Journal of Cognition and Culture*, *5*(1–2), 118–142.

Borgia, G. (1994). The scandals of San Marco. *The Quarterly Review of Biology*, *69*(3), 373–375.

Boyer, P. (2001). *Religion explained: The evolutionary origins of religious thought*. New York, NY: Basic Books.

Boyer, P., & Bergstrom, B. (2011). Threat-detection in child development: An evolutionary perspective. *Neuroscience and Biobehavioral Reviews*, *35*(4), 1034–1041.

Buss, D. M. (1995). Evolutionary psychology: A new paradigm for psychological science. *Psychological Inquiry*, *6*(1), 1–30.

Buss, D. M., Haselton, M. G., Shackelford, T. K., Bleske, A. L., & Wakefield, J. C. (1998). Adaptations, exaptations, and spandrels. *American Psychologist*, *53*(5), 533–548.

Buss, D. M. (2015). *Evolutionary psychology: The new science of the mind. Fifth edition*. Abingdon, UK: Routledge.

Buss, D. M. (2018). *The evolution of desire: Strategies of human mating*. New York, NY: Basic Books.

Byars, S. G., Stearns, S. C., & Boomsma, J. J. (2014). Opposite risk patterns for autism and schizophrenia are associated with normal variation in birth size: Phenotypic support for hypothesized diametric gene-dosage effects. *Proceedings of the Royal Society B: Biological Sciences*, *281*(1794), 1–9.

Case, T. I., Repacholi, B. M., & Stevenson, R. J. (2006). My baby doesn't smell as bad as yours: The plasticity of disgust. *Evolution and Human Behavior*, *27*(5), 357–365.

Chen, C., Burton, M. L., Greenberger, E., & Dmitrieva, J. (1999). Population migration and the variation of dopamine D4 receptor (DRD4) allele frequencies around the globe. *Evolution and Human Behavior*, *20*(5), 309–324.

Cochran, G., & Harpending, H. (2009). *The 10,000 year explosion: How civilization accelerated human evolution*. New York, NY: Basic Books.

Confer, J. C., Easton, J. A., Fleischman, D. S., Goetz, C. D., Lewis, D. M., Perilloux, C., &

Buss, D. M. (2010). Evolutionary psychology: Controversies, questions, prospects, and limitations. *American Psychologist, 65*(2), 110–126.

Crawford, L. L., Holloway, K. S., & Domjan, M. (1993). The nature of sexual reinforcement. *Journal of the Experimental Analysis of Behavior, 60*(1), 55–66.

Crespi, B. J. (2000). The evolution of maladaptation. *Heredity, 84*(6), 623–629.

Crespi, B. (2014). An evolutionary framework for psychological maladaptations. *Psychological Inquiry, 25*(3–4), 322–324.

Crespi, B., & Badcock, C. (2008). Psychosis and autism as diametrical disorders of the social brain. *Behavioral and Brain Sciences, 31*(3), 241–261.

Curtis, V., Aunger, R., & Rabie, T. (2004). Evidence that disgust evolved to protect from risk of disease. *Proceedings of the Royal Society B: Biological Sciences, 271*(4), S131–S133.

Curtis, V., de Barra, M., & Aunger, R. (2011). Disgust as an adaptive system for disease avoidance behaviour. *Philosophical Transactions of the Royal Society B: Biological Sciences, 366*(1563), 389–401.

Darwin, C. (1859). *On the origin of species by means of natural selection.* London: John Murray.

Dawkins, R. (1976). *The selfish gene.* Oxford, UK: Oxford University Press.

Dawkins, R. (1999). *The extended phenotype: The long reach of the gene.* Oxford, UK: Oxford University Press.

Del Giudice, M. (2018). *Evolutionary psychopathology: A unified approach.* New York, NY: Oxford University Press.

Dennett, D. C. (1996). *Darwin's dangerous idea: Evolution and the meanings of life.* London: Penguin Books.

Dugatkin, L. A., & Trut, L. N. (2018). *How to tame a fox (and build a dog): Visionary scientists and a Siberian tale of jump-started evolution.* Chicago, IL: The University of Chicago Press.

Eisenberg, D. T., Campbell, B., Gray, P. B., & Sorenson, M. D. (2008). Dopamine receptor genetic polymorphisms and body composition in undernourished pastoralists: An exploration of nutrition indices among nomadic and recently settled Ariaal men of northern Kenya. *BMC Evolutionary Biolology,* 8:173.

Eisner, T., & Aneshansley, D. J. (1999). Spray aiming in the bombardier beetle: Photographic evidence. *Proceedings of the National Academy of Sciences, 96*(17), 9705–9709.

Fan, S., Hansen, M. E., Lo, Y., & Tishkoff, S. A. (2016). Going global by adapting local: A review of recent human adaptation. *Science, 354*(6308), 54–59.

Faulkner, J., Schaller, M., Park, J. H., & Duncan, L. A. (2004). Evolved disease-avoidance mechanisms and contemporary xenophobic attitudes. *Group Processes & Intergroup Relations, 7*(4), 333–353.

Fenneman, J., & Frankenhuis, W. E. (2020). Is impulsive behavior adaptive in harsh and unpredictable environments? A formal model. *Evolution and Human Behavior, 41*(4), 261–273.

Fessler, D. M., Eng, S. J., & Navarrete, C. D. (2005). Elevated disgust sensitivity in the first trimester of pregnancy: Evidence supporting the compensatory prophylaxis hypothesis. *Evolution and Human Behavior, 26*(4), 344–351.

Frankenhuis, W. E., & Panchanathan, K. (2011). Balancing sampling and specialization: An adaptationist model of incremental development. *Proceedings of the Royal Society B: Biological Sciences, 278*(1724), 3558–3565.

Futuyma, D. J., & Kirkpatrick, M. (2017). *Evolution. Fourth edition.* Sunderland, MA: Sinauer Associates.

Gangestad, S. W., & Buss, D. M. (1993). Pathogen prevalence and human mate preferences. *Ethology and Sociobiology, 14*(2), 89–96.

Gangestad, S. W., Haselton, M. G., & Buss, D. M. (2006). Evolutionary foundations of cultural variation: Evoked culture and mate preferences. *Psychological Inquiry, 17*(2), 75–95.

Gernsbacher, M. A., & Yergeau, M. (2019). Empirical failures of the claim that autistic people lack a Theory of Mind. *Archives of scientific psychology, 7*(1), 102–118. https://doi.org/10.1037/arc0000067

Goetz, A. T., & Shackelford, T. K. (2006). Modern application of evolutionary theory to psychology: Key concepts and clarifications. *The American Journal of Psychology, 119*(4), 567–584.

Gould, S. J., & Lewontin, R. C. (1979). The spandrels of San Marco and the Panglossian paradigm: A critique of the adaptationist programme. *Proceedings of the Royal Society of London. Series B: Biological Sciences*, *205*(1161), 581–598.

Gould, S. J., & Vrba, E. S. (1982). Exaptation: A missing term in the science of form. *Paleobiology*, *8*(1), 4–15.

Gould, S. J. (1991). Exaptation: A crucial tool for an evolutionary psychology. *Journal of Social Issues*, *47*(3), 43–65.

Haig, B. D., & Durrant, R. (2000). Theory evaluation in evolutionary psychology. *Psychological Inquiry*, *11*(1), 34–38.

Haig, D. (1993). Genetic conflicts in human pregnancy. *The Quarterly Review of Biology*, *68*(4), 495–532.

Haig, D. (1997). Parental antagonism, relatedness asymmetries, and genomic imprinting. *Proceedings of the Royal Society of London. Series B: Biological Sciences*, *264*(1388), 1657–1662.

Haselton, M. G., & Buss, D. M. (2000). Error management theory: A new perspective on biases in cross-sex mind reading. *Journal of Personality and Social Psychology*, *78*(1), 81–91.

Haselton, M. G., & Nettle, D. (2006). The paranoid optimist: An integrative evolutionary model of cognitive biases. *Personality and Social Psychology Review*, *10*(1), 47–66.

Henningsen, D. D., & Henningsen, M. L. M. (2010). Testing error management theory: Exploring the commitment skepticism bias and the sexual overperception bias. *Human Communication Research*, *36*(4), 618–634.

Herzner, G., Schlecht, A., Dollhofer, V., Parzefall, C., Harrar, K., Kreuzer, A., Pilsl, L., & Ruther, J. (2013). Larvae of the parasitoid wasp *Ampulex compressa* sanitize their host, the American cockroach, with a blend of antimicrobials. *Proceedings of the National Academy of Sciences*, *110*(4), 1369–1374.

Jackson, R. E., & Cormack, L. K. (2007). Evolved navigation theory and the descent illusion. *Perception & Psychophysics*, *69*(3), 353–362. doi:10.3758/BF03193756

Jackson, R. E., & Cormack, L. K. (2008). Evolved navigation theory and the environmental vertical illusion. *Evolution and Human Behavior*, *29*(5), 299–304.

Jacob, F. (1977). Evolution and tinkering. *Science*, *196*(4295), 1161–1166.

Johnson, K. E., & Voight, B. F. (2018). Patterns of shared signatures of recent positive selection across human populations. *Nature Ecology & Evolution*, *2*(4), 713–720.

Ketelaar, T., & Ellis, B. J. (2000). Are evolutionary explanations unfalsifiable? Evolutionary psychology and the Lakatosian philosophy of science. *Psychological Inquiry*, *11*(1), 1–21.

Kirkpatrick, L. A. (2009). An attachment-theory approach to the psychology of religion. *The International Journal for the Psychology of Religion*, *2*(1), 3–28.

Krasnow, M., & Truxaw, D. (2017). The adaptationist program. In T. K. Shackelford & V. A. Weekes-Shackelford (Eds), *Encyclopedia of evolutionary psychological science*. New York, NY: Springer.

Kurzban, R., Tooby, J., & Cosmides, L. (2001). Can race be erased? Coalitional computation and social categorization. *Proceedings of the National Academy of Sciences*, *98*(26), 15387–15392.

Laws, D. R., & Marshall, W. L. (1990). A conditioning theory of the etiology and maintenance of deviant sexual preference and behavior. In W. L. Marshall, D. R. Laws & H. E. Barbaree (Eds), *Handbook of sexual assault: Issues, theories and treatment of the offender* (pp. 209–229). New York, NY: Plenum.

Lewis, D. M. G., Al-Shawaf, L., & Buss, D. M. (in press). Evolutionary personality psychology. In P. J. Corr & G. Matthews (Eds), *The Cambridge handbook of personality psychology. Second edition*. Cambridge: Cambridge University Press.

Lewis, D. M. G., Al-Shawaf, L., Conroy-Beam, D., Asao, K., & Buss, D. M. (2017). Evolutionary psychology: A how-to guide. *American Psychologist*, *72*(4), 353–373.

Lieberman, D., Tooby, J., & Cosmides, L. (2007). The architecture of human kin detection. *Nature*, *445*(7129), 727–731.

Lippa, R. A. (2009). Sex differences in sex drive, sociosexuality, and height across 53 nations: Testing evolutionary and social structural theories. *Archives of Sexual Behavior*, *38*(5), 631–651.

LoBue, V., Rakison, D. H., & DeLoache, J. S. (2010). Threat perception across the life span: Evidence for multiple converging pathways. *Current Directions in Psychological Science*, *19*(6), 375–379.

Lukaszewski, A. W., & Roney, J. R. (2011). The origins of extraversion: Joint effects of facultative calibration and genetic polymorphism.

Personality and Social Psychology Bulletin, *37*(3), 409–421.

Makhanova, A., Miller, S. L., & Maner, J. K. (2015). Germs and the out-group: Chronic and situational disease concerns affect intergroup categorization. *Evolutionary Behavioral Sciences*, *9*(1), 8–19.

McConaghy, N. (1974). Penile volume responses to moving and still pictures of male and female nudes. *Archives of Sexual Behavior*, *3*(6), 565–570.

Mortensen, C. R., Becker, D. V., Ackerman, J. M., Neuberg, S. L., & Kenrick, D. T. (2010). Infection breeds reticence: The effects of disease salience on self-perceptions of personality and behavioral avoidance tendencies. *Psychological Science*, *21*(3), 440–447.

Navarrete, C. D., McDonald, M. M., Molina, L. E., & Sidanius, J. (2010). Prejudice at the nexus of race and gender: an outgroup male target hypothesis. *Journal of Personality and Social Psychology*, 98(6), 933–945.

Nesse, R. M., & Williams, G. C. (1994). *Why we get sick: The new science of Darwinian medicine*. New York, NY: Times Books Random House.

Nesse, R. M. (2001). The smoke detector principle: Natural selection and the regulation of defensive responses. *Annals of the New York Academy of Sciences*, *935*, 75–85.

Nesse, R. M. (2004). Cliff-edged fitness functions and the persistence of schizophrenia. *Behavioral and Brain Sciences*, *27*(6), 862–863.

Nesse, R. M. (2005). Natural selection and the regulation of defenses: A signal detection analysis of the smoke detector principle. *Evolution and Human Behavior*, *26*(1), 88–105.

Nesse, R. M. (2009). Evolution at 150: Time for truly biological psychiatry. *The British Journal of Psychiatry*, *195*(6), 471–472.

Nesse, R. M. (2015). Evolutionary psychology and mental health. In D. M. Buss (Ed.), *The handbook of evolutionary psychology. Second edition. Volume 2: Integrations* (pp. 1007–1026). Hoboken, NJ: John Wiley & Sons.

Neuhoff, J. G. (1998). Perceptual bias for rising tones. *Nature*, *395*(6698), 123–124.

Neuhoff, J. G. (2001). An adaptive bias in the perception of looming auditory motion. *Ecological Psychology*, *13*(2), 87–110.

O'Donohue, W., & Plaud, J. J. (1994). The conditioning of human sexual arousal. *Archives of Sexual Behavior*, *23*(3), 321–344.

Olsson, M. J., Lundström, J. N., Kimball, B. A., Gordon, A. R., Karshikoff, B., Hosseini, N., Sorjonen, K., Höglund, C. O., Solares, C., Soop, A., Axelsson, J., & Lekanger, M. (2014). The scent of disease: Human body odor contains an early chemosensory cue of sickness. *Psychological Science*, *25*(3), 817–823.

Ostrom, J. H. (1974). *Archaeopteryx* and the origin of flight. *The Quarterly Review of Biology*, *49*(1), 27–47.

Ostrom, J. H. (1979). Bird flight: How did it begin? *American Scientist*, *67*(1), 46–56.

Park, J. H. (2007). Persistent misunderstandings of inclusive fitness and kin selection: Their ubiquitous appearance in social psychology textbooks. *Evolutionary Psychology*, *5*(4), 860–873.

Penke, L., Denissen, J. J., & Miller, G. F. (2007). The evolutionary genetics of personality. *European Journal of Personality* (Published for the European Association of Personality Psychology), *21*(5), 549–587.

Pfaus, J. G., Kippin, T. E., & Centeno, S. (2001). Conditioning and sexual behavior: A review. *Hormones and Behavior*, *40*(2), 291–321.

Piek, T., Visser, J. H., & Veenendaal, R. L. (1984). Change in behaviour of the cockroach, *Periplaneta americana*, after being stung by the sphecid wasp *Ampulex compressa*. *Entomologia Experimentalis et Applicata*, *35*(2), 195–203.

Pinker, S. (1997). *How the mind works*. New York, NY: W. W. Norton & Co.

Puts, D. A., & Dawood, K. (2006). The evolution of female orgasm: Adaptation or byproduct? *Twin Research and Human Genetics*, *9*(3), 467–472.

Rachman, S., & Hodgson, R. J. (1968). Experimentally-induced 'sexual fetishism': Replication and development. *The Psychological Record*, *18*(1), 25–27.

Schaller, M., Miller, G. E., Gervais, W. M., Yager, S., & Chen, E. (2010). Mere visual perception of other people's disease symptoms facilitates a more aggressive immune response. *Psychological Science*, *21*(5), 649–652.

Schmitt, D. P. (2005). Sociosexuality from Argentina to Zimbabwe: A 48-nation study of sex, culture, and strategies of human mating. *Behavioral and Brain Sciences*, *28*(2), 247–275.

Schmitt, D. P. (2015). The evolution of culturally-variable sex differences: Men and women are not always different, but when they are … it appears *not* to result from patriarchy or sex role socialization. In T. K. Shackelford & R. D. Hansen (Eds), *The evolution of sexuality* (Evolutionary Psychology series). Cham: Springer.

Shackelford, T. K., & Liddle, J. R. (2014). Understanding the mind from an evolutionary perspective: An overview of evolutionary psychology. *Cognitive Science, 5*(3), 247–260.

Shaver, P. R., Hazan, C., & Bradshaw, D. (1988). Love as attachment: The integration of three behavioral systems. In R. J. Sternberg & M. L. Barnes (Eds), *The psychology of love* (pp. 68–99). New Haven, CT: Yale University Press.

Simpson, J. A., & Campbell, L. (2015). Methods of evolutionary sciences. In D. M. Buss (Ed.), *The handbook of evolutionary psychology. Second edition. Volume 1: Foundations* (pp. 115–135). Hoboken, NJ: John Wiley & Sons.

Symons, D. (1979). *The evolution of human sexuality*. New York, NY: Oxford University Press.

Symons, D. (1989). A critique of Darwinian anthropology. *Ethology and Sociobiology, 10*(1–3), 131–144.

Symons, D. (1990). Adaptiveness and adaptation. *Ethology and Sociobiology, 11*(4–5), 427–444.

Symons, D. (1992). On the use and misuse of Darwinism in the study of human behavior. In J. H. Barkow, L. Cosmides & J. Tooby (Eds), *The adapted mind: Evolutionary psychology and the generation of culture* (pp. 137–159). New York, NY: Oxford University Press.

Symons, D. (1995). Beauty is in the adaptations of the beholder. The evolutionary psychology of human female sexual attractiveness. In P. R. Abramson & S. D. Pinkerton (Eds), *Sexual nature/Sexual culture* (pp. 80–118). Chicago, IL: The University of Chicago Press.

Thomas, J. A., & Elmes, G. W. (1998). Higher productivity at the cost of increased host-specificity when *Maculinea* butterfly larvae exploit ant colonies through trophallaxis rather than by predation. *Ecological Entomology, 23*(4), 457–464.

Tinbergen, N. (1963). On aims and methods of ethology. *Zeitschrift für Tierpsychologie, 20*(4),410–433.

Tooby, J., & Cosmides, L. (1990a). The past explains the present: Emotional adaptations and the structure of ancestral environments. *Ethology and Sociobiology, 11*(4–5), 375–424.

Tooby, J., & Cosmides, L. (1990b). On the universality of human nature and the uniqueness of the individual: The role of genetics and adaptation. *Journal of Personality, 58*(1), 17–67.

Tooby, J., & Cosmides, L. (1992). The psychological foundations of culture. In J. H. Barkow, L. Cosmides & J. Tooby (Eds), *The adapted mind: Evolutionary psychology and the generation of culture* (pp. 19–136). New York, NY: Oxford University Press.

Tooby, J., & Cosmides, L. (July 7, 1997). Letter to the Editor on Stephen Jay Gould's 'Darwinian Fundamentalism' and 'Evolution: The Pleasures of Pluralism'. *The New York Review of Books*.

Tooby, J., & Cosmides, L. (2005). Conceptual foundations of evolutionary psychology. In D. M. Buss (Ed.), *The handbook of evolutionary psychology* (pp. 5–67). Hoboken, NJ: John Wiley & Sons.

Tooby, J., & Cosmides, L. (2015). The theoretical foundations of evolutionary psychology. In D. M. Buss (Ed.), *The handbook of evolutionary psychology. Second edition. Volume 1: Foundations* (pp. 3–87). Hoboken, NJ: John Wiley & Sons.

Trivers, R. L. (1974). Parent–offspring conflict. *Integrative and Comparative Biology, 14*(1), 249–264.

Trut, L. (1999). Early canid domestication: The farm-fox experiment. *American Scientist, 87*(2), 160–169.

van Leeuwen, F., & Petersen, M. B. (2018). The behavioral immune system is designed to avoid infected individuals, not outgroups. *Evolution and Human Behavior, 39*(2), 226–234.

Vercken, E., Wellenreuther, M., Svensson, E. I., & Mauroy, B. (2012). Don't fall off the adaptation cliff: When asymmetrical fitness selects for suboptimal traits. *PLoS One, 7*(4), e34889.

Wiesel, T. N. (1982). Postnatal development of the visual cortex and the influence of environment. *Nature*, *299*(5884), 583–591. doi:10.1038/299583a0

Wilcoxon, H. C., Dragoin, W. B., & Kral, P. A. (1971). Illness-induced aversions in rat and quail: Relative salience of visual and gustatory cues. *Science*, *171*(3973), 826–828.

Wilkins, J. F. (2011). Genomic imprinting and conflict-induced decanalization. *Evolution: International Journal of Organic Evolution*, *65*(2), 537–553.

Willard, A. K., & Norenzayan, A. (2013). Cognitive biases explain religious belief, paranormal belief, and belief in life's purpose. *Cognition*, *129*(2), 379–391.

Williams, G. C. (1957). Pleiotropy, natural selection, and the evolution of senescence. *Evolution*, *11*(4), 398–411.

Williams, G. C. (1966). *Adaptation and natural selection*. Princeton, NJ: Princeton University Press.

Williams, G. C. (1985). A defense of reductionism in evolutionary biology. *Oxford Surveys in Evolutionary Biology*, *2*, 1–27.

Evolved Psychological Mechanisms[1]

David M. G. Lewis, Laith Al-Shawaf,
Matthew B. Thompson and David M. Buss

INTRODUCTION

The cognitive revolution reshaped our understanding of psychology by considering the mind as an assemblage of information-processing mechanisms. A central proposition of this computational theory of mind was that, to understand human behavior, we must attend to the information-processing mechanisms responsible for producing it. Despite the indispensability of the concept of the *psychological mechanism* for understanding psychology, this fundamental idea remains absent from many psychologists' toolkits. We propose that a major hindrance to progress is a confusion about key terms and concepts in cognitive psychology and evolutionary biology.

In this chapter, we first discuss two key terms and concepts: *psychological mechanism* and *human nature*. We then present a three-component model of a psychological mechanism and articulate key properties of evolved psychological mechanisms (EPMs), emphasizing their sensitivity to environmental inputs and their highly flexible outputs. Next, we argue that this central feature of EPMs – their variable behavioral output in response to variable environmental contexts – renders the EPM an invaluable conceptual tool for use in multiple key branches of the psychological sciences. This includes all disciplines in the psychological sciences interested in stable between-individual variation or flexible within-individual variation in response to situational influences: personality, social, developmental, and cross-cultural psychology. We conclude by outlining how the EPM concept can be readily and profitably employed in these key branches of psychology to advance the state of our science.

WHAT IS A PSYCHOLOGICAL MECHANISM?

There are identifiable obstacles that have prevented psychological scientists from integrating the concept of EPMs into their work. First, the term 'mechanism' has been used in numerous, inconsistent ways. This includes using 'mechanism' to refer to a *process*, as a placeholder for *neural pathway*, and to refer to *manifest behavior*. Second, in addition to this lack of consistent use, EPMs are also commonly imagined to be fixed and insensitive to social and environmental circumstances. As this chapter will illustrate, nothing could be further from the truth.

We use the term psychological mechanism to refer to an *information processor*, a concept that we illustrate in multiple ways. Here we illustrate the concept of an information-processing psychological mechanism both as an abstract model and using the metaphor of a smartphone app.[2] Later in the chapter, we provide concrete examples of both physiological and psychological information-processing mechanisms.

The concept of an information-processing mechanism can be illustrated in the abstract with a simple three-component model (Buss, 1991): the first component takes, as *input*, cues from the environment; the second component *processes* these inputs by way of algorithms, decision rules, or other computational procedures; and the third component produces *output*, which can range from internal physiological responses to manifest behavior.

This model highlights several key properties of psychological mechanisms. First, physiological responses and manifest behavior are not psychological mechanisms, but rather are potential outputs of psychological mechanisms. Second, the production of these outputs is not rigid or fixed, but rather is contingent on the inputs – both external and internal to the organism – into the mechanisms. The combination of these properties of psychological mechanisms – first, that they are capable of producing multiple potential outputs, and second, that the production of these outputs is contingent on specific environmental input – renders them capable of producing highly flexible behavior in response to contextual variables.

An alternative way of conceptualizing an information-processing mechanism is by using a smartphone app as a metaphor. Let us imagine that we have a smartphone equipped with an application, *SüperEats*, that enables us to get food delivered to our current location. This metaphor reiterates the same key points as the abstract model, as well as illustrates several other key features of information-processing mechanisms.

First, if *SüperEats* were not sensitive to the specific environmental input of your current location, it could not produce any of its necessary intermediate outputs – such as providing you with a populated list of currently open, local food establishments – and consequently could not produce its final output: the delivery of food to your door. This captures a key feature of any information-processing mechanism, whether a smartphone application or an EPM: in order for the mechanism to solve the task for which it is designed, it must be sensitive to specific environmental input. An information-processing mechanism cannot complete the task for which it is designed (or any task, for that matter) unless it is sensitive to the specific environmental information necessary for successfully completing that task.

Second, the *SüperEats* metaphor reminds us that *outputs* are produced by information-processing mechanisms, but are not themselves mechanisms. The delivery of food to your door is not *SüperEats* itself, but rather is the output of the app. This is equally true of the relationship between psychological mechanisms and behavior: manifest behavior is the output of a psychological mechanism, but it should not be taken to represent the mechanism itself.

Third, *SüperEats* illustrates that an information-processing mechanism shared by all humans can produce rich variation across individuals in manifest output such as observed behavior. Imagine that we all have smartphones equipped with *SüperEats*. Now add a few assumptions that would presumably *decrease* variation across individuals. Imagine that *SüperEats* is an incredibly simple application that is sensitive only to one input: current location. Imagine that we live in a world in which there is only one restaurant in each city, and that each restaurant only serves one food item. In a world in which (1) we all have the exact same information-processing mechanism (*SüperEats*), (2) *SüperEats* is sensitive to only one input (current location), (3) there is only one restaurant in each location, and (4) each restaurant has only food item, we would all be virtual clones of each other *in terms of information-processing*. However, imagine that different food items are available at restaurants in different cities as a consequence of seasonal availability of fresh local produce. In this model, the only source of variation comes from the local ecology. Nonetheless, despite there being variation in only one input, and despite us all being clones of one another in terms of our information-processing mechanisms, we would end up exhibiting great diversity across ecologies; individuals in different geographic regions of the world would be getting very different foods delivered as a simple and direct consequence of variation in just one input into our universally shared information-processing mechanisms.

In summary, psychological mechanisms are three-component information-processing systems, not to be conflated with just one of those components – the output – produced by those systems. These information-processing systems require environmental inputs in order to work, and because that environmental information can vary widely – both between and within individuals across time and space – these information-processing mechanisms, even if identical across all individuals, can produce a great deal of variation in behavior across individuals.

HUMAN NATURE: EVOLVED PSYCHOLOGICAL MECHANISMS

As with the term psychological mechanism, *human nature* has historically been used in diverse and inconsistent ways, ranging from a hierarchy of psychological needs to psychosexual stages and instincts. Although these historical conceptualizations tend to be incongruent with contemporary psychological thinking, their central motivation – to identify universal psychological features – represents a

helpful, clear criterion for defining human nature: *the species-typical characteristics of humans*.

Species-typical characteristics emerge as a consequence of the evolutionary process of selection. Selection refers to the process in which a genetic variant that is associated with greater reproduction, relative to other versions of that gene, is passed down to succeeding generations in greater numbers than other versions of that gene. Iterated over many generations, this process can lead to the extinction of the other genetic variants, the population becoming monopolized by the variant associated with comparatively greater reproduction.[3] In other words, the more reproductively successfully genetic variant is now shared by most or all typically developing members of the species.

This process produces (1) morphological, physiological, and psychological characteristics that (2) interact with the environment in ways that (3) promoted the reproduction of the individuals[4] who possessed those characteristics (Dawkins, 1982; Hamilton, 1964; Williams, 1966). These characteristics are called adaptations, and they are species-typical. *Evolved psychological mechanisms* (a term defined by Buss, 1991: 464, and later elaborated by Buss, 1995a) refers to those adaptations that are psychological in nature.

All adaptations exist in the form that they do because they helped solve a specific problem relevant to survival or reproduction recurrently through evolutionary history (Tooby and Cosmides, 1992; Williams, 1966; see also Lewis et al., 2017). This means that *each adaptation was shaped by a specific survival- or reproduction-related problem*. Consequently, each adaptation is designed (1) to be activated by input signaling the presence of the adaptive problem, and (2) to produce output that typically helped solve that problem in ancestral environments. In other words, adaptations are information-processing systems that produce their output not in rigid, fixed, or invariant fashion, but rather in environmentally sensitive fashion: as responses to environmental information cuing the problem that the adaptation evolved to solve.

Consider a familiar physiological example that illustrates this concept: the production of calluses on the soles of our feet and palms of our hands in response to repeated friction. When asked what causes calluses, people might state that calluses are caused by repeated friction. At best, this is a partial explanation. If repeated friction were a complete explanation for what causes calluses, then we should expect to observe calluses on *any* surface that is exposed to repeated friction. This would include car tires, knife blades, and, surely, our inner thighs. But new car tires do not develop calluses from the wear and tear of the road, the blades of knives wear away with long use, and even our inner thighs chafe rather than produce calluses. This is because tires, knives, and the skin on our inner thighs lack the physiological *mechanism* responsible for producing calluses in response to repeated friction. On the other hand, our palmar and plantar skin does have this physiological mechanism: an adaptation that evolved to solve the problem of potential tissue damage caused by repeated friction (input) by producing cell layers (output) equipped with a keratin-rich network of cross-linked proteins that resist mechanical insults and protect sensitive, underlying tissue layers.

This physiological example illustrates three key implications of understanding human nature at the level of species-typical mechanisms:

> variation in the mechanism's output across individuals, despite the mechanism itself being universal, the mechanism's output is *environmentally contingent* – specifically, the mechanism responds to information cuing the problem that the mechanism evolved to solve, and
>
> the *functional specificity* of the mechanism's output – the output is matched to the problem in order to solve it.

Variation across Individuals – Despite the Universality of the Mechanism

Despite the callus-producing mechanism being shared by all typically developing members of our species, it produces output that varies across individuals: some people have thick calluses on their hands whereas others have virtually none. People are readily familiar with the idea that these differences likely reflect differences in the environments to which these individuals are exposed; our intuitive response to shaking the hand of a laborer with callused hands is to attribute those calluses to the nature of the work that she engages in. Similarly, when we meet a scientist with supple hands, we do not infer that the person altogether lacks the physiological mechanism responsible for producing calluses. These are our intuitions about our physiological mechanisms, and they are correct: these mechanisms are universally shared by all typically developing humans, and they produce their output specifically in response to environmental input indicative of the problem they evolved to solve (Figure 6.1).

Unfortunately, a parallel set of intuitions about species-typical *psychological* mechanisms and their production of differences in *behavior* do not seem to come to us as readily. Unlike our intuitions about callus differences between individuals, our initial intuitions about behavioral differences between individuals are not that those differences reflect differential environmental activation of psychological mechanisms that are identical across individuals. Rather, our intuitive theories about differences in behavior between individuals are that those differences can be attributed to inherent, underlying differences between the individuals themselves. These intuitions are so powerful that they have their own name: the fundamental attribution error (Ross, 1977). We think this name is apt, and emphasize the final word: error. Just as an absence of calluses from a person's hands does not imply that that person lacks the

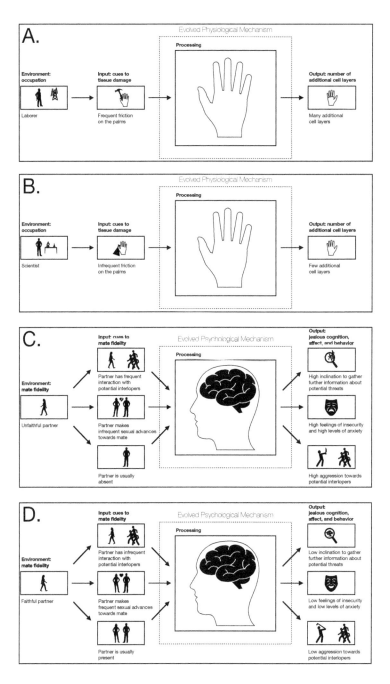

Figure 6.1   Universal human nature can produce differences between individuals. The top two panels illustrate how universal mechanisms can produce individual differences in calluses. The bottom two panels provide a parallel illustration of how universal mechanisms can produce individual differences in jealous cognition, affect, and behavior. The individuals in Panel C and D have identical jealousy mechanisms. However, the individual in Panel C exhibits greater jealousy because he is exposed to more environmental cues to infidelity. *(CC-By-Attribution 4.0 International)*

mechanism capable of producing calluses, the absence of a particular behavior from a person does not necessarily imply that that person lacks the mechanism capable of producing that behavior. The lay person has an intuitive understanding that calluses are the output of a physiological mechanism that all typically developing humans have, but which only produces that output in response to specific environmental cues. This results in species-typical adaptations producing differences in output across individuals. This same understanding needs to be reached for the relationship between species-typical psychological mechanisms and differences in behavior across individuals.

Consider a psychological example that illustrates this principle. Infidelity by one's mate would have been costly for both ancestral men and women. Consequently, selection should have favored anti-infidelity adaptations in all humans: jealousy mechanisms that respond to environmental cues to infidelity (input) by producing outputs to thwart the potential threat.[5] However, just as we should not expect callus mechanisms to produce their output in the absence of friction, we should not expect these mechanisms to produce the output of jealousy in the absence of cues to the problem they were designed to solve (Buss and Shackelford, 1997). If individuals are differentially exposed to cues to infidelity, then we should expect to observe differences in jealousy across individuals – despite jealousy mechanisms being a universal feature of human nature (Figure 6.1).

Universal psychological mechanisms can produce individual differences – and challenge our intuitive theories about differences in behavior. A simple thought experiment illustrates both (1) that we should expect to observe differences in jealousy across individuals – despite the universality of the jealousy mechanism, and (2) that the idea of universal mechanisms producing individual differences violates our intuitive theories of behavior. Here, we provide the thought experiment in two different formats to illustrate these points.

Thought experiment 1

Imagine two clones: Aaron and Daniel. Aaron's mate frequently flirts with other men. These observed flirting behaviors serve as inputs to Aaron's jealousy mechanism, which in turn produces mate guarding behavior as output. Daniel possesses the exact same jealousy-producing mechanism, but Daniel's mate does not flirt with other men. So, there are no inputs activating Daniel's jealousy-producing mechanism. Consequently, Daniel does not exhibit the behavioral outputs of the mechanism. Observers focused on *behavior* might be led to the erroneous conclusions that (1) Aaron has the 'trait' of jealousy, whereas Daniel does not, and (2) jealousy is not a species-typical characteristic. The truth of the matter, however, is that jealousy mechanisms are universal, and the real reason that Aaron and Daniel exhibit different behaviors is that they received different inputs into the identical jealousy mechanism that they share. As with the physiological example, the conclusion is that species-typical mechanisms can produce individual between-individual variation in behavior in response to different environmental inputs.

Thought experiment 2

Imagine two clones: Patrick 1 and Patrick 2. The mate of Patrick 1 frequently flirts with other men. These observed flirting behaviors serve as inputs to Patrick 1's jealousy mechanism, which in turn produces mate guarding behavior as output. Patrick 2 possesses the exact same jealousy-producing mechanism, but Patrick 2's mate does not flirt with other men. So, there are no inputs activating Patrick 2's jealousy-producing mechanism. Consequently, Patrick 2 does not exhibit the behavioral outputs of the mechanism. Observers focused on *behavior* might be led to the erroneous conclusions that (1) Patrick 1 has the 'trait' of jealousy, whereas Patrick 2 does not, and (2) jealousy is not a species-typical characteristic. The truth of the matter, however, is that jealousy mechanisms are universal, and the real reason that Patrick 1 and Patrick 2 exhibit different behaviors is that they received different inputs into the identical jealousy mechanism that they share. As with the physiological example, the conclusion is that species-typical mechanisms can produce individual between-individual variation in behavior in response to different environmental inputs.

The two versions of the thought experiment are identical in structure and content. Both communicate the exact same point that universal psychological mechanisms can produce individual differences in behavior. However, in our laboratory, we have found that the two versions evoke categorically different responses.

When we use different names for the two clones, this appears to activate people's intuitive theories about differences between individuals. Because the example – in which individual differences come from universal mechanisms – violates those intuitive theories, it is more difficult to embrace, but that contradiction also appears to be precisely why the point feels more novel and paradigm-shifting.

The second version does not use different names, and so does not seem to activate people's intuitive theories about differences in behavior between individuals. When uncontaminated by these intuitive theories, people find the idea that universal mechanisms can produce individual differences in behavior to be so straightforward as to be boring: 'Of course clones [i.e., different individuals with identical architectures] will exhibit differences in behavior when exposed to different environments!'

These thought experiments show us two things. First, they demonstrate that our intuitive psychological theories may predictably impair our ability to comprehend evolutionary models of human behavior. Second, they show that, when framed so as *not* to activate these intuitive theories, these evolutionary models feel boringly obvious. We hope that what is currently strongly counterintuitive will eventually become ubiquitously

familiar: universal mechanisms can produce differences in behavior across individuals.[6]

The Environmentally Contingent Production of Output by the Mechanism

The second key property is that these mechanisms produce their outputs specifically in response to environmental inputs that cued the problem they evolved to solve. This stands in contrast to several popular – but scientifically inaccurate – views. One view is that EPMs are rigid, inflexible, and insensitive to context (see Al-Shawaf et al., 2019, for a comprehensive discussion of this misconception). A second view emphasizes the mind's 'plasticity' – the observation that it can flexibly respond to different environmental inputs. EPMs neither invariantly produce their output (as the 'fixed' view would assert) nor respond flexibly to *any* environmental input whatsoever (as implied under certain 'plasticity' views). Rather, each EPM is sensitive to a privileged subset of environmental information: those environmental cues that, ancestrally, were statistically predictive of the problem that they evolved to solve.

This sensitivity to a specific, privileged set of environmental inputs is a key feature of evolved mechanisms. If our callus-producing mechanisms were rigid and produced their output irrespective of environmental input, then all humans would have thickly callused hands, irrespective of whether their skin is exposed to repeated friction. This would be a maladaptive waste of valuable physiological resources. Such rigid or fixed mechanisms are evolutionarily implausible and often non-viable (see Al-Shawaf et al., 2019). This is why we have callus-producing mechanisms that are sensitive to environmental input. However, non-specific environmental sensitivity is also non-viable. If our callus-producing mechanisms were sensitive to *any* environmental input, this, too, would be maladaptive. If our callus-producing mechanisms were so flexible as to be activated by not only cues to the problem they evolved to solve, but also by other environmental inputs, then they would produce calluses in response to irrelevant environmental inputs, such as cues to a lack of hydration. Likewise, if our thirst-producing mechanisms were not designed to be sensitive to a specific subset of environmental inputs – cues to a lack of hydration – then our thirst mechanisms would produce the motivation to drink in response to ... friction on our skin, or other irrelevant inputs. Our callus-producing and thirst-producing mechanisms do not do this. This is because evolved mechanisms are designed to produce their output only in response to the narrow band of environmental cues that were ancestrally predictive of the problem the mechanism evolved to solve.

Implications of the Environmentally Sensitive Nature of EPMs

We now discuss how progress in psychological science could be facilitated by greater integration of the EPM concept. We consider how personality, developmental, social, and cross-cultural psychology could employ this concept, which we argue has the capacity to integrate findings within these disciplines, dissolve boundaries between them, and create novel programs of research.

PERSONALITY PSYCHOLOGY: INDIVIDUAL DIFFERENCES AND UNIVERSAL HUMAN NATURE

One of the central properties of psychological mechanisms – that their output is dependent on environmental input – has the potential to reconcile the observation of individual differences with the proposition of a universal human nature, and to unify them under a single theoretical framework. Most empirical work on

personality deals with individual differences rather than human nature (e.g., McCrae and John, 1992), a restricted focus that has led some to identify personality psychology as 'that branch of psychology which is concerned with ... the ways in which individuals differ from one another' (Wiggins, 1979: 375).

The EPM concept may help to dissolve the unnecessary dichotomy between individual differences and human nature. When human nature is defined at the level of information-processing mechanisms, the idea of a universal human nature is not at odds with differences in behavior between individuals. The fact that individuals experience different environments, coupled with EPMs whose behavioral output is contingent on specific environmental inputs, points to the expectation that universal human nature will produce individual differences. Here, we illustrate how EPMs can lead to both between-sex and within-sex individual differences.

Individual Differences: Between-Sex

Because both sexes faced the adaptive problem of potentially losing their mate to a rival, selection should have equipped both sexes with anti-infidelity adaptations such as sexual jealousy mechanisms.[7] Consistent with this, empirical evidence suggests that men and women exhibit comparable levels of jealousy in terms of both frequency and intensity (Buunk and Hupka, 1987). However, because fertilization occurs internally within women, only ancestral men faced the problem of paternity uncertainty. Since a man's paternity certainty would have been threatened by his mate's sexual infidelity, jealousy mechanisms in men are hypothesized to be particularly sensitive to cues of their partner's sexual infidelity (Buss, 2000). This threat did not exist for ancestral women, but they did face the risk of losing their partner's commitment and support – a concern predicted by their mate's emotional involvement with another woman. As a consequence, jealousy mechanisms in women are hypothesized to be particularly sensitive to cues of their partner's emotional infidelity (Buss and Haselton, 2005; Edlund and Sagarin, 2017).

Diverse forms of evidence support these hypothesized sex differences. Men report that they would experience greater distress in response to a partner's sexual infidelity than to a partner's emotional infidelity, whereas women report the opposite (Buss et al., 1992). This result has been replicated by independent researchers (Wiederman and Allgeier, 1993), using different methods (Buss et al., 1992), and across diverse Western and non-Western cultures (Buunk et al., 1996). This sex difference has also been found using memory tests and physiological measures, along with fMRI results showing different patterns of brain activation in response to sexual versus emotional infidelity (see Buss and Haselton, 2005, and Edlund and Sagarin, 2017, for reviews).

Individual Differences: Within-Sex Differences

Selection would have favored EPMs in the male mind to prevent their mate's infidelity, but we should not expect these jealousy mechanisms to be uniformly activated across all men. Rather, a consideration of women's evolved mating strategies – and the adaptive problems that those strategies posed for men – leads to the expectation that the output of jealousy should vary across men as a function of their differential exposure to infidelity.

Women's mating strategies and the adaptive problems they pose for men

Ancestral women could have increased their reproductive success by both producing high genetic quality offspring and securing long-term investment from their mates. To produce high genetic quality offspring, a woman had to copulate with a man of high genetic quality. High genetic quality men, however, could

have increased their own reproductive success by short-term mating with multiple women. Consequently, some women would have been unable to reliably secure both 'good genes' (Gangestad and Simpson, 2000) and long-term investment from the same man. On this basis, researchers have hypothesized that selection favored mechanisms in the female mind that, in response to circumscribed environmental inputs, produce motivations to engage in sexual relations with high genetic quality men, even when the women themselves are in a committed relationship (see Gangestad and Simpson, 2000, for their seminal proposal of this 'dual mating strategy'). Some empirical evidence is consistent with this hypothesis (e.g., Gangestad et al., 2005), although it has recently been challenged on empirical and conceptual grounds (e.g., Buss et al., 2017; Stern et al., in press; Roney, in press).

An ancestral woman could have reaped genetic and other benefits from sexual affairs (see Greiling and Buss, 2000), but she also would have potentially faced substantial costs from engaging in such liaisons. Selection therefore would have shaped these extra-pair mating mechanisms to (1) be sensitive to situational cues predictive of the costs and benefits of pursuing a sexual affair and (2) be activated only in response to inputs recurrently predictive of the potential costs being outweighed by the potential benefits. A key contextual variable influencing this cost–benefit calculus would have been the mate value of a woman's long-term mate. A woman with a high-value mate would have gained little genetic benefit from a sexual affair, because the 'good genes' she could have obtained from an affair would have been, at best, minimally higher in quality than those of her long-term mate. On the other hand, a woman mated to a low-value man could have reaped substantial benefits by short-term mating with another man who was of high genetic quality. On this basis, we should expect women's EPMs for engaging in extra-pair mating to be activated more frequently, on average, among women mated to lower genetic quality men.

This suggests that, throughout human evolution, low genetic quality men would have been more likely to have had unfaithful mates (see Cerda-Flores et al., 1999). These between-men differences in the likelihood of their partner's infidelity should result in differential activation of men's jealousy mechanisms. Specifically, we should expect lower quality men to experience greater activation of their jealousy mechanisms and therefore exhibit more jealousy than their higher quality counterparts. In short, despite the universality of the jealousy mechanism, we should expect to observe differences in the psychological and behavioral output of that mechanism across individuals. This suggests that a universal human nature – the underlying information-processing mechanisms – can actively produce individual differences.[8]

DEVELOPMENTAL PSYCHOLOGY: SHIFTS IN ADAPTIVE PROBLEMS ACROSS THE LIFESPAN

It is tempting to think that if something is evolved, it has a narrow developmental trajectory – that it must be present at birth, fixed, and insensitive to environmental input. This is a pernicious misconception (Confer et al., 2010). The following section describes how EPMs can be designed to respond to environmental inputs to functionally calibrate their outputs in alignment with the distinct adaptive problems that arise across the lifespan.

Psychological Development Across the Lifespan: EPMs are Latent and Respond to Shifts in Adaptive Problems

EPMs are latent – they do not produce their output until they are activated by environmental input cuing the adaptive problem they were designed to solve. This latency, together with the fact that organisms predictably face

different adaptive problems at different stages of life (Bjorklund and Pellegrini, 2000), has important consequences for psychological development.

Our understanding of psychological development – from infancy to adolescence and through adulthood – might dramatically increase if we consider the onset of distinct adaptive problems across the lifespan. For example, before infants develop the physical capacities necessary to independently explore their environment (e.g., by crawling), they do not face the adaptive problem of encountering dangerous conspecifics while alone – and generally do not exhibit stranger anxiety (see Boyer and Bergstrom, 2011). By the time that children begin to actively explore their environment, however, stranger anxiety reliably appears. The fact that stranger anxiety develops in precise alignment with the onset of an ontogenetically new adaptive problem is consistent with the idea that the mechanisms responsible for producing stranger anxiety remain latent until they receive cues signaling the adaptive problem they are designed to solve. In this way, the EPM concept can increase our understanding of why a particular psychological phenomenon emerges *when* it does.

Even more, it can deepen our understanding of the phenomenon itself. 'Stranger anxiety' would suggest a simple effect: fear of unfamiliar conspecifics. However, this does not accurately describe the phenomenon, which exhibits a nuanced and precise functional match to solve a specific adaptive problem. Evidence from both modern humans and nonhuman primates suggests that genetically unrelated males would have posed the greatest danger to infants (see Daly and Wilson, 1998; Hrdy, 1977). The psychological mechanism responsible for producing stranger anxiety appears to exhibit precise functional specificity to solve this problem: the mechanism produces stranger anxiety in response to unfamiliar and unrelated men, but not in response to women or to familiar, related men (Boyer and Bergstrom, 2011).

Outside of the EPM concept, these features of stranger anxiety remain largely explained, and perhaps inexplicable. The EPM concept illuminates these contingencies as part of a functional pattern of psychological outputs that is precisely matched to the problem that the mechanism evolved to solve.

Our understanding of psychological development at later stages in the lifespan can also be improved by considering the onset of distinct adaptive problems across ontogeny. In adulthood, two distinct adaptive problems that men may face are successfully attracting a fertile mate and taking care of infants. The physiological and psychological mechanisms that help solve one of these adaptive problems may be unhelpful with the other. For example, elevated levels of testosterone are associated with increased success in competing for mates (e.g., Gettler et al., 2011), but also with reduced commitment to one's mate, reduced investment in parenting, and reduced quality of caretaking (see Beall and Schaller, 2017; Burnham et al., 2003; Gray et al., 2006; Weisman et al., 2014).

If we consider the fact that men face different adaptive problems as they transition from mating competition to childrearing, we can generate a priori hypotheses about the shifts that they might be expected to exhibit at this stage in life. As the mechanisms designed to facilitate committed mating and child rearing are activated, and as the mechanisms designed to promote mating effort and competition are deactivated, we would expect to see developmental shifts in the outputs of these mechanisms. Along this line of reasoning, Gettler et al. (2011) hypothesized that men would exhibit increased levels of testosterone during active competition for mates and decreased levels of testosterone during fatherhood. Gettler and colleagues' longitudinal research demonstrated that higher levels of testosterone predicted increased likelihood of mating success; fatherhood, and not merely aging, was associated with a reduction in testosterone; and, among fathers, lower levels of testosterone were associated

with more caregiving. These findings suggest that basing our conceptual models on evolved mechanisms that calibrate their outputs to align with the adaptive problems pertinent to different life phases can both (1) increase our understanding of shifts during ontogeny, and (2) lead to new hypotheses and discoveries about psychological development across the lifespan.

LEARNING AND SOCIAL PSYCHOLOGY: ENVIRONMENTAL INFLUENCES ON BEHAVIOR

Evolved psychological mechanisms' sensitivity to *specific* environmental inputs has important implications for the study of environmental influences on behavior, including learning and social psychology. EPMs are not designed to be activated by just *any* environmental input. Rather, each EPM is designed to be activated by a limited and privileged subset of environmental information – those cues that, ancestrally, were statistically predictive of the problem that the mechanism evolved to solve. Similarly, EPMs are not designed to produce just *any* output. Rather, each mechanism is built to produce physiological, cognitive, affective, and/or behavioral responses that recurrently helped to solve the problem that shaped the mechanism in the first place.

This view has two key implications. First, it indicates that, to understand environmental influences on behavior, and especially to make precise predictions, we must specify the design of the information-processing programs that handle contextual inputs. Second, the influence of evolution and the influence of the situation cannot be separated. In the absence of situational inputs, the mechanisms are not activated, and, in the absence of the mechanisms, there can be no processing of situational inputs. Rather, to understand environmental influences on psychology, including those that fall under the umbrellas of learning and social psychology, we must understand how evolved mechanisms process social and other environmental inputs. The following describes how EPMs drive learning, and how the processing of social inputs by EPMs results in social influences on behavior.

Evolved Learning Mechanisms: EPMs Drive Learning

There is a widespread misconception that 'evolved' and 'learned' are competing explanations. But these two kinds of explanations are not in conflict for two reasons. First, they answer distinct questions at complementary levels of analysis: learning explanations are at the *proximate* level of analysis, whereas evolutionary explanations usually begin at the *distal* or *ultimate* level of analysis (Alcock, 2013; Tinbergen, 1963; see also Lewis et al., 2017, for a discussion of the relationship between these distinct levels of analysis). Second, learning requires evolved learning mechanisms: to explain psychological and behavioral outcomes, it is often necessary to invoke both evolution and learning in the form of *evolved learning mechanisms* (Tooby and Cosmides, 1992; see also Al-Shawaf et al., 2019). To illustrate this point, we present three examples of evolved learning mechanisms: food aversions, learned fears, and incest avoidance.

Learned food aversions

An example of an EPM responsible for food aversion learning is captured by the Garcia Effect (see Garcia and Koelling, 1966). The Garcia effect refers to the fact that rats will readily learn to associate nausea with food, but not with lights or sounds. This occurs because, across the natural environments encountered by rats across their evolutionary history, nausea was caused by toxic or pathogenic food but not by lights or sounds. The Garcia effect suggests that rats have EPMs that are finely attuned to learn some things

more easily than others, such as the evolutionarily recurrent relationship between nausea and having ingested toxic or pathogenic food, but not the ecologically invalid relationship between nausea and buzzers or lights.

Learned fears

EPMs designed to learn specific fears are common among primates. For example, if an observer monkey watches a target monkey react with fear to a snake, the observer monkey will learn a fear of snakes easily and rapidly, sometimes even after a single trial (Mineka et al., 1984). By contrast, if an observer monkey watches a target monkey exhibit the identical fear response to flowers, the observer monkey will usually fail to learn a fear of flowers. It is also harder to get monkeys to *unlearn* a fear of snakes than a fear of flowers (Cook and Mineka, 1990). Both the presence of a snake and the presence of a flower are environmental inputs. However, the presence of a snake is *privileged* input: the presence of a snake (input) posed an adaptive problem (the threat of a venomous bite) to which fear (output) would have been an adaptive response. Flowers did not. It is for this reason that monkeys are 'biologically prepared' to learn a fear of snakes but not flowers. More broadly, the term 'biological preparedness' means that an organism has EPMs designed to learn ancestrally recurrent relationships – for example between food and nausea or between snakes and threat – but typically not relationships that would have been ecologically invalid in ancestral environments, such as between lights and nausea, or between flowers and threat.

Learned incest avoidance

Evolved learning mechanisms also help solve social problems. One example involves the adaptive problem of avoiding incest. We are not born knowing who are genetic relatives are, such as our siblings, so this information must be learned. Our psychological mechanisms responsible for avoiding incest are designed to take, as input, at least two key cues potentially present in the social environment during development: (1) co-residence with another child, and (2) maternal perinatal association (i.e., seeing your mother breastfeed another child). In response to detecting these cues, the EPM in question tags the co-resident as a sibling and produces both a lack of sexual attraction to that person and a disgust response to the thought of having sex with that person (Lieberman et al., 2007; Westermarck, 1891). In short, we avoid having sex with our genetic relatives by way of a learning mechanism that evolved because of its adaptive value in preventing inbreeding depression (Lieberman et al., 2007; Rantala and Marcinkowska, 2011).

The above three examples demonstrate that evolution and learning should not be thought of as separate processes in zero-sum competition with each other for explanatory power. Rather, evolved mechanisms are designed to learn particular things – and learning requires evolved learning mechanisms. The concept of the EPM helps show why evolution and learning are not in conflict, but rather are natural explanatory partners.

The Power of the Situation: EPMs Regulate Their Outputs in Response to Social Inputs

The environment, broadly conceived, includes the social environment (e.g., cultural norms about mating, local male-to-female sex ratio), elements of the ecological environment (e.g., parasite type and prevalence), and the internal environment (e.g., an individual's mutation load, strength of immune function). Because all three of these classes of environmental input carry information pertinent to survival and reproduction, EPMs are designed to process and respond to all of them. Here we present two examples that illustrate this point: emotions and altruism toward kin.

Emotions

Evolutionary psychological thinking suggests that humans have emotion-regulating EPMs that adaptively calibrate their output in response to the problems those emotions evolved to solve. Disgust offers an illustrative example. An adaptive disgust system should be designed to respond to environmental inputs that indicate high pathogen prevalence by reducing exploratory behaviors and intimate interactions with others, thereby decreasing the likelihood of infection. This is exactly what occurs: priming people with pathogen salience reduces levels of extraversion and openness to experience and prompts avoidant motor behavior (Mortensen et al., 2010). Cross-cultural data show a similar pattern: people who live in regions of the world with higher pathogen density tend to be lower in extraversion, lower in openness to experience, and less open to engaging in uncommitted sexual relations (Schaller and Murray, 2008). Research based on the idea that outgroup members tend to carry novel diseases that the immune system is not prepared to deal with also demonstrates that priming people with the situational cue of disease salience results in a more xenophobic response (Faulkner et al., 2004).

These findings illustrate several key features of EPMs. First, EPMs regulate their output specifically in response to environmental cues that indicate the presence of the problem that the mechanism evolved to solve. Second, the mechanism's outputs in response to these cues are not arbitrary or random. Rather, our EPMs adjust our psychological processes and behavior – ranging from our attitudes (e.g., xenophobia) to personality fluctuations (e.g., reduced extraversion) to our manifest behavior (e.g., avoidance) – in response to those cues to help solve the problem being signaled by those cues.

The EPMs responsible for producing social emotions such as the anger response show the same pattern. For example, the welfare-recalibration theory of anger posits that we possess EPMs that are designed to produce anger in response to cues that another individual has not placed sufficient value on our welfare relative to their own (Sell et al., 2009). The output of the EPM – the anger display – is a response designed to attempt to 'convince' the perpetrator to increase the value that he places on the victim's welfare relative to his own. The situational inputs that activate anger-producing EPMs are predictable *a priori* based on this welfare-recalibration theory; the mechanisms responsible for the anger response reliably produce their output when the victim has suffered a large cost, when the perpetrator only gained a small benefit, and when the perpetrator knew exactly whom he was harming (Sell et al., 2017).

These examples illustrate that our emotion-regulating mechanisms (1) are activated by social and environmental inputs – specifically those that signal the adaptive problem the mechanism evolved to solve, and (2) adaptively regulate aspects of motivation and behavior in response to those inputs to help solve that problem. This is true not just of disgust and anger, but also of pride (Sznycer et al., 2017), shame (Sznycer et al., 2016), jealousy (Buss, 2000), envy (Hill and Buss, 2006), sexual arousal (Al-Shawaf et al., 2015), hunger (Al-Shawaf, 2016), gratitude (McCullough et al., 2008), love (Buss, 2006), and, to our knowledge, all emotions (see Al-Shawaf et al., 2015; Al-Shawaf and Lewis, 2017).

Kin-directed altruism

Cues to kinship are situational variables that serve as key inputs into psychological mechanisms that regulate prosocial behavior. We are more likely to provide financial and other aid to kin than non-kin, and to closer than more distant relatives (Smith et al., 1987). When the *victim* of a crime is one of our relatives, we are more willing to incur costs – in terms of both time and money – to pursue perpetrators, and we endorse harsher punishments (Bernhard et al., 2006; Lieberman and Linke, 2007). On the other hand, when the *perpetrator* of a crime is a genetic relative,

we endorse clemency and are more likely to make attributions of remorse (Lieberman and Linke, 2007) – a public signal of non-recidivism that can influence third parties to recommend rehabilitation rather than punishment (Petersen et al., 2012).

Emotions and kinship illustrate that the power of the situation is deeply embedded in the concept of the EPM. Situational inputs are fundamental to the activation of EPMs and are therefore crucial determinants of their outputs. But the phrase 'the power of the situation' can be misleading if unqualified. The mind is not open to influence by just *any* environmental input. Rather, our psychological mechanisms are designed to be activated by a privileged subset of social and environmental cues – those cuing the problem the mechanism is designed to solve – but not necessarily by other social or environmental inputs that were not ancestrally linked to that problem.

Moving forward, research that focuses on the important role of the environment, including social psychology, could profit from investigating social and other environmental influences in a more theoretically principled manner. The catchphrase 'the power of the situation' is so underspecified that it could serve as a post hoc explanation for virtually any observation. This – the ability to explain any observation (or its opposite) – is one of the hallmarks of an unfalsifiable theory (Popper, 2002). Another hallmark of unfalsifiability is if the theory does not 'predict concrete observations that would support or contradict the theory' (Fiske, 2018: 33). What *specific* predictions does the phrase 'the power of the situation' yield? By contrast, the EPM concept is considerably better specified and offers much greater predictive value. By virtue of its integration of (1) environmental inputs with (2) evolved information-processing algorithms to (3) produce specific outputs in specific situations, the EPM concept offers a powerful tool for generating novel and theoretically driven hypotheses about social influences on psychology and behavior.

CROSS-CULTURAL PSYCHOLOGY: UNIVERSAL HUMAN NATURE AND CULTURAL DIFFERENCES

Cultural differences in behavior or psychology are sometimes misinterpreted as evidence against the proposal of a universal human nature. A human nature defined by species-typical mechanisms that process cues from the local environment is not merely compatible with cross-cultural differences, but, more powerfully, can lead to novel

discoveries in cross-cultural psychological research.

Considering EPMs in tandem with variable social, ecological, or other environmental conditions across cultures is a powerful tool for generating theoretically anchored *a priori* hypotheses about cultural differences. Gangestad and Buss (1993) offer an illustrative example of this. They hypothesized that, because parasites can cause morphological perturbations during development, people living in parasite-dense regions of the world

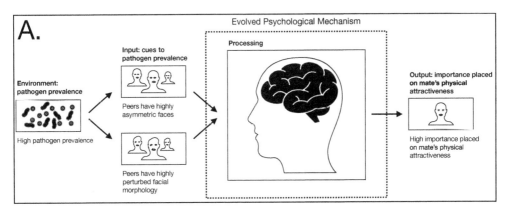

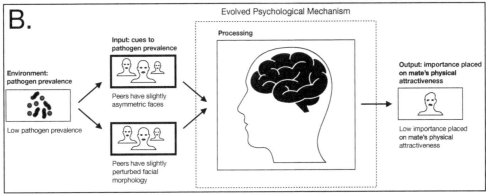

Figure 6.2   Universal human nature can produce differences between cultures. Universal psychological mechanisms process cues to local pathogen prevalence and modify the importance placed on potential mates' physical attractiveness, producing differences between cultures (see Gangestad and Buss, 1993). Culture A is in a geographic region with low pathogen density, whereas Culture B is in a geographic region with high pathogen density. In Culture A, the hypothesized mechanism detects cues to low pathogen density, and downregulates the importance that individuals place on potential mates' physical attractiveness. In Culture B, the mechanism detects cues to high pathogen density and upregulates the importance individuals place on potential mates' attractiveness. (*CC-By-Attribution 4.0 International*)

should place greater importance on physical attractiveness in mates. Selecting a mate with the ability to withstand pathogen exposure without impaired development is beneficial in all environments. But the need to select such a mate is more important in geographical regions with higher levels of pathogens than in regions with lower pathogen prevalence. On this basis, Gangestad and Buss (1993) hypothesized that humans' EPMs should upregulate the importance placed on physical attractiveness in high-pathogen environments relative to low-pathogen environments (see Figure 6.2). Strongly supporting this hypothesis about species-typical mechanisms producing cross-cultural differences, local pathogen prevalence positively predicted valuation of physical attractiveness in potential mates across 29 different cultures drawn from every inhabited continent on the planet.

Scelza and colleagues' recent (2019) work provides another example of how this evolutionary approach can be used to generate and test hypotheses about cross-cultural variation, and in doing so, increase our understanding of cultural differences. The authors reasoned that the costs of sexual infidelity by one's mate are greater for men who engage in high levels of paternal investment (e.g., because this could result in being cuckolded and unwittingly investing in another man's offspring). Based on this, Scelza and colleagues hypothesized that the jealous response to sexual infidelity would be greater in high paternal investment cultures compared to cultures in which there are lower levels of paternal investment. This is exactly what they found: local cultural patterns of paternal investment predicted the magnitude of the jealous response to sexual infidelity across 11 different cultures – including eight non-W.E.I.R.D. small-scale societies – drawn from five different continents around the globe.

In sum, the concept of the universal EPM is not merely compatible with cultural variability, but can lead to theory-driven *a priori* predictions about cross-cultural variation.

The application of the EPM to socioecological conditions that vary across cultures has the potential to yield novel discoveries and reveal the cross-culturally invariant information-processing architecture that defines our shared human nature (see Sell et al., 2017; Sznycer et al., 2016, 2017).

FUTURE DIRECTIONS

We have attempted to clarify the use of the term 'psychological mechanism' and put forth a three-component model: (1) environmental, including social and ecological, inputs; (2) algorithmic processing of those inputs; and (3) physiological, motivational, and behavioral outputs. We then illustrated how EPMs can integrate the notion of a universal human nature with key findings from personality, developmental, social, and cross-cultural psychology (Table 6.1). Because EPMs can underpin individual differences in personality, psychological development across the lifespan, social influences on psychology, and cultural differences, the EPM concept traverses these historically disconnected branches of psychological science and has the potential to facilitate their cross-fertilization. Here, we illustrate how researchers in these domains could fruitfully employ the concept of the EPM in their respective programs of research.

Experiments: Reframing Social Psychology's 'Power of the Situation' and Personality Psychology's 'Importance of the Individual' as Inputs into EPMs

To the extent that there are stable differences across individuals in their exposure to specific adaptive problems (and therefore in their exposure to the inputs that activate their EPMs), we should expect to observe stable differences across individuals in the outputs

Table 6.1 The application of the EPM to personality, developmental, social, and cross-cultural psychology

	The common current view	Limitations on the current view	The EPM View	The result of the EPM view
Personality Psychology: Individual Differences and Universal Human Nature	Individual differences in behavior are attributable to inherent 'trait' differences between people. Between-individual differences in behavior are evidence against a universal human nature.	Universal psychological mechanisms responding to different inputs can produce individual differences in behavior. The cleavage between individual differences and universal human nature is counterproductive.	Define human nature at the level of humans' species-typical information-processing mechanisms rather than at the level of manifest, observed behavior.	Dissolution of the counterproductive cleavage between human nature and individual differences. A powerful tool for generating novel a priori hypotheses about the etiology of individual differences.
Developmental Psychology: Shifts in Adaptive Problems Across the Lifespan	Evolved characteristics must be present at birth, are immutable, and are not associated with flexible developmental trajectories.	Adaptations are often not present at birth. Rather, they reliably appear at the developmentally appropriate stage, and are sensitive to environmental input.	Evolved psychological mechanisms guide development: they respond to environmental inputs to calibrate their output in alignment with the distinct adaptive problems that arise across the lifespan.	An explanation of shifts during ontogeny, and a powerful tool for generating novel o priori hypotheses about psychological development across the lifespan.
Learning and Social Psychology: Environmental Influences on Behavior	Learning and evolution are competing explanations. Situational influences on behavior reflect the 'power of the situation.'	Learning cannot occur in the absence of evolved learning mechanisms. The influence of evolution and the influence of the situation cannot be separated because, in the absence of social inputs, evolved mechanisms are not activated, and, in the absence of the mechanisms, there can be no processing of social inputs.	Evolved mechanisms are designed to be activated by a limited and privileged subset of environmental information. Each mechanism is designed to produce physiological, cognitive, affective, and/or behavioral responses that ancestrally helped to solve the problem cued by the situation.	Better specified hypotheses and greater predictive value. A powerful tool for generating novel a priori hypotheses about learning and situational influences on behavior.
Cross-Cultural Psychology: Universal Human Nature and Cultural Differences	Differences in behavior across cultures are evidence against a universal human nature.	A universal human nature does not imply that behavior must be universal.	Our universal human nature most accurately refers to species-typical psychological mechanisms, not to the manifest behavior those mechanisms produce. A human nature defined by species-typical mechanisms that process cues from the local environment is compatible with cross-cultural differences.	Considering EPMs in tandem with variable social, ecological, and other environmental conditions across cultures is a powerful tool for generating novel a priori hypotheses about cultural differences.

of those mechanisms. For example, above, we outlined why jealousy mechanisms are a species-typical feature of human nature; why cues to infidelity are key inputs that activate these species-typical jealousy mechanisms; why individual differences among men in their mate value should predict differential exposure to cues to infidelity; and, therefore, why we should expect to observe greater jealousy among some men than others. This is just one illustration of the overarching hypothesis that universal EPMs should produce stable individual differences whenever individuals are stably exposed to different levels of cues to the adaptive problem that the relevant EPM evolved to solve.

Individuals can be differentially exposed to a particular adaptive problem when the likelihood of facing that problem is predicted by stable features of the individual's phenotype (i.e., the individual's 'phenotypic condition': Lukaszewski and Roney, 2011; see Tooby and Cosmides, 1990). Such phenotype-linked differences in exposure to specific adaptive problems should lead universal EPMs to produce stable individual differences in psychological processes and behaviors, including those that constitute the major dimensions of human personality (but see Penke et al., 2007; Verweij et al., 2012). Correlational studies (e.g., Lukaszewski, 2013) have shown precisely this pattern. However, when individuals are exposed to contexts that unambiguously indicate that a specific adaptive problem is *not* being faced, the relevant EPM should not be activated – regardless of the individual's phenotypic condition. Similarly, in contexts that unambiguously indicate that the relevant adaptive problem *is* being faced, the EPM should produce its output in all or most individuals – again irrespective of the individual's condition. Finally, it is primarily in circumstances characterized by uncertainty about whether or not the adaptive problem is being faced – which describes most natural settings – that personality-associated psychological processes and behaviors should track individuals' phenotypic condition.

Lewis (2013) used an experimental design to test these hypotheses. His research investigated the hypothesis that EPMs regulate neuroticism levels in response to cues to social exclusion (Denissen and Penke, 2008; Nettle, 2005, 2006). Lewis proposed that neuroticism-regulating EPMs take, as input, cues from the environment – both the social environment and the individual's own condition – that are predictive of social exclusion. However, some of these cues have greater validity than others in predicting social exclusion. Unequivocal indicators of actual social exclusion are the most valid cues, whereas an individual's condition (e.g., physical attractiveness) would have been a less predictive cue of social exclusion (e.g., see Kurzban and Leary, 2001). Based on this, Lewis reasoned that the evolved architecture of the EPM in question should be designed to regulate its outputs according to unequivocal cues when they are available, and to only use condition-based cues when unequivocal indicators of the adaptive problem are unavailable.

Lewis's (2013) constellation of observations align precisely with this hypothesized information-processing architecture. In one experimental scenario, he presented participants with social information unambiguously indicating their social *inclusion*. In this social situation, individuals exhibited lower levels of neuroticism, regardless of their phenotypic condition. This is consistent with the notion that the proposed neuroticism-regulating EPMs were not activated because cues clearly indicated that the adaptive problem of social exclusion was not being faced. In another experimental scenario, participants were exposed to clear indicators of being excluded. In this social situation, individuals exhibited higher levels of neuroticism, irrespective of their phenotypic condition. This is consistent with the idea that the proposed psychological mechanism was activated in *all* individuals when it detected social inputs indicating that the adaptive problem was clearly being faced. Finally, participants were exposed to ambiguous social situations in which they could not be certain of their inclusion or exclusion. In such situations – and only in such situations – individuals' neuroticism systematically tracked their phenotypic condition. This is consistent with the hypothesized evolved information-processing architecture: when the stronger cue indicating the clear presence or absence of the relevant adaptive problem is not available, the mechanism is designed to regulate its output according to a less valid, but still predictive, cue (the participant's phenotypic condition).

Lieberman and colleagues (2003, 2007) observed a similar information-processing architecture in their work on humans' evolved psychological mechanisms for identifying kin. They postulated that our EPMs for learning who are our kin are designed to take, as input, cues recurrently linked to genetic relatedness in ancestral environments (Lieberman et al., 2003, 2007). This kin-identifying EPM (1) takes multiple cues as input (e.g., co-habitation and observing a newborn nursing from one's own mother – Lieberman et al., 2003, 2007; facial resemblance – Lewis, 2011), (2) processes these cues via a decision rule that hierarchically treats these cues according to their ancestral predictive validity (i.e., their correlations with actual genetic relatedness), and (3) regulates kin-directed psychology (e.g., altruistic motivations, anti-incestual sentiment) according to the most valid available cue (Lieberman et al., 2003, 2007).

Generalizing from Lewis (2013) and Lieberman et al. (2003, 2007), selection would have favored EPMs that were designed to (1) take multiple cues as input, (2) hierarchically treat those cues, prioritizing those with the greatest predictive validity, and then (3) produce cognitive, affective, and behavioral outputs to help solve the relevant adaptive problem.

The information-processing structure of EPMs has been a relatively neglected area of research. This gap is not trivial, as the psychological and behavioral output of these mechanisms does not depend on the cues per se, but rather on the computational procedures that the EPMs employ in processing these cues.

To offer a more complete investigation into psychology – whether personality psychology, social psychology, or their intersection – future research could profit from the following. First, research should identify the specific cues that would have been recurrently linked to specific adaptive problems, as these cues are viable candidate inputs into EPMs (Buss, 1991; Tooby and Cosmides, 1990). Second, future research should articulate the hypothesized information-processing architecture of the proposed EPMs. Toward this goal, researchers should consider the different predictive validities of the hypothesized cues. This may yield valuable hypotheses about the EPMs' computational architecture that lead to new discoveries about when, and under what circumstances, they produce their behavioral output.

Longitudinal Studies: Psychological Development in Response to Shifts in Adaptive Problems across the Lifespan

Experimental studies can test for causal relationships between environmental inputs and psychological and behavioral output. However, single-session experimental studies are incapable of testing for psychological and behavioral shifts across the lifespan in response to changes in phenotypic condition, social circumstances, or other environmental inputs (see Buss and Penke, 2015).

A key focus of future research should be longitudinal studies that track within-individual changes in the phenotypic characteristics or social environments hypothesized to serve as input into EPMs. This will enable strong tests of the hypothesis that EPMs regulate our psychological and personality development according to shifts in adaptive problems across the lifespan. This could represent an important step toward the development of a more explanatory framework for both personality and developmental psychology.

CONCLUSION

Evolution by selection is the only known process capable of producing complex organic mechanisms, including the information-processing mechanisms that constitute the human mind. The *evolved psychological mechanism* is a key conceptual tool for the psychological sciences. Integrating the EPM concept into sub-disciplines of psychology yields new predictions and can help make sense of existing findings, while in no way undermining the important past successes or current endeavors of these sub-disciplines.

The definition of human nature that we suggest here focuses not on manifest behavior, but on the underlying mechanisms that produce it. This definitional shift reframes variability in human behavior entirely. Seen in the light of EPMs, human variability is not at odds with the concept of a universal human nature. Rather, our rich individual differences and highly flexible behavior have their roots in our shared human nature.

Because our shared EPMs have evolved to be exquisitely sensitive to environmental context and can produce highly variable output, they are compatible with many key findings in social, personality, developmental, and cross-cultural psychology. Beyond being merely compatible with these findings, the concept of the EPM offers a framework that coherently synthesizes these findings and generates novel hypotheses in these important domains of research. Social psychology's powerful situational influences, personality psychology's stable individual differences, developmental psychology's ontogenetic shifts, and cross-cultural psychology's variation between cultures all depend on underlying psychological mechanisms. The EPM is a common denominator that traverses these different branches of psychology and offers a powerful framework for generating novel discoveries in these multiple important areas of psychological science.

Notes

1 Portions of this chapter were drawn from four sources: (1) Lewis et al., 2017; (2) Al-Shawaf et al., 2019; (3) Lewis, 2015; (4) Lewis et al. (in press).
2 This represents a revised adaptation of metaphors used by Steven Pinker in *How the Mind Works* (1997) and Robert Kurzban in *Why Everyone (Else) is a Hypocrite* (2010). The time appears ripe to reintroduce this metaphor, as the concept of specialized information-processing mechanisms that are designed to serve a specific function is now a ubiquitous household concept: 'There's an app for that.'
3 See Lewis et al. (in press) for a discussion of both (1) forms of selection that do not lead to species-typicality and (2) non-selective evolutionary processes and their products.
4 Most accurately, the process produces characteristics that promoted the reproduction of the *genes* of the individuals who possessed those characteristics (Hamilton, 1964; Williams, 1966).
5 See Lewis et al. (2017) for a theoretical elaboration and computer-based simulation demonstrating that an adaptive problem with a large impact on an individual's reproductive fitness – such as one's mate infidelity – would have created selection pressures for the evolution of adaptations to solve that problem in *all* members of the species, even if the problem was faced only by a small subset of the population.
6 In these thought experiments, between-individual differences in behavior are caused by the differential activation of universal mechanisms in response to environmental cues. However, such differences can also arise from individual differences in the parameters of the mechanisms. For example, some individuals' jealousy mechanisms may have lower thresholds of activation. Such between-individual differences in the parameters of the mechanism may result from critical life events (Buss, 2000) or other forms of developmental calibration (Buss, 2008; Buss and Penke, 2015), genetic variation (e.g., mutation-selection balance; see Verweij et al., 2012), culturally supplied values, environmental perturbations, or other proximate causes.
7 See Buss (1995b) for a meta-theory of both sex differences and similarities; the sexes should be largely similar as a consequence of facing many of the same adaptive problems recurrently through humans' evolutionary past, but also differ in domains in which men and women faced distinct adaptive problems.
8 See Penke et al. (2007) and Lewis et al. (in press) for discussions of five different evolutionary models for the origins of personality differences, including both selective and non-selective models.

REFERENCES

Al-Shawaf, L. (2016). The evolutionary psychology of hunger. *Appetite*, *105*, 591–595.

Al-Shawaf, L., & Lewis, D. M. G. (2017). Evolutionary psychology and the emotions. In V. Zeigler-Hill & T. K. Shackelford (Eds), *Encyclopedia of personality and individual differences*. New York, NY: Springer.

Al-Shawaf, L., Conroy-Beam, D., Asao, K., & Buss, D. M. (2015). Human emotions: An evolutionary psychological perspective. *Emotion Review*, *8*(2), 173–186.

Al-Shawaf, L., Lewis, D. M. G., Wehbe, Y., & Buss, D. M. (2019). Context, environment, and learning in evolutionary psychology. In T. K. Shackelford & V. A. Weekes-Shackelford (Eds), *Encyclopedia of evolutionary psychological science* (pp. 1–12). New York, NY: Springer.

Alcock, J. (2013). *Animal behavior: An evolutionary approach* (10th ed.). Sunderland, MA: Sinauer Associates.

Beall, A. T., & Schaller, M. (2017). Evolution, motivation, and the mating/parenting trade-off. *Self and Identity*, *18*(1), 39–59.

Bernhard, H., Fehr, E., & Fischbacher, U. (2006). Group affiliation and altruistic norm enforcement. *American Economic Review*, *96*(2), 217–221.

Bjorklund, D. F., & Pellegrini, A. D. (2000). Child development and evolutionary psychology. *Child Development*, *71*(6), 1687–1708.

Boyer, P., & Bergstrom, B. (2011). Threat-detection in child development: An evolutionary perspective. *Neuroscience and Biobehavioral Reviews*, *35*(4), 1034–1041.

Burnham, T. C., Chapman, J. F., Gray, P. B., McIntyre, M. H., Lipson, S. F., & Ellison, P. T. (2003). Men in committed, romantic relationships have lower testosterone. *Hormones and Behavior*, *44*(2), 119–122.

Buss, D. M. (1991). Evolutionary personality psychology. *Annual Review of Psychology*, *42*, 459–491.

Buss, D. M. (1995a). Evolutionary psychology: A new paradigm for psychological science. *Psychological Inquiry*, *6*(1), 1–30.

Buss, D. M. (1995b). Psychological sex differences: Origins through sexual selection. *American Psychologist*, *50*(3), 164–168.

Buss, D. M. (2000). *The dangerous passion: Why jealousy is as necessary as love and sex.* New York, NY: The Free Press.

Buss, D. M. (2006). The evolution of love. In R. Sternberg & K. Weis (Eds), *The new psychology of love* (pp. 65–86). New Haven, CT: Yale University Press.

Buss, D. M. (2008). Human nature and individual differences: Evolution of human personality. In O. P. John, R. W. Robins, & L. A. Pervin (Eds), *Handbook of personality: Theory and research* (3rd ed., pp. 29–60). New York, NY: The Guilford Press.

Buss, D. M., & Haselton, M. G. (2005). The evolution of jealousy. *Trends in Cognitive Science*, *9*(11), 506–507.

Buss, D. M., & Penke, L. (2015). Evolutionary personality psychology. In M. Mikulincer & P. R. Shaver (Series Eds) and M. L. Cooper & R. J. Larsen (Vol. Eds), *APA handbook of personality and social psychology: Vol. 4. Personality processes and individual differences* (pp. 3–29). Washington, DC: American Psychological Association.

Buss, D. M., & Shackelford, T. K. (1997). From vigilance to violence: Mate retention tactics in married couples. *Journal of Personality and Social Psychology*, *72*(2), 346–361.

Buss, D. M., Goetz, C., Duntley, J. D., Asao, K., & Conroy-Beam, D. (2017). The mate switching hypothesis. *Personality and Individual Differences*, *104*, 143–149.

Buss, D. M., Larsen, R. J., Westen, D., & Semmelroth, J. (1992). Sex differences in jealousy: Evolution, physiology, and psychology. *Psychological Science*, *3*(4), 251–255.

Buunk, A. P., & Hupka, R. B. (1987). Cross-cultural differences in the elicitation of sexual jealousy. *The Journal of Sex Research*, *23*(1), 12–22.

Buunk, A. P., Angleitner, A., Oubaid, V., & Buss, D. M. (1996). Sex differences in jealousy in evolutionary and cultural perspective: Tests from the Netherlands, Germany, and the United States. *Psychological Science*, *7*(6), 359–363.

Cerda-Flores, R. M., Barton, S. A., Marty-Gonzalez, L. F., Rivas, F., & Chakraborty, R. (1999). Estimation of nonpaternity in the Mexican population of Nuevo Leon: A validation study with blood group markers.

American Journal of Physical Anthropology, *109*(3), 281–293.

Confer, J. C., Easton, J. A., Fleischman, D. S., Goetz, C. D., Lewis, D. M. G., Perilloux, C., & Buss, D. M. (2010). Evolutionary psychology: Controversies, questions, prospects, and limitations. *American Psychologist*, *65*(2), 110–126.

Cook, M., & Mineka, S. (1990). Selective associations in the observational conditioning of fear in rhesus monkeys. *Journal of Experimental Psychology: Animal Behavior Processes*, *16*(4), 372–389.

Daly, M., & Wilson, M. (1998). *The truth about Cinderella: A Darwinian view of parental love*. New Haven, CT: Yale University Press.

Dawkins, R. (1982). *The extended phenotype*. San Francisco: W.H. Freeman.

Denissen, J. J. A., & Penke, L. (2008). Motivational individual reaction norms underlying the Five Factor Model of personality: First steps towards a theory-based conceptual framework. *Journal of Research in Personality*, *42*(5), 1285–1302.

Edlund, J. E., & Sagarin, B. J. (2017). Sex differences in jealousy: A 25-year retrospective. In J. M. Olson (Ed.), *Advances in experimental social psychology* (Vol. 55, pp. 259–302). New York: Academic Press.

Faulkner, J., Schaller, M., Park, J. H., & Duncan, L. A. (2004). Evolved disease-avoidance mechanisms and contemporary xenophobic attitudes. *Group Processes & Intergroup Relations*, *7*(4), 333–353.

Fiske, S. T. (2018). *Social beings: Core motives in social psychology* (4th ed.). New York, NY: Wiley.

Gangestad, S. W., & Buss, D. M. (1993). Pathogen prevalence and human mate preferences. *Ethology & Sociobiology*, *14*(2), 89–96.

Gangestad, S. W., & Simpson, J. A. (2000). The evolution of human mating: Trade-offs and strategic pluralism. *Behavioral and Brain Sciences*, *23*(4), 573–644.

Gangestad, S. W., Thornhill, R., & Garver-Apgar, C. E. (2005). Women's sexual interests across the ovulatory cycle depend on primary partner developmental instability. *Proceedings of the Royal Society of London B*, *272*(1576), 2023–2027.

Garcia, J., & Koelling, R. A. (1966). Relation of cue to consequence in avoidance learning. *Psychonomic Science*, *4*(3), 123–124.

Gettler, L. T., McDade, T. W., Feranil, A. B., & Kuzawa, C. W. (2011). Longitudinal evidence that fatherhood decreases testosterone in human males. *Proceedings of the National Academy of Sciences*, *108*(39), 16194–16199.

Gray, P. B., Yang, C.-F., & Pope, H. G. (2006). Fathers have lower salivary testosterone levels than unmarried men and married non-fathers in Beijing, China. *Proceedings of the Royal Society of London B*, *273*(1584), 333–339.

Greiling, H., & Buss, D. M. (2000). Women's sexual strategies: The hidden dimension of extra-pair mating. *Personality and Individual Differences*, *28*(5), 929–963.

Hamilton, W. D. (1964). The genetical evolution of social behavior. I and II. *Journal of Theoretical Biology*, *7*(1), 1–52.

Hill, S. E., & Buss, D. M. (2006). Envy and positional bias in the evolutionary psychology of management. *Managerial and Decision Economics*, *27*(2–3), 131–143.

Hrdy, S. B. (1977). Infanticide as a primate reproductive strategy. *American Scientist*, *65*(1), 40–49.

Kurzban, R. (2010). *Why everyone (else) is a hypocrite: Evolution and the modular mind*. Princeton, NJ: Princeton University Press.

Kurzban, R., & Leary, M. (2001). Evolutionary origins of stigmatization: The functions of social exclusion. *Psychological Bulletin*, *127*(2), 187–208.

Lewis, D. M. G. (2011). The sibling uncertainty hypothesis: Facial resemblance as a sibling recognition cue. *Personality and Individual Differences*, *51*(8), 969–974.

Lewis, D. M. G. (2013). Individual differences and universal condition-dependent mechanisms (Unpublished doctoral dissertation).

Lewis, D. M. G. (2015). Evolved individual differences: Advancing a condition-dependent model of personality. *Personality and Individual Differences*, *84*, 63–72.

Lewis, D. M. G., Al-Shawaf, L., & Buss, D. M. (in press). Evolutionary personality psychology. In P. J. Corr & G. Matthews (Eds), *The Cambridge handbook of personality psychology* (2nd ed.). Cambridge: Cambridge University Press.

Lewis, D. M. G., Al-Shawaf, L., Conroy-Beam, D., Asao, K., & Buss, D. M. (2017). Evolutionary psychology: A how-to guide. *American Psychologist, 72*(4), 353–373.

Lieberman, D., & Linke, L. (2007). The effect of social category on third party punishment. *Evolutionary Psychology, 5*(2), 289–305.

Lieberman, D., Tooby, J., & Cosmides, L. (2003). Does morality have a biological basis? An empirical test of the factors governing moral sentiments relating to incest. *Proceedings of the Royal Society of London B, 270*(1517), 819–826.

Lieberman, D., Tooby, J., & Cosmides, L. (2007). The architecture of human kin detection. *Nature, 445*(7129), 727–731.

Lukaszewski, A. W. (2013). Testing an adaptationist theory of trait covariation: Relative bargaining power as a common calibrator of an interpersonal syndrome. *European Journal of Personality, 27*(4), 328–345.

Lukaszewski, A. W., & Roney, J. R. (2011). The origins of extraversion: Joint effects of facultative calibration and genetic polymorphism. *Personality and Social Psychology Bulletin, 37*(3), 409–421.

McCrae, R. R., & John, O. P. (1992). An introduction to the five-factor model and its applications. *Journal of Personality, 60*(2), 175–215.

McCullough, M. E., Kimeldorf, M. B., & Cohen, A. D. (2008). An adaptation for altruism: The social causes, social effects, and social evolution of gratitude. *Current Directions in Psychological Science, 17*(4), 281–285.

Mineka, S., Davidson, M., Cook, M., & Keir, R. (1984). Observational conditioning of snake fear in rhesus monkeys. *Journal of Abnormal Psychology, 93*(4), 355–372.

Mortensen, C. R., Becker, D. V., Ackerman, J. M., Neuberg, S. L., & Kenrick, D. T. (2010). Infection breeds reticence: The effects of disease salience on self-perceptions of personality and behavioral avoidance tendencies. *Psychological Science, 21*(3), 440–447.

Nettle, D. (2005). An evolutionary approach to the extraversion continuum. *Evolution and Human Behavior, 26*(4), 363–373.

Nettle, D. (2006). The evolution of personality variation in humans and other animals. *American Psychologist, 61*(6), 622–631.

Penke, L., Denissen, J. J. A., & Miller, G. F. (2007). The evolutionary genetics of personality. *European Journal of Personality, 21*(5), 549–587.

Petersen, M. B., Sell, A., Tooby, J., & Cosmides, L. (2012). To punish or repair? Evolutionary psychology and lay intuitions about modern criminal justice. *Evolution and Human Behavior, 33*(6), 682–695.

Pinker, S. (1997). *How the mind works.* New York, NY: W. W. Norton & Co.

Popper, K. (2002). *The logic of scientific discovery.* New York, NY: Routledge.

Rantala, M. J., & Marcinkowska, U. M. (2011). The role of sexual imprinting and the Westermarck effect in mate choice in humans. *Behavioral Ecology and Sociobiology, 65*(5), 859–873.

Roney, J. R. (in press). On the use of log transformations when testing hormonal predictors of cycle phase shifts: Commentary on Gangestad, Dinh, Grebe, Del Giudice, and Emery Thompson (2019). *Evolution and Human Behavior.* doi:10.1016/j.evolhumbehav.2019.08.006

Ross, L. (1977). The intuitive psychologist and his shortcomings: Distortions in the attribution process. In L. Berkowitz (Ed.), *Advances in experimental social psychology* (Vol. 10, pp. 173–220). New York, NY: Academic Press.

Scelza, B. A., Prall, S. P., Blumenfeld, T., Crittenden, A., Gurven, M., Kline, M., ... McElreath, R. (2019). Patterns of paternal investment explain cross-cultural variance in jealous response. *Nature Human Behaviour.* doi:10.1038/s41562-019-0654-y

Schaller, M., & Murray, D. R. (2008). Pathogens, personality and culture: Disease prevalence predicts worldwide variability in sociosexuality, extraversion, and openness to experience. *Journal of Personality and Social Psychology, 95*(1), 212–221.

Sell, A., Tooby, J., & Cosmides, L. (2009). Formidability and the logic of human anger. *Proceedings of the National Academy of Sciences, 106*(35), 15073–15078.

Sell, A., Sznycer, D., Al-Shawaf, L., Lim, J., Krauss, A., Feldman, A., Rascanu, R.,

Sugiyama, L., Cosmides, L., & Tooby, J. (2017). The grammar of anger: Mapping the computational architecture of a recalibrational emotion. *Cognition*, *168*, 110–128.

Smith, M. S., Kish, B. J., & Crawford, C. B. (1987). Inheritance of wealth as human kin investment. *Ethology and Sociobiology*, *8*(3), 171–182.

Stern, J., Arslan, R. C., Gerlach, T. M., Penke, L. (in press). No robust evidence for cycle shifts in preferences for men's bodies in a multiverse analysis: A response to Gangestad, Dinh, Grebe, Del Giudice, and Emery Thompson (2019). *Evolution and Human Behavior*. doi:10.1016/j.evolhumbehav.2019.08.005

Sznycer, D., Tooby, J., Cosmides, L., Porat, R., Shalvi, S., & Halperin, E. (2016). Shame closely tracks the threat of devaluation by others, even across cultures. *Proceedings of the National Academy of Sciences*, 201514699. doi:10.1073/pnas.1514699113

Sznycer, D., Al-Shawaf, L., Bereby-Meyer, Y., Curry, O. S., De Smet, D., Ermer, E., … & Tooby, J. (2017). Cross-cultural regularities in the cognitive architecture of pride. *Proceedings of the National Academy of Sciences*, *114*(8), 1874–1879.

Tinbergen, N. (1963). On aims and methods of ethology. *Zeitschrift für Tierpsychologie*, *20*(4), 410–433.

Tooby, J., & Cosmides, L. (1990). On the universality of human nature and the uniqueness of the individual: The role of genetics and adaptation. *Journal of Personality*, *58*(1), 17–67.

Tooby, J., & Cosmides, L. (1992). The psychological foundations of culture. In J. H. Barkow, L. Cosmides, & J. Tooby (Eds), *The adapted mind: Evolutionary psychology and the generation of culture* (pp. 19–136). New York, NY: Oxford University Press.

Verweij, K. J. H., Yang, J., Lahti, J., Veijola, J., Hintsanen, M., Pulkki-Råback, L., … Zietsch, B. P. (2012). Maintenance of genetic variation in human personality: Testing evolutionary models by estimating heritability due to common causal variants and investigating the effect of distant inbreeding. *Evolution*, *66*(10), 3238–3251.

Westermarck, E. (1891). *The history of human marriage*. London: Macmillan.

Wiederman, M. W., & Allgeier, R. R. (1993). Gender differences in sexual jealousy: Adaptationist or social learning explanation? *Ethology and Sociobiology*, *14*(2), 115–140.

Weisman, O., Zagoory-Sharon, O., & Feldman, R. (2014). Oxytocin administration, salivary testosterone, and father–infant social behavior. *Progress in Neuro-Psychopharmacology & Biological Psychiatry*, *49*, 47–52.

Wiggins, J. S. (1979). A psychological taxonomy of trait-descriptive terms: The interpersonal domain. *Journal of Personality and Social Psychology*, *37*(3), 395–412.

Williams, G. C. (1966). *Adaptation and natural selection*. Princeton, NJ: Princeton University Press.

PART II

Middle-Level Evolutionary Theories

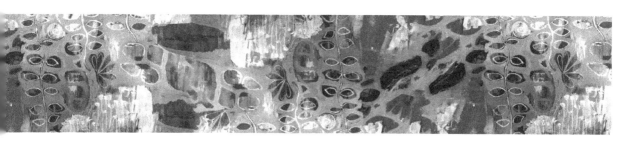

Why Sex?

Mark V. Flinn

INTRODUCTION

Since George C. William's (1966) seminal discussion of evolutionary theory, natural selection is generally accepted as primarily effective at or below the level of the individual (Abott et al., 2011; Alexander and Borgia, 1978; Dawkins, 1982; Leigh, 2010; Lewontin, 1970). The evolution of sex remains a major paradox for this theoretical advance: 'Sexual reproduction must stand as a powerful argument in favor of group selection unless someone can come up with a plausible theory as to how it could be favored by individual selection' (Williams, 1971:161). This issue has deep relevance for key foci of human evolutionary psychology, including mate choice (Buss and Schmitt, 2019; Puts, 2016) and male/female differences (Geary, 2020).

The major difficulty with explaining the evolution of sex by individual selection results from what is termed the 'cost of meiosis'[1] incurred by individuals who provide more parental effort[2] than their mates do. The contribution of parental genes to future generations by an asexual offspring (100% genetic material identical by immediate descent) is double that of a sexual offspring (50% genetic material identical by immediate descent). Hence a 'two-fold cost' is incurred by individuals (usually female) providing all the parental investment for a sexual offspring, because for the same cost (in terms of the calories and risk expended as parental investment), the sexual offspring gives only half the return (in terms of genetic representation). By the logic of inclusive fitness theory (Hamilton, 1964), the benefit/cost ratio of investment in sexual offspring must be at least twice that of investment in asexual offspring, because genetic relatedness with sexual offspring is half that with asexual offspring. A second way of looking at the enigma of sexual reproduction, from the population level, is the two-fold cost of producing males who do not invest resources in offspring compared with the reproductive rate of a population of asexual females (Maynard Smith, 1978). And a third way is to take the gene's eye perspective: how does an allele coding for a sexual phenotype fare in competition with an allele coding for asexuality (Barash, 1976; Hoekstra, 1987; Kondrashov, 1982, 2013 ; Lodé, 2012). Given the huge consequences for the rest of the genome, the logic of the parliament of the genes (Alexander and Borgia, 1978; Van Valen, 1973) would suggest that the individual-level perspective is appropriate (Hartung, 1981; Maynard Smith and Williams, 1976).

The key evolutionary problem with sex is explaining its existence where the sexes provide different amounts of parental effort. Sex would appear disadvantageous for the parent providing the larger share; in effect the genes in males and their sperm seem to be parasitizing the resources females have gathered in their eggs. In species in which males invest parentally, this 'cost of meiosis' incurred by females is reduced. If males and females invest equally, neither incurs a 'cost of meiosis'. And yet despite the apparent huge mathematical reproductive advantage of asexual reproduction, it is rare; only about 0.1% of animal species are asexual (Vrijenhoek, 1998). Sex has been successful for a long time; recombination of genes has an ancient evolutionary history likely dating back over three billion years, and eukaryotic sex one billion years (Maynard Smith, 1978). Here I briefly review several major attempts to resolve this key evolutionary puzzle: (1) recombination that enables 'bad gene' purging or synergistic interactions among deleterious mutations, or antagonistic epistasis among beneficial mutations; (2) advantages from genetically variable progeny in unpredictable environments (Williams, 1975); and (3) red queen host-pathogen arms races (Hamilton, 2002). I then suggest a model for the special circumstances of sexual reproduction with direct mate choice, with an eye toward understanding the psychology of human sexuality.

'BAD GENE' PURGING AND RECOMBINATION SHUFFLING

Recombination generates new genetic mixtures. One potential advantage of sex making numerous genomes is that some of them will not have deleterious mutations that might otherwise accumulate in clonal lineages – termed 'Muller's rachet'. Parthenogenesis involving recombination of parental genes, however, can circumvent this potential disadvantage. The pace of generation of novel combinations is nevertheless much more rapid with sex, potentially providing an advantage in biotic arms races, a key point for the other major theories of the evolution of sex (Birdsell and Wills, 2003; Hartfield and Keightley, 2012; Otto, 2009). Other posited problems for asexuality include synergistic interactions among deleterious mutations, and antagonistic epistasis among beneficial mutations. Recombination makes it easier for selection to act independently on alleles – Hill–Robertson interference (Fisher, 1958; Hill and Robertson, 1966). Although these advantages to sex might be significant in some instances, the power to explain the two-fold cost has not been substantiated by empirical studies.

ADVANTAGES OF SEX IN UNPREDICTABLE ENVIRONMENTS

Williams and Mitton (1973) and Williams (1975) propose that the necessary two-fold advantage for sex can be obtained if unpredictable variability in the environment strongly favors the production of offspring with a wide variety of genetic combinations. If only those offspring with just the right genetic combination survive, and the particular combination is rare, unpredictable, and changing from generation to generation, then sex would be favored if the probability distribution of fitness for sexual offspring is sufficiently greater than for asexual offspring (Williams, 1975:14).

The Williams/Mitton theory (hereafter referred to as the 'variable progeny' theory) depends on two conditions: (1) the environment of a population has sufficient spatial and temporal variability to favor different genotypes each generation; and (2) parents cannot foretell the environmental conditions their offspring will encounter and, therefore, cannot foretell what genetic combinations will be most adaptive for their offspring. In these conditions, according to the variable progeny theory, the best an individual can do is to mate with individuals with different genotypes (outbreed), thereby generating maximum genetic variability among progeny. The evolutionary benefits of genetically variable progeny are posited to outweigh the cost of meiosis. To illustrate such benefits, Williams (1975) draws an analogy with a lottery, noting that a winning ticket is more likely to be obtained by having many tickets with different combinations than by having many tickets with the same combination. Hence, according to the variable progeny theory, an individual is more likely to have some successful offspring (winning tickets) in conditions of environmental uncertainty by maximizing genetic variability among offspring.

Although the variable progeny theory provides an excellent explanation of the evolution of sexuality among high fecundity organisms in environmentally uncertain habitats, several aspects of sexual reproduction remain anomalous. First, Williams (1975) is forced to 'appeal to historical constraints that preserve sexual reproduction when it has ceased to be adaptive' (44) to account for sexuality in low fecundity organisms such as mammals, with humans representing an especially 'maladaptive' case. Second, whereas the variable progeny theory predicts an association between environmental unpredictability and sexual reproduction, asexuality is more common among species that occupy temporary, disturbed habitats with wide fluctuations of environmental conditions (e.g., small fresh-water puddles, marine tidal pools, and high altitude/latitude

regions) (Bell, 1982; Glesener and Tilman, 1978). And third, certain aspects of a critical example used by Williams to support the variable progeny theory, seasonal facultative sexuality (the aphid-rotifer model), may also be anomalous: among several species of facultatively sexual aphids, only one egg is produced by an individual during the sexual generations (Hamilton, 1976). Hence genetic variability among progeny is not being maximized during sexual generations – only one 'lottery ticket' is produced, *contra* the prediction from the variable progeny theory. Similarly, sexual reproduction among prokaryotes involves a unidirectional flow of genetic material and, therefore, does not increase genetic variability of progeny. As Hamilton (1976: 178) concludes: 'Something more general has yet to be shown if we are to understand the near universality and homogeneous properties of sex.'

The variable progeny theory predicts that 'sexuality should occur where there is minimal fitness heritability and maximum likelihood of new genotypes being of greatest fitness' (Williams, 1975: 23). However, if fitness is heritable, or otherwise predictable from one generation to the next, then non-random recombination (mate choice) is favored by natural selection. Non-random recombination is a complementary process that may resolve some of the shortcomings of the variable progeny theory.

TWO ASPECTS OF THE 'COST OF MEIOSIS'

Two factors determine heritable fitness: genetic material and parental investment (Williams, 1966). The phenotypic evidence of these two factors provides adaptive cues for mate choice (Andersson, 1994; Orians, 1969; Parker, 1983). If fitness can be predicted from phenotypic expressions of genetic material from one generation to the next, selection will favor mating with phenotypes that provide offspring with optimal genotypes. This 'choice' may be active, or automatic (Borgia, 1979). If mates invest equally (no cost of meiosis, Maynard Smith, 1978) and sexual offspring are of higher fitness on average than either mates' asexual offspring, then selection will favor sexual reproduction. But if the fitness of sexual offspring is, on average, intermediate between the fitnesses of the two mates' asexual offspring, the mate with higher-fitness asexual offspring incurs a cost from sexual reproduction, even though investment is provided in equal amounts by both mates. This cost is hereafter referred to as the 'genetic fitness cost of meiosis': ΔG_f.

Even if offspring fitness cannot be predicted from parental genetic material, selection may favor mate choice on the basis of parental investment (e.g., choosing mates who provide more investment). An individual who invests more than its mate may not benefit from sexual reproduction. This is the cost associated with sexual reproduction that the variable progeny theory addresses, and is hereafter referred to as the 'investment fitness cost of meiosis': ΔI_f.

This chapter proposes a theory for the maintenance of sexual reproduction involving differential investment based on complementary variations in the 'genetic fitness cost of sex' and the 'investment fitness cost of sex'. Sexual reproduction can be favored by individual selection if these two costs counterbalance. Thus, if an investment fitness cost $(-\Delta I_f)$ is counterbalanced by a genetic fitness gain $(+\Delta G_f)$, or conversely, a genetic fitness loss $(-\Delta G_f)$ is counterbalanced by an investment fitness gain $(+\Delta I_f)$ sufficient to offset mating costs (M_1), sex can become adaptive. This balance of the two costs/benefits of sex is represented by:

$$\Delta G_f + \Delta I_f > M_1$$

If this inequality is satisfied for both potential mates, then a mutually beneficial mate choice exists. Thus, for sexual reproduction (vs. asexual reproduction) to be adaptive:

$$r \times F_s - M_{1,2} > F_a \times I_s / I_a$$

where r = proportion of offspring's genome identical by descent with parent, F_s = fitness of sexual offspring, F_a = fitness of asexual offspring, and I_s/I_a = the ratio of investment by one individual in a sexual vs. an asexual offspring in terms of fitness value. For simplification, I_s/I_a is also considered equal to the proportion of investment an individual provides to a sexual offspring.

With no investment differential between mates, the criterion for favorable sexual reproduction is that sexual offspring have a higher fitness value (F_s) minus the cost of mating (M_1) than the fitness value of asexual offspring (F_a):

$$(.5 \times F_s) - M_1 > F_a \times .5$$
$$= F_s - M_1 > F_a$$

(for simplification, I assume sexual and asexual offspring require the same total amount of investment[3]). For an individual incurring an unfavorable investment differential, the fitness of sexual offspring must be correspondingly greater than that of asexual offspring:

$$(.5 \times F_s - M_1) / Fa > I_s / I_a$$

For a mate providing all the investment $(I_s / I_a = 1.0)$, the fitness of sexual offspring must be at least twice that of asexual offspring:

$$F_s - M_1 > 2 \times F_a$$

And for an individual incurring a genetic fitness cost, a favorable investment differential (i.e., the mate provides a larger share of parental investment) is required for sex to be advantageous:

$$I_s / I_a > (.5 \times F_s - M_1) / F_a$$

If sexual reproduction is to be advantageous for both potential mates, net benefit from sexual reproduction must be greater than mating costs. This net benefit could be a consequence of the benefits asserted by the variable progeny theory (involving, e.g., parasite resistance: Hamilton, 1980; or social competition: West-Eberhard, 1983; or perhaps some minor advantage from heterosis reducing conflict between sub-genomic levels of selection).

The hypothesis developed above (hereafter referred to as the 'heritable fitness' theory) concerns differential investment in a reproductive system with variance in heritable genetic fitness. It suggests that sexual reproduction involving differential investment will be maintained by individual selection, not just 'where there is minimal fitness heritability' (Williams, 1975: 23), but also where predictable fitness heritability leads to adaptive mate choice. I shall now examine how predictable heritable fitness may resolve the aforementioned shortcomings of the variable progeny theory in this special case of sexual reproduction involving adaptive mate choice.

FACULTATIVE SEX: REDUCED FECUNDITY IN SEXUAL GENERATIONS

Facultative sexuality, as found in many species of aphids and rotifers, is a critical life history example used by Williams (1975) to support the variable progeny theory. Some species of aphids and rotifers tend to be asexual throughout the spring and summer (i.e., a stable environment), but become sexual during the fall in preparation for over-wintering (i.e., an unstable environment) (see Williams, 1975; Moran, 1992 – for other possible examples among invertebrates, see Buchsbaum et al., 1987). Consistent with the variable progeny theory, sexual reproduction occurs when environmental uncertainty (e.g., oncoming winter) appears greatest, and producing genetically variable progeny would seem most adaptive. However, as noted by Hamilton (1976), some species of facultatively sexual aphids lay but one egg in the fall

season sexual generation.[4] This clearly contradicts the variable progeny theory. Instead of a great many different 'lottery tickets' being produced, only one genotype is represented among the progeny. In this case, some advantage other than genetic variation must be favoring sex.

RED QUEEN AND BIOTIC ARMS RACES

On the basis of adaptive mate choice, sexuality is most advantageous when variance in heritable fitness is greatest. Environmental change is likely to increase variance in heritable fitness. Therefore, in facultatively sexual organisms, sexuality could be most adaptive when environmental conditions (including biotic interactions: see Bell, 1982; Hamilton et al., 1990) cause higher variance in heritable fitness. Conversely, asexuality could be favored when environmental conditions cause lower variance in heritable fitness. Bell (1982) notes that sexual reproduction in rotifers and cladocerans occurs at or just after peaks in population density. Heritable fitness may be most variable, and hence mate choice most advantageous, during such periods.

Another aspect of the reproductive history of facultatively sexual organisms apparently supporting the variable progeny theory is the association between sexual reproduction and dispersal noted by Bonner (1958) (cf. Williams, 1966: 131–2, 1975: 3–4). In general, sexual offspring are dispersed whereas asexual offspring are not, suggesting that the unpredictable environment of dispersed offspring favors genetic variance (see Williams' 'strawberry-coral' model). However, parental manipulation to reduce competition with genetically non-identical individuals may also be a significant factor. The area around the parent could be viewed as an investment which the parent would rather have utilized by genetically identical individuals. Indeed, asexual clones may provide a useful barrier against invasion by sexual offspring and other more distantly related individuals.

Environmental unpredictability is the critical factor here. Williams, in regard to his strawberry-coral model, assumes that 'environmental gradients behave in such a way that a successful genotype's local fitness has a negligible chance of being higher at any spot likely to be reached by the dispersal stage' noting that this 'seems to propose favorable selection of sexuality as a result of negative heritability of local fitness' (1975: 32–3). His 'triton model' (1975: 50–2) also apparently involves negative heritability of fitness. Williams states that he is unclear whether negative heritability is a necessary assumption for these models (1975: 51). There are several troublesome aspects of this reliance on negative heritability. First, it is not clear to what extent negative heritability in Williams' models implies predictability of offspring environment. In the environmental conditions specified by the triton model, facultative adaptation (i.e., phenotypic plasticity) in response to a consistent, predictable (?) environmental change would seem more likely (West-Eberhard, 2003). Moreover, dispersal entailing negative heritability might select against dispersal for high fitness individuals. If a consistent zygote dispersal pattern (e.g., circular via ocean currents) involves negative heritability, as the triton model presumes, selection for gamete dispersal in the opposite direction from zygote dispersal might be favored. Negative heritability also suggests that low fitness individuals could gain by asexuality, or that they would be attractive mates for high fitness individuals, neither of which appear to be common phenomena.

Genetic recombination in prokaryotes appears contradictory to the variable progeny theory. In the prokaryotic donor-recipient sexual relationship, genetic transfer is unidirectional (Jacob and Wollman, 1961). The result of prokaryotic genetic recombination is not increased genetic variability among subsequent progeny, but only a change in the genotype of the recipient. This genotype change must positively affect recipient fitness or sexuality would not be adaptive for the recipient.[5] There is no investment accompanying transfer of genetic material in prokaryotic sexuality (Jacob and Wollman, 1961), and thus seemingly no 'investment fitness cost of sex' ($-\Delta I_f$). However, this cost is incurred by the recipient because its phenotype represents investment, and a portion of the donor's genome displaces part of the recipient's genome. An increase in genetic fitness ($+\Delta G_f$) must therefore counterbalance this cost proportional to the amount of the genome displaced for sex to be advantageous for the recipient. Note that genes in the recipient might have varying abilities to withstand being replaced by incoming donor genes. Hence the genes within the recipient genome may have different strategies with respect to sexual reproduction by conjugation.

HERMAPHRODITISM AND MATE CHOICE

Sequential hermaphroditism responsive to sexual competition illustrates the importance of mate choice for individual reproductive strategies (Charnov, 1982; Ghiselin, 1974; Warner et al., 1975) and the possible benefits of sex. For example, in the hermaphroditic fish *Thalassoma bifasciatum*, 'The more definite the females tend to be in their choice (that is, the greater the gain of fertility with size in the males), the larger one must be to compete successfully, so the later one should change sex' (Warner et al., 1977: 633). If heritable fitness is correlated with large size, or the ability to achieve it, or whatever other attributes result in successful reproductive competition, the unfavorable investment balance ($-\Delta I_f$) incurred by smaller (potentially lower fitness) individuals (who are facultatively 'female') may be counterbalanced by the probable increase in the genetic fitness of progeny ($+\Delta G_f$). Maximization of genetic variability does not appear to be the sole criterion for mate choice among hermaphroditic species.

GONOCHORISM AND MATE CHOICE

In gonochoristic species, where an individual's sex type is fixed and not facultative, it follows from Fisher's (1958) theory of the sex ratio that fitness per unit of investment has no consistent correlation with sex type (because each sex contributes 50% to the next generation's gene pool (cf. Hamilton, 1967)). Nonetheless, variance in heritable fitness could continue to favor non-random mating and sexual reproduction involving differential investment by the sexes. *If heritable fitness is more variable in one sex than the other, mate choice will be more important for the less variable sex.* The sex with less variance in the genetic component of heritable fitness is predicted to provide a disproportionate share of investment because, if polygamy and adaptive mate choice occur, the sex with less variance in the genetic component will, on average, be choosing a mate with a higher genetic fitness component (Trivers, 1972). This may be, in part, the basis for the evolution of sex differences (i.e., the 'male-female phenomenon', Parker et al., 1972; Alexander and Borgia, 1979).

The variance of the genetic and investment components of heritable fitness determines their importance in mate choice. If variance of the investment component is low compared to variance of the genetic component, selection will favor mate choice based relatively more on the genetic component. Conversely, if variability of the genetic component is negligible, then reproductive variance resulting from mate choice will be determined by variance of the investment component (i.e., differences in parental investment provided by mates affect offspring fitness, but genetic differences among mates do not).

For example, if a species is (hypothetically) polygynous because of variance in the genetic component, and this variance decreases, selection would favor female choice to be based more on the investment component of potential mates. This choice of males providing greater investment would result in monogamy if individual males were unable to control sufficient resources to attract a second mate. Hence the distribution and defensibility of parental resources in the environment may influence variance of the investment component and, consequently, the mating system (Emlen and Oring, 1977; Flinn and Low, 1986; Harrison et al., 2009; Orians, 1969; Wittenberger and Tilson, 2003). Polyandry may develop when variance in heritable fitness becomes higher among females than for males, as might be the case in avian species such as *Jacana spinosa* and *Phalaropus fulicarous*, possibly due to variability in size and quality of female territories (Jenni, 1974). Territories might reflect both genetic and investment heritable fitness.

From the perspective of heritable fitness theory, mating systems are postulated to result in part from mate choice based on the two components of heritable fitness. Variance in potential investment may be concomitant with variance in genetic fitness (i.e., genetic fitness and the ability to invest parentally may be correlated). But the major problem with the evolution of sex is not the maintenance of sexual reproduction in systems with high reproductive variance associated with male resource control (Borgia, 1979; Cronin and Sherman, 1976; Orians, 1969). If both sexes are investing, then the 'investment fitness cost of sex' is reduced, disappearing when investment is equal.

It is the maintenance of sex in systems without apparent choice for investment (such as in most lek breeding species) that is seemingly anomalous. It is here, if there is 'zero investment by males', that a 'two-fold cost of meiosis' is incurred. In such species this cost must be counterbalanced either by an advantage from genetically variable progeny, in which case high fecundity and a highly unpredictable offspring environment are predicted (variable progeny theory), or choice based on the genetic component must entail a counterbalancing benefit (heritable fitness theory), or some combination of the two.

If male parental investment has little effect upon female reproductive success, then sexual selection could drive mate choice based on variance in the genetic component. This might be why leks occur in species with negligible male investment; the congregation of potential mates probably increases the benefits of mate choice while minimizing mating costs for the choosing sex (Alexander, 1975; Bradbury and Gibson, 1983). Phenotypic displays expressing potential heritable genetic fitness are predictably exaggerated in lek species. In such systems, female choice is constantly selected to discriminate, generating high reproductive variance among males (Fisher, 1958). Sexual selection diminishing male parental investment may be irreversible to the extent that selection from female choice based on the genetic component further reduces male ability to invest parentally (Fisher, 1958). Female choice of this sort could rapidly remove genetic variability among males, and thus reduce the benefits from such choice (Williams, 1981), if there was no environmental variability (just as natural selection could diminish genetic variability if selective pressures did not vary from generation to generation, and from one part of a species' habitat to another).

The mate choice behavior of females in low fecundity lek breeding species (e.g., *Centrocercus urophasianus*: Wiley, 1978; *Hypsignathus monstrosus*: Bradbury, 1977) does not suggest that genetic variability among offspring is being maximized. Males apparently are 'chosen' on the basis of phenotypic expression of potentially heritable fitness. Females do not appear to have random multiple matings, which would be expected if mate choice was based on maximizing genetic variability among offspring. However, studies of lek species have yet to document significant advantages of mate choice (cf. Bradbury and Gibson, 1983; Partridge, 1983; Quellar, 1987).

HIGH FITNESS FEMALES

Even if low fitness females gain a two-fold benefit, or more, from selective mating, the advantage of sexual reproduction to high fitness females is not readily apparent. However, to the extent that females are unable to predict the heritable genetic fitness component of asexually produced sons, but are able to do so for sexually produced sons (because of choice based on phenotype of father), only an on-average gain need be achieved, which is inherent in a system with high male reproductive variance. In a system with higher male than female reproductive variance, sons of high phenotypic fitness females are likely to have a higher reproductive potential than daughters (Trivers and Willard, 1973). Thus, for a high fitness female, a sexually produced son may make a larger contribution of his mother's genetic material to future generations' gene pools than an asexually produced daughter. Inbreeding (raising the degree of relatedness between parent and offspring) can also lower the cost of meiosis for high fitness females.[6] Even if sexual reproduction is disadvantageous for females with high heritable fitness, the proximate mechanisms for evaluating this fitness for sons may not be sufficient to make asexuality adaptive. Heritable fitness based on investment, on the other hand, is likely to be more predictable and provide the basis for adaptive sex ratio manipulation (Trivers and Willard, 1973). The inability of females to predict the genetic fitness component of asexual sons would be further compounded by sexually distinct genetic material, such as a 'Y' chromosome (for analysis of the evolutionary significance of sexually distinct genetic material, see Alexander and Borgia, 1978; Beukeboom and Perrin, 2014; Leigh, 1977). High fitness females may be stuck with sex in order to make high fitness sons (male parthenogenesis in haplodiploid systems is an obvious exception).

HISTORICAL CONSTRAINTS AND MATE CHOICE

The variable progeny theory suggests that sex may sometimes be maintained even when it is maladaptive for the investing sex (if that sex is incapable of producing asexual offspring that are half the fitness of sexual offspring, i.e., $F_a > 2F_s - M_1$). However, it is not sex per se that is maladaptive for the investing sex; it is providing a disproportionate share of investment without a counterbalancing benefit that is maladaptive. Mate choice can equal investment (no cost of meiosis) if choice based on the investment component has a greater effect on offspring fitness than choice based on the genetic component. If one sex is incurring an investment fitness cost of meiosis, mate choice based on selecting partners with more investment could eventually reduce or remove this cost.

In a polyandrous system with higher male than female investment (e.g., Syngnathidae), males may incur an investment fitness cost of meiosis, and because they are physically incapable of producing asexual offspring, might be phylogenetically trapped, in a sense. However, in such a polyandrous system, if the variance among females in the parental investment component had a greater effect on the reproductive success of offspring than the genetic component, then selection would favor males that chose females with relatively higher investment. The converse would be true in a polygynous system, with females choosing males on the basis of investment. Consequently, phylogenetic inertia is of limited explanatory value for the maintenance of sex in systems with mate choice. Only if choice is based on the genetic component because of lower variance in the investment component, and the benefits from mate choice do not counterbalance the investment

fitness cost of meiosis, can phylogenetic inertia cause the investing sex to be 'stuck' with maladaptive sexual reproduction.

SEX IN SPECIES WITHOUT MATE CHOICE

All of these possible resolutions to the cost of meiosis dilemma proposed by the heritable fitness theory depend upon selective mating, whether automatic or active (see Borgia, 1979 for discussion of different types of mate choice). Therefore, if mate choice is the basis for maintaining sexual reproduction involving differential investment in species where direct, active mate choice appears likely, then those species where such mate choice is unlikely should be characterized by the criteria postulated by the variable progeny theory. Evidence presented by Williams and Mitton (1973) and Williams (1975) suggests that these criteria (high fecundity and environmental uncertainty) generally are met in species with no apparent direct, active mate selection (e.g., elm-oyster model). Note, however, that such species still benefit from automatic mate choice resulting from gametic selection.

SEX AND ANISOGAMY

Although the variable progeny theory provides an explanation for the maintenance of sexuality involving differential investment in species without direct mate selection, it does not attempt to explain the evolutionary development of differential investment in such species. Parker et al. (1972) and Baker and Parker (1973) have addressed this issue in an analysis of the evolution of gamete dimorphism. Their theory of anisogamy is based on the probability of gamete union (i.e., fertilization), and suggests that divergent selection on gamete size will result from concomitant selection for gamete productivity (perhaps including motility) and zygote viability. This theory (hereafter referred to as the 'productivity theory') does not address the cost of meiosis inherent in differential investment resulting from anisogamy, nor does it address postzygotic differential investment. Nonetheless, the productivity theory provides an important perspective on sexual reproduction.

Divergent selection on gamete size as proposed by the productivity theory is most likely to occur with distant external fertilization (such as in stationary marine organisms). Adaptive sexual specialization in the production of one type of gamete might therefore be a consequence of an individual's microenvironment. Individuals in microenvironments favorable to gamete dispersal could be selected to specialize in the production of the smaller, more motile gametes, whereas individuals in environments favorable to gamete reception (or zygote success, if zygotes are not dispersed far) might be selected to specialize in the production of larger gametes (Togashi and Cox, 2011). Because the predictability of the gamete dispersing quality of an offspring's microenvironment is probably low if zygotes are dispersed, selection might favor microenvironmentally determined facultative sex specialization in such conditions. Life history and sexual competition strategies may also favor facultative sex determination or hermaphroditism (Warner et al., 1975). Because distant fertilization reduces the ability to identify offspring, post-zygotic investment can be affected by this uncertainty, and, secondarily, pre-zygotic investment as well (Alexander, 1974; Alexander and Borgia, 1978).

SUMMARY AND CONCLUSION

In summary, the following aspects of sexual reproduction are consistent with the individual selection theories discussed. Those species with distant fertilization, and therefore little likelihood of direct evaluation of a mate's phenotype (e.g., the plant kingdom

and sessile marine organisms), are in general characterized by:

1 High fecundity (Williams and Mitton, 1973; Williams, 1975)
2 Dispersal of offspring into varied and unpredictable environments (Bell, 1982; Williams, 1975; Williams and Mitton, 1973)
3 High number of mates fertilizing one individual's gametes
4 Potential for facultative asexuality of self-fertilization well developed if environment consistently varies in predictability (Williams, 1975; Williams and Mitton, 1973)
5 Hermaphroditism or environmentally determined sex type
6 Little or no post-zygotic investment (none by mate providing smaller, more motile gamete; Alexander and Borgia, 1979)

In contrast, species with direct proximate distribution of gametes between mates (i.e., potential for direct, active mate choice) are characterized by:

1 Lower fecundity (cf. footnote 6)
2 Selective mating (e.g., Borgia, 1979)
3 Secondary sexual characteristics, resulting from mate choice and sexual competition, in the sex with higher reproductive variance (Fisher, 1958)
4 Number of mates fertilizing one individual's gametes reduced (but number of potential mates is high)
5 Direct competition among sperm high (Ginsburg and Huck, 1989; Smith, 1984)
6 Sex type or progeny sex ratio, if facultative, determined by local sex ratio and potential social position of self (Ghiselin, 1974; Warner et al., 1975) or offspring (Trivers and Willard, 1973)
7 Facultative asexuality or self-fertilization developed in species, where variability of heritable fitness of available mates changes consistently (e.g., in aphids, previously discussed, and in colonizing species; or 'geographic parthenogenesis' in areas with low population densities and hence few opportunities for adaptive mate choice)
8 Mating system influenced by variance in heritable fitness between the two sexes (Borgia, 1979)
9 Post-zygotic investment dependent on proximate mechanisms for identifying offspring (Alexander, 1974; Alexander and Borgia, 1978)

Differential parental investment by the sexes can evolve in systems where variability of heritable fitness favors selective mating. In such systems, the benefits of mate choice may outweigh the 'cost of meiosis' to individuals providing a disproportionate share of investment in sexual offspring. Hence, sexual reproduction with differential investment can evolve and be maintained by individual selection independent of advantages from genetically variable progeny. Sexuality in species with no apparent selective mating is characterized by criteria suggested by the variable progeny theory (Williams, 1975; Williams and Mitton, 1973), so sexuality in species with and without heritable fitness may be parsimoniously explained by natural selection at the level of the individual.

In conclusion, the possible benefits of mate choice appear to resolve some shortcomings of the variable progeny theory. The theory however, is dependent upon identification of factors generating heritable differences in fitness, such as parasite resistance (Hamilton, 1980, 2002; Hamilton et al., 1990; Hamilton and Zuk, 1982) and social competition (Flinn and Alexander, 2007; West-Eberhard, 1983). The relevance to human mating behavior and psychology seems obvious in the general sense – resources and parental care on the one hand, evidence of genetic qualities on the other. But human reproduction in traditional societies involves complex social networks of multi-generational kinship and alliance that generate an extraordinary diversity of mating decisions. As Chagnon (1979: 88) cautions: 'The direct application of theory from evolutionary biology to human marriage behavior and mating strategies … is not possible until the theory is modified to take into consideration the interdependency of individuals … and how their interdependency – coalition alliances – structures human mating behavior.'

Notes

1   'Cost of meiosis' is an imprecise term, because sexual reproduction that does not involve a meiotic process (e.g., prokaryotes; Dougherty, 1955) can entail the same type of cost from unequal investment. Because the usage of the phrase is commonly accepted, it is used here.

2   'Parental effort' is defined in fitness currency as the time, energy, and risk expended in the production of offspring (Fisher, 1958; Low, 1978; Trivers, 1972, 1974; Williams, 1966).

3   The assumption of equal total investment in a sexual and an asexual offspring is made for simplification only. The theory does not depend on this assumption, because the comparison is made between the investment/fitness ratios. Fisher, discussing fecundity, notes: 'In organisms in which that degree of parental expenditure, which yields the highest proportionate probability of offspring survival, is large compared to the resources available, the optimal fertility will be low' (1958: 204).

4   This apparently is a general trend (Bell, 1982). Sexual generations are generally less fecund than asexual generations in seasonal facultatively sexual species.

5   Prokaryotic sexuality may, however, be a parasitic relationship, in some ways analogous to 'forced copulations' in sexual species.

6   Inbreeding can reduce the cost of meiosis only if it does not reduce other mating opportunities for the non-investing sex. It cannot reduce the cost of meiosis on a population wide basis.

REFERENCES

Abbot, P., Abe, J., Alcock, J., Alizon, S., Alpedrinha, J.A., Andersson, M., Andre, J.B., … and Zink, A. (2011). Inclusive fitness theory and eusociality. *Nature* 471(7339): E1–4.

Alexander, R. D. (1974). The evolution of social behavior. *Annual Review of Ecology and Systematics 5*, 325–383.

Alexander, R. D. (1975). The search for a general theory of behavior *Behavioral Science*, 20(2), 77–100. http://dx.doi.org/10.1002/bs.3830200202.

Alexander, R. D. and Borgia, G. (1978). Group selection, altruism and the levels of organization of life. *Annual Review of Ecology and Systematics 9*, 449–474.

Alexander, R. D. and Borgia, G. (1979). The origin and basis of the male-female phenomenon. In M. F. Blum and N. A. Blum (Eds), *Sexual selection and reproductive competition in insects*. Academic Press, pp. 417–440.

Andersson, M. (1994). *Sexual selection*. Princeton, NJ: Princeton University Press.

Baker, R. R. and Parker, G. A. (1973). The origin and evolution of sexual reproduction up to the evolution of the male-female phenomenon. *Acta Biotheoretica 22*(2) 49–77.

Barash, D. P. (1976). What does sex really cost? *The American Naturalist 110*(975), 894–897.

Bell, G. (1982). *The masterpiece of nature: The evolution and genetics of sexuality*. Berkeley: University of California Press.

Beukeboom, L. W. and Perrin, N. (2014). *The evolution of sex determination*. Oxford: Oxford University Press.

Birdsell, J. A. and Wills, C. (2003). The evolutionary origin and maintenance of sexual recombination: A review of contemporary models. In R. J. Macintyre and M. T. Clegg (Eds), *Evolutionary biology 33*. Springer, Boston, pp. 27–137. doi:10.1007/978-1-4757-5190-1_2.

Bonner, J. T. (1958). *The evolution of development: Three special lectures given at University College, London*. Cambridge: Cambridge University Press.

Borgia, G. (1979). Sexual selection and the evolution of mating systems. In M. F. Blum and N. A. Blum (Eds), *Sexual selection and reproductive competition in insects*. Academic Press, pp. 19–80.

Bradbury, J. W. (1977). Lek mating behavior in the hammer-headed bat. *Ethology 45*(3), 225–255.

Bradbury, J. W. and Gibson, R. M. (1983). Leks and mate choice. In P. P. G. Bateson (Ed.), *Mate choice*. Cambridge: Cambridge University Press, pp 109–138.

Buchsbaum, R., Buchsbaum, M., Pearse, J., and Pearse, V. B. (1987). *Animals without backbones*. 3rd edition. Chicago: University of Chicago Press.

Buss, D. M. and Schmitt, D. P. (2019). Mate preferences and their behavioral manifestations. *Annual Review of Psychology 70*, 77–110.

Chagnon, N. A. (1979). Mate competition, favoring close kin, and village fissioning among the Yanomamo Indians. In N. A. Chagnon and W. Irons (Eds), *Evolutionary biology and human social behavior: An anthropological perspective*. North Scituate, MA: Duxbury Press.

Charnov, E. (1982). *The theory of sex allocation*. Princeton University Press.

Cronin, E. W. and Sherman, P.W. (1976). A resource-based mating system: The orange-rumped honeyguide. *Living Bird 15*, 5–32.

Dawkins, R. (1982). *The extended phenotype*. Oxford: Oxford University Press.

Dougherty, E. C. (1955). Comparative evolution and the origin of sexuality. *Systemic Zoology 4*(4), 145–169.

Emlen, S.T., and Oring, L.W. (1977). Ecology, sexual selection, and the evolution of mating systems. *Science 197*(4300), 215–223.

Fisher, R. A. (1958). *The genetical theory of natural selection*. 2nd edition. New York: Dover Publications.

Flinn, M. V., and Alexander, R. D. (2007). Runaway social selection. In S. W. Gangestad and J. A. Simpson (Eds.), *The evolution of mind*, pp. 249–255. New York: Guilford Press.

Flinn, M. V., and Low, B. S. (1986). Resource distribution, social competition, and mating systems in human societies. In R. Wrangham and D. Rubenstein (Eds), *Ecological aspects of social systems*. Princeton, NJ: Princeton University Press, pp. 217–243.

Geary, D. C. (2020). *Male, female: The evolution of human sex differences*. 3rd edition. Washington, DC: American Psychological Association.

Ghiselin, M. (1974). *The economy of nature and the evolution of sex*. Berkeley: University of California Press.

Ginsburg, J. R. and Huck, U. W. (1989). Evolution of sperm competition. *Trends in Ecology and Evolution 4*(3), 74–79.

Glesener, R. R. and Tilman, D. (1978). Sexuality and the components of environmental uncertainty: Clues from geographic parthenogenesis in terrestrial animals. *The American Naturalist 112*(986), 659–673.

Hamilton, W. D. (1964). The genetical evolution of social behaviour. I. *Journal of Theoretical Biology 7*(1), 1–16.

Hamilton, W.D. (1967). Extraordinary sex ratios. *Science 156*, 477–488.

Hamilton, W. D. (1976). Gamblers since life began: Barnacles, aphids, elms. *Quarterly Review of Biology 51*, 407–412.

Hamilton, W. D. (1980). Sex versus non-sex versus parasite. *Oikos 35*(2), 282–290.

Hamilton, W. D. (2002). *Narrow roads of gene land, vol. 2: Evolution of sex*. Oxford: Oxford University Press.

Hamilton, W. D. and Zuk, M. (1982). Heritable true fitness and bright birds: A role for parasites? *Science 218*(4570), 384–387.

Hamilton, W. D., Axelrod, R., and Tanese, R. (1990). Sexual reproduction as an adaptation to resist parasites. *Proceedings of the National Academy of Sciences of the United States of America 87*(9), 3566–3573.

Harrison, F., Barta, Z., Cuthill, I., and Székely, T. (2009). How is sexual conflict over parental care resolved? A meta-analysis. *Journal of Evolutionary Biology 22*(9), 1800–1812.

Hartfield, M., and Keightley, P. D. (2012). Current hypotheses for the evolution of sex and recombination. *Integrative Zoology 7*(2), 192–209.

Hartung, J. (1981). Genome parliaments and sex with the red queen. In R. D. Alexander and D. W. Tinkle (Eds), *Natural selection and social behavior: Recent research and new theory*. New York: Chiron Press, pp. 382–402.

Hill, W.G., and Robertson, A. (1966). The effect of linkage on limits to artificial selection. *Genetics Research 8*(3), 269–294.

Hoekstra, R. F. (1987). The evolution of sexes. In S. C. Stearns (Ed.), *The evolution of sex and its consequences*. Springer Basel AG.

Jacob, F. and Wollman, E. L. (1961). *Sexuality and the genetics of bacteria*. New York: Academic Press.

Jenni, D. (1974). Evolution of polyandry in birds. *Integrative and Comparative Biology 14*(1), 129–144.

Kondrashov, A. S. (1982). Selection against harmful mutations in large sexual and asexual populations. *Genetical Research 40*(3), 325–332.

Kondrashov, A. S. (2013). Genetics: The rate of human mutation. *Nature* 488: 467–468.

Leigh Jr., E. G. (1977). How does selection reconcile individual advantage with the good of the group? *Proceedings of the National Academy of Sciences of the United States of America 74*(10), 4542–4546.

Leigh Jr., E. G. (2010). The group selection controversy. *Journal of Evolutionary Biology 23*(1), 6–10.

Lewontin, R. C. (1970). The units of selection. *Annual Review of Ecology and Systematics 1*, 1–18.

Lodé, T. (2012). Sex and the origin of genetic exchanges. *Trends in Evolutionary Biology 4*(1), e1.

Low, B. S. (1978). Environmental uncertainty and the parental strategies of marsupials and placentals. *The American Naturalist 112*(983), 197–213.

Maynard Smith, J. (1978). *The evolution of sex*. Cambridge: Cambridge University Press.

Maynard Smith, J. and Williams, G. C. (1976). Reply to Barash. *The American Naturalist 110*(975), 897.

Moran, N. A. (1992). The evolution of aphid life cycles. *Annual Review of Entomology 37*, 321–348.

Orians, G. H. (1969). On the evolution of mating systems in birds and mammals. *The American Naturalist 103*(934), 589–603.

Otto, S. P. (2009). The evolutionary enigma of sex. *The American Naturalist 174*(S1), S1–S14.

Parker, G. A. (1983). Mate quality and mating decisions. In P. P. G. Bateson (Ed.), *Mate choice*. Cambridge: Cambridge University Press, pp. 141–164.

Parker, G. A., Baker, R. R., and Smith, V. G. F. (1972). The origin and evolution of gamete dimorphism and the male-female phenomenon. *Journal of Theoretical Biology 36*(3), 529–553.

Partridge, L. (1983). Non-random mating and offspring fitness. In P. Bateson (Ed.), *Mate choice*. Cambridge: Cambridge University Press, pp. 227–256.

Puts, D. (2016). Human sexual selection. *Current Opinion in Psychology 7*, 28–32.

Quellar, D. C. (1987). The evolution of leks through female choice. *Animal Behavior 35*(5), 1424–1432.

Togashi, T. and Cox, P. (Eds) (2011). *The evolution of anisogamy*. Cambridge: Cambridge University Press, pp. 22–29.

Trivers, R. L. (1972). Parental investment and sexual selection. In B. Campbell (Ed.), *Sexual selection and the descent of man, 1871–1971*. Chicago: Aldine, pp.136–179.

Trivers, R. L. (1974). Parent–offspring conflict. *American Zoologist 14*(1), 249–264.

Trivers, R. L. and Willard, D. E. (1973). Natural selection of parental ability to vary the sex ratio of offspring. *Science 179*(4068), 90–92.

Van Valen, L. (1973). A new evolutionary law. *Evolutionary Theory 1*, 1–30.

Vrijenhoek, R. C. (1998). Animal clones and diversity. *BioScience 48*(8), 617–628.

Warner, R. R., Robertson, D. R., and Leigh Jr., E. G. (1975). Sex change and sexual selection. *Science 190*(4215), 633–638.

West-Eberhard, M. J. (1983). Sexual selection, social competition, and speciation. *Quarterly Review of Biology 58*(2), 155–183.

West-Eberhard, M. J. (2003). *Developmental plasticity and evolution*. New York: Oxford University Press.

Wiley Jr., R. H. (1978). Lek mating system of the sage grouse. *Scientific American 238*(5), 114–125.

Williams, G. C. (1966). *Adaptation and natural selection*. Princeton, NJ: Princeton University Press.

Williams, G. C. (Ed.) (1971). *Group selection*. Chicago: Aldine-Atherton.

Williams, G. C. (1975). *Sex and evolution*. Princeton, NJ: Princeton University Press

Williams, G. C. and Mitton, J. B. (1973). Why reproduce sexually? *Journal of Theoretical Biology 39*(3), 545–554.

Wittenberger, J. F. and Tilson, R. L. (2003). The evolution of monogamy: Hypotheses and evidence. *Annual Review of Ecology and Systematics 11*, 197–232.

8

Parental Investment Theory

Justin K. Mogilski

This chapter outlines how Robert Trivers' Parental Investment Theory (PIT) has progressed from its original publication in *Sexual Selection and the Descent of Man* through its expansive application to research in the evolutionary psychological sciences. I begin with an abridged redux of the theory's claims and predictions as they appeared within the original 1972 publication. After, I review groundbreaking research inspired by PIT and evaluate how well the theory has been empirically supported in the past 50 or so years. I then note several major theoretical advancements and address conflicts with other prominent theories of mating and parenting behavior. The chapter closes with several future directions that may help PIT remain a robust and relevant framework for studying human psychology within an increasingly technologically and socially complex world.

PARENTAL INVESTMENT THEORY REDUX

PIT predicts that reproductive behavior and its underlying psychology has been shaped by natural selection to resolve recurrent tradeoffs in offspring investment. Trivers (1972) first outlined PIT as a framework for connecting several key variables of sexual selection which, in prior work (e.g., Bateman, 1948; Fisher, 1958), had not yet been unified or precisely defined. He proposed that parental investment (i.e., any investment into individual offspring that increases the chance of that offspring's survival at the cost of investment into other offspring) systematically differs between males and females within species. This can be attributed to the size of males' and females' reproductive cells (Bateman, 1948). Individuals who produce more numerous, inexpensive, and mobile gametes (e.g., sperm) are better able to increase their reproductive success through multi-partner mating because they are limited by the number of individuals with whom they mate. By comparison, those who produce more expensive and immobile gametes (e.g., eggs) often have a greater minimum obligatory investment in offspring (e.g., gestational resources, early childcare) compared to the other sex, decreasing the value of multi-partner mating. Compared to the opposite sex, then, the less investing sex (e.g., men) benefits more from seeking successive sexual partners whereas the more investing sex (e.g., women) benefits more from enhancing its capacity to support offspring.

Trivers (1972) argues that this asymmetry in minimum parental investment governs sexual selection – the process by which some individuals experience greater reproductive success than others of the same sex. Sexual selection involves two processes: intrasexual competition (i.e., rivalry between same-sex individuals for access to mates) and intersexual mate choice (i.e., differential selection of one sex by members of the opposite sex). Because the reproductive success of the less investing sex is limited by access to the other sex, the sex that contributes more parental investment becomes a limited resource. This yields greater competition among the less investing sex for access to the more investing sex. Likewise, individuals of the more investing sex are choosier when selecting a mate because it is costlier to invest in the offspring of a low quality partner.

This model predicts that discrepancies in parental investment will explain patterns of partner desertion, cuckoldry, and mate guarding behavior. To the extent that the less investing sex may forgo parental investment to enhance reproductive success with little cost, these individuals will be more willing to desert partners for sexual opportunities. In reaction, abandoned parents may desert their offspring, attempt to raise offspring alone, or induce another partner to invest in unrelated offspring (i.e., cuckoldry). Whereas the more investing sex suffers greater cost of desertion, the less investing sex is susceptible to cuckoldry. For example, sperm competition (Parker, 1970) occurs when the gametes of two or more individuals from the less investing sex concurrently occupy the reproductive tract of the more investing sex. Which sperm fertilizes the ovum is unknown and therefore the less investing sex is more uncertain of offspring relatedness relative to the more investing sex. Consequently, the less investing sex will become motivated to territorially aggress against competitors and to restrict a partner's access to extra-pair mating to reduce the risk of cuckoldry.

These sex differences in mating risk are thus predicted to shape within-species features such as mortality rate, reproductive skew, the intensity and strategies of intrasexual competition, and within-sex trait variance. In species where males invest relatively less in offspring, males who outcompete other males have the potential to produce an exceptional number of offspring. This favors intense intrasexual competition via direct aggression and coercion, which leads to greater variance in male reproductive success, mortality, and sex-specific traits. For example, males within promiscuous species will be larger to permit more effective (and deadly) physical contests, have higher metabolic rate to support somatic growth and activity, strategically deploy puberty to manage the costs and benefits of entering the competitive milieu of sexual maturity, and show greater mobility to increase exposure to available mates. By contrast, when males invest more than at least one half the amount that females invest, they yield fewer benefits from direct competition. Where competition exists, males may instead switch to indirect strategies such as clandestine insemination of other males' mates. In turn, if males detect this deception, they may strategically downregulate investment into unrelated offspring and, in extreme cases, kill unrelated offspring to avoid investment.

In species where females are the more investing sex, they will evolve to discriminate potential mates' capacities and exert relatively greater choice than males when deciding with whom to mate. Trivers (1972) argues that female preference will correspond with selection for extreme male traits (i.e., those traits which, through a positive feedback loop, equip males to outcompete less extreme competitors). For example, a female may prefer exaggerated male size to the extent that greater size corresponds to his ability to use that size when defending against predators and competitors. Likewise, preference for features that are clearly sex-typical will reduce the chance of mating errors (i.e., pairing with same-sex individuals who cannot contribute gametes for reproduction). In species where paternal investment is minimal, females will choose mates based on traits that indicate health and genetic robustness because these traits confer a survival advantage independent of parental care. When paternal investment is higher, females will still assess these traits but may compare (and trade off) good gene qualities with good parenting qualities, such as the ability and willingness to provision time and resources. This capacity to provision, however, may not be mutually exclusive with good genes. For example, social dominance may not only index physical health and competence (and therefore genetic quality) but also buffer potential offspring against social threats to survival (e.g., other males). This may thereby favor a strategically pluralistic strategy whereby females adjust their mate preferences according to the adaptive value that a strategy confers to potential offspring given the payoff of each sex's relative investment in offspring.

SUPPORTING EVIDENCE

PIT has generated abundant research, and many of its original claims have been supported by empirical evidence (see Table 8.1 for a brief summary). Buss (1989) provided the first cross-cultural evidence within humans showing that men and women systematically

Table 8.1 Claims from Parental Investment Theory (PIT; see 'Parental Investment Theory Redux') and some findings that support them (see 'Supporting Evidence')

Claims from PIT	Supporting Evidence
The less investing sex will compete for a greater variety of sexual partners; the more investing sex will be choosier about with whom they mate.	Men more than women prefer cues to physical attractiveness and reproductive potential whereas women more than men prefer cues to a partner's willingness and capacity to invest in offspring. Women tend to have higher minimum requirements for their mate's qualities than men. Women are more cautious to engage in casual sex.
The more investing sex suffers greater cost of partner desertion; the less investing sex is more susceptible to cuckoldry.	Mate retention behaviors vary with perceptions of the risk of infidelity and sperm competition. Sex differences in experiences of jealousy correspond to the potential costs associated with a partner's investment of time and resources in others.
Sex differences in mating risk will shape mortality rate, reproductive skew, intensity and strategies of intrasexual competition, and within-sex trait variance.	Men vary more than women in reproductive output and physical/psychological qualities, have higher rates of mortality, and compete more intensely with same-sex rivals.
The more investing sex will strategically adjust their partner preferences according to the adaptive value that a partner's traits provide.	When the sex ratio is disfavorable, women report more interest in casual sex. Women report greater preference for male-typical facial features in harsh environments.

differ in their mate preferences. Men more than women prefer cues to physical attractiveness and reproductive potential whereas women more than men prefer cues to a partner's willingness and capacity to invest in offspring (e.g., social status, generosity, industriousness). To the extent that men optimize their reproductive output by allocating numerous and inexpensive gametes across a variety of partners, men will be relatively less concerned with a partner's commitment and willingness to form a long-term enduring romantic relationship and instead seek traits that indicate a partner's health and ability to successfully nourish and support potential offspring in the absence of paternal investment. Women, by comparison, will place relatively greater importance on cues that indicate whether consortship with a partner will provide her the resources needed to protect and raise their shared offspring.

This preliminary evidence led to a model of human mate preferences termed Sexual Strategies Theory (Buss and Schmitt, 1993). It proposed that men and women evolved mate selection heuristics for navigating sexual conflict in long- and short-term romantic relationships that differed according to men's and women's obligatory minimum offspring investment. This model has been supported in cross-cultural samples (Chang et al., 2011; Fales et al., 2016; Li et al., 2011; Shackelford et al., 2005; de Souza et al., 2016; Sprecher et al., 1994), and using varied methodologies (Conroy-Beam et al., 2015; Fletcher et al., 2004; Li et al., 2002; Mogilski et al., 2014; Thomas et al., 2019). It has been expanded to account for moderating contextual circumstances such as socioeconomic status (Lu et al., 2015; March and Grieve, 2016; Yongxiang and Mengxia, 2018), individual differences (e.g., sociosexuality [Wilbur and Campbell, 2010], antisocial personality [Jonason et al., 2011, 2012]), and cross-cultural variation (Schmitt, 2015) which has advanced the theory's applicability to modern contexts (see Buss and Schmitt, 2019).

Research has documented complementary patterns of mate guarding, jealousy, and cuckoldry that also support predictions from PIT. Mate retention behaviors (i.e., effort devoted to preventing the loss of a romantic partner) were identified in humans by Buss (1988) and formalized into psychometric inventories (i.e., the Mate Retention Inventory [MRI] and MRI-Short Form [MRI-SF]; Buss et al., 2008). Scores on the MRI predict romantic relationship outcomes, behaviors, and attitudes in married (Altgelt and Meltzer, 2019; Buss and Shackelford, 1997) and unmarried couples (Conroy-Beam et al., 2016; Lopes et al., 2018), non-American samples (Atari et al., 2017; Chaudhary et al., 2018; De Miguel and Buss, 2011; Kardum et al., 2006; Lopes et al., 2016), hetero- and homosexual romantic relationships (Brewer and Hamilton, 2014; VanderLaan and Vasey, 2008), and consensually non-monogamous relationships (Mogilski et al., 2017, 2019). Mate retention behaviors vary as predicted with men's perceptions of the risk of infidelity and sperm competition (Starratt et al., 2007), the phase of their female partner's ovulatory cycle (e.g., Gangestad et al., 2002), men's self-esteem (Holden et al., 2014), as well as with both men's and women's self- and partner-evaluations of mate value (Miner et al., 2009; Starratt and Shackelford, 2012) and sociosexuality (Kardum et al., 2006).

Experiences of jealousy likewise correspond to the potential costs associated with a partner's investment of time and resources in others – and therefore away from potential offspring. In societies characterized by greater paternal investment and lower frequencies of extra-pair sex, jealousy is more severe (Scelza et al., 2019). Its activation is sensitive to relationship risks such as mate poaching (Moran and Wade, 2019; Nascimento and Little, 2019; Schmitt and Buss, 2001), mate switching (Buss et al., 2017), cuckoldry (Starratt et al., 2013), intrasexual conflict (Buunk et al., 2019), sperm competition (Pham and Shackelford, 2015; Shackelford and Goetz, 2007), and disinvestment of relationship resources (Campbell and Loving, 2016). Though both men and women get jealous, there are sex differences in the experience of jealousy. Compared to men, women typically report greater distress toward potential loss of a partner's interpersonal support (i.e., extra-pair emotional involvement), whereas men typically report greater distress toward a partner's sexual contact with another person (i.e., extra-pair sexual involvement). Given the risk of cuckoldry for men and partner abandonment for women, these differences in psychological design address the recurrent parental investment challenges that have been relatively more deleterious for men and women, respectively. These differences have been demonstrated across cultures (Bendixen et al., 2015; Fernandez et al., 2006, 2015; Zandbergen and Brown, 2015) using diverse methodologies and measures (Dunn and Ward, 2019; Edlund et al., 2006; Maner and Shackelford, 2008; Sagarin et al., 2012; Wade and Mogilski, 2018) and within some non-heterosexual samples (Bailey et al., 1994; Sagarin et al., 2003; de Souza et al., 2006), though notable exceptions have been observed in nontraditional romantic relationships (see Dijkstra et al., 2001; Frederick and Fales, 2016; Howard and Perilloux, 2017; Mogilski et al., 2019).

Sex differences in within-sex variability of physical and cognitive traits, reproductive skew, and rates of mortality, have also been observed. Men tend to show greater variability in phenotypic qualities such as body mass index and blood parameters (e.g., circulating hemoglobin) (Lehre et al., 2009), muscle mass (Welle et al., 2008), and athletic performance (Handelsman, 2017; Ospina Betancurt et al., 2018). Men also vary more than women across brain structures (Wierenga et al., 2018), and this variation maps onto greater male variability in cognitive and behavioral traits such as academic achievement (Gray et al., 2019; Makel et al., 2016; Reilly et al., 2015), personality (particularly within societies where individuals are less restricted from expressing personality; Borkenau et al., 2013), intelligence (Arden and Plomin, 2006), creativity (Karwowski et al., 2016), language competence (Lange et al., 2016), and mate value qualities (see Archer and Mehdikhani, 2003).

Finally, PIT's prediction that women will exert greater choice and strategically alter their preferences according to features of the mating environment (e.g., operational sex ratio, expected paternal investment) has been supported. Women tend to have higher minimum requirements for their mates than men, whose minimum requirements depend more on their anticipated investment in the relationship (Kenrick et al., 1990). Inasmuch as pregnancy is costlier to women, women are more cautious in accepting an offer of casual sex (Lippa, 2009; Schmitt and ISDP, 2003; Surbey and Conohan, 2000), though this willingness depends on the ratio of men to women within a population (see Maner and Ackerman, 2020). When the sex ratio is disfavorable (i.e., there are more women than men within a population – and therefore more intrasexual competition), women report more interest in casual sex (Moss and Maner, 2016; though, also see Schacht and Borgerhoff Mulder, 2015). Preference for exaggerated male-typical traits also depends on features of the environment that predict paternal investment. When asked to imagine themselves within a more resource scarce environment (i.e., higher competition, lower paternal investment; Hartman et al., 2018), women report greater preference for male-typical facial features in a long-term partner (Little et al., 2007). Likewise, exposure to visual cues of male–male conflict increase women's preferences for facial masculinity (Little et al., 2013), which may index a mate's success during intrasexual competition (Little et al., 2015; Třebický et al., 2015). In this regard, women's preferences have been shown to be strategically pluralistic (Gangestad and Simpson, 2000), whereby preference adaptively shifts in response to women's current mating (and parenting) motives and the constraints imposed by the physical and social environment.

THEORETICAL REFINEMENT

Though PIT has achieved a level of scientific success that places it among the most influential models of natural selection and design, it has had a complex relationship with other theories that attempt to explain how behavior and mental processes are shaped by the natural world. Perhaps most notably, human mating systems are characterized by a high level of paternal investment relative to other mammalian species (Geary, 2015; Marlowe, 2000). Human children tend to have extended dependence on their parents (Montagu, 1960; Zeveloff and Boyce, 1982), and this extended investment translates into later-life advantages for that offspring (Antfolk and Sjölund, 2018; Feldman et al., 2019; Winking and Koster, 2015). The necessity for heavy parental investment within humans is exaggerated within industrialized societies. Modern environments favor more parental investment per child to the extent that investment into the embodied capital of children (e.g., health, skills, social status; Shenke et al., 2016) yields greater payoff within competitive, education-based labor markets that require skilled work (Colleran et al., 2015; Kaplan, 1996; Stulp and Barrett, 2016). Where the extracted value of parental investment is relatively equal for men and women, sex differences due to parental investment should be relatively smaller (Geary, 2000).

In this regard, the complexity of human social living makes it difficult to neatly predict human cognition and behavior using strictly biological attributes like gamete size and minimum obligatory offspring investment. Several prominent, and at times competing (e.g., Archer, 1996; Eagly and Wood, 1999; Fox and Bruce, 2001; Schmitt, 2015), models have posited that sex differences result from the distribution of men and women into social roles that are perpetuated by intergenerational cultural transmission, socialization, and gendered norm enforcement (Eagly and Wood, 2016; Hogg, 2016). Because humans rely on culture to transmit learned knowledge (Dunbar, 2006), these theories have been valuable for characterizing the social systems by which gendered information is spread via culture and integrated into identity (Wood and Eagly, 2015). However, relative to evolutionary predictions derived from PIT, these theories have had difficulty explaining certain patterns, such as the observation that sex differences become more exaggerated in societies with greater gender egalitarianism (Lippa, 2009, 2010; Schmitt et al., 2017). Likewise, sex differences in personality are greater in countries with more gender equality (Kaiser, 2019; Schmitt et al., 2017) and economic development (Falk and Hermle, 2018), suggesting that when people are free to express individual differences without the constraints of social pressure and stigma, people are more likely to embody sex-typical preferences and attitudes. To this end, several researchers have suggested that parental investment theory should be complemented with models that account for social and coevolutionary feedback systems (Alonzo, 2010; Durante et al., 2016; Fromhage and Jennions, 2016).

Life History Theory (LHT) is an exemplar for successfully expanding and integrating predictions from PIT with other theories of psychosocial development. LHT is a framework for understanding individual variation in sexual, reproductive, parental, familial, and social behaviors across the lifespan (reviewed in Figueredo et al., 2006; see also Del Giudice et al., 2015). It predicts that organisms vary adaptively in how they allocate limited time and resources toward growth and reproduction. This variation can be meaningfully divided into two predominant strategies: a slow life history, whereby individuals delay sexual development and reproduction (i.e., invest more in relatively fewer offspring), and a fast life history, in which individuals experience earlier sexual maturity and produce a greater quantity of offspring (i.e., invest less in relatively more offspring). Though recent work has criticized the validity of applying LHT to trait variation within humans (e.g., Nettle and Frankenhuis, 2019; Zietsch and Sidari, 2019), this predictive lens has been useful for studying psychosocial developmental plasticity within unstable and underprivileged environments (see Kuzawa and Bragg, 2012). Relative to a slow life history strategy, people with faster life history strategies prefer immediate over delayed rewards (Griskevicius et al., 2011), reproduce earlier (Boothroyd et al., 2013; Hehman and Salmon, 2019), have more casual sex (Dunkel et al., 2015; Salmon et al., 2016), are more likely to practice consensual non-monogamy (Mogilski et al., 2020), experience earlier sexual debut and report greater sexual risk-taking (James et al., 2012), pursue social status via dominance rather than prestige (Lukaszewski, 2015), score higher on measures of psychopathy (e.g., boldness, aggression, and disinhibition; Međedović, 2018) and dark personality (i.e., impulsivity, antisociality, entitlement/exploitativeness, Machiavellianism, and aggression; McDonald et al., 2012), and are more likely to use psychoactive substances (Richardson et al., 2014).

LHT provides adaptationist logic for why parental investment varies across individuals in response to environmental pressure. If the future is relatively unpredictable, dividing investment among children may be a more successful reproductive strategy than high quality investment in any given child (Ellis and Del Giudice, 2019; Frankenhuis and Nettle, 2019; Pepper and Nettle, 2017). Parenting behavior and investment appears to conform to this prediction (de Baca and Ellis, 2017). Children raised in impoverished communities receive less parental investment (Hampson et al., 2016) and parents in nations with high pathogen loads (i.e., an indicator of environmental harshness) have more children and at a younger age (Pelham, 2019). Family size influences offspring investment, such that children receive less individual investment with increasing family size, suggesting greater competition among children for parental resources (Lawson and

Mace, 2009). Conversely, parenting styles that require investment (i.e., affection and sensitivity) appear to buffer the development of fast life history traits (Dunkel et al., 2018) whereas harsh styles exacerbate it (Belsky et al., 2012; Hentges and Wang, 2018). Furthermore, the quality of received parental care predicts pubertal timing and other features of life history variation (Ellis and Essex, 2007). This type of data generated by LHT has provided a novel perspective from which to examine how parental investment and psychosocial features interact to produce human trait variation.

FUTURE DIRECTIONS

PIT has shaped the theoretical landscape guiding research within evolutionary biology and psychology. However, there are yet improvements to be made to the implementation of PIT in research and unaddressed questions about its applicability to modern human social systems (summarized in Table 8.2). First, research on human sexuality and mate preferences shaped by PIT has predominantly focused on sex differences in mating among non-parents, and relatively less effort has been invested into studying sex differences among those with children. Recent work has shown that mating behavior differs between parents and non-parents (e.g., Barbaro et al., 2016; Flegr et al., 2019) and within pregnant women (Magginetti and Pillsworth, 2019). Furthermore, the relationship between parents and their offspring has been shown to shape parenting behavior (e.g., parent–offspring conflict; see Salmon, 2015). Conflict between the strategic interests of parents and their offspring will influence evolutionary equilibria that shape behavior predicted by parental investment theory (Uller, 2008). For example, parents should modulate their investment depending on a child's developing capacity to provision for itself; however, children should continue

Table 8.2   Summary of future directions and limitations of the implementation of PIT

Limitations	Future Directions
Research predominantly samples non-parents and assesses romantic preference, behavior, and decision-making absent the influence of offspring.	How are sex differences in mate preference and behavior modulated by parenthood? How do men and women differ in the strategies they use to negotiate offspring investment?
Non-normative reproductive and gendered strategies such as homosexuality, transgenderism, and consensual non-monogamy are relatively understudied.	How does the absence of cross-sex negotiation within same-sex relationships alter partner conflict? To the extent that those who are homosexual or transgender develop a more diverse combination of sex-normative and non-normative male- and female-typical psychological characteristics, are sexually selected traits more mosaicked within these individuals than within cisgender and heterosexual people? How do patterns of parental investment vary within non-monogamous mating systems, and how does this variation influence partner preference and conflict?
How morality, social attitudes toward sexual behavior, and willingness to condemn non-normative sexual behaviors (e.g., age-discrepant relationships, consensual non-monogamy) intervene on sexual conflict is poorly understood.	Does moral intuition adaptively vary with obligatory parental investment? Which moral intuitions safeguard against unequal parental investment? Why are some sexual behaviors subject to greater condemnation than others, and how does this condemnation alter sexual strategies and norms? Are the intuitions that motivate condemnation mismatched to modern environments?

to solicit parental resources insofar as excess support advantages the child (Plooij and van de Rijt-Plooij, 1989). Negotiation over how much effort each parent invests into offspring will also shape the nature of sexual conflict between mothers and fathers (Lessells and McNamara, 2012).

PIT also does not directly address non-normative reproductive and gendered strategies such as homosexuality and transgenderism. Though romantic relationship processes have been predominantly shaped by a history of sexual conflict among opposite-sex partners (though also see Monk et al., 2019), modern environments are increasingly permissive of same-sex sexual relationships. Studies examining PIT predictions within homosexual populations have reported mixed results. For example, Dijkstra et al. (2001) examined whether gay men's and lesbian's reactions to emotional and sexual infidelity resemble those of their heterosexual counterparts. They found that homosexuals' reactions to each type of infidelity resembled heterosexuals of the opposite sex (i.e., lesbians were more likely to report upset toward sexual infidelity

whereas gay men were more upset by emotional infidelity). Others have reported sex differences between hetero- but not homo- or bisexual men and women (Frederick and Fales, 2016). Bailey et al. (1994) found that homosexual individuals' mating psychology resembled same-sex heterosexuals. Likewise, Howard and Perilloux (2017) report that sex, rather than the sex to whom a person is attracted, is a better predictor of mating psychology. Aristegui et al. (2019) found that transgender individuals are more likely to respond to relationship threats (e.g., the presence of a romantic competitor) according to their gender identity rather than their sex assigned at birth. It is possible that the absence of cross-sex negotiation between homosexual partners' mating motives (e.g., two gay men will more often have a similar interest in casual sex compared to a man and a woman; Schmitt, 2007) influences how sex-typical psychological mechanisms are expressed within same-sex romantic relationships. It may also be that homosexual and transgender sex and gender development is more mosaicked than in heterosexual individuals.

To the extent that homosexual and transgender individuals develop a diverse combination of sex-normative and non-normative male- and female-typical psychological characteristics, then sexually selected traits may not manifest as clearly as they do within cisgender and heterosexual people.

Similarly, most PIT predictions have been tested within nominally monogamous relationships. Though PIT does account for the possibility that parental investment and sex differences may differ across mating systems (i.e., polygynous mating systems may be characterized by greater intrasexual competition for mates and therefore less paternal investment relative to monogamous systems), these predictions have not been as clearly or frequently tested within human non-monogamous populations. Mogilski et al. (2019) examined reactions to a partner's emotional and sexual extradyadic involvement within monogamous and consensually non-monogamous relationships (CNM) (i.e., romantic relationships wherein people form consensually non-exclusive romantic or sexual partnerships) and found that men and women within monogamous, but not CNM, relationships reacted to sexual and emotional jealousy in a sex-typical fashion. Yet, CNM individuals discriminate between primary and secondary partners when performing mate retention behavior (Mogilski et al., 2017, 2019), suggesting that the challenges of long-term investment and partner loss are still salient within these relationships. Discrepancies in the predictive success of PIT within monogamous and non-monogamous populations may be explained by differences in social opportunities and patterns of offspring resource acquisition that these mating systems provide. For example, Jankowiak and Woodman (2001) point out that polygynously married women have the option to circumvent low paternal investment by earning status among co-wives and soliciting resources from them for her offspring. Future research on non-monogamous mating systems will likely reveal patterns of parental investment

that have yet to be examined within human populations (e.g., the evolutionary dynamics of alloparenting; Kuhle and Radtke, 2013; Quinlan and Quinlan, 2008).

Finally, PIT may provide insight into the evolution of human moral psychology. Moral psychology has been shaped by the selective pressures introduced by group living (see Enke, 2019; Shackelford and Hansen, 2015; Tomasello and Vaish, 2013). Moral intuitions (e.g., prejudices, values) help individuals to manage fitness-relevant threats and opportunities that arise within cooperative contexts (Neuberg and Schaller, 2016; also see DeScioli and Kurzban, 2009, 2013), and intuitions about sexual behavior and cooperation between romantic partners are among the most abundant and intense. They appear to differ between men and women in a manner consistent with PIT. For example, both men and women condemn sexually promiscuous women, but women are more willing than men to inflict costly punishment toward them (Muggleton et al., 2018). To the extent that female promiscuity reduces the value of sex, women may condemn (and wish to punish) promiscuity in other women to preserve sex as a resource to be leveraged when negotiating with their male partner. Similarly, people (especially women) tend to condemn age-discrepant relationships (e.g., an older man with a younger women), and this condemnation appears to be, in part, driven by attitudes about the acceptability of soliciting sex for pay (e.g., prostitution; Sela et al., 2018). Among parents, individuals with higher parenting motives report being more vigilant of moral violations and higher on social conservativism, suggesting that parental investment is associated with the motive to produce more cohesive and uniform social groups (Kerry and Murray, 2018). Researchers who wish to understand the evolved design of moral systems that regulate interpersonal violations will likely benefit from considering how moral intuitions have been shaped by the recurrent adaptive problems introduced by sexual conflict due to unequal parental investment.

CONCLUSION

PIT has transformed the study of sexual selection and revealed the evolutionary pressures that shaped male and female characteristics. Its luminary value within the evolutionary psychological sciences has been substantial, and it has successfully generated a rich and well-substantiated literature documenting how sexual conflict caused by differences in men's and women's minimum obligatory investment in offspring has guided natural selection of psychological traits and capacities. Most importantly, as research has tested its predictions, PIT integrated with other prominent theories within the psychological sciences and provided a biological foundation for phenomena that had previously been attributed solely to culture and social ephemera. The future of PIT will need to continue this trajectory of unifying theory under an integrative framework that accounts for the psychological diversity observed within human populations and novel environmental challenges of an increasingly complex world.

REFERENCES

Alonzo, S. H. (2010). Social and coevolutionary feedbacks between mating and parental investment. *Trends in Ecology & Evolution*, *25*(2), 99–108.

Altgelt, E. E., & Meltzer, A. L. (2019). Mate-retention behaviors mediate the association between spouses' attachment insecurity and subsequent partner satisfaction. *Personality and Individual Differences*, *151*, 109534.

Antfolk, J., & Sjölund, A. (2018). High parental investment in childhood is associated with increased mate value in adulthood. *Personality and Individual Differences*, *127*, 144–150.

Archer, J. (1996). Sex differences in social behavior: Are the social role and evolutionary explanations compatible? *American Psychologist*, *51*(9), 909–917.

Archer, J., & Mehdikhani, M. (2003). Variability among males in sexually selected attributes. *Review of General Psychology*, *7*(3), 219–236.

Arden, R., & Plomin, R. (2006). Sex differences in variance of intelligence across childhood. *Personality and Individual Differences*, *41*(1), 39–48.

Arístegui, I., Solano, A. C., & Buunk, A. P. (2019). Do transgender people respond according to their biological sex or their gender identity when confronted with romantic rivals? *Evolutionary Psychology*, *17*(2), 1474704919851139.

Atari, M., Barbaro, N., Shackelford, T. K., & Chegeni, R. (2017). Psychometric evaluation and cultural correlates of the Mate Retention Inventory-Short Form (MRI-SF) in Iran. *Evolutionary Psychology*, *15*(1), 1474704917695267.

Bailey, J. M., Gaulin, S., Agyei, Y., & Gladue, B. A. (1994). Effects of gender and sexual orientation on evolutionarily relevant aspects of human mating psychology. *Journal of Personality and Social Psychology*, *66*(6), 1081–1093.

Barbaro, N., Shackelford, T. K., & Weekes-Shackelford, V. A. (2016). Mothers and fathers perform more mate retention behaviors than individuals without children. *Human Nature*, *27*(3), 316–333.

Bateman, A. J. (1948). Intra-sexual selection in *Drosophila*. *Heredity*, *2*(3), 349–368.

Belsky, J., Schlomer, G. L., & Ellis, B. J. (2012). Beyond cumulative risk: Distinguishing harshness and unpredictability as determinants of parenting and early life history strategy. *Developmental Psychology*, *48*(3), 662–673.

Bendixen, M., Kennair, L. E. O., & Buss, D. M. (2015). Jealousy: Evidence of strong sex differences using both forced choice and continuous measure paradigms. *Personality and Individual Differences*, *86*, 212–216.

Boothroyd, L. G., Craig, P. S., Crossman, R. J., & Perrett, D. I. (2013). Father absence and age at first birth in a Western sample. *American Journal of Human Biology*, *25*(3), 366–369.

Borkenau, P., McCrae, R. R., & Terracciano, A. (2013). Do men vary more than women in personality? A study in 51 cultures. *Journal of Research in Personality*, *47*(2), 135–144.

Brewer, G., & Hamilton, V. (2014). Female mate retention, sexual orientation, and gender identity. *Evolutionary Behavioral Sciences*, *8*(1), 12–19.

Buss, D. M. (1988). From vigilance to violence: Tactics of mate retention in American undergraduates. *Ethology and Sociobiology*, *9*(5), 291–317.

Buss, D. M. (1989). Sex differences in human mate preferences: Evolutionary hypotheses tested in 37 cultures. *Behavioral and Brain Sciences*, *12*(1), 1–14.

Buss, D. M., Goetz, C., Duntley, J. D., Asao, K., & Conroy-Beam, D. (2017). The mate switching hypothesis. *Personality and Individual Differences*, *104*, 143–149.

Buss, D. M., & Schmitt, D. P. (1993). Sexual strategies theory: An evolutionary perspective on human mating. *Psychological Review*, *100*(2), 204–232.

Buss, D. M., & Schmitt, D. P. (2019). Mate preferences and their behavioral manifestations. *Annual Review of Psychology*, *70*, 77–110.

Buss, D. M., & Shackelford, T. K. (1997). From vigilance to violence: Mate retention tactics in married couples. *Journal of Personality and Social Psychology*, *72*(2), 346–361.

Buss, D. M., Shackelford, T. K., & McKibbin, W. F. (2008). The mate retention inventory-short form (MRI-SF). *Personality and Individual Differences*, *44*(1), 322–334.

Buunk, A. P., Massar, K., Dijkstra, P. D., & Fernandez, A. M. (2019). Intersexual and intrasexual competition and their relation to jealousy. In Welling, L. & Shackelford, T. K. (Eds), *The Oxford handbook on evolutionary psychology and behavioral endocrinology* (pp. 225–236). New York: Oxford University Press.

Campbell, L., & Loving, T. J. (2016). Love and commitment in romantic relationships. In Buss, D. M. (Ed.), *The handbook of evolutionary psychology, 2nd edition, volume 1 foundations* (pp. 482–498). Hoboken, NJ: John Wiley & Sons.

Chang, L., Wang, Y., Shackelford, T. K., & Buss, D. M. (2011). Chinese mate preferences: Cultural evolution and continuity across a quarter of a century. *Personality and Individual Differences*, *50*(5), 678–683.

Chaudhary, N., Al-Shawaf, L., & Buss, D. M. (2018). Mate competition in Pakistan: Mate value, mate retention, and competitor derogation. *Personality and Individual Differences*, *130*, 141–146.

Colleran, H., Jasienska, G., Nenko, I., Galbarczyk, A., & Mace, R. (2015). Fertility decline and the changing dynamics of wealth, status and inequality. *Proceedings of the Royal Society of London. B: Biological Sciences*, *282*(1806), 20150287.

Conroy-Beam, D., Buss, D. M., Pham, M. N., & Shackelford, T. K. (2015). How sexually dimorphic are human mate preferences? *Personality and Social Psychology Bulletin*, *41*(8), 1082–1093.

Conroy-Beam, D., Goetz, C. D., & Buss, D. M. (2016). What predicts romantic relationship satisfaction and mate retention intensity: Mate preference fulfillment or mate value discrepancies? *Evolution and Human Behavior*, *37*(6), 440–448.

de Baca, T. C., & Ellis, B. J. (2017). Early stress, parental motivation, and reproductive decision-making: Applications of life history theory to parental behavior. *Current Opinion in Psychology*, *15*, 1–6.

De Miguel, A., & Buss, D. M. (2011). Mate retention tactics in Spain: Personality, sex differences, and relationship status. *Journal of Personality*, *79*(3), 563–586.

de Souza, A. A. L., Conroy-Beam, D., & Buss, D. M. (2016). Mate preferences in Brazil: Evolved desires and cultural evolution over three decades. *Personality and Individual Differences*, *95*, 45–49.

de Souza, A. A. L., Verderane, M. P., Taira, J. T., & Otta, E. (2006). Emotional and sexual jealousy as a function of sex and sexual orientation in a Brazilian sample. *Psychological Reports*, *98*(2), 529–535.

Del Giudice, M., Gangestad, S. W., & Kaplan, H. S. (2015). Life history theory and evolutionary psychology. In Buss, D. M. (Ed.), *The handbook of evolutionary psychology, vol. 1 foundations* (pp. 88–114). Hoboken, NJ: John Wiley & Sons.

DeScioli, P., & Kurzban, R. (2009). Mysteries of morality. *Cognition*, *112*(2), 281–299.

DeScioli, P., & Kurzban, R. (2013). A solution to the mysteries of morality. *Psychological Bulletin*, *139*(2), 477–496.

Dijkstra, P., Groothof, H. A., Poel, G. A., Laverman, E. T., Schrier, M., & Buunk, B. P. (2001). Sex differences in the events that elicit jealousy among homosexuals. *Personal Relationships*, *8*(1), 41–54.

Dunbar, R. I. (2006). Brains, cognition and the evolution of culture. In Levinson, S. & Jaisson, P. (Eds), *Evolution and culture* (pp. 169–180. Cambridge, MA: MIT Press.

Dunkel, C. S., Summerville, L. A., Mathes, E. W., & Kesserling, S. N. (2015). Using the California Q-sort measure of life history strategy to predict sexual behavioral outcomes. *Archives of Sexual Behavior*, *44*(6), 1705–1711.

Dunkel, C. S., Nedelec, J. L., & van der Linden, D. (2018). Using monozygotic twin differences to examine the relationship between parental affection and personality: A life history account. *Evolution and Human Behavior*, *39*(1), 52–58.

Dunn, M. J., & Ward, K. (2019). Infidelity-revealing snapchat messages arouse different levels of jealousy depending on sex, type of message and identity of the opposite sex rival. *Evolutionary Psychological Science*, 1–9. doi:10.1007/s40806-019-00210-3.

Durante, K. M., Eastwick, P. W., Finkel, E. J., Gangestad, S. W., & Simpson, J. A. (2016). Pair-bonded relationships and romantic alternatives: Toward an integration of evolutionary and relationship science perspectives. In Olson, J. M. & Zenna, M. P. (Eds), *Advances in experimental social psychology* (Vol. 53, pp. 1–74). Academic Press.

Eagly, A. H., & Wood, W. (1999). The origins of sex differences in human behavior: Evolved dispositions versus social roles. *American Psychologist*, *54*(6), 408–423.

Eagly, A. H., & Wood, W. (2016). Social role theory of sex differences. In Naples, N., Hoogland, R. C., Wickramasinghe, M., & Wong W. C. A. (Eds), *The Wiley Blackwell encyclopedia of gender and sexuality studies*, 1–3. New York: Wiley.

Edlund, J. E., Heider, J. D., Scherer, C. R., Farc, M. M., & Sagarin, B. J. (2006). Sex differences in jealousy in response to actual infidelity. *Evolutionary Psychology*, *4*(1), 147470490600400137.

Ellis, B. J., & Del Giudice, M. (2019). Developmental adaptation to stress: An evolutionary perspective. *Annual Review of Psychology*, *70*, 111–139.

Ellis, B. J., & Essex, M. J. (2007). Family environments, adrenarche, and sexual maturation: A longitudinal test of a life history model. *Child Development*, *78*(6), 1799–1817.

Enke, B. (2019). Kinship, cooperation, and the evolution of moral systems. *The Quarterly Journal of Economics*, *134*(2), 953–1019.

Fales, M. R., Frederick, D. A., Garcia, J. R., Gildersleeve, K. A., Haselton, M. G., & Fisher, H. E. (2016). Mating markets and bargaining hands: Mate preferences for attractiveness and resources in two national US studies. *Personality and Individual Differences*, *88*, 78–87.

Falk, A., & Hermle, J. (2018). Relationship of gender differences in preferences to economic development and gender equality. *Science*, *362*(6412), eaas9899.

Feldman, R., Braun, K., & Champagne, F. A. (2019). The neural mechanisms and consequences of paternal caregiving. *Nature Reviews Neuroscience*, *20*(4), 205–224.

Fernandez, A. M., Muñoz, J. A., Dufey, M., Pavez, P., Baeza, C. G., & Kinkead, P. (2015). Sex differences in jealousy are not explained by attachment style in men and women from Chile. *Human Ethology Bulletin*, *30*, 138–150.

Fernandez, A. M., Sierra, J. C., Zubeidat, I., & Vera-Villarroel, P. (2006). Sex differences in response to sexual and emotional infidelity among Spanish and Chilean students. *Journal of Cross-Cultural Psychology*, *37*(4), 359–365.

Figueredo, A. J., Vásquez, G., Brumbach, B. H., Schneider, S. M. R., Sefcek, J. A., Tal, I. R., Hill, D., Wenner, C. J., & Jacobs, W. J. (2006). Consilience and life history theory: From genes to brain to reproductive strategy. *Developmental Review*, *26*(2), 243–275.

Fisher, R. A. (1958). *The genetical theory of natural selection*. New York: Dover Publications.

Flegr, J., Kroupa, S., Nekola, O., & Blum, A. E. (2019). What people prefer and what they think they prefer in short- and long-term partners: The effects of the phase of the menstrual cycle, hormonal contraception, pregnancy, and the marital and the parenthood status on partner preferences. *Evolution and Human Behavior*, *40*(1), 112–125.

Fletcher, G. J., Tither, J. M., O'Loughlin, C., Friesen, M., & Overall, N. (2004). Warm and homely or cold and beautiful? Sex differences in trading off traits in mate selection.

Personality and Social Psychology Bulletin, *30*(6), 659–672.

Fox, G. L., & Bruce, C. (2001). Conditional fatherhood: Identity theory and parental investment theory as alternative sources of explanation of fathering. *Journal of Marriage and Family*, *63*(2), 394–403.

Frankenhuis, W. E., & Nettle, D. (2019). The strengths of people in poverty. *Current Directions in Psychological Science*, 0963721419881154.

Frederick, D. A., & Fales, M. R. (2016). Upset over sexual versus emotional infidelity among gay, lesbian, bisexual, and heterosexual adults. *Archives of Sexual Behavior*, *45*(1), 175–191.

Fromhage, L., & Jennions, M. D. (2016). Coevolution of parental investment and sexually selected traits drives sex-role divergence. *Nature Communications*, *7*(1), 12517.

Gangestad, S. W., & Simpson, J. A. (2000). The evolution of human mating: Trade-offs and strategic pluralism. *Behavioral and Brain Sciences*, *23*(4), 573–587.

Gangestad, S. W., Thornhill, R., & Garver, C. E. (2002). Changes in women's sexual interests and their partner's mate–retention tactics across the menstrual cycle: Evidence for shifting conflicts of interest. *Proceedings of the Royal Society of London. Series B: Biological Sciences*, *269*(1494), 975–982.

Geary, D. C. (2000). Evolution and proximate expression of human paternal investment. *Psychological Bulletin*, *126*(1), 55–77.

Geary, D. C. (2015). Evolution of paternal investment. In Buss D. M. (Ed.), *The handbook of evolutionary psychology, vol 1. Foundations* (pp. 483–505). Hoboken, NJ: John Wiley & Sons.

Gray, H., Lyth, A., McKenna, C., Stothard, S., Tymms, P., & Copping, L. (2019). Sex differences in variability across nations in reading, mathematics and science: A meta-analytic extension of Baye and Monseur (2016). *Large-scale Assessments in Education*, *7*(1), 2.

Griskevicius, V., Tybur, J. M., Delton, A. W., & Robertson, T. E. (2011). The influence of mortality and socioeconomic status on risk and delayed rewards: A life history theory approach. *Journal of Personality and Social Psychology*, *100*(6), 1015–1026.

Hampson, S. E., Andrews, J. A., Barckley, M., Gerrard, M., & Gibbons, F. X. (2016). Harsh environments, life history strategies, and adjustment: A longitudinal study of Oregon youth. *Personality and Individual Differences*, *88*, 120–124.

Handelsman, D. J. (2017). Sex differences in athletic performance emerge coinciding with the onset of male puberty. *Clinical Endocrinology*, *87*(1), 68–72.

Hartman, S., Sung, S., Simpson, J. A., Schlomer, G. L., & Belsky, J. (2018). Decomposing environmental unpredictability in forecasting adolescent and young adult development: A two-sample study. *Development and Psychopathology*, *30*(4), 1321–1332.

Hehman, J. A., & Salmon, C. A. (2019). Sex-specific developmental effects of father absence on casual sexual behavior and life history strategy. *Evolutionary Psychological Science*, *5*(1), 121–130.

Hentges, R. F., & Wang, M. T. (2018). Gender differences in the developmental cascade from harsh parenting to educational attainment: An evolutionary perspective. *Child Development*, *89*(2), 397–413.

Hogg, M. A. (2016). Social identity theory. In McKeown S., Haji R., & Ferguson N. (Eds), *Understanding peace and conflict through social identity theory* (pp. 3–17). Cham: Springer.

Holden, C. J., Shackelford, T. K., Zeigler-Hill, V., Miner, E. J., Kaighobadi, F., Starratt, V. G., Jeffrey, A. J., & Buss, D. M. (2014). Husband's esteem predicts his mate retention tactics. *Evolutionary Psychology*, *12*(3), 147470491401200311.

Howard, R. M., & Perilloux, C. (2017). Is mating psychology most closely tied to biological sex or preferred partner's sex? *Personality and Individual Differences*, *115*, 83–89.

James, J., Ellis, B. J., Schlomer, G. L., & Garber, J. (2012). Sex-specific pathways to early puberty, sexual debut, and sexual risk taking: Tests of an integrated evolutionary–developmental model. *Developmental Psychology*, *48*(3), 687–702.

Jankowiak, W., & Woodman, C. (2001). Paternal investment or maternal investment? A critique of the parental investment hypothesis in an American polygamous community. In Holcomb, H. R. (Ed.), *Conceptual Challenges in Evolutionary Psychology* (pp. 271–290). Dordrecht: Springer.

Jonason, P. K., Luevano, V. X., & Adams, H. M. (2012). How the Dark Triad traits predict relationship choices. *Personality and Individual Differences, 53*(3), 180–184.

Jonason, P. K., Valentine, K. A., Li, N. P., & Harbeson, C. L. (2011). Mate-selection and the Dark Triad: Facilitating a short-term mating strategy and creating a volatile environment. *Personality and Individual Differences, 51*(6), 759–763.

Kaiser, T. (2019). Nature and evoked culture: Sex differences in personality are uniquely correlated with ecological stress. *Personality and Individual Differences, 148*, 67–72.

Kaplan, H. (1996). A theory of fertility and parental investment in traditional and modern human societies. *American Journal of Physical Anthropology: The Official Publication of the American Association of Physical Anthropologists, 101*(S23), 91–135.

Kardum, I., Hudek-Knežević, J., & Gračanin, A. (2006). Sociosexuality and mate retention in romantic couples. *Psihologijske teme, 15*(2), 277–296.

Karwowski, M., Jankowska, D. M., Gajda, A., Marczak, M., Groyecka, A., & Sorokowski, P. (2016). Greater male variability in creativity outside the WEIRD world. *Creativity Research Journal, 28*(4), 467–470.

Kenrick, D. T., Sadalla, E. K., Groth, G., & Trost, M. R. (1990). Evolution, traits, and the stages of human courtship: Qualifying the parental investment model. *Journal of Personality, 58*(1), 97–116.

Kerry, N., & Murray, D. R. (2019). Politics and parental care: Experimental and mediational tests of the causal link between parenting motivation and social conservatism. *Social Psychological and Personality Science*, 1948550619853598.

Kuhle, B. X., & Radtke, S. (2013). Born both ways: The alloparenting hypothesis for sexual fluidity in women. *Evolutionary Psychology, 11*(2), 147470491301100202.

Kuzawa, C. W., & Bragg, J. M. (2012). Plasticity in human life history strategy: Implications for contemporary human variation and the evolution of genus Homo. *Current Anthropology, 53*(S6), S369–S382.

Lange, B. P., Euler, H. A., & Zaretsky, E. (2016). Sex differences in language competence of 3- to 6-year-old children. *Applied Psycholinguistics, 37*(6), 1417–1438.

Lawson, D. W., & Mace, R. (2009). Trade-offs in modern parenting: A longitudinal study of sibling competition for parental care. *Evolution and Human Behavior, 30*(3), 170–183.

Lehre, A. C., Lehre, K. P., Laake, P., & Danbolt, N. C. (2009). Greater intrasex phenotype variability in males than in females is a fundamental aspect of the gender differences in humans. *Developmental Psychobiology: The Journal of the International Society for Developmental Psychobiology, 51*(2), 198–206.

Lessells, C. M., & McNamara, J. M. (2012). Sexual conflict over parental investment in repeated bouts: Negotiation reduces overall care. *Proceedings of the Royal Society of London. B: Biological Sciences, 279*(1733), 1506–1514.

Li, N. P., Bailey, J. M., Kenrick, D. T., & Linsenmeier, J. A. (2002). The necessities and luxuries of mate preferences: Testing the tradeoffs. *Journal of Personality and Social Psychology, 82*(6), 947–955.

Li, N. P., Valentine, K. A., & Patel, L. (2011). Mate preferences in the US and Singapore: A cross-cultural test of the mate preference priority model. *Personality and Individual Differences, 50*(2), 291–294.

Lippa, R. A. (2009). Sex differences in sex drive, sociosexuality, and height across 53 nations: Testing evolutionary and social structural theories. *Archives of Sexual Behavior, 38*(5), 631–651.

Lippa, R. A. (2010). Sex differences in personality traits and gender-related occupational preferences across 53 nations: Testing evolutionary and social-environmental theories. *Archives of Sexual Behavior, 39*(3), 619–636.

Little, A. C., Cohen, D. L., Jones, B. C., & Belsky, J. (2007). Human preferences for facial masculinity change with relationship type and environmental harshness. *Behavioral Ecology and Sociobiology, 61*(6), 967–973.

Little, A. C., DeBruine, L. M., & Jones, B. C. (2013). Environment contingent preferences: Exposure to visual cues of direct male–male competition and wealth increase women's preferences for masculinity in male faces. *Evolution and Human Behavior*, *34*(3), 193–200.

Little, A. C., Třebický, V., Havlíček, J., Roberts, S. C., & Kleisner, K. (2015). Human perception of fighting ability: Facial cues predict winners and losers in mixed martial arts fights. *Behavioral Ecology*, *26*(6), 1470–1475.

Lopes, G. S., Holanda, L. C., DeLecce, T., Holub, A. M., & Shackelford, T. K. (2018). Sexual coercion, mate retention, and relationship satisfaction in Brazilian and American romantic relationships. *Journal of Interpersonal Violence*, 0886260518821458.

Lopes, G. S., Shackelford, T. K., Santos, W. S., Farias, M. G., & Segundo, D. S. (2016). Mate retention inventory–short form (MRI-SF): Adaptation to the Brazilian context. *Personality and Individual Differences*, *90*, 36–40.

Lu, H. J., Zhu, X. Q., & Chang, L. (2015). Good genes, good providers, and good fathers: Economic development involved in how women select a mate. *Evolutionary Behavioral Sciences*, *9*(4), 215–228.

Lukaszewski, A. W. (2015). Parental support during childhood predicts life history-related personality variation and social status in young adults. *Evolutionary Psychological Science*, *1*(3), 131–140.

Magginetti, J., & Pillsworth, E. G. (2019). Women's sexual strategies in pregnancy. *Evolution and Human Behavior*, *41*(1), 76–86.

Makel, M. C., Wai, J., Peairs, K., & Putallaz, M. (2016). Sex differences in the right tail of cognitive abilities: An update and cross cultural extension. *Intelligence*, *59*, 8–15.

Maner, J. K., & Ackerman, J. M. (2020). Ecological sex ratios and human mating. *Trends in Cognitive Sciences*, *24*(2), 98–100.

March, E., & Grieve, R. (2016). Social-economic theory and short-term mate preferences: The effects of gender roles and socioeconomic status. *Australian Journal of Psychology*, *68*(4), 241–250.

Marlowe, F. (2000). Paternal investment and the human mating system. *Behavioural Processes*, *51*(1–3), 45–61.

Maner, J. K., & Shackelford, T. K. (2008). The basic cognition of jealousy: An evolutionary perspective. *European Journal of Personality*, *22*(1), 31–36.

McDonald, M. M., Donnellan, M. B., & Navarrete, C. D. (2012). A life history approach to understanding the Dark Triad. *Personality and Individual Differences*, *52*(5), 601–605.

Međedović, J. (2018). Exploring the links between psychopathy and life history in a sample of college females: A behavioral ecological approach. *Evolutionary Psychological Science*, *4*(4), 466–473.

Miner, E. J., Starratt, V. G., & Shackelford, T. K. (2009). It's not all about her: Men's mate value and mate retention. *Personality and Individual Differences*, *47*(3), 214–218.

Mogilski, J. K., Memering, S. L., Welling, L. L., & Shackelford, T. K. (2017). Monogamy versus consensual non-monogamy: Alternative approaches to pursuing a strategically pluralistic mating strategy. *Archives of Sexual Behavior*, *46*(2), 407–417.

Mogilski, J. K., Mitchell, V. E., Reeve, S. D., Donaldson, S. H., Nicolas, S. C. A., & Welling, L. L. M. (2020). Life history and multi-partner mating: A novel explanation for moral stigma against consensual nonmonogamy. *Frontiers in Psychology, section Evolutionary Psychology*, *10*, 3033.

Mogilski, J. K., Reeve, S. D., Nicolas, S. C., Donaldson, S. H., Mitchell, V. E., & Welling, L. L. (2019). Jealousy, consent, and compersion within monogamous and consensually non-monogamous romantic relationships. *Archives of Sexual Behavior*, *48*(6), 1911–1828.

Mogilski, J. K., Wade, T. J., & Welling, L. L. (2014). Prioritization of potential mates' history of sexual fidelity during a conjoint ranking task. *Personality and Social Psychology Bulletin*, *40*(7), 884–897.

Monk, J. D., Giglio, E., Kamath, A., Lambert, M. R., & McDonough, C. E. (2019). An alternative hypothesis for the evolution of same-sex sexual behaviour in animals. *Nature Ecology & Evolution*, *3*(12), 1622–1631.

Montagu, M. F. A. (1960). Time, morphology, and neoteny in the evolution of man. In Montagu, M. F. A. (Ed.), *An introduction to physical anthropology, 3rd ed.* (pp. 295–316). Springfield, IL: Charles C Thomas.

Moran, J. B., & Wade, T. J. (2019). Perceptions of a mismatched couple: The role of attractiveness on mate poaching and copying. *Evolutionary Behavioral Sciences*. doi:10.1037/ebs0000187.

Moss, J. H., & Maner, J. K. (2016). Biased sex ratios influence fundamental aspects of human mating. *Personality and Social Psychology Bulletin*, *42*(1), 72–80.

Muggleton, N. K., Tarran, S. R., & Fincher, C. L. (2019). Who punishes promiscuous women? Both women and men are prejudiced towards sexually-accessible women, but only women inflict costly punishment. *Evolution and Human Behavior*, *40*(3), 259–268.

Nascimento, B. S., & Little, A. (2019). Mate retention behaviours and jealousy in hypothetical mate-poaching situations: Measuring the effects of sex, context, and rivals' attributes. *Evolutionary Psychological Science*. doi:10.1007/s40806-019-00207-y.

Nettle, D., & Frankenhuis, W. E. (2019). The evolution of life-history theory: A bibliometric analysis of an interdisciplinary research area. *Proceedings of the Royal Society B: Biological Sciences, 286*(1899), 20190040.

Neuberg, S. L., & Schaller, M. (2016). An evolutionary threat-management approach to prejudices. *Current Opinion in Psychology*, *7*, 1–5.

Ospina Betancurt, J., Zakynthinaki, M. S., Martínes-Patiño, M. J., Cordente Martinez, C., & Rodríguez Fernández, C. (2018). Sex-differences in elite-performance track and field competition from 1983 to 2015. *Journal of Sports Sciences*, *36*(11), 1262–1268.

Parker, G. A. (1970). Sperm competition and its evolutionary consequences in the insects. *Biological Reviews*, *45*(4), 525–567.

Pelham, B. (2019). Life history and the cultural evolution of parenting: Pathogens, mortality, and birth across the globe. *Evolutionary Behavioral Sciences*. doi:10.1037/ebs0000185.

Pepper, G. V., & Nettle, D. (2017). The behavioural constellation of deprivation: Causes and consequences. *Behavioral and Brain Sciences*, *40*, e314.

Pham, M. N., & Shackelford, T. K. (2015). Sperm competition and the evolution of human sexuality. In Shackelford, T. K. & Hansen, R. (Eds), *The Evolution of Sexuality* (pp. 257–275). Cham: Springer.

Plooij, F. X., & van de Rijt-Plooij, H. H. (1989). Evolution of human parenting: Canalization, new types of learning, and mother–infant conflict. *European Journal of Psychology of Education*, *4*(2), 177–192.

Quinlan, R. J., & Quinlan, M. B. (2008). Human lactation, pair-bonds, and alloparents. *Human Nature*, *19*(1), 87–102.

Reilly, D., Neumann, D. L., & Andrews, G. (2015). Sex differences in mathematics and science achievement: A meta-analysis of National Assessment of Educational Progress assessments. *Journal of Educational Psychology*, *107*(3), 645–662.

Richardson, G. B., Chen, C. C., Dai, C. L., Hardesty, P. H., & Swoboda, C. M. (2014). Life history strategy and young adult substance use. *Evolutionary Psychology*, *12*(5), 147470491401200506.

Sagarin, B. J., Becker, D. V., Guadagno, R. E., Nicastle, L. D., & Millevoi, A. (2003). Sex differences (and similarities) in jealousy: The moderating influence of infidelity experience and sexual orientation of the infidelity. *Evolution and Human Behavior*, *24*(1), 17–23.

Sagarin, B. J., Martin, A. L., Coutinho, S. A., Edlund, J. E., Patel, L., Skowronski, J. J., & Zengel, B. (2012). Sex differences in jealousy: A meta-analytic examination. *Evolution and Human Behavior*, *33*(6), 595–614.

Salmon, C. (2015). Parental investment and parent-offspring conflict. In Buss D. M. (Ed.), *The handbook of evolutionary psychology, vol 1. Foundations* (pp. 506–527). Hoboken, NJ: John Wiley & Sons.

Salmon, C., Townsend, J. M., & Hehman, J. (2016). Casual sex and college students: Sex differences and the impact of father absence. *Evolutionary Psychological Science*, *2*(4), 254–261.

Scelza, B. A., Prall, S. P., Blumenfield, T., Crittenden, A. N., Gurven, M., Kline, M., … & McElreath, R. (2019). Patterns of paternal investment predict cross-cultural variation in jealous response. *Nature Human Behaviour*. doi:10.1038/s41562-019-0654-y.

Schacht, R., & Borgerhoff Mulder, M. (2015). Sex ratio effects on reproductive strategies in humans. *Royal Society Open Science*, *2*(1), 140402.

Schmitt, D. P. (2007). Sexual strategies across sexual orientations: How personality traits and culture relate to sociosexuality among gays, lesbians, bisexuals, and heterosexuals. *Journal of Psychology & Human Sexuality*, *18*(2–3), 183–214.

Schmitt D. P. (2015). The evolution of culturally-variable sex differences: Men and women are not always different, but when they are … It appears *not* to result from patriarchy or sex role socialization. In Shackelford, T. & Hansen, R. (Eds), *The evolution of sexuality* (pp. 221–256). Cham: Springer.

Schmitt, D. P., & Buss, D. M. (2001). Human mate poaching: Tactics and temptations for infiltrating existing mateships. *Journal of Personality and Social Psychology*, *80*(6), 894–917.

Schmitt, D. P. & International Sexuality Description Project (2003). Universal sex differences in the desire for sexual variety: Tests from 52 nations, 6 continents, and 13 islands. *Journal of Personality and Social Psychology*, *85*(1), 85–104.

Schmitt, D. P., Long, A. E., McPhearson, A., O'Brien, K., Remmert, B., & Shah, S. H. (2017). Personality and gender differences in global perspective. *International Journal of Psychology*, *52*, 45–56.

Sela, Y., Pham, M. N., Mogilski, J. K., Lopes, G. S., Shackelford, T. K., & Zeigler-Hill, V. (2018). Why do people disparage May–December romances? Condemnation of age-discrepant romantic relationships as strategic moralization. *Personality and Individual Differences*, *130*, 6–10.

Shackelford, T. K., & Goetz, A. T. (2007). Adaptation to sperm competition in humans. *Current Directions in Psychological Science*, *16*(1), 47–50.

Shackelford, T. K., & Hansen, R. D. (Eds) (2015). *The evolution of morality*. New York: Springer.

Shackelford, T. K., Schmitt, D. P., & Buss, D. M. (2005). Universal dimensions of human mate preferences. *Personality and Individual Differences*, *39*(2), 447–458.

Shenk, M. K., Kaplan, H. S., & Hooper, P. L. (2016). Status competition, inequality, and fertility: Implications for the demographic transition. *Philosophical Transactions of the Royal Society B: Biological Sciences*, *371*(1692), 20150150.

Sprecher, S., Sullivan, Q., & Hatfield, E. (1994). Mate selection preferences: Gender differences examined in a national sample. *Journal of Personality and Social Psychology*, *66*(6), 1074–1080.

Starratt, V. G., McKibbin, W. F., & Shackelford, T. K. (2013). Experimental activation of anti-cuckoldry mechanisms responsive to female sexual infidelity. *Personality and Individual Differences*, *55*(1), 59–62.

Starratt, V. G., & Shackelford, T. K. (2012). He said, she said: Men's reports of mate value and mate retention behaviors in intimate relationships. *Personality and Individual Differences*, *53*(4), 459–462.

Starratt, V. G., Shackelford, T. K., Goetz, A. T., & McKibbin, W. F. (2007). Male mate retention behaviors vary with risk of partner infidelity and sperm competition. *Acta Psychologica Sinica*, *39*(3), 523–527.

Stulp, G., & Barrett, L. (2016). Wealth, fertility and adaptive behaviour in industrial populations. *Philosophical Transactions of the Royal Society B: Biological Sciences*, *371*(1692), 20150153.

Surbey, M. K., & Conohan, C. D. (2000). Willingness to engage in casual sex. *Human Nature*, *11*(4), 367–386.

Thomas, A. G., Jonason, P. K., Blackburn, J., Kennair, L. E. O., Lowe, R., Malouff, J., … & Li, N. P. (2019). Mate preference priorities in the East and West: A cross-cultural test of the mate preference priority model. *Journal of Personality*, *88*(3), 606–620.

Tomasello, M., & Vaish, A. (2013). Origins of human cooperation and morality. *Annual Review of Psychology*, *64*, 231–255.

Třebický, V., Fialová, J., Kleisner, K., Roberts, S. C., Little, A. C., & Havlíček, J. (2015). Further evidence for links between facial width-to-height ratio and fighting success: Commentary on Zilioli et al. (2014). *Aggressive Behavior*, *41*(4), 331–334.

Trivers, R. (1972). Parental investment and sexual selection. In Campbell, B. (Ed.), *Sexual Selection and the Descent of Man* (pp. 136–179). New York: Aldine de Gruyter.

Uller, T. (2008). Developmental plasticity and the evolution of parental effects. *Trends in Ecology & Evolution*, *23*(8), 432–438.

VanderLaan, D. P., & Vasey, P. L. (2008). Mate retention behavior of men and women in heterosexual and homosexual relationships. *Archives of Sexual Behavior*, *37*(4), 572–585.

Wade, T. J., & Mogilski, J. (2018). Emotional accessibility is more important than sexual accessibility in evaluating romantic relationships – especially for women: A conjoint analysis. *Frontiers in Psychology*, *9,* 632.

Welle, S., Tawil, R., & Thornton, C. A. (2008). Sex-related differences in gene expression in human skeletal muscle. *PloS ONE*, *3*(1), e1385.

Wierenga, L. M., Sexton, J. A., Laake, P., Giedd, J. N., Tamnes, C. K., & Pediatric Imaging, Neurocognition, and Genetics Study (2018). A key characteristic of sex differences in the developing brain: Greater variability in brain structure of boys than girls. *Cerebral Cortex*, *28*(8), 2741–2751.

Winking, J., & Koster, J. (2015). The fitness effects of men's family investments. *Human Nature*, *26*(3), 292–312.

Wilbur, C. J., & Campbell, L. (2010). What do women want? An interactionist account of women's mate preferences. *Personality and Individual Differences*, *49*(7), 749–754.

Wood, W., & Eagly, A. H. (2015). Two traditions of research on gender identity. *Sex Roles*, *73*(11–12), 461–473.

Yongxiang, C., & Mengxia, Y. (2018). The influence of quantity of resources on college students' mate preferences. *Journal of Psychological Science*, *41*(3), 674–679.

Zandbergen, D. L., & Brown, S. G. (2015). Culture and gender differences in romantic jealousy. *Personality and Individual Differences*, *72*, 122–127.

Zeveloff, S. I., & Boyce, M. S. (1982). Why human neonates are so altricial. *The American Naturalist*, *120*(4), 537–542.

Zietsch, B. P., & Sidari, M. J. (2019). A critique of life history approaches to human trait covariation. *Evolution and Human Behavior*. doi:10.1016/j.evolhumbehav.2019.05.007.

9

Parent–Offspring Conflict

Menelaos Apostolou

INTRODUCTION

Parents and children are genetically related but they are not genetically identical and, as a consequence, their genetic interests do not completely overlap (Trivers, 1974). We can better see how this works with reference to Hamilton's (1964) rule, which states that altruistic behavior, meaning behavior which benefits one individual at the expense of the one who performs it, will be favored by natural selection when rB > C: The net benefit the recipient receives (B), discounted by the genetic relatedness between the two parties (r), exceeds the fitness cost to the actor (C). The 'r' represents the probability that, through common descent, two individuals share the same allele at any given locus, and can range from '0' to '1', with '0' meaning that two individuals share no alleles by common descent, and '1' that they share all their alleles that is, that they are genetically identical. In diploid species (i.e., in species which have two sets of chromosomes), the

coefficient of genetic relatedness between a parent and an offspring is '0.5', because an allele that one of the parents carries has a 50% chance to end up in a given offspring. Simply put, parents and offspring can be expected to share the same alleles about 50% of the time (Schlomer et al., 2011).

The more closely genetically related two individuals are, the more they will be selected to behave altruistically toward one another. In particular, if an individual allocates its resources in helping a genetically unrelated individual (r = 0), it receives no direct genetic benefits and so this behavior will not be selected. In terms of Hamilton's rule (0*B = 0), any behavior that results in the allocation of any positive amount of resource in helping a genetically unrelated individual will not be favored by selection forces. On the other hand, if the individual chooses to divert the same amount of resources to a genetically related individual, say a child (r = 0.5), these resources will increase the chance that 50% of the parents' alleles pass to future generations. Accordingly, this altruistic behavior would bring benefits to the parent, and consequently, it is likely to be selected.

In this respect, we can see that parents and children have common genetic interests, and thus, mechanisms which motivate one party to help the other are likely to be favored by selection forces. For instance, children in our species require considerable resources for securing a good mate, and selection forces would favor mechanisms which would motivate parents to divert part of their resources in helping their daughters and sons to succeed in this endeavor. The reason is that, if children succeed, their fitness will increase, as they have an elevated probability to pass their alleles to future generations, but 50% of their alleles are also their parents' alleles who, as a consequence, will also receive substantial fitness benefits. To put it differently, alleles that predispose for mechanisms that motivate parents to divert resources in assisting their children with their mating effort will be selected over alleles that do not, because they have higher chances to be represented in future generations by increasing the probability of success in mating of the individuals who are likely to carry them.

Nevertheless, the degree of genetic relatedness indicates that, apart from vested genetic interests and the potential for cooperation, there are diverging genetic interests and the potential for conflict between parents and children. In the example above, both parties are motivated for the offspring to be successful in mating, but may disagree on the amount of parental resources mobilized in pursuit of mating opportunities. In particular, children benefit more from succeeding in mating as they are more closely related to themselves than to their parents. Consequently, the support that parents divert to each child will be adjusted to take into consideration the genetic benefits they would receive, opening a window for disagreement: since children have the potential to pass 50% of their alleles to future generations by attracting a mate, they would attempt to secure more help from their parents for this purpose than

their parents are willing to provide because they have the potential of passing only 25% of their alleles to future generations by virtue of their child's reproduction.

In sum, disagreement between parents and offspring is expected when the fitness payoffs of a specific outcome are different for each party. There are two areas where this outcome is likely to have different payoffs for each party, namely parental investment and mating. I have briefly addressed mating here, and I will return to it after I examine parent–offspring conflict over parental investment.

PARENT–OFFSPRING CONFLICT OVER PARENTAL INVESTMENT

Children receive considerable investment from their parents, which is critical for their survival, especially during a young age when they have limited capacity to get food and protect themselves from external dangers. Parents control a limited amount of resources and, thus, must be selective in how they allocate them to their offspring. Accordingly, if parents have two children with similar characteristics (health, age, etc.), because they are equally related to each one, it would pay for them to divide their parental investment equally between the two. However, from an offspring's point of view, such division is not optimal, because the coefficient of genetic relatedness with itself is '1' but the coefficient of genetic relatedness with its sibling is '0.5'. Consequently, the parental investment a child receives makes a bigger positive contribution to its fitness than the parental investment its sibling receives.

More specifically, a unit of parental investment a child receives increases the chances that 100% of its genetic material survives and, thus, becomes likely to pass to future generations, while a unit its sibling receives increases the chances that 50% of its genetic material survives and, thus, becomes likely to be represented in future generations.

Consequently, it would be optimal for the child to extract from its parents more than the even split of parental investment, while it would be optimal for its parents to give to their offspring only their fair share of parental investment. In effect, conflict is likely to arise, with children attempting to extract more resources from their parents, and parents attempting to prevent their children from doing so.

The differential fitness benefits result in selection pressures that would reward mechanisms that would enable children to extract more than their fair share of resources from their parents and for parents to become resistant to such attempts. One possibility is that mechanisms may have evolved to make children effective in manipulating their parents to allocate more resources to them. For example, as parents have vested genetic interests in their children, daughters and sons may threaten their parents that they will harm themselves (e.g., refusing to eat) unless they yield to their demands. Parents, on the other hand, would evolve resistance to such manipulation attempts; for instance, their mechanisms would become effective in distinguishing true threats from manipulation. I will proceed to discuss next two further areas where parent–offspring conflict over parental investment is manifested: maternal–fetal conflict and conflict over weaning.

Maternal–Fetal Conflict

Following conception, not all fetuses develop normally; so, from a mother's point of view, it would not be optimal to divert substantial parental investment to a child that would be unhealthy and unlikely to survive adulthood. Consequently, mothers have evolved adaptations that detect chromosomal or other developmental abnormalities, and to abort the embryo within the first 12 weeks after conception, at a point when the mother has not yet invested heavily in it (Haig, 1993). From the embryo's point of view however, abortion involves a high fitness cost: being aborted

will bring inclusive fitness benefits to the embryo by increasing the fitness of its mother; yet, it will bring considerable fitness costs to itself, because it has only one chance to live, which is lost if it is aborted. As the embryo is more closely related to itself than to its mother and her future progeny, abortion would be less optimal than non-abortion, which predicts that it would evolve adaptations that would prevent abortion. It has been proposed that such an adaptation is the production and release of human chorionic gonadotropin (hCG) by the fetus into the mother's bloodstream, which prevents the mother menstruating, allowing the fetus to remain implanted (Haig, 1993, 1998).

In the same vein, Haig (1993) argued that selection forces would favor fetal genes to draw more resource from the mother than would be optimal for her to provide. The placenta, which is part of the fetus, secretes human placental lactogen hormone inducing insulin resistance to the mother. The decrease in the sensitivity to insulin results in the mother mobilizing a larger supply of blood sugar, which is then available to the fetus. As a counter measure, the mother increases the level of insulin in her blood, and in order to withstand this response, the placenta has insulin receptors which enable the production of insulin-degrading enzymes. The spontaneous abortion case discussed above, constitutes as a rather extreme example of conflict, where fetal resource allocation can be subtler, and thus, more accurately reflect the costs/benefits of each party. That is, even if given control over material provisioning, it is not in the best interest of the fetus to drain the mother completely nor would it be in the mother's best interest to deny resources to the fetus.

Conflict Over Weaning

Conflict over weaning constitutes another case of parent–offspring conflict over parental investment. In particular, the more parents invest in the current offspring, the less they have available to invest in future offspring. Consequently, parents are selected to continue to invest in their offspring up to the point when the cost in terms of reduced future reproductive success starts to outweigh the fitness benefits to the current offspring. Yet, from the offspring's point of view, such discontinuation of parental investment is not optimal, because it is more closely related to itself than to any future siblings. Accordingly, it has been selected to demand more parental investment in terms of weaning than its parents are willing to provide (Maestripieri, 2002; Trivers, 1974).

Consistent with this argument, it has been observed that baboon mothers increasingly rejected their infants upon resumption of estrus, while the rejected infants gave loud cries and intensified their attempts to cling to their mothers and to nurse (DeVore, 1963). Rejection was occasionally accompanied by aggression from infants, which according to Nash (1978) occurred in three contexts, namely weaning of suckling, resistance to the infant's riding, and mating activity. Maternal aggression, rejection, and tantrums peaked at the same time, with conflict being most intense in conjunction with the mother's mating activity. The strength of parent–offspring conflict over parental investment is not constant, and I will move on to examine the different factors which are likely to affect it.

Factors Affecting Parent–Offspring Conflict Over Parental Investment

One factor which is likely to have an effect on parent–offspring conflict over parental investment is the age of parents. In particular, younger parents who have many additional opportunities to reproduce, would be more inclined to save resources to allocate to future reproductive effort, and thus, divert less parental investment to their offspring than older parents. Accordingly, conflict over parental investment is expected to be more intense when parents are younger (Salmon

and Malcolm, 2011). For instance, it has been found that the age of mothers is a significant predictor of maternal infanticide in humans. Young women with many future opportunities to reproduce, would be more inclined to sacrifice a current child than older women who may not have the opportunity to have another child. In effect, across cultures, younger mothers are more likely to commit infanticide than older ones (Daly and Wilson, 1995; Lee and George, 1999; Overpeck et al., 1998).

Another factor which is likely to influence parent–offspring conflict over parental investment is the number of children parents have. In particular, the more children they have, the higher the conflict over parental investment would be (Salmon and Malcolm, 2011). Parents control limited resources, so when a child is added to the family, these resources need to be divided, so they will be in shorter supply when there are multiple children. This is one reason why existing children are often resistant to adding another child to the household (Michalski and Euler, 2008).

This argument could be generalized to other genetic relatives. In particular, parents usually have genetic relatives, such as nephews and nieces, to whom it would be beneficial, in terms of their fitness, to assist in surviving and reproducing. For instance, if parents have a niece, it would pay to divert resources to her to assist with her survival, because by doing so they assist 25% of their alleles (the coefficient of genetic relatedness between individuals and their nieces is 0.25) to be represented in future generations. Nevertheless, doing so will benefit only 12.5% of their child's alleles (the coefficient of genetic relatedness between cousins is 0.125), so the child would require its parents to divert to it resources in excess of eight times the value of those directed towards cousins. In effect, the fewer genetic relatives, including children, parents have, the less intense the parent–offspring conflict over parental investment would be.

It needs to be said that, if parents have only one child, it does not mean that there would be no parent–offspring conflict over parental investment. One reason is that, when allocating their investment, parents would consider not only their existing child but also the probability of having more children in the future. In particular, parents are likely to have more children, so it would not pay for them to allocate all their resources to their current child. On the other hand, from the current child's point of view, any future sibling would be less related to it than it is to itself. Consequently, parents would limit the resources they allocate to it in order to save for their future offspring, while the child would attempt to extract more resources than its parents are willing to allocate.

A further factor relevant to conflict over parental investment is a child's future prospects. Natural selection would be unlikely to favor mechanisms that direct investment toward a child who has reduced chances to survive and reproduce, as parents are better off, from a fitness perspective, if they terminate investment early (Haig, 2009), and start investing in a different offspring (Salmon and Malcolm, 2011). Consistent with this argument, infants born with severe physical deformities are more likely than healthy ones to fall victims of infanticide (Daly and Wilson, 1984, 1988). Still, from the child's point of view, discontinuation of parental investment or infanticide is not optimal as it has only one chance to live and reproduce. It needs to be said that infanticide could be optimal in the scenario where trading off investment in self vs. investment in 10 siblings, should that investment be necessary for the latter's survival. Yet, such a scenario is probably quite rare. Overall, conflict is more intense when the child experiences reduced prospects of survival and reproduction.

PARENT–OFFSPRING CONFLICT OVER MATING

Parent–offspring conflict is also manifested in the area of mating (Apostolou, 2007; Trivers, 1974). To begin with, in sexually reproducing species, in order to pass copies of their genes to future generations, individuals need to gain access to the reproductive capacity of a member of the opposite sex. Furthermore, since children in our species require considerable and long-term investment before they reach sexual maturity, it would be beneficial for individuals not only to attract mates, but also to retain them and form a family in which their offspring would receive adequate parental investment. Accordingly, success in mating is likely to have substantial fitness benefits for children. Because their alleles are also their parents' alleles, children's mating success is of high fitness-importance to parents – if children fail in their mating effort, parents' chances of passing their alleles to future generations are considerably compromised.

In effect, parents and children have vested interests in the latter's mating success. The fitness at stake favors the evolution of adaptations that would enable parents to divert considerable resources in helping their children to succeed in this endeavor. Such mechanisms have not been adequately studied, but they can take the form of parents diverting resources to their children in order to increase their children's mate value and render them more attractive as mates, using their experience to provide advice to their children about best mates, and diverting their resources in supporting their children to keep a relationship (for instance, buying a house for the newlywed couple). Yet, because parents and children are not genetically identical, the fitness costs and benefits arising from children's mating is not the same for parents and their children, and conflict between the two is likely to arise.

Before moving on to discuss conflict over mating in more detail, it needs to be noted that, one important difference between parent–offspring conflict over parental investment and parent–offspring conflict over mating, is that the latter may be unique in our species. More specifically, to my knowledge, there has not been any manifestations of parent–offspring conflict over mating in non-human species. One reason is that, in most species, when they reach sexual maturity, individuals are independent from their parents, and as a consequence, the latter cannot exercise any influence over their mate choices.

Conflict Over Parental Support in Mating Effort

As discussed above, it would pay for parents to divert considerable support to their children's mating effort, which can take the form of material wealth and advice that would enable them to succeed in their mating effort. Similarly to parental investment, parental support in mating effort also involves parental resources, but there is a conceptual difference between the two: the former involves resources which enable children to survive and reach sexual maturity, and the latter involves resources which enable children to attract and retain mates. As in the case of parental invest-ment, there is parent–offspring conflict over parental support in mating effort.

More specifically, if an offspring is suc-cessful in mating (i.e., attracts and retains a high quality mate) and has say, one child, it passes 50% of its alleles to future genera-tions. Nevertheless, if its sibling succeeds in mating and also has one child, only 25% of its alleles are passed to the next generation. Accordingly, one unit of parental support allocated to it would increase its fitness more than one unit of parental resources allocated to its sibling. Parents are equally related to each of their children, so the fitness benefits they derive from allocating one unit of sup-port to the mating success of one child is equal to the fitness benefits they derive from allocating it to the other child. Therefore, a child would desire more than its fair share of parental support, and conflict between the two parties is likely to arise.

Overall, differential fitness benefits in mating success select for mechanisms that would motivate children to attempt to extract more support than their parents are willing to provide in helping them with their mating effort, and for parents to resist such attempts and allocate their resources in maximizing their own and not their children's fitness. For instance, such mechanisms may give rise to manipulation – a son may attempt to manipu-late his parents into buying him a fancy car: 'Unless you buy me this car, I will run away from home,' and parents have mechanisms to resist such manipulation, if the threat is not real: 'Feel free to leave home anytime.' Or parents could use manipulation tactics on their own in order to appear, for instance, to their children as having fewer resources in their control than they actually do, so as to constrain their sons' and daughters' demands.

Parent–Offspring Conflict Over Traits

Prospective mates differ in traits such as attractiveness, health, age, family back-ground, and so they differ in their fitness contribution as mates. For instance, mating candidates who suffer from poor health would make a much lower contribution to a mate-seeker's fitness – as they may soon die – than mates who enjoy good health. Accordingly, mate-seekers have evolved mate preferences which enable them to dis-criminate between prospective mates, and divert their mating effort toward the ones with the most fitness-increasing traits (Buss, 2017). In the same vein, as prospective mates for their children differ in desirable qualities, parents have evolved in-law preferences which enable them to discriminate between prospective in-laws, and divert their effort in securing for their children the mates with the most fitness-increasing traits (Apostolou, 2007). Yet, certain traits may give different benefits to parents and their children, result-ing in disagreement between the two.

More specifically, poor genetic quality (i.e., carrying mutations that impair adap-tations so that they cannot deal effectively with the challenges of the environment) compromises individuals' survival success. Individuals of poor genetic quality are more likely to die or become incapacitated, leaving their partners and their children without support. Poor genetic quality is likely to have an effect on attractiveness; for example, people with adaptations that cannot deal effectively with parasites may suffer during their development, which can affect their body's symmetry (Gangestad et al., 1994; Thornhill and Gangestad, 1993). Health status is another important consideration in mate choice, as individuals with poor health may die or become incapacitated and, consequently, may be unable to provide for their family. Health status often reflects on attractiveness; for instance, individuals may have pale skin color or thinning hair. Age is another factor important in mate choice because reproductive capacity declines as people get older (Eskenazi et al., 2003; Nelson et al., 2012). Age reflects also on attractiveness; as people get older, their hair thins, their teeth decay, and their skin becomes rougher.

In sum, there is substantial information about the fitness contribution prospective partners can make, which is largely summarized in their attractiveness, so people tend to ascribe high importance to the looks of a prospective mate and in-law (Apostolou, 2007; Buss, 2017). Still, the fitness contributions of good looks are different in a mate and an in-law (Apostolou, 2008a). More specifically, if individuals' mates die due to, say, poor genetic quality or poor health, the fitness loss will be higher than if their sons- or daughters-in-law die. One reason is that mates contribute more resources to their partners than to their partners' parents. Furthermore, good looks in a partner portend that the individuals' children and grandchildren will enjoy higher fitness as they are likely to inherit good genes. Nonetheless, because individuals are more closely related to their children than to their grandchildren, the fitness contributions of good looks are higher when they are found in a mate than in an in-law.

On this basis, it has been predicted that good looks would be preferred more by children in a mate than by their parents in an in-law (Apostolou, 2007). Different studies using different methods in different samples have provided strong evidence to support this prediction. To begin with, Apostolou (2008a,b) asked British participants who had children to rate how desirable they considered a set of traits, including good looks, in a prospective mate for themselves and in a prospective mate for their children. It was found that participants indicated a higher importance to the good looks of a prospective mate than of a prospective daughter- and son-in-law. Another set of studies asked parents to rate several traits, including good looks, in a prospective partner for their children and their children to rate the same traits in a prospective partner for themselves. Comparisons of scores between the two parties indicated that parents gave lower scores to good looks than their children (Apostolou, 2015b; Apostolou and Wang, 2018; Fugère et al., 2017; Guo et al., 2017; Perilloux et al., 2011).

In a different line of research, participants were asked to rate a set of traits, including good looks, in a partner for themselves, and they were also asked to indicate how they thought that their parents would rate the same traits in a partner for their children (Buunk et al., 2008; Buunk and Solano, 2011; Dubbs and Buunk, 2010; Dubbs et al., 2013). It was found that participants gave higher scores to good looks than they thought their parents would. However, this line of research suffered from validity issues, as it compared the differences between what individuals thought about themselves and their parents, and not the differences between in-law and mate preferences. Another line of research employed facial images that varied in several dimensions, including attractiveness, in order to assess both reproductively-aged daughters' and their parents' preferences in potential mates for the daughters (Lefevre and Saxton, 2017). It was found that the daughters showed stronger preferences for attractive mates than their parents did.

Similarly, Bovet and colleagues (2018) used a naturalistic marriage market design where parents actively search for marital partners for their children. In particular, in China parents gather at a public park in order to advertise the characteristics of their adult children, looking for a potential son or daughter-in-law. The researchers presented parents and young adults from the city of Kunming (Yunnan, China) with hypothetical mating candidates varying in their levels of physical attractiveness. They found that daughters, but not sons, evaluated attractiveness as more important than their parents did.

In sum, there is consistent evidence that in-law and mate preferences diverge over good looks. Disagreement is not confined only to this trait as research indicates that specific personality traits are preferred more in a spouse than in an in-law, while good family background is valued more in an in-law than in a spouse (Apostolou, 2008b, 2015b; Apostolou and Wang, 2018; Perilloux et al., 2011).

Good Looks vs. Other Traits

Individuals establish intimate long-term relationships with the purpose of creating an environmental context in which children can be born and raised to sexual maturity. The nature of this relationship requires close and continuous contact and cooperation between the two parties. Accordingly, individuals interact more closely with their intimate partners than with their intimate partners' in-laws. On this basis, it could be argued that, similarly to good looks, other traits such as wealth, resource provision capacity and kindness are more impactful to the fitness of children than to the fitness of their parents. If we take capacity to generate resources as an example, it is reasonable to assume that individuals would divert more resources in supporting their children and their mates, than in supporting their mates' parents and other relatives. Because individuals are more closely related to themselves than to their

parents, and are also more closely related to their children than their parents to their grandchildren, a high resource acquisition capacity would be more beneficial in a prospective mate for them than in a prospective in-law for their parents.

Yet, resource provision capacity may have important inclusive fitness benefits for parents. In a pre-industrial context, in-laws integrate into the family unit, and the resources they produce diffuse to the different family members. Thus, these resources could benefit parents and their extensive family, including their other children and grandchildren, their siblings, their nephews and nieces and so on. The inclusive fitness potential of the resource acquisition capacity of a prospective in-law would tend to equalize the benefits that parents and their children accrue from this trait. In different words, there would be no parent–offspring disagreement over the resource generating capacity of a prospective mate and in-law.

On the other hand, good looks do not have such an inclusive fitness potential. If we consider that looks predominantly summarize information about genetic quality and fertility, good looks in a prospective in-law would be beneficial because they would enable parents to have more of healthy grandchildren, but this trait will not give them any additional inclusive fitness benefits. That is, good genetic quality and fertility in a prospective daughter- or son-in-law are not useful traits in enabling parents to help their genetic relatives. In consequence, good looks are less beneficial for parents in a prospective in-law than for their children in a prospective mate, so the two parties are likely to disagree over this trait.

Compromises and Conflict

If two parties prefer a trait differently, this difference does not necessarily translate into conflict between the two. For conflict to arise, the preferences of one party need to inflict a cost to the other party, which is the case here, because mating involves compromises and tradeoffs (Apostolou, 2011; Li et al., 2002). More specifically, if mate-seekers could attract mates who scored the maximum in all relevant traits, there would be no conflict between parents and children, because if parents were to choose mates for their children, they would not be able to do any better. Yet, this is unlikely to happen, with one reason being that mate-seekers are constrained by their own mate value in calibrating the value of mate they can attract. In particular, assuming that there are available options, individuals are less willing to settle for long-term mates of lower mate value to their own and, thus, mate-seekers who themselves do not score maximum in all traits would need to make compromises (Li et al., 2002). Because some traits provide different fitness benefits to parents and to their children, the compromises the latter will make will not be deemed optimal to the former. For instance, children would be willing to settle with mates of poor family background who are, however, good looking. This is a compromise which is not optimal for parents who gain less from good looks, so the gains in this trait cannot compensate them for their losses in family background. If parents were to choose mates for their children, they would make different compromises – they would, for instance, compromise more in good looks and less in family background – that would be more optimal for their fitness.

Accordingly, parent–offspring conflict over mating arises because the mate choices of children inflict an opportunity cost to their parents which is equal to the extra fitness benefits they would get if they would exercise choice for their children, and they do not in the case that their children exercise choice on their own. This argument has been examined theoretically (Apostolou, 2017) and tested empirically (Apostolou, 2011). More specifically, in one study parents and children were asked to allocate a fixed number of mate points to several traits in a prospective spouse for themselves and in a prospective spouse for their children (Apostolou, 2011). It was found that children allocated more points to good looks, saving from traits such as good family background, in comparison to their parents who allocated fewer points to good looks and more to good family background. In effect, children's mate choices would cost to their parents in terms of losses in good family background and other desirable traits, and these loses cannot be compensated by gains in good looks, which are less valuable to them.

Conflict Over Age, Mating Strategies, and Divorce

The research discussed above indicates that children's free mate choice is likely to inflict costs to their parents, which in turn, result in conflict in other domains, one being short-term mating strategies. Having casual partners could potentially bring several benefits, including gifts and good genes, so mate-seekers sometimes engage in short-term mating (Buss and Schmitt, 1993, 2019). On the other hand, children's short-term mating is not equally beneficial to their parents, as casual relationships may lead to feelings of love with individuals parents do not approve, compromising in effect parental control over mating. In addition, children who engage in short-term mating may get a reputation for promiscuity that would be damaging for the status and reputation of their family. Also, when engaging in short-term mating, individuals tend to discount other qualities in favor of good looks (Buss and Schmitt, 1993), and if these relationships become long-term commitments or result in pregnancy, parents who gain much less from the good looks of a prospective in-law (see above), will suffer an opportunity cost. On this basis, it has been predicted that people would find short-term mating strategies more acceptable for themselves than for their children (Apostolou, 2009).

In order to test this prediction, one study asked participants who had children to rate how acceptable they considered a set of short-term mating acts, such as 'Have a one night stand', for them and for their children (Apostolou, 2009). It was found that participants considered such acts more acceptable for themselves than for their daughters and sons. A different study asked parents to rate how acceptable they considered these acts for their children, and their children to rate how acceptable they considered these acts for themselves (Apostolou and Georgiou, 2011). It was found that parents rated these behaviors much less acceptable than their children did. However, it needs to be said that the observed difference may be partially explained by the age difference between parents and children. In particular, parents are much more likely than their children to be past reproductive age and also to be of higher status, and they are therefore better able to accommodate the costs associated with short-term mating such as unplanned pregnancies.

Mating age is another area of conflict. In particular, parental influence over mating is inversely related to children's age because, as children grow older, they become more independent of their parents (Apostolou, 2010). On this basis, it has been predicted that children prefer to get married at an older age than their parents would prefer them to do so. In addition, as discussed above, sexual relationships may result in the development of feelings of love or in pregnancy, which could compromise parental attempts to control their children's mate choices. Thus, it has been further predicted that children prefer to start having sexual relationships at an earlier age than their parents would prefer them to do so (Apostolou, 2010). In order to test these predictions, one study asked participants to indicate the preferred age of marriage and of initiating sexual relationships for them and for their children (Apostolou, 2010). It was found that individuals preferred to get married at a later age and start engaging in sexual relationships at a younger age than they preferred their children to do so.

The parental disapproval of short-term mating and the favoring of long-term mating strategies is also likely to lead to parent–offspring disagreement over divorce. In particular, terminating a long-term intimate relationship may be interpreted by parents as an indication that their children are shifting toward a short-term mating strategy, and they are thus, likely to disapprove of it. In this respect, it can be predicted that parents would be more disapproving than their children of the latter getting a divorce. In order to test this prediction, one study asked children to indicate the likelihood of getting a divorce in different scenarios, such as a partner's infidelity, and also asked their parents to indicate their agreement with their children getting a divorce in the same scenarios (Apostolou et al., 2016). It was found that children indicated greater likelihood than their parents of getting a divorce across the different scenarios. It needs to be said however, that the observed difference may partially reflect a cohort effect where divorce was less acceptable in the previous (parents) than it is in the current generation (children).

Factors That Determine the Strength of Parent–Offspring Conflict Over Mating

Conflict over mating is not constant but it is affected by several factors, one being children's mate value. In particular, when mate value is low, children have fewer mate points to allocate to each conflicting trait (i.e., a trait which provides asymmetric benefits to parents and their children), so the cost of forgone traits for parents is small. Yet, as mate value increases, children can afford to secure more conflicting traits, such as good looks, imposing in effect a larger opportunity cost to their parents. Consequently, as children's mate value increases, parent–offspring conflict over mating intensifies. Yet, if children are of very high mate value, they could afford to secure mates who score high in traits they desire, as well as in traits their parents desire, meaning that after a point, further increases in children's mate value would result in lower parent–offspring conflict (Apostolou, 2017).

Another factor which is expected to determine the degree of conflict, is the age of parents. If parents are young and have not concluded their mating career, they would prefer to save resources to allocate to their own mating effort than to their children's mating effort, something that their children would not prefer as they are more closely related to themselves than to their parents. On the other hand, if parents are older and no longer participate in the mating market, they would not need to save resources for their own mating effort, and would thus allocate more resources to their children's mating effort. In effect, *ceteris paribus*, parent–offspring conflict over mating is expected to be higher when parents are younger than when they are older.

For parents, the fitness impact that their resources would have on children's mating success depends also on the specifics of their children. For instance, one child may have already secured a good mate, while the other child may have not; thus, it could pay for parents to divert more support to help the latter than the former child with its mating effort. Or it could be the case that one child has a serious issue, for example a deformity, which dramatically compromises its mating success. Thus, parents may not divert any resources in assisting it with its mating effort, as these resources will make little difference in benefiting its mating success. Similarly, children may also consider their own situation in demanding parental resources for their mating effort. For example, if a child has managed to attract a good mate, and its relationship is going well, while its sibling has not done so, it may pay for it to be less demanding from its parents, allowing them to divert more resources to its sibling. The reason is that, one unit of parental support allocated to its mating effort would increase less its fitness, as it has already succeeded

in mating, than a unit of parental resources allocated to its sibling's mating effort who still needs to succeed in its mating effort.

Manifestations of Parent– Offspring Conflict in Mating

As discussed above, the asymmetric interests over mating indicate that if parents allow their children to exercise choice on their own, they would suffer an opportunity cost which is equal to the additional fitness benefits they could derive if they controlled mate choice and made thus, more optimal for them compromises. This opportunity cost would translate in selection forces shaping parental behavior to motivate parents to place children's mating behavior under their control (Apostolou, 2016). In a pre-industrial context, where children are heavily dependent on their family for survival and reproduction, parents place their children's mating behavior under their control through the institution of arranged marriage. More specifically, parents choose spouses for their daughters and sons in negotiations with other parents, with little input from their children (Apostolou, 2014). Analysis of the anthropological record indicates that arranged marriage is the typical form of mating in pre-industrial societies which base their subsistence on agriculture, animal herding, and hunting and gathering (Apostolou, 2014).

The effort of the older generation to control the mating behavior of the younger generation is also manifested in other social institutions, such as female circumcision, child marriage, and chaperoning (Apostolou, 2013b). For instance, several pre-industrial societies practice female circumcision, which usually involves the removal of the clitoris, aiming to handicap women's capacity to experience sexual pleasure and thereby render her mating behavior more easily controllable by her parents (Apostolou, 2013b). In addition, several societies practice child marriage, where parents arrange the marriages of their children when they are very young, and thus, easier to be controlled (Frayser, 1985).

In post-industrial societies, children at marriage age are less dependent on their families, while individual rights are protected. Thus, parents cannot directly control their children's mate choices, so marriages are not arranged but instead mate choice is freely exercised. Yet, parents can influence mate choice indirectly through manipulation. More specifically, when two parties have conflicting interests, manipulation is likely to emerge, where one party attempts to change the behavior of the other in a way that best serves its own interests (Buss, 1988, 1992; Buss and Shackelford, 1997).

Sussman (1953) reported that parents employ means such as 'cajolery, persuasion, appeals to loyalty, and threats' in order to influence their children's mating behavior. In a more comprehensive study of manipulation, Apostolou (2013a) identified 12 tactics that parents employ on their children, and four tactics that they employ on their children's mates (see also Apostolou and Papageorgi, 2014). Accordingly, when their daughters and sons engage in undesirable relationships, parents attempt to undermine these relationships either by manipulating their children and/or by manipulating their children's mates to terminate the relationship. For example, they may try to bribe their children out of the relationship or threaten their children's mates so as to drive them away (Apostolou, 2013a). One study found that such manipulation can be effective in weakening a relationship parents consider undesirable (Apostolou et al., 2015). Yet, effective manipulation by parents can go against the interests of children, who engage in counter-manipulation with the purpose of aligning their parents to their own mate choices. Accordingly, one study found that children have a battery of seven manipulation tactics they use on their parents to make them accept their mate choices (Apostolou, 2015a). For instance, daughters and sons try to demonstrate to their parents that their current mates make them happy.

SEXUAL SELECTION

In sexually reproducing species such as our own, reproduction requires that individuals gain access to the reproductive capacity of the opposite sex. The fitness stakes associated with mating translates in strong selection pressure on individuals to evolve traits that would enable them to succeed in this endeavor. This selection force is called sexual selection and takes two forms: intersexual selection and intrasexual selection (Darwin, 1871). In intrasexual selection, it is usually the case that men compete with other men in order to monopolize women, so intrasexual selection takes the form of favoring traits such as strong muscles and aggressive behavior, which enable men to fight effectively with other men (Andersson, 1994). In intersexual selection, it is usually the case that males strive to gain access to females, who find themselves in a position to exercise choice. Thus, female choice becomes an important intersexual selection force, driving the evolution of male adaptations, such as the peacock's tail, which are assessed as attractive by female mate preference evaluation systems (Zahavi and Zahavi, 1997).

As discussed above, conflicting interests over mating motivate parents to attempt to control their children's mate choices which, in a pre-industrial context, takes the form of direct control through arranged marriage. Anthropological and historical records indicate that the typical mode of mating in ancestral and contemporary pre-industrial societies is arranged marriage. These records indicate also that parental control is exercised more intensely over daughters, and that fathers have a larger role in the selection process than mothers (Apostolou, 2014). One reason for the asymmetry in parental control over mating is that sons are usually married at a later age than daughters, when they are more independent from their parents and thus, less susceptible to their will. Parental control over daughters is further facilitated by female circumcision, child marriage, and chaperoning (Apostolou, 2013b). Thus, in the pre-industrial context, women's capacity to exercise choice is substantially constrained by parental control, meaning that in this context female choice may be a weak intersexual selection force. As parents, and particularly fathers, exercise considerable control over their children's mate choices, male parental choice becomes the primary intersexual selection force: success in mating depends on whether one would be selected as in-law by parents, especially fathers, which translates into sexual selection pressures to evolve mechanisms that would enable mate-seekers to succeed in this endeavor (Apostolou, 2014, 2016).

In sum, conflicting interests over mating result in parents controlling the mate choices of their children, especially of their daughters, becoming effectively an intersexual selection force. The emergence of parental choice as a sexual selection force is an important consequence of parent–offspring conflict over mating. As discussed above, parent–offspring conflict over mating is unique in our species and thus, parental choice is only found in *Homo sapiens*. Considerable research is necessary to understand this force and its consequences in shaping adaptations involved in human mating.

CONCLUSION

In this chapter, I have argued that because parents and children are not genetically identical, there is potential for conflict to arise between the two. This conflict is manifested in the allocation of parental investment, where children demand more from their parents than they are willing to provide, and in mating, where children tend to make mate choices that are not always to their parents' best interest. Apart from enabling us to understand family dynamics, parent–offspring conflict has more far-reaching

implications such as determining how sexual selection works. These implications have not adequately been studied, and there is a long road ahead before we reach a good understanding of parent–offspring conflict and its implication.

REFERENCES

Andersson, M. (1994). *Sexual selection*. Princeton, NJ: Princeton University Press.

Apostolou, M. (2007). Elements of parental choice: The evolution of parental preferences in relation to in-law selection. *Evolutionary Psychology*, 5(1), 70–83.

Apostolou, M. (2008a). Parent–offspring conflict over mating: The case of beauty. *Evolutionary Psychology*, 6(2), 303–315.

Apostolou, M. (2008b). Parent–offspring conflict over mating: The case of family background. *Evolutionary Psychology*, 6(2), 456–468.

Apostolou, M. (2009). Parent–offspring conflict over mating: The case of mating strategies. *Personality and Individual Differences*, 47(8), 895–899.

Apostolou, M. (2010). Parent–offspring conflict over mating: The case of mating age. *Evolutionary Psychology*, 8(3), 365–375.

Apostolou, M. (2011). Parent–offspring conflict over mating: Testing the tradeoffs hypothesis. *Evolutionary Psychology*, 9(4), 470–495.

Apostolou, M. (2013a). Do as we wish: Parental tactics of mate choice manipulation. *Evolutionary Psychology*, 11(4), 795–813.

Apostolou, M. (2013b). Parent–offspring conflict over mating and the evolution of mating-control institutions. *Mankind Quarterly*, 54(1), 49–74.

Apostolou, M. (2014). *Sexual selection under parental choice: The evolution of human mating behaviour*. Hove, UK: Psychology Press.

Apostolou, M. (2015a). Accept my choices, but I will not accept yours! Children's tactics of mate choice manipulation. *Evolutionary Behavioral Sciences*, 9(2), 129.

Apostolou, M. (2015b). Parent–offspring conflict over mating: Domains of agreement and disagreement. *Evolutionary Psychology*, *13*(3), 1474704915604561.

Apostolou, M. (2016). Sexual selection and the opportunity cost of free mate choice. *Theory in Biosciences*, *135*(1–2), 45–57.

Apostolou, M. (2017). The nature of parent–offspring conflict over mating: From differences in genetic relatedness to disagreement over mate choice. *Evolutionary Psychological Science*, *3*(1), 62–71.

Apostolou, M., & Georgiou, S. (2011). Parent–offspring conflict over short-term mating strategies. *Interpersona*, *5*(2), 134–148.

Apostolou, M., & Papageorgi, I. (2014). Parental mate choice manipulation tactics: Exploring prevalence, sex and personality effects. *Evolutionary Psychology*, *12*(3), 588–620.

Apostolou, M., & Wang, Y. (2018). Parent–offspring conflict over mating in Chinese families: Comparisons with Greek Cypriot families. *Evolutionary Psychology*, *16*(1), 1474704918764162.

Apostolou, M., Kasapi, K., & Arakliti, A. (2015). Will they do as we wish? An investigation of the effectiveness of parental manipulation on mating behavior. *Evolutionary Psychological Science*, *1*(1), 28–36.

Apostolou, M., Chari, I., Lefkides, C., Theophanous, I., & Khalil, M. (2016). Parent–offspring conflict over mating: The case of divorce. *Personality and Individual Differences*, *99*, 286–294.

Bovet, J., Raiber, E., Ren, W., Wang, C., & Seabright, P. (2018). Parent–offspring conflict over mate choice: An experimental study in China. *British Journal of Psychology*, *109*(4), 674–693.

Buss, D. M. (1988). From vigilance to violence: Tactics of mate retention in American undergraduates. *Ethology and Sociobiology*, *9*(5), 291–317.

Buss, D. M. (1992). Manipulation in close relationships: Five personality factors in interactional context. *Journal of Personality*, *60*(2), 477–499.

Buss, D. M. (2017). *The evolution of desire: Strategies of human mating* (4th ed.). New York: Basic Books.

Buss, D. M., & Schmitt, D. P. (1993). Sexual strategies theory: An evolutionary perspective on human mating. *Psychological Review*, *100*(2), 204–231.

Buss, D. M., & Schmitt, D. P. (2019). Mate preferences and their behavioral manifestations. *Annual Review of Psychology*, *70*, 77–110.

Buss, D. M., & Shackelford, T. K. (1997). From vigilance to violence: Mate retention tactics in married couples. *Journal of Personality and Social Psychology*, *72*(2), 346–361.

Buunk, A. P., & Solano, A. C. (2010). Conflicting preferences of parents and offspring over criteria for a mate: A study in Argentina. *Journal of Family Psychology*, *24*(4), 391–399.

Buunk, A. P., Park, J. H., & Dubbs, S. L. (2008). Parent–offspring conflict in mate preferences. *Review of General Psychology*, *12*(1), 47–62.

Daly, M., & Wilson, M. (1984). A sociobiological analysis of human infanticide. In G. Hausfater, & S. B. Hrdy (Eds), *Infanticide: Comparative and evolutionary perspectives* (pp. 487–502). New York: Aldine.

Daly, M., & Wilson, M. (1988). *Homicide*. Hawthorne, NY: Aldine.

Daly, M., & Wilson, M. (1995). Discriminative parental solicitude and the relevance of evolutionary models to the analysis of motivational systems. In M. Gazzaniga (Ed.), *The cognitive neurosciences* (pp. 1269–1286). Cambridge, MA: MIT Press.

Darwin, C. (1871). *The descent of man, and selection in relation to sex*. London: John Murray.

DeVore, I. (1963). Mother–infant relations in free-ranging baboons. In H. L. Rheingold (Ed.), *Maternal behavior in mammals* (pp. 305–335). New York: John Wiley & Sons.

Dubbs, S. L., & Buunk, A. P. (2010). Sex differences in parental preferences over a child's mate choice: A daughter's perspective. *Journal of Social and Personal Relationships*, *27*(8), 1051–1059.

Dubbs, S. L., Buunk, A. P., & Taniguchi, H. (2013). Parent–offspring conflict in Japan and parental influence across six cultures. *Japanese Psychological Research*, *55*(3), 241–253.

Eskenazi, B., Wyrobek, A. J., Sloter, E., Kidd, S. A., Moore, L., Young, S., & Moore D. (2003). The association of age and semen quality in healthy men. *Human Reproduction*, *18*(2), 447–454.

Frayser, S. G. (1985). *Varieties of sexual experience*. New Haven, CT: HRAF Press.

Fugère, M. A., Doucette, K., Chabot, C., & Cousins, A. J. (2017). Similarities and differences in mate preferences among parents and their adult children. *Personality and Individual Differences*, *111*, 80–85.

Gangestad, S. W., Thornhill, R., & Yeo, R. A. (1994). Facial attractiveness, developmental stability, and fluctuating asymmetry. *Ethology and Sociobiology*, *15*(2), 73–85.

Guo, Q., Li, Y., & Yu, S. (2017). In-law and mate preferences in Chinese society and the role of traditional cultural values. *Evolutionary Psychology*, *15*(3), 1474704917730518.

Haig, D. (1993). Genetic conflicts in human pregnancy. *The Quarterly Review of Biology*, *68*(4), 495–532.

Haig, D. (1998). Genetic conflicts of pregnancy and childhood. In S. C. Sterns (Ed.), *Evolution in health and disease* (pp. 77–90). Oxford, UK: Oxford University Press.

Haig, D. (2009). Transfers and transitions: Parent–offspring conflict, genomic imprinting, and the evolution of human life history. *Proceedings of the National Academy of Sciences*, *107*(Suppl_1), 1731–1735.

Hamilton, W. D. (1964). The genetical evolution of social behaviour. I and II. *Journal of Theoretical Biology*, *7*(1), 1–52.

Lee, B. J., & George, R. M. (1999). Poverty, early childbearing and child maltreatment: A multinomial analysis. *Children and Youth Services Review*, *21*(9), 755–780.

Lefevre, C. E., & Saxton, T. K. (2017). Parental preferences for the facial traits of their offspring's partners can enhance parental inclusive fitness. *Evolution and Human Behavior*, *38*(4), 546–551.

Li, N. P., Bailey, J. M., Kenrick, D. T., & Linsenmeier, J. A. W. (2002). The necessities and luxuries of mate preferences: Testing the tradeoffs. *Journal of Personality and Social Psychology*, *82*(6), 947–955.

Maestripieri, D. (2002). Parent–offspring conflict in primates. *International Journal of Primatology*, *23*(4), 923–951.

Michalski, R. L., & Euler, H. A. (2008). Evolutionary perspectives on sibling relationships. In C. A. Salmon, & T. K. Shackelford (Eds), *Family relationships: An evolutionary perspective* (pp. 185–204). New York: Oxford University Press.

Nash, L. T. (1978). The development of the mother–infant relationship in wild baboons (*Papio anubis*). *Animal Behavior*, *26*(3), 746–759.

Nelson, S. M., Telfer, E. E., & Anderson, R. A. (2012). The ageing ovary and uterus: New biological insights. *Human Reproduction Update*, *19*(1), 67–83.

Overpeck, M. D., Brenner, R. A., Trumble, A. C., Trifiletti, L. B., & Berendes, H. W. (1998). Risk factors for infant homicide in the United States. *New England Journal of Medicine*, *339*(17), 1211–1216.

Perilloux, C., Fleischman, D. S., & Buss, D. M. (2011). Meet the parents: Parent–offspring convergence and divergence in mate preferences. *Personality and Individual Differences*, *50*, 253–258.

Salmon, C. A., & Malcolm, J. (2011). Parent–offspring conflict. In C. A. Salmon, & T. K. Shackelford (Eds), *The Oxford handbook of family psychology* (pp. 83–96). New York: Oxford University Press.

Schlomer, G. L., Del Giudice, M., & Ellis, B. J. (2011). Parent–offspring conflict theory: An evolutionary framework for understanding conflict within human families. *Psychological Review*, *118*(3), 496–521.

Sussman, M. B. (1953). Parental participation in mate selection and its effect upon family continuity. *Social Forces*, *32*(1), 76–81.

Thornhill, R., & Gangestad, S. (1993). Human facial beauty: Averageness, symmetry and parasite resistance. *Human Nature*, *4*(3), 237–269.

Trivers, R. (1974). Parent–offspring conflict. *American Zoologist*, *14*(1), 249–264.

Zahavi, A. & Zahavi, A. (1997). *The handicap principle: A missing piece of Darwin's puzzle*. New York: Oxford University Press.

The Theory of Reciprocal Altruism

Gerald Carter, Mu-Hsun Chen and Imran Razik

INTRODUCTION

Human cooperation is unique in scale, complexity, and flexibility (Bowles and Gintis, 2003; Boyd and Richerson, 2009; Fehr and Fischbacher, 2004; Gintis et al., 2005; Kurzban et al., 2015; Tomasello et al., 2012). Modern humans have complex social institutions that allow strangers around the globe to cooperate simultaneously and continuously. Consider, for instance, the degree of cooperation required to obtain the last meal you ate, including the growth and harvesting of raw ingredients, transportation to the grocery store which includes the construction of vehicles and roads, the entire economic system, and so on. A hunter in even the most isolated tribe relies on culturally-acquired tools and skills resulting from a long history of cooperative interactions (Boyd and Richerson, 1985, 2009). Although global cooperation is not the product of genetic evolution alone, it was only possible because humans have evolved a suite of cognitive

traits that were selected for by our ancestral social environments. The most obvious example is language (Pinker, 2010), but there are many others, including social conformity and enforcement of social norms, a capacity for perspective-taking that allows us to navigate complex and nuanced social relationships, and biases that favor competition between tribes and cooperation within tribes (Bowles and Gintis, 2003; Burton-Chellew and West, 2012; Cosmides and Tooby, 2015; Tomasello et al., 2012; Tooby and Cosmides, 2016, 2008; West et al., 2011).

Despite the many unique forms of cooperation in humans, many of the basic functions underlying human cooperative traits exist in other species. For example, many animals, plants, fungi, and microbes engage in some form of conditional trade both within (Borgeaud and Bshary, 2015) and between species (Kiers et al., 2011), and primates have relationships that are functionally and mechanistically similar to human friendship (Brent et al., 2014; Seyfarth and Cheney, 2012).

Insight into cooperation in other species is therefore important for understanding the basis of human cooperation and what makes it unique.

It was not until the 1960s that evolutionary biologists understood that natural selection should not always lead to traits that maximize offspring production (direct fitness). Instead, natural selection rewards increases in *inclusive fitness*, which includes not only direct fitness but also *indirect fitness* gained from aiding the reproduction of genetic relatives (Hamilton, 1964). Hence, even altruistic traits that decrease the actor's lifetime direct fitness could evolve if recipients of altruistic acts are sufficiently genetically related (Hamilton, 1964). However, this process, called kin selection, could not fully explain human cooperation because humans frequently help unrelated individuals. Early explanations for non-kin cooperation often invoked simple group selection arguments that humans act for the good of the whole tribe because cooperative groups outcompete non-cooperative groups. However, these models failed to explain how such traits could persist within each tribe, given that, within each tribe, more reproductively altruistic individuals should suffer a fitness disadvantage compared to the more selfish individuals (Maynard Smith, 1976; West et al., 2007a, 2011). That is, if the altruistic trait were heritable, it would be passed down at a lower frequency than the non-altruistic trait within each group.

The theory of reciprocal altruism (Trivers, 1971) was one of the first explanations for the evolutionary stability of cooperation between non-relatives that did not rely on the notion of group-level adaptations. It explained how conditionally helping others could benefit the long-term interest of each helper. Trivers' theory predicted that individuals should preferentially help individuals that help them in return and reduce help toward partners that do not reciprocate. In the 1980s, reciprocal altruism was defined broadly and was the main explanation for non-kin cooperation (Carter, 2014). Over the next 40 years, many theorists extended, re-defined, and clarified Trivers' ideas to explore a variety of alternative forms of conditional cooperation, including biological market models based on partner choice (Barclay and Willer, 2007; Noë and Hammerstein, 1994, 1995), models of helping as a costly signal of partner or mate quality (Smith et al., 2003), and models based on byproduct benefits, like pseudoreciprocity (Connor, 1986, 2010). Today, the question has largely shifted from 'Why does cooperation evolve?' to 'Which factors are most responsible for the evolutionary stability of this particular cooperative trait?' Before we address current questions, let's first review the basic puzzle.

WHY DOES HUMAN COOPERATIVE BEHAVIOR EVOLVE?

In a human population, a heritable cooperative trait might provide greater motivation to share food with a hungry stranger. This cooperative trait would vary on a continuous scale, would be influenced by a huge number of genes, and would be flexible across contexts. All else being equal, however, if individuals with less cooperative phenotypes could gain all the fitness benefits from others' food-sharing behavior without paying the same fitness costs, then the cooperative trait would disappear over evolutionary time (West et al., 2007a). In other words, cooperative individuals are readily exploited by less cooperative 'free-riders' or 'cheats'.

As non-kin cooperation becomes less costly, it becomes easier to explain through mere byproduct benefits. For example, if two individuals must work together to hunt a large animal, and any lack of cooperation will lead to definite failure of the hunt, then the immediate costs of not cooperating might be worse than the costs of hunting cooperatively. In this case, being selfish leads to a worse outcome for both individuals, so it might not make sense to cheat.

The costs and benefits of cooperating and defecting are often formally described by a payoff matrix – a concept adopted from game theory (Dimand and Dimand, 1996). The payoff matrix specifies the distribution of relative payoffs for each individual for all possible combinations of actions by both the actor and the partner (Table 10.1). In evolutionary game theory, different strategies typically play repeated games with each other and reproduce themselves at rates relative to their accumulated payoffs. A key assumption here is that the short-term costs and benefits (the game payoffs) determine long-term fitness. This line of theory led to the concept of evolutionarily stable strategies, which are strategies that cannot be out-reproduced by a rare alternative strategy (Axelrod and Hamilton, 1981; Maynard Smith, 1982). Even an initially rare evolutionarily stable strategy can eventually displace a more common but less stable strategy, whereas the opposite does not happen.

Table 10.1   Alternative payoff matrices for an example social dilemma (cooperative hunting) *For simplicity, payoffs are shown for only one player (you), and not your partner. In a symmetrical game, the partner faces the same options and consequences. Payoff numbers are shown for comparative purposes only (the exact values are not meaningful, but the relative values define the kind of game).*

A. Payoff matrix for cooperative hunting

	Partner cooperates	Partner defects
You cooperate	Work together and hunt a large animal. **Payoff = 3**	Your partner lets you take all the risk in attacking the animal, greatly decreasing the chance of a successful hunt. **Payoff = 1**
You defect	You defect and let your partner take all the risk in attacking the animal. However, this greatly decreases the chance of a successful hunt. **Payoff = 2**	No success. **Payoff = 0**

If your partner cooperates, the highest payoff is obtained by cooperating. If your partner defects, the best payoff is still obtained through cooperation. You always expect cooperation.

B. Payoff matrix for cooperative hunting as a 'Snowdrift game' or 'Hawk–Dove game'

	Partner cooperates	Partner defects
You cooperate	Work together and hunt a large animal. **Payoff = 2**	Your partner lets you take all the risk in attacking the animal. **Payoff = 1**
You defect	You defect and let your partner take all the risk in attacking the animal. **Payoff = 3**	No success. **Payoff = 0**

If your partner cooperates, the highest payoff is obtained by defecting. If your partner defects, the best payoff is obtained by cooperating.

C. Payoff matrix for cooperative hunting as a 'Prisoner's dilemma'

	Partner cooperates	Partner defects
You cooperate	Work together and hunt a large animal (a risky activity). **Payoff = 2**	Your partner lets you take all the risk in attacking the animal. You are likely to get injured. **Payoff = 0**
You defect	You defect and let your partner take all the risk in attacking the animal. They are likely to get injured, but you will be safe. **Payoff = 3**	No food but no risk of severe injury. **Payoff = 1**

If your partner cooperates, the highest payoff in a prisoner's dilemma is obtained by defecting. If your partner defects, the best payoff is also obtained by defecting. The prisoner's dilemma is often used to depict why cooperation is a puzzle. If the prisoner's dilemma is played repeatedly with an accumulation of payoffs, cooperative strategies (like 'tit-for-tat') can outperform always defecting.

WHAT IS RECIPROCAL ALTRUISM?

This question is not as straightforward as it might seem, because researchers use this term in different ways (Carter, 2014). The term 'reciprocal altruism' can be confusing because many (but not all) evolutionary biologists define 'altruism' as a trait or behavior that decreases direct fitness. Altruism in this sense can only persevere through kin selection, since only increased reproduction by kin can make up for a trait that reduces the lifetime reproductive success of the altruistic individual. By this definition, reciprocal altruism would not be a form of 'altruism' because it directly benefits the actor. It also cannot exist between members of different species. This is consistent with Darwin's (1859) conjecture that, 'If it could be proved that any part of the structure of any one species had been formed for the exclusive good of another species, it would annihilate my theory, for such could not have been produced through natural selection.'

In contrast, Trivers' theory of reciprocal altruism defined 'altruism' based on more immediate, short-term costs. Each act of apparent altruism is an investment that, despite the short-term cost, provides a net positive return to fitness. Some authors have argued that there is no empirical evidence that nonhuman animals help others in a way that decreases direct fitness at the time it is provided (Clutton-Brock, 2009), but this would be almost impossible to demonstrate unambiguously. In behavioral ecology, the typical approach is to assume that helping poses a potential fitness cost when there is an obvious energetic cost, opportunity cost, or increased mortality risk.

Another point of confusion is that Trivers' original notion of reciprocal altruism describes an evolutionary strategy, not a psychological mechanism or motivation. Yet for many psychologists, 'altruism' is inherently connected to motivation. For clarity, we therefore use and advocate the term 'reciprocity' or 'direct reciprocity' instead of reciprocal altruism.

Some definitions of reciprocity are used for both positive and negative behaviors. Positive reciprocity is 'I'll scratch your back if you scratch mine', and negative reciprocity is 'I'll attack you if you attack me'. Many examples of reciprocity in animals take this latter form, such as conditional counter-singing among male songbirds (Carter, 2014). The same evolutionary pathways and cognitive mechanisms can underlie both conditional reward and conditional punishment because punishment can be just as costly as helping, and both actions require recognizing individuals and remembering their previous behavior. In this review, we focus on reciprocal helping to induce mutual benefit rather than reciprocal punishment to prevent mutual harm.

The classic game-theoretic model of reciprocity is the strategy 'tit-for-tat' in a repeated Prisoner's Dilemma game (Axelrod and Hamilton, 1981). In a computer simulation, different strategies can repeatedly face this payoff matrix (Table 10.1c), and their fitness can be calculated based on the sum of their accumulated payoffs. The evolutionarily stable strategy 'tit-for-tat' involves cooperating on the first round, and then copying the partner's previous move in the next round. Tit-for-tat enforces cooperation on two timescales. First, it does not allow itself to be exploited by a partner with a strategy of constant defection on an evolutionary timescale. Second, if the partner can learn and change its strategy over the course of several games, then tit-for-tat can 'train' a partner to cooperate by repeatedly rewarding cooperation and punishing defection.

The concept of tit-for-tat has been hugely influential, but its application to animal and human behavior has also been controversial due to conflicting interpretations of how the model applies to real-life situations (Carter, 2014). Earlier authors considered tit-for-tat to be a general model for conditional cooperation that could be applied equally to humans, songbirds, and microbes, but later interpretations took the tit-for-tat model more literally (Axelrod and Hamilton, 1981;

Carter, 2014). Although virtually everyone agrees that reciprocity plays an important role in human social life, narrower interpretations led authors to disagree about whether reciprocity is important in nonhuman species (Carter, 2014). Understanding this controversy provides important insights into current disagreements in the human literature.

ONLY CERTAIN FORMS OF RECIPROCITY REQUIRE SOPHISTICATED COGNITION

One point of disagreement is whether reciprocity requires a specific cognitive mechanism or is the functional result of any number of different mechanisms. 'Calculated reciprocity' is based on an intentional strategy requiring some understanding of the payoffs (Carter, 2014; de Waal and Luttrell, 1988; de Waal and Suchak, 2010; Stevens et al., 2005). It occurs when an individual explicitly trades one good or service for another and it requires sophisticated cognitive abilities such as the ability to keep score, plan ahead, and delay gratification (Stevens et al., 2005). Not surprisingly, evidence for calculated reciprocity in nonhuman animals is rare.

Other forms of reciprocity require only simple heuristics. For example, 'attitudinal reciprocity' states that reciprocal helping can emerge as two individuals mirror each other's social attitudes (de Waal, 2000; de Waal and Suchak, 2010), and 'emotional book-keeping' posits that individuals help others with whom they have positive emotional experiences (Schino and Aureli, 2009, 2010). These forms of reciprocity can involve acts of helping that feel inherently rewarding (de Waal et al., 2008; Rilling et al., 2002). Although humans are probably the only species that frequently make flexible and calculated economic decisions, many animals have social relationships that appear functionally and mechanistically like friendships (Seyfarth and Cheney, 2012).

A key insight of evolutionary theory is that natural selection produces seemingly strategic behaviors that are economically rational, even if the mechanisms are different from those that facilitate human decision-making (Noë and Hammerstein, 1995). For example, many species that lack cognition provide conditional reward and punishment. When plants and fungi exchange carbon and phosphorus underground, the plant preferentially allocates carbon to fungi that provide greater amounts of phosphorus, and the fungi do the same by preferentially allocating phosphorus (Kiers et al., 2011). This principle of conditional cooperation and partner choice (reciprocity in the broadest sense) is common across many mutualisms in which members of different species trade resources (Carter, 2014).

EVIDENCE FOR EVOLVED COGNITIVE MECHANISMS THAT SUPPORT RECIPROCITY IN HUMANS

Calculated reciprocity assumes that reciprocity must occur from learning the relative payoffs of cooperating and defecting in a given scenario. Some simple forms of reciprocity might occur through associative learning (such as training a dog to perform a helpful behavior), but there is abundant evidence that helping decisions in humans are not just based on which actions were previously rewarded. Rather, helping decisions rely on many context-specific heuristics, which sometimes lead people to make irrational decisions that would otherwise be optimal under more natural social circumstances (Burton-Chellew and West, 2013; Delton et al., 2011; Tooby and Cosmides, 2016). For example, humans treat one-shot economic games as if they might be repeated, which makes sense given that most social interactions in the human ancestral environment would be repeated (Delton et al., 2011). Even in the context of playing experimental economic games, most human decisions to cooperate are fast and intuitive, rather than relying on slow deliberation and strategic self-control (Rand, 2016; Rand et al., 2014).

If decisions were driven solely by payoffs in a Prisoner's Dilemma, then the most inherently rewarding outcome should be defection against a cooperating partner, regardless of whether playing against a computer or a human. However, cooperate–cooperate outcomes activate distinct reward regions in the brain (Rilling et al., 2002), are more psychologically rewarding, and provide greater psychological rewards when the payoffs occur with a human partner than with a computer (Abric and Kahan, 1972; Kiesler et al., 1996). When people defect or are experimentally made to defect in an economic cooperation game, they report guilt, and the level of guilt predicts future cooperation (Ketelaar and Tung Au, 2003). There is also evidence that humans have an evolved cognitive system for both revenge and forgiveness (McCullough et al., 2013). People often feel anger in response to defection and will pay a cost to punish defection, even when this yields no material gain (Fehr and Gachter, 2002). Much of human social behavior follows from heuristics and intuitions that work in most natural situations.

The fact that humans will pay a personal cost to punish defection has been confusingly called 'altruistic punishment' or 'strong reciprocity', and some have claimed that such behaviors deviate from expectations of evolutionary theory (reviewed by West et al., 2011). A simple explanation is that costly punishment of defectors yields a self-serving benefit to the punisher under most real-world conditions (West et al., 2011). We should expect cooperation in one-shot games and costly punishment if humans apply heuristics from direct reciprocity. For example, a person's desire to cooperate can be triggered by cues that are normally associated with conditions in which reciprocity could apply, just as sexual arousal can be triggered by cues normally associated with mating even in contexts in which these cues could no longer serve that purpose. In some studies,

even mere confusion has been misinterpreted as irrationally high levels of cooperation that defy evolutionary explanation (Burton-Chellew and West, 2013). In sum, we should not expect evolutionary explanations for human cooperation to explain behaviors unique to artificial lab settings.

The evolutionary psychologists Cosmides and Tooby have gathered a large body of evidence that the human mind has neurocognitive specializations that facilitate reciprocity via detection of cheating. They have shown that humans are poor at detecting potential violations of conditional logic rules, yet we can easily detect a violation of a rule that involves a social exchange or social cheating (Cosmides et al., 2010; Cosmides and Tooby, 2015). This specialized ability develops by age 3 or 4 and has been demonstrated in college undergraduates in developed nations and in the Shiwiar hunter-horticulturalists of the Ecuadorian Amazon (Cosmides and Tooby, 2015; Sugiyama et al., 2002). These studies show that human proficiency in reasoning about social exchange is not a byproduct of a neurocognitive system that evolved for a different function, such as reasoning about obligations, or for more general functions like logical reasoning (Cosmides and Tooby, 2015).

Tooby and Cosmides first gave subjects a logic quiz called The Wason Selection Task. Here is an example:

Ebbinghaus disease was recently identified and is not yet well understood. So an international committee of physicians who have experience with this disease was assembled. Their goal was to characterize the symptoms, and develop surefire ways of diagnosing it.

Patients afflicted with Ebbinghaus disease have many different symptoms: nosebleeds, headaches, ringing in the ears, and others. Diagnosing it is difficult because a patient may have the disease, yet not manifest all of the symptoms. Dr. Buchner, an expert on the disease, said that the following rule holds:

'If a person has Ebbinghaus disease, then that person will be forgetful.'

Dr. Buchner may be wrong, however. You are interested in seeing whether there are any patients whose symptoms violate this rule.

The cards below represent four patients in your hospital. Each card represents one patient. One side of the card tells whether or not the patient has Ebbinghaus disease, and the other side tells whether or not that patient is forgetful.

Which of the following card(s) would you definitely need to turn over to see if any of these cases violate Dr. Buchner's rule: 'If a person has Ebbinghaus disease, then that person will be forgetful.' Don't turn over any more cards than is absolutely necessary.

Card 1: has Ebbinghaus disease
Card 2: does not have Ebbinghaus disease
Card 3: is forgetful
Card 4: is not forgetful

The correct answer is to turn over only cards 1 and 4. Most people find this difficult. Only 5 to 30% of people give the correct answer, regardless of whether the rule involves unfamiliar or familiar terms, and formal education in logical inference does not seem to boost performance (Cosmides and Tooby, 2015).

The next step is to keep everything else the same but change the task so that people must look for violations of a conditional rule in the context of a social contract. An example is below.

'If you borrow my car, then you have to fill up the tank with gas.'

Card 1: borrowed car
Card 2: did not borrow car
Card 3: filled up tank with gas
Card 4: did not fill up tank with gas

Now 65% to 80% of subjects get the correct answer. The ability to detect violation of a social contract or exchange occurs even when the social contract is unfamiliar. For example, consider the rule, '*If a man eats cassava root, then he must have a tattoo on his face.*' Which cards must be turned over?

At first, it seems puzzling, yet if the subjects are told that cassava root is a rare food that provides a great benefit, they will now have an intuitive understanding that the cost or requirement of getting the cassava root is to have a tattoo on the face. As a result, they will complete the task with equal proficiency as a familiar social exchange.

Finally, consider the following two rules:

'If one is going out at night, then one must tie a small piece of red volcanic rock around one's ankle.'

'If one is taking out the garbage, then one must tie a small piece of red volcanic rock around one's ankle.'

Tooby and Cosmides argued that a 'cheater detection subroutine' in the human mind is designed to find benefits that are taken without paying the cost, so without an obvious benefit, this task becomes difficult. When the action was a chore (e.g., taking out the garbage), the success rate was 44%, but by simply framing the action as a benefit or reward (e.g., getting to go out at night), the success rate increased to 80% (Cosmides et al., 2010; Cosmides and Tooby, 2015).

Humans also excel at using verbal and non-verbal cues to predict levels of cooperation among strangers. The ability to assess cooperation based on cues besides the experience of reciprocal returns goes beyond what is necessary for direct reciprocity, but it provides further support that humans have specialized abilities for social judgment of partners. The idea is that certain personalities or states that correlate with cooperative behavior might correlate with particular cues. One example is the so-called Duchenne smile, a 'genuine' smile that is not under voluntary control and hence difficult to mimic (Mehu, Grammer, et al., 2007; Mehu, Little, et al., 2007; Oda et al., 2009). Humans can use these cues when making cooperative investments: after talking with or merely observing strangers, they can predict their cooperation rates in a Prisoner's Dilemma game at a level better than would be expected by chance (DeSteno et al., 2012; Frank et al., 1993; Stirrat and Perrett, 2010; Verplaetse et al., 2007; Yamagishi et al., 1999, 2003).

THE LIMITS OF THE TIT-FOR-TAT MODEL

In the tit-for-tat model, cooperation occurs in the absence of partner choice, power asymmetries, communication, trust, or any prior experience, but all these factors are common in social life. Social dominance and power asymmetries play important roles in both human and nonhuman species. In many animals, subordinate individuals help dominant individuals in exchange for tolerance (Borgeaud and Bshary, 2015; Bruintjes and Taborsky, 2008; Taborsky et al., 2016; Zöttl et al., 2013). For example, a dominant vervet monkey is more likely to tolerate the presence of a subordinate feeding next to it if it was recently groomed by that subordinate (Borgeaud and Bshary, 2015). In cooperatively breeding cichlid fish, subordinates that do not help with parental care face possible eviction (Bergmüller et al., 2005; Bruintjes and Taborsky, 2008; Zöttl et al., 2013). Dominance and variable access to resources means that reciprocity will not always lead to exchanges that seem fair and equal.

THE IMPORTANCE OF PARTNER CHOICE

Tit-for-tat is a strategy that occurs in the context of a single relationship, but most relationships exist in social networks, where partner choice creates a 'market' of possible partnerships (Borgeaud and Bshary, 2015; Bruintjes and Taborsky, 2008; Taborsky et al., 2016; Schino and Aureli, 2017). Partner choice based on reputation plays an important role in human social life (Barclay, 2016;

Barclay and Willer, 2007; Roberts, 1998; Sylwester and Roberts, 2010, 2013). When humans can choose cooperation partners, then potential partners often compete to be chosen, and this 'competitive altruism' can intensify as the choosing individual becomes more valuable due to generosity, social rank, or access to resources. This market of partners leads people to compete to be more generous, to help even when it is unnecessary, and to attack or suppress the helping efforts of others (Barclay, 2016). Biological market models that make partner choice a central feature of human cooperation are becoming increasingly popular given the ubiquity and importance of partner choice (Barclay, 2016; Noë and Hammerstein, 1994, 1995).

INDIRECT RECIPROCITY VERSUS REPUTATION-BASED PARTNER CHOICE

A concept related to competitive altruism is 'indirect reciprocity' (Nowak and Sigmund, 1998; Roberts, 2008; Sylwester and Roberts, 2013), which is used in contrast to 'direct reciprocity'. Competitive altruism (or reputation-based partner choice) requires direct reciprocity: individuals that develop a reputation for being cooperative are chosen more often as partners, and they also receive higher cooperative investments from those partners (Sylwester and Roberts, 2010, 2013). In contrast, indirect reciprocity is often defined in such a way that direct reciprocity is not required. Like competitive altruism, indirect reciprocity predicts that individuals who cooperate more are also more likely to receive cooperative acts from third parties; however, to remove the effects of direct reciprocity, many models of indirect reciprocity assume that those partners will never meet again. Simulations show that indirect reciprocity becomes unstable with respect to direct reciprocity as the probability of repeated interaction increases (Roberts, 2008).

One disadvantage of indirect reciprocity relative to direct reciprocity is that defections are not necessarily a good reflection of an individual's strategy; even a tit-for-tat strategy will involve defecting against a defector (Roberts, 2008). Most natural situations that might be explained as indirect reciprocity might actually be cases of the more simple mechanism of reputation-based partner choice (Sylwester and Roberts, 2013). Some people also use the term 'indirect reciprocity' to refer to either idea, as long as individuals help those that they observe helping others.

RECIPROCITY IN FRIENDSHIPS

The tit-for-tat strategy has no memory beyond the most recent interaction, but humans clearly integrate many different kinds of social experiences and many encounters with different partners over time. Trivers (1971) considered reciprocity as a basis for human friendship and for understanding emotions such as guilt, shame, gratitude, sympathy, and trust. But, in later years, as reciprocity became associated with literal tit-for-tat, authors began considering reciprocity and friendship as sharply contrasting behaviors. Indeed, friends do not appear to closely track favors, humans report feeling a stronger obligation to reciprocate to strangers than to friends, and explicitly calculated exchanges are often offensive in a close, personal relationship (Boster et al., 1995; Hruschka, 2010; Shackelford and Buss, 1996; Silk, 2002, 2003). Why might this be?

In a market of possible partners, generosity acts as a costly signal of partner quality, so individuals might benefit from making their cooperative investments seem as altruistic as possible, which requires downplaying the expectation of a return. If an individual desires immediate reciprocation, this can signal a lack of trust and add tension to a relationship. Similarly, a desire to immediately 'repay' social debts might signal

that the partner does not expect many future interactions. In general, explicit trade suggests social distance (Tooby and Cosmides, 1996).

People can navigate possible social conflict by concealing expectations of reciprocation (even to themselves). Consider someone who is investing time and energy in being kind toward a friend that they are also interested in as a potential romantic or sexual partner. In this case, we might expect this person to conceal their attraction so that the relationship will not be damaged if the friend is not interested. We might also expect them to emphasize their motivation in tending to their partner's needs ('I'm just trying to help') rather than expectations of a 'return' on their social investments. Similarly, reciprocal social support is a primary benefit of friendship, but individuals are more prone to emphasize their commitment to supporting others ('I'll be there for you') rather than their own need for social support ('You must be there for me'). Trivers (2000) emphasized the potential importance of self-deception in human social life to accomplish this biased self-representation. A good way to develop a relationship that provides cooperative returns is to seem as unconcerned with those returns as possible, and a good way to hide selfish motivations would be to not be aware of them at all.

Humans tolerate short-term imbalances with friends more than with strangers and track the cooperative acts of strangers more than of friends, but they do track the investments of friends (Hruschka et al., 2015; Xue and Silk, 2012). The ability of friends to reciprocate, the availability of alternative friends, and the need for social support can affect social investments (Barclay, 2016; Frank, 1988; Hruschka, 2010; Hruschka et al., 2015; Shackelford and Buss, 1996). However, little work exists on the subtle and hidden conditional strategies in human relationships that emphasize unconditional support, such as parent-offspring bonds, close friendships, and marriages. One reason for this lack of work on these topics is that detecting conditional investments in such relationships would require the ethically questionable practice of manipulating them. Most work on reciprocity in humans therefore relies on experiments outside the context of real, natural social relationships.

RECIPROCITY VERSUS PSEUDORECIPROCITY

Much debate on reciprocity comes from a disagreement about the costs of cooperating that determine the payoff matrix for a given situation (Carter, 2014). It is difficult to simulate all the assumptions of a particular game in a way that is ecologically realistic or to know how animals perceive the payoffs for a given situation in nature (Carter, 2014; Noë, 2006; Trivers, 2006), and this leads to ambiguity about whether cheating is possible. Pseudoreciprocity is an alternative model to reciprocity based on the idea that cooperative investments can lead to byproduct returns (Connor, 1986, 1995, 2010). Reciprocity involves making costly cooperative investments that promote costly cooperative returns, whereas pseudoreciprocity involves a costly investment that promotes a noncostly cooperative return (Bergmüller et al., 2007; Connor, 2010). Because the cooperative return is not costly, there is no reason for the individual to defect. For example, consider the payoff matrix for cooperative hunting in Table 10.1c. In this high-conflict scenario, the hunter benefits most by defecting, because the best outcome is that the partner accepts all the risk of being injured during the hunt, so it is tempting to cheat. However, if the partner was the hunter's sibling or child, the payoff matrix could shift from a Prisoner's Dilemma (Table 10.1c) to a Snowdrift game (Table 10.1b), or to what might be called a 'Prisoner's Delight' (Table 10.1a, Bshary et al., 2016), because kin altruism can eliminate the temptation to cheat. The same can happen if the partner is

valuable to the focal hunter in other ways, a factor called 'fitness interdependence' (Bshary et al., 2016; Roberts, 2005). For example, if an injured partner could no longer help to defend the tribe or help in future hunting, then any injury to the partner would be detrimental to the hunter in the long-term. In these cases, cheating is not possible, and the hunter's investment is described as pseudoreciprocity.

One problem with distinguishing between pseudoreciprocity and reciprocity is that both models can lead to the prediction of conditional helping (Bshary et al., 2016). The only way to distinguish them is to observe or demonstrate the possibility of cheating, but if reciprocity is common and effective, then attempts to cheat might be rare. Due to the difficulty of testing these models, pseudoreciprocity often acts as a null hypothesis for situations in which one individual makes a cooperative investment in another. It is ultimately a subjective question whether the null hypothesis should be the assumption that cheating is possible (reciprocity models) or absent (pseudoreciprocity models).

Although reciprocity and pseudoreciprocity are different models, in the real world, the byproduct benefits of helping and therefore the possibility of cheating can change continuously between situations and partners and over time. A better way to think of reciprocity and pseudoreciprocity are as regions along a continuous spectrum of social conflict (Figure 10.1; Bshary et al., 2016). On one end is the Prisoner's Dilemma in which cheating is likely and cooperation must be enforced. On the other end is a game scenario in which cooperative outcomes emerge as a byproduct of selfish behavior. In between, the risk of cheating can range from low to high, making enforcement (reciprocity) more or less necessary.

Bshary et al. (2016) argued that intermediate amounts of conflict will exist in most real-world forms of cooperation. For a cooperative outcome that results from selfish behavior (byproduct mutualism), even small

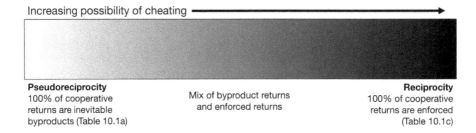

Figure 10.1   Cooperation in the real world can vary on a spectrum where cooperative returns are inevitable (as in pseudoreciprocity and other byproduct models) or entirely enforced (reciprocity models). Many real-world scenarios involve intermediate conflict

Source: Adapted from Bshary et al. (2016).

variation in partner quality can lead to partner choice. For example, consider two hunters that must work together to hunt prey (Table 10.1a). Not all hunters are equally skilled at being hunting partners. The best partners will be preferred, and now we have partner choice selecting for traits such as being good at hunting in the presence of others, coordinating with others, and convincing others to hunt with you. This moves us on the spectrum away from byproduct mutualism toward conditional cooperation. However, this state might also be unstable. Humans typically live in families and stable groups, sometimes in competition with other groups. As a result, interdependence and kin selection can reduce conflict such that a certain amount of cooperation is always self-serving even before we consider the effects of reward and punishment (Bshary et al., 2016).

GENERALIZED RECIPROCITY

When people receive help from one individual, they are more likely to help a different individual (Bartlett and DeSteno, 2006; Berkowitz and Daniels, 1964; Pfeiffer et al., 2005). One potential explanation for this observation is that a positive mood makes people more generous. For example, finding a free coin makes people more likely to help

a stranger (Isen, 1987). An alternative explanation is that receiving help from any partner is a cue of being in a more cooperative social environment, just as receiving help from a specific partner is a cue that the partner is more cooperative. Generalized reciprocity is a strategy of helping others if you have been helped by anyone, and this heuristic has been observed in humans and a variety of other species, including rats (Rutte and Taborsky, 2007, 2008), dogs (Gfrerer and Taborsky, 2017), and nonhuman primates (Leimgruber et al., 2014). Generalized reciprocity in other animals shows that an increase in helping toward others after being helped by anyone cannot always be explained as an increase in the salience of a 'social responsibility norm' (Berkowitz and Daniels, 1964).

Rutte and Taborsky (2008) compared direct and generalized reciprocity in Norway rats. Rats were paired and trained to pull sticks that moved a tray with food into the other rat's compartment; they could not pull for themselves and relied on a partner for access to food. The rats exhibited both direct and generalized reciprocity, but the effect of direct reciprocity was greater – rats pulled more often and sooner for a partner they had previously experienced as a helper than a new one (Rutte and Taborsky, 2007, 2008). Later experiments investigated pulling rates in rats that received food from a remotely controlled food dispenser in either the presence or absence of other rats, and detected no increase in cooperation for a partner (Schmid et al., 2017). This is consistent with the hypothesis that past evidence for generalized reciprocity was not a mere byproduct of a nonsocial positive experience.

RECIPROCITY AND NEPOTISM

Nepotism and reciprocity are not mutually exclusive explanations, because decisions to help others can be influenced by both kinship cues and past experience of reciprocal help. Reciprocity might be more common among relatives than non-relatives, and the degree of reciprocity might be stronger or weaker among kin compared to non-kin (an interaction effect). When nepotism and reciprocity coexist, it is often difficult to disentangle and determine their relative effects (Carter et al., 2019). In correlational studies, evidence of reciprocity is often assessed as the degree to which helping rates are reciprocated by partners, and nepotism is measured as the degree to which helping rates are kin-biased. However, nepotism is often easier to detect for several reasons. First, measures of relatedness, based on maternal pedigrees or genetic markers, are often more precise, easier to measure, and less time-variant than measures of reciprocal helping rates. Second, if individuals decide whether to help based on multiple past experiences with a partner, the history of reciprocity between them can span longer time periods than the study period, so snapshots of observed cooperation might not capture the underlying relationship. Third, if helping behaviors are rare or hard to observe, then estimates of helping and reciprocal helping rates will often be imprecise.

Nepotism and reciprocity between relatives make the same prediction that relatives should help each other reciprocally. The only way to separate these two effects would be to prevent reciprocation among kin, as has

been done with rats and cooperatively breeding cichlid fish. Male rats can discriminate unfamiliar kin, but in food-pulling experiments, they perform direct reciprocity without favoring kin (Schweinfurth and Taborsky, 2018). This result suggests that reciprocity applies to both kin and non-kin. In cichlid fish, both kin and non-kin subordinates must 'pay to stay', but unrelated helpers provide more care for eggs than related helpers. Non-kin helpers also increased their helping when experimenters simulated egg cannibalism, while kin helpers did not (Zöttl et al., 2013). These findings support the hypothesis that the 'pay-to-stay' rule applies more strongly to non-kin, because nepotism causes dominants to be more tolerant of less helpful kin subordinates.

HOW DO NEW RECIPROCAL RELATIONSHIPS FORM?

One unrealistic feature of tit-for-tat is that cooperative investments are binary: individuals can either cooperate or defect. In the real world, investments are often continuous, which can allow individuals to reduce risk by dividing a big investment into a series of smaller investments over time, called 'parceling' (Connor, 1992, 2010), or by spreading investments to a larger number of possible partners, called 'social bet-hedging' (Carter et al., 2017). The idea of making less risky investments underlies one of the theories about how reciprocally cooperative relationships might begin. Strangers can avoid the risk of exploitation via defection if they initially make smaller, low-cost cooperative investments and then adjust the magnitude of their investments based on the subsequent returns (Roberts and Sherratt, 1998). This strategy, called 'raising-the-stakes', has been demonstrated in human strangers playing economic cooperation games (Roberts and Renwick, 2003). It would be interesting to test this theory at the start of more natural relationships, such as courtship, or the formation of new friendships. Social bet-hedging (Carter et al., 2017) predicts how individuals should distribute their cooperative investments across multiple relationships. In an unstable social environment, where partner availability varies greatly, one should distribute cooperative investments across more partners because this reduces the risk of each partner not being present when they are needed. In a more stable social environment, individuals should invest preferentially in the partner yielding the greatest cooperative returns, such as a best friend.

Food-sharing vampire bats provide evidence for social bet-hedging (Carter et al., 2017). Individuals regurgitate food to help starving groupmates who failed to feed. Females always feed their offspring, and female–female food sharing continues into adulthood (adult males leave their natal group). Some females share with many non-kin in their group who have helped them before, whereas others focus their investments in kin groupmates (Carter and Wilkinson, 2013, 2015, 2016; Wilkinson, 1984). Because kin can also perform reciprocity, and helping relatives is supported by kin selection, what is the advantage of investing in non-kin rather than kin? One explanation is that a kin-limited support network is too small and risky. To test this idea, a primary donor of each bat was temporarily removed. The primary donor for most bats was either a mother or daughter, if they were present in the group. When their primary donors were removed, females that previously fed a greater number of non-kin suffered smaller reductions in the amount of food received because they had more donors. The data were consistent with the hypothesis that females investing in quantity over quality do not gain more under normal conditions, but they cope better with partner loss.

In humans, there is evidence that relationship quality is better than relationship quantity at predicting received social support (Franks et al., 2004), but people appear to benefit from a greater number of weaker friendships

in environments where friendships are more transient (Oishi and Kesebir, 2012). More work on this topic from an evolutionary perspective would be exciting. Do individuals that invest preferentially in stronger friendships have fewer friends? Do humans with smaller or less supportive families depend and invest more in friendships? Do investments in established friendships or new friendships yield higher returns? Do humans invest more in forming new friendships after the loss of an important friendship? Female baboons increase their rates of social grooming to others in the group immediately after the death of a close female relative (Engh et al., 2006).

Another reason to have multiple friends is to form alliances in disputes or conflicts with other individuals. There is evidence that human friendship is supported by cognitive mechanisms designed to form such alliances (DeScioli and Kurzban, 2009). Theoretical simulations predict that people would benefit from ranking their friends, hiding these ranks, and adjusting them according to estimates of their own position in the ranks of their friends. Three studies found support for these predictions. How people ranked their closest friends was predicted by how they perceived themselves to be ranked by each friend, and this prediction held true after controlling for a variety of other factors, such as the subject's perception of similarity, familiarity, and benefits received from their friends (DeScioli and Kurzban, 2009).

Alliances might also predict the kinds of new friendships people seek out. For example, if A and B are friends, and B and C are friends, then it is likely that A and C will become friends. However, if A and B are prone to disputes, then A might prefer to build a friendship with the more independent individual D, because C will always be closer to B and be more likely to take B's side in a dispute (DeScioli et al., 2011). The alliance hypothesis for friendship can be considered an alternative to the narrow idea of reciprocity as the direct exchange of benefits, but it still requires reciprocity in the broader sense of cooperative investments that are conditional on a cooperative return (in this case, investing in a friendship can lead to support in a conflict). One interesting future line of work would be to assess the relative importance of different kinds of reciprocal benefits in different types of relationships. Another would be to test how reciprocity changes as relationships form and develop over time.

The theory of reciprocity has led generations of evolutionary biologists to think carefully about the immediate costs and future benefits of cooperative behavior. Gaps in this theory have sparked the creation of more general theories, such as biological market theory, and inspired a large number of theoretical models of cooperation based on the iterated Prisoner's Dilemma and similar games. At its core, the simple notion of conditional cooperation provides the foundation for a more complex and nuanced understanding of human cooperation that also considers the effects of reputation, culture, and group competition.

REFERENCES

Abric JC and Kahan JP (1972) The effects of representations and behavior in experimental games. *European Journal of Social Psychology* 2(2): 129–144. DOI: 10.1002/ejsp.2420020203.

Axelrod R and Hamilton WD (1981) The evolution of cooperation. *Science* 211(4489): 1390–1396.

Barclay P (2016) Biological markets and the effects of partner choice on cooperation and friendship. *Current Opinion in Psychology* 7, Special issue: Evolutionary Psychology: 33–38. DOI: 10.1016/j.copsyc.2015.07.012.

Barclay P and Willer R (2007) Partner choice creates competitive altruism in humans. *Proceedings of the Royal Society B* 274(1610): 749–753.

Bartlett MY and DeSteno D (2006) Gratitude and prosocial behavior: helping when it costs you. *Psychological Science* 17(4): 319–325. DOI: 10.1111/j.1467-9280.2006.01705.x.

Bergmüller R, Heg D and Taborsky M (2005) Helpers in a cooperatively breeding cichlid stay and pay or disperse and breed, depending on ecological constraints. *Proceedings of Royal Society B* 272(1560): 325–331.

Bergmüller R, Johnstone RA, Russell AF and Bshary R (2007) Integrating cooperative breeding into theoretical concepts of cooperation. *Behavioural Processes* 76(2): 61–72.

Berkowitz L and Daniels LR (1964) Affecting the salience of the social responsibility norm: effects of past help on the response to dependency relationships. *The Journal of Abnormal and Social Psychology* 68(3): 275–281. DOI: 10.1037/h0040164.

Borgeaud C and Bshary R (2015) Wild vervet monkeys trade tolerance and specific coalitionary support for grooming in experimentally induced conflicts. *Current Biology* 25(22): 3011–3016.

Boster FJ, Rodríguez JI, Cruz MG and Marshall L (1995) The relative effectiveness of a direct request message and a pregiving message on friends and strangers. *Communication Research* 22(4): 475–484. DOI: 10.1177/009365095022004005.

Bowles S and Gintis H (2003) The Origins of Human Cooperation. In: Hammerstein P (ed.) *Genetic and Cultural Evolution of Cooperation*. Cambridge, MA: MIT Press, pp. 429–444.

Boyd R and Richerson PJ (1985) *The Evolution of Culture*. Chicago: University of Chicago Press.

Boyd R and Richerson PJ (2009) Culture and the evolution of human cooperation. *Philosophical Transactions of the Royal Society B* 364(1533): 3281–3288.

Brent LJ, Chang SW, Gariépy J-F and Platt ML (2014) The neuroethology of friendship. *Annals of the New York Academy of Sciences* 1316(1): 1–17.

Bruintjes R and Taborsky M (2008) Helpers in a cooperative breeder pay a high price to stay: effects of demand, helper size and sex. *Animal Behaviour* 75(6): 1843–1850.

Bshary R, Zuberbühler K and van Schaik CP (2016) Why mutual helping in most natural systems is neither conflict-free nor based on maximal conflict. *Philosophical Transactions of the Royal Society B* 371(1687): 20150091.

Burton-Chellew MN and West SA (2012) Pseudocompetition among groups increases human cooperation in a public-goods game. *Animal Behaviour* 84(4): 947–952.

Burton-Chellew MN and West SA (2013) Prosocial preferences do not explain human cooperation in public-goods games. *Proceedings of the National Academy of Sciences* 110(1): 216–221.

Carter GG (2014) The reciprocity controversy. *Animal Behavior and Cognition* 1(3): 368–386. DOI: 0.12966/abc.08.11.2014.

Carter GG and Wilkinson GS (2013) Food sharing in vampire bats: reciprocal help predicts donations more than relatedness or harassment. *Proceedings of the Royal Society B* 280: 20122573.

Carter GG and Wilkinson GS (2015) Social benefits of non-kin food sharing by female vampire bats. *Proceedings of the Royal Society B* 282(1819): 20152524. DOI: 10.1098/rspb.2015.2524.

Carter GG and Wilkinson GS (2016) Common vampire bat contact calls attract past food-sharing partners. *Animal Behaviour* 116: 45–51. DOI: 10.1016/j.anbehav.2016.03.005.

Carter GG, Farine DR and Wilkinson GS (2017) Social bet-hedging in vampire bats. *Biology Letters* 13(5): 20170112.

Carter GG, Schino G and Farine D (2019) Challenges in assessing the roles of nepotism and reciprocity in cooperation networks. *Animal Behaviour* 150: 255–271.

Clutton-Brock T (2009) Cooperation between non-kin in animal societies. *Nature* 462(7269): 51–57.

Connor RC (1986) Pseudo-reciprocity: investing in mutualism. *Animal Behaviour* 34(5): 1562–1566.

Connor RC (1992) Egg-trading in simultaneous hermaphrodites: an alternative to Tit-for-Tat. *Journal of Evolutionary Biology* 5(3): 523–528.

Connor RC (1995) Altruism among non-relatives: alternatives to the 'Prisoner's Dilemma'. *Trends in Ecology & Evolution* 10(2): 84–86.

Connor RC (2010) Cooperation beyond the dyad: on simple models and a complex society. *Philosophical Transactions of the Royal Society B* 365(1553): 2687–2697.

Cosmides L and Tooby J (2015) Adaptations for reasoning about social exchange. *The Handbook of Evolutionary Psychology*: 1–44. doi.org/10.1002/9781119125563.evpsych225.

Cosmides L, Barrett HC and Tooby J (2010) Adaptive specializations, social exchange, and the evolution of human intelligence. *Proceedings of the National Academy of Sciences* 107(Suppl_2): 9007–9014.

Darwin C (1859) *On the Origins of Species by Means of Natural Selection*. London: John Murray.

de Waal FBM (2000) Attitudinal reciprocity in food sharing among brown capuchin monkeys. *Animal Behaviour* 60(2): 253–261.

de Waal FBM and Luttrell LM (1988) Mechanisms of social reciprocity in 3 primate species: symmetrical relationship characteristics or cognition? *Ethology and Sociobiology* 9(2–4): 101–118.

de Waal FBM and Suchak M (2010) Prosocial primates: selfish and unselfish motivations. *Philosophical Transactions of the Royal Society B* 365(1553): 2711–2722. DOI: 10.1098/rstb.2010.0119.

de Waal FBM, Leimgruber K and Greenberg AR (2008) Giving is self-rewarding for monkeys. *Proceedings of the National Academy of Sciences* 105(36): 13685–13689.

Delton AW, Krasnow MM, Cosmides L and Tooby J (2011) Evolution of direct reciprocity under uncertainty can explain human generosity in one-shot encounters. *Proceedings of the National Academy of Sciences* 108(32): 13335–13340.

DeScioli P and Kurzban R (2009) The alliance hypothesis for human friendship. *PLoS One* 4(6): e5802. DOI: 10.1371/journal.pone.0005802.

DeScioli P, Kurzban R, Koch EN and Liben-Nowell D (2011) Best friends: Alliances, friend ranking, and the MySpace social network. *Perspectives on Psychological Science* 6(1): 6–8. DOI: 10.1177/1745691610393979.

DeSteno D, Breazeal C, Frank RH, Pizarro D, Baumann J, Dickens L and Lee JJ (2012) Detecting the trustworthiness of novel partners in economic exchange. *Psychological Science* 23(12): 1549–1556.

Dimand M-A and Dimand RW (1996) *The History of Game Theory, Volume 1: From the Beginnings to 1945*. Routledge.

Engh AL, Beehner JC, Bergman TJ, Whitten PL, Hoffmeier RR, Seyfarth RM, and Cheney DL (2006) Behavioural and hormonal responses to predation in female chacma baboons

(*Papio hamadryas ursinus*). *Proceedings of the Royal Society B* 273: 707–712.

Fehr E and Fischbacher U (2004) Social norms and human cooperation. *Trends in Cognitive Sciences* 8(4): 185–190.

Fehr E and Gachter S (2002) Altruistic punishment in humans. *Nature* 415(6868): 137–140.

Frank RH (1988) *Passions Within Reason: The Strategic Role of Emotions*. New York: W. W. Norton.

Frank RH, Gilovich T and Regan DT (1993) The evolution of one-shot cooperation: an experiment. *Ethology and Sociobiology* 14(4): 247–256.

Franks HM, Cronan TA and Oliver K (2004) Social support in women with fibromyalgia: is quality more important than quantity? *Journal of Community Psychology* 32(4): 425–438.

Gintis H, Bowles S, Boyd R and Fehr R (2005) *Moral Sentiments and Material Interests: The Foundations of Cooperation in Economic Life*. Cambridge, MA: MIT Press.

Gfrerer N and Taborsky M (2017) Working dogs cooperate among one another by generalised reciprocity. *Scientific Reports* 7(1): 1–6.

Hamilton WD (1964) The genetical evolution of social behavior. *Journal of Theoretical Biology* 7(1): 1–51.

Hruschka DJ (2010) *Friendship: Development, Ecology, and Evolution of a Relationship*. University of California Press.

Hruschka DJ, Hackman J and Macfarlan S (2015) Why Do Humans Help Their Friends? Proximal and Ultimate Hypotheses from Evolutionary Theory. In: Zeigler-Hill V, Welling LLM, and Shackelford TK (eds) *Evolutionary Perspectives on Social Psychology*. Evolutionary Psychology. Cham: Springer, pp. 255–266. DOI: 10.1007/978-3-319-12697-5_20.

Isen AM (1987) Positive Affect, Cognitive Processes, and Social Behavior. In: Berkowitz L (ed.) *Advances in Experimental Social Psychology*. Academic Press, pp. 203–253. DOI: 10.1016/S0065-2601(08)60415-3.

Ketelaar T and Tung Au W (2003) The effects of feelings of guilt on the behaviour of uncooperative individuals in repeated social bargaining games: an affect-as-information interpretation of the role of emotion in social interaction. *Cognition and Emotion* 17(3): 429–453.

Kiers ET, Duhamel M, Beesetty Y, et al. (2011) Reciprocal rewards stabilize cooperation in the mycorrhizal symbiosis. *Science* 333(6044): 880–882.

Kiesler S, Sproull L and Waters K (1996) A prisoner's dilemma experiment on cooperation with people and human-like computers. *Journal of Personality and Social Psychology* 70(1): 47–65.

Kurzban R, Burton-Chellew MN and West SA (2015) The evolution of altruism in humans. *Annual Review of Psychology* 66: 575–99. DOI: 10.1146/annurev-psych-010814-015355.

Leimgruber KL, Ward AF, Widness J, et al. (2014) Give what you get: capuchin monkeys (*Cebus apella*) and 4-year-old children pay forward positive and negative outcomes to conspecifics. *PLoS ONE* 9(1). DOI: 10.1371/journal.pone.0087035.

Maynard Smith J (1976) Group selection. *Quarterly Review of Biology* 52(2): 277–283.

Maynard Smith J (1982) *Evolution and the Theory of Games*. Cambridge: Cambridge University Press.

McCullough ME, Kurzban R and Tabak BA (2013) Cognitive systems for revenge and forgiveness. *Behavioral and Brain Sciences* 36(1): 1–15.

Mehu M, Grammer K and Dunbar RI (2007) Smiles when sharing. *Evolution and Human Behavior* 28(6): 415–422.

Mehu M, Little AC and Dunbar RI (2007) Duchenne smiles and the perception of generosity and sociability in faces. *Journal of Evolutionary Psychology* 5(1): 183–196.

Noë R (2006) Cooperation experiments: coordination through communication versus acting apart together. *Animal Behaviour* 71(1): 1–18.

Noë R and Hammerstein P (1994) Biological markets: supply and demand determine the effect of partner choice in cooperation, mutualism and mating. *Behavioral Ecology and Sociobiology* 35(1): 1–11.

Noë R and Hammerstein P (1995) Biological markets. *Trends in Ecology and Evolution* 10(8): 336–339.

Nowak MA and Sigmund K (1998) Evolution of indirect reciprocity by image scoring. *Nature* 393(6685): 573–577.

Oda R, Yamagata N, Yabiku Y and Matsumoto-Oda A (2009) Altruism can be assessed correctly based on impression. *Human Nature* 20(3): 331–341.

Oishi S and Kesebir S (2012) Optimal social-networking strategy is a function of socio-economic conditions. *Psychological Science*: 0956797612446708.

Pfeiffer T, Rutte C, Killingback T, Taborsky M and Bonhoeffer S (2005) Evolution of cooperation by generalized reciprocity. *Proceedings of the Royal Society B* 272(1568): 1115–1120.

Pinker S (2010) The cognitive niche: coevolution of intelligence, sociality, and language. *Proceedings of the National Academy of Sciences* 107(Suppl_2): 8993–8999. DOI: 10.1073/pnas.0914630107.

Rand DG (2016) Cooperation, fast and slow: meta-analytic evidence for a theory of social heuristics and self-interested deliberation. *Psychological Science* 27(9): 1192–1206.

Rand DG, Peysakhovich A, Kraft-Todd GT, Newman GE, Wurzbacher O, Nowak MA and Greene JD (2014) Social heuristics shape intuitive cooperation. *Nature Communications* 5: 3677.

Rilling JK, Gutman DA, Zeh TR, Pagnoni G, Berns G and Kilts C (2002) A neural basis for social cooperation. *Neuron* 35(2): 395–405.

Roberts G (1998) Competitive altruism: from reciprocity to the handicap principle. *Proceedings of the Royal Society B* 265(1394): 427–431.

Roberts G (2005) Cooperation through interdependence. *Animal Behaviour* 70(4): 901–908.

Roberts G (2008) Evolution of direct and indirect reciprocity. *Proceedings of the Royal Society B* 275(1631): 173–179. DOI: 10.1098/rspb.2007.1134.

Roberts G and Renwick JS (2003) The development of cooperative relationships: an experiment. *Proceedings of the Royal Society B* 270(1530): 2279–2283. DOI: 10.1098/rspb.2003.2491.

Roberts G and Sherratt TN (1998) Development of cooperative relationships through increasing investment. *Nature* 394(6689): 175–179.

Rutte C and Taborsky M (2007) Generalized reciprocity in rats. *PLoS Biology*, 5(7): e196.

Rutte C and Taborsky M (2008) The influence of social experience on cooperative behaviour of rats (*Rattus norvegicus*): direct vs generalised reciprocity. *Behavioral Ecology and Sociobiology* 62: 499–505.

Schino G and Aureli F (2009) Reciprocal altruism in primates: partner choice, cognition, and emotions. *Advances in the Study of Behavior* 39: 45–69. DOI: 10.1016/S0065-3454(09)39002-6.

Schino G and Aureli F (2010) Primate reciprocity and its cognitive requirements. *Evolutionary Anthropology: Issues, News, and Reviews* 19(4): 130–135. DOI: 10.1002/evan.20270.

Schino G and Aureli F (2017) Reciprocity in group-living animals: Partner control versus partner choice. *Biological Reviews* 92(2): 665–672.

Schmid R, Schneeberger K and Taborsky M (2017) Feel good, do good? Disentangling reciprocity from unconditional prosociality. *Ethology* 123(9): 640–647. DOI: 10.1111/eth.12636.

Schweinfurth MK and Taborsky M (2018) Relatedness decreases and reciprocity increases cooperation in Norway rats. *Proceedings of the Royal Society B* 285(1874). DOI: 10.1098/rspb.2018.0035.

Seyfarth RM and Cheney DL (2012) The evolutionary origins of friendship. *Annual Review of Psychology* 63: 153–77. DOI: 10.1146/annurev-psych-120710-100337.

Shackelford TK and Buss DM (1996) Betrayal in mateships, friendships, and coalitions. *Personality and Social Psychology Bulletin* 22(11): 1151–1164. DOI: 10.1177/01461672962211006.

Silk JB (2002) Using the 'F'-word in primatology. *Behaviour* 139(2–3): 421–446.

Silk JB (2003) Cooperation without Counting. In: Hammerstein P (ed.) *Genetic and Cultural Evolution of Cooperation*. Cambridge, MA: MIT Press, pp. 37–54.

Smith EA, Bird RB and Bird DW (2003) The benefits of costly signaling: Meriam turtle hunters. *Behavioral Ecology* 14(1): 116–126. DOI: 10.1093/beheco/14.1.116.

Stevens JR, Cushman FA and Hauser MD (2005) Evolving the psychological mechanisms for cooperation. *Annual Review of Ecology Evolution and Systematics* 36: 499–518.

Stirrat M and Perrett DI (2010) Valid facial cues to cooperation and trust: male facial width and trustworthiness. *Psychological Science* 21(3): 349–354.

Sugiyama LS, Tooby J and Cosmides L (2002) Cross-cultural evidence of cognitive adaptations for social exchange among the Shiwiar of Ecuadorian Amazonia. *Proceedings of the National Academy of Sciences* 99(17): 11537–11542.

Sylwester K and Roberts G (2010) Cooperators benefit through reputation-based partner choice in economic games. *Biology Letters* 6(5): 659–662. DOI: 10.1098/rsbl.2010.0209.

Sylwester K and Roberts G (2013) Reputation-based partner choice is an effective alternative to indirect reciprocity in solving social dilemmas. *Evolution and Human Behavior* 34(3): 201–206. DOI: 10.1016/j.evolhumbehav.2012.11.009.

Taborsky M, Frommen JG and Riehl C (2016) Correlated pay-offs are key to cooperation. *Philosophical Transactions of the Royal Society B* 371(1687): 20150084.

Tomasello M, Melis AP, Tennie C, Wyman E and Hermann E (2012) Two key steps in the evolution of human cooperation: the interdependence hypothesis. *Current Anthropology* 53(6): 673–692.

Tooby J and Cosmides L (1996) Friendship and the Banker's Paradox: Other Pathways to the Evolution of Adaptations for Altruism. In: Runciman, WG, Smith JM and Dunbar RIM (eds) *Proceedings of the British Academy Vol.88. Evolution of Social Behaviour Patterns in Primates and Man*, pp. 119–143. Oxford University Press.

Tooby J and Cosmides L (2008) The Evolutionary Psychology of the Emotions and Their Relationship to Internal Regulatory Variables. In: Lewis M, Haviland-Jones JM, and Barrett LF (eds) *Handbook of Emotions, 3rd Ed*. New York: Guilford Press., pp. 114–137.

Tooby J and Cosmides L (2016) Human cooperation shows the distinctive signatures of adaptations to small-scale social life. *The Behavioral and Brain Sciences* 39: e54. DOI: 10.1017/S0140525X15000266.

Trivers RL (1971) The evolution of reciprocal altruism. *Quarterly Review of Biology* 46(1): 35–57.

Trivers R (2000) The elements of a scientific theory of self-deception. *Annals of the New York Academy of Sciences* 907: 114–131.

Trivers R (2006) Reciprocal altruism: 30 years later. *Cooperation in Primates and Humans* 244(1): 133–140.

Verplaetse J, Vanneste S and Braeckman J (2007) You can judge a book by its cover: the sequel. A kernel of truth in predictive cheating detection. *Evolution and Human Behavior* 28(4): 260–271.

West SA, Griffin AS and Gardner A (2007a) Evolutionary explanations for cooperation. *Current Biology* 17(16): R661–R672. DOI: 10.1016/j.cub.2007.06.004.

West SA, Griffin AS and Gardner A (2007b) Social semantics: altruism, cooperation, mutualism, strong reciprocity and group selection. *Journal of Evolutionary Biology* 20(2): 415–432.

West SA, El Mouden C and Gardner A (2011) Sixteen common misconceptions about the evolution of cooperation in humans. *Evolution and Human Behavior* 32(4): 231–262.

Wilkinson GS (1984) Reciprocal food sharing in the vampire bat. *Nature* 308(5955): 181–184.

Xue M and Silk JB (2012) The role of tracking and tolerance in relationship among friends. *Evolution and Human Behavior* 33(1): 17–25. DOI: 10.1016/j.evolhumbehav.2011.04.004.

Yamagishi T, Kikuchi M and Kosugi M (1999) Trust, gullibility, and social intelligence. *Asian Journal of Social Psychology* 2(1): 145–161.

Yamagishi T, Tanida S, Mashima R, Shimoma E and Kanazawa S (2003) You can judge a book by its cover: evidence that cheaters may look different from cooperators. *Evolution and Human Behavior* 24(4): 290–301.

Zöttl M, Heg D, Chervet N and Taborsky M (2013) Kinship reduces alloparental care in cooperative cichlids where helpers pay-to-stay. *Nature Communications* 4(1): 1341. DOI: 10.1038/ncomms2344.

The Trivers–Willard Hypothesis

Catherine Salmon and Jessica Hehman

INTRODUCTION

While many species do not engage in extensive parental care (Alcock, 2001), for others, including humans, parents contribute substantially to the survival and success of their offspring. Trivers (1972) defined parental investment as any investment by the parent in an individual offspring that increases the offspring's chance of surviving (and reproductive potential) at the expense of the parent's ability to invest in other offspring, current or future. For some species this investment consists mainly of providing food, shelter, and protection from predators. For humans, it involves not only these elements but also the tools for social success including the development of a variety of skills (everything from hunting and weaving to education in the modern world). In general, an offspring's fitness increases with the amount of parental investment it receives. Parental investment has been the target of an extensive amount of research activity from

biologists, psychologists, and anthropologists, among others, in the pursuit of understanding the factors that shape how much and when parents allocate resources toward offspring (for reviews see Geary, 2016; Salmon, 2016). There are many factors that influence the amount of parental investment parents provide and selection has favored mechanisms of parental care that have the effect of increasing the fitness of the parent by favoring offspring who are likely to provide a greater reproductive return on their parents' investment (Daly and Wilson, 1995). These factors that influence the costs and benefits of parental investment include such factors as parental and offspring age (Daly and Wilson, 1988; Salmon and Daly, 1998; Volk and Atkinson, 2013), number of offspring (Daly and Wilson, 1995), paternity uncertainty (Alvergne et al., 2010; Apicella and Marlowe, 2007), offspring expected future prospects (Daly and Wilson, 1988; Trivers and Willard, 1973), offspring need (Beaulieu and Bugental, 2008; Bugental et al., 2010), offspring sex (Trivers and Willard, 1973), and parental resources (Davis et al., 1999; Trivers and Willard, 1973). The Trivers–Willard hypothesis, the focus of this chapter, concerns the interplay between offspring sex, offspring expected future prospects, and parental resources.

The Trivers–Willard hypothesis is based on three assumptions. The first is that parental condition (typically maternal condition) influences offspring condition. The second is that offspring condition persists into adulthood, such that it influences reproductive value. The third is that adult males will benefit more in terms of lifetime reproductive success than adult females by small advantages in condition. Trivers and Willard (1973) suggested that when one sex has a greater variance in lifetime reproductive success than the other and parents (specifically mothers) vary in their physical condition or access to resources, differences in preferences for offspring of the two sexes are likely to evolve. When mothers are in good condition, they should prefer the offspring sex with greater variance in reproductive success. When mothers are in poor condition, they should prefer the offspring sex with less variance in reproductive success. Two mechanisms have been proposed to explain how this occurs. In one, mothers in good condition bias the sex ratio of offspring toward males while mothers in poor condition bias their offspring sex ratio toward females. In the second, mothers bias parental care such that mothers in good condition invest more in male offspring, while mothers in poor condition invest more in female offspring.

males obtain more matings than smaller less dominant ones. Males born large, due to well-nourished healthy mothers, are better able to compete for food and other resources and become dominant as adults. Males born smaller due to mothers in poor nutritional condition are likely to be less successful in competition for food and resources and less likely to become dominant as adults. The impact of maternal condition is less substantial for female offspring in terms of their reproductive prospects. Since access to females is a limiting factor on reproductive success for males, the majority of females will have the opportunity to breed, even if of smaller than average size. Such a female would be likely to out-reproduce a similarly smaller than average male. Thus, Trivers and Willard (1973) claimed that when polygynous mammals can produce male offspring that are larger and healthier than average, they should favor them and that when their offspring are likely to be smaller than average and perhaps less healthy, they should favor daughters. Clutton-Brock et al. (1984) tested this hypothesis in a herd of Scottish red deer. They found that socially dominant females, who were in superior physical condition, produced more male than female offspring and that their male offspring produced more offspring in turn than their female offspring. Correspondingly, subordinate females gave birth to more daughters who had greater reproductive success in turn than the sons subordinate females produced. For this mechanism, the favoring of one sex occurs before birth so as to shift the sex ratio of offspring produced.

Sex Ratio Manipulation

Trivers and Willard (1973) suggested that selection should favor parents that produce greater numbers of the sex that is likely to have more offspring than the other, which is condition dependent. For example, in highly polygynous mammals, larger more dominant

Post-Birth Investment Manipulation

This mechanism, rather than influence the sex ratio of offspring born, works via differential investment post-birth. The rationale is similar to that of sex ratio manipulation. When parental resources have a greater impact on male reproductive success, parents should invest more post-birth in male off-spring and if parental resources have a greater benefit for female reproductive success, parental investment should be preferentially directed toward female offspring. An extreme example can be seen in Dickemann's (1979) review of the incidence of infanticide within the Indian caste system. Female infanticide was frequent in the highest castes prior to the 20th century and has been attributed to the highly stratified nature of the caste system such that men could only marry women from a sub-caste equal to or lower than their own (i.e., females could 'marry up' but males could not). This means daughters from the highest caste families would have few options and as a result were sometimes killed shortly after birth. For these high-caste families, investment in males was a better payoff in terms of future grandchildren and so investment was biased toward sons, with some daughters receiving no post-birth investment (e.g., when infanticide was committed). But because lower caste females can marry up, lower caste families often invested more in their daughters who could realize greater reproductive success than their sons, resulting in much lower rates of female infanticide.

The rest of this chapter will review the research testing the Trivers–Willard hypothesis in non-human species and humans as well as examine the evidence that relates to these two proposed mechanisms. While some studies have demonstrated maternal condition as a predictor of sex biases in infant mortality and parental investment, effect sizes have tended to be small. In addition, a number of studies have also failed to find effects in humans altogether. Some of the difficulties in testing the Trivers–Willard hypotheses in large industrialized societies will be discussed, as the strongest evidence in humans for Trivers–Willard effects comes from small-scale societies. The contradictory nature of sex ratio results in non-human mammals will also be explored with regard to the assessment of maternal condition.

TESTS OF THE HYPOTHESIS IN NON-HUMAN ANIMALS

The non-human animal research that examines the Trivers–Willard hypothesis tends to focus on several questions. One is whether it is possible or not for mammalian mothers to adaptively control the sex of their offspring? If they do so, is it dependent on maternal condition or environmental variables? And what mechanisms might allow for such sex ratio biases? Much of the research is on mammals which will also be the focus of this section of the chapter. However, research on haplodiploid insects has clearly shown facultative adjustment of offspring sex ratio in response to factors influencing offspring future reproductive success (Gullan and Cranston, 2010; West and Sheldon, 2002). The mechanism is clear here as well. Females can control the sex of their offspring by either fertilizing their eggs (producing females) or leaving them unfertilized (producing males). Mammals have a bit of a different problem due to chromosomal sex determination and thus a lot of attention has been paid recently to possible mechanisms for maternal allocation of sex in such species. Many mammalian species have been examined in search of Trivers–Willard effects with mixed results. Some reasons for these discrepant findings are discussed later in the chapter, including how and when maternal condition is assessed and whether offspring fitness is measured.

Perhaps the species most associated with early tests of the Trivers–Willard hypothesis and the role of maternal condition is *Cervus elaphus*, or red deer (Clutton-Brock et al., 1984). This is a polygynous species of ungulate where maternal investment results in increased offspring quality extending into adulthood. As a result, Trivers–Willard would predict that mothers in superior condition should invest more in male offspring because only high quality males will be successful in competition with other males and have high reproductive success, while reproductive success in female offspring will be less variable. Studies have shown that mothers in comparatively top condition are more likely to produce male offspring in red deer (Clutton-Brock et al., 1984), reindeer (Trivers and Willard, 1973), and Alaskan moose (Veeroja et al., 2010). More recently, Ceacero and colleagues (2018) examined maternal investment in a captive population of red deer, finding support for Trivers–Willard in maternal investment in male calves. Older mothers with a greater body mass produced male calves earlier in the season that were heavier at weaning, a substantial advantage for males. For mothers giving birth to female calves, they only gave birth early when the mothers were in good condition; it was unrelated to maternal age. Another recent study of red deer in a low-density woodland population in northeastern Poland found that while the overall fetal sex ratio did not differ from parity, a mother's probability of having a male offspring increased with her body mass independent of her age (Borowik and Jedrzejewska, 2017). However, the authors noted that they did not track offspring reproductive success, which, in fact, most tests of the Trivers–Willard hypothesis fail to do. So they found support for a bias in favoring sons for heavier mothers but they did not test that these sons produced more grandchildren for their mothers. In addition, a study testing Trivers–Willard in dairy cows (Roche et al., 2006) demonstrated that mothers in poorer condition were less likely to have male calves. For those cows that lost little weight between calving and their next conception, there was a 14% increase in male calves indicating that good physiological condition made male calf production more likely to occur.

Tests of sex ratio bias in wild or feral horses, largely monomorphic but polygynous, have been conducted with respect to mare body condition at conception (Cameron et al., 1999). Kaimanawa horses are a population where male reproductive success is improved with slight advantages in condition. In this population, mares with a female foal

experienced poorer condition at conception than those with a male foal and mares who had different sexes in different years were in poorer condition when they conceived their female foal. An additional study in this New Zealand feral horse population that assessed maternal condition before and after conception in order to measure the change in condition around conception for individual mares revealed an extreme sex ratio bias. Only 3% of mares who lost condition during that time produced a male foal, while 80% that gained condition produced a male foal (Cameron and Linklater, 2007).

While many of these tests of the Trivers–Willard hypothesis are of ungulates, there are studies that examine parental bias of sex ratio in other mammalian species. For example, a study of paroxetine exposure in wild derived mice (*Mus musculus*) found that mothers exposed to paroxetine had female biased litters (Gaukler et al., 2016). Interestingly, this study also compared the reproductive success of the male and female offspring and reported that the reproductive success of sons was reduced more than daughters in these litters. In addition, the sons of the exposed mothers only managed to obtain about half as many territories as the ones born to the control mothers, an indicator of their lack of success in male competition. The researchers also noted that the drug exposed mothers' litters weighed less than controls, as a result of the exposed mothers being in poorer condition. Their interpretation was that the exposed mothers increased their fitness by biasing their litters toward females who were less negatively affected than males.

However, a number of studies have failed to find Trivers–Willard effects (for a review see Sheldon and West, 2004) including some that have found better condition mothers to have more daughters. For example, a study of maternal investment bias in Montana elk indicated that improved maternal condition was associated with producing more daughters (Cunningham et al., 2009). Clancey and Byers (2016) tested the Trivers–Willard hypothesis in a Montana population of pronghorn (*Antilocapra americana*) and reported that while females in good condition or who were socially dominant produced larger fawns that were in better condition, there was no consistent sex bias in offspring favoring males. Some studies also highlight the relevance of the specific adult environment. While one study of mountain goats (*Oreamnos americanus*) (Côté and Festa-Bianchet, 2001) indicated that maternal age strongly correlated with body mass and social rank and had a large effect on sex ratio such that the youngest mothers produced 70% daughters and the oldest ones produced 70% sons, a recent update with a larger sample size and measuring maternal condition at conception revealed a more complicated picture. Now the offspring sex ratio varied with adult ratio but only for mothers in good condition at conception. For these dominant mothers, their bias toward males decreased from 80% males to 20% as the adult sex ratio became more male biased (Hamel et al., 2016). In this case, mothers in good condition produced more of the rarer sex, who presumably would do better in terms of their own reproductive success, though offspring reproductive success was not reported in this study. In a similar vein, a study of sex ratios in impala (*Aepyceros melampus*) and kudu (*Tragelaphus strepsiceros*) over a four-year span in South Africa demonstrated that impala sex ratios across the population as a whole were biased toward females in the absence of predation (O'Kane and Macdonald, 2016). As there was an overabundance of adult males, from a reproductive standpoint, it would be beneficial to produce daughters who are not likely to miss out on chances to reproduce in the same way some males will in such a high male competition environment.

One explanation put forth in some studies for the lack of consistent findings is that in species with male dispersal, daughters increase local competition such that only mothers in top condition can afford to produce daughters (Clutton-Brock et al., 1982).

Cameron's (2004) meta-analysis of mammalian sex ratio studies suggested that studies investigating maternal condition around the time of conception show the strongest support for the prediction that mothers in good condition (relative to the average) bias their litters toward sons. Cameron (2004) also suggested that excess glucose might play a role in a mechanism favoring male blastocysts over female ones. Thus, mothers in superior body condition with abundant food and superior body weight (excess glucose) around the time of conception may produce more male offspring. So mother's condition at implantation may be more relevant to testing the Trivers–Willard hypothesis than condition at birth, for example. This might also indicate that some bias favoring female offspring is actually the result of greater mammalian male vulnerability across the lifespan including at the fetal stage (Geary, 2015). However, a recent study of maternal glucocorticoid levels in black howler monkeys (*Alouatta pigra*) found that variation in glucocorticoid concentrations around conception predicted infant sex such that there were fewer female births under adverse environmental conditions (Rangel-Negrin et al., 2017) due to sex differences in conceptus survival.

One area that has received relatively little attention in the animal literature is the possible role of paternal condition in sex role biases. The majority of research has focused on the ability of the mother to invest in offspring to maximize her fitness. However, Perret (2018) examined the possible role of paternal testosterone on sex ratio biases at birth in the lesser mouse lemur (*Microcebus murinus*) which is a promiscuous monomorphic primate species in which daughters stay in the natal range with their mothers and males disperse. In a captive population, housed in different conditions, the reproductive success of mothers was independent of body condition. However, high male testosterone levels, particularly those of dominant males, were significantly correlated with more infants produced in male-biased litters.

TESTS OF THE HYPOTHESIS IN HUMAN POPULATIONS

In humans, the evidence for Trivers–Willard effects has been mixed. Recent research on Trivers–Willard effects in humans has suggested several proximate mechanisms that lead to biased sex ratios as well as biased parental investment, including factors such as morning sickness (Almond et al., 2016), postnatal depression (Johns and Myers, 2016), and financial investment in education of offspring and setting educational expectations for offspring (Hopcroft and Martin, 2016). However, other research has found no evidence of Trivers–Willard effects in humans (Beaulieu and Bugental, 2008; Freese and Powell, 1999; Keller et al., 2001; Sieff, 1990; Stein et al., 2004). The inconsistency in the findings has been attributed by some researchers to modern, contemporary society where abundant resources do not necessitate the activation of Trivers–Willard effects (Freese and Powell, 1999) and/or a lack of appropriate, reliable and valid measures of parental investment in humans, which is much longer and complex than periods of parental investment in most non-human animals (Sieff, 1990). We first describe tests of the biased sex ratio manipulation and post-birth investment mechanisms in humans, then we address limitations in this line of research that may account for some of the inconsistency in findings.

Tests of Biased Sex Ratios in Humans

Pollet et al. (2009) reported that lower ranking polygynous wives in Rwanda have significantly more daughters than higher ranking polygynous wives or monogamously married women in a population in which male reproductive success is extremely variable and strongly dependent on adult status and access to resources. Bereczkei and Dunbar's (1997, 2002) studies of Hungarian Gypsy populations

also reveal Trivers–Willard effects. Compared to native Hungarians, Gypsies are lower in social status and have substantially more daughters than sons. Gypsy women are also much more likely to marry up the social status scale than are men, and they typically outreproduce their Gypsy brothers. They also, on average, have healthier babies than those Gypsy women who marry within their own group. The same pattern was found among contemporary Chinese peasants with high-status families more likely to have more sons than daughters (Luo et al., 2016). This evidence suggests that higher status individuals produce more male offspring whereas lower status individuals produce more female offspring.

Consistent with high status being linked to having more sons, research has found that the sex ratio favors males in wealthier households. An examination of infant survival in Northern Ghana, a polygynous society where wealthy men have the opportunity to have greater number of offspring via multiple wives, demonstrated that in wealthy households, men have a greater lifetime number of offspring (6.0 versus 3.4) than men from poor households (van Bodegom et al., 2013). In addition, the sex ratio slightly favored males in the rich households (0.52 versus 0.49), and sons had lower mortality (during the first 3 years of life) in rich households compared to poor ones. Cameron and Dalerum's (2009) study of Trivers–Willard effects in the *Forbes'* list of billionaires indicated that people in the top economic bracket have more grandchildren via their sons than daughters and that mothers at this highest socioeconomic status have more sons.

Almond and Edlund's (2007) study of natality data for white females in the United States between 1983 and 2001, found that younger, more highly educated, and married women gave birth to more sons. When they looked at infant deaths, there were more male deaths when the mother was younger and unmarried.

Marital status was also related to sex ratio in a Venezuelan study of demographic registration data from 1988 and 1990 (Chacon-Puignau and Jaffe, 1996). They examined sex ratio at birth as well as fetal and infant deaths and reported finding support for the Trivers–Willard hypothesis in a cross-sectional sample of the Venezuelan population. Factors associated with producing a son included: being married, higher educational levels for both parents, being the first child, and similar socioeconomic statuses for the parents (which was assumed to increase relationship stability). One parent being illiterate and the absence of medical assistance were associated with producing a daughter and considered to be indicators of high levels of poverty.

Kanazawa (2005) proposed a generalized Trivers–Willard hypothesis such that parents that possess any heritable trait (not just those with access to resources or social status, for example) which increases male reproductive success more than female reproductive success in a particular environment will have more sons, while those parents who possess a heritable trait that increases female reproductive success more than that of males will produce more daughters. Note that this is a sex ratio not a post-birth investment model of Trivers–Willard, which has been examined less frequently in humans, though as noted previously, Hungarian Gypsy data has supported a sex ratio manipulation model. Kanazawa (2005) predicted that as physical size (height and weight) is heritable and has been more beneficial to males ancestrally in terms of intrasexual competition, parents who are taller and heavier should produce more sons than daughters and those parents who are shorter and weigh less should produce more daughters. This was tested using follow up samples from the National Child Development Study (NCDS) and the 1970 British Cohort Study (BCS70). When Kanazawa examined the impact of body size of the number of male or female fetuses, height and weight were predictive of fetal sex such that taller and larger parents had more sons than shorter and smaller parents.

Kanazawa followed this up with two additional studies examining the relationship between parental attractiveness and offspring sex ratio. While size and social status tend to benefit males more than females in terms of reproductive success (Betzig, 1986; Hopcraft, 2006), physical beauty has a greater reproductive return for females (Buss, 1989; Symons, 1979). Kanazawa (2007) tested his generalized Trivers–Willard hypothesis prediction that physically attractive parents would have more daughters and less sons as beauty benefits females more than males, based on heritability estimates for attractiveness in twins (McGovern et al., 1996; Rowe et al., 1989). Using data from the U.S. National Longitudinal Study of Adolescent Health (Add Health), he examined the relationship between the sex of first child and a measure of the physical attractiveness of respondents in the study. Respondents in the top attractiveness category ('very attractive') were 26% less likely to have sons as a first child (controlling for education, race, sex, and income among other variables). A follow up study (Kanazawa, 2011), using the prospectively longitudinal NCDS data in the UK, replicated the results of the previous study. British children who were rated by their teachers as attractive at age 7 had 23% higher odds of having a daughter 40 years later, while those rated as unattractive had 25% higher odds of having a son as their firstborn.

In addition to individual social status, wealth, and other heritable traits that may influence reproductive success of offspring and therefore influence the sex ratio, several studies have shown that mothers who experience a variety of different social and/or economic stressors during the gestational period are more likely to have daughters. Evidence demonstrating this effect includes a comparison of births in East and West Germany following the economic collapse of East Germany (Catalano, 2003), in the United States following the 9/11 terrorist attack (Catalano et al., 2006), following the Kobe earthquake in Japan (Fukuda et al., 1998), in the United States for African American mothers diagnosed with anxiety disorders relative to healthy controls (Subbaraman et al., 2010), and in Slovenia following a 10-year war (Zorn et al., 2002).

Another factor that has been associated with sex of offspring is maternal diet and nutritional status before conception as well as during gestation. In a rural, food-stressed community in southern Ethiopia, there was a strong association between the sex of a mother's most recent offspring and maternal nutritional status, indexed by measures of fat and muscle mass, such that the stronger mothers gave birth to more sons than weaker mothers (Gibson and Mace, 2003). Mathews et al. (2008) suggested that maternal preconception diet influences fetal sex in humans and that high resource availability around the time of conception is linked to differential production of male offspring (as has been demonstrated in some non-human mammalian species). They tested this in a cohort of over 700 white nulliparous women recruited from a hospital in the south of England early in their pregnancies. These pregnant women were blind to the sex of their gestating offspring and gave a retrospective diary of their usual diet over the year prior to conception. Their results indicated that women in the highest third of nutritional energy intake had 11% more sons than those in the lowest third. This suggests that when resources are abundant (i.e., nutrition is good), sex ratios may be biased toward producing more costly male offspring.

Although morning sickness during pregnancy is fairly common, Almond and colleagues (2016) proposed that severe morning sickness, known as *hyperemesis gravidarum* (HG) and which can be fatal, is a proximate mechanism that may influence sex ratios. In a large Swedish sample, not only was HG found to be more common among less educated women (a proxy for poor maternal condition), HG in the first few weeks of gestation was associated with having more female offspring (Almond et al., 2016). Although

34% of spontaneous abortions were linked to HG, live births were more likely to occur when the woman was more educated and live births from HG pregnancies were more likely to result in female offspring. Together, these findings suggest that the number of male offspring is being limited by differential mortality rates of male and female fetuses as a function of early maternal gestational condition (Almond et al., 2016). Using data collected from the 2001 and 2006 Demographic and Health Surveys (DHS) of developing countries, Valente (2015) tested Trivers–Willard predictions of sex ratio bias following a period of civil conflict in Nepal. Civil conflict increased the likelihood of spontaneous abortion, with male fetuses more likely to be spontaneously aborted relative to female fetuses, and was more likely to result in a female live birth. The consistent finding of disproportionate loss of male fetuses as a function of maternal condition suggests the mechanism regulating sex ratios in humans as a function of maternal condition is acting post-fertilization rather than at conception (Almond et al., 2016; Valente, 2015).

This point of sex biased retention (or loss) before birth versus sex biased conception is reinforced by the fact that males exhibit more genetic vulnerability (in terms of susceptibility to threats to development) beginning at conception and continuing throughout the life span, including greater variation in male growth, health, and mortality relative to females (Geary, 2015). Therefore, if male growth and mortality are more sensitive to energetic conditions during gestations, it could be that mothers (especially those in resource-limited environments) experience higher spontaneous loss of male fetuses than female fetuses. Indeed, recent research has found that, globally, human sex ratios are related to mortality and life expectancy such that countries with longer and healthier life expectancy were found to have significantly more sons than those with lower life expectancy (Dama, 2011).

As mentioned previously, the evidence for Trivers–Willard effects on the sex ratio in humans has been mixed. Stein and colleagues' (2004) historical study of the impact of acute undernutrition during the Dutch Hunger Winter of 1944–45 (a 7-month famine) did not find support for Trivers–Willard. Specifically, undernutrition was not associated with an increased number of female births. Similarly, a recent large cohort study in Japan found no effect of maternal condition (including age, body mass index, job status, education level, medical history, or income) on sex of offspring suggesting no Trivers–Willard effect on sex ratio (Morita et al., 2017). It is important to point out caveats of measuring human sex ratio that may contribute to the inconsistent findings (especially relative to the non-human literature). Specifically, some populations may engage in selective infanticide that is not being captured in the human studies. For example, in the Dama (2011) global sex ratio study, several countries were excluded from analysis due to known widespread practice of medical termination of female fetuses (e.g., Afghanistan, Bangladesh, China, India, and others). Another consideration is that (many) humans in the modern environment do not face the energetic constraints that may have resulted in loss of a male fetus in our ancestral environment.

Tests of Biased Parental Investment in Humans

Several studies have shown sex-biased investment (Gaulin and Robbins, 1991; Hopcroft, 2005; Kanazawa, 2005), while others have found no such effects (Beaulieu and Bugental, 2008; Freese and Powell, 1999; Keller et al., 2001; Sieff, 1990). Studies in the United States (Gaulin and Robbins, 1991) and Kenya (Cronk, 1989) have suggested that female infants from low-income families are nursed more than males. A more recent study in Kenya, however, found that in drought-ridden areas only mothers who had insufficient nutrition breastfed their daughters more than their sons with no difference in breastfeeding of sons and daughters when the mothers had adequate nutrition (Fujita et al., 2012).

Like the earlier classic example of the lower caste Indians (Dickemann, 1979), Hungarian Gypsy parents (again, who are of lower status than native Hungarians) invest more heavily in their daughters than their sons (Bereczkei and Dunbar, 1997). Bereczkei and Dunbar (1997) also found that Gypsy women spent more time nursing their firstborn daughters than sons, when compared to native Hungarians, and provided more education for their daughters (their education was not free and came at a significant cost to the parents). Interestingly, daughter-biased investment has also been reported in Hutterite colonies (Margulis et al., 1993), where daughters were nursed longer than sons, leading to a longer interbirth interval after the birth of a daughter.

As was the case for Almond and Edlund's (2007) highly educated married mothers, there are times when investment favors sons over daughters. In societies in which the possession of resources significantly improves male reproductive success (such as India's caste system), a preference for sons, or for investing heavily in them, will be seen among the wealthy (as it has been in India). This was also the case in 18th-century northern German villages (Voland, 1998) and has been noted in the records of probated wills in British Columbia (Smith et al., 1987).

Johns and Myers (2016) suggested that postnatal depression may be a proximate mechanism by which maternal investment is withdrawn from an offspring when that investment is less likely to pay off in terms of the offspring's future reproductive success. Consistent with Trivers–Willard effects, postnatal depression was found to be more common with mothers of sons when mothers have less social support and when there was a complicated birth that may signal bleak future reproductive outcomes (Johns and Myers, 2016). Another proximate mechanism that has received consistent cross-cultural support is that of parental investment in educational attainment of their offspring. In Kenya, richer families were found to invest more in their sons' educations, while poorer families invested more in their daughters' educations (Borgerhoff Mulder, 1998). The same pattern was found among contemporary Chinese peasants such that high-status families' sons obtained higher education than what was obtained by the daughters (Luo et al., 2016). Studies in the United States have also found that whereas sons of high-status men obtain higher education, daughters of low-status men obtain higher education (Hopcroft, 2005). High-status parents were more likely to send their sons to private school and set higher educational expectations for their sons, while low-status parents were more likely to send their daughters to private school and set higher educational expectations for their daughters (Hopcroft and Martin, 2016). Another study found that high-status fathers provided more financial support during college to their sons than their daughters, and low-status fathers showed the opposite pattern of support by providing more financial support to their daughters than to their sons (Pink et al., 2017).

However, as mentioned earlier, documentation of Trivers–Willard effects in humans has been inconsistent. In a large sample of children from the United States, there was no evidence that high-status parents invested more in sons and low-status parents invested more in daughters (Keller et al., 2001). Likewise, Ellis and Bonin (2002) also found no evidence of Trivers–Willard effects in contemporary North America. Freese and Powell's (1999) test of the Trivers–Willard hypothesis in the United States via the National Educational Longitudinal Study of 1988 (NELS), a survey of over 24,000 eighth and tenth grade students, and a 1990 follow-up also found little evidence of the predicted Trivers–Willard parental investment biases. An investigation of differential maternal investment as a function of health status of offspring as well as

maternal resources found that low resource mothers were more likely to heavily invest in the low-risk child, while high-resource mothers were more likely to heavily invest in the high-risk child, but found no reliable support for Trivers–Willard effects (Beaulieu and Bugental, 2008). A study in rural Dominica also revealed no evidence for Trivers–Willard effects in that age of weaning was not related to household wealth or other maternal support variables (Quinlan et al., 2003).

Limitations of Testing the Hypothesis in Humans

There are several limitations in the existing research that may help explain the inconsistent support for Trivers–Willard effects in humans, including what is actually being measured and when it is being measured. As pointed out by Veller et al. (2016), investigations of Trivers–Willard effects that have focused on biased sex ratios have found more consistent evidence, whereas studies that have focused on biased parental investment have found more inconsistent results. One possible explanation for this is that measuring parental investment is more complex than measuring sex ratios. Specifically, parental investment, compared to sex ratios, (1) is not as readily observable as an outcome of Trivers–Willard effects and (2) can be measured many different ways (Veller et al., 2016). Grant (2003) suggested the lack of consensus among researchers regarding valid measures of parental investment could be one reason for the inconsistent findings of Trivers–Willard effects on parental investment. Indeed, not only is the lack of consensus a problem, but also the numerous ways in which parental investment has been measured for testing the Trivers–Willard hypothesis, including how long the child/parent relationship is observed following birth, investment behaviors that are observed (e.g., time spent holding, nursing, interacting with the child, etc.), outcome variables (e.g, health of offspring, resource allocation, education, etc.), as well as parental self-report measures (Cronk, 2007). It appears that more subjective measures (e.g., self-report, diaries) tend to find no support for Trivers–Willard effects (Keller et al., 2001); whereas more objective measures (e.g., birth intervals and length of breastfeeding) have tended to find (at least limited) support for Trivers–Willard effects (Koziel and Ulijaszek, 2001). As pointed out by Cronk (2007), what is missing from the operationalization of parental investment is a direct measure of the effect (or payoff) of the investment in terms of the child's reproductive success.

A recent study (Song, 2018) reflected on the challenges of testing the Trivers–Willard hypothesis in humans, citing the problems of measuring parental investment, and arguing for using alternatives to self-report for assessing investment. Instead Song (2018) looked at sales of student backpacks in China using online purchasing data with parental investment measured by how much money parents spent on their children's backpacks. The results indicated the existence of daughter preference and son preference in contemporary China such that daughter preference (indexed by the amount of money spent on backpacks) was only present in those with low economic status, while son preference was present among those with the highest economic status. There was also a middle economic status group that invested equally in sons and daughters. This study highlights the research opportunities big data may provide in this area.

Another issue surrounding the measurement of parental investment concerns who is being compared. Schnettler (2009) identified two main problems with between-family comparisons employed by some studies: (1) the studies tend to have relatively small sample sizes (making it more difficult to detect any differences in investment); and (2) The families being compared tend to be gender homogeneous families in which families with only sons are compared to families with only

daughters. Given that parental investment is multifaceted, parents may withdraw investment in one area and compensate by increasing investment in another area. Therefore, Schnettler (2009) suggested that researchers use within-family designs and compare investment across different areas in mixed-sex sibling dyads for a more robust test of Trivers–Willard effects.

However, the largest limitation facing this area of research may be the lack of understanding of the proximate mechanisms underlying Trivers–Willard effects (Douhard, 2017; Kolk and Schnettler, 2013; Lynch et al., 2018). While there are no known physiological mechanisms that allow mammals to maternally alter the sex of their offspring (Douhard, 2017), it is also true that the current methodologies being employed to investigate Trivers–Willard effects on parental investment present a mismatch to the underlying psychological mechanism which presumably was designed to work largely on an unconscious level (Lynch et al., 2018). The proposed mismatch here would be between the self-reported measures of parental investment that have been most commonly used in investigations of Trivers–Willard effects on parental investment and actual behavioral measures of parental behavior. In one of the few studies to use an experimental manipulation to investigate Trivers–Willard effects in humans, Lynch and colleagues (2018) primed individuals to feel either wealthy or poor and then used a behavioral measure to identify whether the *condition prime* led to behavioral preferences for having sons versus daughters (i.e., whether they choose to make a donation to a boys' versus a girls' charity). While they did find a trend suggesting findings consistent with Trivers–Willard effects (i.e., men from low socioeconomic status showed a slight preference to adopt girls rather than boys before the wealthy/poor prime), overall there was only limited support for Trivers–Willard predictions (Lynch et al., 2018). Similarly, Du and Mace (2017) interviewed adult males and females from five villages in Tibet and found a mismatch between parents' subjective stated preference for offspring sex and objective behavioral measures of parental investment, including breastfeeding and interbirth intervals. This suggests that offspring sex preference may not map onto actual biases in parental investment and highlights that there are a multitude of factors beyond prenatal energetic conditions that may be relevant to understanding biases in post-birth investment.

Another complication that arises from the lack of understanding of the underlying mechanisms is that researchers are also lacking understanding of *when* it is best to measure factors that would influence Trivers–Willard effects (for example, maternal condition; Kolk and Schnettler, 2013). Without knowing what the mechanism is, it is difficult to determine when that mechanism is most likely to be activated. Is the best time to measure maternal condition pre-conception or during gestation? If during gestation, when during gestation? Perhaps around the time of birth, maternal condition or resources may be more relevant in humans if their main mechanisms are post-birth ones. These questions still remain to be answered and are confounded with the issue of *how* to measure maternal condition. For example, some researchers have suggested that most measurements of maternal condition have been inadequate, especially measurements that were not taken around the time of conception (Douhard, 2017). Measures of maternal condition that have been used in past studies include individual factors such as weight, body mass, age, parity, social status, change in body condition from pre-conception to post-conception, exposure to stress, female testosterone levels, as well as measures of environmental condition (Douhard, 2017; Kolk and Schnettler, 2013; Veller et al., 2016). In fact, some researchers have proposed the lack of an adequate measure of maternal condition is one of the largest obstacles in investigations of Trivers–Willard effects (Veller et al., 2016).

Finally, it is important to note the lack of complete tests of the Trivers–Willard hypothesis. As described earlier, the Trivers–Willard hypothesis rests on three assumptions: (1) parental condition, typically maternal, influences offspring condition; (2) offspring condition persists into adulthood, such that it influences reproductive value; and (3) adult males will benefit more in terms of lifetime reproductive success than adult females by small advantages in condition. Many studies, however, fail to test the third assumption and do not assess offspring fitness or their reproductive outcomes (Cronk, 2007; Douhard, 2017). All of the above discussed limitations may contribute not only to the discrepancy in the findings, but also the small effect sizes that are typically found (Hopcroft and Martin, 2016; Kolk and Schnettler, 2013).

CONCLUSION

The Trivers–Willard hypothesis suggests that selection has shaped a mechanism (or mechanisms) to direct parental investment toward the offspring most likely to increase their fitness. In non-human animals this has frequently been tested in mammals where good maternal condition is associated with greater success on the part of male offspring with the assumption that the sex ratio of offspring can be skewed to favor greater parental fitness. In the human animal, research has focused more often on a variety of measures of parental investment in male and female offspring with the assumption that when males benefit more from investment and parents can provide it, they receive more with the same being true of circumstances where female offspring may achieve greater reproductive success. This chapter attempts to summarize some of this work and the limitations of what has been done so far. The general conclusion is that the evidence is still mixed with the most support for Trivers–Willard being found in biased sex ratios in non-human animals though more extensive models and tests of local competition versus Trivers–Willard are needed. In humans, the results are even more equivocal and are attenuated by the problem of detecting small effect sizes.

In future research, we would recommend a number of approaches that might help to clarify the current picture. The first focuses on examining possible mechanisms for sex selective investment in humans, including the possible role of spontaneous miscarriages as a way of skewing the sex ratio at birth. Are spontaneous miscarriages associated with maternal condition, particularly in circumstances where it would be more beneficial to invest in one sex versus the other? In this case, would the best timing for assessing maternal condition be conception? For post-birth differential investment would maternal condition be best assessed at the birth of offspring? What about paternal condition – is there any evidence of a male contribution to Trivers–Willard effects (i.e., a cue or signal contingent on paternal status or resources that can predict sex ratios at birth)? In addition, there is the question of how to best measure parental investment. As seen earlier, there are many different approaches to this across studies, making it difficult to compare results. It may be that a multifactorial measure of parental investment, capturing a variety of parental behaviors from breastfeeding to skill teaching to financial investment, would be a more useful way to try to sum up the wide range of behaviors that parents engage in that increase offspring fitness.

Two more limitations of the work in this area that need to be addressed include the examination of the basic assumptions of the model, in particular the assumption of the impact on offspring lifetime reproductive success. This is something few human or non-human animal studies examine. Along with this is the taking into account of the range of offspring factors that influence their expected future fitness, including local competition which has been examined in the non-human animal literature but not so much considered in research with humans.

REFERENCES

Alcock, J. (2001). *Animal Behavior: An Evolutionary Approach*, 7th ed. Sunderland, MA: Sinauer Associates.

Almond, D., & Edlund, L. (2007). Trivers–Willard at birth and one year: evidence from US natality data 1983–2001. *Proceedings of the Royal Society of London. Series B: Biological Sciences*, 274(1624), 2491–2496.

Almond, D., Edlund, L., Joffe, M., & Palme, M. (2016). An adaptive significance of morning sickness? Trivers–Willard and *hyperemesis gravidarum*. *Economics and Human Biology*, 21, 167–171.

Alvergne, A., Faurie, C., & Raymond, M. (2010). Are parents' perceptions of offspring facial resemblance consistent with actual resemblance? Effects on parental investment. *Evolution and Human Behavior*, 31(1), 7–15.

Apicella, C. L., & Marlowe, F. W. (2007). Men's reproductive investment decisions: mating, parenting and self-perceived mate value. *Human Nature*, 18(1), 22–34.

Beaulieu, D. A., & Bugental, D. (2008). Contingent parental investment: an evolutionary framework for understanding early interaction between mothers and children. *Evolution and Human Behavior*, 29(4), 249–255.

Bereczkei, T., & Dunbar, R. I. M. (1997). Female-biased reproductive strategies in a Hungarian Gypsy population. *Proceedings of the Royal Society of London. Series B: Biological Sciences*, 264(1378), 17–22.

Bereczkei, T., & Dunbar, R. I. M. (2002). Helping-at-the-nest and sex-biased parental investment in a Hungarian Gypsy population. *Current Anthropology*, 43(5), 804–809.

Betzig, L. L. (1986). *Despotism and Differential Reproduction: A Darwinian View of History*. New York: Aldine.

Borgerhoff Mulder, M. (1998). The demographic transition: are we any closer to an evolutionary explanation? *Trends in Ecology and Evolution*, 13(7), 266–270.

Borowik, T., & Jędrzejewska, B. (2017). Heavier females produce more sons in a low-density population of red deer. *Journal of Zoology*, 302(1), 57–62.

Bugental, D. B., Beaulieu, D. A., & Silbert-Geiger, A. (2010). Increases in parental investment and child health as a result of an early intervention.

Journal of Experimental Child Psychology, 106(1), 30–40.

Buss, D. M. (1989). Sex differences in human mate preferences: evolutionary hypotheses tested in 37 cultures. *Behavioral and Brain Sciences*, 12(1), 1–49.

Cameron, E. Z. (2004). Facultative adjustment of mammalian sex ratios in support of the Trivers–Willard hypothesis: evidence for a mechanism. *Proceedings of the Royal Society of London. Series B: Biological Sciences*, 271(1549), 1723–1728.

Cameron, E. Z., & Dalerum, F. (2009). A Trivers–Willard effect in contemporary humans: male-biased sex ratios among billionaires. *PLoS ONE*, 4(1), e4195.

Cameron, E. Z., & Linklater, W. L. (2007). Extreme sex ratio variation in relation to change in condition around conception. *Biology Letters*, 3(4), 395–397.

Cameron, E. Z., Linklater, W. L., Stafford, K. J., & Veltman, C. J. (1999). Birth sex ratios relate to mare condition at conception in Kaimanawa horses. *Behavioral Ecology*, 10(5), 472–475.

Catalano, R. (2003). Sex ratios in the two Germanies: a test of the economic stress hypothesis. *Human Reproduction*, 18(9), 1972–1975.

Catalano, R., Bruckner, T., Marks, A., & Eskenazi, B. (2006). Exogenous shocks to the human sex ratio: the case of September 11, 2001 in New York City. *Human Reproduction*, 21(12), 3127–3131.

Ceacero, F., Komárková, M., García, A. J., & Gallego, L. (2018). Different maternal investment strategies for male and female calves in a polygynous mammal. *Current Zoology*, 1–9. doi:10.1093/cz/zoy049.

Chacon-Puignau, G. C., & Jaffe, K. (1996). Sex ratio at birth deviations in modern Venezuela: the Trivers–Willard effect. *Social Biology*, 43(3-4), 257–270.

Clancey, E., & Byers, J. A. (2016). A comprehensive test of the Trivers–Willard hypothesis in pronghorn (*Antilocapra americana*). *Journal of Mammalogy*, 97(1), 179–186.

Clutton-Brock, T. H., Albon, S. D., & Guinness, F. E. (1982). Competition between female relatives in a matrilocal mammal. *Nature*, 300(5888), 178–180.

Clutton-Brock, T. H., Albon, S. D., & Guinness, F. E. (1984). Maternal dominance, breeding success and birth sex ratio in red deer. *Nature*, 308(5957), 358–360.

Côté, S. D., & Festa-Bianchet, M. (2001). Offspring sex ratio in relation to maternal age and social rank in mountain goats (*Oreamnos americanus*). *Behavioral Ecology and Sociobiology*, 49(4), 260–265.

Cronk, L. (1989). Low socioeconomic status and female-based parental investment: the Mukogodo example. *American Anthropologist*, 91(2), 414–429.

Cronk, L. (2007). Boy or girl: gender preferences from a Darwinian point of view. *Reproductive Biomedicine Online*, 15(Suppl_2), 23–32.

Cunningham, J. A., Hamlin, K. L., & Lemke, T. O. (2009). Fetal sex ratios in southwestern Montana elk. *The Journal of Wildlife Management*, 73(5), 639–646.

Daly, M., & Wilson, M. (1995). Discriminative parental solicitude and the relevance of evolutionary models to the analysis of motivational systems. In *The Cognitive Neurosciences*, M. Gazzaniga, ed., pp. 1269–1286. Cambridge, MA: MIT Press.

Daly, M., & Wilson, M. (1988). *Homicide*. Hawthorne, NY: Aldine.

Dama, M. S. (2011). Sex ratio at birth and mortality rates are negatively related in humans. *PLoS ONE*, 6(8), e23792.

Davis, J. N., Todd, P. M. & Bullock, S. (1999). Environment quality predicts parental provisioning decisions. *Proceedings of the Royal Society of London. Series B: Biological Sciences*, 266(1430), 1791–1797.

Dickemann, M. (1979). Female infanticide, reproductive strategies, and social stratification: a preliminary model. In *Evolutionary Biology and Human Social Behavior*, N. A. Chagnon & W. Irons, eds, pp. 321–367. North Scituate, MA: Duxbury Press.

Douhard, M. (2017). Offspring sex ratio in mammals and the Trivers–Willard hypothesis: in pursuit of unambiguous evidence. *Bioessays*, 39(9), 1700043.

Du, J., & Mace, R. (2017). Parental investment in Tibetan populations does not reflect stated cultural norms. *Behavioral Ecology*, 29(1), 106–116.

Ellis, L., & Bonin, S. (2002). Social status and the secondary sex ratio: new evidence on a lingering controversy. *Social Biology*, 49(1–2), 35–42.

Freese, J., & Powell, B. (1999). Sociobiology, status, and parental investment in sons and daughters: testing the Trivers–Willard Hypothesis. *American Journal of Sociology*, 104(6), 1704–1743.

Fujita, M., Roth, E. A., Lo, Y-J., Hurst, C., Vollner, J., & Kendell, A. (2012). Low serum vitamin A mothers breastfeed daughters more often than sons in drought-ridden northern Kenya: a test of the Trivers–Willard hypothesis. *Evolution and Human Behavior*, 33(4), 357–364.

Fukuda, M., Fukuda, K., Shimizu, T., & Moller, H. (1998). Decline in sex ratio at birth after Kobe earthquake. *Human Reproduction*, 13(8), 2321–2322.

Gaukler, S. M., Ruff, J. S., & Potts, W. K. (2016). Paroxetine exposure skews litter sex ratios in mice suggesting a Trivers–Willard process. *Behavioral Ecology*, 27(4), 113–1121.

Gaulin, S. J. C., & Robbins, C. J. (1991). Trivers–Willard effect in contemporary North American society. *American Journal of Physical Anthropology*, 85(1), 61–69.

Geary, D. C. (2015). *Evolution of Vulnerability: Implications for Sex Differences in Health and Development*. Cambridge, MA: Academic Press.

Geary, D. (2016). Evolution of paternal investment. In *The Handbook of Evolutionary Psychology* (2nd edition), D. Buss, ed., pp. 524–541. Hoboken, NJ: John Wiley & Sons.

Gibson, M. A., & Mace, R. (2003). Strong mothers bear more sons in rural Ethiopia. *Proceedings of the Royal Society of London. Series B: Biological Sciences*, 270(Suppl_1), S108–S109.

Grant, V. J. (2003). The maternal dominance hypothesis: questioning Trivers and Willard. *Evolutionary Psychology*, 1(1), 96–107.

Gullan, P. J., & Cranston, P. S. (2010). *The Insects: An Outline of Entomology* (4th edition). Wiley-Blackwell.

Hamel, S., Festa-Bianchet, M., & Côté, S. D. (2016). Offspring sex in mountain goat varies with adult sex ratio but only for mothers in good condition. *Behavioral Ecology and Sociobiology*, 70(1), 123–132.

Hopcroft, R. L. (2005). Parental status and differential investment in sons and daughters: Trivers–Willard revisited. *Social Forces*, 83(3), 1111–1136.

Hopcroft, R. L., & Martin, D. O. (2016). Parental investments and educational outcomes: Trivers–Willard in the U.S. *Frontiers in Sociology*, 1, 1–12. doi.org/10.3389/fsoc.2016.00003.

Johns, S. E., & Myers, S. (2016). Male infants, risk, and postnatal depression: evidence supporting the Trivers–Willard hypothesis in a contemporary low-fertility context. European Human Behaviour and Evolution Association (EHBEA) Conference. LHSTM, London, UK.

Kanazawa, S. (2005). Big and tall parents have more sons: further generalizations of the Trivers–Willard Hypothesis. *Journal of Theoretical Biology*, 235(4), 583–590.

Kanazawa, S. (2007). Beautiful people have more daughters: a further implication of the generalized Trivers–Willard hypothesis (gTWH). *Journal of Theoretical Biology*, 244(1), 133–140.

Kanazawa, S. (2011). Beautiful British parents have more daughters. *Reproductive Sciences*, 18(4), 353–358.

Keller, M. C., Nesse, R. M., & Hofferth, S. (2001). The Trivers–Willard hypothesis of parental investment: no effect in the contemporary United States. *Evolution and Human Behavior*, 22(5), 343–366.

Kolk, M. & Schnettler, S. (2013). Parental status and gender preferences of children: is differential fertility stopping consistent with the Trivers–Willard hypothesis? *Journal of Biosocial Science*, 45(5), 683–704.

Koziel, S. & Ulijaszek, S. J. (2001). Waiting for Trivers and Willard: do the rich really favour sons? *American Journal of Physical Anthropology*, 115(1), 71–79.

Luo, L., Zhao, W., & Weng, T. (2016). Sex-biased parental investment among contemporary Chinese peasants: testing the Trivers–Willard hypothesis. *Frontiers in Psychology*, 7, 1215.

Lynch, R., Wasielewski, H., & Cronk, L. (2018). Sexual conflict and the Trivers–Willard hypothesis: females prefer daughters and males prefer sons. *Scientific Reports*, 8(1), 15463.

Margulis, S. W., Altmann, J., & Ober, C. (1993). Sex-biased lactational duration in a human population and its reproductive costs. *Behavioral Ecology and Sociobiology*, 32(1), 41–45.

Mathews, F., Johnson, P. J., & Neil, A. (2008). You are what your mother eats: evidence for maternal preconception diet influencing foetal sex in humans. *Proceedings of the Royal Society of London. Series B: Biological Sciences*, 275(1643), 1661–1668.

McGovern, R. J., Neale, M. C., & Kendler, K. S. (1996). The independence of physical attractiveness and symptoms of depression in a female twin population. *The Journal of Psychology*, 130(2), 209–219.

Morita, M., Go, T., Hirabayaski, K., & Heike, T. (2017). Parental condition and infant sex at birth in the Japan Environment and Children's Study: a test of the Trivers–Willard hypothesis. *Letters on Evolutionary Behavioral Science*, 8(2), 40–44.

O'Kane, C. A., & Macdonald, D. W. (2016). An experimental demonstration that predation influences antelope sex ratios and resource-associated mortality. *Basic and Applied Ecology*, 17(4), 370–376.

Perret, M. (2018). Revisiting the Trivers–Willard theory on birth sex ratio bias: role of paternal condition in a Malagasy primate. *PloS ONE*, 13(12), e0209640.

Pink, K. E., Schaman, A., & Fieder, M. (2017). Sex differences in intergenerational income transmission and educational attainment: testing the Trivers–Willard hypothesis. *Frontiers in Psychology*, 8, 1879.

Pollet, T. V., Fawcett, T. W., Buunk, A. P., & Nettle, D. (2009). Sex-ratio biasing toward daughters among lower-ranking co-wives in Rwanda. *Biology Letters*, 5(6), 765–768.

Quinlan, R. J., Quinlan, M. B., & Flinn, M. V. (2003). Parental investment and age at weaning in a Caribbean village. *Evolution and Human Behavior*, 24(1), 1–16.

Rangel-Negrin, A., Coyohua-Fuentes, A., Canales-Espinosa, D., Chavira-Ramirez, D. R., & Dias, P. A. D. (2017). Maternal glucocorticoid levels affect sex allocation in black howler monkeys. *Journal of Zoology*, 304(2), 124–131.

Roche, J. R., Lee, J. M., & Berry, D. P. (2006). Pre-conception energy balance and secondary sex ratio – partial support for the Trivers–Willard hypothesis in dairy cows. *Journal of Dairy Science*, 89(6), 2119–2125.

Rowe, D. C., Clapp, M., & Wallis, J. (1989). Physical attractiveness and the personality resemblance of identical twins. *Behavior Genetics*, 17(2), 191–201.

Salmon, C. (2016). Parental investment and parent–offspring conflict. In *The Handbook of Evolutionary Psychology* (2nd edition), D. Buss, ed., pp. 542–560. Hoboken, NJ: John Wiley & Sons.

Salmon, C. A., & Daly, M. (1998). Birth order and familial sentiment: middleborns are different. *Evolution and Human Behavior*, 19(5), 299–312.

Schnettler, S. (2009). A structured overview of 50 years of small-world research. *Social Networks*, 31(3), 165–178.

Sheldon, B. C., & West, S. A. (2004). Maternal dominance, maternal condition, and offspring sex ratio in ungulate mammals. *The American Naturalist*, 163(1), 40–54.

Sieff, D. F. (1990). Explaining biased gender ratios in human populations. *Current Anthropology*, 31(1), 25–48.

Smith, M. S., Kish, B. J., & Crawford, C. B. (1987). Inheritance of wealth and human kin investment. *Ethology and Sociobiology*, 8(3), 171–182.

Song, S. (2018). Spending patterns of Chinese parents on children's backpacks support the Trivers–Willard hypothesis: results based on transaction data from China's largest online retailer. *Evolution and Human Behavior*, 39(3), 336–342.

Stein, A. D., Zybert, P. A., & Lumey, L. H. (2004). Acute undernutrition is not associated with excess of females at birth in humans: the Dutch Hunger Winter. *Proceedings of the Royal Society of London. Series B: Biological Sciences*, 271(Suppl_4), S138–S141.

Subbaraman, M., Goldman-Mellor, S., Anderson, E., LeWinn, K., Saxton, K., Shumway, M., & Catalano, R. (2010). An exploration of secondary sex ratios among women diagnosed with anxiety disorders. *Human Reproduction*, 25(8), 2084–2091.

Symons, D. (1979). *The Evolution of Human Sexuality*. New York: Oxford University Press.

Trivers, R. L. (1972). Parental investment and sexual selection. In *Sexual Selection and The Descent of Man: 1871–1971*, B. Campbell, ed., pp. 136–179. Chicago: Aldine-Atherton.

Trivers, R. L., & Willard, D. (1973). Natural selection of parental ability to vary the sex-ratio of offspring. *Science*, 179(4068), 90–92.

Valente, C. (2015). Civil conflict, gender-specific fetal loss, and selection: a new test of the Trivers–Willard hypothesis. *Journal of Health Economics*, 39, 31–50.

Van Bodegom, D., Rozing, M. P., May, L., Meij, H. J., Thomese, F., Zwaan, B. J., & Westendorp, R. G. J. (2013). Socioeconomic status determines sex-dependent survival of human offspring. *Evolution, Medicine, and Public Health*, 2013, 37–45.

Veeroja, R., Kirk, A., Tilgar, V., Säde, S., Kreitsberg, M., & Tõnisson, J. (2010). Conception date affects litter type and foetal sex ratio in female moose in Estonia. *Journal of Animal Ecology*, 79(1), 169–175.

Veller, C., Haig, D., & Nowak, M. A. (2016). The Trivers–Willard hypothesis: sex ratio or investment? *Proceedings of the Royal Society of London. Series B: Biological Sciences*, 283(1830), 20160126.

Voland, E. (1998). Evolutionary ecology of human reproduction. *Annual Review of Anthropology*, 27, 347–374.

Volk, A. A., & Atkinson, J. A. (2013). Infant and child death in the human environment of evolutionary adaptation. *Evolution and Human Behavior*, 34(3), 182–192.

West, S. A., & Sheldon, B. C. (2002). Constraints in the evolution of sex ratio adjustment. *Science*, 295(5560), 1685–1688.

Zorn, B., Sucur, V., Stare, J., & Meden-Vrtovec, H. (2002). Decline in sex ratio at birth after 10-year war in Slovenia. *Human Reproduction*, 17(12), 3173–3177.

Life History Theory

Daniel J. Kruger

INTRODUCTION

Evolutionary biologists have long recognized that organisms are limited in their capacities to invest in important aspects of life such as maintenance of the body and reproduction, and that forms of investment are shaped by environmental conditions (Fisher, 1930). Life history traits include gestation length, maturation rate, age of sexual reproduction, level of investment in mating effort, number of offspring, level of investment in parenting effort, age-specific mortality rates, and life expectancy. Time orientation, tendencies for risk taking, and complexity of social organization are also considered life history attributes among humans. Variations in life history strategies have been documented across many species (e.g., Oli, 2004; Promislow and Harvey, 1990; van Schaik and Isler, 2012).

Early formulations of life history theory focused on the contrast between environments with high unpredictability of future events and those with greater stability and predictability. Greater levels of unpredictability in extrinsic mortality accelerate both development and reproduction, resulting in higher fertility rates (Schmalhausen, 1949, as cited in Dobzhansky, 1950). Organisms that cannot predict important conditions such as the availability of resources (Weinrich, 1977) and death from predation need to accelerate growth and reproduction, evolving trait clusters related to rapid and prolific breeding with relatively lower parental investment in offspring (MacArthur and Wilson, 1967; Pianka, 1970). Parental investment in offspring is lower in foraging cultures where high pathogen load leads to higher offspring mortality, regardless of parental investment (Quinlan, 2007).

Organisms developing in environments with greater stability and predictability can invest more in the somatic effort that is necessary for longer intergenerational times, and lower reproductive rates foster greater investment in parenting effort to enhance outcomes for offspring. These relative allocations of life efforts are products of functional adaptations designed to maximize average lifetime inclusive fitness in the experienced developmental environment (Gadgil and Bossert, 1970). Greater environmental stability and predictability fosters greater investment in somatic and parental effort, with lower reproductive rates and longer intergenerational times. Thus, life histories strategies can be thought of as varying along a fast to slow continuum, based on the relative valuation of immediate and future consequences in accelerated and decelerated reproductive patterns.

Because of its broad scope and integration of evolutionary, ecological, and socio-developmental perspectives, life history theory is a powerful organizing framework and is increasingly integrated into models of and research on human psychology and behavior. Life history theory can serve as the key to integrating research focusing on the proximate levels of causation with a deeper explanatory framework. Some scholars may resist adopting an evolutionary framework for understanding humans due to perceptions that explanations rooted in evolutionary adaptation are equivalent to genetic determinism (e.g., Rose and Rose, 2000). Life history theory explicitly refutes these simplistic accounts (Kruger, 2011), as it recognizes that phenotypes are flexible within a range of reaction norms and are shaped by complex interactions between genetic inheritance and developmental environments (Kaplan and Bock, 2001; Schlichting and Pigliucci, 1998). Life history theorists recognize that there is no single best strategy for survival and reproduction in most species because the success of each strategy depends on environmental parameters (Crawford and Anderson, 1989). Variation in individuals' physiological and behavioral strategies reflect adaptations to developmental conditions, and strategies are only better or worse in promoting reproductive success contingent on the environment (Gadgil and Bossert, 1970; Roff, 1992; Stearns, 1992).

HUMAN LIFE HISTORY VARIATION

Life history theory emerged as a framework for explaining differences in life patterns across non-human species. Rushton (1985) proposed that life history theory could be useful in understanding individual differences in human behavioral strategies and physiological functioning, and variations within our own species are now extensively documented (e.g., Belsky et al., 1991; Ellis et al., 1999; Figueredo et al., 2004; Hawkes and Paine, 2006; Heath and Hadley, 1998; Quinlan, 2007). Life history theory may be crucial for understanding human variation and is a powerful guide for research on psychological and behavioral adaptations (Chisholm, 1993; Kaplan and Gangestad, 2005).

Because resources are limited, organisms (including humans) must make trade-offs between different types of effort in various aspects of life. These trade-offs can be conceptualized as a pattern of nested sets, most fundamentally between one's own somatic effort and the reproductive effort of producing successful offspring. Somatic effort includes trade-offs between growth and physiological maintenance, for example, resistance to pathogens and parasites. Reproductive effort includes trade-offs between the mating effort of acquiring reproductive partners and the parental effort directed toward offspring. Parental effort includes trade-offs between investment in current offspring and conservation of resources for potential future offspring (Roff, 1992; Stearns, 1992). The number of offspring produced from one pregnancy is less variable in humans than it is for other species. As seen with the example of offspring number per pregnancy, human life history strategies are constrained by physiology (Heath and Hadley, 1998), though they are also influenced by environmental circumstances such as socio-economic, ecological, developmental, and cultural conditions.

Those facing higher risks of extrinsic mortality, deaths that cannot be predicted or avoided through investment, develop accelerated life patterns characterized by earlier menarche, earlier ages of reproduction, higher reproductive rates, lower birthweights, shorter breast-feeding, lower paternal investment, reduced alloparenting support from extended family members, and higher levels of violence (Chisholm, 1999; Copping and Campbell, 2015; Copping et al., 2013; Kim et al., 1997; Nettle, 2010). Those living in environments where mortality rates are low and predictable and access to resources is stable tend to experience the opposite pattern of outcomes as a slower life history is optimal when one has the luxury of extended time horizons. As life history relates to fundamental aspects of life, there are a host of related psychological constructs relevant to life history variation and processes.

Life history variation is often described along a unidimensional continuum from 'fast' (accelerated) to 'slow' (decelerated); all humans are near the slow end of the cross-species life history continuum, and individual variation is within a subset of this range (Hawkes and Paine, 2006; Low, 1998). Human life histories contrast considerably with those of other primates in several important ways: we have relatively long lifespans, an extended period of juvenile dependence and overlapping dependency among offspring, multi-generational transfers of resources including transfers with post-reproductive age individuals, extensive investment in reproductive partners and offspring, and extensive investment in brain size and development (Kaplan and Lancaster, 2003).

Early models of human life history variation are also unidimensional (e.g., Figueredo et al., 2006; Rushton, 1985), though there is growing evidence for multi-dimensionality. When controlling for overall body size, there appear to be separate dimensions of reproductive timing and reproductive quantity (i.e., an inverse relationship between offspring size and number), both across and within mammalian clades (Bielby et al., 2007). Research on human life history variation has identified mating competition as a dimension

independent of general life history speed ('Differential K') indicators (e.g., Richardson et al., 2017), and mating effort and parenting effort as two inversely related but distinct dimensions of reproductive effort, consistent with theoretical models of nested sets of trade-offs (Kruger, 2017).

Nettle and Frankenhuis (2019) note the recent divergence of life history literatures between humans and other species. Articles on the human fast–slow unidimensional life history continuum form their own cluster separate from other life history literature. Biological literature on other species has a much stronger focus on formal mathematical modelling. Also, life history research in psychology focuses on individual variation resulting from differential developmental environments and life history research in biology focuses on population differences based on evolutionary processes in differential ecologies (Nettle and Frankenhuis, 2019). However, the notion of psychological differences across human populations that are based on ecological differences in ancestral conditions is extremely controversial in contemporary academia (e.g., Kelly and Littlejohn, 2019).

BIODEMOGRAPHIC AND PSYCHOMETRIC APPROACHES TO ASSESSING HUMAN LIFE HISTORY VARIATION

Psychometric assessments of human life history are complementary to the biometric assessments of the developmental parameters used across species, such as spacing of births, length of gestation, weight at birth, length of juvenile dependency, and age at sexual maturity. These biological and demographic indicators bring considerable value, although some may be difficult to interpret in technologically advanced societies because of relatively novel factors such as caloric surplus and artificial control of fertility.

Different types of indicators may be most powerful when used in combination. Psychological measures add value in identifying and describing the proximal mental processes or mechanisms guiding behavioral strategies (see Cosmides and Tooby, 1994). As described above, human life history variation has been represented in psychological and behavioral research in several ways, including indicators of conditions in the developmental environment, indicators of conditions in the current environment, indicators of maturation and life milestones (e.g., menarche, initial sexual activity, first pregnancy), and in self-report survey scale measures. Survey scale measures have included constructs such as a general index of life history speed (*K*-factor), mating effort, parenting effort, time perspective and future discounting. Human life history researchers have emphasized the need to clearly determine what is being measured by life history indicators and have expressed a preference for precise measurement over conceptual complexity (e.g., Copping et al., 2014).

LIFE HISTORY THEORY INFORMS PSYCHOLOGICAL VARIATION

Time Orientation

Time orientation, representing the degree to which behaviors are oriented toward immediate versus future goals, is fundamental to life history theory and human psychology. Researchers in various fields have developed related constructs such as time horizons, future discounting, planning, (low) impulsivity, and high self-control. Time perspective is a pervasive, powerful, and underrecognized influence on human behavior (Zimbardo and Boyd, 1999) and an important predictor in risky behaviors such as adult alcohol, tobacco, and other drug use (Keough et al., 1999). Conscientiousness, a personality dimension including future orientation and

planning, is fundamental in the selection and pursuit of social goals (Carstensen et al., 1999). Future-oriented self-control predicts a wide range of outcomes such as social competence, educational achievement, and resilience to frustration and stress (e.g., Mischel et al., 1989).

Those living in unpredictable environments develop behavioral strategies relatively more oriented toward immediate outcomes and with greater variation in success (Chisholm, 1999; Wilson and Daly, 1997), discounting the future more and acting more impulsively (Frankenhuis and de Weerth, 2013; Frankenhuis et al., 2016). These riskier, more present-oriented strategies help individuals take advantage of transient opportunities that facilitate early reproduction. Such behavioral patterns are functional as adaptations, as they have historically promoted reproductive success in adverse environments, even if they have detrimental consequences for the majority of individuals who enact them (Wilson and Daly, 1997).

Urban adolescents living in neighborhoods with low levels of safety and social capital have time preferences for more immediate rewards and lesser orientations toward long-term goals, which in turn predict their rates of committing interpersonal violence and property crimes (Kruger et al., 2008). Community college students took risks more frequently when they estimated their lifespans to be shorter and their futures to be less predictable (Hill et al., 1997). Shorter average life expectancies at birth and greater levels of income inequality predicted five-year neighborhood homicide rates as well as higher overall mortality rates across Chicago neighborhoods (Wilson and Daly, 1997). Those who live in chronically risky and uncertain environments are more likely to have earlier menarche, earlier ages of reproduction, and higher overall rates of reproduction (Chisholm, 1999; Johns, 2010; Kim et al., 1997).

Those with slower life history strategies (i.e., higher parenting effort, lower mating effort) have greater relationship stability, higher investment in children, lower impulsivity, lower levels of risk taking, and greater regard for social rules (Figueredo et al., 2006). These traits may be considered to be good for individuals or desirable for society, yet it is important to make the distinction between explanatory frameworks for, and value judgements of, behavioral patterns (Kruger, 2011). From an evolutionary perspective, slower life history strategies are not inherently advantageous, as success is contingent on environmental conditions. Future-oriented slower strategies will be outcompeted by more present-oriented faster strategies in less predictable environments with higher variation in mortality and reproductive success. Environmental factors promoting riskier behavioral strategies are usually interpreted under a framework of psychopathology; however, these responses may be adaptive in terms of promoting reproductive success in ancestral environments (Ellis and Bjorklund, 2012).

Heightened attention-shifting in present-oriented cognition may enable individuals to take advantage of fleeting opportunities in rapidly changing environments (Mittal et al., 2015). A reconfiguration of Mischel's Delay of Gratification Tasks demonstrated that children are less likely to delay gratification when the experimenter has proven unreliable, suggesting the unpredictability of future rewards (Kidd et al., 2013). It is also important to note that psychological well-being is not equivalent to an individual's fitness in an evolutionary sense, which is based on reproductive success (Frankenhuis and Del Giudice, 2012).

Romantic Attachment Style

Bowlby (1969) originally conceptualized the attachment system as an evolved survival strategy for protecting infants from predators. Belsky et al. (1991) reframed the psychological attachment process as a product of evolved psychological mechanisms designed to evaluate one's environment and pursue a reproductive strategy that would be more likely to succeed in the given circumstances. In this model, insecure attachment is a consequence of responses to environmental cues that suggest pursuing long-term monogamous relationships would not be a viable strategy. There is now considerable empirical evidence documenting the relationship between attachment styles and reproductive strategies (see Del Giudice, 2009). Women who grow up without substantial paternal involvement exhibit earlier sexual activity, as well as a lack of interest or ability to form and/or maintain, long-term monogamous relationships (Belsky et al., 1991; Chisholm, 1999). A recent review indicates that the association between father absence and daughters' accelerated maturation may be stronger in Western countries where nuclear families are normative than in other cultures with more extensive alloparenting from extended families (Sear et al., 2019). Also, some (e.g., Barbaro et al., 2017) argue that the relationship between father absence and age at menarche may be a spurious phenotypic correlation and product of shared genes.

Decades of research has revealed that there are two dimensions of romantic attachment, and two forms of insecure attachment (Brennan et al., 1998).

Those high in attachment avoidance are uncomfortable with being emotionally close to relationship partners and hide their true feelings from them. Those high in attachment anxiety worry about being abandoned by relationship partners and that the feelings they have for their partner are not reciprocated. Del Giudice (2009) proposed that highly avoidant attachment styles are a component of high mating effort reproductive strategies that emphasize short-term and uncommitted mating. Those high in attachment anxiety may behave in ways to elicit expressions of relationship commitment and additional investment (Del Giudice, 2009). Among university students in the United States, higher attachment avoidance predicted a general indicator of accelerated life history, higher self-reported mating effort, and was inversely related to inclinations for future parenting effort (Kruger, 2017). Attachment anxiety was not related to these constructs, despite a highly powered analysis.

Sociosexuality

The concept of sociosexuality was originally developed to describe individual differences in the willingness to engage in uncommitted sexual behaviors (Kinsey et al., 1948). This concept was the basis for a brief self-report measure developed by evolutionary psychologists, the Sociosexual Orientation Inventory (SOI; Simpson and Gangestad, 1991). The SOI predicts mate choice preferences, courtship behaviors, and the stability and quality of romantic relationships (Simpson et al., 2004). The original measure contained one dimension related to short-term mating motivations. A revised instrument was developed that distinguished between Short-Term Mating Orientation (STMO) and Long-Term Mating Orientation (LTMO; Jackson and Kirkpatrick, 2007). STMO, which is highly correlated with the original scale (Jackson and Kirkpatrick, 2007), represents interest in uncommitted sexual behaviors and strongly predicts self-reported mating effort (Kruger, 2017), with weaker predictions of accelerated general life history and lower self-reported parenting effort (Kruger, 2017). LTMO is a largely independent dimension representing interest in long-term, committed, romantic relationships. LTMO directly predicts parenting effort, decelerated general life history, and inversely predicts mating effort (Kruger, 2017).

Penke and Asendorpf (2008) made an explicit life history-based argument that sociosexual behaviors are related to allocations of mating effort and also developed a revised inventory. Although their SOI-R inventory includes three dimensions (past sexual behaviors, attitudes toward uncommitted sex, and

sociosexual desire), Penke and Asendorpf (2008) hold that only behavioral differences ultimately matter for evolutionary models of human mating, following Kinsey's original model. The behavioral subscale of the SOI-R strongly predicts self-reported mating effort, weakly predicts accelerated general life history, and is unrelated to self-reported parenting effort (Kruger, 2017).

Personality Traits

Figueredo and Rushton (2009) argued that a General Factor of Personality (GFP), good mental and physical health, and slower or decelerated life history form a common superordinate factor (Super-K) underlying human life history variation. The GFP encompasses altruism, agreeableness, conscientiousness, emotional intelligence, extraversion, life satisfaction, neuroticism (inversely to other dimensions), and self-esteem. Cross-national twin studies show high (50%) heritability for GFP variance (Figueredo et al., 2004). Accelerated life history also predicts higher levels of neuroticism and psychoticism (Figueredo et al., 2006). The Super-K is believed to be a coordinated suite of traits produced by directional selection for a slower life history strategy because of the benefits of cooperative sociality (Figueredo and Rushton, 2009).

'Dark Triad' personality traits (Paulhus and Williams, 2002), Machiavellianism, Narcissism, and Psychopathy, are associated with short-term mating and social strategies involving the exploitation of other individuals (Jonason and Webster, 2010). People who are high in Machiavellianism see other people as instrumental tools, as they have a stronger tendency to manipulate and exploit others. They have a focus on self-interest at the expense of morality and will often use deception. Individuals high in Narcissism have an unrealistic sense of superiority, lack empathy (an understanding or feeling of what others are experiencing), and are highly motivated to maintain and enhance favorable views of themselves. Those high in Psychopathy have a disregard of others and display patterns of behavior that are antisocial, impulsive, and selfish. They may lack interest in long-term social and romantic relationships. These personality traits are considered part of an accelerated life history strategy focused on securing immediate rewards and gratification (Jonason et al., 2012) and predict favorable attitudes toward uncommitted sex and short-term mating orientation (Jonason et al., 2010; Jonason and Webster, 2010). Psychopathy is also inversely related to long-term mating orientation (Jonason and Webster, 2010). All Dark Triad traits predict self-reported mating effort, and Psychopathy has a weak inverse relationship to self-reported parenting effort (Kruger, 2017).

LIFE HISTORY AND HEALTH PATTERNS

Scientific research and intervention have dramatically improved human health conditions and average life expectancy through advances in medicine, pharmacology, public health, and sanitation. This is especially true in affluent technologically advanced societies. Historically prevalent sources of mortality such as infectious diseases, serious accidents, and pregnancy and childbirth complications have been dramatically reduced. In affluent societies, the scope of pressing health challenges has shifted toward later onset diseases such as hypertension, type 2 diabetes, and cancer (Lopez, 1998). This epidemiological transition presents both challenges to and promise for life history-based approaches to health. The landscape of health-related factors is quite different between technologically advanced and foraging populations, requiring sophistication in life history models to account for novel aspects of the environment. Those living in modern societies have far less regular exercise than foragers, and the resulting imbalance between energy intake and expenditure is

a major contributor to the modern obesity epidemic (Broyles et al., 2015). Although intense strength training exercises are often the focus of modern physical fitness, our modern exercise deficits are primarily in low-impact aerobic exercises such as walking (Katzmarzyk, 2014). Industrialization and advanced technology have reduced or eliminated needs for fetching water, foraging and hunting for food, agricultural labor, and many other activities that are built into daily activities in less developed areas. Despite the technological and cultural changes, we retain a physiological need for considerable levels of low-impact aerobic exercise.

Medical technologies continue to advance, enhancing abilities to save lives in acute crises and improving prospects for chronic conditions. However, contemporary medical and public health concerns have large behavioral components, and efforts to promote healthy behaviors and discourage unhealthy behaviors struggle with diminishing returns. Evolutionary principles provide an ultimate explanation for patterns of health outcomes, and establishing a deep theoretical framework may enhance the effectiveness of health interventions. Life History Theory, in particular, brings considerable power to understanding variation in behavioral patterns related to health and why they vary with environmental conditions. We may be reaching a limit in the returns from traditional educational and motivational health-promoting practices, which assume that if people only had the relevant information and opportunity, they would make health-promoting choices consistently (Bentley and Aunger, 2008; Kruger, 2011). Health education and health resource availability can shape patterns of health behavior, but they are not the only determinants of health behaviors and outcomes.

The motivational systems which enabled our ancestors to successfully survive and reproduce did not evolve to optimize mental and physical health, but to promote reproductive success (Gluckman and Hanson,

2007). Despite comprehensive environmental changes, the legacy of goals and motivations from longer spans of human evolutionary history shape our psychological and behavioral patterns. Even 'non-evolutionary' researchers have recognized the need to understand people's motivations and preferences, and that people do not always act in their best long-term health interests (Hancock and Garrett, 1995). For example, health messaging based on cognitive processes (e.g., reporting the disease risks associated with certain behaviors) have not been particularly successful (Bentley and Aunger, 2008).

Demographically representative community health surveys show that rates of both health promoting behaviors (e.g., exercise, fruit and vegetable consumption, preparation for emergencies) and health adverse behaviors (c.g., smoking tobacco, alcohol consumption, binge alcohol consumption, behaviors that increase risk for HIV infection, physical fights) are substantially related to life history variation, even when controlling for life history-related sociodemographic factors such as age, gender, and education (Kruger and Kruger, 2016; Kruger, 2018). Wilson and Daly (1997) argued that patterns of extremely risky behaviors result from steep future discounting in response to environments where the probability of receiving delayed benefits is uncertain or low and the expected benefits of safer courses of action are negligible. In such environments, extreme risk taking may be necessary to achieve reproduction before mortality. The future-oriented strategies that health promotion efforts encourage are facilitated by long-term stability in environmental conditions. Environments where personal safety, social support, and access to important resources are unpredictable will lead to tendencies to discount future health in favor of immediate rewards (Kruger and Kruger, 2016; Kruger, 2018). Longer-term, more risk averse strategies will be encouraged by the perception and reality that current efforts will lead to substantial future pay offs.

SEX DIFFERENCES IN LIFE HISTORY AND CONSEQUENCES FOR HEALTH

Being male is the most powerful demographic risk factor for early mortality in technologically advanced societies (Kruger and Nesse, 2006a). Stable aggregate sex differences result from sexual selection, the processes of intrasexual competition and intersexual selection, which substantially shape the life histories of females and males. There is a cascade of factors responsible for aggregate differences between females and males, originating from divergence in gamete size and extending to social norms. By definition, females invest more than males in gametes and are more limited in the quantity of offspring they can produce. Females usually invest considerably more than males in offspring, particularly in placental mammals, and thus are selected to be choosier in selecting reproductive partners (Bateman, 1948; Trivers, 1972). Male reproductive success is more dependent on securing mating opportunities than it is for females, both through intrasexual competition with other males and intersexual selection from female choice based on the attractiveness of their traits and displays (Darwin, 1871). Male strategies promoting reproductive success have been selected for, even if they increase risk of injury, sickness, and early death (Daly and Wilson, 1978; Møller et al., 1999). This results in life histories that are substantially different for mammalian males compared to those of females of the same species, including higher male investment in reproductive effort at the expense of somatic maintenance, and higher male investment in mating effort at the expense of parenting effort. In our own species, men on average have greater height and weight, more upper-body strength, higher metabolic rates, and later sexual maturity compared to women (Miller, 1998).

Across cultures, men have higher mortality rates than women from both external (direct behavioral) causes such as accidents, homicides, and suicides, and behaviorally mediated internal causes of death, such as cardiovascular disease, diabetes, and cancer (Kruger and Nesse, 2006a). The similarity of sex differences in mortality across different cultures requires explanation based in our common evolutionary heritage. Excess male mortality is a result of a trade-off between competitiveness and longevity (Kruger and Nesse, 2004). The greater variation and skew in male reproductive success selected for higher investments in mating effort and competition, producing behavioral and physiological strategies that are riskier than those for women. There are occasionally calls for greater attention to men's health and health disparities (e.g., Treadwell and Young, 2013). However, such calls often ignore human biology and search for explanations based on social norms (Treadwell and Young, 2013: 5).

Sex differences in mortality rates vary predictably by age, within populations, and across populations based on the intensity of male mating competition. Across the lifespan, sex differences in mortality rates are highest in late adolescence and young adulthood, corresponding with the onset and peak of mating competition (Kruger and Nesse, 2004, 2006a). Both boys and girls exhibit risky behavior, though there are considerable aggregate sex differences. The relatively riskier behavioral strategies of young males were selected for because they tended to aid in mating competition over our evolutionary history (Wilson and Daly, 1992). In most populations, there is a dramatic decline in mortality sex differences in adulthood as men shift from mating effort toward parenting effort. This decline is not observed in populations where male mating competition remains high throughout adulthood (Kruger and Nesse, 2006a). Male social status and economic power predicts reproductive success across a wide variety of societies (Hopcroft, 2006). Within populations, those of lower status (as well as the unmarried) exhibit greater sex differences in mortality rates (Kruger and Nesse, 2006a), suggesting greater risk taking associated with higher

levels of mating competition. Across societies, the degree of inequality in male social and reproductive outcomes strongly predicts the level of excess male mortality (Kruger, 2010). Changes in socio-economic conditions associated with the intensity of male mating competition can influence sex differences on a relatively short time scale, for example the Eastern European transition to market economies in the 1990s (Kruger and Nesse, 2007). The ratio of male to female mortality rates appears to be an important life history indicator, and is related to other life history indicators such as the percentage of newborns with low birthweight, the adolescent fertility rate, the average maternal age at birth of first child (inversely), and the average age of both men and women at first marriage (Kruger, 2008).

SENSITIVE PERIODS AND MECHANISMS FOR SHAPING HUMAN LIFE HISTORY

Sensitive Periods for Life History Plasticity

Identifying critical sensitive periods for shaping life history variation, and determining reaction norms of life history plasticity, are important goals both for theory and practical applications which seek to alter behavioral patterns related to life history. Sensitive periods, when environmental influences have disproportionate effects in shaping life trajectories, are widespread across species (West-Eberhard, 2003). Many life history derived frameworks propose sensitive periods early in development that shape variation in physiology and behavior for the remainder of the lifespan (Frankenhuis and Fraley, 2017). Considerably more research is needed, however, to produce a comprehensive portrait of developmental sensitivity based on the costs and benefits of maintaining plasticity during different portions of the lifespan (Frankenhuis and Fraley, 2017).

Developmental programming (e.g., Barker, 1992) proposes a critical period in gestation and/or early infancy with substantial consequences for adult health conditions. Bodily systems and processes are influenced by maternal stressors such as poor nutrition, multiple pregnancy, gynecological immaturity, as well as environmental stressors such as prenatal steroid exposure, high temperature, and low oxygen and air pressure from high altitudes. These stressors impair offspring growth and functioning throughout their lifespan, results which are interpreted in a deficit model rather than as contingent adaptive response. Belsky et al.'s (1991) model of the psychological attachment process as an evolved psychological mechanism which shapes adult reproductive strategy considers one's experiences with attachment figures in middle childhood to be the critical period.

Mathematical modelling indicates there are benefits for extended life history plasticity because of the geometric decay in the predictive power of environmental experiences (Nettle et al., 2013). Recent research supports the notion that facultative adjustments may also occur much later in the lifespan. Delinquency in adolescence was, at least temporarily, reduced by interventions promoting the consideration of the status of one's future self (Van Gelder et al., 2013, 2015). An individual's parental attachment security was more affected by parental divorces in the recent past than in the distant past, beyond the sensitive period before four years of age (Fraley and Heffernan, 2013). Among adults who experienced an acute toxic contamination of the municipal water supply, those who experienced lower tap water quality had lower general tendencies for future planning (Kruger, 2018). Tendencies for future planning mediated the relationships between poor tap water quality and health-related behaviors including fruit and vegetable consumption, sugar-sweetened beverage consumption, rates of vigorous exercise, and preparations taken for responses to emergencies. Lower water quality

experiences also directly predicted higher likelihoods of health adverse behaviors, such as being a tobacco smoker, having higher self-reported HIV risk, and a higher likelihood of being involved in a physical fight. All associations were independent of individual differences in socio-demographics related to life history variation. Additionally, during the Croatian 1991–1995 War of Independence, the sudden increase in environmental unpredictability and harshness increased the level of risky behavior and physiological susceptibility to disease, especially for men. The increase in the sex differences in mortality rates from accidents, suicide, and homicide (all unrelated to deaths from military combat) peaked during the most intense phase of the war (Kruger and Nesse, 2006b).

These findings suggest that there may be bidirectional effects in extended life history plasticity, but it is not known whether these effects would be symmetrical in magnitude or form. An acute threat may be a stronger influence than acute improvements in condition, as a rapid response may be necessary in ensuring immediate survival, whereas the duration of improved conditions may be unknown. Improvements may need to be maintained over time to foster both longer time horizons and future oriented behaviors. Future research could systematically examine the effects of sudden windfalls and steady improvements on the degree of planning behavior and other aspects of life history variation.

External and Internal Prediction Mechanisms

The investigation of prediction mechanisms is another direction for future research to elaborate and clarify. Some life history theorists have proposed a differentiation between external and internal mechanisms of prediction in shaping life history variation (e.g., Nettle et al., 2013; Rickard et al., 2014). Initial life history models proposed external predictions, analogous to a weather forecast, where individuals develop a phenotype adapted to the conditions of the local environment. For example, perceptions of greater environmental uncertainty would result in faster life history strategies favoring immediate outcomes (Chisholm, 1999). Belsky et al.'s (1991) model of the psychological attachment system describes the calibration of relationship strategies based on one's adult social environment. The acceleration in reproductive strategy is seen as the cause of riskier behaviors which lead to somatic damage. In contrast, internal prediction models base the calibration of strategies based on one's own somatic state. Perceptions of somatic damage lead to an accelerated reproductive strategy in response to likely reductions in lifespan and health quality. The relationship between the external and internal prediction mechanisms are not clear and they may not be mutually exclusive. Circumstantial evidence supports the possibility of both mechanisms being involved in the aftermath of the municipal water supply contamination incident (Kruger, 2018).

Harsh versus Unpredictable Environments

Early life history models (MacArthur and Wilson, 1967; Pianka, 1970) proposed selection of strategies based on population density. When population density was low, conditions would favor a high reproductive rate, though there was little need to invest in competitive abilities for contests over resources as resources were thought to be abundant in these environments (Pianka, 1970). Low population density would promote 'r selection', named after the coefficient for the maximum reproductive rate. When population densities were high, resources would be more limited, and organisms would need to invest in competitive abilities. This form of selection was named 'K selection' after the coefficient for the population carrying capacity of the environment. Although some aspects of this model were supported by empirical research, factors such

as age-specific mortality and environmental variability were found to be stronger predictors of life history variation than population density (Roff, 2002). The terms 'r selection' and 'K selection' were used in early applications of life history theory to human variation, though these terms have largely been replaced by the terms 'fast' or 'accelerated' and 'slow' or 'decelerated', partly in recognition that all humans would be considered strongly K-selected and vary within the upper range (Hawkes and Paine, 2006; Low, 1998).

Ellis et al. (2009) proposed a differentiation between extrinsic levels of morbidity and mortality that could not be predicted or ameliorated by investment ('harshness') and variation in harshness over time and space ('unpredictability'). High levels of adult-specific morbidity and mortality would lead to faster life histories, and high levels of juvenile-specific morbidity and mortality would lead to faster life histories if they are relatively extrinsic (insensitive to parental investment and juvenile quality). Fast growth and development serve to minimize time in the vulnerable juvenile stage. If higher parental investment can improve juvenile morbidity and mortality risk, then slower life histories with greater parental effort and greater effort in somatic maintenance will be selected. Low environmental harshness will select for slower life histories when population density and resource competition are high, but faster life histories if population density is low. Ellis et al. acknowledge that juvenile and adult extrinsic mortality risk are strongly correlated and have comparably powerful effects across mammals (Promislow and Harvey, 1990) and in small-scale human societies (Walker et al., 2006). High levels of unpredictability in adult mortality (high variation in threats from predators, extreme weather, etc.) will also select for faster life histories, whereas high levels of unpredictability in juvenile mortality are predicted to increase fertility and diversity of reproductive partners if environmental changes are on a shorter time scale and a smaller number of offspring with greater parental investment if environmental changes are on a longer time scale (Ellis et al., 2009).

APPLICATION OF LIFE HISTORY INSIGHTS

Contemporary policy makers and applied professionals may value low mortality rates, high life expectancy, lower levels of behavioral risk taking, stable parental relationships, high investment in children, and high degrees of helping and social support among kin and neighbors. Life history theory provides a powerful framework guiding the generation of environments that encourage cautious, long-term strategies that engender healthy lifestyles. The implications of evolutionary insights often converge with recommendations for social and environmental conditions that facilitate health, though originating from a deeper understanding of the causal framework behind social and health patterns. This framework also provides a more realistic account of the limits of shorter-term changes. Psychological time horizons are often unsuitably brief for maintaining health behaviors whose benefits are not seen in the short term, and individual values and motivations may deprioritize long-term health outcomes. Facilitating stable access to necessary resources, personal safety, social support, and community cohesion will foster longer-term strategies based on perceptions that current efforts will be rewarded in the future. Creating and enhancing safe public and family-friendly social space may increase perceptions of safety and decrease levels of interpersonal crime. Public areas that embrace the architectural properties of defensible space may contribute to social capital and cohesion. Neighborhoods where important resources are within walking distance and are well-serviced by public transportation will encourage greater levels of exercise. In addition to providing supportive structures for those most in need, reducing both perceived and actual differentials in social

status may benefit the vast majority of the population. It may be impossible to eliminate all social status differentials; however, relatively egalitarian foraging societies exist (e.g., the Tsimané of Bolivia) and may serve as a model for more equitable societies (Kaplan et al., 2009). Life history theory has already contributed to better understandings of important social issues beyond the usual domains of evolutionary psychology, such as the degree of preparations made for emergencies (Kruger et al., 2019) and community members' attitudes toward, and cooperation with, the police (Kruger et al., 2015, 2018).

CONCLUSION

The principles of life history evolution provide a systematic and ultimate explanation for patterns of individuals, differences in psychology and behavior. Researchers and practitioners could benefit considerably from an understanding of life-history trade-offs, life history related motivations, time orientation, and other relevant constructs, even if they are not explicitly testing evolutionary hypotheses. Life history theory is also a powerful framework that can help promote understanding of variation in health behaviors, health outcomes, and other important social issues, and why these behaviors vary consistently with environmental conditions. Efforts to actively integrate the evolutionary perspective of life history theory into human research and intervention have considerable potential to exceed the benefits of current efforts.

REFERENCES

Bateman, A. J. (1948). Intra-sexual selection in drosophila. *Heredity*, *2*(3), 349–368.
Barbaro, N., Boutwell, B. B., Barnes, J. C., & Shackelford, T. K. (2017). Genetic confounding of the relationship between father

absence and age at menarche. *Evolution and Human Behavior*, *38*(3), 357–365.

Barker, D. J. (1992). *Fetal and infant origins of adult disease*. London: British Medical Journal.

Belsky, J., Steinberg, L., & Draper, P. (1991). Childhood experience, interpersonal development, and reproductive strategy: An evolutionary theory of socialization. *Child Development*, *62*(4), 647–670.

Bentley, G. R., & Aunger, R. (2008). Practical aspects of evolutionary medicine. In S. Elton & P. O'Higgins (Eds.), *Medicine and evolution: Current applications, future prospects* (pp. 217–239). Boca Raton, FL: CRC Press.

Bielby, J., Mace, G. M., Bininda-Emonds, O. R., Cardillo, M., Gittleman, J. L., Jones, K. E., Orme, C. D., & Purvis, A. (2007). The fast–slow continuum in mammalian life history: An empirical reevaluation. *The American Naturalist*, *169*(6), 748–757.

Bowlby, J. (1969). *Attachment. Attachment and loss, vol. 1*. New York: Basic Books.

Brennan, K. A., Clark, C. L., & Shaver, P. R. (1998). Self-report measurement of adult attachment: An integrative overview. In J. A. Simpson, & W. S. Rholes (Eds.), *Attachment theory and close relationships* (pp. 46–76). New York: Guilford Press.

Broyles S. T., Denstel, K. D., Church, T. S., Chaput, J.-P., Fogelholm, M., Hu, G., Kuriyan, R., Kurpad, A., Lambert, E. V., Maher, C., Maia, J., Matsudo, V., Olds, T., Onywera, V., Sarmiento, O. L., Standage, M., Tremblay, M. S., Tudor-Locke, C., Zhao, P., and Katzmarzyk P. T. for the ISCOLE Research Group (2015). The epidemiological transition and the global childhood obesity epidemic. *International Journal of Obesity Supplements*, *5*(Suppl_2), S3–S8.

Carstensen, L. L., Isaacowitz, D. M., & Charles, S. T. (1999). Taking time seriously: A theory of socioemotional selectivity. *American Psychologist*, *54*(3), 165–181.

Chisholm, J. S. (1993). Death, hope, and sex: Life-history theory and the development of reproductive strategies. *Current Anthropology*, *34*(1), 1–24.

Chisholm, J. S. (1999). *Death, hope and sex: Steps to an evolutionary ecology of mind and morality*. Cambridge, UK: Cambridge University Press.

Copping, L. T., & Campbell, A. (2015). The environment and life history strategies: Neighborhood and individual-level models. *Evolution and Human Behavior*, *36*(3), 182–190.

Copping, L. T., Campbell, A., & Muncer, S. (2013). Violence, teenage pregnancy, and life history. *Human Nature*, *24*(2), 137–157.

Copping, L. T., Campbell, A., & Muncer, S. (2014). Psychometrics and life history strategy: The structure and validity of the High K Strategy Scale. *Evolutionary Psychology*, *12*(1), 200–222.

Cosmides, L. & Tooby, J. (1994). Origins of domain specificity: The evolution of functional organization. In L. A. Hirschfeld & S. A. Gelman (Eds.), *Mapping the mind: Domain specificity in cognition and culture* (pp. 85–116). Cambridge, UK: Cambridge University Press.

Daly, M., & Wilson, M. (1978). *Sex, evolution, and behavior: Adaptations for reproduction*. North Scituate, MA: Duxbury Press.

Darwin, C. (1871). *The descent of man and selection in relation to sex*. London: John Murray.

Del Giudice, M. (2009). Sex, attachment, and the development of reproductive strategies. *Behavioral and Brain Sciences*, *32*(1), 1–67.

Dobzhansky, T. (1950). Evolution in the tropics. *American Scientist*, *38*(2), 209–221.

Ellis, B. J., & Bjorklund, D. F. (2012). Beyond mental health: An evolutionary analysis of development under risky and supportive environmental conditions: An introduction to the special section. *Developmental Psychology*, *48*(3), 591–597.

Ellis, B. J., Figueredo, A. J., Brumbach, B. H., & Schlomer, G. L. (2009). Fundamental dimensions of environmental risk: The impact of harsh versus unpredictable environments on the evolution and development of life history strategies. *Human Nature*, *20*(2), 204–268.

Ellis, B. J., McFadyen-Ketchum, S., Dodge, K. A., Pettit, G. S., & Bates, J. S. (1999). Quality of early family relationships and individual differences in the timing of pubertal maturation in girls: A longitudinal test of an evolutionary model. *Journal of Personality and Social Psychology*, *77*(2), 387–401.

Figueredo, A. J., & Rushton, J. P. (2009). Evidence for shared genetic dominance between the general factor of personality, mental and physical health, and life history traits. *Twin Research and Human Genetics*, *12*(6), 555–563.

Figueredo, A. J., Vásquez, G., Brumbach, B. H., & Schneider, S. M. (2004). The heritability of life history strategy: The K-factor, covitality, and personality. *Social Biology*, *51*(3–4), 121–43.

Figueredo, A. J., Vásquez, G., Brumbach, B. H., Schneider, S. M., Sefcek, J. A., Tal, I. R., Hill, D., Wenner, C. J., & Jacobs, W. J. (2006). Consilience and Life History Theory: From genes to brain to reproductive strategy. *Developmental Review*, *26*(2), 243–275.

Fisher, R. A. (1930). *The genetical theory of natural selection*. New York: Dover.

Fraley, R. C., & Heffernan, M. E. (2013). Attachment and parental divorce: A test of the diffusion and sensitive period hypotheses. *Personality and Social Psychology Bulletin*, *39*(9), 1199–1213.

Frankenhuis, W. E., & de Weerth, C. (2013). Does early-life exposure to stress shape, or impair, cognition? *Current Directions in Psychological Science*, *22*(5), 407–412.

Frankenhuis, W. E., & Del Giudice, M. (2012). When do adaptive developmental mechanisms yield maladaptive outcomes? *Developmental Psychology*, *48*(3), 628–642.

Frankenhuis, W. E., & Fraley, R. C. (2017). What do evolutionary models teach us about sensitive periods in psychological development? *European Psychologist*, *22*(3), 141–150.

Frankenhuis, W. E., Panchanathan, K., & Nettle, D. (2016). Cognition in harsh and unpredictable environments. *Current Opinion in Psychology*, *7*, 76–80.

Gadgil, M., & Bossert, W. H. (1970). Life historical consequences of natural selection. *The American Naturalist*, *104*(935), 1–24.

Gluckman, P. D., & Hanson, M. A. (2007). Developmental plasticity and human disease: Research directions. *Journal of Internal Medicine*, *261*(5), 461–471.

Hancock, T., & Garrett, M. (1995). Beyond medicine: Health challenges and strategies in the 21st century. *Futures*, *27*(9–10), 935–951.

Hawkes, K., & Paine, R. (Eds) (2006). *The evolution of human life history*. Santa Fe, NM: School of American Research Press.

Heath, K., & Hadley, C. (1998). Dichotomous male reproductive strategies in a polygynous human society: Mating versus parental effort. *Current Anthropology*, *39*(3), 369–374.

Hill, E. M., Ross, L. T., & Low, B. S. (1997). The role of future unpredictability in human risk-taking. *Human Nature*, *8*(4), 287–325.

Hopcroft, R. L. (2006). Sex, status and reproductive success in the contemporary U.S. *Evolution and Human Behavior*, *27*(2), 104–120.

Jackson, J. J., & Kirkpatrick, L. A. (2007). The structure and measurement of human mating strategies: Toward a multidimensional model of sociosexuality. *Evolution and Human Behavior*, *28*(6), 382–391.

Johns, S. E. (2010). Perceived environmental risk as a predictor of teenage motherhood in a British population. *Health & Place*, *17*(1), 122–131.

Jonason, P. K., Li, N. P., & Buss, D. M. (2010). The costs and benefits of the Dark Triad: Implications for mate poaching and mate retention tactics. *Personality and Individual Differences*, *48*(4), 373–378.

Jonason, P. K., & Webster, G. D. (2010). The Dirty Dozen: A concise measure of the Dark Triad. *Psychological Assessment*, *22*(2), 420–432.

Jonason, P. K., Webster, G. W., Schmitt, D. P., Li, N. P., & Crysel, L. (2012). The antihero in popular culture: Life History Theory and the Dark Triad personality traits. *Review of General Psychology*, *16*(2), 192–199.

Kaplan, H. S., & Bock, J.A. (2001). Fertility theory: Embodied-capital theory of life history evolution. In N.J. Smelser & P.B. Baltes (Eds.), *International Encyclopedia of the Social and Behavioral Sciences* (pp. 5561–5568). Oxford, UK: Elsevier.

Kaplan, H. S., & Gangestad, S. W. (2005). Life History Theory and Evolutionary Psychology. In D. M. Buss (Ed.), *The handbook of evolutionary psychology* (pp. 68–95). Hoboken, NJ: John Wiley & Sons.

Kaplan, H. S., & Lancaster, J. B. (2003). An evolutionary and ecological analysis of human fertility, mating patterns, and parental investment. In K. W. Wachter & R. A. Bulatao (Eds.), *Offspring: Human fertility behavior in biodemographic perspective* (pp. 170–223). Washington, DC: National Academies Press.

Kaplan, H. S., Hooper, P. L., & Gurven, M. (2009). The evolutionary and ecological roots of human social organization. *Philosophical*

Transactions of the Royal Society – Series B, *364*(1533), 3289–3299.

Katzmarzyk, P. T. (2014, 18 February). Personal communication.

Kelly, J., & Littlejohn, A. (2019, 7 November). Evolution Working Group on hosting Bo Winegard: 'It was our mistake'. *The Crimson White*. Tuscaloosa, AL: University of Alabama.

Keough, K. A., Zimbardo, P. G., & Boyd, J. N. (1999). Who's smoking, drinking, and using drugs? Time perspective as a predictor of substance use. *Basic and Applied Social Psychology*, *21*(2), 149–164.

Kidd, C., Palmeri, H., & Aslin, R. N. (2013). Rational snacking: Young children's decision-making on the marshmallow task is moderated by beliefs about environmental reliability. *Cognition*, *126*(1), 109–114.

Kim, K., Smith, P. K., & Palermiti, A. L. (1997). Conflict in childhood and reproductive development. *Evolution and Human Behavior*, *18*(2), 109–142.

Kinsey, A. C., Pomeroy, W. B., & Martin, C. E. (1948). *Sexual behavior in the human male*. Philadelphia: Saunders.

Kruger, D. J. (2008). Human life history variation and sex differences in mortality rates. *Journal of Social, Evolutionary, and Cultural Psychology*, *2*(4), 281–288.

Kruger, D. J. (2010). Socio-demographic factors intensifying male mating competition exacerbate male mortality rates. *Evolutionary Psychology*, *8*(2), 194–204.

Kruger, D. J. (2011). Evolutionary theory in Public Health and the public health of evolutionary theory. *Futures*, *43*, 762–770.

Kruger, D. J. (2017). Brief self-report scales assessing life history dimensions of mating and parenting effort. *Evolutionary Psychology*, *15*(1), 1–9.

Kruger, D. J. (2018). Facultative adjustments in future planning tendencies: Insights on life history plasticity from the Flint Water Crisis. *Evolutionary Psychological Science*, *4*(4), 372–383.

Kruger, D.J., & Kruger, J.S. (2016). Psychometric assessment of human life history predicts health related behaviors. *Psychological Topics*, *25*(1), 19–28.

Kruger, D. J., & Nesse, R. M. (2004). Sexual selection and the Male:Female Mortality Ratio. *Evolutionary Psychology*, *2*, 66–77.

Kruger, D. J., & Nesse, R. M. (2006a). An evolutionary life-history framework for understanding sex differences in human mortality rates. *Human Nature*, *17*(1), 74–97.

Kruger, D. J., & Nesse, R. M. (2006b). Understanding sex differences in Croatian mortality with an evolutionary framework. *Psychological Topics*, *15*(2), 351–364.

Kruger, D. J., & Nesse, R. M. (2007). Economic transition, male competition, and sex differences in mortality rates. *Evolutionary Psychology*, *5*(2), 411–427.

Kruger, D. J., Fernandes, H. B. F., Cupal, S., & Homish, G. G. (2019). Life history variation and the preparedness paradox. *Evolutionary Behavioral Sciences*, *13*(3), 242–253.

Kruger, D. J., Köster, M., Nedelec, J. L., & Murphy, S. F. (2018). A life history framework advances the understanding of intentions for police cooperation. *Evolutionary Behavioral Sciences*, *12*(2), 87–98.

Kruger, D. J., Nedelec, J. L., Reischl, T. M., & Zimmerman, M. A. (2015). Life history predicts perceptions of procedural justice and crime reporting intentions. *Evolutionary Psychological Science*, *1*(3), 183–194.

Kruger, D.J., Reischl, T.M., & Zimmerman, M.A. (2008). Time perspective as a mechanism for functional developmental adaptation. *Journal of Social, Evolutionary, and Cultural Psychology*, *2*(1), 1–22.

Lopez, A. D. (1998). Morbidity and mortality, changing patterns in the twentieth century. In P. Armitage and T. Colton (Eds.). *Encyclopedia of biostatistics* (pp. 2690–2701). New York: John Wiley and Sons.

Low, B. (1998). The evolution of human life histories. In C. Crawford & D. Krebs (Eds.) *Handbook of evolutionary psychology: Issues, ideas, and applications* (pp. 131–161). Mahwah, NJ: Lawrence Erlbaum Associates.

MacArthur, R., & Wilson, E. O. (1967). *The theory of island biogeography*. Princeton, NJ: Princeton University Press.

Miller, G. F. (1998). How mate choice shaped human nature: A review of sexual selection and human evolution. In C. Crawford & D. Krebs (Eds.), *Handbook of evolutionary psychology: Ideas, issues, and applications* (pp. 87–129). Mahwah, NJ: Lawrence Erlbaum Associates.

Mischel, W., Shoda, Y., & Rodriguez, M. L. (1989). Delay of gratification in children. *Science*, *244*(4907), 933–938.

Mittal, C., Griskevicius, V., Simpson, J. A., Sung, S., & Young, E. S. (2015). Cognitive adaptations to stressful environments: When childhood adversity enhances adult executive function. *Journal of Personality and Social Psychology*, *109*(4), 604–621.

Møller, A. P., Christe, P., & Lux, E. (1999). Parasitism, host immune function, and sexual selection. *Quarterly Review of Biology*, *74*(1), 3–20.

Nettle, D. (2010). Dying young and living fast: Variation in life history across English neighbourhoods. *Behavioral Ecology*, *21*(2), 387–95.

Nettle, D., & Frankenhuis, W. E. (2019). The evolution of life-history theory: A bibliometric analysis of an interdisciplinary research area. *Proceedings of the Royal Society B – Biological Sciences*, *286*(1899), 20190040.

Nettle, D., Frankenhuis, W. E., & Rickard, I. J. (2013). The evolution of predictive adaptive responses in human life history. *Proceedings of the Royal Society of London. Series B: Biological Sciences*, *280*(1766), 20131343.

Oli, M. K. (2004). The fast–slow continuum and mammalian life-history patterns: An empirical evaluation. *Basic and Applied Ecology*, *5*(5), 449–463.

Paulhus, D. L., & Williams, K. M. (2002). The Dark Triad of personality. *Journal of Research in Personality*, *36*(6), 556–563.

Penke, L., & Asendorpf, J. B. (2008). Beyond global sociosexual orientations: A more differentiated look at sociosexuality and its effects on courtship and romantic relationships. *Journal of Personality and Social Psychology*, *95*(5), 1113–1135.

Pianka, E. R. (1970). On *r*- and *K*-selection. *The American Naturalist*, *104*(940), 592–596.

Promislow, D. E. L., & Harvey, P. H. (1990). Living fast and dying young: A comparative analysis of life-history variation among mammals. *Journal of Zoology*, *220*(3), 417–437.

Quinlan, R. J. (2007). Human parental effort and environmental risk. *Proceedings of the Royal Society of London. Series B: Biological Sciences*, *274*(1606), 121–125.

Richardson, G. B., Sanning, B. K., Lai, H. C., Copping, L. T., Hardesty, P. H., & Kruger, D. J. (2017). On the psychometric study of human life history strategies: State of the science and evidence of two independent dimensions. *Evolutionary Psychology*, *15*(1), 1–24.

Rickard, I. J., Frankenhuis, W. E., & Nettle, D. (2014). Why are childhood family factors associated with timing of maturation? A role for internal state. *Perspectives on Psychological Science*, *9*(1), 3–15.

Rushton, J. P. (1985). Differential K theory: The sociobiology of individual and group differences. *Personality and Individual Differences*, *6*(4), 441–452.

Roff, D. A. (1992). *The evolution of life histories: Theory and analysis*. New York: Chapman & Hall.

Roff, D. A. (2002). *Life history evolution*. Sunderland, MA: Sinauer Associates.

Rose, H., & Rose, S. (2000). *Alas Poor Darwin: Arguments against Evolutionary Psychology*. New York: Harmony Books.

Schlichting, C. D., & Pigliucci, M. (1998). *Phenotypic evolution: A reaction norm perspective*. Sunderland, MA: Sinauer.

Schmalhausen, I. I. (1949). *Factors of evolution*. Philadelphia: Blakiston.

Sear, R., Sheppard, P., & Coall, D. A. (2019). Cross-cultural evidence does not support universal acceleration of puberty in father-absent households. *Philosophical Transactions of the Royal Society – Series B*, *374*(1770). doi.org/10.1098/rstb.2018.0124.

Simpson, J. A., & Gangestad, S. W. (1991). Individual differences in sociosexuality: Evidence for converging and discriminant validity. *Journal of Personality and Social Psychology*, *60*(6), 870–883.

Simpson, J. A., Wilson, C. L., & Winterheld, H. A. (2004). Sociosexuality and romantic relationships. In J. H. Harvey, A. Wenzel, & S. Sprecher (Eds.), *Handbook of sexuality in close relationships* (pp. 87–111). Mahwah, NJ: Lawrence Erlbaum Associates.

Stearns, S. C. (1992). *The evolution of life histories*. Oxford, UK: Oxford University Press.

Treadwell, H. M., & Young, A. M. (2013). The right US men's health report: High time to adjust priorities and attack disparities. *American Journal of Public Health*, *103*(1), 5–6.

Trivers, R. (1972). Parental investment and sexual selection. In B. Campbell (Ed.), *Sexual selection and the descent of man: 1871–1971* (pp. 136–179). Chicago: Aldine.

Van Gelder, J. L., Hershfield, H. E., & Nordgren, L. (2013). Vividness of the future self reduces delinquency. *Psychological Science*, *24*(6), 974–980.

Van Gelder, J. L., Luciano, E. C., Kranenbarg, M. W., & Hershfield, H. E. (2015). Friends with my future self: Longitudinal vividness intervention reduces delinquency. *Criminology*, *53*(2), 158–179.

van Schaik, C. P., & Isler, K. (2012). Life-history evolution. In J. C. Mitani, J. Call, P. M. Kappeler, R. Palombit, & J. B. Silk (Eds.), *The evolution of primate societies* (pp. 220–244). Chicago: University of Chicago Press.

Walker, R., Gurven, M., Hill, K., Migliano, A., Chagnon, N., De Souza, R., et al. (2006). Growth rates and life histories in twenty-two small-scale societies. *American Journal of Human Biology*, *18*(3), 295–311.

Weinrich, J. D. (1977). Human sociobiology: Pair-bonding and resource predictability (effects of social class and race). *Behavioral Ecology and Sociobiology*, *2*(2), 91–118.

West-Eberhard, M. J. (2003). *Developmental plasticity and evolution*. Oxford, England: Oxford University Press.

Wilson, M., & Daly, M. (1992). The man who mistook his wife for chattel. In J. H. Barkow, L. Cosmides & J. Tooby (Eds.), *The adapted mind* (pp. 289–322). Oxford, UK: Oxford University Press.

Wilson, M., & Daly, M. (1997). Life expectancy, economic inequality, homicide, and reproductive timing in Chicago neighbourhoods. *British Medical Journal*, *314*(7089), 1271–1274.

Zimbardo, P., & Boyd, J. (1999). Putting time in perspective: A valid, reliable individual differences metric. *Journal of Personality and Social Psychology*, *77*(6), 1271–1288.

Sperm Competition Theory

Tara DeLecce and Michael N. Pham

Sperm competition occurs when one female copulates with two or more males within a sufficiently brief time period, resulting in sperm of the different males competing to fertilize ova (Parker, 1970). Among socially monogamous species – animals that form long-term bonds and occasionally pursue extra-pair copulations – sperm competition most commonly occurs when females pursue extra-pair copulations (Smith, 1984). A paternally investing male whose regular partner pursues extra-pair copulations is at risk of cuckoldry – unwitting investment of resources into offspring to whom he is genetically unrelated. The costs of cuckoldry may have driven the evolution of male sperm competition tactics – strategic adjustments in psychology, behavior, and physiology that increase sperm competition success. Because males have finite resources for survival and reproduction, males judiciously deploy sperm competition tactics: males attend to specific sperm competition cues and adjust accordingly their sperm competition tactics.

AN EVOLUTIONARY HISTORY OF SPERM COMPETITION IN HUMANS

Cuckoldry is likely to have recurred over human evolution. Current estimates document non-zero rates of discrepant social and genetic fatherhood (Anderson, 2006; Bellis et al., 2005; Larmuseau et al., 2016; Wolf et al., 2012). A meta-analysis of 32 published studies documented that 3.1% of children are genetically unrelated to their social father (Voracek et al., 2008). Anderson (2006) showed that 29.8% of men with low paternity confidence (e.g., those disputing paternity), compared to 1.7% of men with high paternity confidence, are genetically unrelated to their child. These results suggest that men's perceived cuckoldry risk may reasonably predict their actual cuckoldry risk.

Additionally, male sexual jealousy is considered evidence that cuckoldry recurred over human evolution. Jealousy motivates men to minimize the risk of their partner's extra-pair copulations, and jealousy is so strong, in fact, that it is a leading cause of partner-killing and interpersonal violence across cultures (Buss, 2006; Daly and Wilson, 1988). Male sexual jealousy could not have evolved without the evolutionary recurrence of cuckoldry (Buss, 2013).

MATING THAT PROMOTES SPERM COMPETITION

Human sperm competition occurs when a woman 'double-mates' or copulates with two or more men within about five days (sperm remain alive in the female reproductive tract for about five days; Baker and Bellis, 1995). Using data collected from a nationwide survey of British women, Baker and Bellis (1995) reported the percentage of women who ever double-mated as a function of their sexual experience, operationalized as lifetime number of copulations. For women reporting fewer than 50 lifetime copulations, 17.5% reported having double-mated at least once. This percentage sharply increases with sexual experience: 71.8% of women reporting more than 1,000 lifetime copulations reported double-mating at least once. Among American college women, 13.4% reported having copulated with two men within a 24-hour period at least once, and 8.3% reported having copulated with two men simultaneously at once.

The temporal window for human sperm competition may extend beyond the temporal window for sperm viability. For example, dead sperm may block cervical pathways for sperm of subsequent ejaculates (Baker and Bellis, 1995). Additionally, research has yet to investigate the extent to which non-sperm substances in semen (e.g., spermicidals; Baker and Bellis, 1995) might influence the outcome of human sperm competition or the duration that these substances remain potent in the female reproductive tract. For example, it has been speculated that hormones in seminal fluid (namely follicle-stimulating

hormone and luteinizing hormone) in the female reproductive tract may trigger ovulation (reviewed in Burch and Gallup, 2006; Gallup et al., 2012).

Additional information about women's propensity for (or at least attitudes to) double-mating can be gleaned from reports of their sexual fantasies. Price and Miller (1984) ranked the content of women's sexual fantasies by popularity, and found that sexual fantasies involving sperm competition were among the top 10 most popular fantasies. Specifically, women claimed to fantasize about having sex with more than one male simultaneously, which definitively involves sperm competition. They also commonly reported fantasies of having sex with someone other than their current partner, which also might imply sperm competition.

COMPARATIVE TESTIS SIZE

Relative testis size – the ratio of testis weight to body weight – is a reliable proxy both for sperm count and for sperm competition level. A species' level of sperm competition typically correlates with its relative testis size (see Baker and Shackelford, 2018; Simmons and Fitzpatrick, 2012). Additionally, experimentally increasing sperm competition level also increases relative testis size (and, therefore, sperm count; Hosken and Ward, 2001). Although relative testis size in humans is smaller than in highly polyandrous primates, it is larger than in relatively monogamous primates (Short, 1981), indicating that sperm competition may have occurred over human evolution.

Genetic Markers

Research investigating genes that encode seminal fluid proteins suggests a moderate history of sperm competition in humans. In many non-human species (including other primates such as the gorilla and chimpanzee), proteins in seminal fluid function to form a 'mating plug' within the female reproductive tract. One of the hypothesized functions of this plug is to block sperm from rival males in subsequent matings (Leivers and Simmons, 2014), and the rate of evolution of a certain gene involved in the production of the proteins necessary to form the mating plug is positively correlated with the level of sperm competition within a species (Clark and Swanson, 2005). Among primates, the rate of evolution of this gene is moderate in humans compared to the highly promiscuous chimpanzee (Dorus et al., 2004).

Prudent Sperm Allocation

Sperm are 'tickets' for the 'lottery prize' of fertilizing ova (Parker, 1970; Wedell et al., 2002). Males at greater sperm competition risk ejaculate more sperm to increase the probability that their sperm – and not rival sperm – fertilize ova (Wedell et al., 2002). For example, among many avian species, males at greater sperm competition risk ejaculate more sperm at the next copulation (Nicholls et al., 2001; Pizzari et al., 2003). Human males at greater 'objective' sperm competition risk – the proportion of time they spend apart from their regular partner since their last in-pair copulation – ejaculate more sperm at their next in-pair copulation (Baker and Bellis, 1993a). Males may also adjust other semen parameters in response to sperm competition risk. Human males produce masturbatory ejaculates containing a greater percentage of motile sperm when viewing male-male-female (MMF) pornography (i.e., indexing sperm competition), than when viewing female-female-female (FFF) pornography (i.e., indexing the absence of sperm competition; Kilgallon & Simmons, 2005).

Whether humans can adjust their ejaculate (engage in prudent sperm allocation) in a manner predicted by sperm competition theory remains debated. For example, critics have cited the decline in semen quality during recent decades as evidence against the existence of human sperm competition (e.g., Auger et al., 1995; Bostofte et al., 1982). In terms of direct empirical evidence, a recent study by Pham and colleagues (2018) revealed that there were no significant differences in ejaculate quality between men primed with sperm competition and those in a control condition via written vignettes. While these findings appear to contradict ejaculate adjustment as predicted by sperm competition theory, it could be that written vignettes are not the appropriate stimuli to evoke such expected differences in ejaculates in the way that audiovisual stimuli might. The fact that Kilgallon and Simmons (2005) found differences in ejaculates between conditions using visual stimuli supports this speculation. Further research should incorporate such stimuli in priming studies for ejaculate adjustment.

In-pair Copulatory Interest

Males may possess a sperm competition psychology – a set of information-processing mechanisms that motivate males to strategically deploy sperm competition tactics. These mechanisms are activated when males perceive sperm competition cues (e.g., female attractiveness: Cornwallis and O'Connor, 2009; presence of rival males: Nicholls et al., 2001), and produce outputs that motivate them to perform sperm competition tactics (Goetz et al., 2007).

Among many non-human species, males attend to the presence of rival males and adjust accordingly their sperm competition tactics (Candolin and Reynolds, 2002; Gage and Barnard, 1996; Nicholls et al., 2001). Human males at greater objective sperm competition risk report greater in-pair copulatory interest, and greater distress (e.g., anger, upset, frustration, and persistence) if their regular partner denies their in-pair copulation request (Shackelford et al., 2002, 2007), but only among men who perceive that she spends more time with male friends (i.e., sexual rivals; Pham and Shackelford, 2013a; DeLecce et al., 2017). Men assess greater sperm competition risk when their regular partner is absent because it is during her absence that they cannot account for her sexual behavior with other men. Additionally, men experimentally primed with thoughts of partner infidelity reported distress if their regular partner denies their copulatory request (Starratt et al., 2013). These studies suggest a male sperm competition psychology that regulates in-pair copulatory interest as a function of sperm competition risk.

In-pair Sexual Coercion

Males at greater sperm competition risk may perform sexual coercion to force their sperm into competition with rival sperm that may be, or will be, in her reproductive tract. Human females whose regular partner is unattractive report lower sexual desire toward their regular and greater interest in extra-pair copulations during periods of conception risk (Gangestad et al., 2005). Thus, males may sexually coerce their regular partner as a sperm competition tactic. This is a result of sexual conflict – when male mating strategies and female mating strategies are at odds (Shackelford and Goetz, 2012).

Among socially monogamous birds, forced in-pair copulations occur predictably (and immediately) following events that index cuckoldry risk (e.g., intrusion of rival males, female absence, partner-observed female extra-pair copulations; Barash, 1997; Cheng et al., 1983; reviewed in Goetz and Shackelford, 2006). Human males who engage in sexual coercion also are more likely to accuse their regular partner of extra-pair copulations around the time they engage in this act (Finkelhor and Yllo, 1985; Russell, 1982). According to both men's reports and women's reports, men who are sexually coercive toward their regular partner also are more likely to accuse her of sexual infidelity

(Starratt et al., 2008). Among physically abused women, those whose regular partner performed forced copulations also report that he is more sexually jealous (Frieze, 1983; Gage and Hutchinson, 2006). Men who report sexually coercing their regular partner also report greater suspicion of her having committed sexual infidelity, and women who report a greater likelihood of pursuing extra-pair copulations also report that their regular partner is more sexually coercive (Arnocky et al., 2015; Goetz and Shackelford, 2006, 2009). Among men convicted of physically assaulting their regular partner, those who engaged in sexual coercion – relative to those who did not – experienced greater cuckoldry risk events prior to the assault (Camilleri and Quinsey, 2009). Men at greater objective sperm competition risk are more likely to engage in sexual coercion, but only those men who perceive a greater likelihood of partner infidelity (McKibbin et al., Starratt et al., 2011; reviewed in Goetz et al., 2008).

In-pair Copulation Frequency

Frequent in-pair copulations may function as a sperm competition tactic. A male who performs frequent in-pair copulations maintains large numbers of viable sperm in his partner's reproductive tract to increase his chances of success in sperm competition across her fertility cycle. In many avian species, males at greater sperm competition risk copulate frequently with their regular partner. For example, male Montagu's harriers (*Circus pygagus*) experimentally exposed to a rival male – relative to no rival males – performed more frequent in-pair copulations (Mougeot et al., 2001). Thus, males may strategically adjust copulation frequency according to sperm competition risk.

In humans, frequent in-pair copulations also may function as a sperm competition tactic. For example, a man copulates more frequently with his regular partner if she is more attractive (Kaighobadi and Shackelford, 2008), if she has more male friends and male coworkers (i.e., potential sexual rivals; Pham et al., 2014), and if he performs more mate guarding behaviors (Shackelford et al., 2006). Additionally, frequent copulation as a sperm competition tactic may explain why men (but not women) report continued sexual desire toward their regular partner over the duration of a romantic relationship (Klusmann, 2002, 2006).

Frequent in-pair copulations also may function to solve male adaptive problems associated with concealed fertility status. Because human females do not display obvious signs of ovulation in the way that other female primates do (Alexander and Noonan, 1979), frequent in-pair copulations may function as a male strategy to maintain large numbers of viable sperm in his partner's reproductive tract across her fertility cycle, ensuring that his sperm are present to fertilize her ova. Although men may detect fertility cues (Haselton and Gildersleeve, 2011), frequent copulations minimize the likelihood of missing fertilizations, and also may explain why copulation frequency decreases during menses – a time during which ova cannot be fertilized (reviewed in Brewis and Meyer, 2005).

Semen Displacement

Among several non-human species, males have adaptations to displace rival semen from a female's reproductive tract. For example, male tree crickets (*Truljalia hibinosis*) can remove nearly 90% of a rival's ejaculate from a female's reproductive tract during copulation (Ono et al., 1989). Humans also may have adaptations for semen displacement. Using artificial human penises, artificial female reproductive tracts, and semen-like fluid, Gallup et al. (2003) provided evidence that the human penis may be able to displace semen from the female reproductive tract during copulatory thrusting. Men perform more semen-displacing copulatory behaviors (e.g., deeper and more thrusts, as reported by both men and their partners) when they are at a greater recurrent risk of sperm competition (Goetz et al., 2005; Pham et al., 2017), and when they accuse their regular partner of infidelity (Gallup et al., 2003). Additionally, men experience post-ejaculatory events that prevent them from displacing their own semen, including decreased copulatory interest with the same woman (reviewed in Gallup and Burch, 2004), but not with novel women (i.e., Coolidge Effect; O'Donohue and Plaud, 1991).

An alternative explanation is that men who suspect partner infidelity may be engaging in such copulatory behaviors as a way to facilitate their partner's orgasm, as increasing their partner's orgasm frequency may be a way to increase her sexual satisfaction and thus decrease her motivation to seek extra-pair partners. Additionally, Baker and Bellis (1993b) provided evidence that women who experience orgasm near the time of their partner's ejaculation retain more of his sperm in their reproductive tract, potentially increasing his chances of success in sperm competition. However, Pham and colleagues (2017) accounted for this possibility with the finding that the deeper thrusts were not associated with the likelihood of female orgasm. Additionally, men were generally poor at knowing if their partner had a copulatory orgasm or not. These data support the explanation that the purpose of deeper copulatory thrusts are indeed for semen displacement. Deeper thrusts need not coincide with female reproductive interests, but surely with male reproductive interests. This notion has also been supported by Borgerhoff Mulder and Rauch (2009).

Male Sexual Arousal

Male sexual arousal may proximately cause the deployment of sperm competition tactics. Men's pornography preferences provide insight into male sexual arousal because pornography is produced largely to facilitate or enhance male sexual arousal (Mosher, 1988). Therefore, more sexually arousing pornography is likely more popular and prevalent. Pound (2002) documented that MMF pornography (i.e., indexing sperm competition) is more prevalent than male-female-female (MFF) pornography (i.e., indexing the decreased sperm competition). These findings are consistent with men's reports of their preferences in pornography (Pound, 2002; cf. Hald, 2006). McKibbin et al. (2013) found that the frequency of images on adult DVD covers depicting MMF pornography predicted the DVD's sales rank, whereas the frequency of images on adult DVD covers depicting MFF pornography did not predict the DVD's sales rank. Consistent with these findings from Pound (2002) and from McKibbin et al., (2013), men produce more competitive ejaculates when viewing MMF pornography than when viewing FFF pornography (as this type of pornography depicts a complete absence of sperm competition; Kilgallon and Simmons, 2005).

An alternative explanation is that men prefer MMF pornography because they are super-stimulated by witnessing simultaneous, multiple, sexual acts (e.g., oral sex, vaginal sex). However, Pound (2002) and McKibbin et al. (2013) found that MMF pornography was more arousing than pornography depicting multiple males and multiple females – scenes which likely contained the most frequent representation of simultaneous, multiple, sexual acts. Thus, men likely prefer MMF pornography because of adaptations to sperm competition, and not because of male hypersexuality.

Still, there exists other research that contradicts this preference for sperm competition cues. Hughes and colleagues (2004) documented that men overwhelmingly (97%) self-report a preference for sexual fantasies in which they have sex with more than one woman. In this case, men prioritize their desire for sexual variety over sperm competition cues. Another study revealed that when faced with a forced choice paradigm, men have the strongest preference for pornography depicting moderate levels of sperm competition (1

woman and 1 man). Pornography depicting a high level of sperm competition (1 woman with 2 men) were the least popular (Prokop, 2015). Future research should aim to clarify the sexual scenarios that men find the most sexually arousing. Along this same vein, research should also investigate the contexts and/or individual differences associated with greater sexual arousal from sperm competition cues versus those associated with greater sexual arousal from sexual variety.

Male sexual arousal causes behavioral and physiological adjustments that may function as sperm competition tactics. For example, men who are more sexually aroused express greater copulatory interest (Ariely and Loewenstein, 2006) and produce more competitive ejaculates (Zavos, 1985; Zavos and Goodpasture, 1989). Furthermore, men who are experimentally sexually aroused report a greater likelihood of performing sexually aggressive behaviors (Ariely and Loewenstein, 2006). Sufficient evidence suggests that men are sexually aroused when viewing sperm competition cues, and because their sexual arousal causes deployment of sperm competition tactics, assessing men's sexual arousal provides insight into human sperm competition psychology.

Oral Sex

Here, we define oral sex as oral stimulation of the genitals. Individuals report performing oral sex for many reasons. Cornell and Halpern-Fisher (2006) surveyed 425 young men and women who reported that they perform oral sex to retain virginity (because oral sex is sometimes not perceived as 'real' sex; Sanders and Reinisch, 1999), to increase their sexual reputation, to sexually satisfy their partner, and to avoid the risk of pregnancy and sexually transmitted infections. Much evidence suggests a human evolutionary history of oral sex. Oral sex occurs in many cultures (e.g., Guadamuz et al., 2010; Iwawaki and Wilson, 1983; Lurie et al., 1995), indicating that oral sex may not be a culture-specific practice. Pornography frequently involves oral sex, and pornography appeals to evolved mechanisms: humans do not possess adaptations to experience sexual arousal in response to viewing computer images, but to viewing live humans with whom they can copulate (Malamuth, 1996). Oral sex is depicted in ancestral cave paintings (Angulo and Garcia, 2005). Oral sex also occurs across many species (Nishimura et al., 1991; Maruthupandian and Marimuthu, 2013; Palagi et al., 2003; Soini, 1987), and behaviors that occur across species indicate the possibility of convergent adaptations. Next, we review how oral sex performed by men on women (cunnilingus) may be related to sperm competition.

Mate retention

Mate retention behaviors reduce the risk of a regular partner's extra-pair copulations (Buss, 1988; Buss and Shackelford, 1997). Men may perform cunnilingus on their regular partner to minimize their sperm competition risk. Women who receive cunnilingus are more sexually satisfied (Richters et al., 2006), and women who are more satisfied with their regular partner are less likely to commit sexual infidelity (Santtila et al., 2007). Pham and Shackelford (2013b) found that men who report greater interest in and spend more time performing cunnilingus on their regular partner also report more frequent performance of other types of mate retention tactics.

The infidelity detection hypothesis

Men may perform cunnilingus to assess sperm competition risk. Because some semen remains in the reproductive tract following insemination (Baker and Bellis, 1993b), men may assess their sperm competition risk by smelling and tasting the presence of rival semen that may be in or near their regular partner's genitals (Thornhill, 2006). The infidelity detection hypothesis may explain why men typically perform cunnilingus before

(but not after) they ejaculate (Halpern and Sherman, 1979): men's own semen might 'mask' the odor of rival semen. However, it could be that men are simply repulsed by their own semen. Indirect evidence indicates that humans can smell the semen of others. For example, fertility clinicians record the odors they smell from semen as part of semen quality analysis (e.g., Mauras et al., 2005). Pham and Shackelford (2013c) found that men with more attractive regular partners – with attractiveness being a sperm competition cue – also report greater interest in and spend more time performing cunnilingus on her.

Fertility status assessment

Males may perform cunnilingus to assess a female's fertility by sniffing and licking (i.e., oral sex) her genitals to gather scent cues to her fertility status. For example, male cotton-top tamarins (*Saguinus oedipus*) that smell a female's scent marks produced at high-fertility – relative to at low-fertility – experience more frequent penile erections and perform more mounting behaviors (Ziegler et al., 1993). Gathering scent cues to fertility status also may explain why non-human males of several species more frequently perform cunnilingus on high-fertility females than on low-fertility females (Dunbar, 1977; Johnston, 1974; Kiddy et al., 1978; Murphy, 1973; Nishimura et al., 1991; Palagi et al., 2003; Sankar and Archunan, 2004; Soini, 1987). In humans, men may also detect a female's fertility status through scent cues. For example, men rate vaginal odors that are produced during high-fertility (relative to low-fertility) as more pleasant smelling (Cerda-Molina et al., 2013; Doty et al., 1975).

Increased sexual arousal

Cunnilingus may be related to male sexual arousal and, therefore, to other sperm competition tactics. Maruthupandian and Marimuthu (2013) found that male Indian flying foxes (*Pteropus giganteus*) that spend more time performing cunnilingus on a female also copulate with her for longer durations, and they have interpreted this relationship with respect to sperm competition theory. Males typically perform cunnilingus before they copulate and ejaculate (Halpern and Sherman, 1979), suggesting that cunnilingus may influence sexual arousal and consequent sperm competition tactics (e.g., copulatory thrusting, ejaculate adjustment). Pham et al. (2013) found that men who spend more time performing oral sex on their regular partner also spend more time copulating with her, perform more semen-displacing copulatory behaviors, and report greater sexual arousal (e.g., more forceful ejaculation, greater orgasm intensity). Additionally, Cerda-Molina et al. (2013) found that men who smell vaginal odors produced at high-fertility (relative to low-fertility) also experience heightened testosterone and report greater sexual desire.

These findings from Cerda-Molina et al. (2013) support both the fertility detection function and the sexual arousal function of cunnilingus. This implies that each of these proposed functions of oral sex are not necessarily mutually exclusive. Rather, all of the proposed functions of cunnilingus support the broader hypothesis that cunnilingus minimizes cuckoldry risk for the in-pair male.

Research on the function of oral sex is preliminary, and several directions exist for future research. For example, Pham et al. (2013) provide preliminary evidence that men may perform cunnilingus on their regular partner to promote her orgasm, which may increase the number of sperm retained in her reproductive tract (Baker and Bellis, 1993b; reviewed in King and Belsky, 2012). Because women experience greater satisfaction when receiving cunnilingus (Richters et al., 2006), future research should also explore the reproductive benefits for females. Additionally, oral sex performed by females on males (fellatio) is common in humans, though less common among non-human species. Tan et al. (2009) documented that female short-nosed fruit bats (*Cynopterus sphinx*) that spend more time performing

fellatio on a male also spend more time copulating with him, and Koelman et al. (2000) found that a woman is less likely to experience pre-eclampsia if her partner ejaculates into her mouth – and especially if she ingests his semen – prior to conception. Future work on oral sex could benefit from sperm competition theory as a guide.

Remaining Issues and Future Research Directions

Male precedence

Male precedence refers to the order in which a male copulates with a female – relative to other males – and how that order influences sperm competition success. In some species (e.g., stalk-eyed flies [*Cyrtodiopsis whitei*]), the first male that copulates with a female fertilizes the largest proportion of her ova ('first male precedence'; Lorch et al., 1993). In other species (e.g., fruit flies [*Drosophila melanogaster*]), a male that copulates with a female after all other rival males copulate with her fertilizes the largest proportion of her ova ('last male precedence'; Wilson et al., 1997).

Indirect evidence suggests that human males may exhibit last male precedence (Gallup and Burch, 2004). For example, men have anatomical (Gallup et al., 2003) and physiological (Gallup and Burch, 2004) adaptations to displace rival semen – but not their own semen. Additionally, substances in seminal fluid once in the female reproductive tract from one ejaculate may create a more hospitable environment for subsequent ejaculates (reviewed in Gallup et al., 2012).

The in-pair copulation proclivity model proposes that women manipulate the time between their in-pair copulations and their extra-pair copulations. Gallup et al. (2006) found that 64.1% of women delayed indefinitely an in-pair copulation following an extra-pair copulation and suggested that women may be actively avoiding sperm competition. However, if women do not delay an extra-pair copulation following an in-pair copulation, then not only do women actively promote sperm competition, but they also actively ensure that an extra-pair partner secures a competition advantage associated with last male precedence (e.g., semen displacement). Either possibility (of female avoidance of sperm competition or of female manipulation of male precedence) provides further evidence of an evolutionary history of sperm competition in humans.

Sperm competition intensity

Sperm competition risk refers to the likelihood that a female has copulated or will copulate with two or more males during a given time period. Sperm competition intensity refers to the number of males that a female copulates with during a given time period, and is common in species in which females are highly promiscuous. There is evidence in non-human animals that males adjust the number of sperm they ejaculate in response to sperm competition intensity. For example, subdominant red junglefowl (*Gallus gallus*) males ejaculate the largest number of sperm in the presence of one rival male (i.e., low-intensity sperm competition), a moderate number of sperm when rivals are absent (i.e., zero-intensity sperm competition), and the lowest number of sperm when two or more rivals are present (i.e., high-intensity sperm competition), whereas dominant males ejaculate more sperm as the number of rivals increases (Pizzari et al., 2003).

In humans, contexts of high-intensity sperm competition (e.g., orgies, gang rapes) are less common than the contexts of low-intensity sperm competition (e.g., female infidelity; Smith, 1984). For instance, Gallup et al. (2006) found that 3.1% of college women copulated with three or more men simultaneously at least once. There is indirect evidence to suggest that men are sensitive to sperm competition intensity. For example, men prefer short-term mating with a woman who has several sexual partners (i.e., high-intensity sperm competition)

than with a woman who is in a committed relationship (i.e., low-intensity sperm competition; Shackelford et al., 2004). Pound (2002) found that men prefer viewing MMF pornography (higher-intensity sperm competition) over male-female (MF) pornography (lower-intensity sperm competition). Because men are 'witnessing' a woman copulating with another man, both conditions present an equally high risk of sperm competition, but the two conditions differ in the number of men, and, therefore, the intensity of sperm competition. This line of research suggests that sperm competition intensity models in humans mirror sperm competition intensity models in dominant male *Gallus gallus* (Pizzari et al., 2003). Men facing greater sperm competition intensity may deploy more sperm competition tactics (e.g., produce more competitive ejaculates; experience greater sexual arousal; Kilgallon and Simmons, 2005; McKibbin et al., 2013; Pound, 2002).

An evolutionary history of forced copulations by multiple males (i.e., gang rape) may have generated high-intensity sperm competition. Gang rapes have been documented in several non-human species. For example, in lesser snow geese (*Anser caerulescens caerulescens*), a female is often gang raped during her regular partner's absence, and her regular partner is absent because he is likely participating in a gang rape of a different female (Mineau and Cooke, 1979).

In humans, some evidence suggests that rapists more frequently target women at high-fertility than women at low-fertility (Gottschall and Gottschall, 2003). Some research suggests that women at high-fertility dress more provocatively (Haselton et al., 2007) and walk more sexually (Guéguen, 2012), and individuals generally agree on the 'ease of rape' when judging the walk of featureless avatars (Gunns et al., 2002). However, other evidence suggests that women take less sexual risks during the high-fertility phase of their cycle (e.g., Chavanne and Gallup, 1998).

One-third of rape complaints and one-fifth of confirmed rape cases in the United

States are gang rapes (Ullman, 1999). Gang rapes are more prevalent in some populations than others. For example, men in urban townships in the former Transkei region of South Africa invite their male friends to rape a woman, and under many circumstances (e.g., the victim supposedly deserved the rape; the victim did not vocally refuse the rape) this behavior is often legitimized (Wood, 2005). These men may recruit their male friends to forcefully copulate with their regular partner if they suspect or know of her extra-pair copulations (Wood, 2005). Among those who serve in the military, 5% of women report experiencing gang rape during their military service (Sadler et al., 2005). There are numerous case studies documenting the occurrence of gang rape perpetrated by college fraternity men (Sanday, 2007). This research suggests that contexts that promote strong male coalitions may also be the contexts that promote gang rape (e.g., friendships, fraternities, military; Gottschall, 2004).

Gang rape occurs in modern hunter-gatherer tribes, providing further evidence that gang rape may have recurred over human evolutionary history. Gang rape of women by men in the Xingu tribes of South America is so prevalent that the behavior is ritualized (McCallum, 1994). Among the Yanomamo of South America, men gang rape women who are captured from a defeated, neighboring tribe (Sanday, 1981). Gang rape may have been a recurrent context selecting over evolutionary history for adaptations to high-intensity sperm competition in humans.

Kamikaze sperm hypothesis

Although sperm competition is traditionally considered to function via a 'lottery' process (Parker, 1990), there has been some debate in the literature on the exact mechanism of sperm competition. Reports on human sperm quality routinely find up to 40% of sperm in a given ejaculate to be deformed in healthy men (Wren, 1985). Even among sperm without morphological abnormalities and in carefully controlled conditions for in vitro fertilization,

sperm have a remarkably low ability to fertilize ova, with some estimates being less than .001% for fertilization rate (Lee, 1988).

Such findings have led to questions about the lottery principle of sperm competition. Baker and Bellis (1988) proposed the Kamikaze sperm hypothesis, which suggests that not all sperm are designed to find and fertilize ova, but rather that there are three sperm types with different task specializations. The first of these are known as blockers, and these would most likely consist of the morphologically abnormal sperm that seem to comprise 40% of an average ejaculate. Their hypothesized function is to coagulate to form a copulatory plug to make it more difficult for subsequent sperm from rival males to enter the reproductive tract. Such plugs have been observed in most mammals, including primates (Ramm et al., 2005). The second sperm type are known as seek-and-destroyers, or 'kamikaze' sperm, that are able to distinguish between self and non-self and seek out sperm from other males. They then would destroy non-self sperm via premature acrosome reaction. The third sperm type are referred to as egg-getters, and they would be the ones that are actually able to fertilize ova.

The kamikaze sperm hypothesis is a controversial one, and it has been met with theoretical opposition. Harcourt (1989) argues that the kamikaze sperm hypothesis is unlikely to be true and evidence that there are positive associations between polyandry and both testis and ejaculate size are more supportive of the lottery principle proposed by Parker (1990). He also supports the proposal by Cohen (1973) that defective sperm numbers are the result of random errors in spermatogenesis, and that in some species numbers of defective sperm increase with inbreeding.

There have only been two empirical tests of the kamikaze sperm hypothesis in humans. Baker and Bellis (1995) compared sperm from the same male to a mixture of sperm from two different males. They observed that the sperm mixture from two different males was more likely to contain dead sperm and sperm with decreased motility in comparison to the condition in which there was only sperm from one male. This was interpreted as indicative of kamikaze sperm activity. However, Moore and colleagues (1999) also compared sperm from one male to sperm from two males mixed together and they did not observe significant differences in sperm parameters in either condition.

Beyond these empirical tests, Kura and Nakashima (2000) used mathematical modeling to conclude that kamikaze sperm (or soldier sperm classes, which is the term they use) could plausibly evolve even when there are low levels of sperm competition in a given species. Additionally, Holman and Snook (2006) proposed the possibility that different types of sperm with different functions (sperm heteromorphism) have been observed in numerous species from very distantly related taxa, and that non-fertile sperm could have evolved to perform more than one function depending on the context (e.g., to affect subsequent mating behavior in females or to attack fertile sperm from rival males) and that empirical tests examining only one of these possibilities at a time might miss a more nuanced picture of non-fertile sperm activity.

Taken together, sperm heteromorphism and the possibility that different sperm types evolved to increase paternity certainty in the context of sperm competition remains poorly understood and in need of further research. Future research should empirically test the kamikaze sperm hypothesis using enhanced technology that would improve the methodology that was used in previous attempts.

Relationship between phenotype and ejaculate quality

Some literature has put forth the idea that non-human males give cues to their ejaculate quality via other phenotypic traits. This has led to the formation of the phenotype-linked fertility hypothesis (Sheldon, 1994) which suggests that females assess male fertility

through secondary sexual characteristics that provide honest cues of a male's probability of fertilizing ova. This could be useful for females seeking to promote sperm competition by only mating with males of the highest phenotypic quality to ensure the best of that already high-quality pool of males fertilizes ova. For example, larger, more colorful male guppies, who are preferred as mating partners, also have larger, more abundant, and more motile sperm than their smaller rivals (Locatello et al., 2006). In humans, who are relatively more monogamous, this would likely function differently, such that women could easily pick extra-pair copulation partners via phenotypic cues as fertility insurance in the event that her regular partner fails to fertilize her ova (Jeffrey et al., 2016). There is limited research testing this idea in humans, but the extant literature has yielded conflicting results. In humans, the secondary sexual characteristics that have been commonly studied are intelligence (Arden et al., 2009), physical attractiveness (Soler et al., 2014), voice pitch (Simmons et al., 2011), and masculinity (often measured by 2D:4D ratio; Manning et al., 1988). A recent meta-analysis examining the relationship between all of these markers of phenotypic quality and ejaculate quality revealed that there is inconclusive evidence for the phenotype-linked fertility hypothesis in humans, suggesting that future research on the subject should attempt to standardize methodologies for measuring both phenotypic traits and ejaculate quality (Jeffery et al., 2016).

In contrast to the phenotype-linked fertility hypothesis, another line of research suggests there is a different theory that can be applied to explain the relationship between phenotypic traits and ejaculate quality; specifically, that there exists a trade-off between secondary sexual characteristics and ejaculate quality (Simmons et al., 2017). This trade-off posits that animals have a finite amount of metabolic energy, and that which is spent on secondary sexual characteristics is at the expense of ejaculate quality and vice versa. Experimental manipulations in insects that involve interference in the development of secondary sexual characteristics (e.g., horns on beetles) have resulted in larger testes in the affected individuals (Simmons and Emlen, 2006; Somjee et al., 2018).

This theory has been applied to humans as well and it has found some support. In one study, a negative correlation was revealed between men's ejaculate quality and their perceived physical strength (assessed via ratings from static photographs; Foo et al., 2018). Perhaps this tradeoff can also manifest itself in the form of behaviors, as Leivers and colleagues (2014) found that men who invest more of their time engaging in mate guarding behaviors (e.g., being vigilant of their mate's whereabouts, spending a lot of free time with their mate, buying gifts for their mate) tend to have lower sperm concentration and motility compared to men who report relatively little time in mate guarding.

The relationship between ejaculate quality and secondary sexual characteristics is complex, with some evidence supporting the phenotype-linked hypothesis and some evidence supporting the trade-off hypothesis. Further research is required to disentangle this complex relationship, which may also depend on individual difference and/or contextual factors.

CONCLUSION

In this chapter, we reviewed evidence that human and many non-human males attend to similar cues of sperm competition (e.g., female attractiveness, regular partner's absence, presence and number of rival males) and deploy similar sperm competition tactics (e.g., ejaculate adjustment, sexual coercion, frequent in-pair copulations). In particular, many human sperm competition adaptations are analogous to those in birds. Convergent evolution may explain these cross-species similarities, because humans and most birds have similar mating systems (i.e., social monogamy) that require solutions to similar adaptive problems (e.g., cuckoldry). The substantial body of research documenting physiological anatomical, behavioral, and psychological adaptations to sperm competition in birds and many other non-human animals provides evidence that sperm competition was a recurrent adaptive problem for these animals. Research on humans also provides evidence that sperm competition was a recurrent feature of human evolutionary history and still warrants further research to reach a better understanding of both its prevalence and its effects on mating behavior.

ACKNOWLEDGEMENTS

The structure of this chapter was inspired by a literature review by Pham and Shackelford (2014).

REFERENCES

Alexander, R. D., & Noonan, K. M. (1979). Concealment of ovulation, parental care, and human social evolution. In N. A. Chagnon & W. Irons (Eds), *Evolutionary biology and human social behavior: An anthropological perspective* (pp. 436–453). North Scituate, MA: Duxbury Press.

Anderson, K. (2006). How well does paternity confidence match actual paternity? Evidence from worldwide nonpaternity rates. *Current Anthropology*, *47*(3), 513–520.

Angulo, J., & García, M. (2005). *Sex in stone: Sexuality, reproduction, and eroticism in the Paleolithic epoch*. Madrid: Luzán.

Arden R., Gottfredson, L. S., Miller, G. F., & Pierce, A. (2009). Intelligence and semen quality are positively correlated. *Intelligence*, *37*(3), 277–282.

Ariely, D., & Loewenstein, G. (2006). The heat of the moment: The effect of sexual arousal on sexual decision making. *Journal of Behavioral Decision Making*, *19*(2), 87–98.

Arnocky, S., Sunderani, S., Gomes, W., & Vaillancourt, T. (2015). Anticipated partner infidelity and men's intimate partner violence: The mediating role of anxiety. *Evolutionary Behavioral Sciences*, *9*(3), 186–196.

Auger, J., Kunstmann, J. M., Czyglik, F. & Jouannet, P. (1995). Decline in semen quality among fertile men in Paris during the past 20 years. *New England Journal of Medicine*, *332*(5), 281–285.

Baker, R. R., & Bellis, M. A. (1988). 'Kamikaze' sperm in mammals? *Animal Behaviour*, *36*(3), 936–939.

Baker, R. R., & Bellis, M. A. (1993a). Human sperm competition: Ejaculate adjustment by males and the function of masturbation. *Animal Behaviour*, *46*(5), 861–885.

Baker, R. R., & Bellis, M. A. (1993b). Human sperm competition: Ejaculate manipulation by females and a function for the female orgasm. *Animal Behaviour*, *46*(5), 887–909.

Baker, R., & Bellis, M. A. (1995). *Human sperm competition: Copulation, masturbation and infidelity*. London: Chapman & Hall.

Baker, R. R., & Shackelford, T. K. (2018). A comparison of paternity data and relative testes size as measures of level of sperm competition in the Hominoidea. *American Journal of Physical Anthropology*, *165*(3), 421–443.

Barash, D. P. (1977). Sociobiology of rape in mallards (*Anas platyrhynchos*): Responses of the mated male. *Science*, *197*(4305), 788–789.

Bellis, M. A., Hughes, K., Hughes, S., & Ashton, J. R. (2005). Measuring paternal discrepancy and its public health consequences. *Journal of Epidemiology & Community Health*, *59*(9), 749–754.

Borgerhoff Mulder, M., & Rauch, K. L. (2009). Sexual conflict in humans: Variations and solutions. *Evolutionary Anthropology*, *18*(5), 201–214.

Bostofte, E., Serup, J., & Rebbe, H. (1983). Has the fertility of Danish men declined through the years in terms of semen quality? A comparison of semen qualities between 1952 and 1972. *International Journal of Fertility*, *28*(2), 91–95.

Brewis, A., & Meyer, M. (2005). Demographic evidence that human ovulation is undetectable (at least in pair bonds). *Current Anthropology*, *46*(3), 465–471.

Burch, R. L., & Gallup, G. G. (2006). The psychobiology of human semen. In S. M. Platek & T. K. Shackelford (Eds), *Female infidelity and paternal uncertainty* (pp. 141–172). New York: Cambridge University Press.

Buss, D. M. (1988). From vigilance to violence: Tactics of mate retention in American undergraduates. *Ethology and Sociobiology*, *9*(5), 291–317.

Buss, D. M. (2006). *The murderer next door: Why the mind is designed to kill*. New York: Penguin.

Buss, D. M. (2013). Sexual jealousy. *Psychological Topics*, *22*(2), 155–182.

Buss, D. M., & Shackelford, T. K. (1997). From vigilance to violence: Mate retention tactics in married couples. *Journal of Personality and Social Psychology*, *72*(2), 346–361.

Camilleri, J. A., & Quinsey, V. L. (2009). Testing the cuckoldry risk hypothesis of partner sexual coercion in community and forensic samples. *Evolutionary Psychology*, *7*(2), 147470490900700203.

Candolin, U., & Reynolds, J. D. (2002). Adjustments of ejaculation rates in response to risk of sperm competition in a fish, the bitterling (*Rhodeus sericeus*). *Proceedings of the Royal Society of London. Series B: Biological Sciences*, *269*(1500), 1549–1553.

Cerda-Molina, A. L., Hernández-López, L., Claudio, E., Chavira-Ramírez, R., & Mondragón-Ceballos, R. (2013). Changes in men's salivary testosterone and cortisol levels, and in sexual desire after smelling female axillary and vulvar scents. *Frontiers in Endocrinology*, *4*, 159.

Chavanne, T. J., & Gallup Jr, G. G. (1998). Variation in risk taking behavior among female college students as a function of the menstrual cycle. *Evolution and Human Behavior*, *19*(1), 27–32.

Cheng, K. M., Burns, J. T., & McKinney, F. (1983). Forced copulation in captive mallards III. Sperm competition. *The Auk*, *100*(2), 302–310.

Clark, N. L., & Swanson, W. J. (2005). Pervasive adaptive evolution in primate seminal proteins. *PLoS Genetics*, *1*(3), e35.

Cohen, J. (1973). Crossovers, sperm redundancy, and their close association. *Heredity*, *31*(3), 408–413.

Cornell, J. L., & Halpern-Felsher, B. L. (2006). Adolescents tell us why teens have oral sex.

Journal of Adolescent Health, *38*(3), 299–301.

Cornwallis, C. K., & O'Connor, E. A. (2009). Sperm: Seminal fluid interactions and the adjustment of sperm quality in relation to female attractiveness. *Proceedings of the Royal Society of London B: Biological Sciences*, *276*(1672), 3467–3475.

Daly, M. & Wilson, M. (1988). *Homicide*. Hawthorne, NY: Aldine.

DeLecce, T., Barbaro, N., Mohamedally, D., & Shackelford, T. K. (2017). Husband's reaction to his wife's sexual rejection is predicted by the time she spends with her male friends, but not her male coworkers. *Evolutionary Psychology*, *15*(2), 1–5.

Dorus, S., Evans, P. D., Wyckoff, G. J., Choi, S. S., & Lahn, B. T. (2004). Rate of molecular evolution of the seminal protein gene SEMG2 correlates with levels of female promiscuity. *Nature Genetics*, *36*(12), 1326–1329.

Doty, R. L., Ford, M., Preti, G., & Huggins, G. R. (1975). Changes in the intensity and pleasantness of human vaginal odors during the menstrual cycle. *Science*, *190*(4221), 1316–1318.

Dunbar, I. F. (1977). Olfactory preferences in dogs: The response of male and female beagles to conspecific odors. *Behavioral Biology*, *20*(4), 471–481.

Finkelhor, D., & Yllo, K. (1985). *License to rape: Sexual abuse of wives*. New York: Holt, Rinehart and Winston.

Foo, Y. Z., Simmons, L. W., Peters, M., & Rhodes, G. (2018). Perceived physical strength in men is attractive to women but may come at a cost to ejaculate quality. *Animal Behavior*, *142*, 191–197.

Frieze, I. H. (1983). Investigating the causes and consequences of marital rape. *Signs: Journal of Women in Culture and Society*, *8*(3), 532–553.

Gage, A. J., & Hutchinson, P. L. (2006). Power, control, and intimate partner sexual violence in Haiti. *Archives of Sexual Behavior*, *35*(1), 11–24.

Gage, A. R., & Barnard, C. J. (1996). Male crickets increase sperm number in relation to competition and female size. *Behavioral Ecology and Sociobiology*, *38*(5), 349–353.

Gallup Jr, G. G., & Burch, R. L. (2004). Semen displacement as a sperm competition strategy in humans. *Evolutionary Psychology*, *2*(1), 147470490400200105.

Gallup Jr, G. G., & Burch, R. L. (2006). The semen-displacement hypothesis: Semen hydraulics and the intra-pair copulation proclivity model of female infidelity. In S. Platek and T. Shackelford (Eds), *Female infidelity and paternal uncertainty: Evolutionary perspectives on male anti-cuckoldry tactics* (pp. 129–140). Cambridge, UK: Cambridge University Press.

Gallup, G. G., Burch, R. L., & Mitchell, T. J. B. (2006). Semen displacement as a sperm competition strategy: Multiple mating, self-semen displacement, and timing of in-pair copulations. *Human Nature*, *17*(3), 253–264.

Gallup Jr, G. G., Burch, R. L., & Petricone, L. R. (2012). Sexual conflict, infidelity, and vaginal/semen chemistry. In T. K. Shackelford & A. T. Goetz (Eds), *The Oxford handbook of sexual conflict in humans* (pp. 217–231). New York: Oxford University Press.

Gallup Jr, G. G., Burch, R. L., Zappieri, M. L., Parvez, R. A., Stockwell, M. L., & Davis, J. A. (2003). The human penis as a semen displacement device. *Evolution and Human Behavior*, *24*(4), 277–289.

Gangestad, S. W., Thornhill, R., & Garver-Apgar, C. E. (2005). Women's sexual interests across the ovulatory cycle depend on primary partner developmental instability. *Proceedings of the Royal Society of London B: Biological Sciences*, *272*(1576), 2023–2027.

Goetz, A. T., & Shackelford, T. K. (2006). Sexual coercion and forced in-pair copulation as sperm competition tactics in humans. *Human Nature*, *17*(3), 265–282.

Goetz, A. T., & Shackelford, T. K. (2009). Sexual coercion in intimate relationships: A comparative analysis of the effects of women's infidelity and men's dominance and control. *Archives of Sexual Behavior*, *38*(2), 226–234.

Goetz, A. T., Shackelford, T. K., & Camilleri, J. A. (2008). Proximate and ultimate explanations are required for a comprehensive understanding of partner rape. *Aggression and Violent Behavior*, *13*(2), 119–123.

Goetz, A. T., Shackelford, T. K., Platek, S. M., Starratt, V. G., & McKibbin, W. F. (2007). Sperm competition in humans: Implications for male sexual psychology, physiology, anatomy, and behavior. *Annual Review of Sex Research*, *18*(1), 1–22.

Goetz, A. T., Shackelford, T. K., Weekes-Shackelford, V. A., Euler, H. A., Hoier, S.,

Schmitt, D. P., & LaMunyon, C. W. (2005). Mate retention, semen displacement, and human sperm competition: A preliminary investigation of tactics to prevent and correct female infidelity. *Personality and Individual Differences*, *38*(4), 749–763.

Gottschall, J. (2004). Explaining wartime rape. *Journal of Sex Research*, *41*(2), 129–136.

Gottschall, J. A., & Gottschall, T. A. (2003). Are per-incident rape-pregnancy rates higher than per-incident consensual pregnancy rates? *Human Nature*, *14*(1), 1–20.

Guadamuz, T. E., Kunawararak, P., Beyrer, C., Pumpaisanchai, J., Wei, C., & Celentano, D. D. (2010). HIV prevalence, sexual and behavioral correlates among Shan, Hill tribe, and Thai male sex workers in Northern Thailand. *AIDS Care*, *22*(5), 597–605.

Guéguen, N. (2012). Gait and menstrual cycle: Ovulating women use sexier gaits and walk slowly ahead of men. *Gait & Posture*, *35*(4), 621–624.

Gunns, R. E., Johnston, L., & Hudson, S. M. (2002). Victim selection and kinematics: A point-light investigation of vulnerability to attack. *Journal of Nonverbal Behavior*, *26*(3), 129–158.

Hald, G. M. (2006). Gender differences in pornography consumption among young heterosexual Danish adults. *Archives of Sexual Behavior*, *35*(5), 577–585.

Halpern, J. & Sherman, M. A. (1979). *Afterplay: A key to intimacy*. New York: Pocket Books.

Harcourt, A. H. (1989). Deformed sperm are probably not adaptive. *Animal Behaviour, 37*(5), 863–865.

Haselton, M. G., & Gildersleeve, K. (2011). Can men detect ovulation? *Current Directions in Psychological Science*, *20*(2), 87–92.

Haselton, M. G., Mortezaie, M., Pillsworth, E. G., Bleske-Rechek, A., & Frederick, D. A. (2007). Ovulatory shifts in human female ornamentation: Near ovulation, women dress to impress. *Hormones and Behavior*, *51*(1), 40–45.

Holman, L., & Snook, R. R. (2006). Spermicide, cryptic female choice and the evolution of sperm form and function. *Journal of Evolutionary Biology*, *19*(5), 1660–1670.

Hosken, D. J., & Ward, P. I. (2001). Experimental evidence for testis size evolution via sperm competition. *Ecology Letters*, *4*(1), 10–13.

Hughes, S. M., Harrison, M. A., & Gallup, G. G. Jr. (2004). Sex differences in mating strategies: Mate guarding, infidelity and multiple concurrent sex partners. *Sexualities, Evolution & Gender*, *6*(1), 3–13.

Iwawaki, S., & Wilson, G. D. (1983). Sex fantasies in Japan. *Personality and Individual Differences*, *4*(5), 543–545.

Jeffery, A. J., Pham, M. N., Shackelford, T. K., & Fink, B. (2016). Does human ejaculate quality relate to phenotypic traits? *American Journal of Human Biology*, *28*(3), 318–329.

Johnston, R. E. (1974). Sexual attraction function of golden hamster vaginal secretion. *Behavioral Biology*, *12*(1), 111–117.

Kaighobadi, F., & Shackelford, T. K. (2008). Female attractiveness mediates the relationship between in-pair copulation frequency and men's mate retention behaviors. *Personality and Individual Differences*, *45*(4), 293–295.

Kiddy, C. A., Mitchell, D S., Bolt, D. J., & Hawk, H. W. (1978). Detection of estrus-related odors in cows by trained dogs. *Biology of Reproduction*, *19*(2), 389–395.

Kilgallon, S. J., & Simmons, L. W. (2005). Image content influences men's semen quality. *Biology Letters*, *1*(3), 253–255.

King, R., & Belsky, J. (2012). A typological approach to testing the evolutionary functions of human female orgasm. *Archives of Sexual Behavior*, *41*(5), 1145–1160.

Klusmann, D. (2002). Sexual motivation and the duration of partnership. *Archives of Sexual Behavior*, *31*(3), 275–287.

Klusmann, D. (2006). Sperm competition and female procurement of male resources as explanations for a sex-specific time course in the sexual motivation of couples. *Human Nature*, *17*(3), 283–300.

Koelman, C. A., Coumans, A. B., Nijman, H. W., Doxiadis, I. I., Dekker, G. A., & Claas, F. H. (2000). Correlation between oral sex and a low incidence of preeclampsia: A role for soluble HLA in seminal fluid? *Journal of Reproductive Immunology*, *46*(2), 155–166.

Kura, T., & Nakashima, Y. (2000). Conditions for the evolution of soldier sperm classes. *Evolution*, *54*(1), 72–80.

Larmuseau, M. H., Matthijs, K., & Wenseleers, T. (2016). Cuckolded fathers rare in human populations. *Trends in Ecology & Evolution*, *31*(5), 327–329.

Lee, S. (1988). Sperm preparation for assisted conception. *Conceive*, *12*, 4–5.

Leivers, S., & Simmons, L. W. (2014). Human sperm competition: Playing a defensive strategy. *Advances in the Study of Behavior*, *46*(2), 1–44.

Leivers, S., Rhodes, G., & Simmons, L. W. (2014). Sperm competition in humans: Mate guarding behavior negatively correlates with ejaculate quality. *PLoS One*, 9(9), e108099.

Locatello, L., Rasotto, M. B., Evans, J. P., & Pilastro, A. (2006). Colourful male guppies produce faster and more viable sperm. *Journal of Evolutionary Biology*, *19*(5), 1595–1602.

Lorch, P. D., Wilkinson, G. S., & Reillo, P. R. (1993). Copulation duration and sperm precedence in the stalk-eyed fly *Cyrtodiopsis whitei* (Diptera: Diopsidae). *Behavioral Ecology and Sociobiology*, *32*(5), 303–311.

Lurie, P., Fernandes, M. E. L., Hughes, V., Arevalo, E. I., Hudes, E. S., Reingold, A., & Hearst, N. (1995). Socioeconomic status and risk of HIV-1, syphilis and hepatitis B infection among sex workers in São Paulo State, Brazil. *AIDS*, *9*(Suppl_1), S31–S37.

Malamuth, N. M. (1996). Sexually explicit media, gender differences and evolutionary theory. *Journal of Communication*, *46*(3), 8–31.

Manning, J. T., Scutt, D., Wilson, J., & Lewis-Jones, D. I. (1998). The ratio of 2nd to 4th digit length: A predictor of sperm numbers and concentration of testosterone luteinizing hormone and oestrogen. *Human Reproduction*, *13*(11), 3000–3004.

Maruthupandian, J., & Marimuthu, G. (2013). Cunnilingus apparently increases duration of copulation in the Indian flying fox, *Pteropus giganteus*. *PLoS One*, *8*(3), e59743.

Mauras, N., Bell, J., Snow, B. G., & Winslow, K. L. (2005). Sperm analysis in growth hormone-deficient adolescents previously treated with an aromatase inhibitor: Comparison with normal controls. *Fertility and Sterility*, *84*(1), 239–242.

McCallum, C. (1994). Ritual and the origin of sexuality in the Alto Xingu. In P. Harvey & P. Gow (Eds), *Sex and violence: Issues in representation and experience* (pp. 90–114). New York: Routledge.

McKibbin, W. F., Pham, M. N., & Shackelford, T. K. (2013). Human sperm competition in postindustrial ecologies: Sperm competition cues predict adult DVD sales. *Behavioral Ecology*, *24*(4), 819–823.

McKibbin, W. F., Starratt, V. G., Shackelford, T. K., & Goetz, A. T. (2011). Perceived risk of female infidelity moderates the relationship between objective risk of female infidelity and sexual coercion in humans (*Homo sapiens*). *Journal of Comparative Psychology*, *125*(3), 370–373.

Mineau, P., & Cooke, F. (1979). Rape in the lesser snow goose. *Behaviour*, *70*(3–4), 280–291.

Moore, H. D. M., Martin, M., & Birkhead, T. R. (1999). No evidence for killer sperm or other selective interactions between human spermatozoa in ejaculates of different males in vitro. *Proceedings of the Royal Society of London. Series B: Biological Sciences*, *266*(1436), 2343–2350.

Mosher, D. L. (1988). Pornography defined: Sexual involvement theory, narrative context, and goodness-of-fit. *Journal of Psychology & Human Sexuality*, *1*(1), 67–85.

Mougeot, F., Arroyo, B. E., & Bretagnolle, V. (2001). Decoy presentations as a means to manipulate the risk of extrapair copulation: An experimental test of paternity assurance strategies in a semi-colonial raptor, the Montagu's Harrier (*Circus pygargus*). *Behavioural Ecology*, *12*(1), 1–7.

Murphy, M. R. (1973). Effects of female hamster vaginal discharge on the behavior of male hamsters. *Behavioral Biology*, *9*(3), 367–375.

Nicholls, E. H., Burke, T., & Birkhead, T. R. (2001). Ejaculate allocation by male sand martins, *Riparia riparia*. *Proceedings of the Royal Society of London. Series B: Biological Sciences*, *268*(1473), 1265–1270.

Nishimura, K., Utsumi, K., Okano, T., & Iritani, A. (1991). Separation of mounting-inducing pheromones of vaginal mucus from estrual heifers. *Journal of Animal Science*, *69*(8), 3343–3347.

O'Donohue, W., & Plaud, J. J. (1991). The long-term habituation of sexual arousal in the human male. *Journal of Behavior Therapy and Experimental Psychiatry*, *22*(2), 87–96.

Ono, T., Siva-Jothy, M. T., & Kato, A. K. I. (1989). Removal and subsequent ingestion of rivals' semen during copulation in a tree cricket. *Physiological Entomology, 14*(2), 195–202.

Palagi, E., Telara, S., & Tarli, S. B. (2003). Sniffing behavior in *Lemur catta*: Seasonality, sex, and rank. *International Journal of Primatology, 24*(2), 335–350.

Parker, G. A. (1970). Sperm competition and its evolutionary consequences in the insects. *Biological Reviews, 45*(4), 525–567.

Parker, G. A. (1990). Sperm competition games: Raffles and roles. *Proceedings of the Royal Society of London. Series B: Biological Sciences, 242*(1304), 120–126.

Pham, M. N., & Shackelford, T. K. (2013a). The relationship between objective sperm competition risk and men's copulatory interest is moderated by partner's time spent with other men. *Human Nature, 24*(4), 476–485.

Pham, M. N., & Shackelford, T. K. (2013b). Oral sex as mate retention behavior. *Personality and Individual Differences, 55*(2), 185–188.

Pham, M. N., & Shackelford, T. K. (2013c). Oral sex as infidelity-detection. *Personality and Individual Differences, 54*(6), 792–795.

Pham, M. N. & Shackelford, T. K. (2014). Human sperm competition: A comparative evolutionary analysis. *Animal Behavior and Cognition, 1*(3), 410–422.

Pham, M. N., DeLecce, T., & Shackelford, T. K. (2017). Sperm competition in marriage: Semen displacement, male rivals, and spousal discrepancy in sexual interest. *Personality and Individual Differences, 105*, 229–232.

Pham, M. N., Shackelford, T. K., Sela, Y., & Welling, L. L. (2013). Is cunnilingus-assisted orgasm a male sperm-retention strategy? *Evolutionary Psychology, 11*(2), 147470491301100210.

Pham, M. N., Shackelford, T. K., Holden, C. J., Zeigler-Hill, V., Hummel, A., & Memering, S. L. (2014). Partner attractiveness moderates the relationship between number of sexual rivals and in-pair copulation frequency in humans (*Homo sapiens*). *Journal of Comparative Psychology, 128*(3), 328–331.

Pham, M. N., Shackelford, T. K., Welling, L. L., Ehrke, A. D., Sela, Y., & Goetz, A. T. (2013). Oral sex, semen displacement, and sexual arousal: Testing the ejaculate adjustment hypothesis. *Evolutionary Psychology, 11*(5), 147470491301100515.

Pham, M. N., Barbaro, N., Holub, A., Holden, C. J., Mogilski, J. K., Lopes, G. S., Nicolas, S.

C. A., Sela, Y., Shackelford, T. K., Zeigler-Hill, V., & Welling, L. L. M. (2018). Do men produce higher-quality ejaculates when primed with thoughts of partner infidelity? *Evolutionary Psychology, 16*(1), 1–7.

Pizzari, T., Cornwallis, C. K., Løvlie, H., Jakobsson, S., & Birkhead, T. R. (2003). Sophisticated sperm allocation in male fowl. *Nature, 426*(6962), 70–74.

Pound, N. (2002). Male interest in visual cues of sperm competition risk. *Evolution and Human Behavior, 23*(6), 443–466.

Price, J. H., & Miller, P. A. (1984). Sexual fantasies of Black and of White college students. *Psychological Reports, 54*(3), 1007–1014.

Prokop, P. (2015). Perception of intensity of sperm competition on the part of males. *Personality and Individual Differences, 76*, 99–103.

Ramm, S. A., Parker, G. A., & Stockley, P. (2005). Sperm competition and the evolution of male reproductive anatomy in rodents. *Proceedings of the Royal Society for Biological Sciences of London. Series B: Biological Sciences., 272*(1566), 949–955.

Richters, J., de Visser, R., Rissel, C., & Smith, A. (2006). Sexual practices at last heterosexual encounter and occurrence of orgasm in a national survey. *Journal of Sex Research, 43*(3), 217–226.

Russell, D. E. H. (1982). *Rape in marriage*. New York: Macmillan Press.

Sadler, A. G., Booth, B. M., & Doebbeling, B. N. (2005). Gang and multiple rapes during military service: Health consequences and health care. *Journal of the American Medical Women's Association, 60*(1), 33–41.

Sanday, P. R. (1981). The socio-cultural context of rape: A cross-cultural study. *Journal of Social Issues, 37*(4), 5–27.

Sanday, P. (2007). *Fraternity gang rape: Sex, brotherhood, and privilege on campus*. New York: NYU Press.

Sanders, S. A., & Reinisch, J. M. (1999). Would you say you 'had sex' if …? *Journal of the American Medical Association, 281*(3), 275–277.

Sankar, R., & Archunan, G. (2004). Flehmen response in bull: Role of vaginal mucus and other body fluids of bovine with special reference to estrus. *Behavioural Processes, 67*(1), 81–86.

Santtila, P., Wager, I., Witting, K., Harlaar, N., Jern, P., Johansson, A. D. A., Varjonen, M. & Sandnabba, N. K. (2007). Discrepancies between sexual desire and sexual activity: Gender differences and associations with relationship satisfaction. *Journal of Sex & Marital Therapy*, *34*(1), 31–44.

Shackelford, T. K., & Goetz, A. T. (Eds) (2012). *The Oxford handbook of sexual conflict in humans.* New York: Oxford University Press.

Shackelford, T. K., Goetz, A. T., Guta, F. E., & Schmitt, D. P. (2006). Mate guarding and frequent in-pair copulation in humans. *Human Nature*, *17*(3), 239–252.

Shackelford, T. K., Goetz, A. T., McKibbin, W. F., & Starratt, V. G. (2007). Absence makes the adaptations grow fonder: Proportion of time apart from partner, male sexual psychology, and sperm competition in humans (*Homo sapiens*). *Journal of Comparative Psychology*, *121*(2), 214–220.

Shackelford, T. K., Goetz, A. T., LaMunyon, C. W., Quintus, B. J., & Weekes-Shackelford, V. A. (2004). Sex differences in sexual psychology produce sex-similar preferences for a short-term mate. *Archives of Sexual Behavior*, *33*(4), 405–412.

Shackelford, T. K., LeBlanc, G. J., Weekes-Shackelford, V. A., Bleske-Rechek, A. L., Euler, H. A., & Hoier, S. (2002). Psychological adaptation to human sperm competition. *Evolution and Human Behavior*, *23*(2), 123–138.

Sheldon, B. C. (1994). Male phenotype fertility and the pursuit of extra-pair copulations by female birds. *Proceedings of the Royal Society of London. B: Biological Sciences*, *257*(1348), 25–30.

Short, R. V. (1981). Sexual selection in man and the apes. In C. E. Graham (Ed.), *Reproductive biology of the great apes* (pp. 319–341). New York: Academic Press.

Simmons, L. W., & Emlen, D. J. (2006). Evolutionary trade-off between weapons and testes. *Proceedings of the National Academy of Sciences of the United States of America*, *103*(44), 16349–16351.

Simmons, L. W., & Fitzpatrick, J. L. (2012). Sperm wars and the evolution of male fertility. *Journal of Reproduction and Fertility*, *144*(5), 519–534.

Simmons, L. W., Lüpold, S., & Fitzpatrick, J. L. (2017). Evolutionary trade-off between secondary sexual traits and ejaculates. *Trends in Ecology & Evolution*, *32*(12), 964–976.

Simmons, L. W., Peters, M. P., & Rhodes, G. (2011). Low pitched voices are perceived as masculine and attractive but do they predict semen quality in men? *PLoS One*, *6*(12), e29271.

Smith, R. L. (1984). Human sperm competition. In R. L. Smith (Ed.), *Sperm competition and the evolution of animal mating systems* (pp. 601–659). New York: Academic Press.

Soini, P. (1987). Sociosexual behavior of a free-ranging *Cebuella pygmaea* (Callitrichidae, platyrrhini) troop during postpartum estrus of its reproductive female. *American Journal of Primatology*, *13*(3), 223–230.

Soler, C., Kekäläinen, J., Núñez, M., Sancho, M., Alvarez, J.G., Núñez, J., Yaber, I., & Gutiérrez, R. (2014). Male facial attractiveness and masculinity may provide sex- and culture-independent cues to semen quality. *Journal of Evolutionary Biology*, *27*(9), 1930–1938.

Somjee, U., Miller, C., Tatarnic, N. J. & Simmons, L. W. (2018). Experimental manipulation reveals a trade-off between weapons and testes. *Journal of Evolutionary Biology*, *31*(1), 57–65.

Starratt, V. G., Goetz, A. T., Shackelford, T. K., McKibbin, W. F., & Stewart-Williams, S. (2008). Men's partner-directed insults and sexual coercion in intimate relationships. *Journal of Family Violence*, *23*(5), 315–323.

Starratt, V. G., McKibbin, W. F., & Shackelford, T. K. (2013). Experimental activation of anti-cuckoldry mechanisms responsive to female sexual infidelity. *Personality and Individual Differences*, *55*(1), 59–62.

Tan, M., Jones, G., Zhu, G., Ye, J., Hong, T., Zhou, S., Zhang, S., & Zhang, L. (2009). Fellatio by fruit bats prolongs copulation time. *PLoS One*, *4*(10), e7595.

Thornhill, R. (2006). Foreword: Human sperm competition and women's dual sexuality. In T. K. Shackelford & N. Pound (Eds), *Sperm competition in humans: Classic and contemporary readings* (v–xix). New York: Springer.

Ullman, S. E. (1999). A comparison of gang and individual rape incidents. *Violence and Victims*, *14*(2), 123–133.

Voracek, M., Haubner, T., & Fisher, M. L. (2008). Recent decline in nonpaternity rates:

A cross-temporal meta-analysis. *Psychological Reports*, *103*(3), 799–811.

Wedell, N., Gage, M. J., & Parker, G. A. (2002). Sperm competition, male prudence and sperm-limited females. *Trends in Ecology & Evolution*, *17*(7), 313–320.

Wilson, N., Tubman, S. C., Eady, P. E., & Robertson, G. W. (1997). Female genotype affects male success in sperm competition. *Proceedings of the Royal Society of London. Series B: Biological Sciences*, *264*(1387), 1491–1495.

Wolf, M., Musch, J., Enczmann, J., & Fischer, J. (2012). Estimating the prevalence of nonpaternity in Germany. *Human Nature*, *23*(2), 208–217.

Wood, K. (2005). Contextualizing group rape in post-apartheid South Africa. *Culture, Health & Sexuality*, *7*(4), 303–317.

Wren, B. G. (1985). *Handbook of obstetrics and gynaecology*. London: Chapman & Hall.

Zavos, P. M. (1985). Seminal parameters of ejaculates collected from oligospermic and normospermic patients via masturbation and at intercourse with the use of a Silastic seminal fluid collection device. *Fertility and Sterility*, *44*(4), 517–520.

Zavos, P. M., & Goodpasture, J. C. (1989). Clinical improvements of specific seminal deficiencies via intercourse with a seminal collection device versus masturbation. *Fertility and Sterility*, *51*(1), 190–193.

Ziegler, T. E., Epple, G., Snowdon, C. T., Porter, T. A., Belcher, A. M., & Küderling, I. (1993). Detection of the chemical signals of ovulation in the cotton-top tamarin, *Saguinus oedipus. Animal Behaviour*, *45*(2), 313–322.

Sexual Conflict Theory: Concepts and Empirical Tests

Wayne G. Rostant, Emily K. Fowler
and Tracey Chapman

FUNDAMENTAL CONCEPTS

It has been recognised for many decades that the evolutionary interests of males and females (Parker, 1979), or of different sex functions within hermaphrodites (Charnov, 1979), may often diverge. This realisation originally stemmed from observations that, in addition to mutually coordinated and seemingly highly co-operative courtship displays (Krebs and Davies, 1987), reproductive interactions can also result in mortal injuries (Chapman et al., 2003a). This is a manifestation of the concept that males and females may ultimately maximise their fitness in different ways, for example, by breeding promiscuously and often, versus choosily at longer intervals (Hamilton, 1964; Trivers, 1972; Dawkins, 1976; Parker, 1979; Chapman et al., 2003a). However, as the fitness of each sex is ultimately realised through shared reproductive processes, maximum fitness for both sexes cannot be simultaneously achieved, revealing the underlying evolutionary tension at the heart of sexual conflict. An important component of this tension arises because the costs of each mating are often higher for females than males (Bell and Koufopanou, 1986; Chapman et al., 2003a; Partridge and Harvey, 1988; Partridge and Hurst, 1998). Hence the combination of life history traits that maximise the fitness of each sex often differs and one way in which the expression of sexual conflict can be minimised is via the evolution of sex-specific lifespans and reproductive schedules (Bonduriansky et al., 2008; Duxbury et al., 2017).

Sexual conflict was originally defined as 'conflict between the evolutionary interests of the two sexes' (Parker, 1979) and subsequently broadened to the more inclusive 'sexually antagonistic selection on shared traits' (Rowe and Day, 2006). It is now recognised to be a powerful and pervasive evolutionary selective force (Partridge and Hurst, 1998; Arnqvist and Rowe, 2005; Chapman, 2009). It can shape reproductive processes from the molecular level to behaviour and is recognised as a key component of understanding selective forces. Sexual conflict can occur in principle across all species that engage in sexual reproduction and does not require the existence of separate sexes (Charnov, 1979).

The evolutionary tension between the fitness interests of the sexes or sex functions is intriguing and has attracted wide interest because it can select for strategies in which one sex can gain, even if these result in the expression of costs in the other (Parker, 1979; Rice, 1992, 1996, 1998; Rice and Holland, 1997; Holland and Rice, 1998, 1999; Chapman et al., 2003a; Chapman, 2006; Rice et al., 2006). This can result in adaptations in one sex or sex function being followed by selection for counter-adaptation in the other (Rice, 1992; Arnqvist and Rowe, 2002a) and it creates the evolutionary back and forth that constitutes sexually antagonistic coevolution (Holland and Rice, 1998; Arnqvist and Rowe, 2005). This is important, as sexual conflict can act as a fundamental driver for generating evolutionary change and maintaining genetic variation (Rice, 2000; Chippindale et al., 2001; Fiumera et al., 2006). Hence, the ultimate significance of sexual conflict is its potential to generate the fuel to lead to divergence within and between species and result in reproductive isolation and even speciation (Chapman and Partridge, 1996; Arnqvist et al., 2000; Gavrilets, 2000; Gavrilets et al., 2001; Kokko et al., 2002; Kokko and Rankin, 2006; Hayashi et al., 2007; Paterson et al., 2010). It is this capacity of sexual conflict to maintain and generate genetic variation upon which we focus in this chapter. We consider, in particular, recent theory and data that reflect an increased understanding of how the expression of sexual conflict interacts with biotic and key environmental factors (Arbuthnott et al., 2014).

INTRA VERSUS INTERLOCUS SEXUAL CONFLICT

Sexual conflict can be mediated through the actions of the same (intra) or different (inter) loci in males and females (Holland and Rice, 1998). As recently emphasised, differences in these underlying modes are important, as each can result in a distinct evolutionary outcome of conflict (Schenkel et al., 2018). For example, a different expression level of the same gene could be favoured in each sex (Civetta and Singh, 1999; Ellegren and Parsch, 2007; Parisi et al., 2004) or a single shared trait might be influenced by genes showing sex-specific regulation. However, exactly how intra and inter locus sexual conflict differentially influence the rate and extent of evolutionary change across the genome is not yet clear and represents a key topic for further study (Schenkel et al., 2018).

(i) *Intralocus sexual conflict.* Conflicts mediated by loci expressed by each sex may be manifested in differences in the optimum level of gene expression of the same allele, or by sex-specific optima of different alleles, for each sex. A well-known example is that of adult locomotory activity in the fruit fly *Drosophila melanogaster*. There is a positive genetic correlation between movement levels in males and females, which indicates that the same gene or genes influence adult locomotion in both sexes. However, it is observed that a high level of activity benefits males as it increases female encounters, leading to increased reproductive success. Yet, high activity in females reduces fitness as such females spend less time feeding and egg laying (Long and Rice, 2007). Clear evidence for intralocus sexual conflict at the underlying genomic level has been gleaned from experiments conducted in fruit flies using cytogenetic techniques (Chippindale et al., 2001; Ruzicka et al., 2019) in which the 'same' genome is expressed in both sexes and fitness then measured. This type of experiment has provided data consistent with the idea that fitness differences between the sexes are low during larval development, but that at the adult stage, genomes that confer high fitness for males result in low fitness when expressed in females, and vice versa (Chippindale et al., 2001; Ruzicka et al., 2019). Quantitative genetic studies in wild populations have also highlighted the abundance of sexually antagonistic variation segregating in genomes (e.g., Foerster et al., 2007). Experimental evolution experiments have, by various techniques, allowed the genomes of either males or females to evolve free of the

constraint of passage through the other sex (Rice, 1992, 1996; Holland and Rice, 1999). This invariably results in the evolution of a genome that is 'better suited' to either male or female interests and less suited to the opposite sex. The outcome of these intralocus sexual conflicts is predicted to be an evolutionary to and fro depending on the presence of specific alleles, or extent of sex-biased gene expression currently operating in males or females (Parker, 1979; Hayashi et al., 2007).

Mechanistically, resolution of intralocus sexual conflict is predicted to occur via the evolution of gene duplication (facilitating neo-functionalisation) or sex limitation (the silencing of expression of the gene subject to conflict in one sex but not the other) (Ellegren and Parsch, 2007; Connallon and Clark, 2011; Parsch and Ellegren, 2013; Connallon and Clark, 2014; Wright et al., 2018). A nice example of how gene duplication can apparently resolve sexual antagonism via the evolution of sex-specific gene expression, is found in the *Artemis* (*Arts*) and *Apollo* (*Apl*) genes in *Drosophila* (VanKuren and Long, 2018). These genes arose by a duplication event and subsequent changes led *Apl* expression to become limited to males with functions in spermatid maturation, and *Arts* expression limited to females with functions in egg development. Interestingly, the effects of each gene are sexually antagonistic: *Apl* expression is essential for male fertility, but reduces that of females, while *Arts* is required for female fertility but harms that of males. Thus, the antagonistic effects of each gene have been eliminated by their testis- vs ovary-specific expression. It follows from this, that a potential signature of the existence, or indeed resolution, of intralocus sexual conflict is the extent and location of sex-biased gene expression within the genome (Ellegren and Parsch, 2007; Parsch and Ellegren, 2013; Wright et al., 2018). That such genes may contribute to the maintenance of genetic variation in sexual conflict is also suggested by the finding that they may show elevated rates of evolutionary change (Ellegren and Parsch, 2007; Parsch and Ellegren, 2013; Wright et al., 2018).

The type of coevolutionary dynamics predicted to emerge from the operation of intralocus sexual conflict are not yet clear (Schenkel et al., 2018), though recent studies highlight there may be constraints present, due to balancing selection (Ruzicka et al., 2019). However, the evolution of sex limitation by gene duplication or via the evolution of sex-limited gene expression is not necessarily an end point of conflict resolution. The expression of sex-limited genes can result in fitness costs in the other sex and become subject to subsequent interlocus sexual conflict (Chapman et al., 2003a; Chapman, 2006), which is outlined below.

(ii) *Interlocus sexual conflict* can occur between different loci in each sex that influence the expression of shared traits (e.g., mating frequency; Arnqvist and Rowe, 2005). Extensive evidence for this mode of sexual conflict has been provided by 'economic studies' of sex-specific costs and benefits, whereby manipulating the values of such shared traits reveals divergence in sex-specific optima (Arnqvist and Rowe, 2005). Classic examples have been described in studies of pondskaters, in which the grasping adaptations of males that aid in mating attachment become less effective following experimental manipulations of anti-grasping adaptations in females (Arnqvist and Rowe, 1995).

The mechanistic routes by which interlocus sexual conflict can be resolved have not yet received extensive attention. It is thought that there could be selection for sex-specific gene regulatory systems to reduce the expression or effects of sexually antagonistic loci expressed in a sex-limited fashion in the other sex. One potential example of this is found in the fruit fly *D. melanogaster*. Here, females may frequently suffer costs of mating as a side-effect of male adaptations to competition in this multiply-mating species (Chapman, 1992, 2006; Chapman et al., 2003a). The actions of seminal fluid proteins (SFPs) transferred from males to females can benefit both sexes but can incur costs in females, reflecting the actions of interlocus sexual conflict (Chapman et al., 1995; Wigby and Chapman, 2005;

Fricke et al., 2009b). However, mating and the receipt of SFPs also stimulates the expression of several regulatory microRNAs in females (Fricke et al., 2014). The actions of these miRNA 'guards' can buffer the costly effects of SFPs (Fricke et al., 2014; Green et al., 2016; Figure 14.1). In this manner, sexual conflict can occur over the effects and level of expression of adaptations in males and the mechanisms that apparently regulate their activity in females. The predicted coevolutionary outcomes of intersexual conflict are varied and include evolutionary chases, equilibrium, and divergence (Hayashi et al., 2007; Brockhurst et al., 2014), as well as reduction

of the conflict (Arnqvist and Rowe, 2005; Rowe et al., 2005) reflecting a kind of conflict resolution. As noted above, reduction of conflict in one arena does not necessarily resolve ultimate conflicts, which can continue via alternative routes (Rowe et al., 2005).

BRIEF SUMMARY OF SUPPORTING EVIDENCE

As is evident from the studies listed above, a strong theory base predicts the outcomes and significance of intra and inter locus sexual

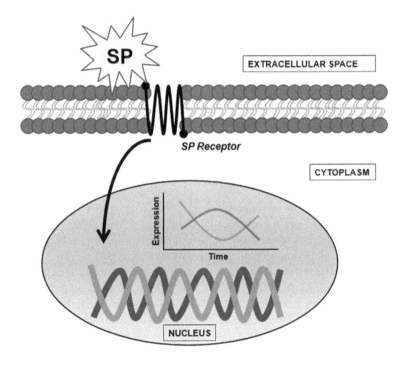

Figure 14.1   Example of potential resolution of interlocus sexual conflict by gene regulatory mechanisms in fruit flies (*Drosophila melanogaster*). Sex peptide (SP), one of ~130 male seminal fluid proteins (SFPs) is transferred into the female during mating and activates the SP receptor in the female genital tract and central nervous system. The activated SP receptor initiates intracellular signalling that alters the transcription of genes involved in behaviour, embryology, immunity and ageing. Deleterious fluctuations of miRNA expression in the female, facilitated by receipt of SP and other male ejaculate proteins, are smoothed and dampened by synchronous expression of miRNAs by females as a potential defence mechanism to reduce costs.

conflict. These studies predict the outcomes of short and longer term antagonistic interactions (Alonzo and Warner, 2000; Rowe et al., 2005; Kokko and Rankin, 2006; Rowe and Day, 2006; Mokkonen et al., 2011), the effects of sexual conflict on population density (Kokko and Rankin, 2006), female mate choice (Gavrilets et al., 2001), sex allocation (Alonzo and Sinervo, 2007), mating systems (Alonzo, 2007), extent of male effects on females (Cameron et al., 2007; Alonzo and Pizzari, 2009) and evolutionary dynamics arising from coevolutionary processes fuelled by sexual antagonism (Rowe et al., 2005; Hayashi et al., 2007). Key to the ultimate significance is that sexual conflict can contribute to speciation (Gavrilets, 2000; Gavrilets and Waxman, 2002; Gavrilets and Hayashi, 2005; Hayashi et al., 2007).

As also described above, many types of data provide support for the existence of sexual conflict (Arnqvist and Rowe, 2005). Among the strongest is from studies that provide data on the fitness effects of the sexually antagonistic trait on both sexes (Rowe and Day, 2006). Evidence from experimental evolution studies of selection and counterselection in males and females (Rice, 1992) and of the fitness consequences of the arrest of evolutionary processes in one sex but not the other (Rice, 1996) provide good evidence for intralocus sexual conflict (Chippindale et al., 2001). Genome-wide investigations are increasingly highlighting the existence of abundant sexually antagonistic genetic variation, offering the potential to result in intralocus sexual conflict (Chippindale et al., 2001; Foerster et al., 2007; Brommer et al. 2012; Ruzicka et al., 2019). Patterns of sex-biased gene expression across species can also provide key signatures of sexual antagonism and the involvement of sex-specific gene regulation (Wright and Mank, 2013; Mank, 2017) in resolving conflicts (Wright et al., 2018).

Studies of the molecular evolution and functions of reproductive proteins (Swanson and Vacquier, 1995, 1998; Swanson et al., 2001a,b; Swanson and Vacquier, 2002; Swanson et al., 2003; Levitan and Ferrell, 2006; Haerty et al., 2007; Hart et al., 2014) have provided evidence for positive selection that is at least partly driven by antagonistic effects (e.g., Levitan and Ferrell, 2006; Sirot et al., 2014). Reproductive genes, some of which are implicated in mediating sexual conflict, can show rapid evolutionary change (e.g., Begun et al., 2000; Swanson et al., 2001a; Kern et al., 2004; Begun and Lindfors, 2005; Clark and Swanson, 2005; Wagstaff and Begun, 2005; Haerty et al., 2007). There are also examples of reproductive gene turnover among very closely related species as well as recruitment of such genes *de novo* (Begun and Lindfors, 2005; Begun et al., 2006). Evidence for coevolution between male and female reproductive proteins is also starting to be uncovered (Clark et al., 2009), and further mechanistic studies should resolve the extent to which this is driven by sexually antagonistic coevolution (Sirot et al., 2014).

The taxonomic spread of species providing evidence for sexual conflict is broad but detailed. Experimental studies remain dominated by those conducted in invertebrates such as dungflies (*Scathophaga stercoraria* and *Sepsis cynipsea,* e.g., Parker, 1970a,b,c; Martin and Hosken, 2003), fruit flies (*D. melanogaster*; e.g., Chapman et al., 1995; Rice, 1996; Chapman, 2006), abalone (*Haliotis* spp., e.g., Clark et al., 2009), *Callosobruchus* beetles (e.g., Ronn et al., 2007; Berg and Maklakov, 2012; Grieshop and Arnqvist, 2018) and various pondskater species (*Aquarius*, *Gerris* spp., e.g., Arnqvist and Rowe, 2002a,b; Perry et al., 2017). Key sexual conflict research in vertebrates has been conducted in dunnocks (*Prunella modularis*, e.g., Davies, 1992), red deer (*Cervus elaphus,* e.g., Foerster et al., 2007) and various species of wrasse (Warner et al., 1995; Alonzo and Warner, 2000). Authors such as Haig (e.g., Haig and Wilczek, 2006) have emphasised the potential for sexual conflict in plants, emphasising the key role of relatedness among the interacting parties. These and many further examples of sexual conflict in action have been synthesised in greater detail in multiple reviews (e.g., Chapman et al., 2003a; Arnqvist and Rowe, 2005; Chapman, 2006, 2018).

SEXUAL CONFLICT AND THE MAINTENANCE OF GENETIC VARIATION

In the rest of this chapter we consider an emerging body of theory and research that indicates how genetic variation subject to sexual conflict can be generated and maintained (e.g., Linder and Rice, 2005; Foerster et al., 2007; Bonduriansky and Chenoweth, 2009; Hall et al., 2010). This important research theme is increasingly showing that sexual conflict can interact with key ecological factors such as population density, environmental complexity, female quality, encounter rates, and resource availability (Linder and Rice, 2005; Connallon and Hall, 2016; Yun et al., 2017; Zajitschek and Connallon, 2017; MacPherson et al., 2018; Rostant et al., 2019). These interactions can alter evolutionary outcomes and trajectories and can act to maintain phenotypic and genetic variation within populations, leading to enhanced persistence of sexually antagonistic variation. In this way, our understanding of sexual conflict is maturing as we explore its effects in ever more realistic environments. It is also relevant to the wider recognition of the importance of incorporating life history theory and ecology into the study of sexual conflict (Perry and Rowe, 2018).

Interaction of Sexual Conflict Genotypes with High and Low Mating Environments

In a pedigree study of *D. melanogaster*, Brommer et al. (2012) measured the reproductive fitness of 639 individual males and 1062 females across four generations. The opportunity for sexual conflict in these focal female individuals across generations was manipulated by giving them high or low exposure to males. A quantitative genetic approach was then taken and an animal model was used to estimate the extent of genotype by sexual conflict environment interactions for female fitness, as well as any indirect benefits gained across generations through sons and daughters that might offset costs arising from sexual conflict (Kokko and Brooks, 2003). The key results of the study were that there was a consistent 10% reduction in female fitness under high conflict environments, regardless of maternal history across generations. Though high conflict mothers produced sons with increased fitness, their grandsons were less fit. This opposing effect suggests there were no consistent fitness gains through sons for females that experienced elevated sexual conflict. There were no indirect benefits through daughters. This confirmed the importance of conflict in shaping selection and that, in this context (though see Head et al., 2005; Priest et al., 2008), there were no indirect genetic benefits that could offset costs of sexual conflict (Orteiza et al., 2005; Galliard et al., 2008). However, it was also found that some female genotypes achieved higher fitness under low, in comparison to high, conflict environments and vice versa (Figure 14.2). This finding of a female genotype by sexual conflict interaction shows that no single female genotype was fittest across all environments and is noteworthy, as it shows how this scenario can maintain and thus slow the erosion of genetic variation (Brommer et al., 2012).

Interaction of Sexual Conflict Genotypes with Environmental Complexity

Much of the experimental research, particularly in fruit flies, has been conducted in simple environments in which opportunities

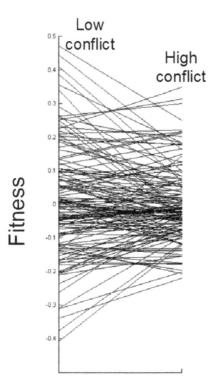

Figure 14.2   Interaction of female genotypes with sexual conflict environment can maintain genetic variation for fitness in *D. melanogaster*. Female fitness (Y-axis, predicted breeding value) for females subjected to low and high conflict environments (X-axis, low and high mating frequency, respectively). The figure shows that some female genotypes do better in low, others in high conflict environments

Source: Adapted and reproduced, with permission, from Brommer et al. (2012).

for interactions have been manipulated in standard food vials lacking environmental variation. As such the opportunities for variation in encounter rates, choice, and resistance in females is limited. An important step forward in assessing the importance of this type of environmental complexity has been to experimentally manipulate and test its effects over generations. Taking this approach and using different levels of male–female interactions in straws, vials, and more spatially

complex cup environments, the interactions of choice and harm levels can be more accurately assessed. In one of a series of studies using this approach, Yun et al. (2017) show that the sexual interactions between the sexes are less frequent in the more complex environments and, more importantly, that the differential targeting by males of high and low quality females diminished. However, when male choice was permitted, selection on high quality females was again strengthened in the complex environment. A further study using these lines showed that the extent of male harm on females was contingent upon environmental heterogeneity and, in fact, was greatest overall for low quality females in complex environments (MacPherson et al., 2018). These results are important as they show how even simple variation in environmental complexity, which presumably offers greater opportunities for each sex to vary how and when they interact with the other, can alter the intensity of sexual conflict.

Interaction of Sexual Conflict Genotypes with Resource Levels and Resource Acquisition

The ultimate expression of sexual conflict depends upon an individual's condition and their ability to express phenotypes or mount responses to them (Chapman, 2006). In particular, a better understanding is needed of the influence of resource levels (van Noordwijk and de Jong, 1986; Arbuthnott et al., 2014; Perry et al., 2017; Perry and Rowe, 2018), condition dependence (Rowe and Houle, 1996; Chen and Maklakov, 2012; Zajitschek and Connallon, 2017) and stress (Berger et al., 2014). The theory shows that the extent to which sexual conflict is evident when resources vary will depend upon: genetic variance and between-sex covariance for resource acquisition and allocation; the extent of condition-dependent expression of resource allocation; and sex differences in selection for resource allocation to different fitness components (Zajitschek and Connallon, 2017). Variation in resource levels is important as it can alter or and even reverse sexual conflict outcomes (Poissant et al., 2010; Adler and Bonburiansky, 2014; Connallon and Clark, 2014; Connallon and Hall, 2016; Han and Dingemanse, 2017). A key point to recognise is that interactions of sexual conflict with resource levels may go undetected, as placing individuals in different resource environments may subject them to directional selection to respond to the novel test conditions, hence obscuring evidence for the underlying conflict present (Connallon and Hall, 2016).

The extent of sexual conflict is closely linked to both resource availability and resource acquisition. Layered on top of this is the potential for either availability or acquisition to show sex specificity. There are good examples whereby the expression of traits subject to selection arising from sexual conflict, or female responses to them, are impacted by nutritional resources. For example, as noted above, in the fruit fly *D. melanogaster*, there is sexual conflict over the actions of SFPs transferred from males to females during mating (Chapman, 2001, 2018). These SFPs direct the reproductive responses of females to mating including reproductive investment in egg production and behavioural decisions influencing when to remate (Chapman et al., 2003b; Liu and Kubli, 2003). While these responses can coordinate reproductive decisions they can also tip over into the zone in which they become costly for females (Chapman et al., 1995; Wigby and Chapman, 2005). As such effects involve both signalling by ejaculate components and changes to reproductive investment it would be expected that both of these components should be nutritionally sensitive. The data support this expectation, as both the ability of males to effect post-mating receptivity and egg production responses in females, and the female's ability to respond to a standard SFP signal delivered by males, show nutritional dependence

(Fricke et al., 2008, 2010). Hence as would be predicted, this nutritional sensitivity also impacts upon the actual expression of costs in females arising from the transfer of cost-inducing ejaculate components from males (Fricke et al., 2010).

Another example from the same system illustrates nutritional dependence in the evolution of female resistance responses to sexual conflict (Wigby and Chapman, 2004). In an experimental evolution study in which the level of sexual conflict was varied from high through medium to low, it was found that within a few tens of generations females from the high conflict lines had evolved resistance to the costly effects of elevated rates of mating with males. However, under nutritional resource limitation these responses were absent (Rostant et al., 2019). Hence, despite similar selection pressures under poor and good dietary environments, resistance could be expressed only when resources were in abundance (Wigby and Chapman, 2004; Rostant et al., 2019).

Variation in the manifestation of sexual conflict could also be influenced by sex differences in the way in which resources are acquired by each sex, by sex-specific dietary preferences, or by the effects of a given type of nutrient on each sex. Male and female lifespan and reproductive success can be maximised on different ratios of proteins to carbohydrates (Maklakov et al., 2008, 2009; Jensen et al., 2015; Camus et al., 2017; Duxbury and Chapman, 2019) and adult males and female dietary preferences do not necessarily map onto these (Jensen et al., 2015; Camus et al., 2017).

Diet has a sex-specific (Maklakov et al., 2008, 2009; Duxbury et al., 2017; Griffin et al., 2018) influence on lifespan, with female lifespan being more sensitive to nutrition (Simon et al., 2003; Magwere et al., 2004; Regan and Partridge, 2013). Because males are usually selected to be competitive in reproductive competitions, investment in secondary sexual traits may be promoted over that into the soma (Stearns, 1992; Brooks, 2000;

Lemaître et al., 2015). However, there are also fitness benefits for males, over that of females, reaching a large body size (Fox et al., 1995; Fairbairn et al., 2007). Hence males should be selected to acquire proteins to gain large body size, but also carbohydrates specifically in adulthood to fuel reproductive activity (South et al., 2011; Jensen et al., 2015; Camus et al., 2017; Young et al., 2018). Investment in females is expected to be higher in the soma to support fecundity (Chapman et al., 2003a), which depends primarily on the acquisition of a protein-rich adult diet (Maklakov et al., 2008; Jensen et al., 2015; Camus et al., 2017) and may explain the higher feeding rates observed in females (Lee et al., 2013).

Overall, this emerging body of data shows that each sex acquires and requires different types of nutritional resources over their lifetimes. While global effects of resource levels on the expression of and responses to sexual conflict are known, the exact interplay between the sex-specific effects described here and the outcome of sexual conflict is not yet known. Differences in the interactions of sexual conflict expression with resource availability and acquisition are important as they show that, provided there is variation in resource levels within environments, this will act to maintain variation in the phenotypic expression of sexual conflict and thus selection for or against its effects.

Maintenance of Genetic Variation in Sexual Conflict Genotypes via Alternative Mating Tactics

At least some of the expression of costs arising from sexual conflict in females appears to be a byproduct of male–male competition. For instance, in *D. melanogaster*, females incur costs due to receipt of SFPs from males (Chapman et al., 1995; Mueller et al., 2007). It is the actions of SFPs to maximise female reproductive investment into current versus future reproductive episodes that appears to

result in costly 'over investment'. Hence part of the variation in the expression of sexual conflict will depend upon variation in the types and strength of reproductive competition from males. If reproductive success in males can be achieved by different routes, then this will automatically provide fuel to maintain variation in sexual conflict expression.

An illustrative example is the mechanism used by males in achieving success when in sperm competition with other males. There is abundant evidence of variation in many aspects of sperm competition including those directly influenced by SFPs subject to sexual conflict (Clark et al., 1995, 1999, 2000; Fiumera et al., 2005, 2006, 2007; Chow et al., 2010). Of key importance is evidence of associations between the competitiveness of males and the expression of harm to females (Civetta and Clark, 2000; Pitnick and García-González, 2002). Fricke and Chapman (2017) used selection analysis of the fitness of the first of two males mated to a female in series. They constructed fitness landscapes to illustrate the different routes by which male reproductive success can be achieved (Figure 14.3). This showed that males can be good direct sperm competitors and apparently trade this off against the ability to prevent females from remating, or they can be very good at switching off female remating receptivity and hence have less requirement for direct sperm competition. The analyses show there is abundant variation in how males achieve success in competition, which retains variability in the types and strength of conflictual interactions with females and thus contributes to the maintenance of genetic variation in sexual conflict.

An alternative strategy by which sexual conflict may be maintained is in the mechanism deployed by males to influence the speed and likelihood of resistance to sexual conflict in females (Chapman, 2018). This hypothesis follows from one of the striking features of sexual conflict, namely the variety of adaptations and processes whose evolution can be shaped by it. For example, in

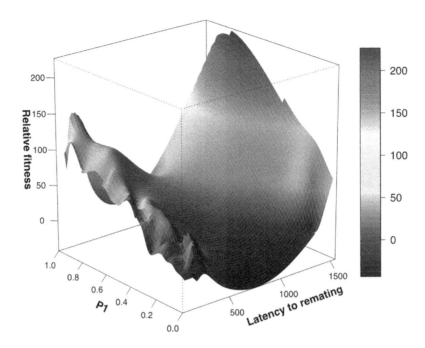

Figure 14.3   Phenotypic variation in traits influencing sexual conflict is maintained by different routes to male reproductive success in *D. melanogaster*. Shown is relative male fitness for the first of two males to mate with a female (number of offspring sired) against his sperm competitive ability (proportion of offspring sired, or P1) and the latency to remating with a second male. Relative fitness is highest for first mating males that induce a long latency to remating and have high sperm competitive ability. However, there is a second lower peak of fitnesses at very short remating latencies for males across the whole range of sperm competitive abilities. This semi-bimodal distribution shows alternative routes to male reproductive success, maintaining variation in sexual selection and sexual conflict

Source: Reproduced, with permission, from Fricke and Chapman (2017).

the sexual conflict that can occur over the sexually antagonistic effects of SFPs in *D. melanogaster*, an unanswered question is why there are so many SFPs of so many different forms and functions. One possibility is that this complexity is at least partly driven by male 'resistance proofing', that is, selection for the strategies used by males to lower the likelihood of broad scale, strong resistance evolution in females. Observations of variation in the expression of mating costs across populations (Fiumera et al., 2006; Arbuthnott et al., 2014) could represent a signature of the deployment of different resistance strategies. This process parallels thinking on how to prevent the evolution of resistance

to insecticides, antimicrobials and vaccines (Consortium, 2010).

Maintenance of Genetic Variation in Sexual Conflict Genotypes Due to Genetic Architecture

That there is substantial sexually antagonistic genetic variation residing within genomes is increasingly reported (e.g., Foerster et al., 2007; Grieshop and Arnqvist, 2018; Ruzicka et al., 2019). In addition to some of the factors outlined above, the maintenance of such variation, and the maintenance of loci under balancing selection, in particular, could be fostered if there were sex-specific patterns of dominance and recessivity. An example of this phenomenon was recently described in *Callosobruchus maculatus* seed beetles. In this study, fitness (measured as lifetime reproductive success) was scored in the F1 individuals of diallel crosses of isogenic, naturally derived lines of the beetles. Decomposition of the structure of the genetic variation underlying reproductive success showed contributions of dominance and, more importantly, sex-specific dominance variance. In particular, among the fixed allelic differences between the strains, there were many examples where alleles were dominant in their effects in one sex but recessive in the other. This pattern of mixed dominance/recessivity effects will represent a substantial mechanism that can maintain genetic variation in populations (Grieshop and Arnqvist, 2018). It will be interesting now to discover the extent of this pattern across a broader range of species.

Maintenance of Genetic Variation in Sexual Conflict Genotypes Due to Interactions with Ecology

The increasing interest in testing for the existence and importance of sexual conflict under more realistic conditions is welcome (Fricke et al., 2009a; Arbuthnott et al., 2014; Perry et al., 2017; Perry and Rowe, 2018) as it aids in determining the relative importance of selection arising from antagonistic processes in the face of variation in ecologically-relevant factors such as food availability and climatic variation, as well as neutral processes such as drift and bottlenecks. Perry et al. (2017) conducted a study of the patterns of correlated evolution in *Gerris incognitus* pondskaters from 19 localities in Canada. The aim was to measure mother–offspring correlations in morphology of female and male structures with sexually antagonistic functions, and to distinguish the relative contributions of ecological variation,

coancestry, and spatial variation to sexual covariation. The results indicated little support for the presence of a genetic correlation in the sexually antagonistic spines in females and pre-genital structures in males. Interestingly, a role for ecological processes in determining female spines and body size was also detected. Importantly, once all the ecological and spatial variation was accounted for, a strong positive correlation between female spines and male pre-genital structures remained. This shows that, despite the presence of ecologically-selected and neutral variation, there was a strong role in natural populations for sexually antagonistic coevolution (Perry et al., 2017).

CONCLUSION AND FUTURE DIRECTIONS

In this chapter, we have covered the main theoretical concepts underpinning sexual conflict and reviewed supporting evidence. We have focussed the review on our increasing understanding of the main factors that can explain how variation in sexual conflict is maintained and thus why it represents such a potential fuel for driving evolutionary change.

We covered variation in the biotic environment such as female genotypes that have high fitness in some mating environments but not others (Brommer et al., 2012). Studies of nutritional ecology in the laboratory have increased our understanding of the different nutritional responses and requirements of each sex and seem set to provide an enhanced understanding of how nutritional responses can maintain substantial phenotypic variation in the expression of sexual conflict (Zajitschek and Connallon, 2017; Rostant et al., 2019). We also covered explanations for the extreme variation that resides within reproductive proteins and the contribution to fitness variation of different routes to reproductive success in males (Fricke and Chapman, 2017) and the resulting promotion of heterogeneity in female responses. An intriguing role for genetic architecture and of dominance, in particular, to the maintenance of sexually antagonistic loci under balancing selection is of great interest if it proves to be widespread.

The continually expanding use of clonal-type lines in combination with genome-wide analyses of single nucleotide polymorphisms (SNPs) is proving particularly powerful in dissecting the imprint of sexual antagonism within the genome and to detect its nature (Ruzicka et al., 2019). For example, the scoring of sex-specific fitness to identify candidate 'antagonistic' SNPs in *D. melanogaster* and the subsequent detection that these loci were often subject to balancing selection represents an advance, as it suggests that much sexually antagonistic variation can be maintained within genomes because sexual conflicts operating on such loci cannot be resolved (Grieshop and Arnqvist, 2018; Ruzicka et al., 2019). From this we conclude that sexual conflict can result in widespread imprints within the genome.

The intersection of ecology and sexual conflict in driving divergence has been neglected (Arbuthnott et al., 2014). This is an important omission because it has been shown that both the effect of males on female lifespan and of female resistance to male effects can evolve alongside adaptation to different ecological environments (Arbuthnott et al., 2014). Hence the evolution of sexual conflict traits can occur in parallel with ecology, leading to the interesting outcome that ecological context might predict the outcome of sexual conflict. That there are differences in the extent and nature of sexually antagonistic genetic variation across different populations with different ecologies is also indicated by the existence of population-specific resistance to sexual conflict that is observed in studies across a number of different vertebrate and invertebrate taxa (Arnqvist and Rowe, 2005). The importance of ecological and neutral processes is starting to be addressed (Perry et al., 2017) and the tools and analyses to detect the operation of sexual conflict in non-model systems in nature now exist to fuel further studies in ever-more realistic contexts.

ACKNOWLEDGEMENTS

We thank the UK's Biotechnology and Biological Sciences Research Council, BBSRC (BB/L003139/1) and the Natural Environment Research Council, NERC (NE/R010056/1, NE/R000891/1, NE/J024244/1, NE/K004697/1) for funding the research that fuelled the discussions that fed into this review.

REFERENCES

Adler, M. I., and R. Bonburiansky. 2014. Sexual conflict, life span, and ageing. *Cold Spring Harbor Perspectives in Biology* 6(8): a017566.

Alonzo, S. H. 2007. Conflict between the sexes and cooperation within a sex can alter classic predictions of mating systems theory. *Evolutionary Ecology Research* 9(1):145–156.

Alonzo, S. H., and T. Pizzari. 2009. Male fecundity stimulation: conflict and cooperation within and between the sexes: model analyses and coevolutionary dynamics. *American Naturalist* 175(2):174–185.

Alonzo, S. H., and B. Sinervo. 2007. The effect of sexually antagonistic selection on adaptive sex ratio allocation. *Evolutionary Ecology Research* 9(7):1097–1117.

Alonzo, S. H., and R. R. Warner. 2000. Dynamic games and field experiments examining intra- and intersexual conflict: explaining counterintuitive mating behaviour in a Mediterranean wrasse, *Symphodus ocellatus*. *Behavioral Ecology* 11(1):56–70.

Arbuthnott, D., E. M. Dutton, A. F. Agrawal, and H. D. Rundle. 2014. The ecology of sexual conflict: ecologically dependent parallel evolution of male harm and female resistance in *Drosophila melanogaster*. *Ecology Letters* 17(2):221–228.

Arnqvist, G., M. Edvardsson, U. Friberg, and T. Nilsson. 2000. Sexual conflict promotes speciation in insects. *Proceedings of the National Academy of Sciences, USA* 97(19):10460–10464.

Arnqvist, G., and L. Rowe. 1995. Sexual conflict and arms races between the sexes: a morphological adaptation for control of mating in a female insect. *Proceedings of the Royal Society B* 261(1360):123–127.

Arnqvist, G., and L. Rowe. 2002a. Antagonistic coevolution between the sexes in a group of insects. *Nature* 415(6873):787–789.

Arnqvist, G., and L. Rowe. 2002b. Correlated evolution of male and female morphologies in water striders. *Evolution* 56(5):936–947.

Arnqvist, G., and L. Rowe. 2005. *Sexual conflict*. Princeton University Press, Princeton, NJ.

Begun, D. J., and H. A. Lindfors. 2005. Rapid evolution of genomic Acp complement in the melanogaster subgroup of *Drosophila*. *Molecular Biology and Evolution* 22(10):2010–2021.

Begun, D. J., H. A. Lindfors, M. E. Thompson, and A. K. Holloway. 2006. Recently evolved genes identified from *Drosophila yakuba* and *D. erecta* accessory gland expressed sequence tags. *Genetics* 172(3):1675–1681.

Begun, D. J., P. Whitley, B. L. Todd, H. M. Waldrip-Dail, and A. G. Clark. 2000. Molecular population genetics of male accessory gland proteins in *Drosophila*. *Genetics* 156(4):1879–1888.

Bell, P. D., and V. Koufopanou. 1986. *The cost of reproduction*. Oxford, Oxford University Press, UK.

Berg, E. C., and A. A. Maklakov. 2012. Sexes suffer from suboptimal lifespan because of genetic conflict in a seed beetle. *Proceedings of the Royal Society B* 279(1745):4296–4302.

Berger, D., K. Grieshop, M. I. Lind, J. Goenaga, A. A. Maklakov, and G. Arnqvist. 2014. Intralocus sexual conflict and environmental stress. *Evolution* 68(8):2184–2196.

Bonduriansky, R., and S. F. Chenoweth. 2009. Intralocus sexual conflict. *Trends in Ecology and Evolution* 24(5):280–288.

Bonduriansky, R., A. Maklakov, F. Zajitschek, and R. Brooks. 2008. Sexual selection, sexual conflict and the evolution of ageing and life span. *Functional Ecology* 22(3):443–453.

Brockhurst, M. A., T. Chapman, K. C. King, J. E. Mank, S. Paterson, and G. D. D. Hurst. 2014.

Running with the Red Queen: the role of biotic conflicts in evolution. *Proceedings of the Royal Society B* 281(1797):20141382.

Brommer, J. E., C. Fricke, D. A. Edward, and T. Chapman. 2012. Interactions between genotype and sexual conflict environment influence transgenerational fitness in *Drosophila melanogaster*. *Evolution* 66(2):517–531.

Brooks, R. 2000. Negative genetic correlation between male sexual attractiveness and survival. *Nature* 406(6791):67–70.

Cameron, E., T. Day, and L. Rowe. 2007. Sperm competition and the evolution of ejaculate composition. *American Naturalist* 169(6):E158–E172.

Camus, M. F., K. Fowler, M. D. W. Piper, and M. Reuter. 2017. Sex and genotype effects on nutrient-dependent fitness landscapes in *Drosophila melanogaster*. *Proceedings of the Royal Society B* 284(1869):20172237.

Chapman, T. 1992. A cost of mating with males that do not transfer sperm in female *Drosophila melanogaster*. *Journal of Insect Physiology* 38(3):223–227.

Chapman, T. 2001. Seminal fluid-mediated fitness traits in *Drosophila*. *Heredity* 87(5):511–521.

Chapman, T. 2006. Evolutionary conflicts of interest between males and females. *Current Biology* 16(17):R744–R754.

Chapman, T. 2009. Sexual conflict and sex allocation. *Biology Letters* 5(5):660–662.

Chapman, T. 2018. Sexual conflict: mechanisms and emerging themes in resistance biology. *American Naturalist* 192(2):217–229.

Chapman, T., G. Arnqvist, J. Bangham, and L. Rowe. 2003a. Sexual conflict. *Trends in Ecology and Evolution* 18(1):41–47.

Chapman, T., J. Bangham, G. Vinti, B. Seifried, O. Lung, M. F. Wolfner, H. K. Smith, and L. Partridge. 2003b. The sex peptide of *Drosophila melanogaster:* female post-mating responses analyzed by using RNA interference. *Proceedings of the National Academy of Sciences, USA* 100(17):9923–9928.

Chapman, T., L. F. Liddle, J. M. Kalb, M. F. Wolfner, and L. Partridge. 1995. Cost of mating in *Drosophila melanogaster* females is mediated by male accessory gland products. *Nature* 373(6511):241–244.

Chapman, T., and L. Partridge. 1996. Sexual conflict as fuel for evolution. *Nature* 381(6579):189–190.

Charnov, E. L. 1979. Simultaneous hermaphroditism and sexual selection. *Proceedings of the National Academy of Sciences, USA* 76(5):2480–2484.

Chen, H., and A. A. Maklakov. 2012. Longer life span evolves under high rates of condition-dependent mortality. *Current Biology* 22(22):2140–2143.

Chippindale, A. K., J. R. Gibson, and W. R. Rice. 2001. Negative genetic correlation for adult fitness between sexes reveals ontogenetic conflict in *Drosophila*. *Proceedings of the National Academy of Sciences, USA* 98(4):1671–1675.

Chow, C. Y., M. F. Wolfner, and A. G. Clark. 2010. The genetic basis for male × female interactions underlying variation in reproductive phenotypes of *Drosophila*. *Genetics* 186(4):1355–1365.

Civetta, A., and R. S. Singh. 1999. Broad-sense sexual selection, sex gene pool evolution, and speciation. *Genome* 42: 1033–1041.

Civetta, A., and A. G. Clark. 2000. Correlated effects of sperm competition and postmating female mortality. *Proceedings of the National Academy of Sciences, USA* 97(24):13162–13165.

Clark, A. G., M. Aguade, T. Prout, L. G. Harshman, and C. H. Langley. 1995. Variation in sperm displacement and its association with accessory gland protein loci in *Drosophila melanogaster*. *Genetics* 139(1):189–201.

Clark, A. G., D. J. Begun, and T. Prout. 1999. Female x male interactions in *Drosophila* sperm competition. *Science* 283(5399):217–220.

Clark, A. G., E. T. Dermitzakis, and A. Civetta. 2000. Nontransitivity of sperm precedence in *Drosophila*. *Evolution* 54(3):1030–1035.

Clark, N. L., J. Gasper, M. Sekino, S. A. Springer, C. F. Aquadro, and W. J. Swanson. 2009. Coevolution of interacting fertilization proteins. *PLoS Genetics* 5(7):e1000570.

Clark, N. L., and W. J. Swanson. 2005. Pervasive adaptive evolution in primate seminal proteins. *PLoS Genetics* 1(3):335–342.

Connallon, T., and A. G. Clark. 2011. The resolution of sexual antagonism by gene duplication. *Genetics* 187(3):919–937.

Connallon, T., and A. G. Clark. 2014. Evolutionary inevitability of sexual antagonism. *Proceedings of the Royal Society B* 281(1776):20132123.

Connallon, T., and M. D. Hall. 2016. Genetic correlations and sex-specific adaptation in changing environments. *Evolution* 70(10):2186–2198.

Consortium, R. 2010. The skill and style to model the evolution of resistance to pesticides and drugs. *Evolutionary Applications* 3(4):375–390.

Davies, N. B. 1992. *Dunnock behaviour and social evolution*. Oxford University Press, Oxford.

Dawkins, R. 1976. *The selfish gene*. Oxford University Press, Oxford.

Duxbury, E. M. L., and T. Chapman. 2019. Sex-specific responses of lifespan and fitness to variation in developmental versus adult diets in *Drosophila melanogaster*. *Journals of Gerontology: Biological Sciences* https://doi.org/10.1093/gerona/glz175.

Duxbury, E., W. R. Rostant, and T. Chapman. 2017. Evolutionary manipulation of feeding regime alters sexual dimorphism for lifespan and reduces sexual conflict in the fruit fly, *Drosophila melanogaster*. *Proceedings of the Royal Society B* 284(1854):20170391.

Ellegren, H., and J. Parsch. 2007. The evolution of sex-biased genes and sex-biased gene expression. *Nature Reviews Genetics* 8(9):689–698.

Fairbairn, D. J., W. U. Blanckenhorn, and T. Székely. 2007. *Sex, size and gender roles: evolutionary studies of sexual size dimorphism*. Oxford University Press, Oxford.

Fiumera, A. C., B. L. Dumont, and A. G. Clark. 2005. Sperm competitive ability in *Drosophila melanogaster* associated with variation in male reproductive proteins. *Genetics* 169(1):243–257.

Fiumera, A. C., B. L. Dumont, and A. G. Clark. 2006. Natural variation in male-induced 'cost-of-mating' and allele-specific association with male reproductive genes in *Drosophila melanogaster*. *Philosophical Transactions of the Royal Society B* 361(1466):355–361.

Fiumera, A. C., B. L. Dumont, and A. G. Clark. 2007. Associations between sperm competition and natural variation in male reproductive genes on the third chromosome of *Drosophila melanogaster*. *Genetics* 176(2):1245–1260.

Foerster, K., T. Coulson, B. C. Sheldon, J. M. Pemberton, T. H. Clutton-Brock, and L. E. B. Kruuk. 2007. Sexually antagonistic genetic variation for fitness in red deer. *Nature* 447(7148):1107–1111.

Fox, C. W., L. A. McLennan, and T. A. Mousseau. 1995. Male body size affects female lifetime reproductive success in a seed beetle. *Animal Behaviour* 50(1):281–284.

Fricke, C., A. Bretman, and T. Chapman. 2008. Adult male nutrition and reproductive success in *Drosophila melanogaster*. *Evolution* 62(12):3170–3177.

Fricke, C., A. Bretman, and T. Chapman. 2010. Female nutritional status determines the magnitude and sign of responses to a male ejaculate signal in *Drosophila melanogaster*. *Journal of Evolutionary Biology* 23(1): 157–165.

Fricke, C., and T. Chapman. 2017. Variation in the post-mating fitness landscape in fruit flies. *Journal of Evolutionary Biology* 30(7):1250–1261.

Fricke, C., D. Green, D. T. Smith, T. Dalmay, and T. Chapman. 2014. MicroRNAs influence reproductive responses by females to male sex peptide in *Drosophila melanogaster*. *Genetics* 198(4):1603–1619.

Fricke, C., J. Perry, T. Chapman, and L. Rowe. 2009a. Conditional economics of sexual conflict. *Biology Letters* 5(5): 671–674.

Fricke, C., S. Wigby, R. Hobbs, and T. Chapman. 2009b. The benefits of male ejaculate sex peptide transfer in *Drosophila melanogaster*. *Journal of Evolutionary Biology* 22(2):275–286.

Galliard, J-F. Le, J. Cote, and P. S. Fitze. 2008. Lifetime and intergenerational fitness consequences of harmful male interactions for female lizards. *Ecology* 89(1):56–64.

Gavrilets, S. 2000. Rapid evolution of reproductive barriers driven by sexual conflict. *Nature* 403(6772):886–889.

Gavrilets, S., G. Arnqvist, and U. Friberg. 2001. The evolution of female mate choice by sexual conflict. *Proceedings of the Royal Society B* 268(1466):531–539.

Gavrilets, S., and T. I. Hayashi. 2005. Speciation and sexual conflict. *Evolutionary Ecology* 19(2):167–198.

Gavrilets, S., and D. Waxman. 2002. Sympatric speciation by sexual conflict. *Proceedings of the National Academy of Sciences, USA* 99(16):10533–10538.

Green, D., T. Dalmay, and T. Chapman. 2016. Microguards and micromessengers of the genome. *Heredity* 116(2):125–134.

Grieshop, K., and G. Arnqvist. 2018. Sex-specific dominance reversal of genetic variation for fitness. *PLoS Biology* 16(12):e2006810.

Griffin, R. M., A. D. Hayward, E. Bolund, A. A. Maklakov, and V. Lummaa. 2018. Sex differences in adult mortality rate mediated by early life environmental conditions. *Ecology Letters* 21(2):235–242.

Haerty, W., S. Jagadeeshan, R. J. Kulathinal, A. Wong, K. R. Ram, L. K. Sirot, L. Levesque, C. G. Artieri, M. F. Wolfner, A. Civetta, and R. S. Singh. 2007. Evolution in the fast lane: rapidly evolving sex-related genes in *Drosophila*. *Genetics* 177(3):1321–1335.

Haig, D., and A. Wilczek. 2006. Sexual conflict and the alternation of haploid and diploid generations. *Philosophical Transactions of the Royal Society B* 361(1466):227–386.

Hall, M. D., S. P. Lailvaux, M. W. Blows, and R. Brooks. 2010. Sexual conflict and the maintenance of multivariate genetic variation. *Evolution* 64(6):1697–1703.

Hamilton, W. D. 1964. The genetical evolution of social behaviour I, II. *Journal of Theoretical Biology* 7(1):1–52.

Han, C. S., and N. J. Dingemanse. 2017. Protein deprivation decreases male survival and the intensity of sexual antagonism in southern field crickets *Gryllus bimaculatus*. *Journal of Evolutionary Biology* 30(4):839–847.

Hart, M. W., J. M. Sunday, I. Popovic, and C. M. Konrad. 2014. Incipient speciation of sea star populations by adaptive gamete recognition coevolution. *Evolution* 68(5):1294–1305.

Hayashi, T. I., M. Vose, and S. Gavrilets. 2007. Genetic differentiation by sexual conflict. *Evolution* 61(3):516–529.

Head, M., J. Hunt, M. Jennions, and R. Brooks. 2005. The indirect benefits of mating with attractive males outweigh the direct costs. *PLoS Biology* 3(2):e33.

Holland, B., and W. Rice. 1998. Chase-away sexual selection: antagonistic seduction versus resistance. *Evolution* 52(1):1–7.

Holland, B., and W. R. Rice. 1999. Experimental removal of sexual selection reverses intersexual antagonistic coevolution and removes a reproductive load. *Proceedings of the National Academy of Sciences, USA* 96(9):5083–5088.

Jensen, K., C. McClure, N. K. Priest, and J. Hunt. 2015. Sex-specific effects of protein and carbohydrate intake on reproduction but not lifespan in *Drosophila melanogaster*. *Aging Cell* 14(4):605–615.

Kern, A. D., C. D. Jones, and D. J. Begun. 2004. Molecular population genetics of male accessory gland proteins in the *Drosophila simulans* complex. *Genetics* 167(2):725–735.

Kokko, H., and R. Brooks. 2003. Sexy to die for? Sexual selection and the risk of extinction. *Annales Zoologici Fennici* 40(2):207–219.

Kokko, H., R. Brooks, J. M. McNamara, and A. I. Houston. 2002. The sexual selection continuum. *Proceedings of the Royal Society B* 269(1498):1333–1340.

Kokko, H., and D. J. Rankin. 2006. Lonely hearts or sex in the city? Density-dependent effects in mating systems. *Philosophical Transactions of the Royal Society B* 361(1466):227–386.

Krebs, J. R., and N. B. Davies. 1987. Sexual conflict and sexual selection. In *An introduction to behavioural ecology*, 2nd edition. Sinauer Associates, Sunderland, Massachusetts, pp.161–190.

Lee, K. P., J-S. Kim, and K-J. Min. 2013. Sexual dimorphism in nutrient intake and life span is mediated by mating in *Drosophila melanogaster*. *Animal Behaviour* 86(5): 987–992.

Lemaître, J-F., V. Berger, C. Bonenfant, M. Douhard, M. Gamelon, F. Plard, and J-M. Gaillard. 2015. Early-late life trade-offs and the evolution of ageing in the wild. *Proceedings of the Royal Society B* 282(1806):20150209.

Levitan, D. R., and D. L. Ferrell. 2006. Selection on gamete recognition proteins depends on sex, density, and genotype frequency. *Science* 312(5771):267–269.

Linder, J. E., and W. R. Rice. 2005. Natural selection and genetic variation for female resistance to harm from males. *Journal of Evolutionary Biology* 18(3):568–575.

Liu, H., and E. Kubli. 2003. Sex peptide is the molecular basis of the sperm effect in *Drosophila melanogaster*. *Proceedings of the National Academy of Sciences, USA* 100(17):9929–9933.

Long, T. A. F., and W. R. Rice. 2007. Adult locomotory activity mediates intralocus sexual conflict in a laboratory-adapted population of *Drosophila melanogaster*. *Proceedngs of the Royal Society B* 274(1629):3105–3112.

MacPherson, A., L. Yun, T. S. Barrera, A. F. Agrawal, and H. D. Rundle. 2018. The effects of male harm vary with female quality and environmental complexity in *Drosophila melanogaster*. *Biology Letters* 14(8): 20180443.

Magwere, T., T. Chapman, and L. Partridge. 2004. Sex differences in the effect of dietary restriction on lifespan and mortality rates in female and male *Drosophila melanogaster*. *Journal of Gerontology: Biological Sciences* 59(1):3–9.

Maklakov, A. A., M. D. Hall, S. J. Simpson, J. Dessmann, F. J. Clissold, F. Zajitschek, S. P. Lailvaux, D. Raubenheimer, R. Bondurianasky, and R. C. Brooks. 2009. Sex differences in nutrient-dependent reproductive ageing. *Aging Cell* 8(3):324–330.

Maklakov, A. A., S. J. Simpson, F. Zajitschek, M. D. Hall, J. Dessmann, F. Clissold, D. Raubenheimer, R. Bondurianasky, and R. C. Brooks. 2008. Sex-specific fitness effects of nutrient intake on reproduction and lifespan. *Current Biology* 18(14):1062–1066.

Mank, J. E. 2017. Population genetics of sexual conflict in the genomic era. *Nature Reviews Genetics* 18(12):721–730.

Martin, O. Y., and D. J. Hosken. 2003. The evolution of reproductive isolation through sexual conflict. *Nature* 423(6943):979–982.

Mokkonen, M., H. Kokko, E. Koskela, J. Lehtonen, T. Mappes, H. Martiskainen, and S. C. Mills. 2011. Negative frequency-dependent selection of sexually antagonistic alleles in *Myodes glareolus*. *Science* 334(6058):972–974.

Mueller, J. L., J. L. Page, and M. F. Wolfner. 2007. An ectopic expression screen reveals the protective and toxic effects of *Drosophila* seminal fluid proteins. *Genetics* 175(2):777–783.

Orteiza, N., J. E. Linder, and W. R. Rice. 2005. Sexy sons from re-mating do not recoup the direct costs of harmful male interactions in the *Drosophila melanogaster* laboratory model system. *Journal of Evolutionary Biology* 18(5):1315–1323.

Parisi, M., R. Nuttall. P. Edwards, J. Minor, D. Naiman, J. N. Lu, M. Doctolero, M. Vainer, C. Chan, J. Malley, S. Eastman, and B. Oliver. 2004. A survey of ovary-, testis-, and soma-biased gene expression in *Drosophila melanogaster* adults. *Genome Biology* 5: R40.

Parker, G. A. 1970a. The reproductive behaviour and nature of sexual selection in *Scathophaga stercoraria* L. (Diptera: Scatophagidae). VII. The origin and evolution of the passive phase. *Evolution* 24(4):774–788.

Parker, G. A. 1970b. The reproductive behaviour and the nature of sexual selection in *Scathophaga stercoraria* L. (Diptera: Scatophagidae). II. The fertilisation rate and the spatial and temporal relationships of each sex around the site of mating and oviposition. *Journal of Animal Ecology* 39(1):205–228.

Parker, G. A. 1970c. The reproductive behaviour and the nature of sexual selection in *Scathophaga stercoraria* L. (Diptera: Scatophagidae) IV. Epigamic recognition and competition between males for the possession of females. *Behaviour* 37(1–2):113–139.

Parker, G. A. 1979. *Sexual selection and sexual conflict*. Academic Press, New York.

Parsch, J., and H. Ellegren. 2013. The evolutionary causes and consequences of sex-biased gene expression. *Nature Reviews Genetics* 14(2):83–87.

Partridge, L., and L. D. Hurst. 1998. Sex and conflict. *Science* 281(5385):2003–2008.

Paterson, S., T. Vogwill, A. Buckling, R. Benmayor, A. J. Spiers, N. R. Thomson, M. Quail, F. Smith, D. Walker, B. Libberton, A. Fenton, N. Hall, and M. A. Brockhurst. 2010. Antagonistic coevolution accelerates molecular evolution. *Nature* 464(7286):275–278.

Perry, J. C., C. J. Garroway, and L. Rowe 2017. The role of ecology, neutral processes and antagonistic coevolution in an apparent sexual arms race. *Ecology Letters* 20(9):1107–1117.

Perry, J. C., and L. Rowe. 2018. Sexual conflict in its ecological setting. *Philosophical Transactions of the Royal Society B* 373(1757): 20170418.

Pitnick, S., and F. García-González. 2002. Harm to females increases with male body size in *Drosophila melanogaster*. *Proceedings of the Royal Society B* 269(1502):1821–1828.

Poissant, J., A. J. Wilson, and D. W. Coltman. 2010. Sex-specific genetic variance and the evolution of sexual dimorphism: a systematic review of cross-sex genetic correlations. *Evolution* 64(1):97–107.

Priest, N. K., L. F. Galloway, and D. A. Roach. 2008. Mating frequency and inclusive fitness in *Drosophila melanogaster*. *American Naturalist* 171(1):10–21.

Regan, J. C., and L. Partridge. 2013. Gender and longevity: Why do men die earlier than women? Comparative and experimental evidence. *Best Practice & Research Clinical Endocrinology & Metabolism* 27(4):467–479.

Rice, W. R. 1992. Sexually antagonistic genes: experimental evidence. *Science* 256(5062):1436–1439.

Rice, W. R. 1996. Sexually antagonistic male adaptation triggered by experimental arrest of female evolution. *Nature* 381(6579):232–234.

Rice, W. R. 1998. Intergenomic conflict, interlocus antagonistic coevolution and the evolution of reproductive isolation. In D. J. Howard and S. H. Berlocher (Eds), *Endless forms species and speciation*. Oxford University Press, Oxford, pp. 261–270.

Rice, W. R. 2000. Dangerous liaisons. *Proceedings of the National Academy of Sciences, USA* 97(24):12953–12955.

Rice, W. R., and B. Holland. 1997. The enemies within: intergenomic conflict, interlocus contest evolution (ICE), and the intraspecific Red Queen. *Behavioural Ecology and Sociobiology* 41(1):1–10.

Rice, W. R., A. D. Stewart, E. H. Morrow, J. E. Linder, N. Orteiza, and P. G. Byrne. 2006. Assessing sexual conflict in the *Drosophila melanogaster* laboratory model system. *Philosophical Transactions of the Royal Society B* 361(1466):287–299.

Ronn, J., M. Katvala, and G. Arnqvist. 2007. Coevolution between harmful male genitalia and female resistance in seed beetles. *Proceedings of the National Academy, USA* 104(26):10921–10925.

Rostant, W. G., J. S. Mason, J.-C. de Coriolis, and T. Chapman. 2019. Evolution of lifespan and ageing in response to sexual conflict is sex-specific and condition-dependent. *Evolution Letters*, in press.

Rowe, L., E. Cameron, and T. Day. 2005. Escalation, retreat, and female indifference as alternative outcomes of sexually antagonistic coevolution. *American Naturalist* 165(5):S5–S18.

Rowe, L., and T. Day. 2006. Detecting sexual conflict and sexually antagonistic coevolution. *Philosophical Transactions of the Royal Society B* 361(1466):277–285.

Rowe, L., and D. Houle. 1996. The lek paradox and the capture of genetic variance by condition dependent traits. *Proceedings of the Royal Society B* 263(1375):1415–1421.

Ruzicka, F., M. S. Hill, T. M. Pennell, I. Flis, F. C. Ingleby, R. Mott, K. Fowler, E. H. Morrow, and M. Reuter. 2019. Genome-wide sexually antagonistic variants reveal long-standing constraints on sexual dimorphism in fruit flies. *PLoS Biology* 17(4):e3000244.

Schenkel, M. A., I. Pen, L. W. Beukeboom, and J. C. Billeter. 2018. Making sense of intralocus and interlocus sexual conflict. *Ecology and Evolution* 8(24):13035–13050.

Simon, A. F., C. Shih, A. Mack, and S. Benzer. 2003. Steroid control of longevity in *Drosophila melanogaster*. *Science* 299(5611):1407–1410.

Sirot, L. K., A. Wong, T. Chapman, and M. F. Wolfner. 2014. Sexual conflict and seminal fluid proteins: a dynamic landscape of sexual interactions. In W. R. Rice and S. Gavrilets (Eds), *The sexual conflict of sexual conflict*. Cold Spring Harbor Laboratory Press, Cold Spring Harbor, New York.

South, S. H., C. M. House, A. J. Moore, S. J. Simpson, and J. Hunt. 2011. Male cockroaches prefer a high carbohydrate diet that makes them more attractive to females: implications for the study of condition dependence. *Evolution* 65(6): 1594–1606.

Stearns, S. C. 1992. *The evolution of life histories*. Oxford University Press, Oxford.

Swanson, W. J., C. F. Aquadro, and V. D. Vacquier. 2001a. Polymorphism in abalone fertilisation proteins is consistent with neutral evolution of the egg's receptor for lysin (VERL) and positive Darwinian selection of sperm lysin. *Molecular Biology and Evolution* 18(3):376–383.

Swanson, W. J., A. G. Clark, H. M. Waldrip-Dail, M. F. Wolfner, and C. F. Aquadro. 2001b. Evolutionary EST analysis identifies rapidly evolving male reproductive proteins in *Drosophila*. *Proceedings of the National Academy of Sciences, USA* 98(13): 7375–7379.

Swanson, W. J., R. Nielsen, and Q. F. Yang. 2003. Pervasive adaptive evolution in mammalian fertilization proteins. *Molecular Biology and Evolution* 20(1):18–20.

Swanson, W. J., and V. D. Vacquier. 1995. Extraordinary divergence and positive Darwinian selection in a fusagenic protein coating the acrosomal process of abalone spermatozoa. *Proceedings of the National Academy of Sciences, USA* 92(11):4957–4961.

Swanson, W. J., and V. D. Vacquier. 1998. Concerted evolution in an egg receptor for a rapidly evolving abalone sperm protein. *Science* 281(5377):710–712.

Swanson, W. J., and V. D. Vacquier. 2002. The rapid evolution of reproductive proteins. *Nature Reviews Genetics* 3(2):137–144.

Trivers, R. L. 1972. Parental investment and sexual selection. In B. Campbell (Ed.), *Sexual selection and the descent of man 1871–1971*. Chicago: Aldine.

VanKuren, N. W., and M. Long. 2018. Gene duplicates resolving sexual conflict rapidly evolved essential gametogenesis functions. *Nature Ecology and Evolution* 2(4):705–712.

van Noordwijk, A. J., and G. de Jong. 1986. Acquisition and allocation of resources: their influence on variation in life-history tactics. *American Naturalist* 128(1):137–142.

Wagstaff, B. J., and D. J. Begun. 2005. Comparative genomics of accessory gland protein genes in *Drosophila melanogaster* and *D. pseudoobscura*. *Molecular Biology and Evolution* 22(4):818–832.

Warner, R., D. Shapiro, A. Marcanato, and C. Petersen. 1995. Sexual conflict: males with highest mating success convey the lowest fertilization benefits to females. *Proceedings of the Royal Society B* 262(1364):135–139.

Wigby, S., and T. Chapman. 2004. Female resistance to male harm evolves in response to manipulation of sexual conflict. *Evolution* 58(5):1028–1037.

Wigby, S., and T. Chapman. 2005. Sex peptide causes mating costs in female *Drosophila melanogaster*. *Current Biology* 15(4):316–321.

Wright, A. E., M. Fumagalli, C. R. Cooney, N. I. Bloch, F. G. Vieira, S. D. Buechel, N. Kolm, and J. E. Mank. 2018. Male-biased gene expression resolves sexual conflict through the evolution of sex-specific genetic architecture. *Evolution Letters* 2(2):52–61.

Wright, A. E., and J. E. Mank. 2013. The scope and strength of sex-specific selection in genome evolution. *Journal of Evolutionary Biology* 26(9):1841–1853.

Young, Y., N. Buckiewicz, and T. A. Long. 2018. Nutritional geometry and fitness consequences in *Drosophila suzukii*, the Spotted-Wing Drosophila. *Ecology and Evolution* 8(5):2842–2851.

Yun, L., P. J. Chen, A. Singh, A. F. Agrawal, and H. D. Rundle. 2017. The physical environment mediates male harm and its effect on selection in females. *Proceedings of the Royal Society B* 284(1858):20170424.

Zajitschek, F., and T. Connallon. 2017. Partitioning of resources: the evolutionary genetics of sexual conflict over resource acquisition and allocation. *Journal of Evolutionary Biology* 30(4):826–835.

15

Attachment Theory: A Behavioral Systems Approach for Studying Species-Universal and Individual-Differences Aspects of the Social Mind

Mario Mikulincer and Phillip R. Shaver

Attachment theory (Bowlby, 1973, 1980, 1982) has proven to be one of the most useful and influential contemporary theories in social/ personality, developmental, and clinical psychology (Cassidy and Shaver, 2016). The theory has generated an enormous research and intervention literature, in part because Bowlby combined ideas and insights from psychoanalysis, cognitive-developmental psychology, and ethology, especially primate ethology. He can reasonably be considered one of the first evolutionary psychologists, because his conception of human infancy, social development, and close interpersonal relationships (colored by a history of loves and losses) was strongly affected by Darwinian and ethological concepts. Interestingly, his final book, finished shortly before he died (Bowlby, 1991), was a clinical biography of Darwin.

In this chapter, we consider a core construct in Bowlby's attachment theory – *behavioral system* – and evaluate its usefulness for studying the social mind. We begin by explaining the behavioral system construct, including its

evolutionary basis and its species-universal and individual-differences aspects. Next, we discuss the behavioral systems that have been studied to date within Bowlby's theoretical framework: attachment, exploration, caregiving, sex, and power. We place more emphasis on the attachment system than on the other behavioral systems because it has received more research attention, but we also summarize recent research related to the other behavioral systems. We then briefly review research on the adaptive benefits of optimal behavioral-system functioning. Finally, we suggest avenues for further research and integration of attachment theory with other approaches within evolutionary psychology – leading, we hope, to a more comprehensive and deeper understanding of the social mind.

THE CONCEPT OF BEHAVIORAL SYSTEMS

In thinking about the motivational bases of human behavior, Bowlby (1982) was strongly influenced by his training as a psychoanalyst and his interest in control systems theory (an early form of cognitive psychology and cognitive neuroscience), Piaget's theory of cognitive development, Harlow's studies of infant–mother attachment in rhesus monkeys, primate ethology more generally (e.g., the work of Lorenz and Tinbergen), and community psychiatrists' studies of grief and depression. Much of his thinking remarkably anticipated contemporary work in evolutionary psychology (see, e.g., other chapters in this *Handbook*). Specifically, like other evolutionary approaches, Bowlby (1982) discussed human behavior in the context of homologous animal behavior and argued that behavioral patterns are shaped by natural selection in response to adaptive challenges that a species faced throughout its evolutionary history.

Moreover, like Tooby and Cosmides (1992), Bowlby (1982) claimed that these psychological adaptations are *functionally domain-specific* (i.e., different adaptations are required to solve different problems) and were 'designed' (i.e., evolved) as solutions to challenges that existed when a particular adaptation evolved (what Bowlby, 1982, called the *environment of evolutionary adaptedness*, EEA). In some respects, Bowlby's proposal of domain-specific adaptations, which is derived from ethological ideas about feedback-regulated control systems (e.g., Hinde, 1966; Lorenz, 1952), is similar to the evolutionary psychological construct of a mental 'module' (Tooby and Cosmides, 1992). However, 'module' is a generic construct that may apply to behavioral systems as well as many other kinds of psychological mechanisms.

Bowlby (1982) noted that although some evolved psychological adaptations are designed in a very simple way (e.g., reflexes, fixed-action patterns), others are more complex and flexible and have a continuing influence on social behavior and adjustment across the lifespan. Borrowing from ethological theory, Bowlby (1982) called these complex adaptations *behavioral systems* – species-universal,

dynamic information-processing neural programs that organize behavior in ways that increase the likelihood of survival and reproductive success. For example, the attachment behavioral system evolved in response to helpless infants' problem, after being born prematurely (compared to other mammals), of coping with predators and other dangers. Similarly, the exploration behavioral system evolved in response to threats related to novelty, uncertainty, and ambiguity.

Distinct but interrelated behavioral systems (e.g., attachment, exploration, caregiving, sex) evolved in the EEA, each with its own functions and characteristic behavioral strategies (Bowlby, 1982). For example, the attachment behavioral system was 'designed' to organize a person's proximity-seeking bids when faced with threats (e.g., vocalizing distress, clinging to a caregiver) and relaxing once support is provided. Similarly, the caregiving behavioral system evolved as a response to a needy other's (often a child's) bids for care and protection. This system involves innate empathy and compassion as well as rewarding feelings associated with effectively reducing another person's distress.

According to Kirkpatrick (2012), Bowlby's construct of the behavioral system provides a basis for an evolutionary explanation of the modularity of the social mind. In Kirkpatrick's words, Bowlby views the human social mind as 'characterized by a species-universal psychology that comprises highly numerous, functionally domain-specific mechanisms and systems – analogous to the many specialized organs and systems in the human body – that collectively constitute "human nature"' (235–6).

NORMATIVE PARAMETERS

Bowlby (1982) viewed each behavioral system as having a particular biological function and a general 'set-goal' related to that function – for example, maintaining a sense of safety and security, curiously exploring and learning about the environment, or promoting the safety and welfare of others. The word 'set' in set-goal referred to the fact that the general goals could be adjusted slightly to fit the situation at hand. Bowlby viewed each goal as a desired change in the person–environment relationship that, if achieved, would terminate or 'deactivate' the system, making way for other goals and activities. (This way of thinking was inspired by ethologists who developed cybernetic models of animal and human behavior.) Each system was assumed to respond to a particular set of activating triggers – internal bodily or mental states or environmental demands and opportunities – that made a particular goal salient (e.g., loud noises signaling danger and instigating a desire for safety and protection; exposure to a new object or situation that arouses curiosity). Each system was thought to include a set of interchangeable, functionally equivalent behaviors that constitute the primary strategy for attaining a particular goal – for example, maintaining proximity to a supportive other in times of need; competing for and controlling precious resources; having sex with an attractive mate, which in the environment of evolutionary adaptation signaled a healthy, fertile partner.

According to Bowlby (1982), behavior is best defined functionally, in terms of its goal. A particular action, such as moving physically closer to another person, is viewed as an attachment behavior if it is intended to secure comfort, support, or relief from threat. The same action is viewed as sexual if it moves a person toward a sexual relationship, and it can be viewed as a product of the power behavioral system if it occurs in the service of gaining or controlling resources in competitive contexts. Similarly, termination of one kind of behavior and initiation of another kind are not defined primarily in terms of particular motor or physical processes but by the motivation to seek out, attain, or control a particular goal. For example, when an infant encounters what Bowlby (1982) called 'natural clues of danger' (e.g., unexpected

noises, an approaching stranger), the child terminates whatever activity is in progress (e.g., playing with new toys) and attempts to gain physical proximity to a caregiver as a means of attaining protection and support – the main goal of the attachment behavioral system. If the caregiver provides adequate security, the attachment system is deactivated and the infant typically becomes interested again in exploratory play, in which case he or she may signal a desire to be put down amid interesting toys (Ainsworth et al., 1978). This dynamic balance between attachment and exploration is the focus of the famous Strange Situation assessment procedure created by Ainsworth and her associates.

According to Bowlby's (1982) conceptual framework, mental processes related to a behavioral system – for example, a person's chronic and context-specific access to a system's goal or goal-related feeling states – govern the activation and termination of particular behavioral sequences. Moreover, the psychological meaning of a motor or perceptual act is determined by the behavioral system's goal that instigates, organizes, and governs the act. Behavior, in turn, can recursively influence these mental processes. For example, moving physically closer to a relationship partner and being comforted by him or her often enhances security and allows other non-attachment goals to arise in the comforted person's mind and guide behavior. Moreover, failure of a behavioral system's primary strategy to attain a goal (e.g., seeking support from a non-responsive and rejecting other) can foster the adoption of alternative strategies, which is the basis of individual differences in the activation and functioning of the system.

INDIVIDUAL-DIFFERENCES COMPONENTS

According to Bowlby (1973), the ability of a behavioral system to achieve its set-goal depends on the extent to which its operational parameters can be corrected to fit with demands and opportunities encountered in particular social-relational contexts. From birth, behavioral systems are receptive to environmental feedback concerning progress toward goal attainment and can be affected or shaped by this information. Over time, repeated activation of a behavioral system in a given environmental context can mold the activation and functioning of the system, and thereby a person's general neural/behavioral capacities become 'programmed' to fit with the repeatedly encountered context so as to create more effective context-specific action sequences. According to Bowlby (1982), this flexible, goal-corrected adjustment is a hard-wired feature of behavioral systems, which takes advantage of the evolution of cortical capacities for monitoring and appraising the course of behavior and the utility of a chosen line of action in a particular situation. Moreover, it is the basis of individual differences in the functioning of the behavioral systems. To the extent that different people encounter different contexts (e.g., different relationship partners, such as parents or lovers), the parameters of their behavioral systems – their neural, cognitive, and behavioral subroutines – will become different as well.

Bowlby (1973) claimed that the residues of impactful experiences are stored in the form of episodic memories and mental representations of person–environment transactions, which he called *internal working models of self and others*. In his view, each behavioral system, once it has been repeatedly activated in particular social contexts, includes representations of responses of other people to one's attempts to attain a goal (these complex representations forming working models of others) as well as representations of one's own efficacy and social value or lack thereof (working models of self). These models presumably operate mainly at a cortical level and in a relatively reflective and intentional manner. Nevertheless, with repeated use they can become automatic and may sometimes

be held out of awareness either by habit or by defensive maneuvers (e.g., repression or deliberate inattention; Bowlby, 1980). These models become parts of a behavioral system's programming and are responsible for within-person continuity over time. However, these well-rehearsed mental representations can be updated and revised based on subsequent social experiences and relationships, including psychotherapy (Bowlby, 1988).

When a behavioral system's primary strategy repeatedly leads to goal attainment, the working models that are constructed in relation to it allow the system to function well. If the primary strategy repeatedly fails to attain its goal, the resulting working models (e.g., 'When I try to rely on others, they prove either unreliable or outright punishing') will vary from the norm, and the person in question will increasingly adopt what Main (1990) called secondary strategies. Attachment theorists (e.g., Cassidy and Kobak, 1988; Mikulincer and Shaver, 2016) have proposed that secondary strategies can be characterized in terms of hyperactivation vs. deactivation of a behavioral system. Hyperactivating strategies can be conceptualized as 'fight' (persist or protest) responses that intensify a system's primary strategy, to the point where it no longer works adaptively (e.g., it may drive other people away rather than attracting their social support) Deactivating strategies can be conceptualized as 'flight' (escape, avoid) responses that suppress or down-regulate a system's primary strategy.

Both hyperactivation and deactivation of a behavioral system are well-organized, perhaps once-effective adaptations to a non-optimal environment. However, when generalized beyond that specific context and transferred to other contexts, hyperactivated and deactivated strategies tend to be problematic and put a person at risk for emotional disorders and maladjustment. For example, hyperactivation often entails heightened agitation, distress, self-related worries, and interpersonal conflicts, which can endanger emotional balance, interfere with goal-oriented activities, and destroy important relationships. Deactivation often results in a narrowing of experiences and behavior (e.g., avoiding affection, not being curious about the world, not being interested in caring for others) which makes life seem less interesting, engaging, and meaningful. Moreover, deactivating strategies prevent a person from realizing that there are social contexts in which a behavioral system's primary strategy would be effective.

Although attachment theory places strong emphasis on the history of positive and negative outcomes of system activation across the lifespan, it is also important to recognize the role of genetic factors in explaining individual differences in the functioning of a behavioral system (see Barbaro et al., 2017, for a review). These genetic factors may contribute to the adoption of either deactivation or hyperactivation strategies when the system fails to attain its goal. For example, a more agitated, distress-prone child might be more likely to adopt hyperactivation strategies following frustrating experiences, whereas a more introverted, shy child might be more likely to deactivate the system and forego certain personal goals. Also of importance, genetic differences in infant temperament and reactivity to stress might elicit different parental responses, which affect the outcome of system activation and thereby contribute to subsequent individual differences in the system's functioning. The behavior of a highly irritable infant, for example, might make it more difficult for parents to respond sensitively to the infant's needs, disrupting the smooth functioning of the infant's behavioral system, thereby leading to the adoption of secondary attachment strategies. In addition, children differ genetically in their susceptibility to positive or negative social experiences (Belsky and Pluess, 2009), which can moderate the role of these experiences in shaping the functioning of behavioral systems. Finally, a parent's genetic factors contribute to his or her responsiveness to their infants (Wertz et al., 2019), thereby having an effect on individual differences in attachment system functioning among infants.

CONCEPTUALIZING SPECIFIC BEHAVIORAL SYSTEMS

For purposes of illustration, we focus here on five behavioral systems: attachment, exploration, caregiving, sex, and power. We describe their normative parameters (goals, triggers, primary strategies); the major individual differences in their functioning, conceptualized in terms of hyperactivation and deactivation; and the ways of assessing these individual differences.

The Attachment Behavioral System

According to Bowlby (1982), one of the earliest behavioral systems to appear in human development is the attachment system, whose inferred biological function is to protect a person (especially during infancy) from danger by assuring that he or she maintains proximity to supportive others (*attachment figures*). Attachment figures are not just ordinary relationship partners. They are special individuals to whom a person turns in times of need to attain two main provisions – *safe haven* and *secure base*. Bowlby argued that a relationship partner can become an attachment figure if he or she provides a physical and emotional safe haven (i.e., alleviates distress and is a source of relief and comfort) as well as a secure base from which one can explore, learn, and thrive. Proximity to these figures is a source of positive emotions (e.g., joy, gratitude, relief), whereas separation and distance from these figures is a source of distress.

The set-goal of the attachment system is to sustain a sense of security, rooted in beliefs that the world is generally safe, that one is competent and lovable, and that key people will be supportive in times of need. This system is activated by events that threaten the sense of security, such as encounters with actual or symbolic threats and noticing that an attachment figure is not sufficiently near, interested, or responsive. Under these conditions, a person is automatically motivated to seek and reestablish actual or symbolic proximity to an attachment figure (the system's primary strategy). These bids for proximity persist until security is attained. The attachment system is then deactivated and the person can calmly return to other activities. Although the attachment system is most important early in life (where protection and support are matters of life or death), Bowlby (1988) believed it is active across the life span and is manifest in thoughts and behaviors related to seeking support in times of need.

During infancy, primary caregivers (usually parents) are likely to occupy the role of attachment figure. During adolescence and adulthood, other relationship partners also become providers of safe haven and secure base, including close friends and romantic partners. Teachers and supervisors in academic settings, managers in work settings, or therapists in clinical settings can also serve as potential sources of security, and therefore can be viewed as attachment figures. Moreover, groups, institutions, and symbolic personages (e.g., God, the Buddha, the Virgin Mary) can also be recruited as attachment figures. All of these real and symbolic care providers form what Bowlby (1982) called a person's *hierarchy of attachment figures.*

In addition to their actual physical presence, mental representations of caring and loving attachment figures can serve as symbolic sources of security (Mikulincer and Shaver, 2004). They can also provide models of effective, loving behavior that influence the way a person regards and treats him- or herself in the temporary absence of an actual attachment figure. Nonetheless, although Bowlby (1982, 1988) assumed that age and psychological development result in an increased ability to gain comfort from attachment-related mental representations, he also assumed that no one of any age is completely free of reliance on actual others when confronting illness, death of loved others, aging, and other disasters and traumas.

Bowlby's ideas about the predisposition to seek proximity to others to obtain care and protection have received extensive empirical support. In times of need, infants show a clear preference for their familiar caregiver, engage in intense proximity seeking, and are soothed by a caregiver's presence and support (e.g., Ainsworth, 1991). Conceptually parallel research with adults has shown that people are likely to turn to key others for support while, or immediately after, encountering stressors (see Mikulincer and Shaver, 2016, for an extensive review).

Using cognitive research techniques, we (e.g., Mikulincer et al., 2002) have found that adults react to even minimal threat cues with activation of mental representations of security-providing attachment figures. In these studies, subliminal priming with a threat word (e.g., illness, failure) was found to heighten the cognitive accessibility of attachment-related mental representations, indicated by faster lexical-decision times for the names of people nominated as providing protection and security (e.g., the name of a parent, spouse, or close friend). Interestingly, these effects were not found for the names of people other than attachment figures, including family members who were not nominated as security providers. Similar findings have been obtained in subsequent studies, where threat primes have automatically increased representations of symbolic sources of attachment security, such as a person's pet or God (Granqvist et al., 2012; Zilcha-Mano et al., 2012). These findings support Bowlby's core claim that the mind turns automatically to attachment figures when threats loom.

Following up this line of research, Beckes et al., (2010) reasoned that the repeated automatic activation of representations of a comforting relationship partner following encounters with threats would be enough to transform this partner into a security-enhancing attachment figure. Beckes et al. used a classical conditioning procedure to test whether participants would be more likely to develop security-related associations with the faces of people who displayed genuine smiles if those faces were repeatedly paired with subliminally presented threatening stimuli (e.g., a picture of a striking snake) rather than with neutral stimuli. As compared to smiling faces paired with neutral stimuli, smiling faces paired with threatening stimuli did indeed decrease lexical decision response times for security-related words (e.g., 'belong') while lengthening lexical decision response times to insecurity-related words (e.g., 'betray'). Importantly, the learning process did not have this effect when neutral, unresponsive faces were used. Thus, responsive faces preceded by potential threats promote implicit associations between those responsive faces and mental representations of security.

This evidence fits with Panksepp's (1998, 2011) ideas concerning the linkage between stress-related neural systems and attachment-system activation in rodents and other mammals. Panksepp proposed that the mammalian brain contains an integrated social emotion system that includes both a separation-distress circuitry (PANIC) and a social-reward/contact-comfort circuitry (SEEKING). The PANIC circuitry overlaps with the physical-pain circuitry, elicits distress-related responses, and activates the SEEKING circuitry, which fosters proximity seeking – a key component of attachment. When a sought figure is available and responsive, the SEEKING circuitry down-regulates the PANIC circuitry and elicits opiod- and oxytocin-mediated relief and social pleasure (Panksepp, 1998, 2011). In this way, a responsive attachment figure becomes associated with both distress down-regulation and feelings of comfort and relief, setting the neural basis for the conditioning process observed by Beckes et al. (2010).

There is also extensive evidence that separation from and loss of attachment figures is a powerful source of pain and distress.

Observation of infants separated from their mothers (e.g., Robertson and Bowlby, 1952) revealed early in the history of attachment research that absence of an attachment figure causes intense distress, anger, and yearning. In adulthood, bereavement research has also found that death of a close relationship partner is one of the most painful experiences a person can endure, one that typically elicits extreme sorrow, despair, and painful longing for the deceased partner (see Fraley and Shaver, 2016, for a review). Similar emotional reactions have also been observed following experiences of others' disapproval, criticism, or rejection (see Rotge et al., 2015, for a review and meta-analysis) and the break-up of romantic relationships (see Sbarra, 2012, for a review).

Researchers have also documented at a neurological level the positive effects of gaining proximity to attachment figures. For example, Coan et al., (2006) scanned the brains (using functional magnetic resonance imaging) of married women undergoing a laboratory stressor (threat of electric shock) while either holding their husband's hand, the hand of an otherwise unfamiliar male experimenter, or no hand at all. The findings indicated that spousal handholding reduced physiological stress responses, as seen in brain regions associated with distress (e.g., right anterior insula, superior frontal gyrus, and hypothalamus). Moreover, Eisenberger and colleagues (Eisenberger et al., 2011; Master et al., 2009) found that holding the hand of a romantic partner or viewing his or her photograph reduced pain-related brain responses to heat stimuli.

Conceptually similar findings were obtained when experimentally priming security-related mental representations (security priming). For example, Mikulincer et al., (2001) found that subliminal presentation of the names of participants' security providers, compared with the names of close others or mere acquaintances who were not nominated as attachment figures, led to greater liking of previously unfamiliar Chinese ideographs even in a threatening context. Subsequent studies have found that security priming, as compared to neutral priming, reduces negative thoughts after recalling an upsetting event (Selcuk et al., 2012), inhibits the intrusion of traumatic memories (Bryant and Chan, 2017), and attenuates activation in brain areas, such as the hypothalamus and amygdala, implicated in the experience of social threats, (Karremans et al., 2011; Norman et al., 2015). Moreover, security priming increases parasympathetic responses to stress stimuli – a physiological indicator of ease and relaxation (Bryant and Hutanamon, 2018).

Besides these normative processes related to attachment security and insecurity, there are major individual differences in tendencies to hyperactivate or deactivate the attachment system following repeated failure to sustain a sense of security. Hyperactivation of the attachment system is characterized by energetic, insistent attempts to induce a relationship partner, viewed as insufficiently available or responsive, to pay more attention and provide better care and support. Hyperactivating strategies include clinging, controlling, and coercive responses; cognitive and behavioral efforts to establish physical contact and a sense of 'oneness'; and overdependence on relationship partners as a source of protection (Shaver and Mikulincer, 2002). Deactivation refers to inhibition of proximity-seeking inclinations and actions, suppression or discounting of threats that might activate the attachment system, and determination to handle stresses alone (a stance Bowlby, 1982, called compulsive self-reliance). These strategies involve maintaining physical and emotional distance from others, being uncomfortable with intimacy and interdependence, ignoring or downplaying threat- and attachment-related cues, and suppressing threat- and attachment-related thoughts (Cassidy and Kobak, 1988).

Partly because of their clinical significance, these individual differences have received more research attention than the normative functioning of the system. In studying these individual differences in adolescence and adulthood, researchers have focused on the construct of attachment orientations or styles – patterns of relational expectations, emotions, and behaviors that result from internalizing a particular history of attachment experiences (Fraley and Shaver, 2000). Research, beginning with Ainsworth et al. (1978) and continuing through hundreds of studies by social and personality psychologists (reviewed by Mikulincer and Shaver, 2016), indicates that attachment orientations are located in a two-dimensional space defined by roughly orthogonal factors which we call attachment-related anxiety and avoidance (e.g., Brennan et al., 1998). The avoidance dimension reflects the extent to which a person distrusts relationship partners' good will and relies on deactivating strategies. The anxiety dimension reflects the extent to which a person worries that a partner will not be available in times of need and relies on hyperactivating strategies. People who score low on both dimensions are relatively secure with respect to attachment.

The two attachment-style dimensions can be measured with the 36-item Experiences in Close Relationships inventory (ECR; Brennan et al., 1998), which is reliable in both the internal-consistency and test-retest senses and has high construct, predictive, and discriminant validity (see Crowell et al., 2016, for a review). This scale can be used to assess a person's global attachment orientations in a range of close relationships as well as his or her attachment orientation in a particular relationship or on a particular occasion (e.g., Fraley et al., 2011; Gillath et al., 2009).

These two basic dimensions of adult attachment orientations have been found in multiple cultures (Shaver et al., 2010). For example, Schmitt et al. (2003, 2004) found cross-cultural similarities in attachment scores and correlates of these scores in 62 cultures. Moreover, people worldwide seem to view secure attachment as the ideal for a mating partner (Schmitt et al., 2003, 2004), and security seems to be more common than the different kinds of insecurity in different societies, except under unusual circumstances (e.g., living under extreme life-threatening conditions; Schmitt et al., 2004).

Studies using self-report measures of adult attachment orientations have found them to be predictably related to cognitions, feelings, and behaviors that characterize hyperactivation or deactivation of the attachment system (see Mikulincer and Shaver, 2016, for an extensive review). Anxious attachment has been associated with increased emotionality, vigilance regarding partner availability and commitment, jealousy, hurt feelings, self-doubts, intrusiveness, and coercive violence. Avoidant attachment has been associated with suppression of negative thoughts, denial of vulnerability and hurt feelings, lack of self-disclosure, sexual infidelity, and lack of compassion. Thus, the same concepts that are used to understand the attachment behavioral system as an innate motivational system can also be used to characterize important individual differences in attachment behavior. Importantly, these attachment-related variations are usually not well explained by more global personality traits such as extraversion, neuroticism, or self-esteem, although there are predictable and meaningful associations between attachment orientations and personality traits and they share some common genetic basis (see Mikulincer and Shaver, 2016, for a review).

It is important to mention that although the vast majority of studies assess variations in attachment orientations along the anxiety and avoidance dimensions, some scholars have suggested that it would be better to rotate the axes of the measurement space and assess individual differences in security vs. insecurity and anxiety vs. avoidance strategies (e.g., Asendorpf et al., 1997; Stein et al., 2002). In response to this criticism, researchers have developed unidimensional scales designed to measure the sense of security similar to scales designed to measure other inner resources or strengths, such as optimism, hope, mastery, and self-efficacy (e.g., Lopez et al., 2018).

Such scales are particularly valuable in studies in which the main goal is to understand the antecedents, correlates, and outcomes of the sense of security. However, in studies where the main issue is the functioning and effects of a particular kind of 'organized' or 'strategic' attachment insecurity, it is still valuable to assess individual variations along the two main dimensions of attachment anxiety and avoidance.

The Exploration Behavioral System

In their discussions of the attachment behavioral system in infancy, Bowlby (1982) and Ainsworth (1967) recognized that infants possess an innate propensity to explore and learn about the world, even at the cost of temporarily distancing themselves from attachment figures. Bowlby attributed this motivation, which Harlow (1955) called an 'exploratory drive', to an innate exploration behavioral system. Panksepp (1998, 2011) proposed that both the attachment and exploration behavioral systems reflect different manifestations of the SEEKING neural circuitry. According to Panksepp, the SEEKING neural circuitry not only drives animals to seek comforting attachment figures in times of need, but also

> provokes animals to become intensely energized to explore the world and also promotes learning … it leads animals to become excited about the mundane, and the system conditions rapidly to yield vigorous approach, exploration, and, eventually, various consummatory behaviors when there are predictable associations between external events and the things animals need to survive. (Panksepp, 2011:1798)

The set-goal of the exploration system is to promote and sustain a person's sense of mastery and competence and the primary strategy for achieving this goal is to seek, learn, and master new information about oneself and the world. This strategy is activated whenever a person encounters novel situations, objects, or people, or experiences novel internal states that cannot be easily assimilated to existing knowledge. The exploration system can also be activated by environmental affordances (Gibson, 1977), which provide opportunities to acquire new knowledge and skills. The exploratory system is deactivated when the desired knowledge or skill is acquired, resulting in a temporary sense of mastery.

Just as happens in the attachment domain, there are major individual differences in tendencies to hyperactivate or deactivate the exploration system following repeated failure to sustain a sense of mastery due to personal shortcomings or environments that inhibit or frustrate exploratory attempts. Hyperactivation of the system is characterized by engagement in exploratory activities even in situations where no exploration is needed and, instead, rapid decisions and actions are required, and by difficulties in deactivating the system once new information is acquired and digested. Moreover, because of past negative experiences with exploration, hyperactivation arouses doubts and worries about one's ability to explore and master new tasks and environments, thereby reducing self-esteem and strengthening fear of failure. In contrast, deactivation of the exploration system is characterized by inhibition and avoidance of exploratory activities and defensive evasion of situations or internal states that might activate the system. Such deactivation is manifested in cognitive closure, intolerance of ambiguity and novelty, and preference for known stimuli and environments over complex or novel ones.

The Caregiving Behavioral System

According to Bowlby (1982), humans are born with a caregiving behavioral system that fosters empathy and compassion for others and care for them when they are in need (see also Brown et al., 2012, for similar ideas). This caregiving system seems to be organized around what Panksepp (1998, 2011) called the CARE neural circuitry. This circuitry presumably emerged over the course of evolution because it increased humans' inclusive fitness (Hamilton, 1964; West and Gardner, 2013) by heightening the transmission of genes to future generations. Today, although people probably still care disproportionately for others with whom they are closely related, either psychologically or genetically, the caregiving system can be activated by anyone in need and is a key contributor to prosocial behavior (e.g., Feeney and Woodhouse, 2016).

The set-goal of the caregiving system is to alleviate others' suffering, protect them from harm and foster their well-being and growth (e.g., Feeney and Woodhouse, 2016; Shaver et al., 2010). This goal is typically made salient when one realizes that another person is confronting a danger or challenge and is directly or indirectly asking for a safe haven or secure-base support (Feeney and Woodhouse, 2016). In order to accomplish this goal, the primary strategy of the system, what Batson (2010) called empathic concern, involves sensitivity and responsiveness to another person's signals and needs. Sensitivity includes attunement to, and accurate interpretation of, another person's signals, and responding appropriately to his or her support-seeking behavior. Responsiveness includes validating another person's needs and feelings, respecting his or her beliefs and values, and helping the person feel understood and cared for (Feeney and Woodhouse, 2016).

Although we assume that everyone is born with the potential to provide care, there are genetic-influenced individual differences in caregiving and prosocial behavior (e.g., Knafo-Noam et al., 2018). Moreover, the quality of care can be impaired by a person's history of inefficient and frustrating caregiving attempts, due to personal shortcomings or others that reject or devalue these attempts. Such a negative history tends to sustain secondary strategies of hyperactivation and deactivation that dampen or conflict with sensitivity and responsiveness (Shaver et al., 2010). Hyperactivated caregiving is intrusive, poorly timed, anxious, and effortful and may be motivated by a wish to make oneself indispensable to a relationship partner, or a wish to feel competent and admirable as a caregiver. These goals are served by exaggerating others' needs or coercing others to accept one's help. In contrast, deactivated caregiving involves avoidance of caregiving, inhibition of responsiveness, lack of a desire to help, offering only half-hearted assistance, and insisting on emotional distance when someone seeks care and comfort.

The Sexual Behavioral System

In line with the preceding analyses, we view sexual motivation and behavior, and individual differences in sexual attitudes and activities, as reflecting, in part, the activation and functioning of a sexual behavioral system (Birnbaum, 2015), which seems to be organized around what Panksepp (1998, 2011) called the LUST neural circuitry. From an evolutionary perspective, the ultimate function of the sexual system is to pass genes from one generation to the next, and its main goal is to have sexual intercourse with an opposite-sex partner and either become pregnant oneself (in the case of women) or impregnate a partner (in the case of men). As evolutionary psychologists have explained, however, the proximal motivation for an act (i.e., wishing to have sex with an attractive person) need not be the same as the evolutionary reason for the existence of the motives involved. People can seek sexual pleasure without hoping that pregnancy will result, and modern methods of birth control, as well as homosexuality, make it possible to separate the two goals. Nevertheless, many aspects of sexual motivation and attraction (e.g., being attracted to people whose qualities suggest fertility or 'good genes'; Gangestad et al., 2004) are governed by neural and hormonal systems that evolved for reproductive purposes.

The sexual system is automatically activated by noticing and appraising an attractive, sexually interested, and (in the case of heterosexual attraction) presumably fertile partner (Birnbaum, 2015). The primary strategy for achieving the sexual system's goal is to approach a potential partner, entice or persuade him or her to have sex, and then engage in intercourse (Birnbaum, 2015). However, problems in coordinating sexual interests and behavior with a partner, a partner's rejecting responses, or experiencing frustrating intercourse can lead to a failure of the primary strategy of the sexual system and the adoption of secondary hyperactivating or deactivating strategies (Birnbaum et al., 2014). Hyperactivation of the sexual system includes effortful, mentally preoccupying, sometimes intrusive, and sometimes even coercive attempts to persuade a partner to have sex or to acknowledge one's sexual value (Birnbaum et al., 2014). When adopting these strategies, a person overemphasizes the importance of sex, exaggerates appraisals of a partner's sexual interest, and is overly focused on the partner's signals of sexual arousal or disinterest. In contrast, deactivation of the sexual system is characterized by inhibiting or deemphasizing sexual desire and attempting to avoid sex (Birnbaum et al., 2014). It may include dismissal of sexual needs, distancing from or disparaging a partner when he or she expresses interest in sex, suppressing sexual thoughts and fantasies, and blocking sexual arousal and discounting orgasmic pleasure.

The Power Behavioral System

Bowlby (1982), who focused mainly on infant-parent attachment when creating attachment theory, said relatively little about power or aggression. In our efforts to create a behavioral systems approach to human motivation, we perceived a need for an additional behavioral system related to power and dominance, perhaps motivated in part by what Panksepp (1998, 2011) called the RAGE neural circuitry. We (Shaver et al.,

2011) have therefore proposed that human beings are born with the rudiments of a behavioral system (the power behavioral system) that is designed to facilitate the acquisition and control of material and social resources (e.g., food, shelter, social status, followers, sexual partners). Although differing in terminology, several authors have proposed a similar behavioral system with the ultimate goal of maintaining control over social and material resources, such as the rank regulation system (Zuroff et al., 2010), the hierarchical domain (Bugental, 2000), or the dominance behavioral system (Johnson et al., 2012).

The main function of the power system is to remove threats and obstacles that interfere with a sense of influence and control (e.g., Keltner et al., 2010), and its set-goal is to achieve both actual influence and control as well as an inner sense of power and efficacy. The triggers of power-system activation include (a) noticing that other people are attempting to acquire one's valuable psychological or physical resources and (b) perceiving that other people are constraining one's access to such resources (Shaver et al., 2011). In either case, the power system is activated, causing a person to engage in behaviors aimed at protecting or restoring a sense of influence of the kind that Parker (1974) called 'resource-holding power' (the power system's primary strategy). These behaviors include asserting one's dominance, authority, rights, or competence; expressing confidence in one's strengths, values, and opinions; deterring others from competing for or exerting control over one's resources; and verbally or physically attacking (or threatening to attack) others until power is restored. This does not mean that the primary strategy of the power system necessarily involves aggression. Although aggression presumably evolved because it facilitates acquisition and control over resources (Buss and Duntley, 2006), there are many cases in which one's sense of power can be restored simply by asserting one's position, rights, or authority.

As with the other behavioral systems, repeated failure to gain a sense of power due to personal disabilities or social contexts that preclude or constrain competition, severely punish assertiveness or aggression, or demand submission or self-abasement (e.g., Gilbert et al., 2009) can encourage either hyperactivation or deactivation of the power system. Hyperactivation involves a dramatic increase in efforts to restore a sense of power despite adverse circumstances, and despite doubts and worries about failure or retaliation (Shaver et al., 2011). Hyperactivation results in indiscriminate attempts to use force; frequent anger, hostility, and aggression toward anyone viewed as a potential rival; and a proclivity to attack others following even minimal or ambiguous signs of competition or provocation. When extreme, hyperactivation can lead to flagrant vindictiveness and destructive, even murderous behavior. Deactivation, in contrast, involves giving up on the possibility of using the system's primary strategies to defend against threats and damages to one's sense of power (Shaver et al., 2011). Deactivation is evident in submissiveness, self-abasement, and the absence of resource-holding power strategies. Deactivation also involves avoiding situations that call for assertion of one's rights, values, or opinions, such as competitions, arguments, disputes, and actual fights.

MEASURING INDIVIDUAL DIFFERENCES IN EXPLORATION, CAREGIVING, SEX, AND POWER SYSTEMS

During the last decade, we have begun a long-term research project aimed at creating and validating new self-report measures that, like the ECR inventory, are specifically designed to assess individual differences in the functioning of the other behavioral systems. On this basis, we constructed for each behavioral system (exploration, caregiving, sex, and power), a self-report scale that assesses both anxious hyperactivation and avoidant deactivation of the system. We now have four such measures: the Caregiving System Scale (CSS; Shaver et al., 2010), the Sexual System Functioning Scale (SSFS; Birnbaum et al., 2014), the Exploration System Scale (ESS; Doron, 2009), and the Power Behavioral System Scale (PBSS; Shaver et al., 2011). Of course, this is just a first step in measuring these individual differences. Future studies should be undertaken to develop unidimensional scales to measure the feelings and cognitions resulting from succeeding and failing in attaining the goals of each system (similar to scales assessing attachment security).

Factor analyses conducted in the US and Israel, and in English and Hebrew, with each of the fours scales have yielded the intended two factors for each set of items. Moreover, the correlations between the hyperactivation and deactivation scores for each scale are relatively weak, indicating that the two strategies are roughly independent, as in the ECR measure of attachment anxiety and avoidance. These scales have good test-retest reliability and high correlations between self-reports and relationship partners' reports. This correspondence implies that the self-report scales concern, at least in part, social behaviors that can be observed by relationship partners. We have also examined the convergent validity of each of the new scales by correlating them with preexisting self-report measures tapping various aspects of exploration, caregiving, sex, and power. In general, the findings indicate that hyperactivation scores are associated with preexisting measures tapping intense but anxious activation of the targeted behavioral tendency, and deactivation scores are associated with inhibition of the tendency. For example, Shaver et al. (2011) found that hyperactivation scores on the Power Behavioral System Scale were associated with reports of physical aggression, verbal aggression, outbursts of anger, hostility,

a tendency to engage in violent behavior, abusive behavior in intimate relationships, and angry rumination. In contrast, power deactivation was associated with measures of submissiveness, lack of assertiveness, giving up during interpersonal conflicts, a tendency to withdraw in response to interpersonal transgressions, and higher levels of internalized anger in response to provocations (Shaver et al., 2011).

PSYCHOLOGICAL CORRELATES OF INDIVIDUAL DIFFERENCES IN BEHAVIORAL SYSTEM FUNCTIONING

Since a behavioral system accomplishes a specific biological function, individual variations in the functioning of a system have important implications for a person's psychosocial functioning, mental health, and quality of life. Consider the case of the attachment system. It is activated by perceived threats and dangers, which cause a threatened person to seek proximity to a protective other (Bowlby, 1982). An attachment figure who is responsive to the person's proximity-seeking bids facilitates the smooth functioning of the attachment system, infuses feelings of security, and promotes positive working models of self and others. Bowlby (1988) considered this cascade of mental events to be crucial for sustaining resilience and effective coping with life's adversities, promoting adjustment and mental health, and facilitating the smooth functioning of other behavioral systems. In contrast, failure to consolidate a solid sense of security can erode a person's mental health and interfere with the functioning of other behavioral systems. In this section, we briefly review research on the ways in which these individual differences in behavioral-system functioning are correlated with emotion regulation and mental health. We also review evidence concerning the dynamic interplay among the various behavioral systems. We place more emphasis on self-reports of attachment anxiety and avoidance, because they have been more thoroughly studied than the hyperactivation and deactivation of the other behavioral systems.

ATTACHMENT, EMOTION REGULATION, AND MENTAL HEALTH

According to attachment theorists (e.g., Cassidy and Kobak, 1988), secondary attachment strategies can bias emotion regulation and alter, obstruct, or suppress the experience and expression of emotions. The deactivating strategies used by avoidant individuals are intended to defuse or suppress negative emotions, because these emotions can activate unwanted attachment-related needs and are viewed as signs of weakness or vulnerability incompatible with the desire for self-reliance. Unlike avoidant people, people who score high on attachment-related anxiety tend to perceive negative emotions as congruent with their goal of attachment-system hyperactivation (Mikulincer and Shaver, 2016). As a result, such people tend to generate and intensify negative emotional states that activate the attachment system (e.g., fear, anxiety, distress) and emphasize their weaknesses, incompetence, and neediness (e.g., sadness, shame, guilt). This strategy can create a self-amplifying cycle of distress, maintained by ruminative thoughts even after a threat subsides.

These tendencies have been extensively documented in empirical studies of attachment insecurities and reactions to stressful events (see Mikulincer and Shaver, 2016, for a review). In these studies, higher avoidance scores are associated with higher scores on measures of coping by distancing, and higher scores on attachment anxiety are associated with higher scores on measures of emotion-focused coping. Moreover, attachment-related individual differences have been found in brain responses to stressful events (see Mikulincer and Shaver, 2016,

for a review). For example, Lemche et al. (2006) found that self-reports of attachment anxiety or avoidance were associated with heightened activation in bilateral amygdalae to a stressful stimulus – a neural indication of distress-related arousal. Vrtička et al. (2012) scanned the brains of people who were asked to attend naturally or cognitively reappraise their emotional responses to unpleasant scenes and found that avoidant participants showed increased prefrontal and anterior cingulate activation to unpleasant scenes and exhibited increases in dorsolateral prefrontal cortex and left amygdala activity during reappraisal. These results suggest that avoidant people may be less efficient in using reappraisal strategies and need to engage in more effortful control for dealing with distress. Anxious participants showed increases in the right amygdala across the conditions – another sign of their heightened reactivity.

Bowlby (1988) viewed secondary attachment strategies as risk factors that reduce resilience in times of stress and contribute to emotional problems and poor adjustment. Although these strategies are initially adaptive, in the sense that they adjust a child's behavior to the requirements of a non-responsive or inconsistently available attachment figure, they can become maladaptive when applied to later relationships in which support-seeking and comfortable interdependence could be rewarding and help a person maintain a sense of well-being. Indeed, many studies have shown that self-reports of attachment anxiety are associated with global distress, depression, anxiety, eating disorders, substance abuse, conduct disorders, and severe personality disorders (see Mikulincer and Shaver, 2016, for an extensive review). Several studies also indicate that avoidant attachment is associated with particular patterns of emotional and behavioral problems, such as a pattern of depression characterized by perfectionism, self-punishment, and self-criticism (e.g., Chen et al., 2015), somatic complaints (e.g., Martin et al., 2012), conduct disorders (e.g., Ogilvie et al., 2014), and schizoid and avoidant personality disorders (e.g., Crawford et al., 2007). Of course, all of these findings are correlational and so do not provide direct evidence about the implied causal role of attachment insecurities.

PSYCHOLOGICAL CORRELATES OF INDIVIDUAL DIFFERENCES IN OTHER BEHAVIORAL SYSTEMS

In our research program (Birnbaum et al., 2014; Doron, 2009; Shaver et al., 2010, 2011), we have begun to explore the psychological correlates of individual differences in the functioning of the caregiving, sex, exploration, and power systems. These preliminary findings indicate that hyperactivation or deactivation of each of these systems, like attachment anxiety and avoidance, are associated with lower scores on scales measuring self-control, negative mood regulation, and social skills, and higher scores on scales measuring threat appraisal and interpersonal problems. Our studies also reveal that both hyperactivation and deactivation of caregiving, sex, exploration, and power are associated with lower scores on measures of self-esteem, mastery, coherence, optimism, and psychological well-being. Moreover, these secondary strategies are associated with greater psychological distress and with heightened levels of anxiety, depression, and other emotional problems.

The Dynamic Interplay of Behavioral Systems

Bowlby (1982) assumed that different behavioral systems are connected by excitatory or inhibitory links and that activation of one system can activate or deactivate other systems (see Panksepp, 1998, for similar ideas). For example, activation of the sexual system by a new potential partner can activate the

exploration system and result in mutual self-disclosure and exploration of interests and desires, which may facilitate the formation of a sexual relationship. However, due to their focus on the infant-parent bond as a basis for socioemotional development, Bowlby (1982) and Ainsworth et al. (1978) were especially interested in the ways in which attachment-system functioning contributes to the functioning of other systems. In addition, most of the studies conducted with adolescents and adults have focused on ways in which individual differences in attachment orientations shape other non-attachment cognitions and behavior. In Bowlby's view, interactions with a security-enhancing figure and the resulting sense of being loved and protected set the foundation for the smooth functioning of other systems, because a child or adult who feels secure has more courage and conflict-free mental resources to fully engage and enjoy exploration and learning, caregiving, sex, and assertion of power. In contrast, when a person is frightened and insecure, he or she is mainly focused on his or her own distress and in defending against the pain of being rejected rather than on other non-attachment activities.

With regard to the attachment-exploration link, several studies have shown that both forms of attachment insecurity, anxiety and avoidance, are associated with lower trait curiosity, less willingness to explore new environments, weaker endorsement of mastery-approach goals in achievement settings, and lower cognitive openness and more dogmatic thinking (e.g., Bourne et al., 2014; Lattifian and Delavarpour, 2012; Mikulincer, 1997). Research on the attachment-caregiving link have also shown that self-reports of attachment insecurity are associated with lower scores on measures of responsiveness to a relationship partner's needs and with less supportive behavior toward a distressed partner or toward a partner who is exploring personal plans (e.g., Feeney and Thrush, 2010; Monin et al., 2012). In addition, Mikulincer et al., (2013) found that experimental priming of security-enhancing mental representations increased behavioral responsiveness toward a distressed romantic partner.

Attachment research has also revealed how attachment insecurities are associated with sexual system functioning. For example, attachment insecurities in adolescence and adulthood are associated with more negative sexual experiences (Birnbaum et al., 2006) and more negative sexual fantasies (Birnbaum et al., 2011). There is also evidence that adults scoring high on avoidant attachment report relatively low sexual drive, are less likely to have and enjoy sex, and tend to be motivated by self-enhancement and public reputation rather than concern for their partners (e.g., Birnbaum et al., 2006; Schachner and Shaver, 2004). Attachment-anxious individuals are more likely to report sexual dissatisfaction and to use sex as a means for achieving emotional intimacy and reassurance, eliciting a partner's caregiving behaviors, and defusing a partner's anger (e.g., Birnbaum et al., 2006; Schachner and Shaver, 2004). Attachment researchers have also found that attachment insecurities are associated with the functioning of the power system. For example, attachment anxiety is associated with outbursts of anger, aggression, and violence during couple interactions (e.g., Diamond and Hicks, 2005; Simpson et al., 1996). In addition, numerous studies have found that attachment insecurities are associated with measures of domestic violence, antisocial behavior, and intergroup aggression (see Mikulincer and Shaver, 2016, for a review).

All of these studies illustrate the various ways in which individual differences in attachment system functioning can affect other behavioral systems. Bowlby (1982) began his theorizing by portraying attachment security as a 'secure base for exploration', which suggested that the attachment system comes first in development and forms either a solid or shaky foundation for the functioning of other behavioral systems. However, changes in the functioning of the other systems (e.g., failure to learn new skills and then doubting one's competence and value;

volunteering to help others and becoming more self-confident as a result) can feed back on attachment security. At present, we know little about the extent to which other behavioral systems affect the attachment system, but Mizrahi et al. (2016) found that more displays of sexual interest at the earliest stage of a couple relationship contributed to a prospective decline in partners' attachment anxiety eight months later. Moreover, Gillath et al. (2008) found that subliminal exposure to pictures of sexually attractive naked members of the opposite sex, as compared to neutral pictures, increased self-disclosure in couple relationships, the tendency to sacrifice for a partner, and endorsement of constructive conflict resolution strategies, presumably reflecting a more secure and caring attitude toward relationship partners. Future research should explore more systematically the ways in which other systems shape the functioning of the attachment system as well as reciprocal relations between caregiving, power, exploration, and sex.

CONCLUSION AND FUTURE DIRECTIONS

Bowlby's attachment theory is an extremely valuable evolutionary framework for studying and explaining social behavior. Although he did not mean to propose a broad theory of the social mind (he was trying mainly to propose an alternative to the Freudian concept of drive and to understand the evolutionary significance of close relationships), our reading of his work suggests that the theory can be applied to a wide variety of social behaviors. For example, the attachment behavioral system has been shown to underlie general features of close relationships (e.g., love, support seeking, grief), as well as individual variations in the ways people form and maintain emotional bonds, manage distress, cope with threats, and regulate goal-oriented behavior (see Mikulincer and Shaver, 2016, for a review). Similarly, the caregiving system is important for understanding altruistic behavior in general and the way particular people behave in specific caregiving contexts (e.g., parenthood, leadership), and the exploration system provides a framework for understanding a person's behavior in learning and achievement settings and ways of dealing with novelty and uncertainty. Behavioral systems are also important for understanding social cognition, because they involve mental representations of self and others that can shape a person's social attitudes and judgments (Collins and Read, 1994).

Attachment theory is also useful for integrating research on personality, interpersonal relations, and group processes, and can provide bridges between various levels of analysis (individual, dyadic, and group). At the individual level, consolidation of a relatively stable working model is the most important psychological process that explains the transition from context-tailored variations in the functioning of a behavioral system to person-tailored variations. What began as representations of specific person–environment transactions become core personality characteristics and tend to be applied in new situations where they explain variations in social cognition and behavior. However, a person's responses in a given context are also affected by the quality of interactions he or she has with others in that context. For example, Arriaga et al. (2014) have described how a supportive romantic partner can induce greater felt-security (and its associated benefits), even in generally insecure individuals, and Rom and Mikulincer (2003) showed how a highly cohesive group improved the functioning of chronically attachment-anxious group members. In this way, attachment theory provides a foundation for a systemic evolutionary model of social behavior in which one person's cognitions, emotions, and behaviors are determined partly by the functioning of the behavioral systems of relationship partners or group members.

To date, most research on the behavioral systems has been conducted at individual and dyadic levels. Future studies should examine behavioral-system functioning at family, small group, and community levels, while integrating personality research with social network analysis.

Future studies should also attempt to integrate attachment theory with other evolutionary approaches to human behavior. For example, researchers can deepen our understanding of the interplay between support seeking, the primary attachment strategy, and ancestral fight-or-flight responses governed by the fear system (e.g., Tovote et al., 2015). According to Social Defense Theory (Ein-Dor et al., 2010) – an extension of attachment theory – attachment-related avoidance reflects heavy reliance on fight-or-flight responses and deactivation of support seeking, whereas attachment-related anxiety implies exclusive reliance on the primary attachment strategy for dealing with threats and challenges. Moreover, there is growing evidence that a contextual infusion of attachment security inhibits fear conditioning and the resulting escape or avoidance responses (e.g., Hornstein and Eisenberger, 2017). Future studies should follow these lines of theorizing and research and provide a more comprehensive picture of the neural, cognitive, and behavioral substrates of the fear-attachment link and its consequences for the functioning of other behavioral systems.

Another important topic for future work is the integration of attachment theory with other evolutionary approaches to explaining the developmental sources and trajectories of individual differences in behavioral-system functioning. On one hand, attachment theory emphasizes parental caregiving as a major developmental source of a person's internal working models (e.g., Thompson, 2015). On the other hand, Life History Theory (e.g., Del Giudice et al., 2016; Ellis et al., 2009), an evolutionary approach that deals with the tradeoffs people make when allocating limited resources to various, often competing life tasks, proposes that harsh and unpredictable childhood environments can bias the developmental trajectory of social cognition and behavior. Although attachment researchers pay attention to what Belsky (2005) called the 'broad ecology of attachment security', more research is needed on the ways in which harsh and unpredictable childhood environments interact with parenting and other sources of security in shaping a person's working models and motivational orientations in adulthood (Szepsenwol and Simpson, 2019). More research is also needed on integrating these environmental factors with the genetic basis of individual differences in behavioral-system functioning.

In conclusion, the behavioral system construct is clearly a useful conceptual tool for evolutionary psychologists studying species-universal and individual-differences aspects of the social mind. We hope this chapter, which merely scratches the surface of several large bodies of research on attachment theory, inspires researchers to use the behavioral systems construct in their attempts to study social cognition and behavior and to understand the evolutionary basis of the social mind and social behavior. We look forward to further integrations of literature on evolutionary, cognitive, and psychodynamic approaches to psychology that would benefit researchers interested in the complex interplay of evolution, physiology, culture, individual development in a relational context, and larger social contexts.

REFERENCES

Ainsworth, M. D. S. (1967). *Infancy in Uganda: Infant care and the growth of love*. Baltimore: Johns Hopkins University Press.

Ainsworth, M. D. S. (1991). Attachment and other affectional bonds across the life cycle. In C. M. Parkes, J. Stevenson-Hinde, & P. Marris (Eds), *Attachment across the life cycle* (pp. 33–51). New York: Routledge.

Ainsworth, M. D. S., Blehar, M. C., Waters, E., & Wall, S. (1978). *Patterns of attachment: Assessed in the strange situation and at home*. Hillsdale, NJ: Lawrence Erlbaum Associates.

Arriaga, X. B., Kumashiro, M., Finkel, E. J., VanderDrift, L. E., & Luchies, L. B. (2014). Filling the void: Bolstering attachment security in committed relationships. *Social Psychological and Personality Science*, 5(4), 398–406.

Asendorpf, J. B., Banse, R., Wilpers, S., & Neyer, F. J. (1997). Relationship-specific attachment scales for adults and their validation with network and diary procedures. *Diagnostica*, 43(4), 289–313.

Barbaro, N., Boutwell, B. B., Barnes, J. C., & Shackelford, T. K. (2017). Rethinking the transmission gap: What behavioral genetics and evolutionary psychology mean for attachment theory: A comment on Verhage et al. (2016). *Psychological Bulletin*, 143(1), 107–113.

Batson, C. D. (2010). Empathy-induced altruistic motivation. In M. Mikulincer & P. R. Shaver (Eds), *Prosocial motives, emotions, and behavior: The better angels of our nature* (pp. 15–34). Washington, DC: American Psychological Association.

Beckes, L., Simpson, J. A., & Erickson, A. (2010). Of snakes and succor: Learning secure attachment associations with novel faces via negative stimulus pairings. *Psychological Science*, 21(5), 721–728.

Belsky, J. (2005). Attachment theory and research in ecological perspective: Insights from the Pennsylvania Infant and Family Development Project and the NICHD Study of Early Child Care. In K. E. Grossmann, K. Grossmann, & E. Waters (Eds), *Attachment from infancy to adulthood: The major longitudinal studies* (pp. 71–97). New York: Guilford Press.

Belsky, J., & Pluess, M. (2009). Differential susceptibility to rearing experience: The case of childcare. *Journal of Child Psychology and Psychiatry*, 50(4), 396–404.

Birnbaum, G. E. (2015). On the convergence of sexual urges and emotional bonds: The interplay of the sexual and attachment systems during relationship development. In J. A. Simpson & W. S. Rholes (Eds), *Attachment theory and research: New directions and emerging themes* (pp. 170–194). New York: Guilford Press.

Birnbaum, G. E., Mikulincer, M., & Gillath, O. (2011). In and out of a daydream: Attachment orientations, daily relationship quality, and sexual fantasies. *Personality and Social Psychology Bulletin, 37*(10), 1398–1410.

Birnbaum, G. E., Mikulincer, M., Szepsenwol, O., Shaver, P. R., & Mizrahi, M. (2014). When sex goes wrong: A behavioral systems perspective on individual differences in sexual attitudes, motives, feelings, and behaviors. *Journal of Personality and Social Psychology, 106*(5), 822–842.

Birnbaum, G. E., Reis, H. T., Mikulincer, M., Gillath, O., & Orpaz, A. (2006). When sex is more than just sex: Attachment orientations, sexual experience, and relationship quality. *Journal of Personality and Social Psychology, 91*(5), 929–943.

Bourne, K., Berry, K., & Jones, L. (2014). The relationships between psychological mindedness, parental bonding and adult attachment. *Psychology and Psychotherapy: Theory, Research and Practice, 87*(2), 167–177.

Bowlby, J. (1973). *Attachment and loss: Vol. 2. Separation: Anxiety and anger*. New York: Basic Books.

Bowlby, J. (1980). *Attachment and loss: Vol. 3. Sadness and depression*. New York: Basic Books.

Bowlby, J. (1982). *Attachment and loss: Vol. 1. Attachment* (2nd ed.). New York: Basic Books. (Original ed. 1969).

Bowlby, J. (1988). *A secure base: Clinical applications of attachment theory*. London: Routledge.

Bowlby, J. (1991). *Charles Darwin: A new life*. New York: W. W. Norton.

Brennan, K. A., Clark, C. L., & Shaver, P. R. (1998). Self-report measurement of adult romantic attachment: An integrative overview. In J. A. Simpson & W. S. Rholes (Eds), *Attachment theory and close relationships* (pp. 46–76). New York: Guilford Press.

Brown, S. L., Brown, R. M., & Preston, S. D. (2012). The human caregiving system: A neuroscience model of compassionate motivation and behavior. In S. L. Brown, R. M. Brown, & L. A. Penner (Eds), *Moving beyond self-interest: Perspectives from evolutionary biology, neuroscience, and the social sciences* (pp. 75–88). New York: Oxford University Press.

Bryant, R. A., & Chan, I. (2017). Activating attachment representations during memory retrieval modulates intrusive traumatic memories. *Consciousness and Cognition, 55*, 197–204.

Bryant, R. A., & Hutanamon, T. (2018). Activating attachments enhances heart rate variability. *PLoS ONE, 13*(2), e0151747.

Bugental, D. B. (2000). Acquisition of the algorithms of social life: A domain based approach. *Psychological Bulletin, 126*(2), 187–219.

Buss, D. M., & Duntley, J. D. (2006). The evolution of aggression. In M. Schaller, J. A. Simpson, & D. T. Kenrick (Eds), *Evolution and social psychology* (pp. 263–285). Madison, CT: Psychosocial Press.

Cassidy, J., & Kobak, R. R. (1988). Avoidance and its relationship with other defensive processes. In J. Belsky & T. Nezworski (Eds), *Clinical implications of attachment* (pp. 300–323). Hillsdale, NJ: Lawrence Erlbaum Associates.

Cassidy, J., & Shaver, P. R. (2016). *Handbook of attachment: Theory, research, and clinical applications* (3rd edition). New York: Guilford Press.

Chen, C., Hewitt, P. L., & Flett, G. L. (2015). Preoccupied attachment, need to belong, shame, and interpersonal perfectionism: An investigation of the perfectionism-social disconnection model. *Personality and Individual Differences, 76*, 177–182.

Coan, J. A., Schaefer, H. S., & Davidson, R. J. (2006). Lending a hand: Social regulation of the neural response to threat. *Psychological Science, 17*(12), 1032–1039.

Collins, N. L., & Read, S. J. (1994). Cognitive representations of attachment: The structure and function of working models. In K. Bartholomew & D. Perlman (Eds), *Advances in personal relationships: Attachment processes in adulthood* (Vol. 5, pp. 53–92). London: Jessica Kingsley.

Crawford, T. N., Livesley, W. J., Jang, K. L., Shaver, P. R., Cohen, P., & Ganiban, J. (2007). Insecure attachment and personality disorder: A twin study of adults. *European Journal of Personality, 21*(2), 191–208.

Crowell, J. A., Fraley, R. C., & Roisman, G. I. (2016). Measurement of individual differences in adult attachment. In J. Cassidy & P. R.

Shaver (Eds), *Handbook of attachment: Theory, research, and clinical applications* (3rd edition, pp. 598–637). New York: Guilford Press.

Del Giudice, M., Gangestad, S. W., & Kaplan, H. S. (2016). Life History theory and evolutionary psychology. In D. M. Buss (Ed.), *The handbook of evolutionary psychology: Foundations* (2nd edition, pp. 88–114). Hoboken, NJ: John Wiley & Sons.

Diamond, L. M., & Hicks, A. M. (2005). Attachment style, current relationship security, and negative emotions: The mediating role of physiological regulation. *Journal of Social and Personal Relationships*, *22*(4), 499–518.

Doron, Y. (2009). *Conceptualization and operationalization of individual differences in the functioning of the exploration behavioral system*. Unpublished Doctoral Dissertation, Bar-Ilan University, Ramat-Gan, Israel.

Ein-Dor, T., Mikulincer, M., Doron, G., & Shaver, P. R. (2010). The attachment paradox: How can so many of us (the insecure ones) have no adaptive advantages? *Perspectives on Psychological Science*, 5(2), 123–141.

Eisenberger, N. I., Master, S. L., Inagaki, T. K., Taylor, S. E., Shirinyan, D., Lieberman, M. D., & Naliboff, B. D. (2011). Attachment figures activate a safety signal-related neural region and reduce pain experience. *Proceedings of the National Academy of Sciences, USA*, *108*(28), 11721–11726.

Ellis, B. J., Figueredo, A. J., Brumbach, B. H., & Schlomer, G. L. (2009). Fundamental dimensions of environmental risk: The impact of harsh versus unpredictable environments on the evolution and development of life history strategies. *Human Nature*, *20*(2), 204–268.

Feeney, B. C., & Thrush, R. L. (2010). Relationship influences on exploration in adulthood: The characteristics and function of a secure base. *Journal of Personality and Social Psychology*, *98*(1), 57–76.

Feeney, B. C., & Woodhouse, S. S. (2016). Caregiving. In J. Cassidy & P. R. Shaver (Eds), *Handbook of attachment: Theory, research, and clinical applications* (3rd edition, pp. 827–851). New York: Guilford Press.

Fraley, R. C., & Shaver, P. R. (2000). Adult romantic attachment: Theoretical developments, emerging controversies, and unanswered questions. *Review of General Psychology*, *4*(2), 132–154.

Fraley, R. C., & Shaver, P. R. (2016). Attachment, loss, and grief: Bowlby's views, new developments, and current controversies. In J. Cassidy & P. R. Shaver (Eds), *Handbook of attachment: Theory, research, and clinical applications* (3rd edition, pp. 40–62). New York: Guilford Press.

Fraley, R. C., Heffernan, M. E., Vicary, A. M., & Brumbaugh, C. C. (2011). The Experiences in Close Relationships–Relationship Structures Questionnaire: A method for assessing attachment orientations across relationships. *Psychological Assessment*, *23*(3), 615–625.

Gangestad, S. W., Simpson, J. A., Cousins, A. J., Garver-Apgar, C. E., & Christensen, P. N. (2004). Women's preferences for male behavioral displays. *Psychological Science*, *15*(3), 203–206.

Gibson, J. J. (1977). The theory of affordances. In R. Shaw & J. Bransford (Eds), *Perceiving, acting, and knowing: Toward an ecological psychology* (pp. 67–82). Hillsdale, NJ: Lawrence Erlbaum Associates.

Gilbert, P., McEwan, K., Bellew, R., Mills, A., & Gale, C. (2009). The dark side of competition: How competitive behavior and striving to avoid inferiority are linked to depression, anxiety, stress and self-harm. *Psychology and Psychotherapy*, *82*(2), 123–136.

Gillath, O., Hart, J., Noftle, E. E., & Stockdale, G. D. (2009). Development and validation of a state adult attachment measure (SAAM). *Journal of Research in Personality*, *43*(3), 362–373.

Gillath, O., Mikulincer, M., Birnbaum, G., & Shaver, P. R. (2008). When sex primes love: Subliminal sexual priming motivates relationship goal pursuit. *Personality and Social Psychology Bulletin*, *34*(8), 1057–1069.

Granqvist, P., Mikulincer, M., Gurwitz, V., & Shaver, P. R. (2012). Experimental findings on God as an attachment figure: Normative processes and moderating effects of internal working models. *Journal of Personality and Social Psychology*, *103*(5), 804–818.

Hamilton, W. D. (1964). The genetic evolution of social behavior. *Journal of Theoretical Biology*, *7*(1), 1–52.

Harlow, H. F. (1955). Exploratory drives in primates. *Acta Psychologica*, *11*, 152–153.

Hinde, R. (1966). *Animal behavior: A synthesis of ethology and comparative psychology*. New York: McGraw-Hill.

Hornstein, E. A., & Eisenberger, N. I. (2017). Unpacking the buffering effect of social support figures: Social support attenuates fear acquisition. *PLoS ONE, 12*(5). Article ID e0175891

Johnson, S. L., Leedom, L. J., & Muhtadie, L. (2012). The dominance behavioral system and psychopathology: Evidence from self-report, observational, and biological studies. *Psychological Bulletin, 138*(4), 692–743.

Karremans, J. C., Heslenfeld, D. J., van Dillen, L. F., & Van Lange, P. A. M. (2011). Secure attachment partners attenuate neural responses to social exclusion: An FMRI investigation. *International Journal of Psychophysiology, 81*, 44–50.

Keltner, D., Gruenfeld, D., Galinsky, A., & Kraus, M. W. (2010). Paradoxes of power: Dynamics of the acquisition, experience, and social regulation of social power. In A. Guinote & T. K. Vescio (Eds), *The social psychology of power* (pp. 177–208). New York: Guilford Press.

Kirkpatrick, L. A. (2012). Attachment theory and the evolutionary psychology of religion. *International Journal for the Psychology of Religion, 22*(3), 231–241.

Knafo-Noam, A., Vertsberger, D., & Israel, S. (2018). Genetic and environmental contributions to children's prosocial behavior: brief review and new evidence from a reanalysis of experimental twin data. *Current Opinion in Psychology, 20*, 60–65.

Lattifian, M., & Delavarpour, M. A. (2012). An investigation into the relationship between attachment style and mental health by the mediating role of emotional creativity. *Advances in Cognitive Science, 14*(2), 45–62.

Lemche, E., Giampietro, V. P., Surguladze, S. A., Amaro, E. J., Andrew, C. M., Williams, S. C., Brammer, M. J., Lawrence, N., Maier, M. A., Russell, T. A., Simmons, A., Ecker, C., Joraschky, P., & Phillips, M. L. (2006). Human attachment security is mediated by the amygdala: Evidence from combined fMRI and psychophysiological measures. *Human Brain Mapping, 27*(8), 623–635.

Lopez, F. G., Ramos, K., & Kim, M. (2018). Development and initial validation of a measure of attachment security in late adulthood. *Psychological Assessment, 30*(9), 1214–1225.

Lorenz, K. Z. (1952). *King Solomon's ring.* New York: Crowell.

Main, M. (1990). Cross-cultural studies of attachment organization: Recent studies, changing methodologies, and the concept of conditional strategies. *Human Development, 33*(1), 48–61.

Martin, L. A., Vosvick, M., & Riggs, S. A. (2012). Attachment, forgiveness, and physical health quality of life in HIV + adults. *AIDS Care, 24*(11), 1333–1340.

Master, S. L., Eisenberger, N. I., Taylor, S. E., Naliboff, B. D., Shirinyan, D., & Lieberman, M. D. (2009). A picture's worth: Partner photographs reduce experimentally induced pain. *Psychological Science, 20*(11), 1316–1318.

Mikulincer, M. (1997). Adult attachment style and information processing: Individual differences in curiosity and cognitive closure. *Journal of Personality and Social Psychology, 72*(5), 1217–1230.

Mikulincer, M., Gillath, O., & Shaver, P. R. (2002). Activation of the attachment system in adulthood: Threat-related primes increase the accessibility of mental representations of attachment figures. *Journal of Personality and Social Psychology, 83*(4), 881–895.

Mikulincer, M., Hirschberger, G., Nachmias, O., & Gillath, O. (2001). The affective component of the secure base schema: Affective priming with representations of attachment security. *Journal of Personality and Social Psychology, 81*(2), 305–321.

Mikulincer, M., & Shaver, P. R. (2004). Security-based self-representations in adulthood: Contents and processes. In W. S. Rholes & J. A. Simpson (Eds), *Adult attachment: Theory, research, and clinical implications* (pp. 159–195). New York: Guilford Press.

Mikulincer, M., & Shaver, P. R. (2016). *Attachment patterns in adulthood: Structure, dynamics, and change* (2nd edition). New York: Guilford Press.

Mikulincer, M., Shaver, P. R., Sahdra, B. K., & Bar–On, N. (2013). Can security-enhancing interventions overcome psychological barriers to responsiveness in couple relationships? *Attachment & Human Development, 15*(3), 246–260.

Mizrahi, M., Hirschberger, G., Mikulincer, M., Szepsenwol, O., & Birnbaum, G. E. (2016).

Reassuring sex: Can sexual desire and intimacy reduce relationship-specific attachment insecurities? *European Journal of Social Psychology*, *46*(4), 467–480.

Monin, J. K., Feeney, B. C., & Schulz, R. (2012). Attachment orientation and reactions to anxiety expression in close relationships. *Personal Relationships*, *19*(3), 535–550.

Norman, L., Lawrence, N., Iles, A., Benattayallah, A., & Karl, A. (2015). Attachment-security priming attenuates amygdala activation to social and linguistic threat. *Social, Cognitive, and Affective Neuroscience*, *10*(6), 832–839.

Ogilvie, C. A., Newman, E., Todd, L., & Peck, D. (2014). Attachment and violent offending: A meta-analysis. *Aggression and Violent Behavior*, *19*(4), 322–339.

Panksepp, J. (1998). *Affective neuroscience: The foundations of human and animal emotion.* New York: Oxford University Press.

Panksepp, J. (2011). The basic emotional circuits of mammalian brains: do animals have affective lives? *Neuroscience & Biobehavioral Reviews*, *35*(9), 1791–1804.

Parker, G. A. (1974). Assessment strategy and the evolution of fighting behavior. *Journal of Theoretical Biology*, *47*(1), 223–243.

Robertson, J., & Bowlby, J. (1952). Responses of young children to separation from their mothers. *Courier of the International Children's Center, Paris, 2*, 131–140.

Rom, E., & Mikulincer, M. (2003). Attachment theory and group processes: The association between attachment style and group-related representations, goals, memories, and functioning. *Journal of Personality and Social Psychology*, *84*(6), 1220–1235.

Rotge, J.-Y., Lemogne, C., Hinfray, S., Huguet, P., Grynszpan, O., Tartour, E., George, N., & Fossati, P. (2015). A meta-analysis of the anterior cingulate contribution to social pain. *Social Cognitive and Affective Neuroscience*, *10*(1), 19–27.

Sbarra, D. A. (2012). Marital dissolution and physical health outcomes: A review of mechanisms. In L. Campbell, J. La Guardia, J. Olson, & M. Zanna (Eds), *The science of the couple: The Ontario Symposium* (Vol. 12, pp. 205–227). Florence, KY: Psychology Press.

Schachner, D. A., & Shaver, P. R. (2004). Attachment dimensions and sexual motives. *Personal Relationships*, *11*(2), 179–195.

Schmitt, D. E., et al. (2003). Are men universally more dismissing than women? Gender differences in romantic attachment across 62 cultural regions. *Personal Relationships*, *10*(2), 307–331.

Schmitt, D. E., et al. (2004). Patterns and universals of adult romantic attachment across 62 cultural regions: Are models of self and of other pancultural constructs? *Journal of Cross-Cultural Psychology*, *35*(4), 367–402.

Selcuk, E., Zayas, V., Günaydin, G., Hazan, C., & Kross, E. (2012). Mental representations of attachment figures facilitate recovery following upsetting autobiographical memory recall. *Journal of Personality and Social Psychology*, *103*(2), 362–378.

Shaver, P. R., & Mikulincer, M. (2002). Attachment-related psychodynamics. *Attachment & Human Development*, *4*(2), 133–161.

Shaver, P. R., Mikulincer, M., Alonso-Arbiol, I., & Lavy, S. (2010). Assessment of adult attachment across cultures: Conceptual and methodological considerations. In P. Erdman, K.-M. Ng, & S. Metzger (Eds), *Attachment: Expanding the cultural connections* (pp. 89–108). New York: Routledge/Taylor & Francis.

Shaver, P. R., Mikulincer, M., & Shemesh-Iron, M. (2010). A behavioral-systems perspective on prosocial behavior. In M. Mikulincer & P. R. Shaver (Eds), *Prosocial motives, emotions, and behavior: The better angels of our nature* (pp. 73–91). Washington DC: American Psychological Association.

Shaver, P. R., Segev, M, & Mikulincer, M. (2011). A behavioral-systems perspective on power and aggression. In P. R. Shaver & M. Mikulincer (Eds), *Understanding and reducing aggression and their consequences* (pp. 71–88). Washington DC: American Psychological Association.

Simpson, J. A., Rholes, W. S., & Phillips, D. (1996). Conflict in close relationships: An attachment perspective. *Journal of Personality and Social Psychology*, *71*(5), 899–914.

Stein, H., Koontz, A., Fonagy, P., Allen, J. G., Fultz, J., Brethour, J. R., Allen D., & Evans, R. B. (2002). Adult attachment: What are the underlying dimensions? *Psychology and Psychotherapy*, *75*(1), 77–91.

Szepsenwol, O., & Simpson, J. A. (2019). Attachment within life history theory: An evolutionary perspective on individual differences in attachment. *Current Opinion in Psychology*, *25*, 65–70.

Thompson, R. A. (2015). Relationships, regulation, and early development. In M. E. Lamb & R. M. Lerner (Eds), *Handbook of child psychology and developmental science: Socioemotional processes* (pp. 201–246). Hoboken, NJ: John Wiley & Sons.

Tooby, J., & Cosmides, L. (1992). The psychological foundations of culture. In J. H. Barkow, L. Cosmides, & J. Tooby (Eds), *The adapted mind: Evolutionary psychology and the generation of culture* (pp. 19–136). New York: Oxford University Press.

Tovote, P., Fadok, J. P., & Lüthi, A. (2015). Neuronal circuits for fear and anxiety. *Nature Reviews Neuroscience*, *16*(6), 317–331.

Vrtička, P., Bondolfi, G., Sander, D., & Vuilleumier, P. (2012). The neural substrates of social emotion perception and regulation are modulated by adult attachment style. *Social Neuroscience*, *7*(5), 473–493.

Wertz, J., Belsky, J., Moffitt, T. E., Belsky, D. W., Harrington, H., Avinun, R., Poulton, R., Ramrakha, S., & Caspi, A. (2019). Genetics of nurture: A test of the hypothesis that parents' genetics predict their observed caregiving. *Developmental Psychology*, *55*(7), 1461–1472.

West, S. A., & Gardner, A. (2013). Adaptation and inclusive fitness. *Current Biology*, *23*(13), R577–R584.

Zilcha-Mano, S., Mikulincer, M., & Shaver, P. R. (2012). Pets as safe havens and secure bases: The moderating role of pet attachment orientations. *Journal of Research in Personality*, *46*(5), 571–580.

Zuroff, D. C., Fournier, M. A., Patall, E. A., & Leybman, M. J. (2010). Steps toward an evolutionary personality psychology: Individual differences in the social rank domain. *Canadian Psychology*, *51*(1), 58–66.

PART III

Research Methods and Strategies

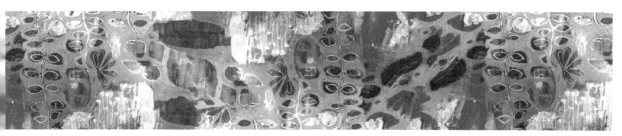

16

Cross-Species Comparisons: When Comparing Apples to Oranges Is Fruitful

Jennifer Vonk, Jared Edge, Jacob Pappas, Audrey Robeson and Amity Jordan

INTRODUCTION

Within psychology generally, and human evolutionary psychology specifically, the goal has been to advance understanding of human behavior and cognition. Animals are referenced primarily to the extent that differences and similarities across species can shed light on possible selection pressures giving rise to uniquely human traits, or to illuminate the shared history or lineage of a trait through evolutionary history. Sometimes the study of animals can be brought to bear on issues related to the ubiquity of traits. For instance, if fish, amphibians, reptiles, birds, and mammals alike demonstrate the capacity to estimate quantity, and evidence in fish and humans converges on the notion that there are two distinct systems for representing small versus large quantities (Agrillo et al., 2012), then the trait can be recognized as evolutionarily ancient and widely shared. In contrast, if little evidence for particular traits exists outside of the great apes, it is assumed that the trait arose sometime after the extant apes split from their last common ancestor (as with abilities such as self-awareness/meta-cognition, e.g., Anderson and Gallup, 2011; Smith et al., 2009).

Rather than being focused on better understanding the selection pressures driving (potentially) uniquely human evolved traits, comparative psychology would be better modeled after evolutionary biology in which the goal is to understand each species in its own right. Therefore, we recommend a bottom-up process whereby researchers explore as many different species as possible to gain a better understanding of their own unique attributes and abilities (see Eaton et al., 2018; Vonk, in press; Vonk and Shackelford, 2012) rather than a top-down process where scientists begin by making assumptions about what abilities are important (often from an anthropocentric perspective) and comparing species somewhat atheoretically. In top-down approaches, researchers seek evidence for a particular behavior or trait, whereas in bottom-up approaches, researchers attempt to identify the mechanism that is operating without a priori expectations. From a bottom-up approach, one can then begin to piece together which traits are shared among various taxa, and the selection pressures that may have been present in the history of organisms that share common abilities or evolved unique solutions to adaptive problems. In this way, we can search for the presence or absence of abilities along a continuum rather than in an all or none fashion. In order to paint a complete portrait, comparative psychologists must shift their focus from species of convenience (e.g., laboratory rat, pigeon, or chimpanzee) and examine less studied species. In what follows, we outline some ideas about which species comparisons will be most germane to a better understanding of the evolution of cognition.

SELECTION PRESSURES FOR THE EVOLUTION OF COGNITION

In the most basic terms, evolution of a particular trait requires two things: a series of random mutations and a set of environmental factors that select for that trait. Organisms are shaped by the environment they inhabit; those that are best equipped to interact successfully with the environment will receive the most opportunities to reproduce and be most likely to confer traits that allow their offspring to survive to reproductive age. These advantages confer inclusive fitness such that the most adaptive traits are the ones passed on and represented in the population. Psychologists often work backwards, identifying interesting traits, and then attempting to re-trace the evolutionary origins of the trait. Comparative approaches are particularly helpful in this regard, as they allow us to trace the history of the trait within evolutionary lineages, using extant species.

The construct of theory of mind (ToM) serves a powerful example, as it constitutes one of the most hotly contested, potentially uniquely human abilities in comparative

psychology. ToM is defined as the ability to ascribe mental states to others (Premack and Woodruff, 1978). If ToM is unique to humans, then researchers must answer questions regarding the unique pressures or combinations of pressures in the evolutionary history of humans since they diverged from their last common ancestor (LCA) with their closest extant relatives – chimpanzees. If ToM is shared with great apes but not with other primates, then we must examine pressures present before the split with the LCA of great apes and other primates, and so on. If ToM is present in distantly related species, such as corvids, then we must consider that convergent evolutionary forces may be at play and we must still seek commonalities in the evolutionary environments of these distantly related species. Two broad categories of factors are considered important as selection pressures impacting cognition: sociality and foraging problems faced by a particular species (Milton, 1981).

Sociality

Alison Jolly (1966) argued that lemurs provide insight regarding the role of social complexity in selecting for cognitive complexity. The lemurs of Madagascar display similar social structure and inhabit similar ecological niches to that of monkeys in other locales. Jolly noted that lemurs performed similarly to monkeys on tasks requiring social learning but not on object manipulation tasks. It was proposed that differences in sensory motor intelligence (hereafter SMI) account for why lemurs underperform monkeys on object manipulation tasks. SMI refers to the cognitive functions that rely on perception and motor activities to manipulate objects in the environment. This divergence in SMI abilities make sense because lemurs are most reliant on their olfactory faculties, whereas monkeys rely more heavily on their enhanced visual abilities (Tattersall et al., 1999). Species that rely primarily on visual or tactile information are afforded a benefit in SMI tasks because these modalities provide rich information on the orientation of the object, which is not the case for olfactory sensations. Because lemurs share social cognitive skills with monkeys, it may be that lemurs split from other primates after they began group living, but before the development of other types of cognitive complexity, such as that involving SMI. Thus, sociality may contribute to advanced social cognitive abilities, but not to more sophisticated physical cognitive abilities.

Another seminal contribution to the study of sociality and the evolution of cognition came when Humphrey (1976) suggested that the intelligence displayed by humans, as well as other great apes, and to a lesser degree monkeys, evolved in response to the complexity involved in the lives of social animals. In essence, his argument was that an individual of a social species was confronted with the problem of meeting its own needs through manipulation of conspecifics without irreparably damaging the social structure of the group by breaking the social contract that allows groups to exist. Humphrey compared social interactions to a game of chess. Much like a game of chess, social interactions are fluid and have many moving pieces. An organism can interact with a conspecific but cannot be certain how that conspecific will respond. This uncertainty requires a social organism that interacts with a group member to be prepared for a multitude of outcomes. A social organism would benefit from the ability to predict the behaviors of others, which requires a specific form of social intelligence. The transactional nature of social life requires that individuals constantly strategize in considering their next interaction with a conspecific. This requires social species to consider the costs and benefits of their actions in social situations, which they may then apply to inanimate objects.

As an example of how humans apply this transactional thinking to inanimate objects, Humphrey describes the human tendency to bargain with objects that cannot respond. Consider, for instance, any time your car has not started after multiple attempts. You may find yourself saying 'Come on, come on! Just start already!' Yet you know that your car is inanimate, has no mechanism by which to hear your pleas and, therefore, no amount of pleading will cause it to start. Such animacy attributions may not be unique to humans: anecdotally, chimpanzees have been known to display aggressively toward the sky at the onset of storms. Whether the displaying chimpanzees attribute animacy to the storm is unknown, but this example calls to mind the transactional thinking that Humphrey describes.

Humphrey (1976) conceded that sociality is not entirely advantageous. Sociality allowed for longer rearing periods, meaning that individuals could explore and experiment with their environment (opportunities that would facilitate the evolution of intelligence), as well as the ability for older and infirm conspecifics to be cared for. Retention of older members of the group allows juveniles to learn through observation, but for every juvenile, elderly, or infirm member that a social group retains, the able-bodied members must shoulder that much more of a burden to provide for them. It is important to bear in mind that any investment in skill or brain structure typically results in a trade-off with other abilities/structures. To reap many benefits of sociality, an individual must trade off certain other advantages, such as impulse and freedom.

The social brain hypothesis

The social brain hypothesis (Dunbar, 1998), also called the Machiavellian Intelligence hypothesis (Byrne and Whiten, 1988), builds on the theorizing of Jolly (1966) and Humphrey (1976), and states that sociality and cognitive complexity go hand in hand; that is, species with more complex social systems display more complex cognition. This hypothesis provides an alternative to the view that primates developed relatively large brains and complex cognition to cope with the ecological demands of their habitats (see below, Milton, 1981). However, it is important that the two hypotheses are not viewed as mutually exclusive as both social and foraging demands contribute to enhanced cognition, and can exert differential influence over different taxa. Indeed, most species that have demonstrated complex cognition, such as primates and corvids, exhibit high levels of both foraging and social complexity, making it difficult to disentangle the contribution of these two factors to the evolution of cognition.

The social brain hypothesis takes two forms that diverge with regard to which problem is the most limiting factor of survival for social species (Dunbar, 2009). One camp holds that predation is the most significant selective pressure faced by social species and the primary reason that apes display the complexity of cognition that they do; essentially, predation necessitates larger group sizes, creating more complex social dynamics, in turn, creating selective pressures for complex cognition (Alexander, 1974). The other camp implicates foraging ecology as the primary selective pressure for cognitive complexity in apes (Reader and Laland, 2002). Learning socially is adaptive because a newborn organism needs to learn to survive in its environment rapidly (Galef and Laland, 2005). An organism that learns to forage by trial-and-error risks the consumption of toxins, whereas organisms that learn acceptable foods from more experienced conspecifics can learn quickly and without the risk of trial-and-error. This line of thought suggests that the transmission of foraging techniques between individuals selects for cognitive complexity. This latter version of the social brain hypothesis indicates the lack of independence between sociality and foraging complexity as selective pressures for cognition.

Adaptive Problems in Foraging

In line with this second camp among Social Brain proponents, some researchers have theorized that environmental factors, such as foraging ecology, are the primary selection pressures for cognitive complexity (Byrne, 1997; Milton, 1981). However, these theorists do not focus on the interplay between social and foraging complexity. For example, Milton implicated the variety of food, in tandem with its spatial and temporal distribution, for the evolution of primate cognition. Animals that rely on a diverse array of foods have to remember where these foods grow, as well as when they are suitable for consumption. Various factors related to foraging have since been proposed as important selection pressures for cognition.

Hunting

If one wonders about the evolutionary importance of cooperation in social animals, one only needs to look so far as the Taï Forest of Côte d'Ivoire. The chimpanzees that inhabit the Taï Forest display remarkably complex group hunting behavior (Boesch, 2002). Chimpanzees hunt red colobus monkeys by chasing them through the forest canopy. Although the chimpanzees are much larger than the colobus monkeys, and therefore can easily kill their quarry when caught, this advantage turns to disadvantage when the monkeys jump to branches much too small to support the weight of an adult chimpanzee. The chimpanzees work through this problem in one of two ways. In locales other than Taï, the chimpanzees will simply chase their prey into a break in the forest canopy. The cornered monkey has nowhere to go, and the chimpanzees have their meal. The canopy of the Taï Forest, however, is remarkably continuous (Boesch, 2002). With no option to corner their prey, the chimpanzees must resort to other means. In response, these apes have developed a system in which an individual chimpanzee chases a small group of monkeys across the canopy while other chimpanzees lie in wait, attempting to predict not only the actions of the monkey, but their own effect on the prey's trajectory. These chimpanzees run along the ground and climb up the tree they anticipate the prey will be passing. Once in the trees, they block its escape or capture it, depending on their role in the hunt.

Clearly, individuals could maximize the sustenance gained from a single prey if they did not have to share it with other members of a hunting party. However, because of the environmental constraints of a continuous canopy, it is more beneficial to work together, which necessitates sharing the reward, than to waste energy unsuccessfully hunting alone. In fact, with regard to individual hunts, Taï chimpanzees take five times longer than chimpanzees of other locales (Boesch and Boesch-Achermann, 2000). Meat is rewarded on the basis of merit in these hunts: the individuals that contribute the most to the capture receive more meat than those with less important roles, with individuals who do not participate in the hunt receiving less meat (Boesch, 1994). This necessity provides a possible model, from a closely related species, of how humans may have developed cooperation. Perhaps early humans, with relative lack of speed and offensive measures, fared poorly as individual hunters, and resorted to cooperation to meet their needs (Vonk and Aradhye, 2015).

As social groups grew, hunting and gathering was no longer efficient, resulting in a need to innovate (Harner, 1970). The pressure of group size acting on the development of agriculture is known as population pressure. Faced with a once successful method of subsistence becoming obsolete, neolithic humans turned to agriculture to meet their growing food needs. This innovation was especially adaptive because, instead of having to rely on the potentially variable windfall afforded by nature, humans could rely on a consistent food source. A further consequence of this development was the development of more complex societies. The development of agriculture temporarily lessened competition between neolithic humans, with individuals

no longer monopolizing resources. However, it also led to further population growth. It is thought that, as social groups continued to grow, the requisite resources of agriculture became scarce, leading to alliances and more complex societies.

Generalist Diets

Humans are a classic example of generalists, as they consume multiple types of food (e.g., meat, grains, fruit, vegetation, seeds, and nuts). This flexibility means that they can adapt to changing environmental conditions but it also means that they likely must learn how to exploit multiple food sources during ontogeny. If meat is not available, humans can subsist on a vegetarian diet, but they have also developed agriculture to yield crops and to process food like wheat and other grains that would not be available naturally. Generalist feeders might display greater behavioral flexibility and problem-solving skills relative to more specialist feeders (Lefebvre et al., 2004). Specialists do not need to actively solve foraging problems because they may be morphologically and behaviorally sculpted to exploit a plentiful food source (e.g., grazers, anteaters).

Comparing the cognition of omnivores to obligate carnivores and herbivores can help elucidate the possible role of diet in selecting cognitive traits. We have focused on studying cognition in bears (e.g., Johnson-Ulrich et al., 2016; Vonk and Beran, 2012; Vonk and Jett, 2018; Vonk et al., 2012, 2015; Zamisch and Vonk, 2012) because the bear family presents the opportunity to study closely related species that vary in the extent to which they are generalists (e.g., brown bears, black bears, sun bears) and specialists (polar bears are carnivorous whereas giant pandas subsist solely on bamboo). Brown bears exhibit the largest relative brain size of all the bears (Gittleman, 1986) so it is hard to disentangle the relative importance of diet versus brain size and which factor preceded the other.

At the same time, bears are relatively less social than more commonly studied carnivores like canids and pinnipeds, so sociality is controlled for. At the other end of the spectrum, most chiropterans are highly social, but also vary in diet. Chiropterans include frugivorous and insectivorous bats, as well as vampire bats, which are hematophagorous. Some frugivores eat fruit, whereas others subsist on nectar. Interestingly, although not generalists, vampire bats exhibit the largest relative brain size of all the bats (Bhatnagar, 2008). To date, there are no studies systematically comparing the cognition of various bat species in the same tasks, but these would be useful. Other groups of closely related species that vary significantly in diet and foraging strategy will be useful for further study of cognition. Earlier we mentioned that environmental factors may be equally important to phylogenetic relationships in predicting cognitive abilities. It should not be assumed that animals within the same taxon have the same abilities. Rather, it can be informative to compare individuals within a family or order when genetics and morphology are similar, and examine how cognitive capacities differ as a function of some of the factors we have identified above (such as foraging ecology and social structures). For example, Dobson (2012) has examined variability in facial displays as a function of social tolerance, which varies among macaques.

Extractive Foraging

An additional component of foraging that is hypothesized to influence cognition is the extent to which food must be extracted from, for example, hard exterior shells (e.g., coconuts, Durian fruit) or substrate (such as termite mounds). Extractive foraging is a naturally occurring behavior that utilizes problem solving, tool use, and manual dexterity. Melin et al. (2014) present the jungles of Costa Rica as a natural laboratory in which to examine the potential link between extractive foraging and intelligence. The native

capuchin monkeys are frugivores but fall back on embedded insects when fruit is scarce, demonstrating flexibility. Capuchins are also known for their ability to use tools (Soluto et al., 2011). Melin et al. suggest that foraging demands may predict, for example, SMI. Proficiency in the manipulation of objects and, as a result, SMI, is associated with problem solving, tool use, and manual dexterity.

There were two major forks in the evolutionary lineage of primates that Melin et al. (2014) implicate in the development of cognition. The most recent is the development of sociality, which agrees with the Machiavellian Intelligence hypothesis. To understand the other, one must begin with the point at which primates developed larger bodies. Early primates are thought to have foraged for surface dwelling insects and the fruit of angiosperms (Sussman et al., 2013). The evolution of larger bodies, however, allowed primates to specialize in frugivory or folivory. Although data regarding the association between body mass and diet quality appears complex, the general pattern suggests that larger herbivores can forage on low quality foods exclusively, whereas smaller herbivores can exploit any forage they can manage (Clauss et al., 2013). During times when fruit is not abundant, frugivorous apes fall back on leaves or embedded invertebrates. Those that fell back on leaves evolved specialized digestive processes, while those that relied on embedded invertebrates evolved skills such as tool use, problem solving, and manual dexterity, leading to an increase in general SMI. Frugivores are also thought to have evolved a more complex brain to cope with the challenges of such a diet, leading to more advanced sensorimotor systems. One of these challenges may be that fruit, unlike foliage, is patchily distributed in time and space.

Patchy Food Distribution

The extent to which primary food sources are clumped or patchy (distributed over a wide range spatially and available intermittently) predicts differences in the use of long-term, spatial, and working memory. Organisms that need to maximize energy intake in relation to expenditure with regard to travel time would face selection pressures to evolve superior spatial memory whereas those whose food is spread relatively evenly throughout their habitat or consistently available would not face similar pressures. Rosati (2017) suggests that differences in spatial memory between chimpanzees and bonobos (Rosati and Hare, 2012) are due to differences in foraging ecology; chimpanzees rely on patchily distributed foods, whereas bonobos do not (Malenky and Wrangham, 1993). By examining memory differences in the two species most closely related to humans, we can more accurately hypothesize about the origin of spatial memory in humans and our LCA with these species (Rosati and Hare, 2012). However, exploring differences in memory processes outside of the primate order is necessary to determine the importance of ecological factors in shaping cognition more broadly.

Much of the work on spatial memory as a function of ecological factors has been conducted on birds that vary in the extent to which they must remember the location of food stores over time and space (Shettleworth, 2003). Birds that cache food to be available during harsh winter months have larger hippocampi than those that do not cache (Sherry and Hoshooley, 2010). There is also evidence of a seasonal increase in the size of hippocampi in birds that cache during the winter. This is presumably related to the need to remember the location of distantly placed caches (Male and Smulders, 2007; Sherry and Hoshooley, 2010). Healy and Krebs (1992) corroborate this theory by comparing hippocampal size in seven corvid species categorized with regard to their reliance on caching food. Reliance on caching was positively correlated with hippocampal volume.

Sex differences in spatial memory may also emerge as males of some species (e.g., giant panda) tend to have larger home ranges than females. As expected, sex differences in spatial memory in experimental tests emerge for pandas but not for Asian small-clawed otters for which males and females have similar home range sizes (Perdue et al., 2011). This work supports the idea that spatial memory may be selected for by home range size, which is correlated with species' mating systems. This example also makes clear the point that foraging and social pressures are unlikely to operate independently.

Territoriality

Related to the issue of home range size, territoriality, or the tendency to defend a territory, also confers obvious benefits and may require particular cognitive specializations. In addition to the resources contained within an individual's territory, guarding territories allows an individual to control access to potential mates and protect offspring. In addition to depleting necessary resources, an invading competitor could reproduce with the organism's potential mates as well as kill their offspring, substantially reducing the organism's inclusive fitness. Thus, individuals with the capacity to maintain territories have an additional tool in their arsenal with which to maintain reproductive benefits. In addition to physical skills and attributes necessary to defend one's territory, a species might require the capacity to detect invaders by reading olfactory or acoustic signals and to distinguish between familiar neighbors and newcomers – the classic 'Dear Enemy' phenomenon (for review, see Christensen and Radford, 2018). Some birds even respond differently to neighbors' calls when those calls come from the expected territory border compared to when the calls originate in an unexpected location, indicating that these birds track where particular individuals are located in the surrounding environment (e.g., cuckoos: Moskat et al., 2017).

Some researchers implicate territoriality in the evolution of communication (Scott et al., 2010). In engaging a competitive conspecific, an organism risks injury or even death, so communication offers a mechanism to run off rivals without the risks associated with physical engagement. Scott et al. (2010) found that caterpillars successfully defended their nest from invading conspecifics over 90% of the time by acoustic means. By advertising that the leaf was occupied, they turned away the invading conspecific. The Beau Geste hypothesis states that some male birds will defend territory by utilizing varying songs in their repertoire while moving between posts (Yasukawa and Searcy, 1984). This creates the sense of their territory being more densely populated by males than it actually is, deterring invading males from establishing territories in their vicinity. Empirical support for this hypothesis has been mixed. Smith and Reid (1979) found that 80% of song changes in the red-winged blackbird *(Agelaius phoeniceus)* were immediately preceded by a change in post. On the other hand, Dawson and Jenkins (1983) found that chaffinches *(Fringilla coelebs)* did not synchronously change their songs and post. Specific primate calls have also been recruited to aid in territorial defense. For example, gibbon pairs engage in duetting that presumably indicates that a territory is off-limits to potential invaders (Marshall and Marshall, 1976), and males may use graded signals to discourage rivals (Mitani, 1988). Although it is worth considering whether communication in humans evolved similarly, from a need to defend territory without the risk of injury or death, or an attempt to appear more numerous to various threats, communication is also prevalent in nomadic species (including humans) and in animals that do not defend territories, so it seems more likely that territory defense led to the evolution of a specific type of call rather than communication more broadly.

Cooperative Breeding

The defense of territories can also permit the formation of groups to share in resources and other group benefits, such as cooperative breeding. Cooperative breeding occurs when non-parent conspecifics contribute to the care of a dependent infant or juvenile (Hatchwell and Komdeur, 2000). Cooperative breeding is of particular interest to evolutionary psychologists because it seems a detriment to the helping organism's fitness (Lukas and Clutton-Brock, 2012). One possible explanation for cooperative breeding is kin selection. Because related organisms share genes, organisms benefit their own inclusive fitness by helping to rear the young of related conspecifics. It has also been suggested that there are individual fitness increases involved in cooperative breeding, such as an increased chance to mate with the mother, or group augmentation (Clutton-Brock, 2002; Cockburn, 1998). However, considering the possible benefits does not reveal the reasons why the behavior may have evolved in the first place. Instead, we should examine the factors that were present when this parenting strategy first emerged to better understand its evolution. In the absence of historical data, we might examine factors present in the environment of extant species that exhibit this behavior in comparison to those that do not. It is possible that the strategy exists when there are few mating opportunities for all members of a species or when there are not enough resources to support multiple births within a group (e.g., Culot et al., 2011). In examining behavior that, on the surface, seems to run counter to the best interests of the actor, we can glean useful information about its origins. In this case, a further examination of the origins of cooperative breeding may shed light on the emergence of altruism and cooperation more broadly.

NEUROLOGICAL AND MORPHOLOGICAL STRUCTURES THAT SUPPORT COGNITION

Brain size is interconnected with selection pressures in that ecological factors likely support advanced cognition through the evolution of larger and/or more complex brain structures. The Cognitive Buffer Hypothesis holds that species that experience extreme variability in climate and ecology have larger brains than those that do not experience environmental fluctuations; essentially, that animals that live year-round in locales with variable climates should have evolved larger brains to cope with the adaptive issues faced by such change (e.g., Sayol et al., 2016; Sol, 2009). For instance, in places that experience significant snowfall during the winter, animals not only have to find nourishment at a time of year when food is scarce, but have less daylight in which to do so (Roth et al., 2010). This results in selection pressures that make traits such as behavioral flexibility and persistence adaptive. Animals that can flexibly change their behaviors and persist when confronted with a novel obstacle are better equipped to adapt to variable environments. The individuals that most successfully navigate this variability should survive longer and receive more opportunities to reproduce, leading to offspring that display this flexibility. Larger brains likely support more complex problem solving, inhibition and innovation.

Sayol et al. (2016) found that, indeed, birds that inhabited locales in which the climate varied significantly tended to have larger brains relative to their bodies compared to birds that inhabited less variable locales. Birds with larger brains are better able to establish themselves in novel environments and are more predisposed to innovation (Sol et al., 2005). Behavioral flexibility has also been shown to play a part in invasion for species such as house sparrows *(Passer domesticus:* Martin and Fitzgerald, 2005). When an invading population of sparrows was compared to a population of sparrows that had occupied its range for over 150 years, the invading sparrows were more behaviorally flexible, as measured by consumption of novel food sources. A meta-analysis comparing successful and unsuccessful invasions of New Zealand found similar results: successful invading species had larger brains and displayed significantly more instances of innovation than did unsuccessful invaders. Evolutionarily, this all makes sense. Organisms that have larger brains, and as a result, an enhanced ability to innovate, should be better able to adapt to novel environments. Organisms that adapt to their environment continue to reproduce and thrive. The Cognitive Buffer Hypothesis has not been explicitly tested in non-bird species, which leaves open a fruitful direction for future research.

Brain size is an important component of the Cognitive Buffer Hypothesis. Many hypotheses have neglected to focus on the brain morphology that would be necessary to support various aspects of cognition. If species that display similar levels of cognitive complexity have brains that are radically different from a morphological perspective, this would provide evidence that different structures can support the same aspects of complex cognition. A noteworthy example is the comparison of apes with corvids; both corvids and apes display an impressive array of cognitive capacities, including causal reasoning, flexibility, and prospection (Emery and Clayton, 2004b). One might assume, based on this, that corvid and ape brains have similar structure. On the contrary, although the structure thought to be responsible for advanced cognition is enlarged in both species, the structures themselves are different; apes possess neocortex and corvids possess a nidopallium. If we understand which species share cognitive traits but diverge on brain structure, we will have a better understanding of the origins of those traits.

Brain structure is a common source when making inferences about intelligence because brain size, especially when compared to total body mass, has been connected with more advanced cognitive capabilities (Harvey and Krebs, 1990). This link between relative brain size and cognitive capabilities has been demonstrated in many mammals, with primates, cetaceans, and elephants possessing relatively large brains and cognitive capabilities that are impressive when viewed through an anthropocentric lens (Shultz and Dunbar, 2010). This trend has also been observed among mammalian carnivores and some birds, with corvids and psittaciformes displaying a similar relationship between cognitive capabilities and relative brain size as has been identified in primates (Benson-Amram et al., 2016; Emery and Clayton, 2004a; Iwaniuk et al., 2005). Whereas relative brain size has been the typical predictor for human-like sophisticated cognitive capabilities, the importance of overall brain size has also been supported. Only a few mammals have brains heavier than 700 grams and exhibit the capacity for complex cognition (Manger et al., 2013). Considering the increased metabolic costs of these proportionately larger brains (Armstrong, 1983), there should be equally powerful adaptive benefits.

Similarities in brain size have been identified as a predictor of cognitive capabilities, but similarities in brain functions have also been found between primates and corvids/psittaciformes. In both groups, higher cognitive functions have been connected to specific portions of the brain, the prefrontal cortex in primates and the avian nidopallium caudolaterale, located in the forebrain, in corvids/psittaciformes (Güntürkün, 2012). Whereas brain structures similar to those in primates have been found in cetaceans and elephants, any connection with cognitive capabilities is still unclear (Jacobs et al., 2011). Further work identifying these similarities can help us understand the adaptive benefits of these structures.

Energy Expenditure

Brain tissue is costly to develop and maintain, relative to other organs (Mink et al., 1981). This is important for two reasons, both of which are a matter of biological economics. Because brain tissue is expensive, larger brains should evolve only in circumstances where the advantages outweigh the

costs of maintaining them (Humphrey, 1976). An important evolutionary question is how generations of some organisms met the metabolic needs of their increasingly complex brains. Organisms are theorized to budget energy, meaning that any energy allocated to an enhanced brain must come from elsewhere in the organism's budget (Pontzer et al., 2013). Hypotheses regarding how organisms partition energy to maintain their brains include a focus on reduction in production (which entails growth and reproduction), reduction in size of the gut, and dietary change (Aiello and Wheeler, 1995; Pontzer et al., 2013). There is evidence that non-carnivorous mammal species with larger brains show reduced reproduction in comparison to their smaller-brained relatives, as well as evidence that humans moved from low mass of high-quality foods to reduce the cost of digestion, whereas the data on reduction of gut is less conclusive (Zhao et al., 2016). Understanding the changes that allowed species to budget energy to their costly brains can help us reconstruct the evolutionary changes that allowed humans to do the same.

WHICH PHYLOGENETIC COMPARISONS ARE MOST INFORMATIVE?

To this point, we have reviewed several factors that can inform an understanding of the evolution of cognition. Although we have reviewed topics relevant to various taxa, we have not focused on particular study species from the point of view of phylogenetic comparisons. In what follows we hope to make a case for particularly enlightening comparisons.

Understudied Groups

As has likely become evident thus far, comparative psychologists have relied heavily on the study of a small number of familiar species (see Shettleworth, 2009). This is particularly true with regard to laboratory experiments and perhaps less true of fieldwork. To propel evolutionary and comparative psychology forward, psychologists must continue to expand their study to species that have previously been neglected (Eaton et al., 2018; Macrì and Richter, 2015; Vonk and Shackelford, 2012). Researchers should not be reluctant to study species because of the potential challenges associated with novelty, accessibility, and husbandry. Matsubara et al. (2017) argued that comparative psychology must utilize a diverse group of vertebrates to properly study cognitive evolution; however, in order to understand the evolution of cognition, researchers must study both vertebrates and invertebrates. No single taxonomic group should be prioritized over others in the study of the evolution of cognition, which will require a complete grasp of the many similarities and differences expressed both across and within taxa. These differences occur in basic behavior, but also in morphology, brain structure and function, and information processing.

Less social species

As noted, the Social Intelligence Hypothesis has been a highly generative theory, inspiring researchers to produce reams of data on the many amazing cognitive abilities of social species. However, psychologists have neglected to seek potentially disconfirming evidence by studying less social species to examine whether they may possess the same traits. This oversight violates a fundamental principle of behavioral science; a good hypothesis is one that can be falsified. That is, one must show that sociality correlates with cognitive ability, but one must also show that the same cognitive abilities are absent (or least deficient) in species lacking sociality, in order to draw conclusions regarding the importance of sociality for the evolution of cognition.

Secondly, sociality can be (and is) defined in a number of ways (Barrett and Rendall, 2007). The multiple interpretations of the Social Intelligence Hypothesis along with

the multiple operationalizations of sociality are problematic and likely the cause of apparently conflicting conclusions in the literature. We could simply determine a species' social status on the basis of whether it lives in pairs, groups, or large colonies rather than individually. Alternatively, we can estimate social complexity using a variety of indicators. For example, we can determine whether the groups are stable or dynamic and the extent to which they are composed of kin. We can examine which sex is philopatric. We can determine the extent to which the group exhibits fission–fusion organization and whether it is composed of multiple smaller family units. Although it is simplistic to determine whether an animal is solitary or shares a territory or den with conspecifics, this type of classification would be incomplete as even animals sometimes considered to be solitary may overlap in territory or converge at food sources periodically (e.g., grizzly bears). Others, like giant pandas, may rarely come in contact even with members of the opposite sex. Some species deemed solitary in the wild are quite compatible in social groups in captivity (e.g., orangutans). Sociality may be better defined in concrete terms such as the number of individuals one is likely to come into contact with in one's lifetime, and the extent to which a species exhibits dominance hierarchies whether in a group setting or when converging infrequently at food sources. Treating sociality as a continuous rather than a dichotomous variable will be more useful in determining which aspects of sociality are associated with different traits and behaviors. Only once researchers have agreed upon appropriate aspects of sociality to assess and how to quantify these aspects, can they properly determine the contribution of sociality to the evolution of cognition. Furthermore, only by studying species that exhibit the full range of sociality when measured in this way can one adequately verify or falsify the Social Intelligence Hypothesis.

Although less commonly considered as a rationale for studying less social animals, such research may present a model of asocial cognition that will benefit the study of humans that are asocial (ranging from psychiatric diagnoses of neurodevelopmental, depressive, anxiety, and personality disorders to acute social withdrawal, such as *hikikomori*: Kato et al., 2018; Tamaki, 2015). Studies of less social species will enable researchers to learn more about nonsocial cognition and how it differs from social cognition. There are numerous less social animals that have not been subjected to psychological study to date, such as snails, praying mantises, black rhinoceroses, aardvarks, Tasmanian devils, owls, male white-nosed coatis, platypuses, sea turtles, and numerous others. Studying less social animals affords psychologists the opportunity to explore the influence of sociality on cognitive processes.

Additionally, by extending our studies of animal cognition to non-group-living species, we may have more opportunities to study animals that have various mating strategies. For example, monogamous primates (e.g., Indriidae, Lemuridae, Lepilemuridae, Tarsiidae, Callitrichidae, Cebidae, Cercopithecidae, and Hylobatidae: Fuentes, 1998) are surprisingly neglected compared to their more social relatives. Although a variety of birds with different social structures have been well-studied, current research interest is focused on group-living species such as corvids. By studying the cognition of species that are monogamous, researchers will be able to determine possible associations between mating strategies and cognitive specializations. For example, pair-bonded animals may not need skills associated with tracking the interactions of group members but may benefit from skills associated with maintaining long-term relationships such as conflict resolution, reciprocity, and cooperation. Similar to our discussion of cooperative breeding above, studying monogamous and non-monogamous species may reveal factors significant to the evolution of monogamy. Related to our point about how cognition in asocial species may present appropriate models for disorders of sociality in humans,

studying monogamous species may inform our understanding of human relationships and romantic attachment.

Little psychological research has been conducted on marsupials, which is disappointing given their uniqueness within the animal kingdom. One of the most widely-studied marsupials is the Virginia opossum, the only marsupial native to North America. It is considered one of the brightest species studied in a lab (Wynne and McLean, 1999) despite its relatively short lifespan (Gipson and Kamler, 2001; Harmon et al., 2005; Hossler et al., 1994; MacDonald, 2006). In spatial learning tasks (Doolittle and Weimer, 1968; James and Turner, 1963), opossums have demonstrated visual discrimination (James, 1960) and aversive learning (Cheney and Eldred, 1980). On a fixed interval schedule of reinforcement (Cone and Cone, 1970), and tests of the negative contrast effect (Papini et al., 1988), marsupials perform at levels equal to or greater than that of eutherians, including humans (Wynne and McLean, 1999). Wynne and McLean (1999) argued that further study of marsupials could aid in conservation, providing information that will assist management of so-called nuisance species. Studying ecological pressures and physiological skills, convergence in bodily forms and how ecological convergence impacts behavioral convergence, as well as neural development, will fill a gap in knowledge about this unique infraclass. Bonney and Wynne (2004) showcased the value of studying marsupials from different ecological niches in which resources fluctuate on tasks that are dependent on processing information quickly. As noted, the Cognitive Buffer Hypothesis posits that variability of environments may contribute to the process of learning-to-learn. An animal, such as the dunnart, that lives in environments in which resources fluctuate, predation must be avoided, and food must be hunted, may exhibit important cognitive differences from other members of the same order like the quokka, a grazer with no natural predators. Both dunnarts and quokkas have small encephalization quotients, with dunnarts having small absolute brain size; yet, they performed well in visual discrimination tests and learning, and outperformed quokkas, presumably due to the varying niches and environments they occupy (Bonney and Wynne, 2008).

Other understudied and unique solitary mammals are monotremes, which include duck-billed platypuses and echidnae (spiny-backed anteater). These unique mammals allow for comparisons with other taxa based on surprising similarities such as that they are the only mammals that lay eggs, as do avians, amphibians, reptiles, and some fish. Like reptiles, they actively adjust their body temperatures and hibernate. They also appear to possess relatively large brains (Nicol, 2013). For all of these reasons, the study of monotremes may be informative both in terms of better understanding why they evolved their unique combination of traits, and the role of environmental factors in shaping traits, in general.

Less Studied Members of Highly Studied Groups

Even among rodents, many species remain understudied. Most of the current information on rodent cognition is based on rats and mice that have been bred for the lab. Animals bred in laboratories may usefully serve as a model of basic cognitive processes and allow for the study of invasive techniques applicable to but not permittable in humans, but given their unnatural genetic background and controlled environment, they would not be ideal subjects to understand the questions we have posed in this chapter. As far back as 1974, Dewsbury suggested that a variety of muroid rodents, including voles, lemmings, deer mice, wood rats, dormice, mice, rats, zokors, mole-rats, gerbils, and hamsters, should be included in psychology. The Rodentia order includes species that inhabit several diverse ecological niches (e.g., tree and ground squirrels, beavers, capybara, gophers, zokors, agouti, porcupines). As rodents are indigenous to every continent except Antarctica, study of more rodent species would have great utility for the study of the evolution of cognition.

Non-mammals

As identified, there is plenty of uncharted territory within mammals alone, but other groups have been even more grievously neglected. For example, non-avian reptiles and amphibians comprise an understudied group of terrestrial and aqueous coldblooded species that inhabit every continent except Antarctica. The literature on reptiles is growing, primarily with thanks to a handful of laboratories (e.g., Matsubara et al., 2017; Waters et al., 2017), but many topics remain unstudied. Furthermore, whereas the literature on reptiles is growing, there are relatively few experiments on amphibian cognition. A few of the limited amphibian studies examine numerical ability in salamanders and basic learning processes in frogs, as well as communication and play (reviewed in Burghardt, 2013). As past studies have found that there is evidence of reptile spatial memory, researchers should not be quick to assume that animals lacking a hippocampus, like reptiles (Wilkinson and Huber, 2012), lack the ability to perform spatial memory tasks. However, it is important to consider that tasks designed for mammals may not be appropriate for expressing the capacities of reptiles and amphibians. Furthermore, reptiles often wait long intervals between feedings, which can pose a challenge for motivating them to perform well in cognitive tasks. Another important note is that phenotypic traits of reptiles are influenced by external factors such as incubation temperature, which may influence their cognitive abilities (Matsubara et al., 2017; Siviter et al., 2017). This aspect of reptile ontogeny provides an avenue to investigate a particular environmental aspect (gestational temperature) and its influence on cognitive development, which would not be possible in other species.

Birds

Even among classes more commonly studied, there are orders and families that are relatively neglected. Among bird populations, a single order has been used for a large majority of studies. Columbiformes (pigeons and doves) have been incredibly popular as a classic lab animal, with thousands of studies published, primarily due to the fact that they have been domesticated to serve many different functions (Jerolmack, 2007), and have demonstrated impressive cognitive abilities (Castro and Wasserman, 2017). Although not as common, corvids and psittaciformes have captured the attention of the scientific community recently by demonstrating cognitive capabilities that are comparable to the great apes (Auersperg et al., 2015). In contrast, songbirds, raptors, and many other species of birds have received much less attention, or are studied primarily with respect to a single aspect of cognition such as vocal communication in songbirds (Njegovan and Weisman, 1997; Sturdy et al., 2007; Zollinger, 2007). A recent meta-analysis by Ducatez and Lefebvre (2014) found that bird species native to North America and Europe had been studied much more than species native to other continents. Ducatez and Lefebvre (2014) also found that species that were not at risk of extinction have been studied significantly more than species that are threatened. By focusing current studies on species that are easily accessible, we may lose the chance to study species that might not be available in the future.

A focus on a small number of convenient or exceptional species has prevented researchers from studying a wide range of birds that display unusual behaviors or those that live in harsh climates. One such species is the penguin. The unique habitat and social structure of penguins can provide us with a wealth of knowledge, but studies with these birds are scarce. The few studies that have been performed tend to focus on the strong pair bonds that many species develop (Keddar et al., 2013; Pincemy et al., 2010). Other large flightless birds such as cassowaries, emus, and ostriches have also been largely ignored, with most existing studies focusing on their potential as livestock (Bonato et al., 2015; Hunt, 2011).

Aquatic Species

Many aquatic animals have also been ignored in comparative psychology research. With over 25,000 freshwater and marine fish species (Borski and Hodson, 2003) that inhabit almost every corner of the Earth, under various ecological constraints, there is much we can learn about how fish have adapted to their habitats, how their habitats affect their behavior and cognition, and how they compare to other cold-blooded animals. Zebrafish have recently become one of the most popular laboratory animal models (Khan and Echeverria, 2017), and other fish species have a reasonably long history of experimentation in the lab, but there are many unstudied species – particularly deep sea species that are difficult to acquire and house. Regardless, recent innovations with fish have indicated that fish feel pain (Bjørge et al., 2011; Sneddon, 2015; Sneddon et al., 2014, 2018), estimate quantities (Agrillo et al., 2008; Brown, 2015; Lucon-Xiccato et al., 2015), perform mental rotations (Gierszewski et al., 2013; Schluessel et al., 2014), and may fall prey to visual illusions (Brown, 2015; Kelley and Kelley, 2014; Salva et al., 2014). An exciting avenue of research has revealed evidence for personality in sharks (Byrnes and Brown, 2016; Jacoby et al., 2014). These studies have revolutionized our understanding of fish cognition and will have profound implications for discussions of animal ethics (Brown, 2015; Sneddon, 2015; Sneddon et al., 2018). Recently, a study purporting to reveal evidence of mirror self-recognition in a wrasse set the scientific community scrambling to adjust their expectations of fish cognition, or their acceptance of the mirror test as a test of self-awareness (de Waal, 2019;

Kohda et al., 2019; Vonk, 2019). As fish are compared to other species traditionally considered more cognitively sophisticated, researchers and lay people alike may have to reconsider historical notions of animal intelligence.

Along these lines, cephalopods, in particular, octopuses, have recently captured the imagination of scientists and non-scientists as reports of astonishing cognitive feats begin to proliferate. Octopi have been found to exhibit behavioral flexibliity (Kovács and Mather, 2008). They have also been observed to play, rotate objects to solve a simple problem, use tools and engage in extractive foraging. Cephalopods present an interesting inter-group study comparison based on their social structure, sensory systems, aptitude to learn, de-centralized brain, vision, abilities and relatively short lifespan (reviewed in Mather, 2008, 2019). Given the vast differences between cephalopods and other species in view of their de-centralized nervous system and other unique adaptations, further study of their mental lives would be valuable for understanding the evolution of cognition.

Insects

There is not adequate space here to describe the many fascinating advances in the area of insect cognition. However, it is of note that species such as bees have demonstrated abilities as complex as relational matching (Giurfa et al., 2001), navigation, and communication (Gould, 1990; Menzel and Giurfa, 2006; Srinivasan et al., 2006). Ant-lions demonstrate fascinating rescue behavior (Hollis and Nowbahari, 2013) and spiders astound researchers with their abilities (Cross and Jackson, 2005). As with the claim of mirror self-recognition in fish, claims of emotion states in bees have forced a debate about the paradigms in use with other species (Baracchi et al., 2017). Thus, testing more distantly removed species can sometimes be a good test-case for a paradigm, so long as researchers are

not biased against demonstrations of cognition in species that do not fit the expected mold (Vonk, 2019). Ants have also been championed as passing tests of self-awareness, although this has also been contested (Gallup and Anderson, 2018). It should be noted that use of the mirror test has been controversial, even within primates (de Veer and Van den Bos, 1999). The hymenoptera are unique in their complex social systems and patterns of genetic relatedness. Indeed, much of what we know about sociobiology is owed to E. O. Wilson's fascination with social insects (Wilson, 2013). Therefore, unlike some of the other taxa we have discussed, there is already a long study of insect cognition (e.g., Srinivasan et al., 2006), but, as with the other species, much remains to be discovered and a more serious consideration of what insect cognition can tell us about the evolution of cognition has yet to emerge.

Comparing Distantly Related Species

As discussed above, comparing species that are closely related can be particularly informative with regard to how environmental differences are connected to differences in behavior or cognition. In contrast, by comparing distantly related species we can determine what aspects of the environment likely influenced these similarities. By focusing on traits that emerge through convergent evolution, scientists have managed to identify many of these similarities, including some, such as tool use, that have been attributed to higher cognition. The emergence of these similarities among distantly related species may help us determine how certain environmental pressures can trigger these adaptations.

Convergent evolution occurs when distantly related species evolve similar adaptations, whether physical or cognitive, in response to similar socio-ecological challenges rather than due to phylogenetic similarities. When species are distantly related, any similarities are more likely to have evolved as a result of convergent evolution. Any similarities are typically biological, but convergent evolution has been used to explain cognitive similarities (Emery, 2004). However, we must be cautious when applying convergent evolution to cognition. Whereas biological similarities can be identified by examining bone structures or other organic systems, cognitive abilities are intangible and require inferences based on behaviors or brain structure.

Given some success comparing brain structures between vastly different species, it would be worthwhile to identify associations between cognitive abilities and ecology. Some of the most common comparisons have been between primates and corvids. Several ecological similarities may have resulted in certain cognitive capabilities arising via convergent evolution. Both taxa have a generalized omnivorous diet, which may have evolved in response to unpredictable food sources (Lefebvre et al., 2004). Under this particular pressure, animals may need to evolve more flexible, and potentially innovative, behaviors, which could lead to the increase in brain size that has been found among corvids and primates. Finding similarities between distantly related species that utilize the same sources of food can tell us much about how certain traits evolved. This is one example, but there are many other selection pressures, such as sociality, that can explain how a trait evolved.

The extent to which the Social Intelligence Hypothesis is supported across species may reflect the adequacy of the definition of social complexity. Rather than the size of a social group, the quality of relationships may better predict complex cognition in birds, with long-term monogamous birds possessing the largest relative brain sizes (Emery et al., 2007). Borrego and Gaines (2016) found that social carnivores (lions) significantly outperformed their nonsocial relatives (tigers) on both social and nonsocial cognitive tasks. However, Benson-Amram et al. (2016) found that brain size rather than sociality predicted

problem solving after testing a much larger group of carnivores. Birds and mammals are far from the only animals that live in social groups. Comparing the cognitive capabilities of social fish and insects with other well-researched animal populations may give us greater insight into some of the origins of sociality. There are many cases of parallel cognitive skills among distantly related species. The ability to use tools has been a topic of great interest for many psychologists with many studies conducted using primates and corvids. Many species have demonstrated the ability to use tools, but only some species of primates, with chimpanzees and capuchins being the most prolific (van Schaik et al., 1999), New Caledonian crows, and woodpecker finches have been observed to regularly use and even manufacture tools in the wild (van Horik et al., 2012). This focus on species that habitually use tools may have restricted what we can learn. If we expand our focus to include species that have demonstrated the capability to use tools we might be able to determine what ecological pressures trigger this capability.

Species that have displayed complex cognitive capabilities have been the primary focus for many psychologists. We can learn much from these comparisons, but this narrow view can blind us to other comparisons. We might be able to learn more about selection pressures by investigating cognitive capabilities that can be found in many distantly related species, not just ones that are found in a select few. It is unlikely that complex cognition evolved in response to one particular ecological problem, but if we can identify similarities between distantly related species, cataloging the ecological cocktail may become just a little bit easier.

Comparing Domestic to Wild Species

A seldom-attended comparison that could nonetheless be informative is the comparison of wild to domestic species. Such comparisons focus on the influence of environmental factors and selective breeding in closely related species. Researchers have compared domestic dogs to their wild counterparts (e.g., Brubaker et al., 2017; Marshall-Pescini et al., 2017; Range et al., 2012), but few other species have benefitted from such comparisons. Domestic animals have different foraging strategies than their wild relatives. For example, wild varieties of the Suidae family congregate into larger group sizes than domesticated varieties: collared peccaries in Venezuela have a mean group size of 6.5 pigs (Robinson and Eisenberg, 1985); wild warthogs congregate into groups with 8 or fewer individuals (White, 2010) whereas free-range domestic pigs cluster into groups of 4 or less (Rodríguez-Estévez et al., 2010). However, there are some similarities in foraging behavior as well. For example, peccaries (Nogueira et al., 2011, 2014) and domestic pigs (Gustafsson et al., 1999) tend to be more active when food sources are unpredictable than when they are predictable. Due to the increased energy expenditure when food is not as reliably available, it is advantageous for both wild and domesticated species to prefer predictability. There is evidence that, in a controlled environment, pigs tend to prefer predictability of their food over unpredictability (de Jonge et al., 2008). Because domesticated species are likely to have food readily available, they will not need to forage in large groups to find food. Thus, they will not have to divide their resources with as many conspecifics as their wild counterparts, who may experience environments where food is scarcer. These differences in foraging ecology between wild and domestic species may relate to cognitive differences such as communication, cooperation, and prediction of conspecifics' behaviors.

Warthogs appear to respond to environmental variability in timing conception to occur in one wet season, and births to occur during the next wet season (Ogutu et al., 2015). This flexibility will likely allow them to maximize foraging intake during their offspring's most critical and vulnerable developmental periods. This ability would be unnecessary in domestic pigs and should no longer be selected for, particularly because domestic species are subject to selective breeding with humans controlling characteristics of value such as fertility, carcass and meat quality and yield, human tolerance, and so on (Edwards et al., 2003; Fabian et al., 2003). Examining features that have been retained and lost through the process of domestication would add to the sparse data available on the large-scale impacts of the domestication process. Furthermore, such data would indicate the extent to which characteristics are under environmental control, and which factors are most critical to the development of particular traits.

Wild animals sometimes exhibit cognitive skills in captivity that would not typically be observed in their natural setting (e.g., Bering, 2004; van de Waal and Bshary, 2011, in primates). For example, wild boars (*Sus scrofa*) from the Wildpark in Leipzig, Germany (large outdoor enclosure 2.6 ha with natural vegetation) that have been fed, during the winter months, by humans throwing feed over the fence, were able to solve a social task in which they followed human points, a gesture that is similar to an arm moving outwards as feed is tossed. Domestic pigs from two different farms (one in Leipzig, Germany, one in Colfiorito, Perugia, Italy) who received their food via chutes were not able to follow such points (Albiach-Serrano et al., 2012).

It is possible that increased experience with humans may hinder cognitive abilities. Cats (*Felis catus*) raised in a laboratory have demonstrated impairment in visual associative learning (Zernicki, 1999) and delayed response to auditory cues (Wikmark and Warren, 1972) as compared to free-roaming cats (Vitale Shreve and Udell, 2015), which indicates that training and rearing history may affect various outcomes, even if not intentional. Therefore, when comparing domestic animals to their wild relatives, it is useful to test in a variety of settings, such as a controlled laboratory setting as well as a naturalistic wild setting in which both domestic animals and their wild relatives are free as possible from human interaction. Doing so will help determine the similarities and differences in what animals are capable of doing versus what they would typically do in the setting that they were bred for. Comparing domestic animals to their wild counterparts in this manner will provide insight as to what environmental features are necessary or sufficient for the development of particular characteristics.

In addition, the comparison of domestic species to their wild counterparts may reveal which abilities have been conserved even though they may no longer be adaptive. For example, numerical competence, which clearly has adaptive value in allowing individuals to pursue larger quantities of food has been demonstrated in both wild and domestic felids. Wild lions discriminate between the vocal recordings of an individual lion versus a group of three lions (Heinsohn, 1997; McComb et al., 1994). Domestic cats have been tested in a paradigm of choosing between arrays presenting different quantities of food that parallels the study of captive primates (Pisa and Agrillo, 2009). Thus, very different methodologies suitable for diverse environments and histories can reveal similar cognitive abilities.

CONCLUSION

Animals that are the last remaining branch of their evolutionary tree can potentially assist researchers in understanding how extinct and extant species from the same phylogenetic tree may have responded differently to the same environmental pressures. Taking the time to research them may provide valuable insights into why some species succeeded within their environment and why some are failing or have failed. Viewing animals as part of a larger ecosystem in which animals are assessed on the basis of shared environments as well as

phylogenies will provide a fuller picture of the evolutionary forces at work than a microscopic focus on a single species or taxon can do. Once we allow ourselves to study a more diverse group of animals, we will be able to create endless opportunities in challenging ourselves to study animals using tasks tailored to the specific sensory and morphological adaptations of the species rather than from the human perspective, using our own sensory modes, social structures, environment, strengths and weaknesses, brain, and way of solving problems (see also Eaton et al., 2018). Once we accept that other animals do not view, sense, or navigate the world in the same way humans do, we can begin to see how each species' problem-solving skills have equipped them to successfully survive, navigate, and problem solve in their natural habitat using the traits that evolution armed them with. Thus, elsewhere we have advocated a bottom-up approach to the study of animal cognition where first we learn about an animal's unique capabilities and then further probe those behaviors and capacities rather than beginning with an expectation of how they might compare to other well-studied species (Eaton et al., 2018; Vonk, in press). We still have so much to learn.

Researchers may need to shift away from a reliance on laboratory studies and venture out into the field in order to gain access to certain species, as Bonney and Wynne (2004) suggested. At the very least, researchers engaged in laboratory studies should invite more cross-talk with field researchers and more interdisciplinary collaborations, such as with biologists, anthropologists, and zoologists (Vonk and Shackelford, 2012). Although it may be easier to create and control for more complicated experiments in a laboratory setting, not all species are suitable for captivity. Researchers need to adjust their frame of thinking and generate new ways to research these understudied species, when everything about them is foreign to us, including how they experience the world.

In conclusion, there are still many unexplored avenues for elucidating the evolution of cognition. Much of the existing literature on animal cognition has been centered around human cognition. With so many species and topics relatively unstudied, it is recommended to examine many species to understand their natural behaviors, thus allowing us to probe the underlying cognitive mechanisms for those behaviors and the possible predictors of such processes. Existing data are useful if examined in the context of what each individual species is able to do relative to other species that either share or differ with regard to specific environmental factors, rather than in the context of human psychology alone.

REFERENCES

Agrillo, C., Dadda, M., Serena, G., & Bisazza, A. (2008). Do fish count? Spontaneous discrimination of quantity in female mosquitofish. *Animal Cognition*, *11*(3), 495–503. doi.org/10.1007/s10071-008-0140-9

Agrillo, C., Piffer, L., Bisazza, A., & Butterworth, B. (2012). Evidence for two numerical systems that are similar in humans and guppies. *PLoS ONE*, *7*(2), 8. doi.org/10.1371/journal.pone.0031923

Aiello, L. C., & Wheeler, P. (1995) The expensive-tissue hypothesis: the brain and the digestive system in human and primate evolution. *Current Anthropology*, *36*(2), 199–221.

Albiach-Serrano, A., Brauer, J., Cacchione, T., Zickert, N., & Amici, F. (2012). The effect of domestication and ontogeny in swine cognition (*Sus scrofa scrofa* and *S. s. domestica*). *Applied Animal Behaviour Science*, *141*(12), 25–35.

Alexander, R. D. (1974). The evolution of social behavior. *Annual Review of Ecology and Systematics*, *5*(1), 325–383.

Anderson, J. R., & Gallup, G. G., Jr (2011). Which primates recognize themselves in mirrors? *PLoS Biology*, *9*(3), e1001024. doi.org/10.1371/journal.pbio.1001024

Armstrong, E. (1983). Relative brain size and metabolism in mammals. *Science*, *220*(4603), 1302–1304.

Auersperg, A. M. I., van Horik, J. O., Bugnyar, T., Kacelnik, A., Emery, N. J., & von Bayern, A. M. P. (2015). Combinatory actions during object play in Psittaciformes (*Diopsittaca nobilis*, *Pionites melanocephala*, *Cacatua goffini*) and corvids (*Corvus corax*, *C. monedula*, *C. moneduloides*). *Journal of Comparative Psychology*, *129*(1), 62–71. doi.org/10.1037/a0038314

Baracchi, D., Lihoreau, M., & Giurfa, M. (2017). Do insects have emotions? Some insights from bumble bees. *Frontiers in Behavioral Neuroscience*, *11*, 157. doi.org/10.3389/fnbeh.2017.00157

Barrett, L., Henzi, P., & Rendall, D. (2007). Social brains, simple minds: does social complexity really require cognitive complexity? In N. Emery, N. Clayton & C. Frith (Eds), *Social intelligence: from brain to culture* (pp. 123–146). New York, NY: Oxford University Press.

Benson-Amram, S., Dantzer, B., Stricker, G., Swanson, E. M., & Holekamp, K. E. (2016). Brain size predicts problem-solving abilities in mammalian carnivores. *Proceedings of the National Academy of Sciences USA*, *113*(9), 2532–2537. doi:10.1073/pnas.1505913113

Bering, J. M. (2004). A critical review of the 'enculturation hypothesis': the effects of human rearing on great ape social cognition. *Animal Cognition*, *7*(4), 201–212. doi.org/10.1007/s10071-004-0210-6

Bhatnagar, K. (2008). The brain of the common vampire bat, *Desmodus rotundus murinus* (Wagner, 1840): a cytoarchitectural atlas. *Brazilian Journal of Biology*, *68*(3), 583–599.

Bjørge, M. H., Nordgreen, J., Janczak, A. M., Poppe, T., Ranheim, B., & Horsberg, T. E. (2011). Behavioural changes following intraperitoneal vaccination in atlantic salmon (*salmo salar*). *Applied Animal Behaviour Science*, *133*(1–2), 127–135. doi:http://dx.doi.org/10.1016/j.applanim.2011.04.018

Boesch, C. (1994). Cooperative hunting in wild chimpanzees. *Animal Behaviour*, *48*(3), 653–657.

Boesch, C. (2002). Cooperative hunting roles among Taï chimpanzees. *Human Nature*, *13*(1), 27–36.

Boesch, C., & Boesch-Achermann, H. (2000). *The chimpanzees of the Taï Forest: behavioural ecology and evolution*. Oxford: Oxford University Press.

Bonato, M., Cherry, M. I., & Cloete, S. W. P. (2015). Mate choice, maternal investment and implications for ostrich welfare in a farming environment. *Applied Animal Behaviour Science*, *171*, 1–7. doi.org/10.1016/j. applanim.2015.08.010

Bonney, K. R., & Wynne, C. D. L. (2004). Studies of learning and problem solving in two species of Australian marsupials. *Neuroscience & Biobehavioral Reviews*, *28*(6), 583–594. doi. org/10.1016/j.neubiorev.2004.08.005

Borrego, N., & Gaines, M. (2016). Social carnivores outperform asocial carnivores on an innovative problem. *Animal Behaviour*, *114*, 21–26. doi:http://dx.doi.org/10.1016/j. anbehav.2016.01.013

Borski, R. J., & Hodson, R. G. (2003). Fish research and the Institutional Animal Care and Use Committee, *ILAR Journal*, *44*(4), 286–294.

Brown, C. (2015). Fish intelligence, sentience and ethics. *Animal Cognition*, *18*(1), 1–17.

Brubaker, L., Dasgupta, S., Bhattacharjee, D., Bhadra, A., & Udell, M. A. R. (2017). Differences in problem-solving between canid populations: do domestication and lifetime experience affect persistence? *Animal Cognition*, *20*(4), 717–723. doi.org/10.1007/ s10071-017-1093-7

Burghardt, G. M. (2013). Environmental enrichment and cognitive complexity in reptiles and amphibians: concepts, review, and implications for captive populations. *Applied Animal Behaviour Science*, *147*(3–4), 286–298. doi.org/10.1016/j.applanim.2013.04.013

Byrne, R. (1997). The Technical intelligence hypothesis: an additional evolutionary stimulus to intelligence? In A. Whiten & R. Byrne (Eds), *Machiavellian intelligence II: Extensions and evaluations* (pp. 289–311). Cambridge: Cambridge University Press. doi.org/10.1017/ CBO9780511525636.012

Byrne, R., & Whiten, A. (Eds) (1988). *Machiavellian intelligence: Social expertise and the evolution of intellect in monkeys, apes, and humans*. Oxford: Oxford University Press.

Byrnes, E. E., & Brown, C. (2016). Individual personality differences in Port Jackson sharks *Heterodontus portusjacksoni*. *Journal of Fish Biology*, *89*(2), 1142–1157. doi.org/10.1111/ jfb.12993

Castro, L., & Wasserman, E. A. (2017). Feature predictiveness and selective attention in pigeons' categorization learning. *Journal of Experimental Psychology: Animal Learning and Cognition*, *43*(3), 231–242. doi.org/ 10.1037/xan0000146

Cheney, C. D., & Eldred, N. L. (1980). Lithium-chloride-induced aversions in the opossum (*Didelphis virginiana*). *Physiological Psychology*, *8*(3), 383–385. doi.org/10.3758/BF03337475

Christensen, C., & Radford, A. N. (2018). Dear enemies or nasty neighbours? Causes and consequences of variation in the response of group-living species to territorial intrusions. *Behavioral Ecology*, *29*(5), 1004–1013.

Clauss, M., Steuer, P., Müller, D. W., Codron, D., & Hummel, J. (2013). Herbivory and body size: allometries of diet quality and gastrointestinal physiology, and implications for herbivore ecology and dinosaur gigantism. *PloS ONE*, *8*(10), e68714. doi.org/10.1371/journal. pone.0068714

Clutton-Brock, T. (2002). Breeding together: kin selection and mutualism in cooperative vertebrates. *Science*, *296*(5565), 69–72.

Cockburn, A. (1998). Evolution of helping behavior in cooperatively breeding birds. *Annual Review of Ecology and Systematics*, *29*, 141–177.

Cone, A. L., & Cone, D. M. (1970). Operant conditioning of Virginia opossum. *Psychological Reports*, *26*(1), 83–86. doi.org/10.2466/ pr0.1970.26.1.83

Cross, F. R., & Jackson, R. R. (2005). Spider heuristics. *Behavioural Processes*, *69*(2), 125–127. doi.org/10.1016/j.beproc.2005.02.010

Culot, L., Lledo-Ferrer, Y., Hoelscher, O., Lazo, F. J. M., Huynen, M. C., & Heymann, E. W. (2011). Reproductive failure, possible maternal infanticide, and cannibalism in wild moustached tamarins, *Saguinus mystax*. *Primates*, *52*(2), 179–186.

Dawson, S. M., and Jenkins, P. F. (1983). Chaffinch song repertoires and the Beau Geste hypothesis. *Behaviour*, *87*(3–4), 259–269.

de Jonge, F. H., Ooms, M., Kuurman, W. W., Maes, J. H. R., & Spruijt, B. M. (2008). Are pigs sensitive to variability in food rewards? *Applied Animal Behaviour Science*, *114*(2), 93–104.

de Veer, M. W., & Van den Bos, R. (1999). A critical review of methodology and interpretation of mirror self-recognition research in nonhuman primates. *Animal Behaviour*, *58*(3), 459–468. doi.org/10.1006/anbe.1999.1166 de Waal, F. B. M. (2019). Fish, mirrors, and a gradualist perspective on self-awareness. *PLoS Biology 17*(2), e3000112. doi.org/10.1371/journal.pbio.3000112

Dewsbury, D. A. (1974). The use of muroid rodents in the psychology laboratory. *Behavior Research Methods & Instrumentation*, *6*(3), 301–308. doi.org/10.3758/BF03210882

Dobson, S. D. (2012). Coevolution of facial expression and social tolerance in macaques. *American Journal of Primatology*, *74*(3), 229–235. doi:http://dx.doi.org/10.1002/ajp.21991

Doolittle, J. H., & Weimer, J. (1968). Spatial probability learning in the Virginia opossum. *Psychonomic Science*, *13*(3), 191. doi.org/10.3758/BF03342476

Ducatez, S., & Lefebvre, L. (2014). Patterns of research effort in birds. *PLoS ONE 9*(2), e89955. doi.org/10.1371/journal.pone.0089955

Dunbar, R. I. M. (1998). The social brain hypothesis. *Evolutionary Anthropology*, *6*, 178–189.

Dunbar, R. I. M. (2009). The social brain hypothesis and its implications for social evolution. *Annals of Human Biology*, *36*(5), 562–572.

Eaton, T., Hutton, R., Leete, J., Lieb, J., Robeson, A., & Vonk, J. (2018). Bottoms-up! Rejecting top-down human-centered approaches in comparative psychology. *International Journal of Comparative Psychology*, *31*, 37589.

Edwards, D. B., Bates, R. O., & Osburn, W. N. (2003). Evaluation of Duroc- vs. Pietrian sired pigs for carcass and meat quality measures. *Journal of Animal Science*, *81*(8), 1895–1899.

Emery, N. J. (2004). Are corvids 'feathered apes'? Cognitive evolution in crows, jays, rooks, and jackdaws. In S. Watanabe (Ed.), *Comparative analysis of minds* (pp. 181–213). Tokyo: Keio University Press.

Emery, N. J., & Clayton, N. S. (2004a). Comparing the complex cognition of birds and primates. In L. J. Rogers & G. Kaplan (Eds), *Comparative vertebrate cognition: are primates superior to nonprimates?* (pp. 3–55). New York, NY: Springer Science+Business Media.

Emery, N. J., & Clayton, N. S. (2004b). The mentality of crows: convergent evolution of intelligence in corvids and apes. *Science*, *306*(5703), 1903–1907.

Emery, N. J., Seed, A. M., von Bayern, A. M. P., & Clayton, N. S. (2007). Cognitive adaptations of social bonding in birds. *Philosophical Transactions of the Royal Society B: Biological Sciences*, *362*(1480), 489–505.

Fabian, J., Chiba, L. I., Kuhlers, D. L., Frobish, L. T., Nadarajah, K., & McElhenney, W. H. (2003). Growth performance, dry matter and nitrogen digestibilities, serum profile, and carcass and meat qualities of pigs with distinct genotypes. *Journal of Animal Science*, *81*(5), 1142–1149.

Fuentes, A. (1998). Re-evaluating primate monogamy. *American Anthropologist*, *100*(4), 890–907.

Galef, B. G, & Laland, K. N. (2005). Social learning in animals: empirical studies and theoretical models. *BioScience*, *5*(6), 489–499.

Gallup, G. G., Jr., & Anderson, J. R. (2018). The 'olfactory mirror' and other recent attempts to demonstrate self-recognition in non-primate species. *Behavioural Processes*, *148*, 16–19. doi.org/10.1016/j.beproc.2017.12.010

Gierszewski, S., Bleckmann, H., & Schluessel, V. (2013). Cognitive abilities in Malawi cichlids (*Pseudotropheus* sp.): matching-to-sample and image/mirror-image discriminations. *PLoS ONE* 8(2), e57363. doi.org/10.1371/journal.pone.0057363

Gittleman, J. R. (1986). Carnivore brain size, behavioral ecology, and phylogeny. *Journal of Mammalogy*, *67*(1), 23–36. doi.org/10.2307/1380998

Giurfa, M., Zhang, S., Jenett, A., Menzel, R., & Srinivasan, M. V. (2001). The concepts of 'sameness' and 'difference' in an insect. *Nature*, *410*(6831), 930–933. doi.org/10.1038/35073582

Gipson, P., & Kamler, J. (2001). Survival and home ranges of opossums in northeastern Kansas. *The Southwestern Naturalist*, *46*(2), 178–182. doi.org/10.2307/3672526

Gould, J. L. (1990). Honey bee cognition. *Cognition*, *37*(1–2), 83–103. doi.org/10.1016/0010-0277(90)90019-G

Güntürkün, O. (2012). The convergent evolution of neural substrates for cognition. *Psychological Research*, *76*(2), 212–219. doi.org/10.1007/s00426-011-0377-9

Gustafsson, M., Jensen, P., de Jonge, F. H., & Schuurman, T. (1999). Domestication effects on foraging strategies in pigs (*Sus scrofa*). *Applied Animal Behaviour Science*, *62*(4), 305–317.

Harmon, L. J., Bauman, K., McCloud, M., Parks, J., Howell, S., & Losos, J. B. (2005). What free-ranging animals do at the zoo: a study of the behavior and habitat use of opossums (*Didelphis virginiana*) on the grounds of the St. Louis Zoo. *Zoo Biology*, *24*(3), 197–213. doi. org/10.1002/zoo.20046

Harner, M. J. (1970). Population pressure and the social evolution of agriculturalists. *Southwestern Journal of Anthropology*, *26*(1), 67–86.

Harvey, P. H., & Krebs, J. R. (1990). Comparing brains. *Science*, *249*(4965), 140–146. doi. org//10.1126/science.2196673

Hatchwell, B. J., & Komdeur, J. (2000). Ecological constraints, life history traits and the evolution of cooperative breeding. *Animal Behaviour*, *59*(6), 1079–1086.

Healy, S. D., & Krebs, J. R. (1992). Food storing and the hippocampus in corvids amount and volume are correlated. *Proceedings of the Royal Society of London. B: Biological Science*, *248*(1323), 241–245.

Heinsohn, R. (1997). Group territoriality in two populations of African lions. *Animal Behaviour*, *53*(6), 1143–1147.

Hollis, K. L., & Nowbahari, E. (2013). Toward a behavioral ecology of rescue behavior. *Evolutionary Psychology*, *11*(3), 647–664. doi.org/10.1177/147470491301100311

Hossler, R. J., McAninch, J. B., & Harder, J. D. (1994). Maternal denning behavior and survival of juveniles in opossums in Southeastern New York. *Journal of Mammalogy*, *75*(1), 60–70. doi.org/10.2307/1382236

Humphrey, N. K. (1976). The social function of intellect. In P. P. G. Bateson and R. A. Hinde (Eds), *Growing points in ethology* (pp. 303–317). Cambridge, UK: Cambridge University Press.

Hunt, J. (2011). Ostrich farming poised for a comeback? *Poultry World*, *165*(12), 34–35.

Iwaniuk, A. N., Dean, K. M., & Nelson, J. E. (2005). Interspecific allometry of the brain and brain regions in parrots (Psittaciformes): comparisons with other birds and primates. *Brain, Behavior and Evolution*, *65*(1), 40–59.

Jacobs, B., Lubs, J., Hannan, M., Anderson, K., Butti, C., Sherwood, C. C., Hof, P. R., & Manger, P. R. (2011). Neuronal morphology in the African elephant (*Loxodonta africana*) neocortex. *Brain Structure and Function*, *215*(3–4), 273–298. doi.org/10.1007/s00429-010-0288-3

Jacoby, D. M. P., Fear, L. N., Sims, D. W., & Croft, D. P. (2014). Shark personalities? Repeatability of social network traits in a widely distributed predatory fish. *Behavioral Ecology and Sociobiology*, *68*(12), 1995–2003. doi.org/10.1007/s00265-014-1805-9

James, W. T. (1960). A study of visual discrimination in the opossum. *The Journal of Genetic Psychology: Research and Theory on Human Development*, *97*(1), 127–130. doi.org/10.1080/00221325.1960.10534318

James, W. T., & Turner, William W., III. (1963). Experimental study of maze learning in young opossums. *Psychological Reports*, *13*(3), 921–922. doi.org/10.2466/pr0.1963.13.3.921

Jerolmack, C. (2007). Animal archaeology: domestic pigeons and the nature–culture dialectic. *Qualitative Sociology Review*, *3*(1), 74–95.

Johnson-Ulrich, Z., Vonk, J., Humbyrd, M., Crowley, M., Wojtkowski, E., Yates, F., & Allard, S. (2016). Picture object recognition in an American black bear (*Ursus americanus)*. *Animal Cognition*, *19*, 1237–1242. doi.org/10.1016/j.beproc.2017.12.010

Jolly, A. (1966). Lemur social behavior and primate intelligence. *Science*, *153*(3735), 501–506.

Kato, T. A., Kanba, S., & Teo, A. R. (2018). Hikikomori: experience in Japan and international relevance. *World Psychiatry: Official Journal of the World Psychiatric Association (WPA)*, *17*(1), 105–106. doi.org/10.1002/wps.20497

Keddar, I., Andris, M., Bonadonna, F., & Dobson, F. S. (2013). Male-biased mate competition in king penguin trio parades. *Ethology*, *119*(5), 389–396. doi.org/10.1111/eth.12076

Kelley, L. A., & Kelley, J. L. (2014). Animal visual illusion and confusion: the importance of a perceptual perspective. *Behavioral Ecology*, *25*(3), 450–463. doi.org/10.1093/beheco/art118

Khan, K. M., & Echevarria, D. J. (2017). Feeling fishy: trait differences in zebrafish (*Danio rerio*). In J. Vonk, A. Weiss, & S. A. Kuczaj (Eds), *Personality in nonhuman animals* (pp. 111–127). New York, NY: Springer International Publishing. doi.org/10.1007/978-3-319-59300-5_6

Kohda, M., Hotta, T., Takeyama, T., Awata, S., Tanaka, H., Asai, J., & Jordan, A. L. (2019). If a fish can pass the mark test, what are the implications for consciousness and self-awareness testing in animals? *PLoS Biology 17*(2), e3000021. doi.org/10.1371/journal.pbio.3000021

Kovács, Á., & Mather, J. A. (2008). Cephalopod cognition, scholastic psychology. *Res Cogitans, 5*(1), 23–38.

Lefebvre, L., Reader, S. M., & Sol, D. (2004). Brains, innovations and evolution in birds and primates. *Brain Behavior & Evolution, 63*(4), 233–246.

Lucon-Xiccato, T., Miletto Petrazzini, M. E., Agrillo, C., & Bisazza, A. (2015). Guppies discriminate between two quantities of food items but prioritize item size over total amount. *Animal Behaviour, 107*, 183–191. doi.org/10.1016/j.anbehav.2015.06.019

Lukas, D., & Clutton-Brock, T. (2012). Cooperative breeding and monogamy in mammalian societies. *Proceedings of the Royal Society of London. B: Biological Sciences, 279*(1736), 2151–2156.

Macdonald, D. (2006). *The encyclopedia of mammals* (3rd ed., pp. 808–813). London: The Brown Reference Group.

Macrì, S., & Richter, S. H. (2015). The snark was a boojum – reloaded. *Frontiers in Zoology, 12*(1), S20. doi.org/10.1186/1742-9994-12-S1-S20

Male, L. H., & Smulders, T. V. (2007). Memory for food caches: not just for retrieval. *Behavioral Ecology, 18*(2), 456–459.

Malenky, R. K., & Wrangham, R. W. (1993). A quantitative comparison of terrestrial herbaceous food consumption by *Pan paniscus* in the Lomako Forest, Zaire, and *Pan troglodytes* in the Kibale Forest, Uganda. *American Journal of Primatology, 32*(1), 1–12.

Manger, P. R., Spocter, M. A., & Patzke, N. (2013). The evolutions of large brain size in mammals: the 'over-700-gram club quartet'. *Brain, Behavior and Evolution, 82*(1), 68–78. doi.org/10.1159/000352056

Marshall, J. T., & Marshall, E. R. (1976). Gibbons and their territorial songs. *Science, 193*(4249), 235–237.

Marshall-Pescini, S., Schwarz, J. F. L., Kostelnik, I., Virányi, Z., & Range, F. (2017). Importance of a species' socioecology: wolves outperform dogs in a conspecific cooperation task. *Proceedings of the National Academy of Sciences USA, 114*(44), 11793–11798. doi.org/10.1073/pnas.1709027114

Martin, L. B., II, & Fitzgerald, L. (2005). A taste for novelty in invading house sparrows, *Passer domesticus*. *Behavioral Ecology, 16*(4), 702–707.

Mather, J. A. (2008). Cephalopod consciousness: behavioural evidence. *Consciousness and Cognition, 17*(1), 37–48. doi.org/10.1016/j.concog.2006.11.006

Mather, J. A. (2019). What is in an octopus's mind? *Animal Sentience, 26*(1).

Matsubara, S., Deeming, D. C., & Wilkinson, A. (2017). Cold-blooded cognition: new directions in reptile cognition. *Current Opinion in Behavioral Sciences, 16*, 126–130. doi.org/10.1016/j.cobeha.2017.06.006

McComb, K., Packer, C., & Pusey, A. (1994). Roaring and numerical assessment in contests between groups of female lions, *Panthera leo*. *Animal Behaviour, 47*(2), 379–387.

Melin, A. D., Young, H. C., Modossy, K. N., & Fedigan, L. M. (2014). Seasonality, extractive foraging and the evolution of primate sensorimotor intelligence. *Journal of Human Evolution, 71*, 77–86.

Menzel, R., & Giurfa, M. (2006). Dimensions of cognition in an insect, the honeybee. *Behavioral and Cognitive Neuroscience Reviews, 5*(1), 24–40. doi.org/10.1177/1534582306289522

Milton, K. (1981). Distribution patterns of tropical plant foods as an evolutionary stimulus to primate mental development. *American Anthropologist, 83*(3), 534–548. doi.org/10.1525/aa.1981.83.3.02a00020

Mink, J. W., Blumenschine, R. J., & Adams, D. B. (1981). Ratio of central nervous system to body metabolism in vertebrates: its constancy and functional basis. *American Journal of Physiology, 241*(3), R203–R212.

Mitani, J. C. (1988). Male gibbon (*Hylobates agilis*) singing behavior: natural history, song variations and function. *Ethology, 79*(3), 177–194. doi.org/10.1111/j.14390310.1988.tb00710.x

Moskat, C., Elek, Z., Ban, M., Geltsch, N., & Hauber, M. E. (2017). Can common cuckoos discriminate between neighbours and strangers by their calls? *Animal Behaviour 126*, 253–260.

Nicol, S. (2013). Behaviour and ecology of monotremes. In K. W. S. Ashwell (Ed.),

Neurobiology of monotremes: brain evolution in our distant mammalian cousins (pp. 17–30). Collingwood, Australia: CSIRO Publishing.

Njegovan, M., & Weisman, R. (1997). Pitch discrimination in field- and isolation-reared black-capped chickadees (*Parus atricapillus*). *Journal of Comparative Psychology*, *111*(3), 294–301. doi.org/10.1037/0735-7036.111.3.294

Nogueira, S. S. C., Abreu, S. A., Peregrino, H., & Nogueira-Filho, S. L. G. (2014). The effects of feeding unpredictability and classical conditioning on pre-release training of white-lipped peccary (Mammalia, Tayassuidae). *PLoS ONE*, *9*(1), 1–6.

Nogueira, S. S. C., Calazans, S. G., Costa, T. S. O., Peregrino, H., & Nogueira-Filho, S. L. G. (2011). Effects of varying feed provision on behavioral patterns of farmed collared peccary (Mammalia, Tayassuidae). *Applied Animal Behaviour Science*, *132*(3–4), 193–199.

Ogutu, J. O., Owen-Smith, N., Piepho, H., & Dublin, H. T. (2015). How rainfall variation influences reproductive patterns of African savanna ungulates in an equatorial region where photoperiod variation is absent. *PLoS ONE*, *10*(8), 1–13.

Papini, M. R., Mustaca, A. E., & Bitterman, M. E. (1988). Successive negative contrast in the consummatory responding of didelphid marsupials. *Animal Learning & Behavior*, *16*(1), 53–57. doi.org/10.3758/BF03209043

Perdue, B. M., Snyder, R. J., Zhihe, Z., Marr, M. J., & Maple, T. L. (2011). Sex differences in spatial ability: a test of the range size hypothesis in the order Carnivora. *Biology Letters*, 7(3), rsbl20101116. doi.org/10.1098/rsbl.2010.1116

Pincemy, G., Dobson, F. S., & Jouventin, P. (2010). Homosexual mating displays in penguins. *Ethology*, *116*(12), 1210–1216. doi.org/10.1111/j.1439-0310.2010.01835.x

Pisa, P. E., & Agrillo, C. (2009). Quantity discrimination in felines: a preliminary investigation of the domestic cat (*Felis silvestris catus*). *Journal of Ethology*, *27*(2), 289–293.

Pontzer, H., Raichlen, D. A., Gordon, A. D., Schroepfer-Walker, K. K., Hare, B., O'Neill, M. C., & Rosso, S. R. (2013). Primate energy expenditure and life history. *Proceedings of the National Academy of Sciences USA*, *111*(4), 1433–1437. doi.org/10.1073/pnas.1316940111

Premack, D., & Woodruff, G. (1978). Does the chimpanzee have a theory of mind? *Behavioral and Brain Sciences*, *1*(4), 515–526. doi.org/10.1017/S0140525X00076512

Range, F., Möslinger, H., & Virányi, Z. (2012). Domestication has not affected the understanding of means–end connections in dogs. *Animal Cognition*, *15*(4), 597–607. doi.org/10.1007/s10071-012-0488-8

Reader, S. M., & Laland, K. (2002). Social intelligence, innovation and advanced brain size in primates. *Proceedings of the National Academy of Sciences USA*, *99*(7), 4436–4441.

Robinson, T. G., & Eisenberg, J. F. (1985). Group size and foraging habits of the collared peccary (*Tayassu tajacu*). *Journal of Mammalogy*, *66*(1), 153–155.

Rodríguez-Estévez, V., Sánchez-Rodríguez, M., Gómez-Castro, A. G., & Edwards, S. A. (2010). Group sizes and resting locations of free range pigs when grazing in a natural environment. *Applied Animal Behaviour Science*, *127*(1–2), 28–36.

Rosati, A. G. (2017). Foraging cognition: reviving the ecological intelligence hypothesis. *Trends in Cognitive Science*, *21*(9), 719–816.

Rosati, A. G., & Hare, B. (2012). Chimpanzees and bonobos exhibit divergent spatial memory development. *Developmental Science*, *15*(6), 840–853.

Roth, T. C., LaDage, L. D., & Pravosudov, V. V. (2010). Learning capabilities enhanced in harsh environments: a common garden approach. *Proceedings of the Royal Society of London. B: Biological Sciences*, *277*(1697), 3187–3193.

Salva, O. R., Sovrano, V. A., & Vallortigara, G. (2014). What can fish brains tell us about visual perception? *Frontiers in Neural Circuits*, 8, 119. doi.org/10.3389/fncir.2014.00119

Sayol, F., Maspons, J., Lapiedra, O., Iwaniuk, A. N., Székely, T. & Sol, D. (2016). Environmental variation and the evolution of large brains in birds. *Nature Communications*, 7, 13971.

Schluessel, V., Kraniotakes, H., & Bleckmann, H. (2014). Visual discrimination of rotated 3D objects in Malawi cichlids (*Pseudotropheus* sp.): a first indication for form constancy in fishes. *Animal Cognition*, *17*(2), 359–371. doi.org/10.1007/s10071-013-0667-2

Scott, J. L., Matheson, S. M., & Yack, J. E. (2010). Variation on a theme: vibrational signaling in caterpillars of the rose hook-tip moth, *Oreta rosea. Journal of Insect Science, 10*(1), 54, 1–15. doi.org/10.1673/031.010.5401

Sherry, D. F., & Hoshooley, J. S. (2010). Seasonal hippocampal plasticity in food-storing birds. *Philosophical Transactions of the Royal Society B: Biological Sciences, 365*(1542), 933–943.

Shettleworth, S. (2003). Memory storing and hippocampal specialization in food-storing birds: challenges for research in comparative cognition. *Brain, Behaviour, and Evolution, 62*(2), 108–116.

Shettleworth, S. J. (2009). The evolution of comparative cognition: is the snark still a boojum? *Behavioural Processes, 80*(3), 210–217. doi.org/10.1016/j.beproc.2008.09.001

Shultz, S., & Dunbar, R. (2010). Species differences in executive function correlate with hippocampus volume and neocortex ratio across nonhuman primates. *Journal of Comparative Psychology, 124*(3), 252–260.

Siviter, H., Deeming, D. C., van Giezen, M. F. T., & Wilkinson, A. (2017). Incubation environment impacts the social cognition of adult lizards. *Royal Society Open Science, 4*(11), 170742.

Smith, D. G., & Reid, F. A. (1979). Roles of the song repertoire in red-winged blackbirds. *Behavioural Ecology and Sociobiology, 5*(3), 279–290.

Smith, J. D., Beran, M. J., Couchman, J. J., Coutinho, M. V. C., & Boomer, J. B. (2009). The curious incident of the capuchins. *Comparative Cognition & Behavior Reviews, 4*, 61–64. doi.org/10.3819/ccbr.2009.40008

Sneddon, L. U. (2015). Pain in aquatic animals. *Journal of Experimental Biology, 218*, 967–976. doi.org/10.1242/jeb.088823

Sneddon, L. U., Elwood, R. W., Adamo, S. A., & Leach, M. C. (2014). Defining and accessing animal pain. *Animal Behaviour, 97*, 201–212.

Sneddon, L. U., Lopez-Luna, J., Wolfenden, D. C. C., Leach, M. C., Valentim, A. M., Steenbergen, P. J., Bardine, N., Currie, A. D., Broom, D. M., & Brown, C. (2018). Fish sentience denial: muddying the waters. *Animal Sentience*, 21(1).

Sol, D. (2009). The cognitive-buffer hypothesis for the evolution of large brains. In R. Dukas & J. M. Ratcliffe (Eds), *Cognitive ecology II*, (pp. 111–136). Chicago: The University of Chicago Press.

Sol, D., Duncan, R. P., Blackburn, T. M., Cassey, P., & Lefebvre, L. (2005). Big brains, enhanced cognition, and response of birds to novel environments. *Proceedings of the National Academy of Sciences USA, 102*(15), 5460–5465.

Soluto, A., Bione, C. B. C., Bastos, M., Bezerra, B. M., Fragaszy, D., & Schiel, N. (2011). Critically endangered blonde capuchins fish for termites and use new techniques to accomplish the task. *Biology Letters, 7*(4), 532–535.

Srinivasan, M., Zhang, S., & Reinhard, J. (2006). Small brains, smart minds: vision, perception, navigation, and 'cognition' in insects. In E. Warrant & D. Nilsson (Eds), *Invertebrate vision* (pp. 462–493). New York, NY: Cambridge University Press.

Sturdy, C. B., Bloomfield, L. L., Farrell, T. M., Avey, M. T., & Weisman, R. G. (2007). Auditory category perception as a natural cognitive activity in songbirds. *Comparative Cognition & Behavior Reviews, 2*(1), 93–110.

Sussman, R. W., Rasmussen, D. T., & Raven, P. H. (2013). Rethinking primate origins again. *American Journal of Primatology, 75*(2), 95–106.

Tamaki, S. (2015). Hikikomori: adolescence without end (*Shakaiteki Hikikomori: Owaranai Shishunki*), *Social Science Japan Journal, 18*(1), 138–141. doi.org/10.1093/ssjj/jyu026

Tattersall, I., & Delson, E. (1999). Primates. In R. Singer (Ed.), *Encyclopedia of paleontology (3rd ed.)*. London: Routledge.

van de Waal, E., & Bshary, R. (2011). Contact with human facilities appears to enhance technical skills in wild vervet monkeys. *Folia Primatologica, 81*(5), 282–291. doi.org/10.1159/000322628

van Horik, J. O., Clayton, N. S., & Emery, N. J. (2012). Convergent evolution of cognition in corvids, apes and other animals. In J. Vonk & T. K. Shackelford (Eds), *The Oxford handbook of comparative evolutionary psychology* (pp. 80–101). New York, NY: Oxford University Press.

van Schaik, C. P., Deaner, R. O., & Merrill, M. Y. (1999). The conditions for tool use in primates: implications for the evolution of material culture. *Journal of Human Evolution, 36*(6), 719–741.

Vitale Shreve, K. R., & Udell, M. A. R. (2015). What's inside your cat's head? A review of cat (*Felis silvestris catus*) cognition research past, present and future. *Animal Cognition*, *18*(6), 1195–1206.

Vonk, J. (2019). A fish eye view of the mirror test. *Learning and Behavior*. doi.org/10.3758/s13420-019-00385-6

Vonk, J. (in press). A stalemate in theorizing about mindreading in nonhuman animals: a bottom-up approach. Invited chapter for *The Mind-Reading Brains*, edited by F. Grasso, J. E. Burgos, Ó. García-Leal, and R. Akram, Springer Publishers.

Vonk, J., Allard, S., Torgerson-White, L., Bennett, C., Galvan, M., McGuire, M., Hamilton, J., Johnson-Ulrich, Z., & Lieb. J. M. (2015). Manipulating spatial and visual cues in a win-stay foraging task in captive grizzly bears (*Ursus arctos horribilus*). In E. A. Thayer (Ed.), *Spatial, long- and short-term memory: functions, differences and effects of injury* (pp. 47–60). Hauppauge, NY: Nova Publishers.

Vonk, J., & Aradhye, C. (2015). Evolution of cognition. In M. Muehlenbein (Ed.), *Basics in human evolution* (pp. 479–488). London: Elsevier.

Vonk, J., & Beran, M. J. (2012). Bears 'count' too: quantity estimation and comparison in black bears (*Ursus americanus*). *Animal Behaviour*, *84*(1), 231–238.

Vonk, J., & Jett, S. E. (2018). 'Bear-ly' learning: limits of abstraction in black bear cognition. *Animal Behavior and Cognition*, *5*(1), 68–78. doi.org/10.26451/abc.05.01.06.2018

Vonk, J., Jett, S. E., & Mosteller, K. W. (2012). Concept formation in American black bears (*Ursus americanus*). *Animal Behaviour*, *84*(4), 953–964.

Vonk, J., & Shackelford, T. K. (2012). Comparative evolutionary psychology: a united discipline for the study of evolved traits. In J. Vonk & T. Shackelford (Eds), *Oxford handbook of comparative evolutionary psychology* (pp. 547–560). New York, NY: Oxford University Press.

Waters, R. M., Bowers, B. B., & Burghardt, G. M. (2017). Personality and individuality in reptile behavior. In J. Vonk, A. Weiss & S. A. Kuczaj (Eds), *Personality in nonhuman animals* (pp. 153–184). Springer, Cham. doi.org/10.1007/978-3-319-59300-5_8

White, A. M. (2010). A pigheaded compromise: do competition and predation explain variation in warthog group size? *Behavioral Ecology*, *21*(3), 485–492.

Wikmark, G., & Warren, J. M. (1972). Delayed response learning by cage-reared normal and prefrontal cats. *Psychonomic Science*, *26*(5), 243–245.

Wilkinson, A., & Huber, L. (2012). Cold-blooded cognition: reptilian cognitive abilities. In T. K. Shackelford & J. Vonk (Eds), *The Oxford handbook of comparative evolutionary psychology* (pp. 130–144). New York, NY: Oxford University Press.

Wilson, E. O. (2013). On human nature. In S. M. Downes & E. Machery (Eds), *Arguing about human nature: contemporary debates* (pp. 7–23) New York: Routledge/Taylor & Francis Group.

Wynne, C. D., & McLean, I. G. (1999). The comparative psychology of marsupials. *Australian Journal of Psychology*, *51*(2), 111–116. doi.org/10.1080/00049539908255344

Yasukawa, K., & Searcy, W. A. (1984). Song repertoires and density assessment in red-winged blackbirds: further tests of the Beau Geste hypothesis. *Behavioral Ecology and Sociobiology*, *16*, 171–175.

Zamisch, V., & Vonk, J. (2012). Spatial memory in captive American black bears (*Ursus americanus*). *Journal of Comparative Psychology*, *126*(4), 372–387.

Zernicki, B. (1999). Visual discrimination learning under switching procedure in visually deprived cats. *Behavioural Brain Research*, *100*(1–2), 237–244.

Zhao, L., Mao, M., & Liao, W. B. (2016). No evidence for the 'expensive-tissue hypothesis' in the dark-spotted frog, *Pelophylax nigromaculatus. Acta Herpetologica*, *11*(1), 69–73.

Zollinger, S. A. (2007). *Performance constraints and vocal complexity in birdsong: evidence from a vocal mimic* (Order No. 3277967). Available from ProQuest Dissertations & Theses Global. (304851865).

Cross-Cultural Research

Menelaos Apostolou

INTRODUCTION

Cross-cultural studies employ data from many societies in order to examine the range of human behavior in different cultural settings (Ember and Ember, 2009). In this chapter, I assess the importance of cross-cultural research for the field of evolutionary psychology. In particular, evolutionary psychology is based on the premise that the mind is the product of adaptations that have evolved in the ancestral human environment, which is different in several ways from the contemporary (Tooby and Cosmides, 2005). Accordingly, in order to understand what adaptations have evolved to do, knowledge of the ancestral human condition is necessary, with cross-cultural anthropological and historical research being valid tools for reconstructing the ancestral human environment. Furthermore, evolutionary psychologists assume that adaptations are shared by most members of our species but the range of responses they produce is contingent on prevailing environmental conditions (Tooby and

Cosmides, 2005, 2015). Accordingly, evolutionary hypotheses on how a mechanism works usually predict consistency as well as variation across cultural contexts, rendering cross-cultural research important for testing the predictions which are derived from these hypotheses.

RECONSTRUCTING THE PAST

One key premise of evolutionary psychology is that mechanisms were designed by natural selection to solve adaptive problems regularly faced by our hunter-gatherer ancestors (Tooby and Cosmides, 2005). As the way of life in contemporary post-industrial societies differs in several ways from the way of life of ancestral hunting and gathering societies, one implication of this argument is that the evolutionary function of these mechanisms cannot be readily understood in reference to the contemporary context. To quote John Tooby and Leda Cosmides (2015: 20), founders of the field of evolutionary psychology:

> Although the behavior generated by our evolved programs would have been, on average, adaptive (reproduction promoting) in ancestral environments, there is no guarantee that it will also be now. Modern environments differ importantly from ancestral ones, particularly when it comes to social behavior. We no longer live in small, face-to-face societies, in seminomadic bands consisting typically of 50 to 150 people, many of whom were close relatives. Yet, our cognitive programs were designed for that social world.

In this perspective, certain aspects of human behavior, which at first do not make sense, do so when this insight is adopted. For instance, a tendency to eat more food than necessary, which leads to becoming overweight, appears to be enigmatic if one attempts to figure out its evolutionary origins in terms of the modern post-industrial environment. That is, there is so much food around, it is not clear why food-intake regulation mechanisms have evolved to motivate people to eat more than they need, with the consequence of becoming obese and facing health issues, such as cardiovascular diseases, diabetes, and cancers associated with excess weight.

Evolutionary thinking gives us a sound answer: the food-intake regulation mechanisms we carry with us today have evolved in an ancestral context where food supply was scarce and unpredictable. When food was available (e.g., a kill was made), the optimum strategy in that context would be to eat more than necessary for that day's needs and store the rest in the form of fat that could be used in the following days when food may be scarce. A strategy where individuals would eat 'just enough' would not be optimal given a high chance of there being no food the next day. Thus, selection forces have shaped food-intake regulation mechanisms to follow the former strategy (Wells, 2006). This strategy is not optimal for the contemporary post-industrial context where food supply is predictable and in ample supply as it leads to

obesity and associated health problems. Yet, the transition from an environment where food supply is scarce and unpredictable to an environment where it is ample and predictable has taken place too recently for selection forces to have been able to adjust food-intake regulation mechanisms to work optimally in modern conditions. Therefore, the food-intake behavior we observe today is optimal for an ancestral environment and not for our own (Wells, 2006).

In sum, in an evolutionary psychological perspective, human behavior is generated by mechanisms which have evolved to solve recurrent problems of survival and reproduction that our ancestors faced. It follows that in order to understand human behavior, we need to understand the specific problems that the underlying mechanisms have evolved to solve in the ancestral environment. However, because the ancestral human environment is different from our own, these problems cannot be understood using the contemporary environment as a model of the ancestral one, and consequently, knowledge of the latter is necessary. Cross-cultural anthropological research is one way to reconstruct the ancestral human environment.

Cross-Cultural Anthropological Research

The hunting and gathering period of human evolution

From the emergence of the *Homo* species about two million years ago until the agropastoral revolution about 10,000 years ago, our ancestors lived in small nomadic groups of 50–150 individuals who based their subsistence on hunting animals and gathering plants (Lee and DeVore, 1968). This was the lengthiest period of human evolution, and because evolutionary change proceeds slowly, it has been assumed that most of human evolution took place during that period (Tooby and Cosmides, 2005). Knowledge about the human condition in this stage of human evolution is difficult to gain, we lack written documents about their patterns of life. Scholars can employ archeological evidence in order to reconstruct ancestral environments. For instance, archeological findings inform us that during the hunting and gathering period, our ancestors lived in small groups, had simple technology, and faced violent conflicts (Arnold, 1996). Still, archeological evidence is limited in what it can tell us about most aspects of the ancestral social environment, because many aspects of human behavior do not leave behind archeological clues that would enable a meaningful reconstruction. For instance, how mate choice took place in ancestral hunter-gatherer societies is difficult to infer from the archeological record, as it does not leave clues that an archeologist can unearth and study.

On the other hand, the anthropological record can provide rich information about the ancestral human condition. More specifically, the agropastoral revolution which took place about 10,000 years ago resulted in human societies shifting their mode of subsistence from hunting animals and gathering plants to herding animals and cultivating plants (Bocquet-Appel, 2011). Yet, not all human societies made the transition to agropastoralism, and several societies still rely for their subsistence on hunting and gathering. The way of life and social organization of these societies is likely to be similar to the way of life of ancestral hunter-gatherer societies, which means that, by studying the former, we can reconstruct the environment of the latter (Lee and DeVore, 1968). Anthropologists have studied these societies in detail, producing a rich anthropological record which can be used for this purpose.

Contemporary hunter-gatherer societies, as all other societies, exhibit considerable variation in their patterns of life. One reason is that they occupy different environmental niches, and their cultural patterns have adjusted to these niches. Another reason is that societies are influenced by other societies (Naroll, 1965). For this reason, if the study of one society reveals an idiosyncratic pattern – for instance, that people are free to choose their own partners – it cannot be inferred that a similar pattern was typical of ancestral hunter-gatherer societies. This pattern may reflect a specific environmental reality or an influence from neighboring groups and may not be indicative of the hunter-gatherer way of life. For example, if in one society women actively engage in hunting small animals and participate in the hunting of large animals (see Stange, 1998), it would be erroneous to infer that this pattern reflects the ancestral human condition, that is, that in ancestral human societies women hunted animals, because this pattern could only be specific to that culture.

On the other hand, if a pattern of interest is typical of contemporary hunter-gatherer societies, it is more likely to reflect the hunter-gatherer way of life and thus, of ancestral hunter-gatherer human societies. To provide an example, if we take a large sample of contemporary hunter-gatherer societies, and we find that in almost all of them hunting is conducted by men with limited or no contribution from women, it is most probably the case that this pattern is characteristic of hunter-gatherer societies, and that it was typical of ancestral ones. Put differently, in the light of the finding that in almost all contemporary hunter-gatherer societies hunting is conducted by men, it is unlikely that in ancestral human societies hunting was conducted by women.

In effect, studying one hunter-gatherer society is far from adequate for figuring out what is typical in such societies, and what is needed is cross-cultural anthropological research. In particular, it is important to study anthropological evidence from different hunter-gatherer societies, and examine whether a pattern of interest is found in most hunter-gatherer societies, and is therefore typical of them. In such a case, there would be good reasons to believe that this pattern was also typical of ancestral hunter-gatherer societies.

The agropastoral period of human evolution

About 10,000 years ago, the agropastoral revolution took place, and most human societies started shifting their subsistence from hunting and gathering to cultivating land and herding animals (Bocquet-Appel, 2011). This transition brought considerable changes to social organization: societies became sedentary and much more populous, and specialization and the use of money emerged. Such changes have altered considerably the selection pressures in several domains, which in turn likely precipitates evolutionary change. Many evolutionary scholars consider this period of human evolution to be relatively short for substantial evolutionary change to have occurred; they argue that when trying to understand the evolutionary origins of an adaptation the emphasis should be placed on the foraging period of human evolution (e.g., Tooby and Cosmides, 2005, 2015) – but evidence indicates that this may not be the case.

More specifically, 10,000 years translates to about 400 generations in our species (Irons, 1998). Experiments with non-human animals have demonstrated that 400 generations are more than enough for substantial evolutionary change to take place. For example, in Galapagos finches, a drought resulted in large changes in beak size in only one generation (Weiner, 1995). Grant (1986) estimated that 23 such episodes of evolution could transform one species of finch into another. To provide another example, civil war gripped Mozambique for 15 years ending in 1992. One victim of the war was elephants; about 90% of their population was eliminated to supply the ivory trade. Elephants that did not grow tusks had selective advantage, as they were less likely to be hunted and killed. Under normal circumstances, tusklessness occurs only in about 2–4% of female African elephants. Yet, in Mozambique, of the 200 known adult females, 51% of those that survived the war – animals 25 years or older – are tuskless, and 32% of the female elephants born since the war are tuskless (*National Geographic*, 2018).

In our species, Mekel-Bibrov and colleagues (2005) have shown that a variant of a gene that regulates brain size appeared about 5,800 years ago, and has swept to high frequency under strong positive selection since then. Furthermore, humans have an abundance of rare genetic variants in the protein-encoding sections of the genome (Tennessen et al., 2012). One study investigated when many of those rare variants arose (Fu et al., 2013). In particular, the researchers used deep sequencing to locate and date more than one million single-nucleotide variants – locations where a single letter of the DNA sequence is different from other individuals – in the genomes of 6,500 African and European Americans. The findings indicated that the majority of variants were picked up during the past 5,000–10,000 years. More specifically, the researchers reported that of the 1.15 million single-nucleotide variants found among more than 15,000 protein-encoding genes, 73% arose in the past 5,000 years.

In sum, there are good reasons to believe that the 10,000 years of human evolution following the agropastoral revolution has probably not been a long enough period for complex new adaptations to arise, but may have been more than enough for substantial evolutionary change in the existing adaptations to have occurred. Accordingly, this period, being also the most recent, is especially relevant for enabling us to understand the evolutionary origins of a trait of interest. In turn, reconstructing the ancestral agropastoral environment is important if the nature of human behavior is to be understood. For this purpose, cross-cultural anthropological research can be employed. In particular, the anthropological record is rich in studies of societies which base their subsistence on agriculture and the herding of animals. Cross-cultural research can enable us to identify the patterns of mating typical in contemporary agropastoral societies. If these are typical of the agropastoral way of life, then they are likely to be typical of ancestral agropastoral societies.

Cross-cultural anthropological research also gives us the ability to assess the impact of the agropastoral revolution on the evolutionary trajectory of a trait in question. More specifically, cross-cultural anthropological research on hunter-gatherer societies enables us to reconstruct a specific aspect of interest of the ancestral hunter-gatherer environment. In the same vein, cross-cultural anthropological research on agropastoral societies can enable us to reconstruct this aspect of the environment in those societies. Comparisons between the two can enable us to assess the impact of the agropastoral revolution on this environmental aspect, and consequently, the impact of the agropastoral revolution on adaptations interacting with it (Apostolou, 2010). Accordingly, cross-cultural anthropological research constitutes a powerful tool with which to reconstruct the ancestral human condition and to examine how the ancestral environment has changed across major transition periods.

Limitations of the cross-cultural anthropological research

The most important limitation of anthropological cross-cultural research in reconstructing the ancestral human condition is that it is inferential; that is, we infer that the typical patterns of contemporary hunter-gatherer and agropastoral societies have been typical of the respective ancestral ones. Yet this is only a reasonable inference, and may be in error. The reason is that contemporary hunters and gatherers and agropastoralists may differ from ancestral ones, and, therefore, what is true for the former may not be true for the latter. For instance, contemporary hunters and gatherers live in marginalized areas of the globe, which was not the case for our ancestors (Brody, 2001). Also, contemporary hunters and gatherers and agropastoralists may be influenced by their more advanced neighbors (Wilmsen, 1989). Although these criticisms are to some degree valid, the anthropological record remains a reasonable way to reconstruct the ancestral human condition (Marlowe, 2005).

Cross-Cultural Historical Research

The inference limitation discussed above could be partially addressed by confirming our hypotheses about ancestral human societies using evidence from different sources. In the light of the limitations of the archeological record in helping us to reconstruct the ancestral human condition, and the lack of written records, such an endeavor is not feasible in the ancestral hunter-gatherer context.

On the other hand, we have rich historical records depicting the way of life in ancestral agropastoral societies that can be useful in reconstructing the ancestral human condition, and provide an independent source for confirming the conclusions from cross-cultural anthropological research. More specifically, following the agropastoral revolution, several societies invented forms of writing (Robinson, 1995). Many of their written records have survived today, leaving us with a rich source of valuable information about the ancestral human condition following the move from hunting and gathering to farming. Since ancestral agropastoral societies occupied different areas of the globe at different times, they exhibited considerable variation in their patterns of life. Accordingly, the study of one historical society is insufficient for understanding the condition of all. Thus, cross-cultural historical research could enable us to identify what is typical of ancestral human societies – that is, what is usually found in them.

Limitations of cross-cultural historical research

Cross-cultural research based on historical evidence has the main advantage that it is not inferential – the primary historical records depict what historians observed happening in a specific society at a specific point in time. Yet, such evidence comes with its own limitations – historical records may be incomplete, and therefore unable to provide us with detailed accounts for all aspects of the environments we are interested in. They also suffer from bias which affects the accuracy of the information provided. For instance, almost all historical documents have been written by men, with the effect that women are underreported or inaccurately described.

Reconstructing the Ancestral Environment in the Domain of Mating

In evolutionary terms, what matters most is not the survival of the organism but the perpetuation of the genes that built it (Dawkins, 1989). In sexually reproducing species, passing genes to future generations requires gaining sexual access to the reproductive capacity of the opposite sex, and those who fail to do so experience decreased probability of having their genes represented in future generations. This tremendous evolutionary cost translates into strong selection pressures being exercised on individuals to evolve adaptations that would enable them to succeed in this endeavor. In turn, it is expected that much of human behavior would be motivated by success in mating, which renders the study of mating to be of primary importance in the field of human behavior (Buss, 2017).

Following the principles of evolutionary psychology, psychologists study human mating and the adaptations involved in it, in reference to the ancestral environment. Accordingly, we would expect them to attempt to first reconstruct the ancestral human environment with respect to mating, perhaps by using cross-cultural anthropological research, and subsequently to develop evolutionary theories on human mating. Or they would develop theories and subsequently attempt to examine whether they are consistent with the ancestral human condition as indicated by the anthropological record. Yet, this did not happen, with many scholars assuming that the ancestral human environment in the domain of mating was similar to the modern condition in one key dimension, namely, that mate choice was freely exercised (e.g., Miller, 2000). Cross-cultural

anthropological and historical research depict nevertheless a different story.

More specifically, in order to reconstruct the ancestral human condition with respect to mating during the foraging period of human evolution, one study collected data from a sample of 190 contemporary hunter-gatherer societies, and analyzed their mating patterns (Apostolou, 2007b). It was found that the most frequent mode of long-term mating, in approximately 70% of cases, was arranged marriage, where parents chose spouses for their children, while marriage on the basis of free choice was found in less than 5% of the societies in the sample. Similarly, in order to reconstruct ancestral human condition with respect to mating during the agropastoral period of human evolution, Apostolou (2010) employed anthropological evidence from the Standard Cross-Cultural Sample (SCCS), which included 186 pre-industrial societies of different subsistence types (Murdock and White, 1980). For the societies which based their subsistence on agriculture, it was found that in 7% of the cases women could choose their own spouses with little influence from their parents, in 40.4% they could choose their own spouses but their choices were subject to their parents' approval, in 28.1% marriages were arranged, and finally, in 24.6% of the cases both arranged marriage and free courtship marriage were practiced. For men, in 23.2% of the cases marriage was based on free courtship, in 23.2% on courtship subject to parental approval, in 30.4% marriages were arranged, and in 23.2% of the cases both arranged marriage and courtship marriage were practiced. A different study analyzed the historical records for 16 societies for a time span of approximately 5,000 years (Apostolou, 2012). In all societies, the typical form of mating was arranged marriage. There was only one exception, for which the historical record was inconclusive.

The anthropological and historical records indicate further that individual choice was also present, even in societies where marriages were arranged. In particular, children could accept the spouses that their parents had chosen for them, but would subsequently divorce them, or they could stay married, but find extra-pair partners. Individuals could also exercise choice in relationships prior to marriage. Cross-cultural historical and anthropological research indicated that divorce, pre-marital and extra-marital relationships were common in contemporary and in historical pre-industrial societies (Apostolou, 2017a). For instance, one study employed the SCCS and found that in societies with arranged marriages, extra-marital affairs of women were not uncommon – more than 50% of the cases (Apostolou, 2017a). This evidence indicates that arranged marriage restricts mate choice but not entirely.

Moreover, the Standard Cross-Cultural Sample included pre-industrial societies which based their subsistence on hunting and gathering, as well as societies which based their subsistence on agriculture and animal husbandry, enabling comparisons between the two. Accordingly, one study found that arranged marriage was more common for men in agropastoral than in hunter-gatherer societies (Apostolou, 2010). Thus, the transition from a mode of subsistence based on hunting and gathering to one based on agriculture and the herding of animals is likely to have resulted in the reduction of the freedom for men to exercise choice. One reason is that agropastoral societies produce more wealth than foraging societies, and this is usually inherited through the male line. This in turn augments the ability of parents to control the mate choices of their sons as the latter have more to lose if they disobey the former (Apostolou, 2016).

In sum, cross-cultural anthropological and historical research indicates that in ancestral human societies, free mate choice was constrained and long-term partners were frequently chosen by parents. Individual mate choice was limited but present, manifested in divorce, and pre-marital and extra-marital relationships. The agropastoral revolution

would have resulted in strengthening parental grip over sons' mate choices. The findings from cross-cultural anthropological and historical research need to be integrated in evolutionary research on human mating, which currently proceeds on the assumption that free mate choice was the dominant mode of mating in ancestral human societies.

Such findings can shed light on several phenomena which might not be otherwise understood. For instance, despite mating being of great importance, it appears that a considerable proportion of people today face difficulties in attracting a partner, with the most commonly reported difficulty being poor flirting capacity (Apostolou, 2017b, 2019). If one assumes that in ancestral human societies mate choice was freely exercised, we would expect that selection forces would have selected against poor capacity for flirting, so poor flirting capacity would not be a common problem today. Under the cross-culturally informed assumption that in ancestral human societies mate choice was regulated, this finding is much less enigmatic. People would receive partners predominantly from their parents, so selection forces might be relatively weak in endowing people with a good flirting capacity, which is, however, necessary in contemporary societies where mate choice is freely exercised (Apostolou, 2019).

CROSS-CULTURAL PSYCHOLOGICAL RESEARCH: TESTING EVOLUTIONARY HYPOTHESES

Cross-Cultural Research and Variation

One frequent misunderstanding about evolutionary arguments is that adaptations are inflexible mechanisms which produce the same response across different environments (Confer et al., 2010). This is, however, far from the truth. Most adaptations produce a range of responses which are dependent on environmental conditions (Buss et al., 2001; Pirlott and Schmitt, 2014). Consider human skin as an example; its color is not constant but varies with environmental conditions – it becomes darker during the summer months, when more melanin is produced that absorbs radiation from the sun, protecting the body from possible damage. Similarly, adaptations have evolved to produce responses which are contingent on the environment.

There are good reasons to believe that in ancestral as well as in contemporary human societies, the environment is not stable, with considerable changes occurring throughout an individual's lifetime. For instance, an abnormal weather phenomenon may destroy crops, considerably reducing food supply and giving rise to famine. A war could erupt and many men might be killed, which changes significantly the balance between men and women. Accordingly, adaptations are unlikely to have evolved to be unresponsive to environmental conditions, because this would not be optimal – if the environment changed, a fitness-decreasing response might be produced.

In consequence, we would expect that most adaptations would be responsive to environmental conditions. Because human societies vary considerably in many dimensions – some are more wealthy, egalitarian, tolerant, religious, populous, or technologically advanced than others – we would expect that mechanisms would produce variation in behavioral output across societies. Thus, even if a specific adaptation is shared by all humans, variation is expected in the behavior produced by this adaptations, as not all people live in the same conditions. Accordingly, cross-cultural psychological research is necessary in order to understand how a mechanism produces different behaviors in different environments. A researcher would identify first particular inputs that might be relevant for an adaptation, then make predictions about how variation in those inputs will map onto outputs, and finally test those predictions across cultures.

Operational sex ratio and mating strategies

One aspect of culture that appears to evoke human mating adaptations is the operational sex ratio (Guttentag and Secord, 1983; Pedersen, 1991). The operational sex ratio is the ratio of males and females who are available to mate. The sex ratio is considered 'high' when the number of men significantly outsizes the number of women, and 'low' when there are relatively more women than men in the mating market (Schmitt, 2015).

Following sexual selection theory (Darwin, 1871), when males desire a specific trait in potential mating partners, females of that species tend to respond by competing in the expression and provision of that trait. As discussed above, men more than women tend to prefer short-term mating (Buss and Schmitt, 1993), which predicts that in cultural settings where the sex ratio is low – that is, there are more women than men – men are the scarce reproductive resource and can afford to demand that interested women fulfill their desires for casual sex. In consequence, the culture as a whole would become more short-term mating oriented (Pedersen, 1991). On the other hand, when the sex ratio is high – that is, there are more men available as mates than women – women are the scarce reproductive resource and can afford to demand long-term committed relationships from interested men. In this scenario, the culture as a whole would become more long-term mating oriented (Pedersen, 1991).

In an attempt to test Pedersen's (1991) theory, Schmitt (2005), using a sample of 14,059 participants across 48 nations, examined whether national sex ratios were correlated with direct measures of basic human mating strategies. He found that cultures with more men than women tended toward long-term mating, whereas cultures with more women than men tended toward short-term mating. Thus, human mating strategies appear to be responsive to the balance of men versus women in the local mating pool (Schmitt, 2015).

Operational sex ratio and in-law preferences

As discussed in the previous sections, cross-cultural anthropological research indicates that in ancestral human societies, parents exercised considerable influence over their children's mating decisions. Therefore, it was a common recurrence for parents to find themselves in a position to choose spouses for their children (Apostolou, 2014). Prospective sons- and daughters-in-law differed considerably in their mate value, which exercised considerable selection pressure on parents to evolve preferences that would guide their choices (Apostolou, 2007a).

One study examined in-law preferences in the Greek-Cypriot and in the Chinese cultural contexts (Apostolou and Wang, 2017). An important difference between the two cultures is the operational sex ratio. In the Republic of Cyprus the sex ratio is balanced, with a roughly equal number of men and women available as mates. On the other hand, in China, as a way to combat overpopulation, the 1979 one-child policy was initiated and prevented parents from having more than one child. Chinese parents favored male children, and so, possibly due to means such as selective abortion, sons outnumber daughters, resulting in a high sex ratio, with more men available as grooms and fewer women available as brides (Deng, 2000).

This difference enabled Chinese parents with daughters to be more selective than Chinese parents with sons. Accordingly, when comparing in-law preferences between cultural contexts, a significant interaction between the sex of the in-law and the culture emerged. When shifting from choosing a son-in-law to choosing a daughter-in-law, Chinese parents became considerably less selective (Apostolou and Wang, 2017). In other words, Chinese parents with sons, knowing the shortage of women, lowered their standards considerably in terms of what they would consider desirable for their sons. With no shortage of women in the Greek-Cypriot cultural context, the same thing did not happen for Greek-Cypriot parents with sons.

Cross-Cultural Research and Consistency

As discussed above, one premise of evolutionary psychology is that most human evolution took place in ancestral hunter-gatherer societies in the African continent (Tooby and Cosmides, 2005). Since all contemporary human societies emerged from these ancestral societies, it follows that across the globe, humans share the same adaptations. Still, evolution can progress rapidly when the environment changes considerably, so after leaving Africa most of our ancestors experienced considerable evolutionary change. Yet, several domains may not have been significantly affected by the exodus from Africa, meaning that the specific adaptations which interact with these environmental domains would remain relatively unaffected, and thus, be shared by people around the globe.

Accordingly, evolutionary psychological scholars frequently develop hypotheses about human behavior which have a cross-cultural component: if the aspect of the environment which is relevant in calibrating the adaptation in question is shared across societies, then it is predicted that the output of the adaptation would be more or less identical. Furthermore, psychological mechanisms may respond to environmental conditions; however, if these conditions do not change, it could be hypothesized that these mechanisms would produce similar responses across different human societies. Testing such hypotheses requires cross-cultural psychological research, where the behavior of interest could be measured across different cultures, and consistency could be examined.

Strategies of human mating

Men's and women's approach toward mating can be seen as strategic in the sense that people follow a strategy when engaging in mating that would have enabled their ancestors to have increased their reproductive success or fitness (Buss and Schmitt, 1993). Two such strategies will be discussed here:

short-term and long-term. A short-term mating strategy involves engaging in many casual relationships and investing little in any offspring that may come from them, while a long-term mating strategy involves establishing one or perhaps a few intimate relationships and investing heavily in any offspring that result (Buss and Schmitt, 1993, 2019). A short-term mating strategy is sometimes adopted by both sexes, but it could potentially be more beneficial for men than for women (Buss and Schmitt, 1993, 2019). In particular, following intercourse and successful fertilization of the egg by a sperm, a woman is obliged to divert parental investment to her offspring for about nine months, a period during which she cannot conceive another child. Accordingly, engaging in indiscriminate, short-term sex with numerous partners would bring few reproductive benefits to her. For example, a woman will tend to have only one child by mating with 100 fertile men over the course of a year, the same as a monogamous woman would have with one man during that time. This is not the case for men, however, who can accrue considerable reproductive benefits from adopting such a strategy, as they are not committed by pregnancy (Symons, 1979).

A man can produce 100 offspring by mating with 100 fertile women over the course of a year, whereas a monogamous man, similarly to a monogamous or a polygamous woman, would be able to sire only one child with his partner during that time. This difference translates into a strong selective pressure for men's short-term mating strategy to favor a desire for sexual variety (Buss and Schmitt, 1993, 2019). Moreover, this difference in the fitness benefits across the sexes is expected to have been consistently present during human evolutionary time, as it has been always the case that women got pregnant and men did not. Therefore, the sex difference, with men desiring more sexual variety than women is expected to occur universally, across cultures.

Using evidence from 62 cultural regions in 56 countries of the world, Schmitt and colleagues found that, universally, men agree to have sex after less time has elapsed than women, and that men expend more effort on seeking brief sexual relationships than women (Schmitt et al., 2003). For instance, across all cultures, nearly 25% of married men, but only 10% of married women, reported that they were actively seeking short-term, extra-marital relationships.

Women also engage in short-term mating, with one reason for doing so being to secure good genes for their children (Buss, 2000). More specifically, men are less willing to engage in a long-term intimate relationship with women of lower mate value to their own, but they are more willing to do so for a short-term relationship (Buss, 2017). Women can exploit the latter by entering into a long-term relationship with a man of similar mate value to their own, but they seek better genes in extra-pair intimate relationships. Thus, when engaging in short-term mating, women prefer traits such as good looks which indicate superior genetic quality (Buss, 2017). As a consequence, men who have such traits would be more successful in attracting short-term mates than men who do not. On this basis, it can be predicted that, across cultures, men who consider themselves attractive would be more likely to adopt a short-term mating strategy than men who do not consider themselves attractive (Gangestad and Simpson, 2000). Consistent with this prediction, in a cross-cultural study of 17,804 participants from 62 cultural regions, Schmitt and colleagues (2004) found that, in nearly all cultures, men who considered themselves attractive were more likely than other men to engage in short-term mating strategies.

Mate preferences

Women's fertility typically peaks in their early 20s and shows a sharp decrease with age (Thornhill and Thornhill, 1983). On the other hand, men's fertility is less steeply age-graded from puberty on than female fertility. This difference in fertility translates in differential selection pressures on female and male mate preferences, so that men prefer younger partners as mates than women (Buss, 1989). Across human cultures, female fertility is strongly age dependent, which predicts that this sex difference in preferences would be consistent across cultural contexts.

To test this prediction, Buss (1989) employed a sample of 10,047 participants from 37 samples drawn from 33 countries located on six continents and five islands. In all of the 37 samples, males preferred mates who were younger. In particular, he found that men preferred their spouses to be 2.66 years younger than them, on average. In order to validate this result, he secured demographic statistics of actual age at marriage. Although age at marriage is influenced by several other factors, it should predominantly reflect actual mating decisions. He found that across the 27 countries, the actual age differences between men and women at marriage ranged from 2.17 years (Ireland) to 4.92 years (Greece), all showing the wives to be, on average, younger than their husbands.

CONCLUSION

In conclusion, cross-cultural research is a powerful tool that enables evolutionary-minded scholars to reconstruct the ancestral human condition, and develop testable hypotheses about the evolutionary functions of specific adaptations under consideration. It is also an indispensable tool that enables the testing of specific hypotheses about how the response of an adaptation is likely to be consistent or vary across different cultural contexts.

REFERENCES

Apostolou, M. (2007a). Elements of parental choice: The evolution of parental preferences in relation to in-law selection. *Evolutionary Psychology*, 5(1), 70–83.

Apostolou, M. (2007b). Sexual selection under parental choice: The role of parents in the evolution of human mating. *Evolution and Human Behavior*, 28(6), 403–409.

Apostolou, M. (2010). Sexual selection under parental choice in agropastoral societies. *Evolution and Human Behavior*, 31(1), 39–47.

Apostolou, M. (2012). Sexual selection under parental choice: Evidence from sixteen historical societies. *Evolutionary Psychology*, 10(3), 504–518.

Apostolou, M. (2014). *Sexual selection under parental choice: The evolution of human mating behaviour*. Hove, UK: Psychology Press.

Apostolou, M. (2016). Sexual selection and the opportunity cost of free mate choice. *Theory in Biosciences*, 135(1–2), 45–57.

Apostolou, M. (2017a). Individual mate choice in an arranged marriage context: Evidence from the Standard Cross-Cultural Sample. *Evolutionary Psychological Science*, 3(3), 193–200.

Apostolou, M. (2017b). Why people stay single: An evolutionary perspective. *Personality and Individual Differences*, 111, 263–271.

Apostolou, M. (2019). Why men stay single? Evidence from Reddit. *Evolutionary Psychological Science*, 5(1), 87–97.

Apostolou, M., & Wang, Y. (2017). In-law preferences in China: What parents look for in the parents of their children's mates. *Evolutionary Psychology*, 15(3), 1474704917723913.

Arnold, J. E. (1996). The archaeology of complex hunter-gatherers. *Journal of Archaeological Method and Theory*, 3, 77–126.

Bocquet-Appel, J. P. (2011). When the world's population took off: The springboard of the Neolithic demographic transition. *Science*, 333(6042), 560–561.

Brody, H. (2001). *The other side of Eden*. New York: North Point Press.

Buss, D. M. (1989). Sex differences in human mate preferences: Evolutionary hypotheses tested in 37 cultures. *Behavioral & Brain Sciences*, 12(1), 1–49.

Buss, D. M. (2000). *The dangerous passion: Why jealousy is as necessary as love and sex*. New York: The Free Press.

Buss, D. M. (2017). *The evolution of desire: Strategies of human mating* (4th ed.). New York: Basic Books.

Buss, D. M., & Schmitt, D. P. (1993). Sexual strategies theory: An evolutionary perspective on human mating. *Psychological Review*, *100*(2), 204–231.

Buss, D. M., & Schmitt, D. P. (2019). Mate preferences and their behavioral manifestations. *Annual Review of Psychology*, *70*, 77–110.

Buss, D. M., Shackelford, T. K., Kirkpatrick, L. A., & Larsen, R. J. (2001). A half century of mate preferences: The cultural evolution of values. *Journal of Marriage and Families*, *63*(2), 492–503.

Confer, J. C., Easton, J. A., Fleischman, D. S., Goetz, C. D., Lewis, D. M., Perilloux, C., & Buss, D. M. (2010). Evolutionary psychology: Controversies, questions, prospects, and limitations. *American Psychologist*, *65*(2), 110–126.

Darwin, C. (1871). *The descent of man, and Selection in relation to sex*. London: John Murray.

Dawkins, R. (1989). *The selfish gene* (2nd ed.). Oxford: Oxford University Press.

Deng, G. (2000). The consequences of a low fertility rate and a comparatively high birth sex rate. *Journal of Tsinghua University (Philosophy and Social Sciences)*, *1*, 62–64.

Ember, C. R., & Ember, M. (2009). *Cross-cultural research methods* (2nd ed.). New York: AltaMira Press.

Fu, W., O'Connor, T. D., Jun, G., Kang, H. M., Abecasis, G., Leal, S. M., Gabriel, S., Rieder, M. J., Altshuler, D., Shendure, J., Nickerson, D. A., Bamshad, M. J., NHLBI Exome Sequencing Project, & Akey, J. M. (2012). Analysis of 6,515 exomes reveals the recent origin of most human protein-coding variants. *Nature*, *493*(7431), 216–220.

Gangestad, S. W., & Simpson, J. A. (2000). The evolution of human mating: Trade-offs and strategic pluralism. *Behavioral and Brain Sciences*, *23*(4), 573–644.

Grant, P. R. (1986). *Ecology and evolution of Darwin's finches*. Princeton, NJ: Princeton University Press.

Guttentag, M., & Secord, P. F. (1983). *Too many women? The sex ratio question*. Beverly Hills, CA: Sage.

Irons, W. (1998). Adaptive relevant environments versus the environment of evolutionary adaptedness. *Evolutionary Anthropology*, *6*(6), 194–204.

Lee, R. B., & DeVore, I. (1968). *Man the hunter*. New York: Aldine.

Marlowe, F. W. (2005). Hunter-gatherers and human evolution. *Evolutionary Anthropology*, *14*(2), 54–67.

Mekel-Bobrov, N., Gilbert, S. L., Evans, P. D., Vallender, E. J., Anderson, J. R., Hudson, R. R., Tishkoff, S. A., & Lahn, B. T. (2005). Ongoing adaptive evolution of ASPM, a brain size determinant in *Homo sapiens*. *Science*, *309*(5741), 1720–1722.

Miller, G. (2000). *The mating mind*. London: BCA.

Murdock, G. P., & White, D. R. (1980). Standard cross-cultural sample. In H. Barry & A. Schlegel (Eds), *Cross–cultural samples and codes* (pp. 3–43). Pittsburgh: University of Pittsburgh Press.

Naroll, R. (1965). Galton's problem: The logic of cross cultural research. *Social Research*, *32*(4), 428–451.

National Geographic (November 9, 2018). Under poaching pressure, elephants are evolving to lose their tusks, by D. F. Maron. Retrieved from: www.nationalgeographic.com/animals/2018/11/wildlife-watch-news-tuskless-elephants-behavior-change/

Pedersen, F. A. (1991). Secular trends in human sex ratios: Their influence on individual and family behavior. *Human Nature*, *2*(3), 271–291.

Pirlott, A., & Schmitt, D. P. (2014). Gendered sexual culture. In A. Cohen (Ed.), *New directions in the psychology of culture* (pp. 191–216). Washington, DC: American Psychological Association.

Robinson, A. (1995). *The story of writing*. London: Thames & Hudson.

Schmitt, D. P. (2005). Sociosexuality from Argentina to Zimbabwe: A 48-nation study of sex, culture, and strategies of human mating. *Behavioral and Brain Sciences*, *28*(2), 247–275.

Schmitt, D. P. (2015). Fundamentals of human mating strategies. In D. M. Buss (Ed.), *The handbook of evolutionary psychology, Second edition. Volume 1: Foundations.* (pp. 294–316). Hoboken, NJ: John Wiley & Sons.

Schmitt, D. P., Alcalay, L., Allensworth, M., Allik, J., Ault, L., Austers, I., et al. (2004). Patterns and universals of adult romantic attachment across 62 cultural regions: Are models of self and of other pancultural constructs? *Journal of Cross-Cultural Psychology*, *35*(4), 367–402.

Schmitt, D. P., Alcalay, L., Allik, J., Ault, L., Austers, I., Bennett, K. L., et al. (2003). Universal sex differences in the desire for sexual variety: Tests from 52 nations, 6 continents, and 13 islands. *Journal of Personality and Social Psychology*, *85*(1), 85–104.

Stange, M. Z. (1998). *Woman the hunter*. Boston: Beacon Press.

Symons, D. (1979). *The evolution of human sexuality*. New York: Oxford University Press.

Tennessen, J. A., Bigham, A. W., O'Connor, T. D., Fu, W., Kenny, E. E., Gravel, S., McGee, S., Do, R., Liu, X., Jun, G., Kang, H. M., Jordan, D., Leal, S. M., Gabriel, S., Rieder, M. J., Abecasis, G., Altshuler, D., Nickerson, D. A., Boerwinkle, E., Sunyaev, S., Bustamante, C. D., Bamshad, M. J., Akey, J. M., Broad GO, Seattle GO, NHLBI Exome Sequencing Project (2012). Evolution and functional impact of rare coding variation from deep sequencing of human exomes. *Science*, *337*(6090), 64–69.

Thornhill, R., & Thornhill, N. W. (1983). Human rape: An evolutionary analysis. *Ethology & Sociobiology*, *4*(3), 63–99.

Tooby, J., & Cosmides, L. (2005). Conceptual foundations of evolutionary psychology. In D. M. Buss (Ed.), *The handbook of evolutionary psychology* (pp. 5–67). Hoboken, NJ: Wiley.

Tooby, J., & Cosmides, L. (2015). The theoretical foundations of evolutionary psychology. In D. M. Buss (Ed.), *The handbook of evolutionary psychology, Second edition. Volume 1: Foundations.* (pp. 3–87). Hoboken, NJ: John Wiley & Sons.

Weiner, J. (1995). *The beak of the finch: A story of evolution in our time*. New York: Vintage Books.

Wells, J. C. K. (2006). The evolution of human fatness and susceptibility to obesity: An ethological approach. *Biological Reviews*, *81*(2), 183–205.

Wilmsen, E. N. (1989). *Land filled with flies: A political economy of the Kalahari*. Chicago: Chicago University Press.

Neuroscientific Methods

Jennifer Mundale

INTRODUCTION

It is intuitively obvious that the aims and methods of neuroscience and those of evolutionary psychology should intersect in a mutually productive way. Though intuitively obvious, this interdisciplinary prospect is more challenging, both empirically and conceptually, than is immediately apparent. What follows is an overview of both the challenges and the promise of applying neuroscientific methods to evolutionary psychology and is organized into three main sections: (1) a comparison of narrow vs. broad evolutionary psychology, (2) a re-conception of modularity and the information-processing model as empirically accessible by neuroscience, rather than as guiding assumptions of evolutionary psychology, and (3) an overview of the methods of neuroscience that can further the research goals of evolutionary psychology.

THE LIMITS OF NARROW EVOLUTIONARY PSYCHOLOGY

To discuss the disciplinary relevance of neuroscience to evolutionary psychology it is necessary that an older, yet persistent view about it be clarified and, in part, rejected. In short, it requires a careful distinction between what has come to be called 'narrow' vs. 'broad' evolutionary psychology. The term 'narrow evolutionary psychology' (NEP) was coined by Scher, Raushcer, and Wilson (Scher and Rauscher, 2003: xi). They note that in choosing the term 'narrow', they did not mean to suggest that it 'has an inappropriately narrow point of view, but merely to suggest that the approach adopts a narrower range of assumptions than "broad evolutionary psychology" (or, just "evolutionary psychology" [EP])' (Scher and Rauscher, 2003: 31). For the present purposes, this same understanding of NEP will be assumed. In contrast, a broader evolutionary psychology does not specify any particular approach, framework, or methodology but simply is applied to understanding the general question of how psychological processes evolved (Scher and Rauscher, 2003).

The names most synonymous with NEP are the anthropologist Tooby, the psychologists Cosmides and Buss, along with anthropologists Symons and Barkow, and others; indeed, especially in the case of Tooby and Cosmides, they are widely credited with defining the modern shape of evolutionary psychology. Given these associations, NEP is sometimes referred to as the 'Santa Barbara School'. Since much of the literature remains, whether explicitly or implicitly, influenced by NEP and retains many of its central assumptions, it is not sufficient to simply stipulate that it is the broader conception of evolutionary psychology which is operative in this chapter. The distinction between the two is important because certain assumptions of traditional NEP leave little conceptual space for the methods of neuroscientific investigation, to the detriment of NEP (Bechtel 2003; Mundale, 2003). Only recently have neuroscience and evolutionary psychology come into productive engagement, and much of this remains to be developed.

Neuroscience has been a late entry into evolutionary psychology for reasons that are similar to why it was also a late entry into the cognitive sciences. In both cases, the historical tendency has been to focus on high-level, functional descriptions of an organism's problem-solving capacities and strategies and to largely ignore the level of implementation. Alternatively, the focus of NEP has been almost exclusively on what Dennett terms the *design stance*, as opposed to the *physical stance* (1978), or, as it also is commonly put, the software, rather than the physical hardware. Higher-level descriptions need not be incompatible with physical ones, though the legacy of multiple realizability, another contribution pushed by Fodor (1974), and initiated by Putnam (1967), also served to dampen expectations for what psychology might hope to gain by incorporating

the methods and findings of neuroscience. Though this approach is widely criticized and the conclusion that psychological theories have nothing to gain from the study of neuroscience has largely been discredited, the residue of this thinking remains influential in NEP. Tooby and Cosmides explicitly state, for example, that knowledge of the hardware 'is not necessary for understanding the programs as information-processing systems', and that systems might just as well be made of silicon, since they 'would produce the same behavioral output … in response to the same informational input' (1992: 65). As criticisms of multiple realizability and the lingering legacy of these matters for NEP are argued elsewhere (see, for example, Bechtel and Mundale, 1999; Mundale, 2003), it will suffice to say here that a residue of disciplinary isolation remains in NEP and perhaps in EP more broadly.

MODULARITY AND NEUROSCIENCE

Currently in NEP, an organism's psychological capacities are thought of as special-purpose modules within a cognitive structure that is regarded as an information-processing system. The special-purpose modules evolved as problem-solving adaptations that conferred an advantage on organisms that possessed them. Given the multitude of specific skills needed to successfully navigate one's social and natural environment, the mind is packed with such special-purpose modules, or is said to be *massively modular*. The assumption of massive modularity, so central to NEP, is suspect, as many have argued (Churchland, 1988; Buller and Hardcastle, 2000; Bechtel, 2003; Prinz, 2006 and others). More specifically, both modularity and the information-processing model (the IP model) of cognition, it will be argued, have important, empirically accessible elements, and are more productively seen from this perspective than as a priori guiding assumptions that themselves remain unchallenged. These empirical aspects point the way toward just some of the ways that the tools of neuroscience can be applied to EP.

The version of modularity that is so pervasive in NEP is now just generally assumed, programmatically, with its original justification rarely revisited. As Barrett states, 'Fodor and most psychologists adopt an a priori definition of modularity– as automatic, innate, etc. – and then ask what, if anything, in the mind fits that definition. In contrast, the biologist's approach to modularity is empirical' (2015: 41). Despite these insightful comments, it is nonetheless possible to disentangle some elements of what a modular architecture would predict, and to show the extent to which these elements cohere or conflict with neuroanatomical evidence. Connectivity analysis and its implications for domain specificity and cognitive impenetrability, are examples of this. As more of the brain's cognitive architecture is discovered, it is the empirical approach which should define, or at least constrain, the operative concept of modularity in EP, rather than the reverse approach Barrett describes.

It is not just Fodor, but Cosmides and Tooby who provide an example typical of this a priori approach. In a 2015 paper, for example, they emphasize that 'task analysis of the required computations, social contract theory, specifies what counts as good design in this domain' (Cosmides and Tooby, 2015: 633). This high-level task analysis attempts to reverse engineer the functional components of a system capable of carrying it out, rather than first considering what the methods of neuroscience have so far revealed about the functionally distinct regions of the brain and their interconnection. It should be noted that Cosmides and Tooby do consider their hypothesis for such specialized modules to be empirically testable, though little neurological evidence features in this support. More will be said about this, below.

The kind of modularity most discussed in NEP follows Fodor (1984) in many, but not all respects. The essential elements, for Fodor,

that modular systems may exhibit (at least to some extent) include: (1) domain specificity, (2) informational encapsulation, (3) automatic and obligatory activation, (4) fast processing speed, (5) shallow outputs, (6) limited accessibility, (7) regularity of ontogenetic development, and (8) fixed neural architecture (Fodor, 1984).

One distinction between Fodor's modularity and that assumed by NEP is that he denies modularity for higher-level, cognitive processes, such as those involving belief and reasoning. For Fodor, it is primarily sensory input systems that are modular.

In both philosophical and scientific contexts, the two most important and controversial features of modularity are domain specificity and informational encapsulation. Obviously, both features have implications for the claims of traditional NEP as well as broader approaches. Classic NEP regards modules as essentially content-specialized adaptations, each evolved to solve domain-*specific* problems. It is a massively modular system, rather than any general-purpose reasoning ability, that is responsible for day-to-day functioning and problem solving. These proponents of NEP have consistently maintained this as a central tenet of their research program (Tooby and Cosmides, 1992: 65; Cosmides and Tooby, 2015).

Informational encapsulation is less straightforward. For researchers in Fodor's camp, the important feature of informational encapsulation is that it prevents cognitive interference with perceptual systems. In other words, objectivity of perception is preserved, at some level, and one need not worry that what one is seeing is somehow contaminated by prior thoughts or motivations about that particular perception (Fodor, 1984). Surely crude or simplistic cases of cognitive interference, such as seeing a brown car as red simply because one believes that color makes for a more attractive car, would garner sympathy for Fodor's motivations. As discussed below, the question of cognitive impenetrability is more subtle and complex.

The specific model of modularity required for any variety of EP has been vigorously debated. Carruthers, in fact, argues that much of Fodorian modularity must be rejected. This applies particularly to informational encapsulation and, to a large extent, domain specificity, as well (2006:12, 62). Why, then, have such contentious issues remained central tenets of NEP? The main reason appears to be that they provide a neatly contained solution to the heritability of successful problem-solving abilities and strategies. They are subject to selection pressure and transmitted to offspring (Tooby and Cosmides, 1992). Cosmides and Tooby call this the adaptive specialization hypothesis, which they contrast with the general rationality hypothesis (2015: 630). They argue that these specialized problem-solving capacities are proprietary to a given species, and unlike appeals to general rationality, provide a means by which natural selection can exert differential pressure. But even the necessity of appealing to such task-specific modules has been challenged in the literature. Jaak Panksepp and Jules Panksepp (2000), for example, argue that the specialized problems that modules have been posited to solve can also be solved by appealing to more general-purpose brain capacities, coupled with developmental plasticity and interactions among functionally specialized brain circuits. In other words, a modular architecture is not the only possibility for explaining a species' specialized problem-solving abilities.

The concern here is not to survey competing models of modularity and attempt to adjudicate them. Rather, the point is to show that modularity has been a central, though contentious feature of EP and that its more questionable features, as well as the viability of modularity itself, is accessible to the empirical methods of neuroscience. The importance of this contribution of neuroscientific methods to EP is that it can help to shape understanding of the cognitive architecture of the brain which in turn can help to explain the means by which species-specific, cognitive abilities can be subject to selection pressure. Thus, critics of modularity who challenge its key features on empirical grounds, rather

than on merely conceptual ones, show an important avenue for applying the methods of neuroscience.

Despite the apparent lack of integration with EP, this empirical approach has not been absent from the literature. In 2003, for example, Bechtel discussed the sort of approach that is needed. In summarizing some now classic studies lead by Van Essen and colleagues (Van Essen and deYoe, 1995; Felleman and Van Essen 1991; Van Essen 1997), Bechtel shows how cortical organization is revealed to be much more integrated (hence, less *informationally encapsulated*, less *domain specific*) than is consistent with a modular architecture. He notes, for example, that in the visual system, 'Each component still carries out its own information processing operation but it is highly interconnected and responsive to other components. An often noted important feature of cortical organization is that backwards projections are at least as numerous as forward projections' (2003: 219).

Since then, the neuroscientific evidence against key features of modularity have multiplied, amounting to over 20 years of empirical challenge. The evidential approach cited by Bechtel, of connectivity analysis, or tracing neuronal projections among various functional areas, remains an important method for determining information flow throughout the brain. A recent paper by Newen and Vetter reviews several lines of evidence against informational encapsulation, some of which draws on connectivity analysis: (1) extensive structural feedback organization of the brain, (2) temporally very early feedback loops, and (3) functional top-down processes modulating early visual processes by category-specific information (Newen and Vetter, 2016). With regard to the first, the authors claim that

from a neuroanatomical perspective it is unjustified to speak of impenetrable modules in the brain. Recent evidence shows that cortical brain areas are much more heavily interconnected than previously thought, namely to 66%. That is, each brain area is connected to 66% of the rest of the brain (Markov et al., 2013). While the majority of these connections are short-distance connections between neighbouring areas, the hierarchical structure of the brain implies a cascade of interconnected brain areas across processing levels (29).

The situation grows more complicated when realizing that a functionally defined brain area is itself not well defined, either conceptually or empirically. Newen and Vetter (2017) illustrate this with the example of the fusiform face area, which is generally accepted as an area that selectively processes visual information from faces. In later research, they draw from the work of Çukur et al. (2013) and Gauthier et al. (2000) in pointing out that this same area 'was shown to selectively respond also to cars, birds and other object categories' (Newen and Vetter, 2017: 29). As they admit, these findings do not affect the idea that the fusiform face area mainly processes faces, it just denies that it does this exclusively. An important moral of this finding is that other areas may also have greater functional range than is currently understood:

> Likewise, for many other specialised brain areas, it is well possible that the future will reveal additional functions that we cannot even imagine yet. In the case of V1, despite it being one of the most extensively studied areas in the brain, models can so far explain only up to 40% of its processing variance during natural vision (Carandini et al., 2005; David & Gallant, 2005). That is, there is a lot of remaining unexplained processing function in V1 that may surprise us in the future. Thus, assigning a sole function to a specialised brain area is a risky endeavour as we simply do not know enough about even a single brain area. It is therefore unjustified to speak of a brain area as restricted to one functional role. (Newen and Vetter, 2017: 28–9)

This underscores the importance of Barrett's caution against making the kind of a priori assumptions of modularity mentioned above. It also shows the importance of neuroscientific research in not only identifying specialized, functional processing areas, but in elucidating their full, functional capabilities. It would be premature to conclude that these are modular in any sense that would be meaningful to EP (especially domain-specific)

without knowing what they in fact do, and how they may interact with additional processing areas in carrying out their functions. This understanding, of course, awaits ongoing research in brain mapping. Some of the tools of brain mapping will be discussed further, below.

Newen and Vetter's (2017) second line of evidence, regarding 'temporally very early feedback loops' (32) questions the assumed timeframe for the involvement of higher-level, cognitive processes into the perceptual stream. Typically, it has been assumed that perception takes place fast, first, and in isolation, with higher-level processes becoming involved much later in the processing stream. Evidence the authors cite and interpret suggest otherwise. They argue that evidence favors the early entry of higher-order, cognitive processes, and that these enter

> in a task-specific manner, telling us something about the information conveyed in this feedback: when the task requires face recognition, FEF [frontal eye fields] signals are sent to face-sensitive regions and when the task requires motion discrimination, FEF signals are sent to motion area V5, both within a time frame of 20–40 ms after FEF activity (Morishima et al., 2009). Therefore, top-down signals from a frontal region to earlier visual regions do not occur in a general and unspecific manner. Instead, they carry task-specific, and thus higher-level cognitive information, and are transmitted very quickly. These fast top-down signals from FEF have actual perceptual consequences. (Newen and Vetter, 2017: 30)

As the authors point out, one could explain all this by simply adopting the concept of a very large, functionally complex module, but such a move would weaken the point of assuming a modular architecture in the first place.

Newen and Vetter's (2017) third line of evidence, involving category-specific information, is intriguing because it suggests possibilities about the brain's functional architecture that could not be appreciated within a strictly modular framework. They point to a study (Vetter et al., 2014) involving blindfolded subjects in an MRI being presented with sounds that one might naturally encounter. Since the subjects were blindfolded, no visual information entered the brain. Nonetheless, Newen and Vetter (2017) report that, 'Vetter et al. (2014) showed that neural activity patterns in early visual cortex were distinct depending on the semantic content of the sound. That is, different natural sounds elicited distinct neural activity patterns in early visual cortex in the absence of visual stimulation. Given that there was no feedforward visual stimulation, the content-specific sound information must have been transferred to early visual cortex by feedback from other parts of the brain' (30). The authors also point to what they regard as a further, 'crucial' result of this same study; namely, that 'the information from sounds that ends up in early visual cortex is not only content-specific, but also category-specific' (31), meaning that information about the kind of sound (such as sounds from planes and traffic), rather than its similarity based on auditory qualities (i.e., loud, or roaring sounds), is sent to the visual cortex. They conclude that 'the information that ends up in early visual cortex is categorical and high-level, and thus very likely of semantic nature' (31).

Though there are many critics of modularity, Newen and Vetter (2017) stand out for their careful and subtle appraisal of some key research and its challenging implications for both informational encapsulation and domain specificity. They also show promising avenues for the further application of neuroscientific research to evolutionary psychology, proposing what a 'decisive knock-down experiment' against cognitive impenetrability would look like. Such an experiment would involve a multidisciplinary approach that, among other things, would require 'structural and functional evidence from the neurosciences supporting the modification of perceptual processing' (34).

Turning more directly to domain specificity, this is an especially important feature of modularity for NEP, and one that Cosmides and Tooby have recently (2015) sought to defend by empirical methods that make some

mention of neuroscientific evidence. This recent paper presents what they call 'the high points' of their 25-year research program, so in part it is a summary of previous work. More specifically, and as mentioned above, they seek to defend the *adaptive specialization hypothesis* against the *general rationality hypothesis*. It is not pertinent here to review the entirety of their case, neither is this intended to be a critique of it in its entirety. What is relevant, however, is the kind of neuroscientific evidence they cite (admittedly, not their evidentiary focus) and their interpretation of how it affects their hypothesis.

The adaptive specialization hypothesis is the view that there are 'information processing circuits that are narrowly specialized for understanding, reasoning about, motivating, and engaging in social exchange' and that these circuits are 'neurocognitive adaptations *for* social exchange, evolved cognitive instincts designed by natural selection for that function' (Cosmides and Tooby, 2015: 630). In contrast, the general rationality hypothesis, as the name suggests, is the view that 'social exchange reasoning is a by-product or expression of a neurocognitive system that evolved to perform a more general function – operant conditioning, logical reasoning, rational decision making, or some sort of general intelligence' (630). As mentioned above, the functional description and design features of these specialized circuits are arrived at through a top-down task analysis, one that specifies what such a system would have to be able to do in order to be successful in social exchange (633). One such feature involves cheating detection.

Cheating detection, they claim, is an ability that can be observed and tested by the Wason card selection task (with neuroscientific applications to be explained, shortly). In their 1992 work, Cosmides and Tooby discussed how performance differences on this well-known task depend on whether decisions involved neutral content, such as letters and colors, or social contract content, such as rules about drinking. While subjects are notoriously bad at guessing the correct answer in the former case (typically, cards with numbers on one side and a color on the other), they do substantially better when the rules involve social contracts (such as cards with beverages on one side and ages on the other). So, if the task was, 'Assume every card has a number on one side and a color on the other. Which cards must you turn over to test the rule that if there is an even number on one side, the opposite side is blue?', and the four cards shown were 7, 2, yellow and blue, the correct answer would be that you must turn over the 2 and yellow cards. Most subjects perform poorly on this task. Cosmides and Tooby, however, point to the fact that people do much better if the test is presented in social contract terms. In this case, for example, the task would test a rule such as, 'If you are drinking alcohol, you must be over 18', and the card choices would be soda, beer, age 16, and age 25. In this case, the correct answer would be a beer and 16. They report that fewer than 25% choose correctly when the task is phrased in abstract terms, but that 75% choose correctly when it is put in social contract terms (1992: 182).

For Cosmides and Tooby (1992, 2015), this is evidence of a specific, cheater detection ability that is specialized for social situations and is independent of the formal rules governing the logic of conditionals. In their 2015 work, they argue that not only is it evidence for specialized, social contract reasoning, but that it is also distinct from another kind of deontic reasoning involving precautionary statements. In the case of both social contract statements (e.g., If you accept a benefit, then you must have satisfied a requirement) and precautionary statements (e.g., If there is a hazard, then you must take precautions), subjects do better on the Wason task than when presented with neutral or abstract content. Cosmides and Tooby (2015) argue that these two kinds of deontic reasoning, social and precautionary, are dissociable both from each other and from formal or content-neutral reasoning. Furthermore, it is their contention that

these content-sensitive reasoning processes constitute distinct, special-purpose modules or mechanisms, and that evidence of their dissociation weakens the *general* rationality hypothesis. In their 2015 paper, which is a summary of past work, they compiled evidence from several different studies, but only a few involved neuroscientific research. These studies involved, 1) single dissociation in a single patient, 2) indirect neuroanatomical evidence, and 3) past fMRI studies.

The single dissociation test was conducted on a patient known as R.M. and was first reported in a 2002 study (Stone et al., 2002). R.M. is a noteworthy experimental subject because of his 'extensive bilateral limbic system damage, affecting orbitofrontal cortex, temporal pole, and amygdala' (2002: 11531). When R.M. was given the Wason task he showed significantly worse performance with social contract content than with precautionary content. This selective impairment is taken as evidence that these tasks engage separate brain resources and, thus, involve two functionally distinct neurocognitive mechanisms (2015: 652). As the authors admit, a double dissociation would provide stronger evidence (2002: 115), and a single dissociation in a single patient, while supportive of their theory, is not decisive.

Stronger criticisms concern the logical implications of the dissociative method and were first identified by Shallice (1988), who refined and promoted the method. These criticisms are explained in detail by Van Orden et al. (2001), and one, in particular, is applicable to the present case. They summarize it as follows:

> An indefinite set of choices exists for operational definitions of cognitive components in laboratory tasks.... Additionally, brain damage produces innumerable variations of change in patients' behavior. Consequently, one may count on finding some task on which a patient performs poorly, and one may count on finding some patient who performs poorly on a given task. This insures the discovery of dissociation patterns in patient performance. Outside of theoretical guidelines, these patterns (dissociations) have no meaning.

Whether dissociations are truly pure cases, and whether combinations of dissociations are truly opposite pure cases, cannot be determined outside one's theory of mind and task. (2001: 114)

The particular example Van Orden et al. had in mind with this criticism was the aphasic dissociation between conceptual (semantic) and syntactic knowledge, often regarded as a kind of 'pure', double dissociation. They do not question that these dissociations exist, but they point out that such dissociations are only meaningful within a theory of language that distinguishes these in the first place. In the single case of R.M., his dissociation (and it was partial, since *some* ability was preserved in the social contract task) only made sense if one first assumed a distinction between social contract and precautionary tasks in the first place. In itself, there is nothing wrong with this; it is of course necessary if one is to construct a processing model at all. But as Van Orden et al. point out, by itself, it indicates only that the dissociation (in this case, of a single patient) *isn't incompatible* with their previously assumed theory of cognitive organization. As they further suggest, had one's task analysis carved along different joints (as seems possible, given the complexity of the social interaction described), it is likely one would have found a dissociation for that, as well. This is not to dismiss the value of dissociative studies as such, but their particular application adds little weight to their claim.

As noted above, two other pieces of neuroscientific evidence were supplied in support of the adaptive specialization hypothesis: indirect neuroanatomical evidence (scant enough to ignore) and past fMRI studies. The latter are summarized as follows: 'Recent functional imaging (fMRI) studies also support the hypothesis that social contract reasoning is supported by different brain areas than precautionary reasoning, and imply the involvement of several brain areas in addition to temporal cortex' (Cosmides and Tooby, 2015: 653). One has to question whether a special-purpose reasoning mechanism that,

by their own admission, is instantiated across *several brain areas* (and, necessarily, through a multiplicity of connections) can be the sort of mechanism for which special-purpose heritability can be explained and domain specificity can be maintained. These are the sorts of questions that, empirically, have yet to be worked out, and that have not been adequately addressed in NEP. The larger difficulty, of course, is NEP advocates largely fail to anchor their theory, which they persist in calling '*neuro*cognitive', in anything that is substantively 'neuro'. As they make clear, and as discussed above, it is the architecture dictated by their task analysis that is conceptually prior, and the question of whether its theoretical constructs map onto any neuroscientific components generally seems to be an afterthought.

NEUROSCIENCE AND THE FUTURE OF EVOLUTIONARY PSYCHOLOGY

In a recent provocative article, 'Why isn't everyone an evolutionary psychologist?', Burke attempts a diagnosis for why evolutionary psychology, and evolutionary approaches generally, have so far failed to have much of an impact in mainstream psychology. As he notes, nearly all 'highly educated people' believe in evolution, and nearly all scientific psychologists 'believe that the neural mechanisms that underpin our psychological abilities and propensities are the product of evolution' (2014: 1), so why isn't evolution more prominent in psychology? He provides several reasons, but two, in particular, are most pertinent here. These Burke names, 'The Identification of Evolutionary Psychology with Particular Versions of it' and 'Just So Story Telling'.

The first insists that, just because the dominant version of EP (what is referred to here as NEP) has insisted on massive modularity and the information-processing model does not, mean that EP generally must continue to insist on such ideas. He claims that neither is necessary in order for one to consider how evolutionary forces have shaped the mind. Furthermore, he predicts that 'the convoluted and interconnected way in which complex adaptations evolve means that we should probably expect some to be quite modular, and others to depend on components of pre-existing mechanisms, or even to co-evolve with other mechanisms' (2). Which architectural arrangement(s) turn out to be best confirmed, of course, is an empirical, rather than programmatic matter, which leads to the second of his reasons.

The second reason he calls, 'Just So Story Telling'. As he explains:

> Perhaps we might make more headway by more frequently acknowledging that evolutionary hypotheses are actually quite difficult to test (as have Confer et al., 2010, for example), and that psychological studies are but one of many lines of converging evidence that are helping to put together the pieces of the puzzle. It is probably a fair criticism of our field that we rely too heavily on uncovering signs of special design of human psychological mechanisms as evidence of their evolution, and too little on examining the mechanism across species (Vonk and Shackelford, 2013: 3). (Burke, 2014)

Both of these reasons seem like good ways to sum up present difficulties as well as good indicators for how the methods of neuroscience can help to strengthen evolutionary psychology. This last section will summarize some selected methods and applications.

Several tools of neuroscience might broadly be regarded as falling under the umbrella of brain mapping techniques. In recent years, functional neuroimaging, such as functional magnetic resonance imaging (fMRI), positron emission tomography (PET) (now largely superseded by fMRI), electroencephalography (EEG), magnetoencephalography (MEG) and other radiographic techniques have allowed researchers to visualize the activity of the living brain as it performs various functions. The purpose of these tools with respect to evolutionary psychology is manifold. They can help to pinpoint which

areas of the brain are active, and which are silent, when subjects perform a given task, thus helping to address the organizational and architectural puzzles discussed above. They can also enable researchers to make comparison across ages, sexes, cultures, and for some techniques, across species.

Connectivity analysis is an important part of brain mapping because it reveals which areas of the brain carry information from, and to, other areas of the brain. Many tools can help to shed light on the brain's connectivity patterns, but it is tracing techniques that are most specifically employed for this purpose. Anterograde tracers show which area(s) neural connections target, while retrograde tracers show the areas from which neurons originate. Another way of saying this is that anterograde tracers trace the path of neurons from their source (their cell body, or soma) to their terminus, at the synapse. Retrograde tracers trace the opposite direction, or from the synapse to the cell body. Connectivity analysis can help assess claims of cognitive impenetrability and domain specificity because it shows which areas send information to other areas, showing how information flows through the brain.

Dissociation methods (Shallice, 1988), like those discussed above in the case of R. M., are used to determine the extent to which two mental functions are distinct. In humans, dissociation experiments often involve impaired subjects. The reasoning behind dissociation tasks can be summarized as follows: if an impaired subject can perform task *a*, but not task *b*, then these tasks are said to be functionally dissociated, and presumably, not part of the same functional processing area. This is an example of single dissociation. If, in addition to the first case, there is also a differently impaired subject who can perform test *b*, but not test *a*, then the tasks are said to be doubly dissociated, and there is stronger evidence that the tasks are carried out by different processing areas of the brain. If an impaired subject shows diminished performance in *both* tasks, then the tasks are said to be associated and to share processing resources. As others have argued (see, for example, Shallice, 1988; Dunn and Kirsner, 2003) dissociation tasks are not, by themselves, conclusive. Tasks may be associated yet show little or no decrement in performance if the processing capacities remain sufficient to the demands of the task. Conversely, selective impairment on one task, but not another, does not prove tasks to be functionally dissociated; they may simply be subtasks that occur at slightly different points in the processing stream of a larger function. This is why a double dissociation provides stronger evidence for functional separation.

Comparative neuroanatomy is another method of obvious relevance and has largely been absent in NEP. Brains and nervous systems of different species are shaped by their evolutionary history and the differing cognitive capacities they enable can lead to better understanding about a given species' adaptations and survival strategies. Evolutionary psychologists can use this information to better understand the cognitive abilities, strengths, weaknesses, and the general nature of various cognitive faculties. Understanding evolutionary relationships among species also enables researchers to make use of anatomical studies from closely related species to draw general conclusions that apply across a given kind. Primates, for example, have comparatively more developed neocortices than other species and share other structural similarities, enabling neuroanatomists to make some general conclusions about human brains as a result of studying other primate brains. Brodmann, for example, was among the first to do cross-species comparisons of the laminar structure of the cortex, the thickness of each of the cortical layers, their cytoarchitectonic structures, and other species-specific features. His studies included several primate species (human, chimpanzee, orangutan, langur, rhesus macaque, squirrel monkey, marmoset, tamarin, and others) as well as a wide variety of other mammalian species (2006 translation of 1909 text: 32–3).

Neuroethology is an important tool for evolutionary psychology because it provides a comparative study of animal behavior in their natural habitat, or the habitat in which the animal evolved to survive. It is a natural showcase of the animal's special skills, abilities, and cognitive adaptations that enabled the animal to survive in its particular environment. Animals studied merely in the lab have little opportunity to display their cognitive adaptations because they are divorced from the environment which requires them to be deployed and which gave shape to them. Patel et al. (2007) point to the work of Konrad Lorenz with the greylag goose as prime examples of this kind of research. Through this ethological research, Lorenz discovered such concepts as imprinting and critical periods. This, and related work by Tinbergen and von Frisch, 'led to the development of a subspecialty of ethology known as neuroethology, an innovative branch of science that seeks to identify the ... neural correlates of naturalistic behavior' (2007: 52). The identification of these neural correlates can then be studied through the lens of comparative neuroanatomy to reveal other important evolutionary connections and forces that shaped the cognitive functions of the species in question.

Many controversies remain, not just between NEP and EP, but about larger issues having to do with the contributions of epigenetics, cortical plasticity, the implications of sex differences in the brain, the actual locus of selection pressure in an organism, the most appropriate way to model human, cognitive architecture, and others. But Ian D. Stephen has managed to find a way to summarize a common point of departure to carry evolutionary psychology into the future: 'The necessary foundational principles are merely that behavior, cognition and perception have fitness consequences, and that selection shapes behavior, perception and cognition; something upon which all researchers adopting evolutionary approaches to psychology can surely agree' (2014: 2).

ACKNOWLEDGEMENTS

I wish to thank Donald Jones for his comments on an earlier draft of this work, Katie Rose Mundale-Jones for her general support and proofreading assistance, and above all, Todd Shackelford for outstanding editorial patience and unwavering civility during the numerous delays in the preparation of this chapter.

REFERENCES

Barrett, H. (2015). Modularity. In V. Zeigler-Hill, L. Welling, and T. Shackelford (Eds), *Evolutionary perspectives on social psychology* (pp. 39–50). Cham: Springer.

Bechtel, W. (2003). Modules, brain parts, and evolutionary psychology. In S. J. Scher and F. Rauscher (Eds), *Evolutionary psychology: Alternative approaches* (pp. 211–228). Boston: Kluwer.

Bechtel, W., and Mundale, J. (1999). Multiple realizability revisited: Linking cognitive and neural states. *Philosophy of Science*, 66(2), 175–207.

Brodmann, K. (1909). *Vergleichende Lokalisationslehre der Grosshirnrinde in ihren Prinzipien dargestellt auf Grund des Zellenbaues*. Leipzig: Barth. [Translated and edited by L. J. Garey, *Brodmann's 'Localisation in the Cerebral Cortex'*, New York: Springer, 1994.]

Buller, D. J., and Hardcastle, V. (2000). Evolutionary psychology, meet developmental neurobiology: Against promiscuous modularity. *Brain and Mind* 1(3), 307–325. doi.org/10.1023/A:1011573226794.

Burke, D. (2014). Why isn't everyone an evolutionary psychologist? *Frontiers in Psychology*, 5, 1–8. doi: 10.3389/fpsyg.2014.00910.

Carandini, M., Demb, J. B., Mante, V., Tolhurst, D. J., Dan, Y., Olshausen, B. A., Gallant, J. L., and Rust, N. C. (2005). Do we know what the early visual system does? *Journal of Neuroscience*, 25(46), 10577–10597.

Carruthers, P. (2006). *The architecture of the mind: Massive modularity and the flexibility of thought*. Oxford: Clarendon Press.

Churchland, P. M. (1988). Perceptual plasticity and theoretical neutrality: A reply to Jerry Fodor. *Philosophy of Science*, 55(2), 167–187.

Confer, J. C., Easton, J. A., Fleischman, D. S., Goetz, C. D., Lewis, D. M. G., Perilloux, C., and Buss, D. M. (2010). Evolutionary psychology: Controversies, questions, prospects, and limitations. *American Psychologist*, 65(2), 110–126. doi:10.1037/a00 18413.

Cosmides, L., and Tooby, J. (2015). Adaptations for reasoning about social exchange. In D. M. Buss (Ed.), *The handbook of evolutionary psychology* (pp. 625–668). Hoboken, NJ: John Wiley & Sons.

Çukur, T., Huth, A. G., Nishimoto, S., and Gallant, J. L. (2013). Functional subdomains within human FFA. *The Journal of Neuroscience*, 33(42), 16748–16766. doi: 10.1523/JNEUROSCI.1259-13.2013.

David, S. V., and Gallant, J. L. (2005). Predicting neuronal responses during natural vision. *Network*, 16(2–3), 239–260.

Dennett, D. (1978). Intentional systems. In D. Dennett, *Brainstorms: Philosophical Essays on Mind and Psychology* (pp. 3–24). Montgomery, VT: Bradford Books.

Dunn, J. C., and Kirsner, K. (2003). What can we infer from double dissociations? *Cortex*, 39(1), 1–7. doi: 10.1016/S0010-9452(08)70070-4.

Felleman, D. J., and van Essen, D. C. (1991). Distributed hierarchical processing in the primate cerebral cortex. *Cerebral Cortex*, 1(1), 1–47.

Fodor, J. (1974). Special sciences (or: The disunity of science as a working hypothesis). *Synthese*, 28(2), 97–115.

Fodor, J. (1984). Observation reconsidered. *Philosophy of Science*, 51(1), 23–43.

Gauthier, I., Skudlarski, P., Gore, J. C., and Anderson, A. W. (2000). Expertise for cars and birds recruits brain areas involved in face recognition. *Nature Neuroscience*, 3(2), 191–197.

Markov, N. T., Ercsey-Ravasz, M., Van Essen, D. C., Knoblauch, K., Toroczkai, Z., and Kennedy, H. (2013). Cortical high-density counterstream architectures. *Science*, 342(6158), 1238406. doi:10.1126/science.1238406.

Morishima, Y., Akaishi, R., Yamada, Y., Okuda, J., Toma, K., and Sakai, K. (2009). Task-specific signal transmission from prefrontal cortex in visual selective attention. *Nature Neuroscience*, 12(1), 85–91.

Mundale, J. (2003). Evolutionary psychology and the information-processing model of cognition. In S. J. Scher and F. Rauscher (Eds), *Evolutionary psychology: Alternative approaches* (pp. 229–241). Boston: Kluwer.

Newen, A., and Vetter, P. (2017). Why cognitive penetration of our perceptual experience is still the most plausible account. *Consciousness and Cognition*, 47, 26–37.

Panksepp, J., and Panksepp, J. (2000). The seven sins of evolutionary psychology. *Evolution and Cognition*, 6(2), 108–131.

Patel, S., Rodak, K. L., Mamikonyan, K. S., and Platek, S. M. (2007). Introduction to evolutionary cognitive neuroscience methods. In S. M. Platek, J. P. Keenan, and T. K. Shackelford (Eds), *Evolutionary Cognitive Neuroscience* (pp. 47–62). Cambridge: MIT Press.

Prinz, J. J. (2006). Is the mind really modular? In R. J. Stainton (Ed.), *Contemporary debates in cognitive science* (pp. 22–36). Malden, MA: Blackwell.

Putnam, H. (1967). Psychological predicates. In W. H. Capitan and D. D. Merrill (Eds), *Art, mind, and religion* (pp. 37–48). Pittsburgh: University of Pittsburgh Press.

Scher, S. J., and Rauscher, F. (Eds) (2003). *Evolutionary psychology: Alternative approaches.* Boston: Kluwer.

Scher, S. J., and Rauscher, F. (2003). Introduction. In S. J. Scher and F. Rauscher (Eds), *Evolutionary psychology: Alternative approaches* (pp. xi–xviii). Boston: Kluwer.

Shallice, T. (1988). *From neuropsychology to mental structure.* Cambridge, UK: Cambridge University Press.

Stephen, I. D. (2014). Putting the theory before the data: Is 'massive modularity' a necessary foundation of evolutionary psychology? *Frontiers in Psychology,* 5, 1158. doi.org/10.3389/fpsyg.2014.01158.

Stone, V. E., Cosmides, L., Tooby, J., Kroll, N., and Knight, R. (2002). Selective impairment of reasoning about social exchange in a patient with bilateral limbic system damage. *Proceedings of the National Academy of Sciences, USA*, 99(17), 11531–11536. doi.org/10.1073/pnas.122352699.

Tooby, J., and Cosmides, L. (1992). The psychological foundations of culture. In J. H. Barkow, L. Cosmides, and J. Tooby, *The adapted mind: Evolutionary psychology and the generation of culture* (pp. 19–136). New York: Oxford University Press.

Van Essen, D. C. (1997). A tension-based theory of morphogenesis and compact wiring in the central nervous system. *Nature,* 385(6614), 313–318.

Van Essen, D.C., and deYoe, E. A. (1995). Concurrent processing in the primate visual cortex. In M. Gazzaniga (Ed.), *The cognitive neurosciences* (pp. 383–440). Cambridge, MA: MIT Press.

Van Orden, G. C., Pennington, B. F., and Stone, G. O. (2001). What do double dissociations prove? *Cognitive Science,* 25(1), 111–172.

Vetter, P., Smith, F., and Muckli, L. (2014). Decoding sound and imagery content in early visual cortex. *Current Biology,* 24(11), 1256. doi: 10.1016/j.cub.2014.04.020.

Vonk, J., and Shackelford, T. K. (2013). An introduction to comparative evolutionary psychology. *Evolutionary Psychology,* 11(3), 459–469.

19

Behavior Genetics

Nicole Barbaro and Lars Penke

IMPORTANCE

Findings from the field of behavioral genetics brought about a substantial paradigm shift in the study of psychological science (Plomin et al., 2013, 2016). It is now beyond reasonable debate that understanding the role of genetic variation for explaining complex phenotypes is necessary for informed study of psychology and behavior. Genetic variation is essential to the process of evolution by natural selection. The idea that heritable variation provides the raw material upon which selection can act has long been acknowledged in the biological life sciences. Humans – and their brains – are not exempt from evolutionary processes. Any approach to understanding psychology that fails to take into consideration that genetic variation underpins the foci of psychological study is, therefore, untenable and not a viable approach to the conduct of psychological science (see Penke, 2011).

The claim that human psychological traits are heritable is supported on a substantial scale (e.g., Plomin et al., 2016; Polderman et al., 2015). Although this basic understanding of the widespread heritability of psychological and behavior traits has been prominent since the rise of the field in the 1970s, the methods used to understand genetic (and environmental) influences on traits has substantially advanced in the era after sequencing the human genome, beginning in the early 2000s (International Human Genome Sequencing Consortium, 2001; Venter et al., 2001). With these methodological advancements came a better understanding of the complex interplay of genes and environment that produce phenotypes. As methods and interpretations have become increasingly complex, however, basic understanding of behavior genetics has become increasing difficult as well.

Our goal in this chapter is to provide readers with a broad overview of the popular methods within the domain of classical family studies (e.g., twin and adoption studies), the foundation of behavior genetics, and within the domain of contemporary approaches using genome-wide approaches, which are leading to exciting and informative insights into the evolutionary history of traits. For each method, when relevant, we provide an overview of the research design, key aspects and terms, and the major interpretations of the results produced by the method. Finally, we conclude with three major implications of behavior genetics for psychological science: inferring causality, inferring developmental processes, and inferring the evolution of traits.

METHODS

The field of behavior genetics uses myriad research designs. Classical behavior genetics, which emerged in the 1970s, uses natural quasi-experiments afforded by twinning and adoption to infer the extent to which observable phenotypes are explained by genic variation and environmental variation. Contemporary behavior genetics also uses genome-wide approaches to identify specific genetic markers associated with phenotypes. The history of these methodologies occurs in parallel with the history of genetics more broadly, beginning with the discovery of DNA structure in 1964, experiencing a paradigm shift with the sequencing of the human genome in 2001, and elevating to public discourse in the current era of personal genomics. Classical approaches and genome approaches to studying the complex relationships between genetic variation and observable phenotypes differ in fundamental aspects regarding design, assumptions, and implications. Each approach, however, is aimed at the same overarching goal: to advance understanding of how our genes contribute to who we are. This section will focus on two major domains of behavior genetic methods – family studies and genetic association approaches – outlining basic design features, assumptions, and reasonable interpretation of results.

Classical Family Studies

Twins are one of nature's greatest experiments, and the foundation of classical behavior genetics. Twins come in two types: monozygotic (MZ) and dizygotic (DZ). Because MZ and DZ twins differ in their average degree of genetic relatedness, the two genetic types of twins allow for inferences about the sources of influence on phenotypes. MZ twins result from a fertilized egg splitting very early in development, which means that their DNA is identical. DZ twins, in contrast, develop from different fertilized eggs, meaning that they are no more alike or different than a random pair of siblings from the same parent; DZ twins are simply siblings born on the same day. MZ twins share 100% of their DNA, whereas DZ twins share approximately 50% of their DNA, on average. Knowing parameters of average genetic relatedness, in combination with natural quasi-experimental situations caused by adoption and twinning, allows for inferences about the contributions of genes and environment to phenotypes of interest.

The contribution of nature (genes) and nurture (environment) to observable phenotypes has been a point of debate for more than a century. Children that grow up in the same family tend to resemble one another in many aspects. For most of psychological science's history, most prominently in psychoanalytic and behavioristic traditions, similarities between family members were presumed to be due primarily to the fact that they shared a family environment – resources, experiences, parenting, or neighborhood, for example. Utilization of twinning and adoption led to simple extrapolation about the likely degree to which nature and nature could account for family resemblance. If family resemblance is largely due to growing up in the same household, then it can be reasoned that (1) adoptive siblings, who are not genetically related, should be just as similar as genetic siblings that grow up in the same house, and (2) MZ twins that grow up in different homes due to adoption in infancy, should be no more similar than two people drawn at random who grow up in different families.

These predictions were not borne out by observation, however. Early studies of twinning and adoption found precisely the opposite of what is predicted based on family environment causing similarity. Twins that are reared apart are nearly as similar on psychological and behavioral measures as twins reared together, and by late adolescence adoptive siblings are no more similar than two randomly selected children reared in different homes. These findings suggest that family resemblance is at least in part due to the contributions of shared genes, rather than to the contributions of shared environment. Twinning and adoption studies comparing the relative similarity between children reared together and apart are useful for understanding in broad strokes the contributions of genes and environment, but more precise estimates are produced from quantitative models utilizing MZ and DZ twins.

A fundamental goal of psychological science is to explain variation. Twin studies explain variation in a phenotypic trait, but in a different and complementary way to standard psychological science methods. Twin, adoption, and family studies, collectively known as quantitative genetic studies, can produce two primary outcomes of interest: (1) partitioning the variation of a trait into (usually) the three components of genetic variation, shared environmental variation, and non-shared environmental variation; and (2) partitioning the covariation between two traits – referred to as a *phenotypic association* – into (usually) the three components of genetic variation, shared environmental variation, and non-shared environmental variation.

Partitioning variance

Correlation comparisons and ACE models (A meaning genetic variance, C meaning shared environmental variance, and E meaning non-shared environmental variance) are common approaches used to partition sources of variance for a particular trait in a given population. That is, given a population of individuals, univariate models can estimate what proportion of individual differences within the population for a phenotypic trait – for instance, extraversion – are attributable to genetic variation within the population, and what proportion is attributable to environmental variation (shared and non-shared) within that population. Phenotypic variance is composed of three factors, two of which are distinct environmental factors. Genetic variance explaining phenotypic variance is referred to as heritability (h^2), which acts to make two individuals who share more genes more similar to one another than two individuals who share fewer genes. Environmental influences on phenotypic variation are comprised of two components: shared environment (c^2) and non-shared environment (e^2). The environmental components (collectively referred to as *environmentality*, $c^2 + e^2$) refer to phenotypic variance accounted for by non-genetic, or 'environmental' experiences, in a broad sense. Shared environmental variation, such as family-level variables, are aspects of the environment that make siblings (or others) reared together more similar to one another. Non-shared environmental variation, such as unique peer groups or stochastic developmental variation, are aspects of the environment that make siblings (or others) reared together dissimilar from one another (the non-shared component usually also includes measurement error).

The classical method to estimating the contributions of genetic and environmental variance to a phenotype is to compare correlations between MZ and DZ twins to produce estimates of variance components: genetic, shared environmental, and non-shared environmental. The only information required is the average correlation between MZ and DZ twin pairs for a particular trait. Calculations can then be made to estimate the degree to which each component explains the phenotypic trait (Purcell, 2016). To calculate the contribution of genetic variation, h^2, one calculates the difference between the MZ correlation and the DZ correlation and then multiply by two, $h^2 = 2\ [r_{mz} - r_{dz}]$. The contribution of shared environmental variation can be calculated by subtracting the MZ twin correlation from the genetic contribution calculated above, $c^2 = r_{mz} - h^2$, or by subtracting half the genetic contribution from the DZ twin correlation, $c^2 = r_{dz} - [h^2/2]$. The non-shared environmental component is then calculated by subtracting the genetic and shared environmental values from one, $e^2 = 1 - [h^2 + c^2]$.

The above method based on the correlation coefficients between MZ and DZ twins will produce only one estimate. For example, a trait with $r_{mz} = .60$ and a $r_{dz} = .35$ will yield only $h^2 = .50$, $c^2 = .10$, and $e^2 = .40$. There is no other answer to the calculations. Structural equation modeling can also be used to estimate heritability and environmentality, applying the popular ACE models. The benefit of using structural equation models is that models can be compared to one another to examine, for example, if the $c^2 = .10$ value significantly contributes to the overall understanding of the trait of interest. Does removing the c^2 value from the model (the equivalent of fixing c^2 to zero) substantially affect the fit of the model to the data? Science favors parsimony, such that the simplest explanation should be accepted. ACE models typically test full models including each component, and additionally specify simpler combinations, AE, AC, CE, A, C, E, and compare the fit of those models to the full model. If, for example, the AE model is a better fit, or does not significantly impact the model fit compared to the full ACE model, the simpler model will be accepted, such that the contribution of shared environmental variance will be specified as 0, thus changing the relative contributions of genetic and non-shared variance.

ACE models, like any statistical model, rely on assumptions to produce estimates of heritability and environmentality for a particular trait. First, the models assume that MZ twins share 100% of their DNA

and that DZ twins share 50% of their DNA. These assumptions of genetic relatedness are reflected in the model specifications, such that the A factors, or genetic latent factors, are set to correlate at 1.0 in MZ twins, and 0.50 in DZ twins. In theory, both of these assumptions are true, but in practice MZ and DZ twins genetic relatedness can vary around these assumed values. MZ twins, for example, are derived from the same fertilized egg, meaning that they start with exactly the same genome, but later mutations, genetic expression, and epigenetic modifications can result in minor genotypic differences between MZ twins, though only in parts of the body (Charney, 2012). The assumption that DZ twins share 50% of their DNA reflects a population average, with specific samples, especially smaller samples, more likely to vary above or below the 50% average. Mathematical simulations to investigate the impact of deviations from genetic relatedness assumptions have shown that they have little impact on accurate estimation of heritability (Liu et al., 2018). Violation of the assumptions appear to have the largest effect on phenotypes of high true heritability, underestimating heritability estimates up to 10%, and correspondingly inflating non-shared environmental estimates; estimates of phenotypes of low true heritability are less likely to be affected (Liu et al., 2018).

Variance partitioning approaches also assume that the environmental experiences of MZ twins are no more alike than the environmental experiences of DZ twins, which is referred to as the *equal environments assumption* (Bhattacharjee and Sarkar, 2017; Scarr, 1968). Critics of twin studies argue that MZ twins are socialized to be more similar, and have more similar experiences because of their zygosity, which may bias heritability estimates upward (e.g., Joseph, 2004). Several types of studies, however, provide support for the equal environments assumption. Results of studies examining the similarities of MZ twins reared apart show that reared-apart MZ twins are just as similar as reared-together MZ twins. Other research has investigated whether true zygosity or perceived zygosity influences similarities between twins (Kendler et al., 1993), finding no association between perceived zygosity on trait similarity. Research utilizing doppelgangers (Segal et al., 2018), who are not genetically related, support this idea, indicating that people are treated similarly because of their heritable traits, not because of their zygosity. That is, people possessing particular heritable traits *evoke* similar reactions from other people. MZ twins are genetically identical and therefore evoke similar reactions from others, rather than others treating them similarly because of their perceived zygosity.

Many highly powered variance partitioning studies have produced robust and replicable results (Plomin et al., 2016; see also Stanley et al., 2018). These results from twin methods have culminated in what are referred to as the laws of behavior genetics (Turkhiemer, 2000). The first law of behavior genetics is that all complex phenotypes are, to some degree, heritable. The strongest evidence in support of this claim comes from a meta-analysis of twin studies on nearly 18,000 traits (e.g., intelligence, personality traits, health, relationships) – the largest behavioral genetic analysis on psychological phenotypes published to date (Polderman et al., 2015). Polderman et al. (2015) reported an average heritability of 49% across all complex human traits evaluated, supporting the first law. The results also showed that, on average, approximately 17% of variation across complex human traits is attributable to shared environmental variance. The finding that shared environment explains relatively less phenotypic variance than does genetic variation supports the second law of behavior genetics: that shared genes largely drive similarities between biological relatives, rather than shared environments. Finally, Polderman et al. show that the remainder of the variance of phenotypic traits, on average, is attributable to non-shared environmental variance. Because shared genetic variation and shared environmental variation function to explain similarities between individuals, that a substantial proportion of phenotypic variation is non-shared implies that unique experiences and random stochastic developmental variation are what explains individual differences, which is known as the third law of behavior genetics.

Partitioning covariance

A foundation of psychological science is to understand associations between two variables, or phenotypes, of interest, for example, understanding the association between early developmental stress and psychosocial outcomes. Such associations are referred to in behavior genetics as *phenotypic associations*. Phenotypic associations are correlational associations or regression coefficients reported in standard psychological research. What behavior genetics can add to standard phenotypic associations is the decomposition of the phenotypic association into the three components of genetic covariation, shared environmental covariation, and non-shared environmental covariation. That is, behavior genetic methods can identify the extent to which a reported correlation is explained by different factors, yielding informative insights into the nature of associations. Several statistical methods, often using structural equation modeling, can be used to partition covariance, and are explained in detail elsewhere (Turkheimer and Harden, 2014). Here, we will focus on the importance of this approach for psychological research, and the interpretation of partitioning covariance outcomes.

Establishing causal relations between traits or behaviors is a laudable goal of psychological research, yet one that is littered with myriad ethical and methodological obstacles. Given these obstacles, the social science model necessitates that three requirements are met to state that evidence is consistent with a causal interpretation: (1) two variables are related; (2) appropriate temporal sequence between the variables; and (3) relevant confounds are accounted for. Such approaches are motivated by a desire to establish a causal effect: that the change in one variable will cause a change in another variable. Behavior genetic methods are more aimed at identifying the causal structure of phenotypic associations (Briley et al., 2018): partitioning the covariance into different components of influence. Both causal goals are related. Once causal structure is identified, more precise investigation of causal effects can be pursued, for instance, by investigating genetic mechanisms or family-level factors.

Because of the first law of behavior genetics – that all complex phenotypes are heritable – it is reasonable to suspect that genes play some role in the architecture of phenotypic associations (Briley et al., 2018). Genetic covariation can affect two traits independently, producing a spurious phenotypic association. This particular problem, known as *genetic confounding*, is akin to the third variable problem in psychology. Identifying genetic confounds of phenotypic associations is necessary to accurately identify causal phenotypic effects. For example, if an association is found between depression and anxiety, but the association is predominantly accounted for by shared genetic covariation as described above, changing levels of depression may not produce reliable changes in anxiety. Controlling for genetic covariation is necessary to identify true effects between phenotypic associations, as is often the goal of mainstream psychology. As the genetic covariation between two traits, r_g, increases, the more likely is it that genetic covariation may be confounding phenotypic associations (Barnes et al., 2014).

The findings of shared and non-shared environmental covariance, r_c and r_e respectively, are more nuanced in their interpretation (Turkheimer and Harden, 2014). A result of a significant proportion of a phenotypic effect being attributed to shared environmental covariance is demonstrating that between-pair differences are accounting for

a proportion of the effect. A robust example of this is the positive association between spanking and physical abuse (Jaffee et al., 2004a). Covariance partitioning indicates that the majority of the phenotypic effect between spanking and physical abuse is attributable to shared environmental covariation, meaning that between-family differences, rather than within-pair (i.e., parent and child) differences account for the association. This contrasts with findings from the same data showing that the association between spanking and externalizing problems is attributable to genetic covariation and non-shared environmental covariation (Jaffee et al., 2004b). What this means is that after accounting for estimated genetic confounds, the remainder of the effect of spanking on subsequent externalizing problems is attributable to within-pair differences via non-shared environmental covariation, and not between-family differences. That within-pair differences, or non-shared environmental covariation, explains substantial proportions of phenotypic effects is, in fact, the strongest evidence for (quasi)causal effects that psychologists are often looking for (Turkheimer and Harden, 2014). One of the most important benefits of behavior genetic methods is the identification of environmental covariance to infer (quasi)causal phenotypic effects from correlational data.

Extended family designs

Extended family designs provide a method to identify environmental sources of variance on outcomes while controlling for genetic relatedness. Such designs allow for partitioning variance into genetic and environmental components to address questions of intergenerational transmission. Just as classical covariance partitioning methods, described above, can decompose the variance between two phenotypic traits, extended family designs have the same purpose, but are focused on phenotypic associations between generations. Phenotypic associations between generations, often between parents and children, are ubiquitous and foundational to many psychological theories of development, making extended family designs valuable to understand the causal architecture and directionality of intergenerational transmission (McAdams et al., 2014).

One popular extended family design is the Children of Twins (CoT) design, for which MZ and DZ twin parents and one child for each parent are assessed. CoT models allow for control of genetic covariation between parents and offspring, with the primary outcome being a path estimate between the parent and offspring phenotype. A limitation of the one-child CoT design is a lack of an estimate for shared environmental covariation on offspring phenotypes given that the offspring are assumed to reside in different environments. A difficulty with the CoT (or, by extension, Children of Siblings) design is the lower power to detect the sources of variation in offspring traits (McAdams et al., 2018). The relatedness coefficients between the targets, the offspring, are cousin-level (0.25 and 0.125), rather than sibling-level (1.00 and 0.50) as in classical twin models, meaning that the coefficients themselves are lower and the difference between them smaller, which causes reduced statistical power to detect effects. Power analyses indicate that nearly 1,000 families are needed to accurately detect a phenotypic association between parent and offspring assuming moderately heritable traits ($h^2 = .35$; McAdams et al., 2018).

Newer models extending the one-child CoT designs can more accurately model relationships between parents and offspring. McAdams et al. (2018) propose using a multiple CoT (MCoT) design, whereby at least two children of each twin parent are assessed. The addition of multiple children allows for modeling shared environmental variation on offspring phenotypes that is not available in the classic CoT model. Moreover, MCoT designs can appropriately model individual relationships between parent variables and offspring variables. Research on parent-child

interactions has shown that children shape parenting behavior, therefore violating the assumption that parent variables that psychologists are most often interested in are invariant across children. For variables such as emotional sensitivity, each child may evoke more or less sensitivity from the same parent. MCoT designs (McAdams et al., 2018) can model such relationships, yielding more accurate estimates of parent-offspring associations. Another benefit of MCoT designs, relative to classic CoT designs, is that fewer families are needed (around 500) to achieve adequate power (McAdams et al., 2018). Although nearly as many individuals are needed (more children per family, for example), the fact that fewer families need to be recruited could be a benefit for executing high-powered extended family designs.

Longitudinal designs

Behavior genetic models assume that genetic and environmental influences operate across development to give rise to observable phenotypes. Gene-environment interplay can take various forms across development (Briley et al., 2019; Scarr and McCartney, 1983). Take the associations between parenting and offspring outcomes. Cross-sectional designs, such as the CoT designs described previously, can partition covariance to identify the true phenotypic association between parent and offspring. The design, however, cannot inform the directionality of the association, or the nature of the association over time. Consider, for example, the association between harsh parenting and offspring externalizing behaviors. A cross-sectional CoT design can yield a phenotypic association between parenting and externalizing behaviors that controls for the genetic relatedness between the parent and offspring, but it does not provide information as to whether the harsh parenting led to externalizing behaviors or whether the child's externalizing behaviors prompted harsh parenting (or both).

Longitudinal designs can offer insight into how parents affect children, and how children affect parents. Children are not born as blank slates on which parents unidirectionally shape child outcomes. Children are born with capacities that shape the parenting they receive. Children are also not randomly allocated to environmental experiences (Plomin et al., 1977; Scarr, 1982). Environments provided by parents are influenced by their heritable qualities, some of which are passed down to offspring (Kendler and Baker, 2007). Finally, mating is non-random, meaning that traits of reproducing partners can be correlated both phenotypically and genetically (Yengo et al., 2018).

That environments are non-randomly distributed across individuals and are correlated among genetically similar individuals is referred to as *gene-environment correlation*, or *r*GE. *r*GE can take several forms across development: active, evocative (or reactive), and passive. *Active r*GE occurs when individuals actively seek out, avoid, or modify their environmental experiences that are non-randomly influenced by their genotype. *Evocative r*GE occurs when organisms receive responses or evoke reactions from others in their environment that are non-randomly influenced by their genotype. *Passive r*GE occurs when the environment that an individual inhabits – such as the neighborhood a child grows up in – is correlated with their genome. Parents endow offspring with an environment in which to live, and a genome comprised of half of each (biological) parent's genes, such that the environments children experience are correlated with the genotypes that they inherit from their parents (Kendler and Baker, 2007).

The dominant type of gene-environment correlation is proposed to change over the course of development (Scarr, 1992). Passive gene-environment correlation has greater explanatory power in infancy and early childhood. Because human infants are heavily dependent on caregivers during the first years of life, evident gene-environment correlations are most likely the passive type given the control caregivers have over

children's environment. The importance of active gene-environment correlation increases with age, as individual decision making and environmental control also increase. The implications of this change in dominant gene-environment correlation type over development can, in part, explain the general increase in heritability estimates of myriad traits (most notably, intelligence) over development (Plomin et al., 2016).

The interplay of genes and environments is not simple or straightforward, but rather complex and dynamic (Briley et al., 2019). A comprehensive understanding of gene-environment interplay for understanding phenotypic associations therefore requires that genetic variance is accounted for in research designs, especially longitudinal designs in which genetically related individuals are the targets of focus. In much developmental psychology research, such targets are often parents and offspring, who share, on average, 50% of their DNA. Failing to account for the genetic relatedness between family members may produce biased phenotypic effects of developmental processes across the lifespan.

Genetically-sensitive longitudinal designs can provide a nuanced understanding of purported parenting effects on child development, for example. The negative developmental impacts of spanking on child developmental outcomes is a contentious topic of research, of which most centers on the negative effects of parenting on children. A behavior genetic perspective, however, offers additional insights into understanding the dynamic nature of such phenotypic associations. A longitudinal twin study conducted by Cecil et al. (2012) is particularly suited to demonstrate evocative child effects of spanking, which are suggested by the results of the above genetically-informed studies. Using cross-lagged panel analyses, Cecil et al. examined whether harsh punishment (i.e., smacking and shouting) was associated with self-control difficulties from early childhood to adolescence. The results indicated bi-directional effects of harsh punishment and self-control; but, interestingly, between 7 and 12 years, only evocative effects were found such that self-control difficulties predicted later harsh punishment, but harsh punishment did not predict later self-control difficulties. Cecil et al. did find long-term effects of harsh punishment on early adolescent conduct problems, but for only boys. These results are consistent with the general notion that children's individual behavior can evoke or exacerbate parental punishment, with the unique contribution that the effects of harsh punishment may be particularly relevant in early childhood, as opposed to later childhood and adolescence (Cecil et al., 2012).

Genetically-sensitive longitudinal designs can be utilized to understand how variance components change over time, and can provide insight into which components are responsible for stability and change over development (Briley and Tucker-Drob, 2017). Each trait investigated is unique in many regards, but common among well-studied traits is the finding that shared environmental variance decreases rapidly across development (Plomin et al., 2016; Briley and Tucker-Drob, 2017), whereas non-shared environmental variance and genetic variance increase or remain relatively stable. Longitudinal behavior genetic designs are also capable of decomposing phenotypic stability into genetic and environmental components. Essentially, these models identify whether the genetic or environmental variance of a phenotype at one time point is the same variance that influences the phenotype at another time point. Specifically, variance components are correlated across time points. If the genetic variance component for a trait at time 1 are highly correlated with the genetic variance component for a trait at time 2, this indicates that genetic variance is, in part, responsible for the observed phenotypic stability of the trait. Collectively, longitudinal behavior genetic designs can provide a wealth of information on phenotypes over development.

Genetic Association Approaches

Classical family studies dominated the behavior genetic literature until the 21st century, largely because such designs were the most accessible to researchers. The sequencing of the human genome in 2001 propelled a new era of behavior genetics research – an era that is rapidly advancing and changing. At the beginning of this transition, scientists worked under what we now know to be false assumptions of how genes are associated with complex phenotypes. The goal was to find 'genes for' a particular trait, with the assumption being that traits would be underpinned by a few genes with relatively large effects, and that these genes would explain the genetic variance for traits that had been indicated by decades of family studies.

The focus on finding 'genes for' a particular trait produced a cascade of research in the early 2000s. Linkage and candidate gene approaches were applied to complex behavioral traits because such approaches had been so successful at identifying genes that contributed to Mendelian disorders – disorders in which a single gene can be identified by following traditional inheritance patterns, which are more common for some medical diseases. The 'genes for' approach to complex phenotypes was bolstered by early high-profile candidate gene studies, such as those on depression (Caspi et al., 2002, 2003). Enthusiasm for candidate gene approaches waned as the number of failed replications increased, including the high-profile candidate gene findings for depression (Border et al., 2019). It is now the consensus view that candidate gene approaches to understanding complex phenotypes are flawed and insufficient given what is now known about the genetic nature of complex phenotypes (Dick et al., 2014). Virtually all phenotypes of relevance for psychologists and behavioral scientists belong in the category of complex phenotypes.

Genome wide association studies (GWAS) became increasingly popular as their cost dropped through the 2000s (Mills and Rahal, 2019). GWAS identify associations between genes and phenotypes, as do candidate gene and linkage approaches, but do so across the entire genome. GWAS utilize genetic markers known as single nucleotide polymorphisms, or SNPs, across the genome to identify genetic regions that are associated with an outcome of interest. SNPs are variations in DNA building blocks (either A, C, T, or G), whereby, say, a C might be replaced by a T at a certain locus in a gene or stretch of DNA. These variations are normal in DNA, but particular variations may be relatively more or less common in populations of individuals. Catalogs of known SNPs (more than 100 million have been identified) are used as reference when correlating SNPs with phenotypes of interest. To date, nearly 4,000 GWAS have been conducted on thousands of traits (Mills and Rahal, 2019), the findings of which have greatly informed the field of behavior genetics.

Genetic associations with phenotypes

Family studies, described above, provided the foundation for what are known as the 'three laws of behavior genetics' (Turkheimer, 2000). GWAS has contributed to what is now known as the 'fourth law' of behavior genetics: complex phenotypic traits are highly polygenic (Chabris et al., 2015). Polygenic means that the phenotypic trait of interest has hundreds to thousands of genetic associations. The thousands of GWAS that have been published over the preceding two decades have revealed approximately 10,000 robust associations between genetic markers and various traits and disorders (Visscher et al., 2017), using a purely exploratory approach. The polygenic nature of complex traits sits in stark contrast to historical assumptions of candidate gene and linkage approaches that predicted just a few genes would be found underpinning each trait.

This fundamental insight to the polygenic nature of complex phenotypes also changed the way in which the effects of genes on complex phenotypes are understood. Whereas candidate gene approaches, for example, assumed that identified genes would have substantial effects and would thus explain the genetic variance estimated from family studies, GWAS approaches were increasingly producing two novel insights: (1) identified genetic variants have very small effects, often with each genetic variant explaining much less than 1% of the variance of a phenotype; and (2) GWAS approaches struggled to explain the genetic variance estimated from family studies, with such approaches yielding proportionately small heritability estimates, a problem referred to as *missing heritability*.

The small effects of individual genetic associations with phenotypes have implications for how behavior genetic research is conducted. Because many genetic loci contribute to the genetic variance of a trait, and thus the effect of each genetic variant is very small, it then implies that GWAS sample sizes must be very large to find reliable and accurate genetic associations. Indeed, the average sample size of GWAS has increased substantially since the first GWAS in the early 2000s, with some of the largest studies using data from over 1 million people (Mills and Rahal, 2019). Because larger samples have greater power to detect small effects, such as the type of effects GWAS are searching for, the number of associations found between genetic loci and complex phenotypes has rapidly increased over time as well. Analyses of the literature show that as sample sizes of GWAS have increased, so too have the number of associations found, and the number of traits studied. SNPs from GWAS can also be used to estimate a heritability based on this genetic data, free of the assumptions underlying family studies (as discussed above) (Yang et al., 2010). This SNP-based heritability forms the natural upper boundary for how much variance of a trait can be explained by SNP associations from GWAS. Currently, there seems to be no plateau of GWAS associations with increasing sample sizes, suggesting that continuing to increase sample sizes will continue to identify novel genetic associations and approach the level of explained variance set by the SNP-based heritability (Visscher et al., 2017).

However, estimates of SNP-based heritability from GWAS are often substantially smaller than heritability estimates from family studies (usually around half as large). This peculiar part of the missing heritability is a gap that cannot be expected to close just by increasing GWAS sample sizes. It is also a consequence of the polygenic nature of complex traits: because SNP catalogs that are used as reference panels for GWAS are by nature not complete, and extraordinary sample sizes are needed to detect effects, by design, substantial portions of heritability estimates from family studies will not be accounted for in average GWAS designs. As sample sizes have increased, and SNP catalogs have expanded, the proportion of additive genetic variance from SNP based GWAS is continuing to increase. New methods are also being developed to 'find' the missing heritability.

Whole genome sequencing

SNPs used in reference panels for GWAS as described above do not cover the entire genome, with many SNPs inferred or imputed based on linkage disequilibrium, which is the correlation of an SNP being associated with another SNP based on its location in the genome. Moreover, the SNPs used in reference panels tend to be 'common' variants found in at least 1% of the population (Visscher et al., 2017). These design features therefore mean that many SNPs will not be analyzed, which includes rare genetic variants occurring in less than 1% (and often much smaller proportions) of the population. Rare variants contribute to the problem of SNP heritability estimates being smaller than family study heritability estimates.

Whole genome sequencing methods are being developed and refined to address these limitations of traditional SNP based GWAS to 'find' the missing heritability of complex phenotypes. Many whole genome sequencing methods have been developed in recent years, with the utility of each depending on the specific genetic nature of the trait being assessed (Evans et al., 2018). Because whole genome sequencing methods can capture more SNPs at lower frequency levels than traditional GWAS approaches, whole genome sequencing studies have found that typical SNP heritability estimates may be underestimated by ~20% for most traits due to non-inclusion of rare variants (Evans et al., 2018).

Rare variants have become increasingly important for understanding and estimating the heritability of complex phenotypes and for explaining substantial amounts of heritability estimates found in family studies. Rare or low frequency variants, in contrast to the common variants tagged as SNPs in typical GWAS, have a greater impact on the outcome of interest, meaning that each rare variant explains a greater proportion of variance in the phenotype than does each common variant. Common variants, for example, often explain less than 0.5% to 1.0% of variance in a phenotype, whereas the effect of rare variants can be up to ten times larger than common variants in some cases (Manolio et al., 2009; Marouli et al., 2017). The heritability of traits such as intelligence and educational attainment has been much more accurately estimated using indirect approaches to capture rare variants, with family-specific (i.e., rare) genetic variants being implied in half of the heritability of these traits (Hill et al., 2018).

GWAS approaches, including whole genome sequencing methods, have unambiguously demonstrated the high polygenic nature of complex phenotypes, such that hundreds or thousands of genetic variants underpin traits of interest. Alternatively, some suggest that rather than polygenic, continued research could reveal that complex phenotypes will be more accurately described as 'omnigenic' with essentially all active genes being associated with every complex trait (Boyle et al., 2017). Whole genome sequencing methods (see Evans et al., 2018) continue to utilize the full breadth of the information available to geneticists to uncover heritability of complex phenotypes and solve the missing heritability problem prompted by earlier genetic association methods (Génin, 2019). It is likely that methods will continue to improve resulting in continually increasing accuracy of heritability.

Polygenic scores

GWAS has demonstrated that many genes of very small effects underpin phenotypes; therefore, using the genome to predict phenotypic outcomes necessarily needs to be based on the effects of multiple genes (Turkheimer, 2015). As GWAS discoveries increased, aggregate genetic 'scores' started being used as predictors of phenotypes. Most commonly referred to as *polygenic scores*, these genetic predictors are aggregate genome-based calculations given to an individual based on their genotype. Polygenic scores are genome-wide weighted averages of significant SNPs from independent GWAS (Belsky and Harden, 2019). Although specific methods for constructing polygenic scores vary, each follow a general approach. First, significant SNP associations from a GWAS are identified and weighted, which is referred to as the discovery sample. Next, using participants that were not included in the discovery sample, individual polygenic scores are calculated by summing the weighted SNP alleles (Belsky and Harden, 2019).

Polygenic scores can be calculated for any phenotypic trait for which GWAS is available. Once polygenic scores are calculated for individuals within a sample, the polygenic scores can be used as a predictor variable in psychological research using standard statistical modeling techniques. Although polygenic scores can be useful at the population level, particularly for understanding

how relatively high or low genetic 'risk' for a trait is associated with outcomes, on average, polygenic scores are so far nearly useless for prediction at the individual level (Belsky and Harden, 2019; Turkheimer, 2015). Polygenic scores are currently capable of explaining a few percentage points of variance in most outcomes, with the highest ranges at 3%-15% variance explained depending on the trait (Visscher et al., 2017). Moreover, because polygenic scores are built from GWAS, the limitations of GWAS for finding genetic associations surrounding sample size, missing heritability, and power, are carried over into the limitations of polygenic scores – the score is only as good as the GWAS it is based on, at best.

Additional problems arise regarding the predictive utility of polygenic scores across heterogeneous populations. Allele frequencies between human populations can vary for many reasons (e.g., genetic drift), leading to what is referred to as *population stratification*, or systematic differences in allele frequencies between populations. Because polygenic score construction relies on a discovery GWAS sample that is different than the test sample, and the majority of GWAS are from European populations (Mills and Rahal, 2019), using European-derived polygenic scores with diverse populations, such as those with Asian or African ancestry, results in poor predictive utility of polygenic scores in the test samples. For example, an analysis by Duncan et al. (2019) showed that the median effect size of polygenic scores in African ancestry samples was only 42% of that in a matched European ancestry sample, demonstrating the limitations of polygenic score generalizability to non-European samples. For polygenic scores to be of use in diverse human samples, GWAS must be representative of human populations.

Genetic correlation between phenotypes

Given that GWAS approaches have demonstrated that complex phenotypes are highly polygenic, there is the logical implication that genetic variants associated with one trait are likely to be associated with another trait. In other words, *pleiotropy* – genetic variants associated with more than one phenotypic trait – is pervasive (Visscher et al., 2017). Evidence for pleiotropy comes from a variety of behavior genetic methods estimating genetic correlations, r_g. Family studies, for example, can calculate r_g by correlating latent genetic factors for two phenotypes in twin models; but these correlations do not speak to the specific genetic variants underpinning the correlation. GWAS approaches can also calculate r_g similarly to family studies, but can also identify specific genetic variants that are associated with multiple phenotypes. As with other GWAS research goals, large sample sizes, approaching 100,000 participants depending on the precise method, are needed to achieve adequate power and produce accurate r_g estimates (van Rheenen et al., 2019).

Additionally, whereas family studies require measurements on both phenotypes of interest from the same participants to calculate r_g, GWAS can estimate genetic correlations and identify underlying genetic variants when phenotypes are measured from different individuals (Visscher et al., 2017). Limitations of family studies for calculating r_g are especially challenging for low frequency phenotypes such as disease traits or psychopathologies. GWAS can overcome this limitation by combining information from large data sets that have been independently collected for specific disease traits. Such approaches to measure pleiotropy using GWAS, in fact, exclude closely related individuals (such as siblings or cousins); excluding close relatives from the datasets have the benefit of largely eliminating shared environmental confounds that are present in family studies, which may bias the genetic variance estimates (van Rheenen et al., 2019).

Whereas GWAS methods for measuring pleiotropy avoid shared environmental confounding, researchers need to be cautious of other potential sources of confounding. Population stratification due to genetic drift, non-random mating, and geographic isolation can lead to differences in allele frequencies between populations. Such population differences can bias genetic correlation estimates between traits. Measuring the same phenotypic traits in two different populations may yield different genetic correlations between two disease traits. Such a finding may be indicative of a gene-environment interaction, whereby genetic variants are expressed differently depending on the environment; or in contrast, the effect could be reflective of the population structure rather than anything to do with the functional associations between the traits themselves (van Rheenen et al., 2019). For example, a disease that is relatively rare in one population may not show the same genetic association with other phenotypes as in a population where the disease is more prevalent. The discrepant genetic correlations, however, may not reflect genetic architecture differences between populations, but instead could simply be a result of the analysis not being able to accurately detect the low frequency genetic variants in the population where the disease is rare.

Genetic correlations provide useful information for researchers. Non-zero genetic correlations between two traits can help identify new risk factors for psychiatric conditions, for example, and yield insights into the genetic architecture between traits that may not have previously been obvious from standard social science methods that measure only phenotypes. For example, the understanding that Bipolar 1 disorder, characterized by mania, is more genetically similar to schizophrenia spectrum disorders than major depressive disorders (Coleman et al., 2019) was instrumental for changing the classification of Bipolar disorders in the fifth edition of the Diagnostic Statistical Manual of Mental Disorders to their own class, rather than a class shared with depressive disorders (APA, 2013).

IMPLICATIONS

Behavior genetic methods have substantively advanced in the preceding decades, most notably in the genomic era. This chapter is not an exhaustive description of all behavior genetic methods used in the social and behavior sciences, but is intended to be informative for a broad scientific audience interested in knowing what behavior genetic methods are available and, importantly, what the results of such methods mean for our understanding of psychology and behavior. In addition to the broader goals of behavior genetics – partitioning variance and covariance, and identifying genetic associations with phenotypes – these diverse methods can address pressing questions in the social sciences, especially regarding causality, development, and evolution, each of which will be briefly discussed.

Inferring Causality

Causal inference is a primary goal of social and behavioral science, although it is one that requires high standards of evidence to achieve. Behavior genetics, more broadly, contributes to improved causal inference in psychological science (although, still imperfect). Inference of causality of an association between two traits, X and Y, can be achieved in two ways. First, by conducting a randomized controlled experiment to remove any confounding influences on the association between X and Y can instill greater confidence that $X \rightarrow Y$. However, not all associations psychologists are interested in can be achieved by such methods. Also, not every individual is equally likely to naturally find themselves in each kind of situation that is simulated by experimental conditions (the very logic of gene-environment correlations), making random assignments to experimental conditions intrinsically artificial (Johnson and Penke, 2014). Causality can also be reasonably inferred by the removal of all

relevant confounds of the association between $X \rightarrow Y$ (Pearl and Mackenzie, 2018). Whereas traditional psychological approaches often strive to include relevant controls in non-experimental designs, oftentimes genetic confounds are not included. Given that on average half of the variance in any trait of interest is genetic (Polderman et al., 2015) and genetic correlations are ubiquitous, this is a major confound to ignore. Behavior genetic methods, such as family designs discussed above, offer a means to partition out genetic variance explaining the covariance between $X \rightarrow Y$ to better understand the phenotypic association and more accurately identify environmentally mediated effects, which are prime targets for interventions.

Behavior genetics knowledge and methods are also relevant for a broad understanding of the ways in which we think about causal models in psychological science. Because genes are the starting point from which phenotypes and behavior are descendant, temporal precedent is a reasonable *baseline assumption* for working with genetic association data (see Briley et al., 2018 for extensive discussion). That is, we can reasonably assume that with association between SNPs and a measured phenotype, generally the direction of causality is SNPs $\rightarrow$ phenotype, and not vice versa. This is an assumption that non-genetic psychological data cannot address (Briley et al., 2018). Temporal precedent of genes in relation to phenotypes is particularly relevant for hypothesized causal chains whereby genes $\rightarrow$ trait 1 $\rightarrow$ trait 2, or as in the case of pleiotropy, trait 1 $\leftarrow$ genes $\rightarrow$ trait 2. However, not all genetic associations identified from GWAS are causal but, in a broad sense, temporal precedence of genes to phenotypes is an informative starting point. Psychologists interested in causal inference of phenotypic models would benefit from considering behavior genetic models to strengthen claims (Briley et al., 2018; Johnson and Penke, 2014; Turkheimer and Harden, 2014).

Inferring Developmental Processes

Although it is a reasonable assumption that, broadly, genes cause phenotypes, genes are not the only cause of phenotypes. Phenotypes are intimately related to developmental processes; and behavior genetics assumes that phenotypes arise from complex interplay between genes and environment across development. Understanding developmental processes are therefore necessary for understanding phenotypes of interest to psychologists and social scientists. Developmental processes underlying behavior genetic models are diverse and complex, making identification of any particular developmental process underlying a particular phenotype of interest a difficult task. Briley et al. (2019) provide extensive discussion of developmental processes underlying behavior genetic models, and the reader is encouraged to consult this text directly.

The most common developmental processes discussed in the behavior genetic literature are gene-environment correlations (see Kendler and Baker, 2007; Scarr and McCartney, 1983), which contribute to similarities between genes and environments, and to amplification of genetic effects overtime; gene-environment interactions (see Tucker-Drob and Bates, 2016), in that genetic or environmental effects can have differing effects given either one's genes or environment, and failure to model such interactions can inflate genetic or environmental estimates depending on the particular interaction type; and simultaneous gene-environment interplay, whereby both correlation and interaction processes (discussed above) are occurring.

Adult phenotypes, which are most often studied in behavior genetics, need to consider the range of developmental processes that can yield the adult phenotype (Briley et al., 2019) despite the immense difficulty involved in modeling such processes with real data. Put differently, knowing that a personality trait in a sample of adults is 40% tells scientists nothing about the developmental processes yielding that estimate, or how the estimate changed over time. Careful examination of potential developmental processes for a phenotype in the hope of eliminating certain processes can narrow the remaining possibilities for a phonotype. Despite the difficulty in modeling behavior genetic developmental processes, such understanding is necessary for a complete understanding of phenotypes, and empirical attention to developmental behavior genetics is an important step forward for the field.

Inferring Evolution of Psychological Traits

Although the fields of behavior genetics and evolutionary psychology both have their historical origins in the 1970s, the fields have developed largely independently with little integration sought between the fields. One reason for this is the historical focus of evolutionary psychology to focus on species-typical adaptations (see Tooby and Cosmides, 1992), whereas behavior genetics has historically focused on sources of individual differences (see Plomin et al., 2013). Despite these disciplinary differences, behavior genetics can be informative for evolutionary psychology and offer important insights as to test evolutionary hypotheses (see Arslan and Penke, 2015; Penke et al., 2007; Penke and Jokela, 2016; and Zietsch et al., 2015 for extended discussions).

First, genetic correlations between traits (discussed above) can be informative for understanding the coevolution of traits, such as those regarding sexual selection hypotheses (e.g., the link between female preferences and male ornamentation), and for supporting by-product hypotheses (e.g., if trait X is a byproduct of trait Y then they should predictably covary genetically). Behavior genetics, and particularly GWAS methods can importantly inform proposed evolutionary processes for traits such as whether the existence of a trait is most likely due to mutation-selection balance, neutral-mutation-drift, or balancing selection, which are each underpinned by differing genetic architecture (Arslan and Penke, 2015; Penke et al., 2007; Zietsch et al., 2015). Schizophrenia is a great example for which behavior genetic methods have yielded insights to the evolution of the disorder. Because the causal variants (i.e., variants found to be associated with schizophrenia in GWAS) underlying schizophrenia explain fractions of a percent of the variance in the disorder suggests that deleterious causal variants with large effects are selected against and are therefore rare (Ripke et al., 2014). Put differently, behavior genetic evidence suggests that schizophrenia is most likely under negative selection and its frequency maintained by mutation-selection balance, therefore rendering adaptationist hypotheses of schizophrenia unlikely to be true. As GWAS increase in size, frequency, and breadth, evolutionary psychology can greatly benefit from its findings.

CONCLUSION

Behavior genetics has revolutionized our understanding of psychology. The big insights from behavior genetics (see Plomin et al., 2016) have demonstrated that all complex phenotypes that psychologists and social scientists are interested in are to some degree heritable (Polderman et al., 2015). To ignore this foundational fact of psychological science is to fundamentally limit our understanding of who we are. Research methods available today, most notably classical family studies and rapidly advancing genome association and sequencing approaches, continue to deliver insights into psychology and behavior. As the field's methodological tool kit advances, however, understanding of behavior genetic findings by scientists and the public need to also advance. Behavior genetics findings are more nuanced in their interpretations than early family studies suggested.

For example, interpretations such as 'the lack of substantial shared environmental effects implies that parents have little effect on their children's outcomes,' and 'substantial heritability of a trait naturally implies support for adaptationist models of traits' are no longer grounded in modern behavior genetics. Our intention with this chapter was to provide a broad introductory overview of the popular methods in the field, what can be inferred from these methods and, importantly, how complex and nuanced such interpretations are for understanding psychology and behavior. Behavior genetics has changed the way we understand psychology, and will continue to alter the landscape of psychological understanding.

REFERENCES

Arslan, R. C., & Penke, L. (2015). Evolutionary genetics. In D. M. Buss (Ed.), *Handbook of evolutionary psychology Vol. 2: Integrations* (2nd ed.) (pp. 1047–1066). New York: Wiley.

Barnes, J. C., Boutwell, B. B., Beaver, K. M., Gibson, C. L., & Wright, J. P. (2014). On the consequences of ignoring genetic influences in criminological research. *Journal of Criminal Justice, 42*(6), 471–482.

Belsky, D. W., & Harden, K. P. (2019). Phenotypic annotation: using polygenic scores to translate discoveries from genome-wide association studies from the top down. *Current Directions in Psychological Science, 28*(1), 82–90.

Bhattacharjee, S., & Sarkar, A. (2017). Equal environments assumption. In J. Vonk & T. K. Shackelford (Eds), *Encyclopedia of animal cognition and behavior*. Springer.

Border, R., Johnson, E. C., Evans, L. M., Smolen, A., Berley, N., Sullivan, P. F., & Keller, M. C. (2019). No support for historical candidate gene or candidate gene-by-interaction hypotheses for major depression across multiple large samples. *American Journal of Psychiatry, 176*(5), 376–387.

Boyle, E. A., Li, Y. I., & Pritchard, J. K. (2017). An expanded view of complex traits: From polygenic to omnigenic. *Cell*, *169*(7), 1177–1186.

Briley, D. A., & Tucker–Drob, E. M. (2017). Comparing the developmental genetics of cognition and personality over the lifespan. *Journal of Personality*, *85*(1), 51–64.

Briley, D. A., Livengood, J., & Derringer, J. (2018). Behaviour genetic frameworks of causal reasoning for personality psychology. *European Journal of Personality*, *32*(3), 202–220.

Briley, D. A., Livengood, J., Derringer, J., Tucker-Drob, E. M., Fraley, R. C., & Roberts, B. W. (2019). Interpreting behavior genetic models: seven developmental processes to understand. *Behavior Genetics*, *49*(2), 196–210.

Caspi, A., McClay, J., Moffitt, T. E., Mill, J., Martin, J., Craig, I. W., Taylor, A., & Poulton, R. (2002). Role of genotype in the cycle of violence in maltreated children. *Science*, *297*(5582), 851–854.

Caspi, A., Sugden, K., Moffitt, T. E., Taylor, A., Craig, I. W., Harrington, H., McClay, J., Mill, J., Martin, J., Braithwaite, A., & Poulton, R. (2003). Influence of life stress on depression: moderation by a polymorphism in the 5-HTT gene. *Science*, *301*(5631), 386–389.

Cecil, C. A., Barker, E. D., Jaffee, S. R., & Viding, E. (2012). Association between maladaptive parenting and child self-control over time: cross-lagged study using a monozygotic twin difference design. *The British Journal of Psychiatry*, *201*(4), 291–297.

Chabris, C. F., Lee, J. J., Cesarini, D., Benjamin, D. J., & Laibson, D. I. (2015). The fourth law of behavior genetics. *Current Directions in Psychological Science*, *24*(4), 304–312.

Charney, E. (2012). Behavior genetics and postgenomics. *Behavioral and Brain Sciences*, *35*(5), 331–358.

Coleman, J. R., Gaspar, H. A., Bryois, J., & Breen, G. (2019). The genetics of the mood disorder spectrum: genome-wide association analyses of over 185,000 cases and 439,000 controls. *Biological Psychiatry*. doi:10.1016/j.biopsych.2019.10.015.

Dick, D. M., Agrawal, A., Keller, M. C., Adkins, A., Aliev, F., Monroe, S., Hewitt, J. K., Kendler, K. S., & Sher, K. J. (2015). Candidate gene–environment interaction research: reflections and recommendations. *Perspectives on Psychological Science*, *10*(1), 37–59.

Duncan, L., Shen, H., Gelaye, B., Meijsen, J., Ressler, K., Feldman, M., Peterson, R., & Domingue, B. (2019). Analysis of polygenic risk score usage and performance in diverse human populations. *Nature Communications*, *10*(1), 1–9.

Evans, L. M., Tahmasbi, R., Vrieze, S. I., Abecasis, G. R., Das, S., Gazal, S., … & Yang, J. (2018). Comparison of methods that use whole genome data to estimate the heritability and genetic architecture of complex traits. *Nature Genetics*, *50*(5), 737–745.

Génin, E. (2019). Missing heritability of complex diseases: case solved? *Human Genetics*, 1–11. doi:10.1007/s00439-019-02034-4.

Hill, W. D., Arslan, R. C., Xia, C., Luciano, M., Amador, C., Navarro, P., Hayward, C., Nagy, R., Porteous, D., McIntosh, A. M., Deary, I. J., Haley, C., & Penke, L. (2018). Genomic analysis of family data reveals additional genetic effects on intelligence and personality. *Molecular Psychiatry*, *23*(12), 2347–2362.

International Human Genome Sequencing Consortium (2001). Initial sequencing and analysis of the human genome. *Nature*, *409*(6822), 860–921.

Jaffee, S. R., Caspi, A., Moffitt, T. E., & Taylor, A. (2004a). Physical maltreatment victim to antisocial child: evidence of an environmentally mediated process. *Journal of Abnormal Psychology*, *113*(1), 44–55.

Jaffee, S. R., Caspi, A., Moffitt, T. E., Polo-Tomas, M., Price, T. S., & Taylor, A. (2004b). The limits of child effects: evidence for genetically mediated child effects on corporal punishment but not on physical maltreatment. *Developmental Psychology*, *40*(6), 1047–1058.

Johnson, W., & Penke, L. (2014). Genetics of social behavior. In B. Gawronski & G. Bodenhausen (Eds), *Theory and explanation in social psychology* (pp. 205–223). New York: Guilford Press.

Joseph, J. (2004). *The gene illusion: Genetic research in psychiatry and psychology under the microscope*. New York: Algora.

Kendler, K. S., & Baker, J. H. (2007). Genetic influences on measures of the environment: a systematic review. *Psychological Medicine*, *37*(5), 615–626.

Kendler, K. S., Neale, M. C., Kessler, R. C., Heath, A. C., & Eaves, L. J. (1993). A test of the equal-environment assumption in twin studies of psychiatric illness. *Behavior Genetics*, *23*(1), 21–27.

Liu, C., Molenaar, P. C., & Neiderhiser, J. M. (2018). The impact of variation in twin relatedness on estimates of heritability and environmental influences. *Behavior Genetics*, *48*(1), 44–54.

Manolio, T. A., Collins, F. S., Cox, N. J., Goldstein, D. B., Hindorff, L. A., Hunter, D. J., ... & Cho, J. H. (2009). Finding the missing heritability of complex diseases. *Nature*, *461*(7265), 747–753.

Marouli, E., Graff, M., Medina-Gomez, C., Lo, K. S., Wood, A. R., Kjaer, T. R., ... & Rüeger, S. (2017). Rare and low-frequency coding variants alter human adult height. *Nature*, *542*(7640), 186–190.

McAdams, T. A., Hannigan, L. J., Eilertsen, E. M., Gjerde, L. C., Ystrom, E., & Rijsdijk, F. V. (2018). Revisiting the children-of-twins design: improving existing models for the exploration of intergenerational associations. *Behavior Genetics*, *48*(5), 397–412.

Mills, M. C., & Rahal, C. (2019). A scientometric review of genome-wide association studies. *Communications Biology*, *2*(1), 1–11.

Pearl, J., & Mackenzie, D. (2018). *The book of why: the new science of cause and effect*. New York: Basic Books.

Penke, L. (2011). Bridging the gap between modern evolutionary psychology and the study of individual differences. In D. M. Buss & P. H. Hawley (Eds), *The evolution of personality and individual differences* (pp. 243–279). New York: Oxford University Press.

Penke, L., Denissen, J. J. A., & Miller, G. F. (2007). The evolutionary genetics of personality (target article). *European Journal of Personality*, *21*(5), 549–587.

Penke, L., & Jokela, M. (2016). The evolutionary genetics of personality revisited. *Current Opinion in Psychology*, *7*, 104–109.

Plomin, R., DeFries, J. C., & Loehlin, J. C. (1977). Genotype–environment interaction and correlation in the analysis of human behavior. *Psychological Bulletin*, *84*(2), 309–322.

Plomin, R., DeFries, J. C., Knopik, V. S., & Neiderhiser, J. M. (2016). Top 10 replicated findings from behavioral genetics. *Perspectives on Psychological Science*, *11*(1), 3–23.

Plomin, R., DeFries, J. C., Knopik, V. S., & Neiderhiser, J. M. (2013). *Behavioral genetics* (6th ed.). New York: Worth Publishers.

Polderman, T. J. C., Benyamin, B., de Leeuw, C. A., Sullivan, P. F., van Bochoven, A., Visscher, P. M., & Posthuma, D. (2015). Meta-analysis of the heritability of human traits based on fifty years of twin studies. *Nature Genetics*, *47*(7), 702–709.

Purcell, S. (2016). Statistical methods in behavioral genetics. In R. Plomin, J. C. DeFries, V. S. Knopik, & J. M. Neiderhiser, *Behavioral Genetics* (6th ed.) (pp. 357–412). New York: Worth Publishers.

Ripke, S., Neale, B. M., Corvin, A., Walters, J. T., Farh, K. H., Holmans, P. A., ... & Pers, T. H. (2014). Biological insights from 108 schizophrenia-associated genetic loci. *Nature*, *511*(1470), 421–427.

Scarr, S. (1968). Environmental bias in twin studies. *Eugenics Quarterly*, *15*(1), 34–40.

Scarr, S. (1992). Developmental theories for the 1990s: development and individual differences. *Child Development*, *63*(1), 1–19.

Scarr, S., & McCartney, K. (1983). How people make their own environments: a theory of genotype ☐ environment effects. *Child Development*, *54*(2), 424–435.

Segal, N. L., Hernandez, B. A., Graham, J. L., & Ettinger, U. (2018). Pairs of genetically unrelated look-alikes. *Human Nature*, *29*(4), 402–417.

Stanley, T. D., Carter, E. C., & Doucouliagos, H. (2018). What meta-analyses reveal about the replicability of psychological research. *Psychological Bulletin*, *144*(12), 1325–1346.

Tooby, J., & Cosmides, L. (1992). The psychological foundations of culture. In J. H. Barkow, L. Cosmides, & J. Tooby (Eds), *The adapted mind: Evolutionary psychology and the generation of culture* (pp. 19–136). New York: Oxford University Press.

Tucker-Drob, E. M., & Bates, T. C. (2016). Large cross-national differences in gene × socioeconomic status interaction on intelligence. *Psychological Science*, *27*(2), 138–149.

Turkheimer, E. (2000). Three laws of behavior genetics and what they mean. *Current Directions in Psychological Science*, *9*(5), 160–164.

Turkheimer, E. (2015). Genetic prediction. *Hastings Center Report*, *45*, S32–S38.

Turkheimer, E., & Harden, K. P. (2014). Behavior genetic research methods: testing quasi-causal hypotheses using multivariate twin data. In H. T. Reis & C. M. Judd (Eds), *Handbook of research methods in social and personality psychology* (2nd ed.). Cambridge University Press.

van Rheenen, W., Peyrot, W. J., Schork, A. J., Lee, S. H., & Wray, N. R. (2019). Genetic correlations of polygenic disease traits: from theory to practice. *Nature Reviews Genetics*, *20*(10), 567–581.

Venter, J. C., Adams, M. D., Myers, E. W., Li, P. W., Mural, R. J., Sutton, G. G., … & Gocayne, J. D. (2001). The sequence of the human genome. *Science, 291*(5507), 1304–1351.

Visscher, P. M., Wray, N. R., Zhang, Q., Sklar, P., McCarthy, M. I., Brown, M. A., & Yang, J. (2017). 10 years of GWAS discovery: biology, function, and translation. *The American Journal of Human Genetics*, *101*(1), 5–22.

Yang, J., Benyamin, B., McEvoy, B. P., Gordon, S., Henders, A. K., Nyholt, D. R., Madden, P. A., Heath, A. C., Martin, N. G., & Goddard, M. E. (2010). Common SNPs explain a large proportion of the heritability for human height. *Nature Genetics*, *42*(7), 565–569.

Yengo, L., Robinson, M. R., Keller, M. C., Kemper, K. E., Yang, Y., Trzaskowski, M., Gratten, J., Turley, P., Cesarini, D., Benjamin, D. J., Wray, N. R., Goddard, M. E., Yang, J., & Wray, N. R. (2018). Imprint of assortative mating on the human genome. *Nature Human Behaviour*, *2*(12), 948–954.

Zietsch, B. P., de Candia, T. R., & Keller, M. C. (2015). Evolutionary behavioral genetics. *Current Opinion in Behavioral Sciences*, *2*, 73–80.

Sex Differences and Sex Similarities

Alastair P. C. Davies

INTRODUCTION

From an individual's physical appearance, we can immediately determine that the individual is human. It is not something that we have to think about. Indeed, our ability to do so appears to be instinctive. Further, typically, an individual's physical appearance allows us to instantly ascertain whether the individual is a woman or a man. Again, doing so appears to be instinctive.

Our ability to determine from an individual's physical appearance that the person is human indicates that certain physical features are reliably similar across women and men. Similarly, our ability to determine from an individual's physical appearance whether the person is a woman or a man indicates that that certain physical features reliably differ across women and men.

These same things can be said in relation to our psychology and behavior. Because there are behaviors that are reliably similar across humans, we can immediately ascertain from an individual's behavior that the individual is human. And, as the behavior of individuals is determined by their psychology, we can immediately ascertain from the behavior of individuals that there must be psychological features that are reliably similar across humans. We can also, typically, ascertain from a person's behavior whether the person is a woman or a man, indicating that there are behaviors that typically differ across women and men and that, therefore, there must also be psychological features that typically differ across women and men.

The Approach of this Chapter

In 1776, Adam Smith's 'An Inquiry into the Nature and Causes of the Wealth of Nations' (Smith, 1776) was published. Smith sought to explain the causes of wealth, not of poverty, because poverty did not need explaining; poverty is the default condition in which humans live, in the sense that it is the condition in which humans lived initially and thereafter the condition in which they lived for millennia. What Smith needed to explain, therefore, were the processes by which some nations had been able to rise out of poverty.

Similarly, as sex similarities constitute the species-typical traits that define a species, they may be seen as the default condition of evolved traits within a species, in the sense that individuals who did not evolve those traits would belong to a different species. That which especially requires explanation, therefore, are the processes by which females and males of a particular species come to evolve differences along traits. For this reason, this chapter will be devoted largely to considering the evolution of sex differences rather than sex similarities.

Adaptive Problems and Adaptations

Adaptive problems are challenges concerning survival and mating that individuals reliably face each generation. Because they concern survival and mating, adaptive problems impact upon the reproductive success of individuals. And because they are recurrent across generations, natural or sexual selection leads individuals to evolve traits to solve them. Bodily, psychological, or behavioral traits that evolve to solve adaptive problems are said to be 'adaptive' and are called 'adaptations'.

Natural Selection and the Evolution of Sex Similarities

Natural selection is the process by which traits evolve that solve adaptive problems related to survival (Darwin, 1859). Adaptive problems related to survival include the metabolizing of food, expulsion of nitrogenous waste, the five senses, respiration, selection of food, and the avoidance of predators. As adaptive problems relating to survival are the same for females and males,

natural selection leads to the evolution of sex similarities.

Natural selection is comprised of variation, selection, and inheritance. Variation refers to the fact that there will be variation or differences between individuals of a population along each bodily, psychological, or behavioral trait. Variation is produced randomly by genetic mutations. Some variations of traits, however, will be more adaptive than others such that they solve adaptive problems related to survival better than do other variations in a particular environment. Individuals who possess these most adaptive variations are likely to have higher survival rates and, therefore, more offspring. Therefore, through non-random selection, a greater proportion of the most adaptive variations than the alternative variations will be inherited from generation to generation. This differential selection and inheritance mean that, each generation, the proportion of the most adaptive variations in the population increases relative to the proportion of other, less adaptive, variations. As, within a population, adaptive problems relating to survival are the same for females and males, both females and males inherit a greater proportion of the most adaptive variations. Consequently, after numerous generations, the most adaptive variations become universal in the population such that they are possessed by all individuals in the population. The most adaptive variations, therefore, become the sex similarities that constitute species-typical traits that define or are uniquely associated with a species.

An example of sex similarities that constitute species-typical traits among humans consists of personality traits. It has become widely accepted that human personality is comprised of the five factors or traits of openness, conscientiousness, extraversion, agreeableness, and neuroticism as captured by the *Five Factor Model* (McCrae and Costa, 1993). Buss (1996) argued that these *Big Five* traits evolved to solve *social adaptive problems* or adaptive problems concerning the navigation through social hierarchies associated with group living. According to this view, the *Big Five* enable humans to enact social strategies to prevent them from moving down or facilitate them moving up social hierarchies. A woman or man lacking or falling extremely low along any of the *Big Five* would be significantly disadvantaged in solving social adaptive problems. In line with this, research indicates the *Big Five* to be a universal across humans such that they have been found in women and men across a wide variety of cultures (e.g., John and Srivastava, 1999).

Other sex similarities that evolved among humans through natural selection and that constitute our species-typical traits include the skeletal and musculature structures, the internal organs, the sensory organs, the skin, and the four lobes of the brain and the cerebellum. Evolved psychological sex similarities include fear of heights, fear of snakes, the *Big Five* personality traits of openness, conscientiousness, extraversion, agreeableness, neuroticism, and disgust in response to the smell or taste of pathogens. Evolved behavioral sex similarities include spoken symbolic language and bipedalism.

As sex similarities constitute the traits that define a species, they overwhelmingly outnumber the sex differences within a species. Indeed, as shall be outlined below, many of the sex differences within a species are the result of certain species-typical traits being subject to the process of sexual selection.

Sex Similarities as Evolutionary By-Products

In addition to sex similarities evolving through natural selection, women and men have evolved similarities along traits that were not themselves subject to selection because they do not serve any adaptive function. Such traits are labelled as evolutionary 'by-products' because, although they do not themselves facilitate survival, they are carried along with adaptations when adaptations evolve through natural selection. For instance, the whiteness of women's and men's teeth and bones was not selected and so is not an adaptation. Rather, it is a by-product of calcium phosphate being selected for its rigidity and hardness. From an evolutionary standpoint, the fact that calcium phosphate happens to be white is irrelevant. Similarly, the red color of women's and men's blood is not an adaptation but is an evolutionary by-product of the adaptation hemoglobin. Hemoglobin was selected because of its ability to bind with iron molecules which, in turn, have the ability to bind with oxygen and so enable blood to transport oxygen around the body. The fact that the chemical bonds between iron and oxygen molecules cause light to be reflected in such a way that blood appears to be red serves no evolutionary function. The belly button is another trait that is similar across the sexes but which is not an adaptation. Rather, it is a by-product of the umbilical cord being selected to solve the adaptive problem of connecting the baby in the womb with the mother's placenta, thereby enabling the baby to receive oxygen and nutrients and the baby's waste products to be taken away from the baby and be disposed of. Because they are concomitants of adaptations that evolved through natural selection, these and other evolutionary by-products are, like adaptations that solve adaptive problems related to survival, possessed by all humans.

Sex Differences as Primary Sexual Characteristics

In a sexually-reproducing species, a number of evolved traits are not typical of the species but, rather, are typical of each sex. Such sex-typical traits that, ontogenetically, develop prenatally are known as primary sexual characteristics. They are comprised of the internal and external reproductive organs that are directly related to reproduction. In women, the internal reproductive organs include the ovaries, fallopian tubes, uterus, and proximal vagina. In men, they include the seminal vesicles, epididymis, and vas deferens. In women, the external reproductive organs or genitalia include the distal vagina, vulva, and clitoris. In men, they include the testes and penis. Primary sexual characteristics are also exhibited in the form of sexually dimorphic neural structures (Jazin and Cahill, 2010; McCarthy and Arnold, 2011).

There is controversy regarding whether the sex differences constituted by primary sexual characteristics have evolved through natural or sexual selection (e.g., Ghiselin, 2010). Notwithstanding this, as they have evolved through selection pressures, primary sexual characteristics are sex differences that are adaptations, not evolutionary by-products.

Sexual Selection and the Evolution of Sex Differences

Sexual selection is the process by which traits evolve that solve adaptive problems related to mating (Darwin, 1871). Adaptive problems related to mating differ across the sexes. This is because, among most species, it is females who have the larger obligatory parental investment (OPI) or the amount of parental investment that each sex must make to produce viable offspring, that is, offspring that will survive to reproductive age (Trivers, 1972). For instance, in reptiles (not including birds), after the female has laid the eggs, it is typically she who deposits them and then, if the species continues to care for them, it is typically she who carries out the incubation or guarding of them. In mammals, as the fertilized egg develops internally, females must gestate the offspring and then provide post-natal care through suckling. In contrast, males must provide only the semen to fertilize the females' eggs. As adaptive problems relating to mating are different for females and males, sexual selection leads to the evolution of sex differences.

Ontogenetically, sexually-selected sex differences develop at puberty and are known

as *secondary sexual* characteristics. Unlike primary sexual characteristics, that evolve as sex-specific traits, secondary sexual characteristics evolve as quantitative differences between females and males along evolved species-typical traits.

Each of the following sub-sections first outlines how sexual selection has led non-humans to evolve sex differences along particular species-typical bodily, psychological, and behavioral traits. It then outlines how sexual selection has led humans to evolve similar sex differences along the same species-typical traits.

INTRA-SEXUAL COMPETITION AND INTER-SEXUAL SELECTION

The sex difference in OPI leads to a sex difference in the two components of sexual selection, namely intra-sexual competition and inter-sexual selection. Intra-sexual competition involves members of one sex competing to gain sexual access to members of the other sex. Inter-sexual selection involves members of one sex choosing members of the other sex with whom to mate.

The female-biased OPI means that at any given time, a proportion of females will not be sexually receptive. As a result, at any one time, there will be a male-biased *operational sex ratio* (OSR) or ratio of the number of sexually receptive males to the number of sexually receptive females (Emlen and Oring, 1977). This means that at any one time there will be a relatively large number of males trying to mate with a relatively small number of females. Consequently, the intra-sexual competition for mates will typically be more intense within males. It is, therefore, typically, males who are the 'competing' sex engaging in intra-sexual competition and females who are the 'choosy' sex engaging in inter-sexual selection.

In species in which the only parental investment made by males is sperm, females should have evolved to base their mate selection on the quality of a male's genes. 'Good' genes would be those that provide the individuals possessing them with resistance to parasites and pathogens (Hamilton and Zuk, 1982). In order to maximize the probability that their relatively large OPI is not wasted due to their offspring dying before reaching reproductive age, females should, therefore, have evolved to prefer males with the best quality genes. In turn, males should have evolved to compete against each other in indicating to females that they possess 'honest' signals of such good genes (e.g., Zahavi, 1975).

This competition among males to display such honest signals takes two forms, namely, display and physical combat. In display, these signals include ornamentation, and, in physical combat, they include strength, size, weapons, and aggressiveness. This leads to an evolutionary arms race among males. As, in each generation, only those males who have the brightest and largest ornamentation or who are the strongest, largest, and most aggressive are chosen as mates by females, each subsequent generation of males has, on average, brighter and larger ornamentation and is stronger, larger, and more aggressive than the previous generation. Consequently, over many generations, species-typical traits that facilitate the winning of intra-sexual competition evolve to be highly exaggerated among males. In contrast, as intra-sexual competition among females is minimal, species-typical traits among females remain similar from one generation to the next. This means that, each generation, there is an increase in the magnitude of the sex differences along species-typical traits that facilitate the winning of intra-sexual competition.

Over many generations these sex differences can become vast. Within a species, the greater the proportion of females to which the most ornamented and larger males monopolise sexual access, the greater will be the proportion of offspring of such males in the subsequent generation. Consequently, from generation to generation, the greater will be the increase in the average ornamentation,

size, and strength of males and the larger will be the size of the sex differences within the species along these traits (e.g., Alexander et al., 1979).

Perhaps the most well-known example of a sex difference resulting from intra-sexual competition is that found between peahens and peacocks. As the only parental investment made by peacocks is their sperm, peahens choose to mate with males based on the quality of their genes. Peacocks indicate their genetic quality through displaying their tails. Petrie et al. (1991) found that females prefer to mate with peacocks with the most eyes on their tails and that the offspring of those peacocks have a greater resistance to parasites. So, each generation, it is the most ornamented peacocks who have the most mates and the most surviving offspring. It is, therefore, through an evolutionary arms race involving each generation of peahens choosing to mate with only the most ornamented peacocks that the magnitude of the sex difference in the tails has incrementally increased from generation to generation to what it is today. So, although today, the difference between the large and brightly ornamented tails of peacocks and the small, dull tails of peahens is vast, this sex difference would have been almost imperceptible among early generations.

Intra-male competition in the form of physical combat is clearly evidenced among elephant seals. Combat among male elephant seals takes the form of head-butting, with the winners gaining control of sexual access to a harem comprised of dozens of females. As well as aggressiveness, size is the most important factor in winning this combat. An evolutionary arms race has, therefore, led to males today being between three and eight times heavier than females (Le Boeuf and Reiter, 1988).

Confirming the explanatory power of the theory of sexual selection, it is found that, in species in which males have the larger OPI, intra-sexual competition is more intense among females and it is males who are the choosy sex. For instance, among a species of shorebird named the red phalarope, it is the dull-plumaged males who provide all the parental care and the larger and brightly-plumaged females who fight among themselves for control of harems of males so as to deposit their eggs in the males' nests.

These same evolutionary forces of sexual selection have led to the evolution of sex differences among humans. It is, of course, women who have the larger OPI because, whereas men must provide only their sperm, women must gestate the child for nine months and, among ancestral humans, would have had to breastfeed the child for the first three to four years of its life (e.g., Clayton et al., 2006). So, intra-sexual competition is expected to be more intense among men. In line with this, on average, men have a larger overall physical size than do women (Tanner, 1990). Moreover, men's upper-body strength is, on average, greater than that of women. Even when controlling for height, men have broader shoulders and greater musculature in the upper body and biceps than do women (Ross and Ward, 1982).

It has, however, been argued that such bodily sex differences are due, not to intra-male competition, but, rather, to division of labor, notably men hunting versus women gathering (e.g., Frost, 1998). Evidence against this argument is provided by findings among primates that are monogamous. Among such species, there is, reliably, little intra-male competition for mates and little difference between the sizes of males and females regardless of the species' foraging strategy (Plavcan and van Schaik, 1997).

Moreover, as in most non-human species, the evidence indicates that, among humans, it is males more than females who have evolved to be psychologically predisposed to engage in physical combat. For every culture for which homicide statistics are available, men are overwhelmingly more likely than women to commit and be the victims of homicides (Daly and Wilson, 1988). For instance, Daly and Wilson (1988) found that

in Chicago between 1965 and 1980, 86% of homicides were committed by men and 80% of homicide victims were men. Moreover, the notion that homicide is associated with intra-male competition for mates is supported by findings indicating that the magnitude of the sex difference in being a victim of homicide begins to increase rapidly around puberty when men are beginning to look for mates. The magnitude of this sex difference reaches a peak around the mid to late 20s when men might be expected to have found a mate and, thereafter, declines steadily (e.g., Wilson and Daly, 1985). The proposition that it is competition for mates that underlies the killing of men by other men is further supported by findings that unmarried men are disproportionately more likely to commit a homicide. For instance, Wilson and Daly (1985) found that of male-on-male homicides in 1982 in Detroit, 73% of the perpetrators and 69% of the victims were unmarried whereas only 43% of men in Detroit of a similar age were unmarried.

DEFINING 'LONG-TERM' AND 'SHORT-TERM' MATINGS

Human matings are typically defined temporally as 'long-term' and 'short-term'. Women's and men's preferences and behaviors in relation to a mating are not, however, determined by the mating's temporal length per se. Rather, they are determined by the level of men's parental investment toward the mating. This is because, whereas women are biologically obliged to provide substantial parental investment, men can choose to provide only their relatively small OPI (i.e., only their sperm) or to provide additional parental investment in the form of reliable economic resources. As shall be discussed in detail below, preferences and behaviors in relation to a mating, therefore, are, for men, determined by whether they are willing to provide reliable economic parental investment for any child that should result from the mating and, for women, determined by whether they expect the man to provide reliable economic parental investment for any child that should result from the mating. It follows that a 'short-term' mating may be defined as one in which the man does not provide reliable economic parental investment and a 'long-term' mating may be defined as one in which the man does provide reliable economic parental investment. As such, defining a mating in terms of its temporal length is not meaningful, because a mating may continue over an extended temporal length but the man would be unwilling to provide reliable economic parental investment for any child that should result from the mating and the woman may not expect the man to do so.

As shall be outlined below, females and males are expected to differ regarding their desire for short-term versus long-term mates. In addition, mate preferences of females and males are expected to differ depending on whether a mating is short-term or long-term.

DESIRE FOR MULTIPLE MATINGS

As the OPI of females is, typically, relatively large, the number of offspring that a female can produce during a particular period is limited. While she is gestating, a female cannot increase that number by re-mating with the male who impregnated her or by mating with other males. In contrast, the relatively small OPI of males means that after a male has impregnated a female, he can possibly immediately go on to impregnate other females. Therefore, in a given time-period, a male may have multiple females who have been impregnated by him and who are producing his offspring. Unlike females, therefore, within a given time-period, males can increase the number of offspring they produce by increasing the number of mates they have. The female-biased OPI means, therefore, that the potential reproductive rate or the number of offspring that each sex can possibly produce

in a given time-period (Clutton-Brock and Vincent, 1991) is male-biased.

The male-biased potential reproductive rate means that the reproductive benefit of each additional mating is greater for males than it is for females. It follows that males more than females should have evolved a psychology that motivates them to attempt to secure multiple mates. For instance, during breeding seasons, male meadow voles roam around home ranges four to five times larger than those of females in order to mate with multiple widely-dispersed females (Gaulin and FitzGerald, 1986). Males among a species of bird named the white-bearded manakin secure multiple mates through a different means. Each male locates himself around a sapling and provides displays for females when they arrive. Males preferred by females have a disproportionately large number of mates. For instance, Lill (1974) found that one male manakin achieved almost 75% of all matings. Disproportionately large numbers of mates are also secured by males who win intra-male competition through physical combat. For instance, male southern elephant seals who defeat other males gain control of sexual access to harems of females numbering in the hundreds. These harem-holders can account for almost 90% of paternities in each harem (Fabiani et al., 2004).

Similarly, as human males have a relatively small OPI, men more than women should have evolved to desire multiple mates. Cross-cultural evidence in support of this was provided by Schmitt et al. (2003). They asked women and men from 52 countries comprising 10 world regions (including the Middle East, Africa, Oceania, North America, South America, and East Asia) how many sexual partners they would ideally like to have over various time-intervals ranging from one month to their entire remaining lifetime. Across all world regions combined, men reported wanting more sexual partners than did women for each time-interval ranging from one month to the next 30 years. Considering each world region separately and looking only at the time-intervals of one month and the next 30 years, Schmitt et al. found that men reliably reported wanting more sexual partners than did women. These findings suggest that men's greater desire than women for having multiple sexual partners is not the product of the mores or conventions of a particular culture.

Evidence of men having a greater desire than women for multiple mates has also been secured through field experiments investigating people's willingness to engage in casual sex. Clark and Hatfield (1989) instructed female and male confederates (research assistants) to approach women and men of the opposite-sex to them on a college campus. They were instructed to introduce themselves by saying, 'I have been noticing you around campus. I find you to be very attractive' and then ask one of a pre-specified set of questions. To the question, 'Would you go out with me tonight?', 50% of women and 56% of men replied 'Yes'. To the question, 'Would you come over to my apartment tonight?', 6% of women and 69% of men replied 'Yes'. To the question, 'Would you go to bed with me tonight?', 0% of women and 75% of men replied 'Yes'. Hald and Høgh-Olesen (2010) secured similar findings through a similar procedure. However, it might be argued that the lower percentages of women than of men being willing to go to bed with the confederate was due to women's fear of being physical harmed rather than an unwillingness to have sex with the confederate. However, this does not appear to be the case, as the percentage of women willing to go to the confederate's apartment was greater than the percentage of women willing to go to bed with him. That a desire for sex was the primary factor motivating men to reply 'yes' is indicated by the percentage of men willing to go to the confederate's apartment being less than the percentage of men willing to go to bed with her. This is because it suggests that some men were unwilling to go to the confederate's apartment because they believed it might not result in them having sex with her.

Evidence of men more than women having a desire for multiple mates is also provided by sexual fantasies. Sexual fantasy provides especially direct insight into women's and men's evolved psychology because, unlike behavior, it is not constrained by the exigencies of the real world. Research has indicated large sex differences in sexual fantasy. Women's sexual fantasies are likely to involve partners with whom the women are familiar and to have the setting and feelings as their focus (e.g., Barclay, 1973). In contrast, men's sexual fantasies are likely to involve multiple partners and partners who are strangers or anonymous (e.g., Barclay, 1973) and to have sexual acts and genitalia as their focus (e.g., Follingstad and Kimbrell, 1986). This is illustrated by the following male fantasy reported by Barclay (1973): 'Being the mayor of a small town filled with nude girls from 20 to 24. I like to take walks, and pick out the best-looking one that day and she engages in intercourse with me. All the women have sex with me any time I want' (209). These findings suggest that the sexual fantasies of women have features typically associated with long-term sexual relationships whereas those of men have features typically associated with short-term sexual relationships and, therefore, with the securing of multiple mates.

Evidence of sexual fantasy indicating men having a greater desire for short-term matings has also been provided in the form of findings concerning private wishes. Ehrlichman and Eichenstein (1992) recruited samples from colleges and from the general population. Participants were presented with a list of 48 private wishes including 'to be with God when I die', 'to deeply love a person who deeply loves me', and 'to live my whole life in perfect health'. Participants were asked to select the 10 wishes they would wish for most. Considering the percentages of men and women selecting each wish, several female-biased and male-biased sex differences emerged. However, by far the largest sex difference was the male-biased one for the wish 'To have sex with anyone I choose' and this was reliable across all ages and samples.

The forgoing findings of a sex difference in the desire for short-term matings have, however, been interpreted by social constructivists as being the product, not of evolutionary forces, but, rather, of cultural norms that legitimize men's and censure women's sexual promiscuity (e.g., Eagly and Wood, 1999). According to these critics of evolutionary accounts, therefore, sex differences in mating preferences should be non-existent or, at least, greatly attenuated among egalitarian cultures. One such egalitarian culture is that of Norway, as it is among the most sexually liberal and progressive cultures in the world (Williams and Best, 1990). Among Norwegian samples, however, Kennair et al. (2009) found that contrary to social constructivist accounts, sex differences in the desire for short-term matings were in line with those outlined above. Men more than women reported a desire for short-term matings; men's reported ideal number of sexual partners was greater than women's for each of various time-intervals ranging from next week to the remaining lifetime; men reported a greater likelihood of engaging in sexual intercourse with someone after knowing the person for each of various time intervals ranging from one minute to 10 years and that this sex difference only begins to decrease around the interval of three months; and men more than women reported fantasizing about someone other than their current partner. These findings, therefore, provide further support for the cultural universality of sex differences in mating preferences and the evolutionary psychological account of them.

MATE PREFERENCES REGARDING PARENTAL INVESTMENT

Although OPI is typically female-biased, among species in which the survival rate of offspring is significantly reduced without parental investment from both parents, males also contribute substantial parental investment (Emlen and Oring, 1977). It is for this reason that among species of birds, for instance, social monogamy is overwhelmingly the most frequent mating system. It involves female and male birds forming pair-bonds over one or more mating seasons to share the raising of offspring (Lack, 1968). The reproductive benefits of such pair-bonds are indicated by findings that, for instance, among starlings 97% of eggs incubated by both parents hatched, whereas the figure was only 75% for eggs incubated solely by mothers (Reid et al., 2002). Similarly, female snow buntings that have been experimentally widowed were found to fledge three or less young, whereas control pairs fledged at least four (Lyon et al., 1987). Even a reduction, rather than a complete absence, of male parental care can have significant consequences for the survival of offspring. Among male spotless starlings, increasing levels of testosterone leads to reduced levels of parental investment. It has been found that the mean number of fledged young per brood was lowest for pairs in which the male had been given extra testosterone and highest for pairs in which the male had been given testosterone blockers (Moreno et al., 1999).

Among mammals, although substantial parental investment from males is rare due to the typically female-biased OPI, it does occur in species in which it leads to increased survival rates of offspring. For instance, males of the Djungarian hamster increase survival rates of offspring by helping deliver their partners' pups (Jones and Wynne-Edwards, 2000). Among California mice, pups have reduced survival rates when males are not present to help their partners keep them warm (Gubernick and Teferi, 2000). And, under laboratory conditions, pairs of California mouse were reliably more able than single females to rear litters of four pups (Cantoni and Brown, 1997).

Among humans, the altricial or highly underdeveloped condition in which babies are born means that they are nutritionally dependent for several years (Kaplan, 1996). Indeed, the prolonged dependency of human children is considered to have led to the evolution through natural selection of breastfeeding's contraception effect (Kaplan, 1996) and an interbirth interval among hunter-gatherers of as long as four years (e.g., Blurton Jones, 1986; Hill and Hurtado, 1996). The difficulty faced by mothers of providing sufficient parental investment to ensure the survival of their children means that over human evolutionary history, the survival rate of children is likely to have been significantly increased if men also provided substantial parental investment. Support for this notion is, for instance, given by the finding that among contemporary Kipsigis agropastoralists in Kenya, the number of children that a woman can successfully rear is directly related to the wealth of her husband (Borgerhoff Mulder, 1989). It follows that although men are expected to have evolved to especially desire multiple mates, as with other species in which paternal investment results in increased survival rates of offspring, men should also have evolved a desire to form long-term relationships with women and provide substantial parental investment for any children produced with them.

Evolutionary reasoning suggests, however, that there will be a sex difference in preferences for a long-term mate. As women are biologically obliged to provide substantial parental investment, men are not expected to have evolved to place a high importance on a woman's level of parental investment when choosing a long-term mate. In contrast, as men can choose whether to provide only a relatively small biological parental investment or to additionally provide a substantial economic parental investment, women should have evolved to place a high importance on a long-term mate's economic parental investment. Cross-cultural evidence supports the existence of this sex difference. Buss (1989) asked women and men from 37 cultures spanning 6 continents and 33 countries, including Japan, Zambia, Yugoslavia, Australia, and

the United States, to rate the importance of 'good financial prospects' when choosing a long-term mate (specifically, someone they might marry). For 36 of the 37 samples, women gave a higher rating than did men and although for one sample women's rating was higher than that of men, that difference was not statistically significant.

Not only is this sex difference consistent across geography, it is also consistent across time. In 1939 (Hill, 1945), 1956 (McGinnis, 1958), 1967 (Hudson and Henze, 1969), 1977 (Hoyt and Hudson, 1981), 1984/85 (Buss et al., 2001), and 1996 (Buss et al., 2001), undergraduates at universities in the United States were asked to rate the importance of several traits in a mate. These included 'good financial prospects', 'ambition', and 'industriousness', all of which are associated with the securing of economic resources. In all samples, women gave the three traits higher ratings than did men.

As greater access to and control of economic resources is typically associated with higher social status, women should also have evolved to place a greater importance than men on a mate's social status. Support for this reasoning was provided by Buss et al. (1990). Across samples from 33 countries from Africa, Asia, Europe, Oceania, and the Americas, they found that women rated 'favorable social status' as more important in a mate than did men. They also found that, among all samples, women gave a higher importance than did men to other characteristics associated with the securing of economic resources including 'good financial prospect', 'good earning capacity', 'ambition and industriousness', and 'education and intelligence'. In line with this, in a cross-cultural investigation into the causes of divorce, Betzig (1989) found that when a lack of economic factors was reported as a cause it was ascribed exclusively to husbands.

Choosing a man who has the ability to provide substantial parental investment for any child that he fathers would, however, be a good mate choice for a woman only if the man is also willing to provide such investment. Indeed, avoiding mating with men who are unwilling to provide substantial parental investment for their children is a problem that women will have reliably faced over human evolutionary history. It is expected, therefore, that women will have evolved a psychology that facilitates their solving of this problem. Such a psychology would be one which motivates a woman to be hesitant to mate with a man until he has convinced her that he is in love with her. Evidence that women have evolved such a psychology is provided by the findings noted in the forgoing that women report being less likely than men to engage in sexual relations after knowing someone for various time intervals and that this sex difference only begins to decrease around the interval of three months (Kennair et al., 2009; Buss and Schmitt, 1993). Further, the importance to women of having a long-term mate who is in love with them is indicated by findings that in contrast to men, women report being more upset by a mate committing an emotional infidelity (i.e., falling in love with someone else) than by a sexual infidelity (Buss et al., 1992, 1999). This suggests that a woman fears that if her mate falls in love with another woman he may direct his parental investment away from any children that he has with her and toward children he has with the other woman.

Contrary to the evolutionary psychological account of why women more than men place importance on a long-term mate's economic resources, is the *Structural Powerlessness Hypothesis* (e.g., Buss and Barnes, 1986). This holds that because women have traditionally been excluded from positions of power and the benefits associated with it, such as the control of and access to economic resources, they seek to gain access to power by mating with powerful men. The *Structural Powerlessness Hypothesis* leads to the prediction that as societies move toward a greater degree of gender equality, the greater importance that women place on a mate's economic resources should disappear, or, at least, diminish. To test this, Gustavsson and Johnsson (2008) used personal advertisements among a population from Sweden, as it is considered to have one of the highest degrees of gender equality in the world (Hausmann et al., 2007). In contradiction of the *Structural Powerlessness Hypothesis*, advertisements placed by significantly more women than men requested that a mate have economic resources. One evolutionary psychological account for this finding would be that women have not been able to secure economic resources of their own for a sufficiently long period of time or with a sufficient prevalence for women's evolved preference for long-term mates with economic resources to no longer be adaptive.

MATE PREFERENCES REGARDING AGE

If one sex possesses traits related to survival or reproduction that vary with age, it is expected that the age of members of that sex will be one of the criteria on which members of the other sex evolve to base its mate selection. For instance, evidence suggests that female chimpanzees may possess a variety of traits concerning survival and reproduction that vary with their age. One is that older females may have relatively high social ranking and, thereby, gain reproductive advantages (Pusey et al., 1997). Another is that relatively old females may have greater experience of mothering and, therefore, their offspring have relatively high survival rates (Weladji et al., 2006). Older females may also be of superior genetic quality due to females of higher genetic quality having a greater likelihood of surviving to relatively old age (Weladji et al., 2006). As female chimpanzees do not appear to experience menopause (Nishida et al., 2003), these age-related features of female chimpanzees have led male chimpanzees to evolve a preference for mating with relatively old females (Muller et al., 2006).

Two features of women that are related to reproduction and that vary with women's age are their fertility and their reproductive value. Fertility is the likelihood that a woman will become pregnant from a single mating. Although the age at which girls experience the onset of menarche varies across time and populations, it is typically considered to be at about age 13 (Shawky and Milaat, 2000). Most girls do not, however, become fertile until at least the first year after menarche (Apter, 1980). Nevertheless, women's fertility increases through their teens, reaches a peak in their mid to late 20s and, thereafter, declines at an increasing rate until menopause (Dunson et al., 2002). Reproductive value is the number of children that a woman is likely to give birth to in the future (Fisher, 1930). A woman's reproductive value is, therefore, greatest at the beginning of the period of her life during which she is fertile, namely when she is in her early teens, because it is then that she has her entire duration of fertility ahead of her. This means that, for instance, a 16-year-old girl would have a relatively high reproductive value and a relatively low level of fertility, whereas a 25-year-old woman would have a relatively low reproductive value and a relatively high level of fertility. The forgoing indicates that when a man is seeking a long-term mate, he is expected to have evolved to prefer to mate with a woman of high reproductive value so as to maximize the potential number of children he can produce with her. In contrast, when a man is seeking a short-term mate (e.g., a one-night stand), he is expected to have evolved to prefer to mate with a woman of high fertility so as to maximise the probability that he will impregnate her.

It follows that, although men are likely to prefer a somewhat younger woman when they are seeking a long-term mate for her reproductive value compared to when they are seeking a short-term mate for her fertility, whichever of these two reproductive characteristics underlies men's mate preferences, men will be especially desirous to mate with women who are in their teens and 20s. In line with this, Kenrick and Keefe (1992) assessed personal advertisements and found that as men increased in age from their 20s to their 60s, they expressed a preference for women who were increasingly younger than themselves. For instance, the oldest and youngest women for whom men expressed a preference was, respectively, about five years older and about five years younger than themselves for men in their 20s, about two years older and about 10 years younger than themselves for men in their 30s, about one year older and about 14 years younger than themselves for men in their 40s, and about five years older and about 16 years younger than themselves for men in their 50s.

Further support for the argument that it is women's reproductive characteristics that underlie men's mate preferences was provided by Kenrick et al. (1996). They asked boys aged from 12 to 18 years what would be the age of the most attractive woman they could imagine. Contrary to older men's preference for women younger than themselves, the boys' preferences regarding their ideal woman comprised of women ranging from about 3 to 6 years *older* than themselves. As girls who are younger or the same age as adolescent boys are likely to have both a reproductive value and a fertility level that are especially low, these findings suggest that underlying the boys' preference for women older than themselves are the reproductive characteristics of such women.

Dunn (2018) provided evidence that it is the most highly fertile women to whom men are especially attracted by assessing the online profiles, including photographs, of independent female escorts (i.e., prostitutes) aged between 20 and 50 years old in the UK, Ireland, United States, Australia, and Europe. He found that younger escorts, especially those in their 20s, overwhelmingly charged significantly higher hourly rates for in-call and out-call sexual services, suggesting that younger woman are in greater demand by men. Further, the Miss Universe competition is also in line with the argument that it is the reproductive characteristics of women that underlie perceptions of their attractiveness. This is because the rules of the competition stipulate that contestants must be between 18 and 28 years of age on the day on which their national pageant competition began (Miss Universe, 2019).

A feature of men related to survival and reproduction that varies with age is the ability to secure economic resources. Among hunter-gatherers, meat is a valued resource comprising more than 50% of subsistence energy (e.g., Cordain et al., 2000). Men do not, however, reach their peak hunting skills till around their mid to late 30s (Collings, 2009; Gurven et al., 2006). A similar relationship between men's age and their ability to secure economic resources is also evident in post-industrial societies. For instance, in the UK and the United States, men's income rises steadily from their teens reaching a peak around the age of 40 years in the UK (Survey of Personal Incomes, 2012–13:13) and around the age of 45 years in the United States (Survey of Consumer Finances, 2016: 3). Given the great importance that women place on a mate's economic resources, it is therefore expected that when women are seeking a long-term mate, they should have evolved a preference for men who are relatively old. Cross-cultural evidence in line with this was provided by Buss et al. (1990) who found that across all 37 cultures they considered, women preferred to marry men who were on average 3.5 years older than themselves.

MATE PREFERENCES REGARDING PHYSICAL ATTRACTIVENESS

Although men are expected to have evolved to be especially attracted to women with high reproductive value and fertility, these characteristics of women cannot be directly observed. Men, therefore, are expected to

have evolved to be able to assess them through observable traits of women that have reliably varied with them over human evolutionary history. Specifically, men are expected to have evolved to be especially attracted to features of women that are reliably associated with women being in their teens and 20s when they are of high reproductive value and fertility (Barber, 1995). These features include facial characteristics such as smoothness of skin and fullness of lips that have been found to be cross-culturally perceived as attractive (e.g., Ford and Beach, 1951). The cross-cultural perception of these features as being attractive is further indicated by women across multiple cultures attempting to re-attain them by undergoing cosmetic surgery procedures such as the hiding of wrinkles through Botox, the removal of eye bags, and the lipofilling of lips.

An observable trait that varies reliably with women's level of fertility is the secondary sexual characteristic of women's breasts. The age at which girls' breasts become fully-developed is similar to the age at which they begin ovulating (e.g., Drife, 1986). Moreover, as women's fertility begins to increasingly decline after their late 20s, the symmetry of women's breasts also increasingly lessens (Manning et al., 1997). In line with this, Singh (1995) found that men rated line drawings of women with relatively large and symmetrical breasts as relatively more attractive and youthful.

The level of women's fertility also reliably varies with their waist-to-hip ratio (WHR), namely the ratio of the circumferences of the waist and the hips. Before puberty, the WHR of girls is similar to that of boys. However, at puberty, girls begin to develop fat deposits on their upper thighs and hips (Marti et al., 1991). Also at puberty, the pelvis of girls begins to widen, reaching its greatest width when women are in their late 20s (Huseynov et al., 2016). These changes in the bodies of women mean that, as women's fertility increases during their teens and 20s, their WHR becomes increasingly lower than that of men, resulting in the WHR of premeno-pausal women being in the range of .67 to .80 whereas that of men of similar ages being in the range of .85 to .95 (e.g., Marti et al., 1991). The magnitude of this sex difference in WHRs is at a maximum when women's fertility peaks in their late 20s for, as women's fertility declines through their 30s and 40s, the fat distribution around their hips and waist changes in such a way as to increase their WHR (Kirschner and Samojilik, 1991). Further, from around the age of 40, the pelvis of women becomes increasingly narrow meaning that by the time women reach menopause when they are around 50 years of age, their pelvis is of a width similar to that of the pelvis of men (Huseynov et al., 2016). The forgoing indicates, therefore, that the falling and rising of women's WHR closely follows the respective rising and falling of their level of fertility. As a result, it is expected that men will have evolved to use women's WHR to assay their level of fertility. Specifically, men are expected to have evolved to be especially attracted to women with a relatively low WHR (e.g., Singh, 1993). This argument has been supported by several studies cross-culturally, including among traditional societies (e.g., Butovskaya et al., 2017; Singh, 2006; Singh and Luis, 1994).

Although the notion that men are especially attracted to women with relatively low WHRs has gained a wide degree of acceptance (Bovet, 2019), recent studies have challenged the notion that the underlying reason for this preference of men is that a relatively low WHR among women is associated with them having relatively high levels of fertility. Lassek and Gaulin (2018a, 2018b) have provided evidence that a lower WHR among women is positively associated, not with a high level of fertility, but, instead, with the brain development of fetuses and infants. This, they argue, is because a low WHR is the product of relatively large amounts of gluteofemoral fat that contains fatty acids important for neural development and relatively small amounts of abdominal fat that inhibits

the synthesising of these fatty acids. In support of this, Lassek and Gaulin (2008) found that children of women with relatively low WHRs had relatively high scores on cognitive test scores. Nevertheless, notwithstanding which particular reproductive quality is indicated by a low WHR, because it is associated with women's reproductive quality it is a feature to which men are especially attracted.

Correctly assessing a woman's reproductive quality is especially important for men in the context of long-term matings. One reason for this is that if a man enters a long-term mating with a woman who is of low reproductive value and fertility, he will be devoting all, or at least most, of his mating effort toward a woman who will be unlikely to provide him with children. Another reason is that while a man is in a long-term mating, he will be forgoing opportunities to secure matings with multiple women.

It follows that, given the importance to men of identifying a long-term mate of high reproductive value and fertility, men are expected to have evolved to place an especially great importance on a woman's attractiveness when seeking a long-term mate. In contrast, as women's main goal in a long-term mating is to ensure the survival of her children, women seeking a long-term mate are expected to have evolved to place an especially great importance on a man's ability and willingness to provide reliable parental investment, not on his attractiveness. Empirical evidence supports this hypothesized sex difference. Across samples from 34 of the aforementioned 37 cultures investigated by Buss (1989), men rated 'good looks' in a long-term mate as significantly more desirable than did women. In the three samples for which the sex difference was not statistically significant, it was in the same direction as in the other samples. Moreover, in those three samples, men rated the characteristic 'physically attractive' as significantly more desirable than did women.

This male-biased sex difference in the importance placed on physical attractiveness in relation to long-term mates may not, however, exist in relation to short-term mates. The reason for this is that although men are expected to place a high importance on physical attractiveness in both a long-term and short-term mate, men's aforementioned evolved desire for securing multiple mates means that, when seeking a short-term mate, they are expected to be willing to lower the level of attractiveness that they require in a mate. This is because that by doing so, men will have a larger number of potential short-term mates and, therefore, an increased likelihood of securing a short-term mating. In support of this reasoning, Kenrick et al. (1993) found that men reported that the minimum percentile of attractiveness in which they would accept a mate to be was lower for a one-night stand than for steady dating and marriage.

In contrast to men, when seeking a short-term mating, women are expected to have evolved to increase the level of attractiveness that they require in a mate. This is because, when seeking a short-term mate, although women may seek *immediate*, rather than reliable, economic resources (e.g., Buss and Schmitt, 1993), women may expect to receive only genetic material from the man in the form of sperm. In such instances, therefore, women are expected to place an especially high importance on a short-term mate's genetic quality.

As discussed above when outlining the process of sexual selection, women's preference for high genetic quality when seeking short-term mates is also observed among females of non-human species. For instance, although in 90% of bird species females and males form long-term pair-bonds (Lack, 1968), females engage in extra-pair copulations with males other than their social mates causing their social mates to unknowingly help in the raising of offspring sired by rival males (e.g., Griffith et al., 2002). Research indicates that the survival rates of offspring resulting through these extra-pair copulations are greater than those of offspring produced

with their social mates (e.g., Sardell et al., 2011), suggesting that when engaging in short-term matings, females are choosing to do so with males who are of a higher genetic quality than that of their social mates.

Moreover, just as females in such non-human species assay the genetic quality of short-term mates through the males' observable characteristics, such as peahens selecting to mate with peacocks based on the ornamentation of their tails, so do women assay the genetic quality of men through men's observable characteristics. One such characteristic of men is their facial and bodily symmetry. Deviations from symmetry are produced by developmental perturbations such as mutations, parasitic infections, and environmental stressors such as lack of nutrition. Some individuals, however, have developmental stability due to having a genotype that enables them to be better able to withstand such perturbations. As such, symmetry would be an honest signal of good genes (e.g., Gangestad and Thornhill, 1997). In support of this, individuals with relatively high levels of symmetry have been found to have a stronger immune system (Thornhill and Gangestad, 1994) and relatively high levels of physiological, psychological, and emotional health (Shackelford and Larsen, 1997; Thornhill and Gangestad, 2006). Men with relatively high levels of symmetry are, therefore, likely to be better able to provide parental resources and less likely to pass on diseases to their children. In addition, such men will pass their good genes onto their children.

When seeking a short-term mate, therefore, women are expected to have evolved to be especially attracted to men who display developmental stability through features such as high levels of symmetry. Support for this reasoning was provided by Gangestad and Thornhill (1997) who found that men with relatively high levels of symmetry were more likely to have had sex with women who were currently in relationships, suggesting that these women preferred to mate with such men when seeking short-term matings. In addition, in contrast to their aforementioned findings regarding men, Kenrick et al. (1993) found that women reported that the minimum percentile of attractiveness in which they would accept a mate to be was higher for a one-night stand than for steady dating and marriage. As a result, Kenrick et al.'s findings indicated that, whereas for steady dating and marriage men required a mate to be in a higher minimum percentile of attractiveness than did women, for a one-night stand it was women who required a mate to be in a higher minimum percentile of attractiveness.

ROMANTIC INFIDELITY, JEALOUSY, AND MATE RETENTION

As outlined in the forgoing, although, typically, males' relatively great potential reproductive rate means that they will have evolved to seek multiple mates, among species in which parental investment from males in addition to sperm increases the survival rate of offspring, males form long-term pair bonds with females such that social monogamy is the species' mating system (Emlen and Oring, 1977). When, however, the fertilizing of females' eggs is internal, males face the adaptive problem of paternity uncertainty such that a male can never be entirely sure that the offspring produced by his social mate is genetically related to him. This is an adaptive problem for males entering long-term pair-bonds because social monogamy does not necessarily mean sexual monogamy. For instance, as outlined in the forgoing, although social monogamy is the mating system among 90% of bird species (Lack, 1968), females frequently engage in extra-pair copulations resulting in their social mates unknowingly directing paternal investment toward the offspring of rival males (Griffith et al., 2002). Indeed, Birkhead and Moller (1992) found that, among bird species, up to 35% of chicks were sired by males other than the females' social mates.

It follows that men in long-term relationships face the adaptive problem of paternity uncertainty. They, therefore, run the risk of directing their economic resources toward children to whom they are not genetically related. Doing so is even more detrimental to men's reproductive success than is dying. This is because, not only does it mean that they are not increasing their own reproductive success, they will also be increasing the reproductive success of rival males. In long-term relationships, therefore, men are expected to have evolved to especially feel sexual jealousy such that they are especially upset by their partners engaging in sexual activity with other men.

As women in long-term relationships have maternity certainty, they face an adaptive problem different from that of men. As discussed in the forgoing, the primary aim of a woman entering a long-term relationship is to secure reliable paternal investment to best ensure the survival of her children. Consequently, the foremost adaptive problem for a woman in a long-term relationship is to avoid her mate redirecting his economic resources toward the children of another woman. As a man is likely to provide reliable parental investment only to the children of women with whom he is in love, women in long-term relationships are expected to have evolved to especially feel emotional jealousy such that they are especially upset by their partners forming an emotional attachment to another woman.

Buss et al. (1992) found support for this evolved sex difference in jealousy in response to the two types of romantic infidelity. They asked women and men to imagine a long-term partner committing a sexual infidelity (i.e., having sex with someone else) or committing an emotional infidelity (i.e., falling in love with someone else) and to report which type of infidelity would upset them more. Results indicated that the majority of men indicated that a sexual infidelity would upset them more, whereas the majority of women reported that an emotional infidelity would upset them more. Buss et al. also assayed participants' levels of upset in response to imagining the two types of infidelity by measuring increases in their physiological responses of frowning, sweating, and heart rate. For men, although no significant differences were found for frowning, they displayed greater increases in sweating and heart rate in response to a sexual infidelity compared to an emotional infidelity. For women, although no significant differences were found for frowning and heart rate, they displayed a greater increase in sweating in response to an emotional infidelity compared to a sexual infidelity.

Buss et al.'s (1992) evolutionary-based interpretation of their findings was, however, challenged by Harris and Christenfeld (1996) and DeSteno and Salovey (1996). They proposed a 'Belief' or 'Double-Shot' hypothesis to account for Buss et al.'s findings that holds that people feel more jealousy in response to the type of infidelity that they have been socialized to believe is more likely to indicate that both types of infidelity have occurred. According to this, women feel more jealousy in response to an emotional infidelity because they believe that a man who is in love with a woman will also be having sex with her (double-shot), whereas women feel less jealousy in response to a sexual infidelity because they believe that a man can have sex with a woman without being in love with her (single-shot). On the other hand, it holds that men feel more jealousy in response to a sexual infidelity because they believe that if a woman has sex with a man she must also be in love with him (double-shot), whereas men feel less jealousy in response to an emotional infidelity because they believe that a woman can be in love with a man but not be having sex with him (single-shot). In support of the 'Double-Shot' hypothesis, Harris and Christenfeld found that women and men had the beliefs proposed by the hypothesis and that women and men reported that the type of infidelity that upset them more was as proposed by the hypothesis.

This led Buss et al. (1999) to test the 'Double-Shot' hypothesis by presenting participants with a series of four scenarios each of which made a sexual and an emotional infidelity mutually exclusive such that, in each, it was clear to participants that their long-term partner had committed only one type of infidelity. In line with the evolutionary-based interpretation but not the 'Double-Shot' hypothesis, across all scenarios, results were in accordance with previous findings indicating that the majority of women were more upset by an emotional infidelity and the majority of men were more upset by a sexual infidelity.

This sex difference in jealousy in response to a sexual versus an emotional infidelity is not confined to US samples. Rather, it has been found cross-culturally, including in Brazil (de Souza et al., 2006), Chile (Fernandez et al., 2006), Korea (Buss et al., 1999), Japan (Buss et al., 1999), and Romania (Brase et al., 2004).

Moreover, the sex difference is indicated by brain activation. Takahashi et al. (2006) used functional magnetic resonance imaging (fMRI) to measure participants' brain activity while reading descriptions of sexual and emotional infidelity. In response to both types of infidelity, they found that men showed greater activation than women of brain areas involved in sexuality and aggression (i.e., the amygdala and hypothalamus), whereas women showed greater activation than men of brain areas involved in detection of trustworthiness and violation of social norms (i.e., the posterior superior temporal sulcus). Takahashi et al. concluded, 'Our fMRI results are in favor of the notion that men and women have different neuropsychological modules to process sexual and emotional jealousy' (1299).

By having a psychology evolved to evoke jealousy most strongly in response to the type of infidelity that is more detrimental to women's and men's respective reproductive success, women and men are more likely to be motivated to enact behaviors to prevent such an infidelity. The behaviors by which women and men are most likely to retain their mates and prevent them from committing an infidelity are expected to be those that involve providing their mates with the attributes their mates most desire from a long-term mate. As outlined in the forgoing, evolutionary psychological reasoning suggests that these attributes are for men, physical attractiveness, and for women, economic resources. In line with this, men more than women reported using the mate-retention tactic 'Resource Display', including the acts 'He spent a lot of money on her' and 'He bought her an expensive gift', whereas women more than men reported using the mate-retention tactic 'Appearance Enhancement', including the acts 'Dressed nicely' and 'Made up my face to look nice' (Buss, 1998; Buss and Shackelford, 1997).

CONCLUSION

This chapter has outlined how bodily, psychological, and behavioral sex similarities and sex differences have evolved through the respective processes of natural selection and sexual selection among both non-humans and humans. Sociocultural theories such as the Biosocial Model (e.g., Eagly and Wood, 1999; Wood and Eagly, 2002, 2012) are not, however, in complete agreement with the forgoing regarding the origin of sex differences among humans. Although the Biosocial Model holds that *bodily* sex differences among humans evolved through sexual selection, it does not hold that psychological and behavioral sex differences among humans evolved through sexual selection. Instead, the Biosocial Model posits that psychological and behavioral sex differences among humans are the product of an interaction between sexually-selected bodily sex differences and social and ecological conditions. According to the Biosocial Model, this interaction leads to a division of labor by which each sex performs the activities that it can more efficiently perform than the other sex. As a result, gender roles emerge in which

each sex adopts the particular psychological attributes that facilitate the performing of these sex-specific activities. In this way, sex-specific psychological attributes become stereotypical of each sex and each sex is expected to possess them. In addition, gender roles, along with the sex-specific activities, guide social behaviour. As Wood and Eagly (2002) state, 'Our biosocial model does not assume that any sexual selection pressures that contributed to physical dimorphism between the sexes are major influences on sex-typed psychological attributes such as men's aggressiveness and competitive dominance' (702).

Although it is true that gender roles exist in human societies, the Biosocial Model's claim that it is they, not sexual selection pressures, that are the origin of psychological and behavioral sex differences among humans, is not reasonable. First, it is not reasonable for proponents of the Biosocial Model to hold that the human body was shaped by sexual selection pressures but the human mind escaped such pressures. Moreover, unless proponents of the Biosocial Model argue that psychological and behavioral sex differences among non-humans are not the result of sexual selection, thereby denying sexual selection as being an evolutionary force, they would have to hold the unreasonable position that, whereas the psychology and behaviour of non-humans have been shaped by sexual selection pressures, the psychology and behaviour of humans have escaped such pressures.

Summation

The only processes known to produce functional traits among organisms are natural selection and sexual selection (Williams, 1966). Until evidence is secured that is in contradiction with this, it is only reasonable to assume that sex similarities and sex differences along functional traits among humans are the products of those two processes.

REFERENCES

Alexander, R. D., Hoogland, J. H., Howard, R. D., Noonan, M., & Sherman, P. W. (1979). Sexual dimorphisms and breeding systems in pinnipeds, ungulates, primates, and humans. In N. A. Chagnon and W. G. Irons (Eds), *Evolutionary biology and human social behavior: An anthropological perspective* (pp. 402–405). North Scituate, MA: Duxbury Press.

Apter, D. (1980). Serum steroids and pituitary hormones in female puberty: A partly longitudinal study. *Clinical Endocrinology*, *12*(2), 107–120.

Barber, N. (1995). The evolutionary psychology of physical attractiveness: Sexual selection and human morphology. *Ethology and Sociobiology*, *16*(5), 395–424.

Barclay, A. M. (1973). Sexual fantasies in men and women. *Medical Aspects of Human Sexuality*, *7*(5), 205–216.

Betzig, L. (1989). Causes of conjugal dissolution: A cross-cultural study. *Current Anthropology*, *30*(5), 654–676.

Birkhead, T. R., & Moller, A. P. (1992). *Sperm competition in birds: Evolutionary causes and consequences*. London: Academic Press.

Blurton Jones, N. G. (1986). Bushman birth spacing: A test for optimal interbirth intervals. *Ethology and Sociobiology*, *7*(2), 91–105.

Borgerhoff Mulder, M. (1989). Reproductive consequences of sex-biased inheritance in Kipsigis. In V. Standen and R. A. Foley (Eds), *Comparative socioecology* (pp. 405–427). Oxford: Blackwell.

Bovet, J. (2019). Evolutionary theories and men's preferences for women's waist-to-hip ratio: Which hypotheses remain? A systematic review. *Frontiers in Psychology*, *10*, doi.org/10.3389/fpsyg.2019.01221.

Brase, G. L., Caprar, D. V., & Voracek, M. (2004). Sex differences in responses to relationship threats in England and Romania. *Journal of Social and Personal Relationships*, *21*(6), 763–778.

Buss, D. M. (1988). From vigilance to violence: Tactics of mate retention in American undergraduates. *Ethology & Sociobiology*, *9*(5), 291–317.

Buss, D. M. (1989). Sex differences in human mate preferences: Evolutionary hypotheses tested in 37 cultures. *Behavioral & Brain Sciences*, *12*(1), 1–49.

Buss, D. M. (1996). Social adaptation and five major factors of personality. In J. S. Wiggins (Ed.), *The Five-Factor Model of Personality: Theoretical perspectives* (pp. 180–207). New York: Guilford Press.

Buss, D. M., Abbott, M., Angleitner, A., Asherian, A., Biaggio, A., et al. (1990). International preferences in selecting mates: A study of 37 societies. *Journal of Cross-Cultural Psychology*, *21*(1), 5–47.

Buss, D. M., & Barnes, M. L. (1986). Preferences in human mate selection. *Journal of Personality and Social Psychology*, *50*(3), 559–570.

Buss, D. M., Larsen, R. J., Westen, D., & Semmelroth, J. (1992). Sex differences in jealousy: Evolution, physiology, and psychology. *Psychological Science*, *3*(4), 251–255.

Buss, D. M., & Schmitt, D. P. (1993). Sexual Strategies Theory: An evolutionary perspective on human mating. *Psychological Review*, *100*(2), 204–232.

Buss, D. M., & Shackelford, T. K. (1997). From vigilance to violence: Mate retention tactics in married couples. *Journal of Personality and Social Psychology*, *72*(2), 346–361.

Buss, D. M., Shackelford, T. K., Kirkpatrick, L. A., Choe, J., Hasegawa, M., Hasegawa, T., & Bennett, K. (1999). Jealousy and beliefs about infidelity: Tests of competing hypotheses in the United States, Korea, and Japan. *Personal Relationships*, *6*(1), 125–150.

Buss, D. M., & Shackelford, T. K., Kirkpatrick, L. A, Larsen, R. J. (2001). A half century of mate preferences: The cultural evolution of values. *Journal of Marriage and Families*, *63*(2), 492–503.

Butovskaya, M., Sorokowska, A., Karwowski, M., Sabiniewicz, A., Fedenok, J., Dronova, D., Negesheva, M., Selivanova, E., & Sorokowski, P. (2017). Waist-to-hip ratio, body-mass index, age and number of children in seven traditional societies. *Scientific Reports*, *7*(1), 1622.

Cantoni, D., & Brown, R. E. (1997). Paternal investment and reproductive success in the California mouse, Peromyscus californicus. *Animal Behaviour*, *54*(2), 377–386.

Clark, R. D., III, & Hatfield, E. (1989). Gender differences in receptivity to sexual offers.

Journal of Psychology and Human Sexuality, *2*(1), 39–55.

Clayton, F., Sealy, J., & Pfeiffer, S. (2006). Weaning age among foragers at Matjes river rock shelter, South Africa, from stable nitrogen and carbon isotope analyses. *American Journal of Physical Anthropology*, *129*(2), 311–317.

Clutton-Brock, T. H., & Vincent, A. C. (1991). Sexual selection and the potential reproductive rates of males and females. *Nature*, *351*(6321), 58–60.

Collings, P. (2009). Birth order, age, and hunting success in the Canadian Arctic. *Human Nature*, *20*(4), 354–374.

Cordain, L., Miller, J. B., Eaton, S. B., Mann, N., Holt, S. H. A., & Speth, J. D. (2000). Plant–animal subsistence ratios and macronutrient energy estimations in worldwide hunter-gatherers. *The American Journal of Clinical Nutrition*, *71*(3), 682–692.

Daly, M., & Wilson, M. (1988). *Homicide*. Hawthorne, NY: Aldine.

Darwin, C. R. (1859). *On the origin of species by means of natural selection*. London: John Murray.

Darwin, C. (1871). *The descent of man, and selection in relation to sex*. London: John Murray.

de Souza, A. A., Verderane, M. P., Taira, J. T., & Otta, E. (2006). Emotional and sexual jealousy as a function of sex and sexual orientation in a Brazilian sample. *Psychological Reports*, *98*(2), 529–535.

DeSteno, D. A., & Salovey, P. (1996). Evolutionary origins of sex differences in jealousy? Questioning the 'fitness' of the model. *Psychological Science*, *7*(6), 367–372.

Drife, J. O. (1986). Breast development in puberty. In *Endocrinology of the breast: Basic and clinical aspects. Annals of the New York Academy of Sciences*, *464*(1), 58–65.

Dunn, M. J. (2018). Younger escorts advertise higher charges online than older escorts for sexual services cross-culturally. *Evolutionary Psychological Science*, *4*(3), 331–339.

Dunson, D. B., Colombo, B., & Baird, D. D. (2002). Changes with age in the level and duration of fertility in the menstrual cycle. *Human Reproduction*, *17*(5), 1399–1403.

Eagly, A. H., & Wood, W. (1991). Explaining sex differences in social behavior: A

meta-analytic perspective. *Personality and Social Psychology Bulletin*, *17*(3), 306–315.

Eagly, A. H., & Wood, W. (1999). The origins of sex differences in human behavior: Evolved dispositions versus social roles. *American Psychologist*, *54*(6), 408–423.

Ehrlichman, H., & Eichenstein, R. (1992). Private wishes: Gender similarities and differences. *Sex Roles: A Journal of Research, 26*(9–10), 399–422.

Emlen, S. T., & Oring, L. W. (1977). Ecology, sexual selection, and the evolution of mating systems. *Science*, *197*(4300), 215–223.

Fabiani, A., Galimberti, F., Sanvito, S., & Hoelzel, A. R. (2004). Extreme polygyny among southern elephant seals on Sea Lion Island, Falkland Islands. *Behavioral Ecology*, *15*(6), 961–969.

Fernandez, A. M., Sierra, J. C., Zubeidat, I., & Vera-Villarroel, P. (2006). Sex differences in response to sexual and emotional infidelity among Spanish and Chilean students. *Journal of Cross-Cultural Psychology*, 37(4), 359–365.

Fisher, R. A. (1930). *The genetical theory of natural selection*. Oxford: Clarendon Press.

Follingstad, D. R., & Kimbrell, C. D. (1986). Sex fantasies revisited: An expansion and further clarification of variables affecting sex fantasy production. *Archives of Sexual Behavior*, *15*(6), 475–486.

Ford, C. S., & Beach, F. A. (1951). *Patterns of sexual behavior*. Oxford: Harper and Paul B. Hoeber.

Frost, P. (1998). Sex differences may indeed exist for 3-D navigational abilities. But was sexual selection responsible? *Behavioural and Brain Sciences*, *21*(3), 443–444.

Gangestad, S. W., & Thornhill, R. (1997). Human sexual selection and developmental stability. In J. A. Simpson & D. T. Kenrick (Eds), *Evolutionary social psychology* (pp. 169–196). Hillsdale, NJ: Lawrence Erlbaum Associates.

Gaulin, S. J. C., & FitzGerald, R. W. (1986). Sex differences in spatial ability: An evolutionary hypothesis and test. *American Naturalist*, *127*(1), 74–88.

Ghiselin, M. T. (2010). The distinction between primary and secondary sexual characteristics. In J. L. Leonard and A. Córdoba-Aguilar (Eds), *The evolution of primary sexual characters in animals* (pp. 9–14). Oxford and New York: Oxford University Press.

Griffith, S. C., Owens, I. P. F., & Human, K. A. (2002). Extra pair paternity in birds: A review of interspecific variation and adaptive function. *Molecular Ecology*, *11*(11), 2195–2212.

Gubernick, D. J., & Teferi, T. (2000). Adaptive significance of male parental care in a monogamous mammal. *Proceedings of the Royal Society of London. B: Biological Sciences*, *267*(1439), 147–150.

Gurven, M., Kaplan, H., & Gutierrez, M. (2006). How long does it take to become a proficient hunter? Implications for the evolution of extended development and long life span. *Journal of Human Evolution*, *51*(5), 454–470.

Gustavsson, L., Johnsson, U. I., & Uller, T. (2008). Mixed Support for Sexual Selection Theories of Mate Preferences in the Swedish Population. *Evolutionary Psychology*, *6*(4), 575–585.

Hald, G. M., & Høgh-Olesen, H. (2010). Receptivity to sexual invitations from strangers of the opposite gender. *Evolution and Human Behavior*, *31*(6), 453–458.

Harris, C. R., & Christenfeld, N. (1996). Jealousy and rational responses to infidelity across gender and culture. *Psychological Science*, *7*(6), 364–366.

Hill, R. (1945). Campus values in mate selection. *Journal of Home Economics*, *37*(9), 554–558.

Hamilton, W. D., & Zuk, M. (1982). Heritable true fitness and bright birds: A role for parasites? *Science*, *218*(4570), 384–387.

Hausmann, R., Tyson, L. D., and Zahidi, S. (2007). *The global gender gap report 2007*. World Economic Forum. www3.weforum.org/docs/WEF_GenderGap_Report_2007.pdf

Hill, K., & Hurtado, A. M. (1996). *Ache life history: The ecology and demography of a foraging people*. New York: Aldine de Gruyter.

Hoyt, L., & Hudson, J. (1981). Personal characteristics important in mate preference among college students. *Social Behavior and Personality: An international journal*, *9*(1), 93–96.

Hudson, J. W., & Henze, L. F. (1969). Campus values in mate selection: A replication. *Journal of Marriage and Family*, *31*(4), 772–775.

Huseynov, A., Zollikofer, C. P. E., Coudyzer, W., Gascho, D., Kellenberger, C., Hinzpeter, R., & Ponce de León, M. S. (2016). Developmental evidence for obstetric adaptation of the human female pelvis. *PNAS*, *113*(19) 5227–5232.

Jazin, E., & Cahill, L. (2010). Sex differences in molecular neuroscience: From fruit flies to humans. *Nature Reviews*, *11*(1), 9–17.

John, O. P., & Srivastava, S. (1999). The Big-Five trait taxonomy: History, measurement, and theoretical perspectives. In L. A. Pervin & O. P. John (Eds), *Handbook of personality: Theory and research* (Vol. 2, pp. 102–138). New York: Guilford Press.

Jones, J. S., & Wynne-Edwards, K. E. (2000). Paternal hamsters mechanically assist the delivery, consume amniotic fluid and placenta, remove fetal membranes, and provide parental care during the birth process. *Hormones and Behavior*, *37*(2), 116–125.

Kaplan, H. (1996). A theory of fertility and parental investment in traditional and modern human societies. *Yearbook of Physical Anthropology*, *39*, 91–135.

Kennair, L. E. O., Schmitt, D. P., Fjeldavli, Y. L., & Harlem, S. K. (2009). Sex differences in sexual desires and attitudes in Norwegian samples. *Interpersona*, *3* (Supplement 1), 1–32.

Kenrick, D. T., Groth, G. E., Trost, M. R., & Sadalla, E. K. (1993). Integrating evolutionary and social exchange perspectives on relationships: Effects of gender, self-appraisal, and involvement level on mate selection criteria. *Journal of Personality and Social Psychology*, *64*(6), 951–969.

Kenrick, D. T., & Keefe, R. C. (1992). Age preferences in mates reflect sex differences in human reproductive strategies. *Behavioural and Brain Sciences*, *15*(1), 75–133.

Kenrick, D. T., Keefe, R. C., Gabrielidis, C., & Cornelius, J. S. (1996). Adolescents' age preferences for dating partners: Support for an evolutionary model of life-history strategies. *Child Development*, *67*(4), 1499–1511.

Kirschner, M. A., & Samojilik, E. (1991). Sex hormone metabolism in upper and lower body density. *International Journal of Obesity*, *15*(Supplement 2), 101–108.

Lack, D. (1968). *Ecological adaptations for breeding in birds*. London: Methuen.

Lassek, W. D., & Gaulin, S. J. (2008). Waist–hip ratio and cognitive ability: Is gluteofemoral fat a privileged store of neurodevelopmental resources? *Evolution and Human Behavior, 29*(1), 26–34.

Lassek, W. D., & Gaulin, S. J. C. (2018a). Do the low WHRs and BMIs judged most attractive indicate better health? *Evolutionary Psychology, 16*(4), 1–13.

Lassek, W. D., & Gaulin, S. J. C. (2018b). Do the low WHRs and BMIs judged most attractive indicate higher fertility? *Evolutionary Psychology, 16*(4), 1–16.

Le Boeuf, B. J., & Reiter, J. (1988). Lifetime reproductive success in northern elephant seals. In T. H. Clutton-Brock (Ed.), *Reproductive success* (pp. 344–362). Chicago: University of Chicago Press.

Lill, A. (1974). Sexual behaviour of the lek-forming white-bearded manakin, (*Manacus manacus trinitatis* Hartert). *Zeitschrift fur Tierpsychologie, 36*(1–5), 1–36.

Lyon, B. E., Montgomerie, R. D., & Hamilton L. D. (1987). Male parental care and monogamy in snow buntings. *Behavioral Ecology and Sociobiology, 20*(5), 377–382.

Manning, J. T., Scutt, D., Whitehouse, G. H., & Leinster, S. J. (1997). Breast asymmetry and phenotypic quality in women. *Evolution and Human Behavior, 18*(4), 223–236.

Marti, B., Tuomilehto, J., Saloman, V., Kartovaara, L., Korhonen, H. J., & Pietinen, P. (1991). Body fat distribution in the Finnish population: Environmental determinants and predictive power for cardiovascular risk factor levels. *Journal of Epidemiology and Community Health, 45*(2), 131–137.

McCarthy, M., & Arnold, A. (2011). Reframing sexual differentiation of the brain. *Nature Neuroscience, 14*(6), 677–683.

McCrae, R. R., & Costa, P. T. (2003). *Personality in adulthood: A five-factor theory perspective.* New York: Guilford Press.

McGinnis, R. (1958). Campus values in mate selection: A repeat study. *Social Forces, 36*(4), 368–373.

Miss Universe (2019). Retrieved from www.missuniverse.com.

Moreno, J., Veiga, J. P., Cordero, P. J., & Mínguez, E. (1999). Effects of paternal care on reproductive success in the polygynous spotless starling (*Sturnus unicolor*). *Behavioral Ecology and Sociobiology, 47*(1–2), 47–53.

Muller, M. N., Thompson, M. E., & Wrangham, R. W. (2006). Male chimpanzees prefer mating with old females. *Current Biology, 16*(22), 2234–2238.

Nishida, T., Corp, N., Hamai, M., Hasegawa, T., HiraiwaHasegawa, M., Hosaka, K., Hunt, K. D., Itoh, N., Kawanaka, K., Matsumoto-Oda, A., Mitani, J. C., Nakamura, M., Norikoshi, K., Sakamaki, T., Turner, L., Uehara, S., & Zamma, K. (2003). Demography, female life history, and reproductive pro- files among the chimpanzees of Mahale. *American Journal of Primatology, 59*, 99–121.

Petrie, M., Halliday, T., & Sanders, C. (1991). Peahens prefer peacocks with elaborate trains. *Animal Behaviour, 41*(2), 323–331.

Plavcan, J. M., & van Schaik, C. P. (1997). Intrasexual competition and body weight dimorphism in anthropoid primates. *American Journal of Physical Anthropology, 103*(1), 37–68.

Pusey, A., Williams, J., & Goodall, J. (1997). The influence of dominance rank on the reproductive success of female chimpanzees. *Science, 277*(5327), 828–830.

Reid, J. M., Monaghan, P., & Ruxton, G. D. (2002). Males matter: The occurrence and consequences of male incubation in starlings (*Sturnus vulgaris*). *Behavioral Ecology and Sociobiology, 51*(3), 255–261.

Ross, W. D., & Ward, R. (1982) Human proportionality and sexual dimorphism. In R. L. Hall (Ed.), *Sexual dimorphism in Homo sapiens: A question of size* (pp. 317–361). New York: Praeger.

Sardell, R. J., Arcese, P., Keller, L. F., & Reid, J. M. (2011). Sex-specific differential survival of extra-pair and within-pair offspring in song sparrows (*Melospiza melodia*). *Proceedings of the Royal Society of London. B: Biological Sciences, 278*(1722), 3251–3259.

Schmitt, DP., Alcalay, L., Allik, J., Ault, L., Austers, I., Bennett, KL., Bianchi, G., Boholst, F., Borg Cunen, MA., Braeckman, J., Brainerd, EG., Caral, LGA., Caron, G., Martina Casullo, M., Cunningham, M., Daibo, I., De Backer, C., De Souza, E., Diaz-Loving, R., Diniz, G., Durkin, K., Echegaray, M., Eremsoy, E., Euler, HA.,

Falzon, R., Fisher, ML., Foley, D., Fry, DP., Fry, S., Arif Ghayur, M., Golden, DL., Grammer, K., Grimaldi, L., Halberstadt, J., Herrera, D., Hertel, J., Hoffmann, H., Hooper, D., Hradile-kova, Z., Hudek-Kene-evi, J., Jaafar, J., Jankauskaite, M., Kabangu-Stahel, H., Kardum, I., Khoury, B., Kwon, H., Laidra, K., Laireiter, AR., Lakerveld, D., Lampert, A., Lauri, M., Lavallée, M., Lee, SJ., Chung Leung, L., Locke, KD., Locke, V., Luksik, I., Magaisa, I., Marcinkeviciene, D., Mata, A., Mata, R., McCarthy, B., Mills, ME., Moreira, J., Moreira, S., Moya, M., Munyae, M., Noller, P., Opre, A., Panayiotou, A., Petrovic, N., Poels, K., Popper, M., Poulimenou, M., P'yatokha, V., Raymond, M., Reips, UD., Reneau, SE., Rivera-Aragon, S., Rowatt, WC., Ruch, W., Rus, VS., Safir, MP., Salas, S., Sambataro, F., Sandnabba, KN., Schulmeyer, MK., Schütz, A., Scrimali, T., Shackelford, TK., Shaver, PR., Sichona, F., Simonetti, F., Sineshaw, T., Speelman, T., Spyrou, S., Sümer, HC., Sümer, N., Supekova, M., Szlendak, T. et al. (2003). Universal sex differences in the desire for sexual variety: Tests from 52 Nations, 6 Continents, and 13 Islands. *Journal of Personality and Social Psychology*, *85*(1), 85–104.

Shackelford, T. K., & Larsen, R. J. (1997). Facial asymmetry as an indicator of psychological, emotional, and physiological distress. *Journal of Personality and Social Psychology*, *72*(2), 456–466.

Shawky, S., & Milaat, W. (2000). Early teenage marriage and subsequent pregnancy outcome. *Eastern Mediterranean Health Journal*, *6*(1), 46–54.

Singh, D. (1993). Adaptive significance of female physical attractiveness: Role of waist-to-hip ratio. *Journal of Personality and Social Psychology*, *65*(2), 293–307.

Singh, D. (1995). Female health, attractiveness, and desirability for relationships: Role of breast asymmetry and waist-to-hip ratio. *Ethology and Sociobiology*, *16*(6), 465–481.

Singh, D. (2006). Universal allure of the hourglass figure: An evolutionary theory of female physical attractiveness. *Clinics in Plastic Surgery*, *33*(3), 359–370.

Singh, D., & Luis, S. (1994). Ethnic and gender consensus for the effect of WHR on judgment

of women's attractiveness. *Human Nature*, *6*(1), 51–65.

Smith, A. (1776). *An inquiry into the nature and causes of the wealth of nations*. London: Strahan and Cadell.

Survey of Consumer Finances (2016). Table 1. Before-tax median and mean family income, by selected characteristics of families, 2013 and 2016 surveys. Retrieved from www.federalreserve.gov/publications/files/scf17.pdf

Survey of Personal Incomes (2012/13). Figure 2.5: Median income before tax by age and gender, 2012–13. Retrieved from: assets.publishing.service.gov.uk/government/uploads/system/uploads/attachment_data/file/399016/tables3_1–3_11.pdf

Takahashi, H., Matsuura, M., Yahata, N., Koeda, M., Suhara, T., & Okubo, Y. (2006). Men and women show distinct brain activations during imagery of sexual and emotional infidelity. *NeuroImage*, *32*(3), 1299–1307.

Tanner, J. M. (1990). *Foetus into man: Physical growth from conception to maturity*. Cambridge, MA: Harvard University Press.

Thornhill, R., & Gangestad, S. W. (1994). Human fluctuating asymmetry and sexual behavior. *Psychological Science*, *5*(5), 297–302.

Thornhill, R., & Gangestad, S. W. (2006). Facial sexual dimorphism, developmental stability, and susceptibility to disease in men and women. *Evolution and Human Behavior*, *27*(2), 131–144.

Trivers, R. L. (1972). Parental investment and sexual selection. In B. Campbell (Ed.), *Sexual selection and the descent of man; 1871–1971* (pp. 136–179). Chicago: Aldine.

Weladji RB, Gaillard JM, Yoccoz NG, Holand Ø, Mysterud A, Loison A, Nieminen M, Stenseth NC (2006) Good reindeer mothers live longer and become better in raising offspring. *Proceedings of the Royal Society London B-Biological Sciences*, *273*, 1239–1244.

Williams, G. C. (1966). *Adaptation and natural selection*. Princeton, NJ: Princeton University Press.

Williams, J. E., & Best, D. L. (1990). *Measuring sex stereotypes: A multination study* (revised ed.). Newbury Park, CA: Sage.

Wilson, M., & Daly, M. (1985) Competitiveness, risk taking, and violence: The young male syndrome. *Ethology and Sociobiology*, 6(1), 59–73.

Wood, W., & Eagly, A. H. (2002). A cross-cultural analysis of the behavior of women and men: Implications for the origins of sex differences. *Psychological Bulletin*, 128(5), 699–727.

Wood, W., & Eagly, A. H. (2012). Biosocial construction of sex differences and similarities in behavior. In J. M. Olson & M. P. Zanna (Eds), *Advances in experimental social psychology* (Vol. 46, pp. 55–123). London: Elsevier.

Zahavi, A. (1975). Mate selection – a selection for a handicap. *Journal of Theoretical Biology*, 53(1), 205–214.

Within-Species Individual Differences

Tim Marsh

The process of natural selection results in the non-random reduction of the genetic variation within a population via the subtraction of alleles that produce reproductively unsuccessful phenotypes from subsequent generations. As such, variation within a species is parochially viewed as a figurative fuel that is 'consumed' by the forces of evolution in the production of creatures more adapted to the survival and reproductive demands of their environments (Darwin, 1859; Sela and Shackelford, 2015). While this summary is true, in the strictest sense, it also fosters one of the central oversimplifications employed by theorists investigating possible adaptations: the assumption that the sole outputs of evolution by natural selection are features so unambiguously favored by their selective advantages as to render them species-typical (Tooby and Cosmides, 2005). This chapter reviews the main ways in which the paradigm of evolutionary psychology can address, interface with, and enhance the study of

individual differences, most notably in areas of personality and cognitive ability.

Although prominent evolutionary psychologists, most famously David Buss (1991), have theorized about the applicability of evolutionary analysis to the domains of individual differences since the paradigm was in its infancy (Tooby and Cosmides, 1990), progress on integrating the two perspectives has been slower than many other topics in psychology (Buss, 2009; Ashton et al., 2014), owing in part to the contrasting conceptual and methodological emphases of differential and evolutionary psychology (Marsh and Boag, 2013; Lewis, 2014). Evolutionary psychology, while conceived as a thoroughly interactionist and developmentally aware paradigm (Tooby and Cosmides, 1990; Stearns, 1992), has had the majority of its research and rhetorical successes (that is, in terms of science communication that captures the imagination of the general public) in constructing theories that address how some directly fitness-enhancing psychological mechanisms appear to have been selected to be ubiquitous in the human population (Buss, 2015). Such theories derive much of their clarity from the ease with which one can picture the survival and reproductive benefits of overt behaviors associated with cooperation (Sugiyama et al., 2002), mate-selection (Conroy et al., 2015), cheating-detection (Price et al., 2002) and the like, and thus one can appreciate why such features would fixate as species-typical aspects of human nature, driving less gifted rivals to extinction. Successes such as these have served to tacitly define evolutionary psychology as an approach primarily concerned with the discovery of a shared human nature, with little acknowledgement of the inherent variability that exists in common human experience (Buss, 2009).

In contrast, the study of personality and individual differences has taken the opposite theoretical approach, in that mainstream differential psychology has placed distinctly less emphasis on explanatory theories in recent history, favoring instead a methodological emphasis on honing the most robust possible descriptive measurement tools (John and Srivastava, 1999). This is not to say that there are no researchers of personality and intelligence still concerned with discovering the underlying causes and character of the phenomena they study (Cervone, 2005), but rather, the field has merely concentrated its efforts around its domains of greatest success, which mostly concern the formulation of robust statistical models of the population variance within factors such as the g factor of general intelligence (van der Maas et al., 2006; Plomin et al., 2016) and the orthogonal 'Big 5' of the Five Factor Model (Digman, 1990; Costa and McCrae, 1992).

These differences in approach and emphasis create some underappreciated difficulties for the integration of existing individual differences and evolutionary psychology research, since in principle, individual difference variables that lack a priori theoretical underpinnings (such as hypothetical mechanisms of action), and instead exist largely as statistical inferences modeled out of abundantly collected response data (Denissen and Penke, 2008), are not the kinds of phenomena adaptationist theories are capable of predicting or explaining (see Borsboom and Dolan, 2006, for an example of this conceptual problem). While the traditional fields of individual differences have descriptive value (which may also provide data necessary to evaluate some signaling theories discussed below), evolutionary psychologists interested in personality or cognitive ability have needed to break new ground in clarifying the mechanisms through which the process of evolution might not only tolerate, but perhaps generate, the kinds of systematic variation and lifetime consistency in traits that define individual differences (Buss, 2009).

The following sections review the main conceptual approaches evolutionary psychologists have examined to explain the kinds of enduring within-species individual differences that differential psychology researchers have documented in modern populations: Selective-Neutrality, Mutation-Selection Balance, Balancing Selection, State- and Condition-Dependent Adaptations, and phenotypes shaped by the demands of Signaling.

VARIATION IN SELECTIVE-NEUTRAL DOMAINS

When taking the aforementioned simplified account of species-typical adaptations at face value, some degree of individual variation is still expected, but only in domains not subject to the subtractive forces of natural selection (Campbell, 2007). Since selection can only act on organisms by virtue of the functional contributions their traits make to the propagation of their genes (Houle, 1998), phenotypic traits which are present but make no positive or negative contributions to fitness are not subject to selection. An archetypal example of this is the precise curvature of the intermediate folds of the human small intestines, which varies from person to person in what appear to be heritable ways (Campbell, 2007). In addition to being invisible to other human beings (short of those performing medical imaging or an autopsy), and thus incapable of impacting even superstitious or aesthetic interpersonal judgements, these variations are also invisible to the forces of natural selection, since the common variants are functionally identical and thus make indistinguishable contributions to overall fitness. Although the evolutionary process ultimately favors design efficiency, since it is a universal shortcoming to invest metabolic and developmental resources in features that do not positively contribute to fitness, selection on the level of individual organisms is sufficiently imprecise as to tolerate moderate amounts of 'noise' in many, if not most, bodily systems so long as more efficient conspecifics are not present to gain advantage from these inefficiencies (Kimura, 1983). Thus, when assessing how much variation we ought to expect when comparing individuals within a species, there is a safe background assumption that we should expect moderate amounts of random variation in most phenotypic domains where, functionally, differences do not make a difference (Lynch and Hill, 1986).

Some theorists, notably Campbell (2007), have advanced the argument that much of the noted individual variation that we classify as dispositional personality traits (and by extension, perhaps some related cognitive abilities that show consistent variation) may be behavioral 'noise' that is maintained because of its negligible impact on individual reproductive fitness (Kimura, 1983). In this view, the existence of sustained variability across generations, despite the moderate heritability of the traits in question, is evidence in favor of Selective-Neutrality, and that alternative explanations (such as those explored later in this chapter) require some compelling counter-evidence of fitness-relevance to move beyond this more conservative stance. While such evidence of meaningful fitness-relevance is lacking for many specific

personality constructs, researchers have built a multifaceted case for the extensive ways in which broad descriptive personality traits such as those in the Five Factor Model (Nettle, 2006; Denissen and Penke, 2008) and the HEXACO Model (de Vries et al., 2016) appear to impact survival, status, and reproductive prospects. These include, most notably, the correlations between levels of Extraversion and mating prospects (Nettle, 2005; Lukaszewski and Roney, 2011), Conscientiousness and longevity (Denissen and Penke, 2008), Neuroticism and mate-guarding (Lewis, 2014), and many more (see Merila and Sheldon, 1999, for a foundational review). Although there is little evidence for how stable these proposed impacts on fitness are over generational time, in part due to how unsuited descriptive tools designed to measure differences within the population are to calculating estimates of inherited variation (see Penke et al., 2007), there is sufficient basis for the exploration for alternative mechanisms through which this degree of sustained, heritable variation may be maintained in the face of selective pressures. The case for Selective-Neutrality as a sufficient explanation of the variability observed is weaker still for the well-documented individual differences in cognitive abilities and general intelligence (Plomin et al., 2006), since the obvious contributions that higher levels of these abilities make to human fitness has been at the core of intelligence research since its inception (Merila and Sheldon, 1999).

VARIATION UNDER DIRECTIONAL SELECTION

All species-typical traits are conventionally understood to be the products of once rare, newly mutated polymorphisms which offered fitness advantages over competing alleles and were therefore favored by the processes of selection until they became ubiquitous in subsequent generations, driving rivals extinct

(Darwin, 1859; Fisher, 1930). Even for traits or features that do not bestow a qualitative fitness advantage, quantitative differences in traits that confer unambiguous (even if small) advantages to those possessing higher or lower levels are similarly subject to Directional Selection, driving gene frequencies towards a species-typical fixation point and average phenotypes towards fitness-maximizing extreme values (Fisher, 1930). As such, for heritable quantitative traits in humans that are unambiguously fitness-enhancing at their higher values (outside of atypical environmental conditions such as extreme food shortages), including health (Neeleman et al., 2002), longevity (Friedman et al., 1995), attractiveness (Eaves et al., 1990) and mental ability (Luxen and Buunk, 2006), the most plausible explanation for the existence of individual variation away from some maximized optimal values is that selective pressures have not operated on the genepool for long enough to eliminate the less fit variants through competition (Penke et al., 2007). Rather than projecting an inevitable and idealized endpoint to Directional Selection, the process is complicated further by the constant addition of new polymorphisms into the genepool via mutation, which owing to their random nature are statistically far more likely to be deleterious or disruptive than functionally beneficial (Eyre-Walker and Keightley, 1999). This not only slows the variation-reducing action of Directional Selection but may ultimately balance out its net influence if the rate of variation-reduction comes to approximately match the rate of mutation, resulting in an ever-cycling genepool that maintains a mostly stable cross-sectional profile of variation over generations. The most widely recognized name for this concept is Mutation-Selection Balance (Zhang and Hill, 2005).

Mutation-Selection Balance

The existence of fixated species-typical traits is evidence that Mutation-Selection Balance is not the inevitable consequence of Directional Selection in quantitative traits. Rather, Mutation-Selection Balance is only possible when the passively accumulating Mutation Load of a species introduces phenotypically disadvantageous polymorphisms at a rate comparable to the removal of low-fitness variants by natural selection (Houle et al., 1994). Species vary in their estimated average rate of accumulating germ-line mutations, with humans appearing to possess a relatively high mutation rate of 1.67 new mutations per individual per generation (Eyre-Walker and Keightley, 1999), but even a rate as high as this poses few problems to selection to maintain competitively low levels of genetic variation in most species-typical features (Zhang and Hill, 2005). The essential prerequisite for Mutation-Selection Balance to maintain significant variation in a quantitative trait appears to depend on how closely the genetic differences in question map onto appreciable differences in fitness on the level of phenotype. For traits and features whose function depends heavily on a small number of essential genes, mutations in those genes are likely to immediately translate into phenotypic changes that directly influence the survival and reproductive prospects of the organism (Keightley and Gaffney, 2003). If, however, the trait in question relies on the cumulative influence of many hundreds or even thousands of genes, individual mutations are likely to have only small incremental effects on overall fitness at the phenotypic level (Merila and Sheldon, 1999). The Cannon and Keller 'watershed model' (2005) plots the mathematical relationships of traits that hierarchically depend on each other, and thus also depend on greater or smaller numbers of individual gene loci. The more 'downstream' a trait is from the gene products and simpler systems it depends on, the more indirect and incremental a relationship the expressed phenotype has with specific polymorphisms, and thus the less capable the forces of selection are in removing disadvantageous polymorphisms until a 'critical mass' of accumulated mutations has been reached (Keller and Miller, 2006). Houle (1998) refers to this property as Mutational Target-Size, wherein a larger target-size translates to depending on a larger number of underlying genes and thus showing more incremental shortcomings due to mutations, but traits with smaller target-sizes are more easily targeted by the forces of selection and thus are capable of maintaining lower overall numbers of deleterious genetic variations (Zhang and Hill, 2005).

Mutational Target-Size

For these reasons, Mutation-Selection Balance is the most viable explanatory framework to account for the persistent individual differences observed in human cognitive abilities, particularly the *g* general factor of intelligence (Penke et al., 2007), since the quantitative vulnerability of manifest cognitive ability to one's overall Mutation Load appears to act as a check on the obvious Directional Selection for higher levels of ability. This account is consistent with the limited success behavioral geneticists have encountered in attempting to identify genes with large proportional influences on expressed cognitive abilities (Plomin et al., 2006), and is also consistent with the results of inbreeding research that identifies predictable declines in intelligence for the offspring of cousins and other close relatives, who are especially vulnerable to the homozygous expression of rare deleterious mutations that emerged earlier in their family lines, as well as its conceptual opposite with outbreeding heterosis predicting higher intelligence in offspring (Jensen, 1998). The theoretically large Mutational Target-Size of cognitive ability traits also offers a possible explanation for the higher-order correlations between measures such as general intelligence and other fitness-predicting traits also thought to possess large Mutational Target-Sizes, such as bodily symmetry (Prokosch et al., 2005),

health (Neeleman et al., 2002) and longevity (Friedman et al., 1995). Since many genes are thought to be pleiotropic, with their products ultimately influencing multiple processes and contributing to many phenotypic features, there is an expected convergence between any phenotypic traits that are sufficiently 'downstream' to necessarily rely on common genes and processes, and thus possess Mutational Target-Sizes that non-trivially overlap (Houle, 1998). Phrased differently, the larger any given trait's Mutational Target-Size is, the closer it is to serving as a stand-in for the overall fitness of the organism, and thus the more representative its quantitative deficits will be to a global assessment of the organism's total Mutation Load (a conservative estimate proposes an average human Mutation Load of around 500, with a standard deviation of 22; Keller and Miller, 2006).

While these correlations open up a range of methodological possibilities for indirectly gauging Mutation Load (and thus predict cognitive ability) with other broad phenotypic indicators such as symmetry (Prokosch et al., 2005), the Mutation-Selection Balance explanation of individual differences in cognitive ability unfortunately suggests that behavioral genetic explorations of the impact of specific genes on manifest intelligence are likely to continue to meet with limited success (Plomin et al., 2006). If the alleles at any given locus are likely to contribute only small incremental amounts to the overall cognitive abilities of humans, then exhaustive genetic analyses of candidate genes are unlikely to yield insights that justify the present cost and difficulty of such investigations. The Mutation-Selection Balance approach has also shown some limited explanatory potential in some ability-adjacent domains of personality research (MacDonald, 1995, 1998), but the precise meaning of these findings remains unclear due to the potential confounds with Condition-Dependent Adaptations that are discussed later in this chapter (Lewis, 2014). Furthermore, some heritable personality traits appear to show the opposite of the transient deleterious mutations predicted by a Mutation-Selection Balance explanation, with sources such as Kidd (2006) and Ebstein (2006) identifying characteristic heritable polymorphisms that track with the personality traits in question, at intermediate prevalence rates in the population. As such, the patterns of systematic variation observed in personality psychology appear to require a separate set of evolutionary explanations for those best suited to differences in cognitive abilities.

INDIVIDUAL DIFFERENCES AS ADAPTIVE STRATEGIES

Intra-species competition serves as one of the primary sources of selective pressure that shape any social species, particularly where sexual selection is concerned. The inherent similarities between members of the same species guarantee direct competition for environmental resources, territory, status, and mates, often with zero-sum, winner-takes-all outcomes (Lund et al., 2007). Competition is necessarily the most intense between those organisms that not only seek the same ultimate goals but pursue said goals via the same means (Buss, 1991). As such, an alternative to the inherent costs of staunch competition is for individuals to attempt to pursue their shared goals via contrasting strategies. Strategic specialization is not limited to complementary divisions of labor, as is seen between sexual morphologies in sexually reproducing species, but also between differently endowed competitors who seek the same ends through alternative means, such as the contrasting domination versus sneaking mate acquisition strategies seen in the males of many 'tournament breeding' species (Kassen, 2002). Variation of this kind is best understood in the language of Evolutionary Game Theory, which focuses on modeling the underlying logic on display in competing biological morphologies, via the central metaphor of

what comprises rationally optimal moves in a game (von Neumann and Morgenstern, 1944).

Game Theoretical models offer insights into population-level trends that emerge spontaneously from innumerable individual agents each pursuing the most favorable outcomes they can secure for themselves. One of the earliest and most influential of these emergent phenomena is the Nash Equilibrium (Nash, 1951), a stable state a population reaches where no individual agent is capable of improving their outcomes by changing from their present strategy (see Gintis, 2009, for a detailed overview). Biologists and ethologists began to apply the logic of Game Theory to the behavior of non-human animals, showing that despite obvious and significant limits on their insight and computational abilities, creatures ranging from mammals to birds to arthropods appeared to strategically coordinate their behavior in ways that rationally maximized their survival and reproductive outcomes (Lewontin, 1961). From these foundational insights, John Maynard Smith and colleagues pioneered and popularized Evolutionary Game Theory (Maynard Smith and Price, 1973; Maynard Smith, 1976, 1982), an extension of classical Game Theory that sought to account for the properties of real-world populations of organisms and the ecosystems they inhabit, by describing the fitness-enhancing strategies that are discovered and maintained by the forces of evolution.

While some Evolutionary Game Theorists insist that employing the language of strategies and rationales are metaphorical shorthand for phenomena that are similar only in our methods of analysis, others employ a philosophical approach popularized by theorists like Daniel C. Dennett, wherein all potential strategies are thought of as abstract properties of the situations themselves (sometimes referred to as 'free-floating rationales', see Dennett, 2014), which can be functionally approximated and embodied in real-world systems in a wide variety of ways, only one of which is full mental representation by specific agents. In this sense, organisms are said to demonstrate 'competence without comprehension' (Dennett, 2017), possessing only the minimal sensory, cognitive and motor abilities needed to implement the strategy most beneficial to them, without any need for apparatus that reflects upon or understands precisely why the behaviors in question are beneficial (Maynard Smith, 1976).

This approach has its limitations, notably in terms of predicting the constraints a species' existing genotype places on its prospects for inter- and intra-generational changes in the future (see McNamara, 2013, for an overview), but it is nonetheless useful in modeling the kinds of behavioral strategies we should expect to be conserved as a stable Nash Equilibrium in diverse real-world populations. Sets of biological strategies and traits that can reach equilibria states which are robust to being overrun by new or rival 'mutant' strategies are known as Evolutionarily Stable Strategies (Maynard Smith, 1982), and are foundational in Evolutionary Game Theory models.

BALANCING AND STABILIZING SELECTION

Genes of intermediate population prevalence that appear to persist in roughly stable ratios over generations relative to their conspecifics are characteristic of multiple coexisting Evolutionarily Stable Strategies (Maynard Smith, 1982). While the specific tensions that maintain these equilibria can take on many forms, they will fall into at least one of two broad categories: Balancing Selection, wherein the relative fitness of each strategy changes as a function of social or environmental conditions that may in turn be influenced by the prevalence of the strategy in question, and Stabilizing Selection, the conceptual opposite of Directional Selection, wherein the optimal fitness payoffs for a quantitative trait are not achieved through its

maximization or minimization, but instead by an intermediate level that is difficult to maintain in a trait with a large Mutational Target-Size.

Antagonistic Pleiotropy

When discussing the application of both Balancing and Stabilizing Selection theories to the observed individual differences in human personality, one concept that is crucial to explaining why the traits in question are not ultimately reshaped by the forces of selection into forms that better maximize fitness across multiple domains is Antagonistic Pleiotropy (Hedrick, 1999). While it is common for gene products to ultimately contribute to innumerable phenotypic traits, Antagonistic Pleiotropy describes those instances where, owing to strategic specialization in specific fitness-relevant domains, the alleles that make positive contributions to the phenotype associated with one strategy also confers a proportional liability to the alternative phenotypes associated with other strategies (Roff, 1997). For example, suppose there were a set of gene loci that directly contributed to how an organism makes decisions when faced with risks. There are two rival strategies to address making these decisions, boldness and caution. While any polymorphisms that could meaningfully improve one's fitness, regardless of whether the bold or cautious strategy where being pursued (by virtue of other genes and developmental factors), those variants would be subject to positive Directional Selection, but a more likely outcome is that particular alleles will demonstrate Antagonistic Pleiotropy, whereby variants that confer fitness advantages if the bold strategy is being pursued also confer fitness penalties if the cautious strategy is being pursued, and vice versa. This hypothetical comparison is a simplified form of theories advanced by Nettle (2010) and others (Buss and Greiling, 1999; De Vries et al., 2016) with relation to personality traits such as

Extraversion or the more specific disposition towards Sensation Seeking (Nettle, 2005). For any behavioral domains where this kind of Antagonistic Pleiotropy applies, selection cannot favor any one generalist strategy that always guarantees high phenotypic fitness, but rather, rival strategies reflect tense trade-offs between non-overlapping means of securing survival and reproductive goals, permitting the coexistence of multiple Evolutionarily Stable Strategies (Maynard Smith, 1982), though perhaps over only a limited number of gene loci without the addition of further Balancing or Stabilizing processes (see Turelli and Barton, 2004, for a review of the limitations of Antagonistic Pleiotropy modeled as a sole explanation for personality variation).

Frequency-Dependent Selection

The best understood process favoring Balancing Selection in competing biological strategies is Frequency-Dependent Selection, or more specifically, negative Frequency-Dependent Selection (Kopp and Hermisson, 2006). To say that the selective pressures acting on a trait are Frequency-Dependent is to observe that the fitness payoffs of possessing said trait vary as a direct function of the number of other individuals possessing the same trait in one's social environment (Schneider, 2006). When the presence of other organisms possessing the same trait or employing the same strategy as oneself directly enhances the associated fitness benefits, as is in the case in Game Theoretic models of prosociality and cooperation (Maynard Smith, 1998; Jeon and Buss, 2007), the positive Frequency-Dependence will result in a Fisherian runaway (akin to the runaway selection characteristic of sexual selection, Fisher, 1930), with the most likely outcome being the trait eventually becoming species-typical (Roff, 1997). Negative Frequency-Dependence, on the other hand, describes instances where the fitness benefits

of possessing a trait proportionally diminish, perhaps to the point of becoming a liability, the more prevalent the trait in question is in the social environment (Burger, 2005). In the classic Game Theory model of Hawks vs. Doves (Maynard Smith, 1998), the predatory Hawk strategy is often modeled as negatively Frequency-Dependent, since individuals who are Hawks (or happen to be employing the Hawk strategy during a prevailing number of social interactions) are mutually antagonistic, and are only likely to experience the maximum fitness payoffs in environments where they are sufficiently outnumbered by Doves to ensure that the vast majority of their interactions will produce one-sided benefits. This same logic of predation has been applied to a range of personality traits associated with the Dark Triad, most notably the predatory interpersonal behaviors associated with psychopathy, lending credence to the possibility that psychopathy can be best understood as a cluster of heritable behavioral tendencies that endure as a low-frequency Evolutionarily Stable Strategy in human populations (Jonason et al., 2010, 2016). More benign personality variants also show some signs of negative Frequency-Dependence, including several Five Factor Model traits (Denissen and Penke, 2008), suggesting Frequency-Dependent Selection is at least partially responsible for the intermediate prevalence rates that have been observed (Ebstein, 2006).

Heterozygous Advantage

The most easily understood mechanism of Stabilizing Selection is Heterozygous Advantage (sometimes known as 'overdominance'), popularized by compelling medical examples such as the benefits of malarial-resistance that coexist with near-normal overall health in individuals who are heterozygous, but not homozygous, for the alleles responsible for Sickle-Cell Anemia (Endler, 1986). For complex behavioral tendencies that are likely to possess large Mutational Target-Sizes, such as broad personality traits, the iterative and cumulative impact of Heterozygous Advantage effects across many gene loci can theoretically account for the Stabilizing Selection hypothesized by Nettle (2010), wherein the ideal levels of personality traits for individual fitness cannot be found at their extremes, but are instead likely to be some nominal amount above (or below) the population mean, which constitutes a kind of 'moving target' for selection as the many relevant genes are shuffled and recombined with each generation of sexual reproduction (Curtisinger et al., 1994).

Environmental Heterogeneity

Theories such as those advanced by Nettle (2006, 2010) do not rely on concepts like Heterozygous Advantage and Antagonistic Pleiotropy in isolation, but also include an additional Stabilizing Selection mechanism in the form of Environmental Heterogeneity. Framed in this way, 'ideal' quantitative trait levels are not only a 'moving target' within each genetic lineage disposed towards a particular adaptive strategy, but the relative merits of each adaptive strategy are themselves constantly changing by virtue of frequently shifting conditions in the environment itself (Roff, 1997). Since the prevailing social and physical conditions of human environments can change exceedingly rapidly relative to generational time (a trend which appears to have endured for most of human evolutionary history, see Dingemanse and Reale, 2005), and since no single personality strategy can realistically confer high relative fitness across all conditions, the selective pressures favoring extreme specialization in particular strategies and personality variants cannot be applied consistently enough across generations to produce the highly clustered multimodal distributions of traits we might otherwise expect to observe (Nettle, 2010). Social and environmental variations such as famines versus times of plenty, wars versus

times of peace, and shifts in the relative dominance of social subgroups, are sufficiently frequent, unpredictable, and consequential to human survival as to generate a disadvantage for any members of the population disposed to overspecializing in specific behavioral strategies, as contrasted with those who may be well-suited to some strategies, but still capable of functionally adopting moderate alternative strategies when developmental conditions call for it (Kassen, 2002).

These processes of Balancing and Stabilizing Selection are largely mutually compatible and are theoretically capable of generating predictions that can be tested with standard behavioral genetics methods, most notably twin studies (Polderman et al., 2015). To that end, there are some complicating limitations on the aforementioned processes that researchers need to keep in mind if they hope to make realistic predictions or models concerning the ratios of rival personality strategies and their associated traits that we expect to see in real populations. Most notably, there are a range of subtle gene-environment correlation (rGE) effects that can blur the boundaries of the simple predictions that models based on Balancing and Stabilizing Selection will otherwise offer (Purcell, 2002). These distinct effects are summarized by Scarr and McCartney (1983) as Active rGE, Evocative rGE, and Passive rGE.

Gene-Environment Correlations

Active rGE, also known as Niche Selection, describes the tendency of individuals who possess endowments particularly well-suited to particular environments to actively seek out those environments over their lifetime (Scarr and McCartney, 1983). This tendency complicates the otherwise simple predictions of the relative fitness of different genotypes subject to Environmental Heterogeneity, unless researchers are capable of tracking niches within the accessible environment that individuals with broadly disfavored traits may be capable of proactively finding to enhance their prospects (Camperio Ciani et al., 2007). For example, individuals with dispositions well-suited to violent conflict may mitigate the disadvantages of these traits during times of peace by moving to more conflict-prone areas or pursuing physically endangering work. Evocative rGE describes instances in which some individuals are exposed to a set of environmental conditions (social in nature) as a result of some genetic traits they have inherited (Buss and Greiling, 1999). For example, individuals who are born with especially warm interpersonal dispositions are likely to experience globally more positive social reactions from their peers, which in turn partially shapes the environment their personality needs to thrive in (Lewis, 2014). When taken to extremes, Evocative rGE effects may constitute a form of Condition-Dependent strategic adaptation, which will be reviewed more closely later in this chapter. Finally, Passive rGE effects extrapolate the impacts of the previous two effects across generations, noting that in addition to the genes that offspring inherit from their parents, they are also disproportionately likely to inherit environments that meaningfully correlate with those same genes (Kendler and Baker, 2007). For example, the children of parents who are high on Openness to New Experiences are not only likely to inherit 30–50% of that trait disposition from their parents (Bouchard, 2004), but by virtue of the Active and Evocative rGE effects that have shaped their parents' lives, are also likely to inherit a stimulating home-life in which someone with high Openness is likely to thrive (Schmitt, 2004). Passive rGE in particular makes the methodological disentanglement of genetic versus environmental heritability estimates exceedingly difficult in all but the most fortuitous of natural experiments (such as twin adoption studies, Purcell, 2002), limiting our ability to correctly gauge the cumulative fitness contributions of various personality traits across generations (Polderman et al., 2015).

STATE-DEPENDENT AND CONDITION-DEPENDENT STRATEGIES

Given that the measured heritability of major traits accounts for somewhere between 30–50% of observed variation in personality (Bouchard, 2004), evolutionary and biopsychological theories of personality-like dispositions most commonly proceed with the reasonable assumption that the genetic contributions to these individual differences are the most pressing elements to explain (Penke et al., 2007). As was discussed above, some degree of noise-like variation is expected in any complex trait (Lynch and Hill, 1986), and it is far from impossible that the non-heritable portions of personality variance may primarily or entirely consist of non-adaptive random variation (environmental in origin) that is simply not consequential enough to fitness outcomes to significantly select against (Campbell, 2007). However, the aforementioned fitness-relevance of many personality-mediated behaviors make this degree of non-adaptive variation appear unlikely, particularly since evolved adaptations are in no way functionally limited to preformationist or genetically-deterministic mechanisms, and forms of adaptive plasticity are, in themselves, broadly fitness-enhancing in the aggregate (Kuzawa and Bragg, 2012).

In addition to more general mechanisms that endow an organism with the ability to calibrate and modify their bodies and behaviors based on ontogenic experience, such as those grouped together under the umbrella of learning (Mesoudi, 2011), more domain-specific adaptations can also demonstrate contextual sensitivity to events and conditions encountered within an organism's life experience, which, as a form of competence without comprehension (Dennett, 2017), can respond to environmental cues that signal which potential strategies are statistically likely to be most beneficial (Gigerenzer and Brighton, 2009). Instances of this kind of adaptive plasticity (sometimes collectively referred to as 'facultative' adaptations) can themselves be thought of as traits with a varying genetic basis, as they ultimately represent a class of gene-environment interaction (GxE) effects, wherein organisms vary in their response to common environmental conditions by virtue of the differential strategic sensitivities they are endowed with (see Moffitt et al., 2006, for a review of the potential adaptive tradeoffs at play for higher and lower degrees of sensitivity to environmental cues, and the implications for psychopathologies that embody the common 'diathesis-stress' GxE presentation). An inclusive umbrella term for adaptive strategies whose activation or calibration depends on signals (either internal or external) in an individual's ontogenic experience is State-Dependent Strategies (or State-Dependent Adaptations, see Nettle, 2019). Within this approach is a subset of hypothetical strategies that depend exclusively on self-assessments of major fitness-related domains, known as Condition-Dependent Strategies, which warrant special focus for the methodological confounds such theories can present for some of the genetic approaches in the preceding sections (Verweij et al., 2012).

State-Dependent Adaptations

The adaptive benefits available to organisms capable of adopting or switching between strategies on the basis of identifiable opportunity cues (Luttbeg and Sih, 2010) are especially pronounced when the fitness payoffs of different strategies vary extensively on timescales shorter than a single generation (McNamara, 2013). This means that while we might expect some theories to conform to the classical psychological model of life-long dispositions being calibrated by early life experiences (Srivastava et al., 2003), the timing and frequency of predicted 'switch points' (Del Giudice, 2009) in the mechanisms of calibration are themselves likely to vary from trait to trait on the basis of when strategic realignments would be most beneficial (Del Giudice et al., 2015). While ethology

research into State-Dependent Strategies has largely focused on situational plasticity that activates short-term behavioral changes in response to temporally urgent environmental cues (such as antipredator behavior and asset-protection behavior, see Clark, 1994), ethologists have also identified developmental mechanisms that appear to support more consistent personality-like variations (known as Behavioral Syndromes or Coping Styles, see Sih, 2011) which may be more instructive in the study of human individual differences. For example, a range of animal Behavioral Syndromes have been modeled as State-Dependent Strategies fixed by the accumulation of critical stressors in early development, subject to profound revision during profound shifts in life history phase later in life (Luttbeg and Sih, 2010; Sih, 2011). Other models, such as the winner–loser aggression dynamic studied by Chase and associates (1994), do not track any single developmentally specified early state, but instead operate on a cumulative 'push your luck' logic where the behavioral outcomes of adopting an initially bold strategy serve to modulate the organism's ongoing commitment to said strategy. More specifically, one initially adopts a tentative Hawkish aggressive interpersonal strategy, and both maintains and enhances that strategy for however long one is capable of sustaining a 'winning streak' in physical contests, only to spontaneously shift to an enduring Dovish strategy following one's first significant defeat (Chase et al., 1994). In principle, the only major a priori limits theorists should expect from the switch points in a State-Dependent Adaptation is the signaling limitations imposed by the need to coordinate with one's peers (Olofsson et al., 2009; Wolf and Weissing, 2010), which is discussed later in this chapter.

In seeking to explain individual differences in human personality through the mechanisms of State-Dependent and Condition-Dependent Adaptations, Lewis (2014) outlines an ambitious range of possibilities. If we were to rely primarily on the full range of reliable and semi-reliable cues that were likely available to ancestral human beings in seeking the optimal calibration of behavioral strategies in the fitness domains identified with personality (an approach to adaptationism sometimes described as 'Panglossian', see Dennett, 1995), Lewis argues that we would expect to see extensive State-Dependent Adaptations that directly respond to unambiguous fitness-relevant cues, complemented by a range of Condition-Dependent Adaptations that fill this calibrating role in the (potentially common) event that unambiguous state information is unavailable (Lewis, 2014). Taking the personality trait of Neuroticism as an example, the behavioral tendencies associated with higher Neuroticism are considered maladaptive, but are potentially contextually valuable to individuals who are vulnerable to social rejection and ostracism (which in human ancestral environments was likely to prove lethal, see Kurzban and Leary, 2001). Neuroticism promotes a habitual vigilance and pessimism towards multiple forms of social rejection, and while seemingly strategically poorly suited to maximizing positive social status, does appear to foster behaviors consistent with loss-minimization for individuals whose social standing is already precarious (Nettle, 2006; Lewis, 2014). State-Dependent Adaptations for strategically adopting higher Neuroticism would thus be expected to respond to concrete cues of important social rejections in one's lived experience, and longitudinal evidence does suggest that individuals are prone to undergo personality shifts towards Neuroticism after having experienced such setbacks, in an approximately 'dose-dependent' relationship (Grant, 2011).

Condition-Dependent Adaptations

In complement to preceding State-Dependent Adaptations, the adaptive benefits of Neuroticism would be underutilized if Neuroticism could only emerge in reaction to having already suffered important social rejections, as the main strategic purpose of neurotic behavior appears to be the mitigation of future unanticipated losses. As such, Lewis proposes that the majority of neurotic behavior in the population ought to be activated prior to any concrete experiences of costly rejection, and will instead be activated by mechanisms that draw on an individual's self-evaluations of their relative social condition, such that individuals who possess traits that make them statistically more likely to experience social rejection in the future (e.g., being unattractive, lacking social skills, poor health, all of which non-trivial correlate with trait Neuroticism, see Mathes and Kahn, 1975) will trigger Condition-Dependent Adaptations to activate a neurotic interpersonal strategy (Lewis, 2014). Similar models can be advanced relative to the identified fitness-relevant domains of other major personality traits, such as Extraversion (Lukaszewski and Roney, 2011), Openness to New Experience (Plomin, 2013) and Conscientiousness (Schmitt, 2004), all of which possess a range of unambiguous life states that would signal opportunities for adaptive strategic personality shifts (such as reliably-kept long term promises for Conscientiousness, see Figueredo et al., 2005), and also a range of condition domains which predict better fitness payoffs for individuals with better endowments (e.g., attractiveness for Extraversion, general intelligence for Openness, response-inhibition for Conscientiousness, see Lewis, 2014). Theories such as these propose means through which a large suite of species-typical adaptations may account for much of the variation observed in human personality, independent of the contributions made by genetically heritable dispositions.

The preceding theory represents only the extreme end of a wide range of viable State-Dependent and Condition-Dependent approaches. While it is possible that such an extensive suite of domain-specific ubiquitous adaptations truly exists, it is just as likely that only some partial subset of them exists, perhaps distributed unevenly across the major personality domains that personality psychologists study (Lewis, 2014). Precisely how large a portion of observable phenotypic variation is attributable to State-Dependent and Condition-Dependent mechanisms, relative to the gene-frequency based theories outlined earlier in this chapter, is a genuinely difficult matter to disentangle methodologically, because on the level of observable behaviors these theories often generate predictions in close lock-step with predictions derived from more genetic theories. A particularly challenging example of this concerns the convergence of empirical predictions (especially when employing standard behavioral genetics methodologies) between theories of Mutation-Selection Balance and theories grounded in Condition-Dependent Strategies (Verweij et al., 2012). Almost all of the condition domains hypothesized to activate various Condition-Dependent Strategies are precisely the kind of broad, fitness-predictive traits that are also hypothesized to possess large enough Mutational Target-Sizes to be subject to Mutation-Selection Balance. If, for example, Openness to New Experience demonstrates Condition-Dependent activation based on one's level of general intelligence, the relevant subdomains of Openness will appear in studies estimating inheritance to follow patterns consistent with Mutation-Selection Balance. How, then, are researchers to know if Openness itself is directly subject to Mutation-Selection Balance, or if it is intimately connected in development to general intelligence, which itself appears to follow Mutation-Selection Balance? Short of extensive analyses of specific gene polymorphisms, which themselves are predicted to yield poor returns for traits with large Mutational Target-Sizes, there would be no reliable way to disambiguate between the two explanations, thus leaving the existence of the hypothesized Condition-Dependent Adaptation in question (Verweij et al., 2012). Evolutionary personality psychologists must keep this ambiguous range of possibilities in mind when conducting their investigations, if they are to have any hope of capitalizing on opportunities to empirically delineate

between these competing explanations when they present themselves.

SIGNALING, STABILITY AND PERCEPTION

Each of the individual differences theories reviewed thus far in this chapter seek to explain patterns of human psychological variation with reference to evolutionary and developmental processes that impact the fitness prospects of the individuals involved. Adopting this kind of explanatory approach is typical in evolutionary psychology, but it bears reiterating that the common approach to this subject matter by personality psychologists and cognitive ability researchers is primarily descriptive (Marsh and Boag, 2013). As interdisciplinary works, each of the aforementioned explanatory theories have based much of their empirical testing on concepts and measures borrowed from the study of personality and individual differences, but since these measures are mostly designed to serve a descriptive function in identifying reliable variation in population, this results in some methodological complications that are easy to miss if care is not taken. One prominent cautionary example of this comes with the theories on general intelligence advanced by Satoshi Kanazawa (2004), wherein he employs a fairly standardized evolutionary psychology approach to a trait of interest, conceptualizing it as a domain-specific adaptation with a wide range of fitness benefits, while simultaneously relying exclusively on background research and measurement tools which regard the same trait as a standardized individual differences variable (Kanazawa, 2010). By embracing these two contradictory stances, Kanazawa was able to propose a theory that regards general intelligence as a specific adaptation for coping with evolutionary novelty, a concept that may seem tenable on face value, given the reified way intelligence is sometimes referenced by virtue of the *g* factor statistical aggregate, but which falls apart when employing a more technically rigorous conceptual analysis of the multiple converging ability domains that the individual difference variable represents (see Borsboom and Dolan, 2006, and Penke et al., 2011, for more exhaustive critiques). To offer a more constructive picture of how problems of this sort can be avoided, it is important to both outline what favorable alternatives to the repurposing of descriptive individual differences variables might look like, and to reflect on why the existing use of descriptive individual differences variables can yield limited domains of success.

Signaling Consistency

The latter issue, concerning why descriptive individual differences variables can be used to limited effect in exploring evolutionary theories of ability and personality variation, appears to depend on the role signaling plays in shaping both the traits in question and the human perception of them (Luxen and Buunk, 2006). Descriptive individual difference variables, particularly the most popularized and successful personality models such as the Five Factor Model, were not historically developed by the testing of predictions from some foundational theory, but rather, were discovered through statistical analysis of voluminous human response data, mostly based on the natural language terms used to describe the intuitively salient aspects of human character (Digman, 1990). As such, it is likely that the loose applicability of these descriptive variables to analyses targeting the shaping of human personality by natural and sexual selection is ultimately derived from the underlying sensitivity of human social intuitions to meaningful forms of variation in other humans (Denissen and Penke, 2008). As was discussed with relation to Mutation-Selection Balance, Frequency-Dependent Selection and Condition-Dependent Adaptations, many of the apparent fitness benefits of possessing favorable abilities and

dispositions are the social benefits that accrue from the recognition of these positive traits by our peers and rivals (Luxen and Buunk, 2006; Nettle, 2010). In much the same way as attraction signals in sexual selection evolve via the mutual benefits of possessing and perceiving indicators of mate quality (Kokko et al., 2003), in social species, traits that confer fitness advantages carry with them a corresponding incentive to signal those advantages to others, which in turn drives the selection pressures favoring receptiveness to said signals (so long as they are trustworthy, as in Costly Signaling; see Grafen, 1990). This argument holds true for cognitive abilities in much the same way as for strategically advantageous personality traits, but as with Mutation-Selection Balance itself, likely involves a directional arms-race-like dynamic between the benefits of seeming high ability versus having high enough ability to recognize reliable signals (Luxen and Buunk, 2006). Signaling theory also offers some justification for the demonstrable stability of dispositional traits, even in instances where more frequent opportunistic switch points are possible. As both Olofsson et al. (2009) and Wolf and Weissing (2010) have modeled, several personality traits embody behavioral strategies that depend on cultivating social benefits such as alliances, future reciprocation and mating opportunities which require trusting coordination between peers. Under these circumstances, it is worthwhile to sacrifice a degree of strategic flexibility in exchange for a consistent interpersonal presentation that can more reliably signal coordination benefits to one's peers, thus favoring a threshold of consistency sufficient to give an impression of stability to other people (Wolf and Weissing, 2010).

Alternative Measures

While the role of signaling in our evolutionary history salvages some of the contemporary uses of descriptive difference variables in adaptationist explorations of individual differences, their many limitations are becoming increasingly clear as researchers attempt to employ a wider range of behavioral and population genetic tools to test evolutionary theories. As Penke et al. (2007) explain: 'Calculating the coefficient of additive genetic variance (CVA) of a trait, which is very informative about its evolutionary history (Houle, 1992; Stirling et al., 2002), requires a ratio-scale measure (i.e., a measure with a meaningful zero point). Personality questionnaires with rating scales fail to reach this standard' (578). A potential solution that they and other evolutionary theorists (Boomsma et al., 1997; Cannon and Keller, 2005) suggest is the expanded use of Endophenotypes as approximate indicators of the higher-order behavioral traits they contribute to. To quote: 'It would be very helpful if valid, ratio-scaled personality measures (e.g., based on quantitative endophenotypes or behaviors measured with regard to their energy output, temporal duration, or act frequency – see Buss and Craik, 1983) could be developed and used in quantitative behavior genetic studies' (Penke et al., 2007: 578). While selected Endophenotypes would not necessarily need to be solely responsible for much of the individual variance in the manifested behavioral traits of interest in order to be useful incremental improvements over the measures currently available, one area in which Endophenotypes hold particular promise is in the possible identification of neurological or endocrine mechanisms that embody State-Dependent switch points, for maladaptive behavioral variants (such as those seen in psychopathological disorder characterized by a diathesis-stress presentation, see Moffitt et al., 2006).

INDIVIDUAL DIFFERENCES WITHIN CATEGORIES OF VARIATION

This chapter has focused on the study of within-species individual differences, in a manner reflective of the overarching cognitive abilities and personality categories that shape the contemporary field of differential psychology. These conceptions of individual differences are conceived in such a way as to evenhandedly apply to any member of the human species, with a particular emphasis on trait definitions that all human beings quantitively vary upon in a Gaussian distribution (Larsen and Buss, 2017). But some of the most significant differences that can be found within a species are, due to reflecting significant divergences in interests and strategies, more comfortably modeled as multimodal distributions, if not as qualitatively distinct categories (Del Giudice, 2016). The most obvious and well-studied examples of these are the broad 'fast and slow' life history strategies (often described as 'low-K' and 'high-K' respectively, see Del Giudice et al., 2015) and the complementary binary sex morphologies of female and male (Geary, 2009). While an exhaustive review of the types of variation predicted by either of these divisions far exceeds the scope of this chapter, the existence of these intra-species categories has been found to exert some systematic effects on the kinds of individual differences that this chapter has focused on.

Life History Strategy

With regards to life history strategies, although there have been some concise critiques of the uncritical generalization of life history trends designed for interspecies comparisons to variation within a single species (see Zietsch and Sidari, 2019, for more detail), researchers have encountered some empirical success in predicting clusters of real-world differences based on the inherent tradeoffs between mating efforts and parenting efforts (Ellis, 2004; Figueredo et al., 2005; 2007). This evidence appeared strongest when life history-relevant trait variance seemed to load onto a single 'K-factor', though more recent work by Richardson and colleagues (2017) supports the separating out of 'mating competition' as an independent factor, calling the fundamental fast–slow framework into question. At present, however, there is evidence supporting correlations between personality traits favoring aggression, risk-taking, and highly sexually-divergent mating priorities in individuals classified as fast or low-K life history strategy, whereas the slow or high-K life history strategy appears to correlate with personality traits oriented towards future-investment and long-term relationship cultivation (Barbaro et al., 2017; Barbaro and Shackelford, 2017). Researchers interested in these individual differences should thus expect a multimodal distribution of these trait values, due to their adaptive clustering with compatible life history commitments.

Sex Differences

As far as sex differences are concerned, some clustering of individual differences is expected due to asymmetric leanings towards short-term and long-term mating orientations, but this matter is more complicated than a simple sex division can cover (see Geary, 2009, for a more in-depth review). The more interesting interaction between individual differences and sex differences emerges as a product of the vastly different average amounts of intra-species competition the two sexes are exposed to by virtue of the behavioral differences predicted by Parental Investment Theory (see Trivers, 1972). The benefits, and indeed occasional necessity, of presenting a highly competitive, above-average phenotype for males (due to partially winner-take-all dynamics in mating opportunity) predict higher overall variability in tradeoff domain traits for males (that is, where traits are shaped by Antagonistic Pleiotropy), as well as higher average susceptibility to environmental signals (when traits are shaped by State-Dependent and Condition-Dependent Adaptations) relative to females (Geary, 1996). Conversely, the relative security of at least minimal reproductive prospects for females is predicted to result in more narrowing selection for those key aspects

of the default 'safe' mating strategy (associated with a youth-beauty-fertility axis of appeal), resulting in fewer females at the phenotypic extremes of the population in any given generation (Arden and Plomin, 2006). Individual difference researchers routinely find evidence for this in the multiple domains of individual differences, where regardless of where the sex-typical averages fall, males can reliably be found to occupy more extreme positions on both the high and low ends of abilities and traits (Wallace, 1975). Any researchers hoping to model the relative frequencies of competing personality strategies, inclusive of extreme variants at the tail-ends of the distributions, must plan for this predictable asymmetry in extreme values on the basis of sex.

CONCLUSION

Evolutionary psychology offers a wide range of promising contemporary theories on the origins, maintenance, and proximate mechanisms of intra-species individual differences, which may assist the field of differential psychology in expanding beyond the atheoretical descriptive focus that dominated its recent history (Buss, 2009; Lewis, 2014; Marsh and Boag, 2013). Successful research projects based on these theories will, however, require an atypically high degree of methodological rigor and epistemic humility, owing to the imperfect fit of existing individual differences measures for the task, as well as the range of competing explanations that can be offered for the same empirical results (Verweij et al., 2012). Evolutionary psychologists have seen their greatest predictive successes in domains of human nature that are amenable to explanation by one-size-fits-all species-typical adaptations, but a mature field of evolutionary differential psychology will require training new researchers to instead develop predictive models of competing Evolutionarily Stable Strategies comprised of both heritable and developmental adaptations.

REFERENCES

Arden, R., & Plomin, R. (2006). Sex differences in variance of intelligence across childhood. *Personality and Individual Differences*, *41*(1), 39–48.

Ashton, M. C., Lee, K., & De Vries, R. E. (2014). The HEXACO honesty-humility, agreeableness, and emotionality factors: A review of research and theory. *Personality and Social Psychology Review*, *18*(2), 139–152.

Barbaro, N., & Shackelford, T. K. (2017). Dimensions of environmental risk are unique theoretical constructs. *Behavioral and Brain Sciences*, *40*, 12–13.

Barbaro, N., Boutwell, B. B., Barnes, J. C., & Shackelford, T. K. (2017). Genetic confounding of the relationship between father absence and age at menarche. *Evolution and Human Behavior*, *38*(3), 357–365.

Boomsma, D. I., Anokhin, A., & De Geus, E. J. C. (1997). Genetics of electrophysiology: Linking genes, brains, and behavior. *Current Directions in Psychological Science*, *6*(4), 106–110.

Borsboom, D., & Dolan, C. V. (2006). Why g is not an adaptation: A comment on Kanazawa (2004). *Psychological Review*, *113*(2), 433–437.

Bouchard Jr, T. J. (2004). Genetic influence on human psychological traits: A survey. *Current Directions in Psychological Science*, *13*(4), 148–151.

Burger, R. (2005). A multilocus analysis of intraspecific competition and stabilizing selection on a quantitative trait. *Journal of Mathematical Biology*, *50*(4), 355–396.

Buss, D. M. (1991). Evolutionary personality psychology. *Annual Review of Psychology*, *42*, 459–491.

Buss, D. M. (2009). How can evolutionary psychology successfully explain personality and individual differences? *Perspectives on Psychological Science*, *4*(4), 359–366.

Buss, D. M. (2015). *Evolutionary psychology* (5th ed.). Abingdon-on-Thames: Routledge.

Buss, D. M., & Craik, K. H. (1983). The act frequency approach to personality. *Psychological Review*, *90*(2), 105–126.

Buss, D. M., & Greiling, H. (1999). Adaptive individual differences. *Journal of Personality*, *67*(2), 209–243.

Campbell, A. (2007). Personality: Does selection see it? (Commentary). *European Journal of Personality*, *21*(5), 591–593.

Camperio Ciani, A. S., Capiluppi, C., Veronese, A., & Sartori, G. (2007). The adaptive value of personality differences revealed by small island population dynamics. *European Journal of Personality*, *21*(1), 3–22.

Cannon, T. D., & Keller, M. C. (2005). Endophenotypes in genetic analyses of mental disorders. *Annual Review of Clinical Psychology*, *2*, 267–290.

Cervone, D. (2005). Personality architecture: Within-person structures and processes. *Annual Review of Psychology*, *56*, 423–452.

Chase, I. D., Bartolomeo, C., & Dugatkin, L. A. (1994). Aggressive interactions and inter-contest interval: How long do winners keep winning. *Animal Behaviour*, *48*(2), 393–400.

Clark, C. W. (1994). Antipredator behavior and the asset-protection principle. *Behavioral Ecology*, *5*(2), 159–170.

Conroy-Beam, D., Buss, D. M., Pham, M. N., & Shackelford, T. K. (2015). How sexually dimorphic are human mate preferences? *Personality and Social Psychology Bulletin*, *41*(8), 1082–1093.

Costa, P. T., Jr., & McCrae, R. R. (1992). Four ways five factors are basic. *Personality and Individual Differences*, *13*(6), 653–665.

Curtisinger, J. W., Service, P. M., & Prout, T. (1994). Antagonistic pleiotropy, reversal of dominance, and genetic polymorphism. *The American Naturalist*, *144*(2), 210–228.

Darwin, C. (1859). *On the origin of species*. London: John Murray.

Del Giudice, M. (2009). Sex, attachment, and the development of reproductive strategies. *Behavioral and Brain Sciences*, *32*(1), 1–67.

Del Giudice, M. (2016). The life history model of psychopathology explains the structure of psychiatric disorders and the emergence of the p factor: A simulation study. *Clinical Psychological Science*, *4*(2), 299–311.

Del Giudice, M., Gangestad, S. W., & Kaplan, H. S. (2015). Life history theory and evolutionary psychology. In D. M. Buss (Ed.), *The handbook of evolutionary psychology* (pp. 88–114). Hoboken, NJ: Wiley.

Denissen, J. J. A., & Penke, L. (2008). Motivational individual reaction norms underlying the five factor model of personality: First steps towards a theory-based conceptual framework. *Journal of Research in Personality*, *42*(5), 1285–1302.

Dennett, D. C. (1995). *Darwin's dangerous idea: Evolution and the meanings of life*. London: Allen Lane and the Penguin Press.

Dennett, D. C. (2014). The evolution of reasons. In B. Bashour & H. D. Muller (Eds), *Contemporary philosophical naturalism and its implications* (pp. 47–62). New York: Routledge.

Dennett, D. C. (2017). *From bacteria to Bach and back: The evolution of minds*. New York: W. W. Norton & Company.

De Vries, R. E., Tybur, J. M., Pollet, T. V., & van Vugt, M. (2016). Evolution, situational affordances, and the HEXACO model of personality. *Evolution and Human Behavior*, *37*(5), 407–421.

Digman, J. M. (1990). Personality structure: Emergence of the five-factor model. *Annual Review of Psychology*, *41*, 417–440.

Dingemanse, N. J., & Reale, D. (2005). Natural selection and animal personality. *Behaviour*, *142*(9–10), 1159–1184.

Eaves, L. J., Martin, N. G., Heath, A. C., Hewitt, J. K., & Neale, M. C. (1990). Personality and reproductive fitness. *Behavior Genetics*, *20*(5), 563–568.

Ebstein, R. (2006). The molecular genetic architecture of human personality: Beyond self-report questionnaires. *Molecular Psychiatry*, *11*(5), 427–445.

Ellis, B. J. (2004). Timing of pubertal maturation in girls: An integrated life history approach. *Psychological Bulletin*, *130*(6), 920–958.

Endler, J. A. (1986). *Natural selection in the wild*. Princeton, NJ: University Press.

Eyre-Walker, A., & Keightley, P. D. (1999). High genomic deleterious mutation rates in hominids. *Nature*, *397*(6717), 344–347.

Figueredo, A. J., Vásquez, G., Brumbach, B. H., & Schneider, S. M. R. (2007). The K-factor, covitality, and personality: A psychometric test of life history theory. *Human Nature*, *18*(1), 47–73.

Figueredo, A. J., Vásquez, G., Brumbach, B. H., Sefcek, J. A., Kirsner, B. R., & Jacobs, W. J. (2005). The K-Factor: Individual differences in life history strategy. *Personality and Individual Differences*, *39*(8), 1349–1360.

Fisher, R. A. (1930). *The genetical theory of natural selection*. Oxford: Clarendon Press.

Friedman, H. S., Tucker, J. S., Schwartz, J. E., Martin, L. R., Tomlinson-Keasey, C., Wingard, D. L., & Criqui, M. H. (1995). Childhood conscientiousness and longevity: Health behaviors and cause of death. *Journal of Personality and Social Psychology*, *68*(4), 696–703.

Geary, D. C. (1996). Sexual selection and sex differences in mathematical abilities. *Behavioral and Brain Sciences*, *19*(2), 229–247.

Geary, D. C. (2009). *Male, female: The evolution of human sex differences*. Washington, DC: American Psychological Association.

Gigerenzer, G., & Brighton, H. (2009). Homo heuristicus: Why biased minds make better inferences. *Topics in Cognitive Science*, *1*, 107–143.

Gintis, H. (2009). *The bounds of reason: Game theory and the unification of the behavioral sciences*. Princeton, NJ and Oxford: Princeton University Press.

Grafen, A. (1990). Biological signals as handicaps. *Journal of Theoretical Biology*, *144*(4), 517–546.

Grant, S. (2011). *Neuroticism*. Hauppauge, NY: Nova Science Publishers.

Hedrick, P. W. (1999). Antagonistic pleiotropy and genetic polymorphism: A perspective. *Heredity*, *82*(2), 126–133.

Houle, D. (1992). Comparing evolvability and variability of quantitative traits. *Genetics*, *130*(1), 195–204.

Houle, D. (1998). How should we explain variation in the genetic variance of traits? *Genetica*, *102/103*(1–6), 241–253.

Houle, D., Hughes, K. A., Hoffmaster, D. K., Ihara, J., Assimacopolous, S., Canada, D., & Charlesworth, B. (1994). The effects of spontaneous mutation on quantitative traits I: Variance and covariance of life history traits. *Genetics*, *138*(3), 773–785.

Jensen, A. R. (1998). *The g-factor: The science of mental ability*. Westport, CT: Praeger.

Jeon J., & Buss, D. M. (2007). Altruism towards cousins. *Proceedings of the Royal Society of London, Series B: Biological Sciences*, *274*(1614), 1181–1187.

John, O. P., & Srivastava, S. (1999). The Big Five trait taxonomy: History, measurement and theoretical perspectives. In L. A. Pervin & O. P. John (Eds.), *Handbook of personality: Theory and research* (pp. 102–138). New York: Guilford Press.

Jonason, P. K., Icho, A., & Ireland, K. (2016). Resources, harshness, and unpredictability: The socioeconomic conditions associated with the Dark Triad traits. *Evolutionary Psychology*, *14*(1), 1–11.

Jonason, P. K., Li, N. P., & Buss, D. M. (2010). The costs and benefits of the Dark Triad: Implications for mate poaching and mate retention tactics. *Personality and Individual Differences*, *48*(4), 373–378.

Kanazawa, S. (2004). General intelligence as a domain-specific adaptation. *Psychological Review*, *111*(2), 512–523.

Kanazawa, S. (2010). Evolutionary psychology and intelligence research. *American Psychologist*, *65*, 279–289.

Kassen, R. (2002). The experimental evolution of specialists, generalists, and the maintenance of diversity. *Journal of Evolutionary Biology*, *15*(2), 173–190.

Keightley, P. D., & Gaffney, D. J. (2003). Functional constraints and frequency of deleterious mutations in noncoding DNA of rodents. *Proceedings of the National Academy of Sciences of the United States of America*, *100*(23), 13402–13406.

Keller, M. C., & Miller, G. F. (2006). Resolving the paradox of common, harmful, heritable mental disorders: Which evolutionary genetic models work best? *Behavioral and Brain Sciences*, *29*(4), 385–404.

Kendler, K. S., & Baker, J. H. (2007). Genetic influences on measures of the environment: A systematic review. *Psychological Medicine*, *37*(5), 615–626.

Kidd, K. K. (2006). ALFRED – the ALlele FREquency Database. Retrieved September 2, 2006, alfred.med.yale.edu.

Kimura, M. (1983). *The neutral theory of molecular evolution*. Cambridge, UK: Cambridge University Press.

Kokko, H., Brooks, R., Jennions, M. D., & Morley, J. (2003). The evolution of mate choice and mating biases. *Proceedings of the Royal Society of London, Series B: Biological Sciences*, *270*(1515), 653–664.

Kopp, M., & Hermisson, J. (2006). Evolution of genetic architecture under frequency-dependent disruptive selection. *Evolution*, *60*(8), 1537–1550.

Kurzban, R., & Leary, M. (2001). Evolutionary origins of stigmatization: The functions of social exclusion. *Psychological Bulletin*, *127*(2), 187–208.

Kuzawa, C. W., & Bragg, J. M. (2012). Plasticity in human life history strategy: Implications for contemporary human variation and the evolution of genus Homo. *Current Anthropology*, *53*(Suppl_6), S369–S382.

Larsen, R., & Buss, D. M. (2017). *Personality psychology*. New York: McGraw Hill.

Lewis, D. M. G. (2014). Evolved individual differences: Advancing a condition-dependent model of personality. *Personality and Individual Differences*, *84*, 63–72.

Lewontin, R. C. (1961). Evolution and the theory of games. *Journal of Theoretical Biology*, *1*(3), 382–403.

Lukaszewski, A. W., & Roney, J. R. (2011). The origins of extraversion: Joint effects of facultative calibration and genetic polymorphism. *Personality and Social Psychology Bulletin*, *37*(3), 409–421.

Lund, O. C. H., Tamnes, C. K., Mouestue, C., Buss, D. M., & Vollrath, M. (2007). Tactics of hierarchy negotiation. *Journal of Research in Personality*, *41*(1), 25–44.

Luttbeg, B., & Sih, A. (2010). Risk, resources and state-dependent adaptive behavioural syndromes. *Philosophical Transactions of the Royal Society: Biological Sciences*, *365*(1560), 3977–3990.

Luxen, M. F., & Buunk, B. P. (2006). Human intelligence, fluctuating asymmetry and the peacock's tail: General intelligence (g) as an honest signal of fitness. *Personality and Individual Differences*, *41*(5), 897–902.

Lynch, M., & Hill, W. G. (1986). Phenotypic evolution by neutral mutation. *Evolution*, *40*(5), 915–935.

MacDonald, K. (1995). Evolution, the five-factor model, and levels of personality. *Journal of Personality*, *63*(3), 525–567.

MacDonald, K. (1998). Evolution, culture, and the five-factor model. *Journal of Cross Cultural Psychology*, *29*(1), 119–149.

Marsh, T., & Boag, S. (2013). Evolutionary and differential psychology: Conceptual conflicts and the path to integration. *Frontiers in Psychology*, *4*, 655.

Mathes, E. W., & Kahn, A. (1975). Physical attractiveness, happiness, neuroticism, and self-esteem. *Journal of Psychology*, *90*, 27–30.

Maynard Smith, J. (1976). Evolution and the theory of games. *American Scientist, 64*(1), 41–45.

Maynard Smith, J. (1982). *Evolution and the theory of games*. Cambridge: Cambridge University Press.

Maynard Smith, J. (1998). *Evolutionary genetics*. Oxford: University Press.

Maynard Smith, J., & Price, G. R. (1973). The logic of animal conflict. *Nature, 246*(5427), 15–18.

McNamara, J. M. (2013). Towards a richer evolutionary game theory. *Journal of the Royal Society Interface, 10*, 20130544.

Merila, J., & Sheldon, B. C. (1999). Genetic architecture of fitness and nonfitness traits: Empirical patterns and development of ideas. *Heredity, 83*(2), 103–109.

Mesoudi, A. (2011). An experimental comparison of human social learning strategies: Payoff-biased social learning is adaptive but underused. *Evolution & Human Behavior, 32*(5), 334–342.

Moffitt, T. E., Caspi, A., & Rutter, M. (2006). Measured gene–environment interactions in psychopathology: Concepts, research strategies, and implications for research, intervention, and public understanding of genetics. *Perspectives on Psychological Science, 1*(1), 5–27.

Nash, J. (1951). Non-cooperative games. *Annals of Mathematics, 54*(2), 286–295.

Neeleman, J., Sytema, S., & Wadsworth, M. (2002). Propensity to psychiatric and somatic ill-health: Evidence from a birth cohort. *Psychological Medicine, 32*(5), 793–803.

Nettle, D. (2005). An evolutionary approach to the extraversion continuum. *Evolution and Human Behavior, 26*(4), 363–373.

Nettle, D. (2006). The evolution of personality variation in humans and other animals. *American Psychologist, 61*(6), 622–631.

Nettle, D. (2010). Evolutionary perspectives on the five-factor model of personality. In D. M. Buss & P. H. Hawley (Eds), *The evolution of personality and individual differences* (pp. 5–28). New York: Oxford University Press.

Nettle, D. (2019). State-dependent cognition and its relevance to cultural evolution. *Behavioural Processes, 161*, 101–107.

Olofsson, H., Ripa, J., & Jonzén, N. (2009). Bet-hedging as an evolutionary game: The trade-off between egg size and number. *Philosophical Transactions of the Royal Society: Biological Sciences, 276*(1669), 2963–2969.

Penke, L., Denissen, J. P., & Miller, G. F. (2007). The evolutionary genetics of personality. *European Journal of Personality, 21*(5), 549–587.

Penke, L., Borsboom, D., Johnson, W., Kievit, R. A., Ploeger, A., & Wicherts, J. (2011). Evolutionary psychology and intelligence research cannot be integrated in the way Kanazawa (2010) suggested. *American Psychologist, 66*(9), 916–917.

Plomin, R. (2013). Commentary: Missing heritability, polygenic scores, and gene–environment correlation. *Journal of Child Psychology and Psychiatry, 54*(10), 1147–1149.

Plomin, R., Kennedy, J. K. J., & Craig, I. W. (2006). The quest for quantitative trait loci associated with intelligence. *Intelligence, 34*(6), 513–526.

Plomin, R., DeFries, J. C., Knopik, V. S., & Neiderhiser, J. M. (2016). Top 10 replicated findings from behavioral genetics. *Perspectives on Psychological Science, 11*(1), 3–23.

Polderman, T. J. C., Benyamin, B., de Leeuw, C. A., Sullivan, P. F., van Bochoven, A., Visscher, P. M., & Posthuma, D. (2015). Meta-analysis of the heritability of human traits based on fifty years of twin studies. *Nature Genetics, 47*(7), 702–709.

Price, M. E., Cosmides, L., & Tooby, J. (2002). Punitive sentiment as an anti-free rider psychological device. *Evolution and Human Behavior, 23*(3), 203–231.

Prokosch, M. D., Yeo, R. A., & Miller, G. F. (2005). Intelligence tests with higher g-loadings show higher correlations with body symmetry: Evidence for a general fitness factor mediated by developmental stability. *Intelligence, 33*(2), 203–213.

Purcell, S. (2002). Variance components models for gene–environment interaction in twin analysis. *Twin Research, 5*(6), 554–571.

Richardson, G. B., Sanning, B. K., Lai, M. H., Copping, L. T., Hardesty, P. H., & Kruger, D. J. (2017). On the psychometric study of human life history strategies: State of the science and evidence of two independent dimensions. *Evolutionary Psychology, 15*(1), 1474704916666840.

Roff, D. A. (1997). *Evolutionary quantitative genetics*. New York: Chapman & Hall.

Scarr, S., & McCartney, K. (1983). How people make their own environments: A theory of genotype → environment effects. *Child Development*, *54*(2), 424–435.

Schmitt, D. P. (2004). The Big Five related to risky sexual behaviour across 10 world regions: Differential personality associations of sexual promiscuity and relationship infidelity. *European Journal of Personality*, *18*(4), 301–319.

Schneider, K. A. (2006). A multilocus-multiallele analysis of frequency-dependent selection induced by intraspecific competition. *Journal of Mathematical Biology*, *52*(4), 483–523.

Sela, Y., & Shackelford, T. K. (2015). Evolution. In R. Cautin & S. Lilienfeld (Eds), *The encyclopedia of clinical psychology* (pp. 1–7). Hoboken, NJ: Wiley-Blackwell.

Sih, A. (2011). Effects of early stress on behavioral syndromes: An integrated adaptive perspective. *Neuroscience & Biobehavioral Reviews*, *35*(7), 1452–1465.

Srivastava, S., John, O. P., Gosling, S. D., & Potter, J. (2003). Development of personality in early and middle adulthood: Set like plaster or persistent change? *Journal of Personality and Social Psychology*, *84*(5), 1041–1053.

Stearns, S. (1992). *The evolution of life histories*. Oxford: Oxford University Press.

Stirling, D. G., Reale, D., & Roff, D. A. (2002). Selection, structure and the heritability of behaviour. *Journal of Evolutionary Biology*, *15*(2), 277–289.

Sugiyama, L. S., Tooby, J., & Cosmides, L. (2002). Cross-cultural evidence of cognitive adaptations for social exchange among the Shiwiar of Ecuadorian Amazonia. *Proceedings of the National Academy of Sciences of the United States of America*, *99*(17), 11537–11542.

Tooby, J., & Cosmides, L. (1990). On the universality of human nature and the uniqueness of the individual: The role of genetics and adaptation. *Journal of Personality*, *58*(1), 17–67.

Tooby, J., & Cosmides, L. (2005). Conceptual foundations of evolutionary psychology. In D. M. Buss (Ed.), *The handbook of evolutionary psychology* (pp. 5–67). Hoboken, NJ: Wiley.

Trivers, R. L. (1972). Parental investment and sexual selection. In B. Campbell (Ed.), *Sexual selection and the descent of man* (pp. 136–179). New York: Aldine.

Turelli, M., & Barton, N. H. (2004). Polygenic variation maintained by balancing selection: Pleiotropy, sex-dependent allelic effects and GxE interactions. *Genetics*, *166*(2), 1053–1079.

van der Maas, H. L. J., Dolan, C. V., Grasman, R. P., Wicherts, J. M., Huizenga, H. M., & Raijmakers, M. E. J. (2006). A dynamical model of general intelligence: The positive manifold of intelligence by mutualism. *Psychological Review*, *113*(4), 842–861.

Verweij, K. J. H., Yang, J., Lahti, J., Veijola, J., Hintsanen, M., Pulkki-Raback, L., et al. (2012). Maintenance of genetic variation in human personality: Testing evolutionary models by estimating heritability due to common causal variants and investigating the effect of distant inbreeding. *Evolution*, *66*(10), 3238–3251.

von Neumann, J., & Morgenstern, O. (1944). *Theory of games and economic behavior*. Princeton, NJ: Princeton University Press.

Wallace, B. (1975). Hard and soft selection revisited. *Evolution*, *29*(3), 465–473.

Wolf, M., & Weissing, F. J. (2010). An explanatory framework for adaptive personality differences. *Philosophical Transactions of the Royal Society: Biological Sciences*, *365*(1560), 3959–3968.

Zhang, X.-S., & Hill, W. G. (2005). Genetic variability under mutation selection balance. *Trends in Ecology and Evolution*, *20*(9), 468–470.

Zietsch, B. P., & Sidari, M. J. (2019). A critique of life history approaches to human trait covariation. *Evolution and Human Behavior*, doi: 10.1016/j.evolhumbehav.2019.05.007.

Social Biogeography

Aurelio José Figueredo, Mateo Peñaherrera-
Aguirre, Steven C. Hertler and
Michael A. Woodley of Menie

INTRODUCTION

Social Biogeography is an emergent research
program, still in its exploratory stages, wherein
biogeographical data are used to predict patterns of human social behavior, both directly
and indirectly. A complete model of Social
Biogeography attempts to reconstruct the
pathways of causal influence: (1) from the
Physical to the Community Ecology; (2) from
the Community and Physical to the Social
Ecology; (3) from the Social, Community, and
Physical to the Cultural Ecology; and (4) from
the Cultural, Social, Community, and Physical
to the Cognitive Ecology. This is an ambitious
task, and many attempts have been made in
the past to reconstruct some of these pathways. Only recently have somewhat more
comprehensive models been constructed, but
even these remain rudimentary compared to
the sheer magnitude of the problem.

With the understanding that the causal
directionalities among these different levels of
ecology are not always that straightforward, it
must be acknowledged that there are doubtless
feedback loops of reciprocal causal influence in the real world. For example, the
Community Ecology might sometimes influence the Physical, as when the action of roots,
bacteria, and earthworms modify the soil.
Similarly, the Cultural and Social Ecologies
might sometimes influence the Community
Ecology, as when different human societies
adopt different patterns of land management or cultivation of plants and animals.
Nevertheless, current Social Biogeography
models establish primary causal directionalities based on the presumed relative mag-
nitudes of these effects. In so doing, these
models only provide an approximation of the
exceedingly complex causal networks that
might actually exist within the real ecological system, which is the obvious place to start
such an ambitious undertaking.

We start by reviewing some prior research
that we consider to be both theoretical and
empirical antecedents of Social Biogeography.
This treatment is by no means exhaustive, but

is meant to illustrate from what intellectual and methodological roots the present research program sprang. Afterwards, we review some more recent attempts to construct more fully social biogeographical models based on both synchronic and diachronic analyses.

ANTECEDENTS OF SOCIAL-BIOGEOGRAPHICAL RESEARCH

Cross-regional comparisons represent a common avenue for evolutionary researchers to examine the consistency of behavioral, cognitive, and affective processes between human groups, as well as the unique ecological influence operating on the expression of these traits. Over the years, several projects have collected demographic, epidemiological, and geographical information to test competing evolutionary hypotheses. Although a detailed description of these studies is beyond the scope of this chapter, this section will provide a brief overview of the following research programs:

Biohistorical antecedents in McNeill, Crosby, and Diamond (reviewed in Hertler et al., 2018)
Murdock's (1967, 1981) Cross-Cultural Psychology
Wilson and Daly's (1985, 1997) evolutionary studies of homicide
Lynn and Vanhanen's (2002) *IQ and the Wealth of Nations*
Schmitt and colleagues' (2003, 2004, 2005) International Sexuality Description Project
You's and Henneberg's examinations into the effects of relaxed selection on various health outcomes (Budnik and Henneberg, 2017; You and Henneberg, 2016, 2018; You et al., 2018)
Thornhill and Fincher's (2014) parasite-stress theory
Van Lange and colleagues' (2017) CLASH model

Biohistorical Antecedents of Social Biogeography

In the late 1990s, Jared Diamond, in his *Guns, Germs, and Steel: The Fates of Human Societies*, attracted popular attention to a cross-section of history and ecology yoked together into something akin to Social Biogeography. Diamond inserted geography back into history as he explained the implications of the north–south axis along which the thin and long American continents run, in contrast to the east–west axis along which wide and expansive Eurasia runs. Culture, cultivars, technologies, and trade traverse broad expanses of longitude better than broad expanses of latitude, giving Eurasian societies manifold advantages that were brought to bear to the detriment of Amerindians within the Age of Exploration. Social Biogeography considers such factors, though it does not confine itself, as does Diamond, to cultural adaptations, but additionally studies differential evolution. Diamond's book of course had antecedents in his own work, but also in two intellectuals more directly related to the pursuit of Social Biogeography: Alfred W. Crosby and William H. McNeill.

As reviewed in Hertler et al. (2018), Crosby details the history of European failures to conquer, capture, or colonize outside their own continent, especially tropical locales so different from the temperate climate of Europe. The Norsemen in America and the Crusaders in the Levant were among the many examples of temporary footholds that survived only in the archaeological and historical records (Crosby, 1986). Crosby contrasts this with the Age of Exploration, wherein Europeans successfully conquered and colonized the Americas. Presaging Diamond's (1997) *Guns, Germs and Steel*, was Crosby's (1993) *Germs, Seeds & Animals: Studies in Ecological History*. There and elsewhere (Crosby, 1986, 2003, 2006), Crosby calls attention to the role of ecology and disease as a factor in historical events, such as the Columbian Exchange (Crosby, 1972) taking place between early modern Europe and the Americas. One import of the Columbian Exchange was European diseases which caused virgin soil epidemics among the Amerindians paving the way for the latter's conquest and demographic collapse. Epidemic disease coming from Europeans being enmeshed within a complex set of domesticates was only part of their portmanteau biota, assemblages of weeds, crops, animals, and pathogens connected with a culture. When Europeans reached the shores of America, they brought their persons and weapons with them, but more importantly they brought their domesticated plants and animals in their holds, and the viruses and bacteria in their blood. Previously, Europeans were more likely to fall victim to the integrated matrix of local adaptations of old world cultures as during the Crusades, but with the Columbian Exchange, these powerful ecological factors transitioned from hindrance to help.

Certainly, the Americas were affected by the Neolithic Revolution, the transition to settled agriculture taking place approximately 10,000 years before the present. However, European societies had transitioned earlier and more fully, as per Crosby. Europeans hunted their megafauna to extinction near the time when Amerindians were just crossing the Bering Strait. Malthusian constraints then dictated the transition to farming and domestication. Trade and cultural exchange augmented the natural wealth of animal species tractable to domestication, which contrasts with the dearth of suitable domesticate species in the Americas. Europeans then took the naturally salubrious temperate environs and anthropogenically saturated them with offal productive of diarrheal disease, and crowding productive of density dependent disease. Adding to the dangers of concentrating in towns amid domesticates, Europeans traded far and wide, which brought diseases such as the plague to national populations through the portal of port towns. Having labored for centuries against a disease ecology they created and eventually acclimated to, Europeans accumulated cultural capital through the medieval university system, while the emerging sciences combined with longstanding trades to create weapons of war. Thus, by degrees, Europeans invented the swords and firearms that joined with their coevolved

portmanteau biota of vegetable and animal domesticates, which sustained them even as it subdued their rivals. Crosby (1972, 1993) fixes 50 to 90 percent as the Amerindian death toll at the hands of European diseases, with forced dispossession, enslavement, and war-related deaths directly at the hands of Europeans serving only as an adjunctive factor.

As described in Hertler et al. (2018), smallpox, chickenpox, measles, rubella, diphtheria, whooping cough, scarlet fever, dysentery, bubonic plague, influenza, malaria, and yellow fever were among the many diseases reviewed by Crosby (1972, 1993), which were subsequently identified as historically significant in the writings of William H. McNeill. McNeill married the epidemiologist to the global historian to produce epidemiological world history, a productive line of inquiry that finds demography and biology at the heart of civilization and politics (McNeill, 1990). The study of evolutionary change that is a cornerstone of the Social Biogeography endeavor is importantly linked to past and prevailing mortality regimes, a concept prominently placed in most of McNeill's major works. Ecology, geography, and population density related to disease prevalence, which related to mortality regime, which, in turn, partially determined historical circumstances, such as the winning or losing of wars, the ceding or colonization of territory, and the conquest or extinction of groups. McNeill (1963, 1974, 1976, 1979, 1983, 1990, 1992) explored these interrelations through a lifetime, before consolidating many in *Plagues and Peoples* (1998).

As do Diamond, Crosby, and McNeill, Social Biogeography utilizes maps, historical texts and timelines, life tables, parish records, and like tools within the context of geography and ecology to found new insights into historical change and cultural trajectories. Though sharing in content and method, Social Biogeography chiefly differs in more consciously considering population level evolutionary change that might ultimately explain the proximate and cultural differences discussed by Diamond, Crosby, and McNeill.

Cross-Cultural Psychology

Social Biogeography assumes sociocultural variation is largely evolved as a response to ecological variation. Latitude and altitude, rainfall and distance from temperature-moderating bodies of water, oceanic currents, and air streams are among the physical eco-logical values shaping prevailing community ecologies, and thus the organisms that help and hinder human survival and reproduction. From thence, comes a bio-ecological basis for cross-cultural variation. Within this social biogeographic framework, one would view cultural similarities, for example, between neighboring sub-Saharan African polities or peoples as extending from their shared ecol-ogy. Yet, there is an alternative hypothesis, which may be taken as the null hypothesis: similarities between contiguous polities and peoples are simply an artifact of propinquity. In other words, cultural diffusion takes place across short distances leading to commonali-ties among neighboring societies. This is the essence of Galton's Problem, as described in Hertler et al. (2018). Critiquing a prototypical foray into Social Biogeography by Sir Edward Burnett Tylor during an 1888 meeting of the Royal Anthropological Society in London, Galton noted that the 350 pre-industrial socie-ties presented by Tylor were treated as inde-pendent data points, when in fact they were contiguous, interacting societies capable of influencing one another (Dow and Eff, 2013). Galton chilled Tylor's blossoming interest such that it was not generally pursued over the following century save for the prominent work of George Murdock.

While producing many interesting works relevant to the field of Social Biogeography (Murdock, 1934, 1970, 1980), it is Murdock's *Ethnographic Atlas* (1967), featuring 862 societies, that ranks highest in relevance. Thereafter, in his *Atlas of World Cultures*, Murdock (1981) went on to organize a large subset of these societies into the follow-ing biogeographical regions, giving prefer-ence to ecological regions above national

boundaries: Africa, Circum-Mediterranean, East Eurasia, Insular Pacific, North America, and South America. Moreover, these regions were operationally defined in a manner sensitive to geographic boundaries within and between continents. For instance, the Saharan desert regions of North Africa were classed with the Circum-Mediterranean rather than with Africa, which was confined to Sub-Saharan Africa. Though these deci-sions were obviously sensitive and logical from an evolutionary-ecological perspective, they only exacerbated Galton's Problem. For instance, one could argue that any Circum-Mediterranean cultural similarities, for instance in matrilineal kin groups and exogamy, cognatic kin groups, cousin mar-riage, or the many other variables across which Murdock coded and classed societies, stemmed not from shared ecological fea-tures between southern Europe and Northern Africa, but from the trade facilitated by the Mediterranean Sea.

So when Murdock reports 92 polygamous societies in Africa, compared with 21 in East Eurasia, Social Biogeography would posit this cultural difference to be rooted in, and influenced by, evolved adaptations to eco-logical conditions. Again, however, Galton's Problem stood as a broad impediment to this class of explanation until it was analyzed. In modern statistical parlance, Galton's Problem represents a species of spatial autocorrelation, a validity threat more generally addressed in the literature (Dow, 1984, 1993; Dow et al., 1984; Dow and Eff, 2013). Following from these methodologies, spatial autocorrelations related to Galton's Problem as it affected Murdock's data were statistically controlled (Hertler et al., 2018). To the extent that such statistical controls err, they err on the side of caution against making type I errors, atten-uating differences which might otherwise appropriately be attributed to evolved differ-ences (Thornhill and Fincher, 2013). Despite variation in method, all manner of statistical controls seem to bias conclusions towards the null assumption as outlined by Galton.

Analyses explained and footnoted in Hertler et al. (2018), and detailed in Peñaherrera-Aguirre et al. (2019), uphold the validity of Murdock's cultural cataloguing and the sociobiogeographical explanations of these differences. To provide a brief example on which these conclusions are founded, one can view national homicide data collected by the United Nations Office on Drugs and Crime (UNODC, 2013) as analyzed by Peñaherrera-Aguirre et al. (2019). Peñaherrera-Aguirre et al. compiled data on homocide rates among 172 nations, analyzing these data using two sequential canonical cascade analyses, general linear models, and multilevel models. The combination of these methods allows one to observe spatial contiguity as well as the possible chain of causal effects beginning with physical and community ecology, and extending to cultural and cognitive ecologies as it might influence homicide rates. Results implicate social ecology as causal, with income inequality and the operational sex ratio directly affecting homicide, while other ecological factors appear to affect homicide indirectly via direct effects on social ecology.

Additional analyses relevant to Galton's Problem find ethno-linguistic diversity partially reducible to evolutionary pressures induced by parasites, and evolutionary differences relating to life history traits (Hertler et al., 2018). Such conclusions are then broadly congruent with the work of Fincher et al. (2008) as well as that of Fincher and Thornhill (2012). Still further, all such empirical findings are consistent with Fincher and Thornhill's (2012) theoretical justification asserting the importance of continuously operating evolutionary, ecological pressures above that of cultural inertia.

Cross-Regional Examinations of Homicide

By the end of the 1980s and the mid 1990s, Martin Daly and Margo Wilson published a series of seminal papers examining the association between several risk factors and homicide in the US cities Chicago and Detroit (Wilson and Daly, 1985, 1997). Their data revealed the presence of significant sex and age differences, whereby young males were more likely to be both the perpetrators and the victims of homicide. Though previous sociological and epidemiological research found similar patterns, Daly and Wilson were among the first to adopt a Darwinian understanding of homicide (1988). According to their perspective, lethal intragroup aggression was an extreme manifestation of male intrasexual competition (Wilson and Daly, 1985; Daly and Wilson, 1988), with males, relative to females, exhibiting greater reproductive variance (some males have a reproductive monopoly, copulating with several females and siring multiple offspring, whereas other males are excluded from the mating market; Daly, 2017). In response to this theoretical gap in the literature, the authors predicted that income and wealth inequality could serve as proxies for resource competition. Environments where some individuals had a monopoly of resources were hypothesized to encourage relatively disadvantaged males to adopt riskier strategies to outcompete rivals.

The evidence suggested income inequality (i.e., Gini coefficient) was a better predictor of homicide rates, instead of other economic indicators such as median household income (Daly et al., 2001). These results replicated across Canadian provinces (Daly et al., 2001; Daly, 2017).

Even though some concerns have been raised concerning the confounding effects of ethnic and racial composition on homicide, Daly and Wilson (2010) found similar results once the data was restricted to white male homicides. The copious amount of publications on the evolutionary correlates of homicide based on cross-regional data gives credence to the significant influence of their work. Though the univariate nature of most of their analyses could be considered a limitation, multivariate examinations further support their predictions (Peñaherrera-Aguirre et al., 2019).

IQ and The Wealth of Nations

Richard Lynn and Tatu Vanhanen, authors of *IQ and the Wealth of Nations* (2002), ask why are some countries so rich and others so poor? Using intelligence as an organizing explanation, they devote the next nine chapters of their book to answering the questions framed in their introductory chapter. After introducing intelligence as a construct, including theories and measurement, Lynn and Vanhanen relate intelligence to earnings and related economic and social metrics, after which they discuss cross-national intelligence and economic development.

Disparities in gross national product and economic development, along with disparities in infrastructure, education, and governmental institutions, have attracted the attention of economists, sociologists, psychologists, and many other social scientists. However, variables like intelligence are almost never invoked as explanatory. Education, in contrast, may be discussed, but to the extent that it is, education is often uncoupled from intelligence and thought a result, rather than a cause, of national wealth. Certainly, the World Bank, the Central Intelligence Agency, or any such organization, publishes gross domestic product data or other relevant economic metrics, easily establishing that some nations are indeed rich while others are very poor. However, possibly as a result of intelligence being ignored as an explanation of cross-national income inequality, Lynn and Vanhanen, to pursue their hypothesis, had to aggregate data on intelligence. Findings suggested significant variation in national intelligence with a broad trend showing Eurasian countries having higher estimated intelligence than African countries. Of course, there was inter-continental variation as well reported across a sample of more than 80 countries and another sampling of more than 180 countries. After reporting their findings, these cross-national intelligence estimates are correlated with per capita income at 0.70. It was thereby concluded that intelligence was an understudied explanation of per capita income that

likely had relationships with additional social economic variables.

As per J. P. Rushton, this is an immense contribution to the economics literature, especially as many economists, in his opinion and in that of Lynn and Vanhanen, are disposed to assume intellectual parity among national populations. Rushton reads Lynn and Vanhanen's *IQ and Global Inequality* (2006) as an extension of *IQ and the Wealth of Nations* (2002). In the second book, Lynn and Vanhanen expand their sample size while producing essentially the same correlation coefficient between intelligence and per capita income. Additionally, path model analysis, allowing for national intelligence to be equally determined by genetics and environment, corresponds with observed rates of economic growth. Factors such as education, literacy, life expectancy, and democratic government are traced back to intelligence by Lynn and Vanhanen, even as some of these factors are sometimes posited as independently causal of per capita income.

For some, the concept of intelligence has proved polarizing at the conceptual level, while also ranking among the brightest flashpoints in prior debates over nature and nurture. The measurement of intelligence adds an additional layer of controversy, though this exists among the laity, with psychologists and psychometricians broadly agreeing on the reliability and validity of intelligence testing. Now, Lynn and Vanhanen, compounding conceptual and psychometric controversies, then added an additional layer of nuance by making cross-national comparisons (Whetzel and McDaniel, 2006). *IQ and the Wealth of Nations* has then drawn criticism from purportedly conflating intelligence with human capital, which is thought to undermine the causal scenario postulated by the authors (Volken, 2003). Some find the hypothesis of this book intriguing, but are unconvinced because of a perceived lack of statistical controls for alternative explanatory variables (Ervik, 2003). Following from the aforementioned concern about statistical controls, and relevant to the complexity of the topic and alternative explanations, some prefer to explain current cross-national economic differences to historical factors such as the timing of agricultural development (Daniele, 2013). By contrast, others have brought advanced statistical methods to bear upon Lynn and Vanhanen's data set, upholding the cross-national endeavor (Gelade, 2008) and the correlations it created (Dickerson, 2006). Still others have replicated Lynn and Vanhanen's cross-national findings within the United States (Kanazawa, 2006).

Certainly, when attempting to explain cross-national economic inequality, whether via intelligence or otherwise, causal chains are erected, the junctures of which can be weak. Additionally, third factors in this complex field of inquiry need to be considered and controlled as critics suggest. Still, Lynn and Vanhanen, with respect to their results and their endeavor, are pursuing something that is congruent with Social Biogeography, such that it can be regarded as an early social biogeographical study. *IQ and the Wealth of Nations* focuses essentially on cognitive ecology as an explanation of cross-national differences in per capita income, with cognitive ecology itself being thought a derivative of physical ecology. Seasonal cold, or *cold winters,* as Lynn and Vanhanen assert, augment environmental challenges, demand future-oriented planning and delay of gratification. Food scarcity during winter months demanded preparation; hunting large game demanded coordination; to sow and reap within the confines of seasonal constraints demanded anticipation. These are evolutionary selective pressures to which increased intelligence is casually related. Current Social Biogeography perspectives rest on a foundation of physical ecology, community ecology, social ecology, and cultural ecology (Figueredo, Cabeza de Baca, Fernandes et al., 2017). Accordingly, Lynn and Vanhanen were bringing together multiple ecological levels to productively explain the important sociological variable of per capita wealth as

it varies across nations. The same topic, if pursued formally within the context of Social Biogeography, would then only differ by placing cognition in the context of foundational levels of ecological influence, such that (1) ultimate causes could be more readily identified, (2) causal arrows could be drawn with more confidence in their supposed direction, and (3) some factors thought to be alternative explanations would more likely be implicitly incorporated into a multifactorial explanation. Still further, Social Biogeography has suggested cross-national differences in life history traits that are themselves likely related to longevity, conscientiousness, risk-taking, delay of gratification, future-oriented planning, and other subordinate factors likely to combine with intelligence in explaining cross-national economic inequality.

Cross-State Analyses of Mating Strategies

David Schmitt, in collaboration with researchers from over 40 different countries, collected questionnaire data on various dimensions of human sexuality (i.e., the International Sexuality Description Project; ISDP) including mate poaching frequency, sociosexual orientation, and sexual desire (2003, 2004, 2005). The project aimed to determine the universality of human sexual behaviors and strategies as well as the consistency of sex differences across nation-states. The cross-regional examinations determined statistically significant sex differences in sociosexual orientation, a continuum ranging from an inclination towards long-term relationships and emotional commitment (i.e., low scores) to short-term relationships and little romantic attachment (i.e., high scores). As predicted by theory, males, relative to females, reported higher scores.

Though this sex difference remained consistent across 48 nation-states, within-sex inter-state variation indicated local factors might influence the mean and variance in sociosexual orientation scores (Schmitt, 2005).

Over the years, several theories provided an array of predictions regarding the association between ecology and human mating strategies. Schmitt and colleagues proceeded to examine three evolutionary theories that could account for the regional variation in sociosexuality: sex ratio theory, developmental-attachment theory, and strategic pluralism theory. According to sex ratio theory, males and females are engaged in a constant tug of war with males preferring short-term associations whereas females prefer long-term relationships. When females are scarcer males are predicted to accept long-term bonds, whereas if males are rarer, females are predicted to accept short-term relationships.

In contrast to this perspective, developmental-attachment theory suggests that harsh environmental circumstances will promote the establishment of insecure attachments, which in turn is predicted to favor short-term liaisons instead of longer-term bonds. Finally, strategic pluralism theory predicts that environments characterized by resource scarcity and lethality will select in favor of biparental care. A long-term monogamous association facilitates the persistence of joint investment.

Intending to compare these perspectives, Schmitt and colleagues (2005) gathered demographic data (i.e., sociocultural factors) such as life expectancy, teen pregnancy rate, fertility rate, mean age at marriage of women, gross domestic product per capita, infant mortality rate, and operational sex ratio, among others. According to the authors, results of the various bivariate correlations supported strategic pluralism theory, with male and female sociosexuality negatively associated with indicators of environmental harshness. Though a detailed account concerning the evidence supporting or contradicting these results is beyond the scope of this chapter, the methodological novelty of this study should not be understated. Few projects have collected this amount of information around the world. Furthermore, this study also provided a new methodological avenue based on the combination of primary and secondary data (e.g., the use of ecological indicators) to examine rival evolutionary hypotheses. A similar approach was employed to examine regional differences in mate poaching (Schmitt, 2004). The analyses with data collected from 53 nations concluded that gross domestic product per capita significantly predicted short-term poaching success. The analyses identified sex differences in the degree to which resource scarcity influenced the prevalence of short-term poaching success: the higher the access to resources, the smaller the sex differences in this phenomenon (Schmitt, 2004).

Demographic and geographical information could also be used to determine the degree of sex differences across nations. In a follow-up study, for example, Schmitt et al. (2008) analyzed the role indicators of human development such as life expectancy, education, and economic growth and wealth. The analyses determined that, contrary to popular conception, greater social equality increased sex differences in characteristics such as personality traits.

Implications of Relaxed Selective Pressures for Health Outcomes across Nation-States

Some critics have raised concerns regarding the limitations of using contemporary cross-regional information to test evolutionary predictions. Two research methodologies provide an alternative to the use of cross-sectional information. If data are available, researchers could collect longitudinal information spanning hundreds of years (Woodley of Menie et al., 2017). This solution, however, should be complemented with analytical procedures accounting for temporal autocorrelations (Woodley et al., 2017). However, it is often the case that demographic data spans a couple of decades, limiting the development of longitudinal designs.

The second alternative is to use demographic information and compute metrics of selection. Piontek and Henneberg (1981), for example, proposed the index of biological state (I_{bs}) as a degree of relaxed selection. To compute this value, data on the age-specific death frequency (found in life tables and represented by d_x) is combined with the age-specific reproductive loss (s_x), whereby s_x is the product of an individual dying at a given age prior to the end of his or her reproductive lifespan (You and Henneberg, 2016). The index indicates the probability that any given individual will have the opportunity to contribute its genes to the subsequent generation. Low probabilities reflect considerable selective pressures, assuming the value of fitness (i.e., *w*) is best represented as the ratio of individuals unable to reproduce relative to those who can (You and Henneberg, 2016, 2018). An I_{bs} score of 0 reflects the maximum level of selection, whereas a value of 1 indicates the absence of selection (Piontek and Henneberg, 1981). According to this perspective, the technical and scientific innovations developed in modern and contemporary nation-states reduced mortality and morbidity rates, thereby relaxing selective pressures. Consequently, lower selective pressures increase the likelihood of mutation accumulation and the rise in prevalence rates of several chronic and terminal pathologies (You and Henneberg, 2016, 2018).

You and Henneberg (2016) discovered a significant effect of I_{bs} and the prevalence of type 1 diabetes (T1D) worldwide, with the partial correlation remaining statistically significant after accounting for gross domestic product per capita, Body Mass Index, and sugar intake. Similarly, Budnik and Henneberg (2017) determined that I_{bs} was also a significant predictor of obesity in a sample of 159 countries. The statistically significant partial correlation between obesity and I_{bs} (accounting for caloric intake and lack of physical activity) suggests relaxed selective pressures allow the persistence of mutations involved in metabolic disorders and energy balance (Budnik and Henneberg, 2017). In later analyses, You and Henneberg

(2018) found significant negative associations linking I_s ($I_s = (1-I_{bs})/ I_{bs}$)) to the incidence rate of 15 forms of cancer across 173 countries. These correlations remained statistically significant after controlling for GDP per capita, the life expectancy of individuals over 50 years old, physical inactivity, smoking, obesity, and level of urbanization.

The Parasite-Stress Theory of Human Sociality

Human societies are often described as problem-solving systems (Tainter, 1990), whereby living in proximity with conspecifics provides benefits such as sharing resources, exchanging information, decreasing predation risk, contributing to cooperative breeding, among numerous others (van Schaik, 2016). However, rather than operating in isolation, societies function in a constant exchange with their local ecologies, modulating the impact of selective pressures. Though by no means is cultural and social variation entirely dependent on environmental circumstances, often evolving as consequence of cognitive biases and drift (Boyd and Richerson, 1988; Richerson and Boyd, 2008), it would also be inaccurate to assume that all social behavior evolves in complete independence of any environmental contingency.

The parasite-stress theory of human sociality proposed the unification of ecological indicators and their association with human social phenomena ranging from cultural values and preferences to standardized demographic indicators such as frequency of wars and homicide rates (Letendre et al., 2010; Thornhill and Fincher, 2014). This perspective relied on the premise that infectious diseases, and their corresponding morbidity and mortality rates, were a significant force during human evolution. Therefore, to avoid the onerous costs associated with infection, humans evolved an array of strategies to reduce the impact of parasites (Thornhill and Fincher, 2011). Although physiological immunocompetency acts as a main line of defense, the theory predicted that individuals could decrease the risk of contagion by modifying their behaviors or adopting certain beliefs (Thornhill and Fincher, 2011). According to this view, individuals living in a region with high parasite-stress should select for acting favorably towards in-group members and negatively towards out-groups. In this light, xenophobia, ethnocentrism, neophobia, and antagonism were behaviors and beliefs selected to avoid contagion (Thornhill and Fincher, 2011, 2014). Alternatively, locations with low parasite stress favored cooperation with out-groups (Thornhill and Fincher, 2011).

Nations with high levels of ethnocentrism and antagonism should also be more prone to developing autocratic regimes. Thornhill et al. (2009) collected data from the Global Infectious Diseases and Epidemiology Online Network (GIDEON), the Global Leadership and Organizational Behavior Effectiveness Research Program (GLOBE), the U.N. Human Development Report, and Vanhanen's Index of Democratization, corresponding to over 150 countries. The analysis supported the predicted negative association between parasite stress and the degree of democratization. Although accounting for the effect of economic indicators such as the Gini coefficient and gross domestic product per capita decreased the size of the effect, it remained significant (Thornhill et al., 2009). Hence, countries with higher parasite stress also displayed more autocratic regimes, high collectivism, and low gender equality.

The CLASH Model

Shortly before Peñaherrera-Aguirre et al. (2019) studied the Social Biogeography of homicide, Van Lange and colleagues (2017) proposed the Climate, Aggression, and Self-Control in Humans (CLASH) model in explanation of cross-cultural differences in violence and aggression. CLASH attempted to explain a negative correlation between violence and absolute latitude. In doing so, Van Lange et al. contrast their CLASH model with the General Aggression Model, where the discomfort occasioned by heat augers aggression, and Routine Activity Theory, wherein increased aggression is a byproduct of increased social interaction afforded by warm climates. In contrast, Van Lange et al. posit low temperature, in concert with temperature variation, to evoke a slower life history, future-oriented thought, and self-control, all of which contribute to decreased violence. The authors believe the CLASH model is specifically pertinent to explaining the cross-cultural prevalence of 'honor' threats. Moreover, climate and temperature, following from Van de Vliert (2009), are understood to be important predictors of violence at the individual and group level.

Van Lange et al. (2017) explore their theory's implications for social communication, trade, and business relations, contrasting increased technology-induced connectivity with ancestral differences across cultures, which are maintained actively. More importantly, they review literature chaining each variable in their model to its neighboring variable. For instance, Van Lange et al. show how self-control determines when and whether anger will translate to aggression, citing empirical findings using self-control-inducing therapeutic interventions. Additionally, all model variables, again life history strategy, time-orientation, self-control, and aggression, are associated with a longer life expectancy and behaviors congruent with long life. In contrast, shortened time horizons associated with shorter life expectancy predict reduced self-control, aggression, violence, short-term mating, and sexual coercion. These short-term time horizons and their associated behaviors, however, are related to harshness and unpredictability within certain climates. In turn, northerly climates are described as predictable in their seasonality, and so are productive of the opposite suite of behaviors as that which is evoked within lower latitudes. All of this is well described by Van Lange et al., though most social biogeographical perspectives would suggest something further, *vis à vis* differences in life expectancy and time horizon do not directly relate to the predictability of climate but to the predictability of mortality, with mortality itself being constrained by parasite burden and other community ecological factors, which are then, finally, constrained by climate and other physical ecological factors.

Climate is positioned as a starting point which then affects group and national level social outcomes after being mediated by psychological processes at the individual level. The CLASH model, Van Lange et al. assert, is especially well positioned to explain interrelations between these levels, from climate to psychology to culture. Though it does not specify evolutionary change even as it discusses life history (Cabeza de Baca et al., 2017), the CLASH model deals in Social Biogeographical data. In this way, the CLASH model is a species of Social Biogeography, even as it appears functionally agnostic with respect to evolution. It does include life history variation, though the authors repeatedly allude to climate inducing the adoption of a particular life history strategy, suggesting a facultative, or at most a developmental, effect of climate, as opposed to an evolved and heritable effect. In contrast, most Social Biogeography research includes all three levels of adaptation – facultative, developmental, and evolved – with the latter emphasized over the former two. The work of J. P. Rushton serves as an example, perhaps an exemplar, of Social Biogeography research having the more expansive scope just described.

Under more traditional models of life history research that fit firmly within the Social Biogeography research program, factors like aggression and self-control would be subsumed under the broad banner of life history, rather than being treated as separate variables, and then the whole of life history would be thought to vary as a function of evolved adaptations to climate. All these factors are found

in Rushton's (1985) Differential K Theory. This theory owes its name to the fact that the fast–slow continuum of life history speed used to be known as the r–K continuum, with K representing the slow pole of this graded dimension. Differential K Theory recognizes that all humans have relatively slow life histories compared to many other species of mammals, but observes that there are substantial quantitative differences in how slow in life history individual humans might be. Further, it posits that different continental populations in our species ('races') evolved different mean values on this dimension in response to systematic differences in regional climates.

Differential K Theory looks to climate as does the CLASH model, both emphasizing distance from the equator and seasonal cold. However, Rushton tracks an evolutionary shift occurring in Eurasian populations as they migrated out of Africa. Violence and aggression are thought to have been selected against in European populations, and even more particularly in Northeast Asian populations. Decreases in violence and aggression are also thought to be related to delay of gratification and the degree of risk assumption. Within a life history perspective, however, these traits are contextualized in broad inter-continental differences in developmental speed, as measured for instance by molar eruption and gestational development, both of which are delayed in Eurasian populations relative to African populations.

CROSS-SECTIONAL STUDIES OF SOCIAL BIOGEOGRAPHY

Plants, Parasites, and People

As each respective part of the name implies, Social Biogeography studies social aggregations, understood as biological entities, varying across geographical conditions. Accordingly, Social Biogeography explains biologically based social variation across populations isolated or insulated by distance, especially when distance is compounded by geographical barriers, such as rivers, channels, and oceans, or otherwise by mountains, deserts, or tundra. Less obviously, however, in addition to explaining biosocial variation between populations, Social Biogeography is also capable of explaining biosocial variation within populations. Anchored in Hutchinson's (1957) niche theory, Social Biogeographic studies look to geographic ecological variation to explain contemporaneous variation in biosocial groups, at the levels of both national and subnational polities (Figueredo, Cabeza de Baca, Fernandes et al., 2017; Cabeza de Baca and Figueredo, 2014, 2017; Black et al., 2017; Fernandes et al., 2017; Fernandes and Woodley of Menie, 2017; Figueredo, Cabeza de Baca and Peñaherrera-Aguirre, 2017). Social Biogeography begins with physical ecology, but understands physical ecology as a foundational constraint upon which is layered community, social, cultural, and cognitive ecology. From these hierarchically nested but interacting ecological levels comes a variegated niche, the micro-niches of which select for intraspecies diversity. Ecological complexity fosters niche-splitting, which effects character displacement. In turn, the resultant evolved variation is often studied within a life history framework, which orders and explains the covariance among lower-order traits, such as longevity, fecundity, parental care, personality, and risk-assumption (Figueredo, Fernandes, and Woodley, 2017).

Sequential canonical analysis (Figueredo and Gorsuch, 2007), essentially an exploratory variety of path analysis, is often used in Social Biogeography and life history research to the end of statistically exploring a hypothesized causal order among ecological variables (physical, community, social, cultural, and cognitive) as they directly and indirectly generate biosocial diversity. Sequential canonical analysis is a 'cascade model' roughly equivalent to a system of hierarchical regression analyses wherein each successive criterion variable is used as a predictor for the next one in the series so as

to statistically control for any indirect effects transmitted through each successive criterion variable from all prior predictors. Only the hypothesized causal ordering of the criterion variables is theoretically specified.

Much research representative of the theory and methods of Social Biogeography has been *synchronic*, being confined to the present or a particular period. Synchronic studies, analyzed by sequential canonical cascade and interpreted via evolutionary ecological theory, suggest a causal chain beginning with physical ecological factors, extending to community ecological factors and thereafter potentiating sociological factors. Relevant physical ecology is parsed between a *brumal factor*, a composite of latitude and altitude and corresponding temperate cold, and a *hydrologic factor*, combining annual precipitation with humidity. When present in parallel, the brumal and hydrologic factors enable the growth of oaks, maples, chestnut, hickory and like trees comprising temperate broadleaf deciduous forest biomes. Directly and by virtue of its associated physical ecology, temperate broadleaf deciduous forest biomes decrease human parasite prevalence while increasing carrying capacity, which then act jointly to enable higher population density. Populations existing within these parameters consequently evolved slower life history strategies. From thence come augmented (1) social equality, (2) within-group peace, (3) between-group peace, (4) sexual equality, (5) strategic differentiation, (6) macroeconomic diversification, (7) embodied human capital, (8) brain volume, and (9) aggregate cognitive ability. Therefore, the aforementioned physical and community ecological factors countenance the slowing of life history, which is ultimately related to increases in these latter nine sociological factors. However, these nine factors should not be conceived of as coequal and contemporaneous consequences of slowing life histories; but rather are listed in approximate order along a causal chain. Each is a consequence of its predecessor, but simultaneously a cause of its successor. For example, the relative social equality prominent amid slow life history populations gives rise to within-group peace, which itself fosters between-group peace. Similarly, the strategic differentiation of slow life history populations fosters macroeconomic diversification, which raises the embodied human capital, and so leads to larger brain volumes and enhanced cognitive abilities. Additionally, those at the end rely on all foregoing factors, not just the one immediately before. For example, augmented brain volume is a precondition for augmented cognitive ability, but so are the other enumerated factors, not to mention slow life history itself, and its pre-conditional community and physical ecological factors.

The Social Biogeography of Homicide

A sequential canonical cascade model (Figueredo and Gorsuch, 2007) examined the effects of physical ecology, community ecology, cultural ecology, and cognitive ecology on homicide rates across 170 countries. The model predicted indicators of physical ecology (a 25-year temperature average, a 25-year precipitation average, and the boreal index, a composite of altitude and latitude) would predict indicators of community ecology (parasite burden and population density). In turn, community ecology would predict social ecology (life history strategies, operational sex ratio, and ethnolinguistic diversity). Indicators of social ecology were hypothesized to have significant effects upon cultural ecology (the Gini coefficient, gross domestic product per capita, and the percentage of employed young males). Finally, cultural ecology was predicted to have significant effects upon cognitive ecology (aggregate national intelligence scores), leading to variation in homicide rates. In addition to examining the influence of different ecological dimensions, this study addressed Galton's problem (confounding effects due to cultural

inertia and geographical proximity) by assigning each country a score in a ranking system starting in the southern regions of the African continent. This approach was validated by correlating the assigned scores with Kanazawa's distance from Africa formula (2008). Standardized studentized residuals were computed based on the effect of geographical proximity and homicide rates.

At the bivariate level, temperature, precipitation, parasite burden, the ethnolinguistic factor, and the Gini coefficient displayed positive and significant correlations with the homicide rate residuals. A slow life history, population density, the operational sex ratio, GDP per capita, the percentage of young males in the labor force, and national intelligence, had a significant negative effect on homicide rate residuals. Although bivariate correlations provide an initial approximation to the link between ecological factors and homicide rates, they lack the depth of multivariate procedures. Furthermore, different from other procedures such as path analyses of structural equation modeling, sequential canonical analysis hierarchically partition the variance-giving, allowing the test of specific hypotheses concerning each step of the analyses.

The sequential canonical cascade model explained 32% of variance and detected that higher temperatures had a significant effect (i.e., semi-partial correlation) on parasite burden which in turn negatively predicted a life history factor (comprised of infant mortality rates, adolescent fertility rates, total fertility rates, and life expectancy). A slower life history had a negative effect on ethnolinguistic diversity and a positive effect upon aggregate values of national intelligence. Higher national intelligence had a negative effect on income inequality which in turn had a negative relation with GDP per capita. The Gini coefficient had a positive and moderate association with homicide rates.

Akin to other multivariate procedures, sequential canonical analyses can contrast competing predictions and determine, based on parsimony, which model best fits the data with the least number of assumptions. The analyses tested two models. The first considered the effect of aggregate national intelligence on the Gini coefficient, whereas the second model placed national intelligence as the penultimate step in cascade, directly predicting homicide rates. Contrasting the number of non-significant paths revealed the second model fitted the data using a lesser number of statistically significant predictors.

Methodological Limitations of Synchronic Models

As with the majority of studies done both in evolutionary psychology and in the evolutionary sciences in general, the synchronic Social Biogeography studies use current data to make inferences about past evolution. The data were then treated as essentially cross-sectional, describing the approximately 'current' (21st-century) state of affairs in each of these national and subnational polities. Using those data, we tested causal theories that hypothesized a sequencing of effects based on evolutionary ecological principles. There was no causal inference, as such, in terms of deriving this sequence of effects from the data; instead there was theory testing against the available data, in a Popperian (1962) sense, to determine whether our predictions were or were not consistent with the empirical observations. In general, we believe that they were, and that our cascade models offer reasonably plausible accounts of this welter of otherwise poorly understood associations.

Nevertheless, a potential limitation of this work concerns the use of proximal-level indicators of constructs (such as temperature and precipitation) that may distally have been quite different due to historical changes in the physical ecology. This is important as historically different levels of these indicators (such as colder or more variable temperatures, or lower precipitation) may have shaped the population means of many of the psychosocial indicators considered here in such a way that might

compromise the present pattern of hypothesized causal influence. For example, historically colder climates may have created selective pressures favouring both slower life history (K) and higher general intelligence (g) independently (Meisenberg and Woodley, 2013). This suggests an alternative pattern of mediation to the one examined in the present analysis.

Testing the robustness of the present pattern of causal inference to possible proximal–distal confounding of levels will eventually require elaborating the model to incorporate historical measures of the relevant physical–ecological variables. These historical measures can then be used to determine the effects of alternative distal-level models (such as Cold-Winters theory; Lynn, 2006) on the present pattern of proximal-level causal inference. Phylogenetic reconstruction methods (for a review, see Nunn, 2011) of the biodemographic traits would also permit estimating ancestral states of variables for which historical data are not available, which could then be used to examine the longitudinal, rather than cross-sectional, associations among the variables studied.

LONGITUDINAL MODELS OF SOCIAL BIOGEOGRAPHY

There have been few studies that are diachronic, and thus capable of viewing change through microevolutionary time. The synchronic–diachronic distinction as made in the Social Biogeographical study of populations mirrors the cross-sectional–longitudinal distinction as made in the developmental study of samples. 'The Rhythm of the West', 'War and Peace', and 'The Ecology of Empire' serve as three studies broadly representative of such diachronic investigation.

The Rhythm of the West

Woodley of Menie et al.'s (2017) monograph entitled, 'The Rhythm of the West: A Biohistory of the Modern Era AD1600 to the Present', contains the Nexus 200 and Nexus 400 analyses, respectively spanning AD1800–AD2010 (approximately 200 years, thus Nexus 200) and AD1600–AD1999 (approximately 400 years, thus Nexus 400). The Nexus 200 studied (g.h) heritable general intelligence, (s.e) specialized intelligences, and (s.m) anthropometric changes, as collectively marked by 15 convergent indicators. These three factors, g.h., s.e., and s.m, were then found to cohere around a common higher-order factor, which is referred to as the Co-Occurrence Nexus. The existence of this diachronic latent variable was validated by the application of hierarchically nested, longitudinal multilevel models, which also controlled statistically for any serial autocorrelations over time. The Co-Occurrence Nexus explains changes across the 15 convergent indicators comprising g.h., s.e., and s.m, as arising from the reversal of selective pressures wherein individual selection was preponderant over group selection within the 200 years under consideration. Within a Social Biogeographical framework, causes were explained ecologically with consequences found in cognitive ecology.

Specifically, the interpretation was that climatic warming and stabilization attenuated between-group conflict, resulting in selective pressures disfavoring general intelligence. Unavailable data afforded an incomplete replication of this diachronic investigation before AD 1800. Nevertheless, relying on the prediction of one of five *g.h.* indicators (a *hard word factor* predictive of vocabulary complexity) by a diachronic biocultural group selection factor, the Nexus 400 replicated and extended the findings of the Nexus 200. This latent common factor measured the strength of biocultural between-group competition, as indicated by three convergent historical measures, one lexicographic and the others biodemographic: (1) the frequencies of use of altruistic words, (2) war mortality, and (3) proportions of world population. The authors' conclusions were that higher

biocultural group selective pressures selected for higher general intelligence (*g.h*), whereas higher individual selective pressures selected for higher specialized intelligences (*s.e*); this presumably accounted for the increase in general intelligence during the early modern era, which encompassed the climatically unstable and conflict-ridden 'Little Ice Age', and its subsequent decrease during the late modern era, characterized by warming climates and greater resource abundance.

'War and Peace' and 'The Ecology of Empire'

Also representative of Social Biogeography studies of human life histories is Figueredo et al.'s (2019a), 'War and Peace: A Diachronic Social Biogeography of Life History Strategy and Between-Group Relations in Two Western European Populations'. Like 'Rhythm of the West' (Woodley of Menie et al., 2017), 'War and Peace' is a diachronic study of Britannic populations, including the successor states of the British Empire such as Australia, Canada, and the United States, but one that yields convergent evidence by incorporating comparative analyses of Gallic populations, including Continental France and its erstwhile overseas departments. With respect to newly analyzed Gallic populations, the latent hierarchical structure of life history strategy was found to vary diachronically in a manner replicating data produced by analyzing Britannic populations, again validating the diachronic latent variable by the application of hierarchically nested, longitudinal multilevel models, and also controlling statistically for any serial autocorrelations over time. In turn, diachronic analyses of both groups corresponded with cross-sectional data on synchronically measured economic output, competition and life history. Results of between-group interactions over hundreds of years were measured via economic productivity and various metrics of life history such as lexicographic indicators, infant mortality rates, total fertility rates, and life expectancies.

Last among the examples of Social Biogeography research is Figueredo et al.'s (2019b), 'The Ecology of Empire: The Dynamics of Strategic Differentiation–Integration in Two Competing Western European Biocultural Groups'. Also studying Britannic and Gallic populations diachronically, 'The Ecology of Empire' found France losing power and prestige to Britain with the effect that the former was becoming more homogeneous (strategic integration) and the latter more heterogeneous (strategic differentiation) across life history traits between AD1800–AD1999. Of course, the rivalry between Britain and France unfolded within a larger historical world of war, trade, and exploration, all of which caution against simple causal inferences. While it was hypothesized that conflict and competition advanced the differentiation of one and integration of the other, an asymmetrical effect was found. More precisely, while competition from Britons appeared causally related to strategic integration among Gallics, the opposite did not appear to be the case. Rather than stemming from Gallic competition, the strategic differentiation of Britannic populations had some unstudied cause, such as the effects of rapid territorial expansion characteristic of its days of empire building. Apparently, it matters much whether one wins or loses the competitive struggle.

One way in which the later peaceful co-existence of Britain and France may have manifested at the level of the biocultural group is *via* the process of *limiting similarity*. The Theory of Limiting Similarity (*TLS*) was first proposed by Hutchinson (1959) and describes the maximum allowable overlap between two ecologically similar species. Hutchinson noticed that among highly similar species that co-exist within the same habitat, the size of individuals of one species would often be 1.3 times bigger than that of individuals of the other species. This relation was subsequently termed *Hutchinson's Ratio*, although that precise ratio has not been subsequently reported to be as universal as Hutchinson initially believed. However, the observation that members of co-existent and morphologically similar species vary in size relative to one another has withstood the test of time (Abrams, 1983).

Hutchinson's ratio may have an analog at the biocultural group level. One candidate Type II group selection characteristic that should illustrate this principle is group population size, and at this level there may be character displacement between groups. As the Gallic biocultural group has become historically less successful in between-group competition over the past 200 years than the Britannic biocultural group, we suspect that the previously more successful Gallic biocultural group should have contracted to a smaller proportion of the world population relative to that of the Britannic biocultural group. A temporal trend should therefore reveal a positive association over time if the Britannic proportion of the world population is compared with the Gallic proportion of world population. An increase in this population ratio over time would indicate the action of the *TLS*-type process in producing an accommodation that ensured the co-existence of the two populations and prevented full competitive exclusion. The results of this analysis supported these predictions, with the Britannic–Gallic population ratio starting at barely over 0.5:1 in AD 1800 and rising to nearly 4:1 by AD 1999. We interpret these relations as supporting our proposal that these results conform, at least qualitatively, to pertinent *TLS* predictions.

CONCLUSION

Social Biogeography did not emerge fully-formed out of an intellectual vacuum; there were many prior research programs that contained some of its basic elements. From those basic building blocks a new and overarching framework is being constructed that is more complete and comprehensive. A few preliminary attempts have so far been made to commence those efforts systematically, both synchronically and diachronically, but much more work remains to be done to fill in the many gaps in this complex nomological network. Although many of the findings so far have been exploratory, very similar patterns of results have been obtained from independent synchronic studies of both national and subnational polities, as well as by the diachronic study of two historically important empires. We therefore see Social Biogeography as a research program with great intellectual promise and an ambitious endeavor well worth undertaking.

REFERENCES

Abrams, P. (1983). The theory of limiting similarity. *Annual Review of Ecology, Evolution, and Systematics, 14*, 359–376.

Black, C. J., Peñaherrera-Aguirre, M., Chavarria Minera, C. E., & Figueredo, A. J. (2017). The influence of life history strategies on regional variation in social and sexual equality in Italy, Spain and Mexico. In Figueredo, A. J., Fernandes, H. B. F., & Cabeza de Baca, T., (Eds), *Part 1: The Evolutionary Dynamics of Social Biogeography. Mankind Quarterly, 57*(3), 338–354.

Boyd, R., & Richerson, P. J. (1988). *Culture and the evolutionary process.* Chicago: The University of Chicago Press.

Budnik, A., & Henneberg, M. (2017). Worldwide increase of obesity is related to the reduced opportunity for natural selection. *PloS ONE, 12*(1), e0170098.

Cabeza de Baca, T., & Figueredo, A. J. (2014). The cognitive ecology of Mexico: Climatic and socio-cultural effects on life history strategies and cognitive abilities. *Intelligence, 47*, 63–71.

Cabeza de Baca, T., & Figueredo, A. J. (2017). Population-level life history in Italy, Spain and Mexico: The impact of regional climate, parasite burden, and population density. In Figueredo, A. J., Fernandes, H. B. F., & Cabeza de Baca, T., (Eds), *Part 1: The*

Evolutionary Dynamics of Social Biogeography. Mankind Quarterly, 57(3), 326–337.

Cabeza de Baca, T., Hertler, S. C., & Dunkel, C. S. (2017). Reply to Van Lange et al.: Proximate and ultimate distinctions must be made to the CLASH model. *Behavioral and Brain Sciences, 40*, e81.

Crosby, A. W. (1972). *The Columbian exchange: Biological and cultural consequences of 1492.* Westport, Connecticut: Greenwood Publishing Group.

Crosby, A. W. (1986). *Ecological imperialism: The biological expansion of Europe, 900–1900.* New York: Cambridge University Press.

Crosby, A. W. (1993). *Germs, seeds & animals: Studies in ecological history.* New York: M.E. Sharpe.

Crosby, A. W. (2003). *America's forgotten pandemic: The influenza of 1918.* Cambridge University Press.

Crosby, A. W. (2006). *Children under the sun: A history of humanity's unappeasable appetite for energy.* New York: W. W. Norton & Company.

Daly, M. (2017). *Killing the competition: Economic inequality and homicide.* New York: Routledge.

Daly, M., & Wilson, M. (1988). *Homicide (Foundations of human behavior series).* Hawthorne, NY: Aldine de Gruyter.

Daly, M., & Wilson, M. (1997). Crime and conflict: Homicide in evolutionary psychological perspective. *Crime and Justice, 22*, 51–100.

Daly, M., & Wilson, M. (2010). Cultural inertia, economic incentives, and the persistence of 'Southern violence'. In Schaller, M., Norenzayan, A., Heine, S. J., Yamagishi, T., & Kameda, T. (Eds), *Evolution, culture, and the human mind* (pp. 229–241). New York: Psychology Press.

Daly, M., Wilson, M., & Vasdev, S. (2001). Income inequality and homicide rates in Canada and the United States. *Canadian Journal of Criminology, 43*(2), 219–236.

Daniele, V. (2013). Does the intelligence of populations determine the wealth of nations? *The Journal of Socio-Economics, 46*, 27–37.

Diamond, J. (1997). *Guns, germs, and steel: The fates of human societies.* New York: W. W. Norton & Company.

Dickerson, R. E. (2006). Exponential correlation of IQ and the wealth of nations. *Intelligence*, *34*(3), 291–295.

Dow, M. M. (1984). A bi-parametric approach to network autocorrelation: Galton's Problem. *Sociological Methods and Research*, *13*(2), 201–217.

Dow, M. M. (1993). Saving the theory: On chi-square tests with cross-cultural survey data. *Cross-Cultural Research*, *27*(3–4), 247–276.

Dow, M. M., & Eff, E. A. (2013). The network autocorrelation approach to comparative method: Monogamy in the pre-industrial world. *The Wiley handbook on comparative methods*. Hoboken, NJ: John Wiley & Sons.

Dow, M., Burton, M., White, D., & Reitz, K. (1984). Galton's problem as network autocorrelation. *American Ethnologist*, *11*(4), 754–770.

Ervik, A. O. (2003). IQ and the wealth of nations. *The Economic Journal*, *113*(488), F406–F408.

Fernandes, H. B. F., & Woodley of Menie, M. A. (2017). Aspects of the physical and social ecology affect human capital and intelligence, directly and indirectly, in Italy, Spain and Mexico. In Figueredo, A. J., Fernandes, H. B. F., & Cabeza de Baca, T., (Eds), *Part 1: The Evolutionary Dynamics of Social Biogeography*. *Mankind Quarterly*, *57*(3), 375–387.

Fernandes, H. B. F., Figueredo, A. J., Garcia, R. A., & Wolf, P. S. A. (2017). Regional relations between phenotypic and economic diversity and their ecological predictors in Italy, Spain and Mexico. In Figueredo, A. J., Fernandes, H. B. F., & Cabeza de Baca, T., (Eds), *Part 1: The Evolutionary Dynamics of Social Biogeography. Mankind Quarterly*, *57*(3), 355–374.

Figueredo, A. J., & Gorsuch, R. (2007). Assortative mating in the jewel wasp: 2. Sequential canonical analysis as an exploratory form of path analysis. *Journal of the Arizona-Nevada Academy of Science*, *39*(2), 59–64.

Figueredo, A. J., Cabeza de Baca, T., & Peñaherrera-Aguirre, M. (2017). Summary of results and conclusions: Regional master cascade of social complexity in Italy, Spain and Mexico. In Figueredo, A. J., Fernandes, H. B. F., & Cabeza de Baca, T., (Eds), *Part 1: The Evolutionary Dynamics of Social Biogeography. Mankind Quarterly*, *57*(3), 388–397.

Figueredo, A. J., Cabeza de Baca, T., Fernandes, H. B. F., Black, C. J., Peñaherrera, M., Hertler, S. C., García, R. A., Meisenberg, G., & Woodley of Menie, M. A. (2017). A sequential canonical cascade model of social biogeography: Plants, parasites, and people. *Evolutionary Psychological Science*, *3*(1), 40–61.

Figueredo, A. J., Fernandes, H. B. F., & Woodley of Menie, M. A. (2017). The quantitative theoretical ecology of life history strategies. In Figueredo, A. J., Fernandes, H. B. F., & Cabeza de Baca, T., (Eds), *Part 1: The Evolutionary Dynamics of Social Biogeography. Mankind Quarterly*, *57*(3), 305–325.

Figueredo, A. J., Peñaherrera-Aguirre, M., Fernandes, H. B. F., Lomayesva, S. L., Woodley of Menie, M. A., Hertler, S. C., & Sarraf, M. A. (2019a). War and peace: A diachronic social biogeography of life history strategy and between-group relations in two Western European populations. *Journal of Methods and Measurement in the Social Sciences*, *10*(1), 36–75.

Figueredo, A. J., Peñaherrera-Aguirre, M., Fernandes, H. B. F., Lomayesva, S. L., Woodley of Menie, M. A., Hertler, S. C., & Sarraf, M. A. (2019b). The ecology of empire: The dynamics of strategic differentiation–integration in two competing Western European biocultural groups. *Journal of Politics and the Life Sciences*, *38*(2), 210–225.

Fincher, C. L., & Thornhill, R. (2012). Parasite-stress promotes in-group assortative sociality: The cases of strong family ties and heightened religiosity. *Behavioral and Brain Sciences*, *35*(2), 61–79.

Fincher, C. L., Thornhill, R., Murray, D. R., & Schaller, M. (2008). Pathogen prevalence predicts human cross-cultural variability in individualism/collectivism. *Proceedings of the Royal Society of London. B: Biological Sciences*, *275*(1640), 1279–1285.

Gelade, G. A. (2008). The geography of IQ. *Intelligence*, *36*(6), 495–501.

Hertler, S. C., Figueredo, A. J., Peñaherrera-Aguirre, M., Fernandes, H. B. F., & Woodley of Menie, M. A. (2018). *Life history evolution: A biological meta-theory for the social sciences*. New York: Palgrave Macmillan.

Hutchinson, G. E. (1957). *A treatise on limnology*. Hoboken, NJ: Wiley.

Hutchinson, G. E. (1959). Homage to Santa Rosalia, or Why are there so many kinds of animals? *The American Naturalist*, *93*(870), 145–159.

Kanazawa, S. (2006). IQ and the wealth of states. *Intelligence*, *34*(6), 593–600.

Kanazawa, S. (2008). Temperature and evolutionary novelty as forces behind the evolution of general intelligence. *Intelligence*, *36*(2), 99–108.

Letendre, K., Fincher, C. L., & Thornhill, R. (2010). Does infectious disease cause global variation in the frequency of intrastate armed conflict and civil war? *Biological Reviews*, *85*(3), 669–683.

Lynn, R. (2006). *Race differences in intelligence: an evolutionary analysis*. Whitefish, Montana: Washington Summit Publishers.

Lynn, R., & Vanhanen, T. (2006). *IQ and global inequality*. Whitefish, Montana: Washington Summit Publishers.

Lynn, R., & Vanhanen, T., with Stuart, M. (2002). *IQ and the wealth of nations*. Westport, Connecticut: Greenwood Publishing Group.

Meisenberg, G., & Woodley, M. A. (2013). Global behavioral variation: A test of differential-K. *Personality and Individual Differences*, *55*(3), 273–278.

McNeill, W. H. (1963). *The rise of the West: A history of the human community*. Chicago: The University of Chicago Press.

McNeill, W. H. (1974). *The shape of European history*. New York: Oxford University Press.

McNeill, W. H. (1979). *A world history* (3rd ed.). New York: Oxford University Press.

McNeill, W. H. (1983). *The great frontier: Freedom and hierarchy in modern times*. Princeton, New Jersey: Princeton University Press.

McNeill, W. H. (1990). *Population and politics since 1750*. Charlottesville, Virginia: University of Virginia Press.

McNeill, W. H. (1992). *The global condition: Conquerors, catastrophes, and community*. Princeton, New Jersey: Princeton University Press.

McNeill, W. H. (1998). *Plagues and peoples*. New York: Anchor Books.

Murdock, G. P. (1934). *Our primitive contemporaries*. New York: MacMillan.

Murdock, G. P. (1967). *Ethnographic atlas: A summary*. Pittsburgh, Pennsylvania: The University of Pittsburgh Press.

Murdock, G. P. (1970). Kin term patterns and their distribution. *Ethnology*, *9*(2), 165–207.

Murdock, G. P. (1980). *Theories of illness: A world survey*. Pittsburgh, Pennsylvania: The University of Pittsburgh Press.

Murdock, G. P. (1981). *Atlas of world cultures*. Pittsburgh, Pennsylvania: The University of Pittsburgh Press.

Nunn, C. L. (2011). *The comparative approach in evolutionary anthropology and biology*. Illinois, Chicago: University of Chicago Press.

Peñaherrera-Aguirre, M., Hertler, S. C., Figueredo, A. J., Fernandes, H. B. F., de Baca, T. C., & Matheson, J. D. (2019). A social biogeography of homicide: Multilevel and sequential canonical examinations of intragroup unlawful killings. *Evolutionary Behavioral Sciences*, *13*(2), 158–181.

Piontek, J., & Henneberg, M. (1981). Mortality changes in a Polish rural community (1350–1972) and estimation of their evolutionary significance. *American Journal of Physical Anthropology*, *54*(1), 129–138.

Popper, K. (1962). *Conjectures and refutations: The growth of scientific knowledge*, New York: Basic Books.

Richerson, P. J., & Boyd, R. (2008). *Not by genes alone: How culture transformed human evolution*. Chicago: The University of Chicago Press.

Rushton, J. P. (1985). Differential K theory: The sociobiology of individual and group differences. *Personality and Individual Differences*, *6*(4), 441–452.

Schmitt, D. P. (2003). Universal sex differences in the desire for sexual variety: Tests from 52 nations, 6 continents, and 13 islands. *Journal of Personality and Social Psychology*, *85*(1), 85–104.

Schmitt, D. P. (2004). Patterns and universals of mate poaching across 53 nations: The effects of sex, culture, and personality on romantically attracting another person's partner. *Journal of Personality and Social Psychology*, *86*(4), 560–584.

Schmitt, D. P. (2005). Sociosexuality from Argentina to Zimbabwe: A 48-nation study of sex, culture, and strategies of human mating. *Behavioral and Brain Sciences*, *28*(2), 247–275.

Schmitt, D. P., Realo, A., Voracek, M., & Allik, J. (2008). Why can't a man be more like a woman? Sex differences in Big Five personality traits across 55 cultures. *Journal of Personality and Social Psychology*, *94*(1), 168–182.

Tainter, J. (1990). *The collapse of complex societies*. Cambridge: Cambridge University Press.

Thornhill, R., & Fincher, C. L. (2011). Parasite stress promotes homicide and child maltreatment. *Philosophical Transactions of the Royal Society B: Biological Sciences*, *366*(1583), 3466–3477.

Thornhill, R., & Fincher, C. L. (2013). The comparative method in cross-cultural and cross-species research. *Evolutionary Biology*, *40*(4):480–493.

Thornhill, R., & Fincher, C. L. (2014). *The parasite-stress theory of values and sociality: Infectious disease, history, and human values worldwide*. New York: Springer.

Thornhill, R., Fincher, C. L., & Aran, D. (2009). Parasites, democratization, and the liberalization of values across contemporary countries. *Biological Reviews*, *84*(1), 113–131.

United Nations Office on Drugs and Crime (2013). *Global study on homicide 2013: Trends, contexts, data*. Vienna, Austria: United Nations Office on Drugs and Crime.

Van de Vliert, E. (2009). *Climate, affluence, and culture*. New York: Cambridge University Press.

Van Lange, P. A., Rinderu, M. I., & Bushman, B. J. (2017). Aggression and violence around the world: A model of CLimate, Aggression, and Self-control in Humans (CLASH). *Behavioral and Brain Sciences*, *40*, e75.

Van Schaik, C. P. (2016). *The primate origins of human nature*. New York: John Wiley & Sons.

Volken, T. (2003). IQ and the wealth of nations. A critique of Richard Lynn and Tatu Vanhanen's recent book. *European Sociological Review*, *19*(4), 411–412.

Whetzel, D. L., & McDaniel, M. A. (2006). Prediction of national wealth. *Intelligence*, *34*(5), 449–458.

Wilson, M., & Daly, M. (1985). Competitiveness, risk taking, and violence: The young male syndrome. *Ethology and Sociobiology*, *6*(1), 59–73.

Wilson, M., & Daly, M. (1997). Life expectancy, economic inequality, homicide, and reproductive timing in Chicago neighborhoods. *BMJ*, *314*(7089), 1271–1274.

Woodley of Menie, M. A., Figueredo, A. J., Sarraf, M. A., Hertler, S., Fernandes, H. B. F., & Peñaherrera-Aguirre, M. (2017). The rhythm of the West: A biohistory of the modern era, AD 1600 to present. *Journal of Social, Political and Economic Studies, Monograph Series, Number 37*. Washington, DC: Council for Social and Economic Studies.

You, W., & Henneberg, M. (2016). Type 1 diabetes prevalence increasing globally and regionally: The role of natural selection and life expectancy at birth. *BMJ Open Diabetes Research and Care*, *4*(1), e000161.

You, W., & Henneberg, M. (2018). Cancer incidence increasing globally: The role of relaxed natural selection. *Evolutionary Applications*, *11*(2), 140–152.

You, W., Rühli, F. J., Henneberg, R. J., & Henneberg, M. (2018). Greater family size is associated with less cancer risk: An ecological analysis of 178 countries. *BMC Cancer*, *18*(1), 924.

You, W., Symonds, I., & Henneberg, M. (2018). Low fertility may be a significant determinant of ovarian cancer worldwide: An ecological analysis of cross-sectional data from 182 countries. *Journal of Ovarian Research*, *11*(1), 68.

23

Cross-Cultural Differences in Cognition and Learning

Alfredo Ardila

INTRODUCTION

Cognitive abilities, usually measured with cognitive tests, represent, at least in their contents, learned abilities whose scores correlate with the subject's learning opportunities and contextual experiences. Cultural variations are evident in test scores, as culture provides us with specific models for ways of thinking, acting, and feeling. Although basic cognitive processes are universal, cultural differences in cognition reside more in the situations to which particular cognitive processes are applied than in the existence of the process in one cultural group and its absence in the other. Culture dictates what should be learned, at what age, in what conditions, and by which gender. Consequently, different cultural environments lead to the development of different patterns of abilities. Cultural and ecological factors play a role in developing different cognitive styles. Cognitive processes, including attention, perception, spatial skills, memory, language, and executive functions vary

depending on the idiosyncrasies of the cultural context. Cultural variables affect cognitive test performance, and these cultural differences result in different styles and patterns of learning. As a matter of fact, cognitive test scores are under the influence of a significant number of variables, such as ecological conditions, previous training history, age, gender, linguistic, and cultural values. Cross-cultural comparisons in intellectual abilities are, in consequence, particularly difficult. Current psychometric testing has been developed departing from the cultural values of competitiveness, high productivity, literacy, speed, and so forth in the societies where the tests were developed. Learning must be linked to context and culture to avoid having our findings reflect an ethnocentric artifact of our methodology.

SOME DEFINITIONS

Culture is a fundamental concept in social sciences. Nonetheless, it is not easy to identify a clear and simple definition of it. In anthropology, frequently it is considered that culture refers to the set of learned traditions and living styles shared by the members of a society. It includes the ways of thinking, feeling, and behaving (Harris, 1983). The minimal definition of culture could be, *culture is the specific way of living of a human group* (Ardila, 2018).

Culture includes three different dimensions: (1) the psychological or internal representation of culture, including values, attitudes, thinking, feeling, knowledge, and beliefs; (2) the behavioral dimension of culture, including the ways of behaving in different contexts and circumstances, ways to relate with others, festivities, patterns of associations, etc., and (3) cultural elements: the physical elements characteristic of that human group such as clothes, ornaments, houses, instruments, symbolic elements, weapons, etc. Cultural evolution and cultural changes are found throughout human history, depending on a diversity of factors, including, (a) new environmental conditions, (b) contact with other cultures, and (c) internal cultural evolution.

A departing question when analyzing the influence of the cultural context on learning is how many cultures can be distinguished. Unfortunately, there is not a clear answer to this question, and what an author considers as a culture can be regarded as a subculture by another. Furthermore, cultures are not discrete categories, but there is a continuum across cultures (Haviland et al., 2011). Sometimes culture has been considered as equivalent to country. For instance, Hofstede (2001) when analyzing cross-cultural differences in some 40 different countries refers to the countries as cultures. Alternatively, culture could be equated with language. Worldwide there are around 7,000 different languages (Ethnologue, 2020). However, the number of speakers in the different languages is quite uneven. Whereas one third of the languages have less than 1,000 speakers, 23 languages account for more than half

the world's population. Thus, language has a clear association with culture, but cannot be considered equivalent to culture. Huntington (2009), when referring to cultural conflicts, distinguished nine major culture groups: Western, Latin America, Orthodox, Buddhist, African, Islamic, Sinic, Hindu, and Japanese. The GLOBE (Global Leadership and Organizational Behavior Effectiveness) study (House et al., 2004) proposed that there are 10 major cultural clusters: Anglo, Latin Europe, Nordic Europe, Germanic Europe, Eastern Europe, Latin America, Sub-Saharan Africa, Middle East, Southern Asia, and Confucian Asia.

Cognition can be defined as 'the mental action or process of acquiring knowledge and understanding through thought, experience, and the senses' (*Oxford Dictionary*; en.oxforddictionaries.com/definition/cognition). Consequently, cognition is an internal, psychological process, not an explicit behavior. Cognitive processes include attention, perception, spatial abilities, memory, language, executive functions, and thought (Matlin, 2009; Sternberg and Sternberg, 2009). Cognitive process can be analyzed not just from the purely psychological perspective, but also from the neurological and social points of view.

Metacognition refers to the ability to control cognition, and to apply cognitive strategies (Metcalfe and Shimamura, 1994). Metacognition is considered as an executive function. A significant amount of research in metacognition deals with educational psychology. It has been shown that increasing metacognitive strategies has a significant impact in learning. Consequently, a major goal of education should be to develop and reinforce metacognitive abilities.

Learning is the process of acquiring new, or modifying existing knowledge, behaviors, skills, values, or preferences (Gross, 2010). There is not a well-defined limit between memory and learning, although in general memory is the acquisition of new information, and learning is defined by an implicit change in perception and motor responses. Nonetheless, sometimes learning is included in the memory classification as a subtype of memory (Tulving and Craik, 2005).

Formal education and school are crucial in the diffusion not only of knowledge, but also in developing and reinforcing some specific cultural values. Indeed, school can be considered a subculture (Ardila et al., 2010; Ardila, 2018) or as a major cultural element (Vygotsky, 1930/1978). School not only provides some common knowledge but also trains some abilities and develops certain attitudes and values. Cognitive abilities measured in common psychometric tests are directly associated with schooling (Ardila et al., 2010), including the years of school, along with the quality and characteristics of the school (Sisco et al., 2015). According to Greenfield (1997), 'A major (probably *the* major) factor that makes a culture more or less different from the culture conventions surrounding ability testing is the degree of formal education possessed by the participants' (1119; emphasis in original).

VARIATIONS OF COGNITIVE ABILITIES IN DIFFERENT CULTURAL CONTEXTS

It is assumed that basic cognitive processes are universal and differences in cognition across cultures reflect the specific situations to which cognitive processes are applied than the existence of the process in one cultural group and its absence in the other (Cole, 1981). Furthermore, culture prescribes what should be learned, at what age, and by which individuals. Different patterns of cognitive abilities are observed in different cultural environments. Berry (1979; Berry et al., 2002) proposed that cultural and ecological factors play a decisive role in developing different cognitive styles. Cultural differences in cognitive abilities are examined in the following sections.

Attention

Attention refers to the process of focusing an individual's awareness on a particular type of information or environmental condition. Some studies indicate that there are significant cross-cultural differences in attention. For instance, research has demonstrated that when processing visual scenes, Western individuals attend to salient objects whereas East Asians attend to the relationships between focal objects and background elements (Nisbett and Miyamoto, 2005). However, East Asians are better than Americans at detecting color changes when a layout of a set of colored blocks is expanded to cover a wider region and worse when it is shrunken. East Asians are also slower than Americans at detecting changes in the center of the screen, suggesting that East Asians allocate their attention more broadly than Americans (Boduroglu et al., 2009). It has been suggested that these differences in attention may be instrumental in shaping cultural differences on other aspects of human cognition.

Individual differences in visual attention have been related to thinking styles: whereas analytic thinking (prevalent in individualistic cultures) is thought to promote attention to details, holistic thinking (most frequently found in collectivist cultures) promotes attention to the global structure of a scene and the relationship between its parts. Alotaibi et al. (2017) compared groups from Great Britain (an individualist culture) and Saudi Arabia (a collectivist culture) on a complex visual search task, using natural scenes. A higher overall number of fixations for Saudi participants, along with longer search times, indicated different visual search behavior styles.

Electrophysiological measures, in particular N400 event-related potential, have been used to analyze cross-cultural differences in attention. An event-related potential is the measured brain response that is the direct result of a specific sensory, cognitive, or motor event; N400 is the negative wave observed 400 milliseconds after the specific event. Goto et al. (2010) developed a N400 event-related potential design to measure the degree to which Asian Americans and European Americans responded to semantic incongruity between target objects and background scenes. As predicted, Asian Americans showed a greater negativity to incongruent trials than to congruent trials. In contrast, European Americans showed no difference in amplitude across the two conditions. Furthermore, smaller magnitude N400 incongruity effects were associated with higher independent self-construal scores. These data suggest that Asian Americans are processing the relationship between foreground and background objects to a greater degree than European Americans, which is consistent with hypothesized greater holistic processing among East Asians.

Cantrell et al. (2015) tested preschool-age American and Japanese children in a match-to-sample task. In this task, number was pitted against cumulative surface area in both large and small numerical set comparisons. It was found that children from both countries were biased to attend to the number of items for small sets. However, relative to the responses for small sets, attention to number decreased both for American and for Japanese children; moreover, both groups showed a significant bias to attend to total amount for difficult numerical ratio distances, but Japanese children shifted attention to total area at relatively smaller set sizes than American children did. These results illustrate how quantity is represented and how such representation is influenced by the specific context – both perceptual and cultural.

Waxman et al. (2016) analyzed how 2-year-olds from the US and China deploy their attention to objects and actions when different scenes are presented. Eye movements were recorded while they observed dynamic scenes. Striking convergences, overall, in patterns of visual attention in the two communities was found, but also a brief period during which their attention reliably diverged was observed. This divergence suggests that 2-year-olds from the US devoted relatively more attention to the objects whereas Chinese children devoted relatively more attention to the actions in which they were involved. These results raise the possibility that attention may be shaped by the culturally-inflected attentional proclivities observed in adults in their cultural groups. In conclusion, a relatively important group of studies support the existence of cultural differences in visual attention between Western (detail-oriented, individualistic cultures) and Eastern (global-oriented, collectivist cultures).

Perception

Cross-cultural differences in perceptual abilities have been extensively studied, particularly during the late 20th century (e.g., Laboratory of Comparative Human Cognition, 1983; Segall, 1986). A diversity of cross-cultural differences in perception has been reported. Perceptual constancy (stability of perception despite changes in the actual characteristics of the stimuli) represents the most fundamental ability in the interpretation of the surrounding spatial environment. Different studies have approached the questions of cross-cultural differences in perceptual constancy (Kenyon and Sen, 2014). It has been reported that perceptual constancy (size and shape constancy) is more accurate in less educated, non-Western societies than in more educated and Westernized societies (Pick and Pick, 1978; Vöhringer et al., 2015). Myambo (1972), for instance, observed almost perfect shape constancy in uneducated Malawi adults, whereas educated Africans and Europeans did not perform as accurately. Size constancy can be crucial when recognizing and interpreting pictorial material and has been demonstrated to be both a contextually and experientially rather than a developmentally acquired characteristic (Turnbull, 1961).

Cultural differences in the susceptibility to visual illusions have also been identified (Fujita et al., 2016). Segall et al. (1966)

compared participants in 14 non-Western and three Western societies in susceptibility to six visual illusions (Sander parallelogram, the Muller-Lyer illusion, two versions of the horizontal–vertical illusion, the Ponzo illusion, and the Poggendorff illusion). Western participants were more illusion-prone that non-Western participants, particularly with regard to the Muller-Lyer illusion and the Sander parallelogram. In addition, participants residing in regions with open vistas were more susceptible to the horizontal–vertical illusion.

Berry (1979; Berry et al., 2002) proposed that hunting people with specific ecological demands usually present good visual discrimination and excellent spatial skills. For instance, cultural groups for whom hunting is important for survival performed better on the Embedded Figures Test. Thus, ecological demands and cultural practices are significantly related to the development of perceptual and cognitive skills.

It has been noted that paintings are different in Eastern and Western cultures. Horizontal landscapes are larger in East Asian pictures than in Western, for example, and figures in portraits are larger in Western pictures (Masuda and Nisbett, 2001). Seemingly, East Asian art looks different from Western art because people of these two cultural groups are seeing the world differently. Art therefore may be reflecting differences in perceptual processes (Nisbett, 2003).

Rosselli et al. (2001) compared the performance of Colombian children (Western, low-industrialized society) with the American normative sample (Western, industrialized society) on several verbal and nonverbal measurements. In most of the tests, the performance of the two cultural groups was similar. However, in the Seashore Rhythm test, the Colombian group performed significantly better, two standard deviations above the mean for American normative data reported by Findelieis and Weight and cited by Nussbaum and Bigler (1997). It may be conjectured that musical learning represents a significant cultural value for Colombian

children. Cultural differences in the Seashore Rhythm test have also been reported among the subcultures in the United States. African American males showed significantly higher scores in the Seashore Rhythm test as compared to European Americans and Hispanics (Bernard, 1989; Evans et al., 2000). The Seashore Rhythm test was originally developed to assess musical ability (Mitrushina et al., 1999) but the perceptual skills this test requires may be shaped by cultural influences. Arnold et al. (1994) documented a significant effect of acculturation on the Seashore Rhythm test in a group of Mexican Americans, with better performance in those who had a higher level of acculturation. Cultural effects on the Seashore Rhythm test are likely associated with familiarity and relevance of tone discrimination task. In summary, cultural differences in perceptual abilities have been shown not only for visual but also for the auditory information.

Spatial Abilities

People living in different environments develop different systems of spatial reference (rivers, mountains, sun position, streets, buildings, etc.). Geographic features affect the terms of local reference systems, and differences in reference systems may, in turn, be related to differences in perception of spatial orientation. The analysis of different reference systems can be illustrative.

In a classic report, Gladwin (1970) analyzed the system used by Puluwat sailors to navigate among clusters of islands in the Western Pacific. He disclosed that many different features of the sea and sky comprise the information on which the navigation system is based. Knowledge of the habits of local seabirds provides cues for one's location. The sailors learn to detect changes in a coral reef's formation depending on the conditions of the weather, sea, and sky. Ability to detect change in the 'feel' of the boat moving through the waves on a particular course is a skill used to maintain a course. There is a complex reference system based on the position and patterns of stars in the night sky, and the rules for navigating between specific islands are described in terms of the star patterns and islands. Parallax information is also explicitly included in the system as descriptions of the way in which the islands 'move' as the boat passes on one or the other side of them (Pick and Pick, 1978).

Amazonian Indians simultaneously use a variety of different types of information to move around in the jungle. They use small rivers, orientation and color of trees, soil characteristics, sun position, animal routes, olfactory cues, and many other signals to move in the jungle. Vegetation is slightly different when closer to rivers, and moss grows differently on trees according to the sun direction. Additionally, when moving in the jungle, they permanently break small bush branches to recognize later that they have already crossed (and approximately how long ago) that particular point. All these environmental signals are simultaneously interpreted for establishing orientation and moving around in the jungle (Ardila, 2018).

Goeke et al. (2015) investigate how gender, age, and cultural background account for differences in reference frame proclivity and performance in a virtual navigation task. Using an online navigation study, the authors recorded reaction times, error rates (confusion of turning axis), and reference frame proclivity (egocentric vs. allocentric reference frame) of 1,823 participants from different world regions. Reaction times were correlated with gender and age but were only marginally affected by cultural background. Error rates exhibited a significant influence of gender and culture, but not age. Participants' cultural background significantly influenced reference frame selection: the majority of North American participants, for example, preferred an allocentric strategy, while the majority of Latin American participants preferred an egocentric navigation strategy. European and Asian groups were in between

these two extremes. Neither age nor gender had a direct impact on participants' navigation strategies. The strong effect of cultural background on navigation strategies, without the influence of gender or age, emphasizes the significance of learning and cultural factors in human navigation.

Spatial representation is correlated with time representation. In many languages, such as English and Spanish, the future is situated ahead, and the past is behind. This front–back axis is hypothesized to arise from the motor and perceptual interactions with the environment: we move forward, and the eyes are located in the front of the head. However, some languages exhibit the opposite pattern. For instance, the Aymara language, spoken in Bolivia, places the past in the front and the future behind (Núñez and Sweetser, 2006); they refer to the 'back day' to mean the next day, and to the 'front day' to mean the past day. De la Fuente et al. (2014) observed that in Arabic the future is 'ahead' and the past is 'behind'. They found, however, that Arabic speakers tend to conceptualize the future as behind and the past as ahead of them, despite using spoken metaphors that suggest the opposite. To explain this incongruence, the authors proposed that people should conceptualize either the future or the past as in front of them to the extent that their culture (or subculture) is future-oriented or past-oriented. They suggest a temporal-focus hypothesis, indicating that the space–time mappings in people's minds are conditioned by their cultural attitudes toward time.

We mentally organize new information using a spatial strategy, significantly depending upon the writing directionality. Guida et al. (2018) selected three different groups of participants (left-to-right Western readers, right-to-left Arabic readers, and Arabic-speaking illiterates) and asked them to memorize random (and non-spatial) sequences of color patches and determine whether a subsequent probe was part of the memorized sequence (e.g., press left key) or not (e.g., press right key). The results demonstrated that Western readers mentally organized the sequences from left to right, Arabic readers spontaneously used the opposite direction, and Arabic-speaking illiterates showed no systematic spatial organization. The authors suggested that cultural conventions shape one of the most 'fluid' aspects of human cognition, namely, the spontaneous mental organization of novel non-spatial information.

Memory

Memory differences between Western and Eastern cultures have been identified: participants from Eastern cultures recall background information more readily, whereas participants from Western cultures are more accurate at recognizing a central object when the background is changed (Masuda and Nisbett, 2001). Furthermore, differences in the strategies used to organize the information have been noted: participants in Western cultures show preferences for sorting by categories, whereas those in Eastern cultures prefer sorting by similarities and relationships (Gutchess et al., 2006).

Australian Aboriginals reportedly can recall virtually every topographical feature of any place that they had ever crossed. Nonetheless, performance in laboratory memory tests is not necessarily good (Lewis, 1976). Ardila and Moreno (2001) found in a group of Aruaco Indians from Colombia that a memory score for the Rey-Osterrieth Complex Figure – a typical clinical neuropsychology test – was extremely low, whereas spatial memory for everyday elements (a leaf, a pebble, etc.), placed in a specific spatial location was higher. These results suggest that memory for familiar elements is significantly higher than memory for unusual information.

Zhu et al. (2015) reported an illustrative study of memory differences across cultures. They analyzed 22 memory colors, which are divided into three types: 12 common colors such as of vegetables, fruits, and flowers, six natural colors such as of sky blue, grass, and skin colors, and four culture-specific colors. Each color was assessed by 25 Chinese observers and 30 German observers in each country. Important memory differences were reported between both groups, supporting the effect of cultural factors in memory.

Findings of cross-cultural differences in memory refer, in general, to the situations in which memory is used. Culturally relevant and significant information is recalled at a higher rate, and performance is greater on those tasks that are considered important and relevant. It is understandable that individuals from psychometric-oriented societies and schooled individuals perform higher in standard psychometric memory tests (Ardila et al., 2010).

A significant difficulty in comparing memory across different cultural groups refers to the limitations in memory testing instruments appropriate for cross-cultural comparisons. Usually, only declarative memory is tested in neuropsychology test batteries (e.g., Wechsler, 2009), whereas procedural memory is ignored. Declarative memory is strongly related to school learning, whereas procedural memory refers to learning how to perform different activities. A significant school attendance effect is observed in declarative memory tests, whereas procedural memory is more dependent on manual motor activities (Anderson, 2000).

Language

Language plays an instrumental role in cognition (Vygotsky, 1962, 1930/1978). As a matter of fact, it represents the major cognitive instrument. Languages differ in phonology, lexicon, semantics, grammar, pragmatic, and writing systems. These differences may affect language test performance. Languages conceptualize the world in different ways (Whorf, 1956). For instance, the notion of time is expressed differently in Latin and German languages. Latin languages have a significantly high number of tenses pointing to temporal nuances. Slavic languages use perfective and non-perfective tenses in verbs. Space and causality are also coded differently in different languages (Yule, 2016). Furthermore, it has been proposed that the language lexicon implies a conceptualization of the environmental conditions, whereas the language grammar contains a reasoning strategy (Ardila, 2015). At least to some extent, we think according to the language that we speak, as suggested some time ago in the so-called 'Whorf-Sapir hypothesis' (Sapir, 1949; Whorf, 1956).

Language usage differs according to the cultural (and subcultural) background and strongly correlates with the educational level. Sometimes, test instructions are presented in a formal language, which may be difficult to understand for individuals with limited education. Formal language represents a sort of academic language, most often found in a written form that many people neither use nor completely understand. A concerted effort is required to make test instructions and, in general, test language understandable for less educated people and appropriate for different cultural and subcultural groups.

The search for universals in language has represented a major endeavor for linguistics (Croft, 2017). Lenneberg (1967) argued that the processes by which language is realized are innate. Humans possess certain basic biologic organizational and cognitive abilities that permit language development. Language universals can be characterized as occurring on different language levels: phonemic, semantic, and grammatical.

It has been assumed that when comparing word meanings, some words are observed universally across languages. Swadesh (1952, 1967) proposed that there is a minimal vocabulary found in every language, further known as the 'Swadesh word list' including some 100–200 words. Every human, regardless of the environmental conditions, time, and cultural conditions is exposed to some constant phenomena and conditions: day, night, sun, moon, leaf, water, etc. Equivalent words to refer to these phenomena and conditions are found in every language. Chomsky (1980), on the other hand, suggested that there is a universal grammar that is innate and that determines the development of human language. He made a basic distinction between the surface structure of a language and its deep structure. The expressed surface structure can vary, but it points to a deep structure of meaning.

The comparative studies of language raise the question of how people in different societies name and classify aspects of their world. Conkin (1971) published a classic bibliography that contains 5,000 entries, describing and comparing the different classification systems. Topics included are kinship, colors, and ethnobiology. This bibliography has become a reference point to compare how different systems function, and how words are selected and assembled to name elements of the external world.

Language disturbances associated with brain pathology, on the other hand, have been studied mainly in a handful of Indo-European languages, primarily French, English, German, Russian, Italian, and Spanish. Our knowledge about language disturbances in other tonal and non-Indo-European languages is limited (Penn and Armstrong, 2017). We do not know yet if our current Indo-European languages aphasia model is applicable to tonal languages. Or rather, to what extent it may be applicable. Evidence, however, seems to suggest that there are some universal principles in the brain organization of language and in the language pathology associated with brain damage (Paradis, 2001). Thus, for any language, language disturbances (aphasias) are associated with left hemisphere pathology; phoneme discrimination defects are found in cases of left superior temporal damage, whereas grammatical impairments result from left posterior frontal pathology. Right hemisphere damage, on the other hand, is associated with emotional language defects, regardless of the idiosyncrasies of the language (Costanzo et al., 2015; Gandour, 1998; Rohr and Rahman, 2018).

Executive Functions

The definition of executive functions usually includes a diversity of cognitive and behavioral abilities, such as the ability to control attention, organize goal-directed behaviors, problem-solving, reasoning, temporality of behavior, inhibitory control, and mental flexibility (Jurado and Rosselli, 2007; Stuss and Knight, 2002). Executive functions have been associated with diverse factors, including educational level (Gómez-Pérez and Ostrosky-Solís, 2006) and bilingualism (Bialystok, 2017; Bialystok et al., 2004). Individuals with a higher educational level obtain better scores on executive functions tests, confirming the assumption that executive functions are, to a significant extent, learned abilities. Bilingual individuals, on the other hand, frequently achieve higher scores in attention control tests, suggesting that using two languages requires complex cognitive control. Executive functions represent higher psychological processes emerging recently in human evolution (Ardila, 2008; Vygotsky, 1930/1978).

Tran and colleagues (2018) investigated how bilingualism and culture might shape the development of executive functions. Studying monolingual and bilingual children at different ages and in different cultures, they found a significant bilingualism effect on cognitive control processes measuring selective attention, switching, and inhibition, whereas an effect of culture was most pronounced on behavioral regulation/response inhibition. Therefore, both language use and living conditions impact the development of executive functions, but in different ways.

Kelkar et al. (2013) examined differences between Eastern and Western cultures on complex cognitive–communicative skills, verbal reasoning, and executive functioning abilities. Twenty-two Indian-born individuals and twenty American-born individuals completed an individualism–collectivism scale, a functional assessment of verbal reasoning and executive strategies, and subtests from the Delis–Kaplan Executive Function System. The

results indicated a significant main effect of culture, with Western participants completing the four tasks of the functional assessment of verbal reasoning and executive strategies more rapidly and with higher scores on the reasoning subtest. Western participants demonstrated significantly higher category switching capabilities and category switching accuracy in a verbal fluency subtest. Eastern participants were significantly faster on all subtests of the Trail Making Test. These findings suggest differences in Eastern and Western cultures that may be explained by analytical cognitive strategies and rule-based categorization employed by Western participants to complete reasoning and category-naming tasks. Eastern participants appeared to allocate holistic attention resources to perform more successfully on tasks such as the Trail Making Test, which require rapid application of perceptual relationships.

Finally, Roos et al. (2018) conducted an integrative review of the extant literature addressing differences in childhood executive functions between diverse cultural groups. Eighteen articles were identified that included at least one domain of executive function (working memory, inhibitory control, cognitive flexibility) measured in a child or adolescent sample and related to culture. Notable findings included advantages in executive functions for young children in East Asian cultures, potentially attributable to intensive memory-based language demands. Taking together all these studies suggest that executive functions are depending on education but also on the patterns of cultural learning.

Thought

The idea that there are differences in thinking style between Western and East Asian people was proposed some time ago (Choi et al., 1997; Nisbett et al., 2001). It was suggested that East Asians are holistic, attending to the entire field and assigning causality to it, making relatively little use of categories and formal logic, and relying on 'dialectical' reasoning, whereas Westerners are more analytical, paying attention primarily to the object and the categories to which it belongs and using rules, including formal logic, to understand behavior. It was speculated that the origin of these differences is traceable to markedly different social systems (Nisbett et al., 2001.

These differences in thinking strategies can be traced to the origins of Western and Eastern cultures. Plato supposed that the world was composed by collection of objects that can be categorized according to universal properties and, in general, Greeks proposed a logic system that uses abstract rules and syllogisms. In ancient China, harmony and interconnectedness assumed that the world was composed by interconnected substances (Heine, 2012).

THE INFLUENCE OF THE CULTURAL CONTEXT ON LEARNING

It has been suggested that culture represents one of the most influential socialization variables impacting the development of learning styles (De Vita, 2001; Hayes and Allinson, 1988; Hofstede, 1997) and that each culture has a preferred learning style. Learning style refers to individual differences in strategies of learning. Four basic learning styles have been proposed (Joy and Kolb, 2009): Diverging (learners prefer to make more use of concrete experience and reflective observation), Assimilating (learners prefer to learn through reflective observation and abstract conceptualization), Converging (learners rely on abstract conceptualization and active experimentation), and Accommodating (learners use active experimentation and concrete experience). Based on these four learning modes, Kolb (1999, 2005) proposed an instrument known as the 'Kolb Learning Style Inventory' designed to measure the degree to which individuals display these four learning styles. This inventory has been used in several cross-cultural studies. This instrument is the most widely accepted learning style measure and has received substantial empirical support, even though it has also been criticized because of the type of measure that is used (Manolis et al., 2013).

The Kolb Learning Style Inventory is based on Kolb's (1981) conceptualization of learning. According to Kolb, learning is considered a four-stage cycle. Immediate concrete experience is the basis for observation and reflection. People use these observations to build an idea, generalization, or 'theory'; departing from generalization, new implications for action can be deduced. These implications or hypotheses then serve as guides to create new experience. The learners consequently need four different types of abilities: Concrete Experience abilities (CE), Reflective Observation abilities (RO), Abstract Conceptualization abilities (AC), and Active Experimentation (AE) abilities.

As an example of the use of this instrument, 353 French, German, and French Canadian (Quebec) students completed the Kolb Learning Style Inventory (Barmeyer, 2004). The results of the four dimensions showed several significant gender differences. Females scored higher than males in the dimension CE, suggesting higher social or emotional competences. The results also showed significant differences for the dimensions RO and AC. Here, male students showed a higher average score than female students. There was no significant difference for the fourth dimension, AE. Comparing national groups, results of the sample showed that differences were found in the CE scores: the scores of French and Quebecois students were significantly higher than of the German students. This could indicate a preference for personal involvement with people and a more intuitive approach to problems and situations. The RO scores did not show significant differences. For the dimension AC, the German students scored higher than the French and the Quebecois students. These results thus indicate learning style differences not only between genders but also across national groups.

Yamazaki (2005) analyzed the association between six dichotomous typologies of cultural differences proposed by different authors, including: high-context vs. low-context, shame vs. guilt, interdependent-self vs. independent-self, strong uncertainty avoidance vs. weak uncertainty avoidance, O-type organization (people-orientated rather than task-orientated) vs. M-type organization (more task-oriented and less people-oriented), field-dependent vs. field-independent, on one hand, and the learning styles using Kolb's learning model, on the other. The author concluded that particular cultures, as categorized in those domains, appear to favor or express certain learning styles or abilities.

Hofstede (2001) introduced the concept of continuous cultural dimensions as the basis for comparison. He identified power distance, uncertainty avoidance, individualism–collectivism, and masculinity–femininity (later long-term versus short-term orientations) as the major aspects on which cultures differ. The GLOBE study (House et al., 2004) further developed this idea and suggested nine dimensions: in-group collectivism, institutional collectivism, power distance, uncertainty avoidance, future orientation, performance orientation, humane orientation, assertiveness, and gender egalitarianism.

Joy and Kolb (2009) examined the role that culture plays in the way that individuals learn. They used the Kolb Learning Style Inventory (2005) to assess differences in learning style. Taking the framework for categorizing cultural differences from the Global Leadership and Organizational Effectiveness (GLOBE) study (House et al., 2004), national cultures were analyzed by cultural clusters and individual cultural dimensions. Initially they assessed the relative influence of culture in comparison to gender, age, and level of education in 533 individuals in seven countries (USA, Italy, Germany, Poland, Brazil, India, and Singapore) across different areas of specialization (Humanities and Social Science,

Natural Sciences, and Mathematics). The authors report that a significant percentage of the variance in the preference for abstract conceptualization was explained by culture, gender, level of education, and area of specialization. The variability in preference for active experimentation over reflective observation was accounted for by age and area of specialization. Later, the authors examined the influence of individual culture dimensions in shaping the learning style preferences. It was found that individuals tend to have a less abstract learning style in countries that are high in in-group collectivism, institutional collectivism, uncertainty avoidance, future orientation, and gender egalitarianism. Individuals may have a more reflective learning style in countries that are high in in-group collectivism, uncertainty avoidance and assertiveness.

Maseleno et al. (2016) reviewed some data related to multicultural education. Responses from 253 students were included. The data included six sections: culture (race, ethnicity, language and identity); learning preferences; cognitive learning styles; creativity skills and problem solving skills; motivation; and students' background knowledge. They observed that cognitive styles are closely associated with personality traits and refer to how students organize and process data that has particular meaning for them. Research suggests that creativity will most likely occur when the three elements of expertise, task motivation and creative thinking overlap.

Sisco and Kao (2018) studied the acculturation and learning style preferences of multicultural students enrolled in a college course in the United States. The ethnic background of these participants were as follows: Hispanic 28%, African 25%, West Indian 16%, Asian 13%, Euro 8%, Arab 2%, and Haitian 2%. The remaining failed to provide this information and were categorized as 'other'. Additionally, 62% of the participants reported English as their native or first language, while 76% reported English as their best language. In addition, 59% of the students reported that English was not the only language they spoke at home. The Learning Style Inventory description inventory (Kolb and Kolb, 2005) and the Abbreviated Multidimensional Acculturation Scale (AMAS) (Zea et al., 2003) were administered. The AMAS is a 42-item scale designed to assess an individual's degree of acculturation to the United States. This scale focuses on three factors: Identity (American, as well as one's origin of heritage), Language Competence (mastery of the English language, along with mastery of one's native/heritage language), and Cultural Competence (knowledge of the American culture along with one's culture of origin). As predicted, the students who identified more strongly with American culture preferred using AC over CE as learning styles for grasping the material. The scores for AC and RO were positively related to academic performance, whereas those for CE and AE were negatively related. The results suggested that the more acculturated the multicultural students were to the specific culture of the United States, the preference for the learning style of grasping information was abstract conceptualization (AC), or the generalizing of logistics of what they are learning. There was a greater likelihood that academic performance is enhanced for these multicultural students utilizing AC for grasping information, and RO for transforming of information during learning.

CONCLUSION

It can be concluded that culture represents a significant variable in the development of diverse cognitive abilities, including attention, perception, spatial skills, memory, language, executive functions, and thought. Culture impacts the development of learning styles and each culture has a preferred learning style.

Cultural interpretation of cognition does not rule out the involvement of genetic factors in human abilities. The field of 'cultural neuroscience' (Chiao and Ambady, 2007) aspires to integrate the mechanisms by which the mutual constitution of culture, brain, and genes occurs. Cultural neuroscience is a new, interdisciplinary field that analyses the bidirectional influence of cultural and genic variables on the brain and cognition. Cultural neuroscience integrates theories and methods from different scientific areas, including cross-cultural psychology, behavioral neurosciences, and genetics. Cultural neuroscience investigates how cultural variables shape brain function, and also how the human brain creates cultural capacities (Chiao, 2009, 2018). It represents a bridge to conciliate genetic and cultural interpretations of human cognition and behavior.

ACKNOWLEDGEMENTS

My gratitude to Adriana Ardila for her editorial support.

REFERENCES

Alotaibi, A., Underwood, G., & Smith, A. D. (2017). Cultural differences in attention: Eye movement evidence from a comparative visual search task. *Consciousness and Cognition*, 55, 254–265.

Anderson, J. R. (2000). *Learning and memory: An integrated approach* (2nd Ed.). New York: John Wiley & Sons.

Ardila, A. (2008). On the evolutionary origins of executive functions. *Brain and Cognition*, 68(1), 92–99.

Ardila, A. (2015). Proposed neurological interpretation of language evolution. *Behavioral Neurology*, Article ID 872487.

Ardila, A. (2018). *Historical development of human cognition: A cultural-historical neuropsychological perspective.* Springer.

Ardila, A., & Moreno, S. (2001). Neuropsychological test performance in Aruaco Indians: An exploratory study. *Journal of the International Neuropsychological Society*, 7(4), 510–515.

Ardila, A., Bertolucci, P. H., Braga, L. W., Castro-Caldas, A., Judd, T., Kosmidis, M. H.,

Matute, E., Nitrini, R., Ostrosky-Solis, F., & Rosselli, M. (2010). Illiteracy: Neuropsychology of cognition without reading. *Archives of Clinical Neuropsychology*, 25(8), 689–712.

Arnold, B. R., Montgomery, G. T., Castaneda, I., & Longoria, R. (1994). Acculturation and performance of Hispanics on selected Halstead-Reitan neuropsychological tests. *Assessment*, 1(3), 239–248.

Barmeyer, C. I. (2004). Learning styles and their impact on cross-cultural training: An international comparison in France, Germany and Quebec. *International Journal of Intercultural Relations*, 28(6), 577–594.

Bernard, L. C. (1989). Halstead-Reitan neuropsychological test performance of black, Hispanic, and white young adult males from poor academic backgrounds. *Archives of Clinical Neuropsychology*, 4(3), 267–274.

Berry, J. W. (1979). Culture and cognition style. In A. J. Marsella, R. G. Tharp, & T. J. Ciborowski (Eds), *Perspectives on cross-cultural psychology* (pp. 117–135). New York: Academic Press.

Berry, J. W., Poortinga, Y. H., Segall, M. H., & Dasen, P. R. (2002). *Cross-cultural psychology: Research and applications* (2nd Ed.). Oxford: Oxford University Press.

Bialystok, E. (2017). The bilingual adaptation: How minds accommodate experience. *Psychological Bulletin*, 143(3), 233–262.

Bialystok, E., Craik, F. I., Klein, R., & Viswanathan, M. (2004). Bilingualism, aging, and cognitive control: Evidence from the Simon task. *Psychology of Aging*, 19(2), 290–303.

Boduroglu, A., Shah, P., & Nisbett, R. E. (2009). Cultural differences in allocation of attention in visual information processing. *Journal of Cross-Cultural Psychology*, 40(3), 349–360.

Cantrell, L., Kuwabara, M., & Smith, L. B. (2015). Set size and culture influence children's attention to number. *Journal of Experimental Child Psychology*, 131, 19–37.

Chiao, J. Y. (2009). Cultural neuroscience: A once and future discipline. *Progress in Brain Research*, 178, 287–304.

Chiao, J. Y. (2018). Developmental aspects in cultural neuroscience. *Developmental Review*, 50(Part A), 77–89.

Chiao, J. Y., & Ambady, N. (2007). Cultural neuroscience: Parsing universality and diversity across levels of analysis. In S. Kitayama &

D. Cohen (Eds), *Handbook of cultural psychology* (pp. 237–254). New York: Guilford Press.

Choi, I., Nisbett, R. E, & Smith, E. E. (1997). Culture, category salience, and inductive reasoning. *Cognition*, 65(1), 15–32.

Chomsky, N. (1980). *Rules and representations*. Oxford: Blackwell.

Cole, M. (1981). Cross-cultural psychology: A combined review. *Contemporary Psychology*, 26(5), 330–334.

Conkin, H. C. (1971). *Folk classification: A topically arranged bibliography of contemporary and background references through 1971*. New Haven, CT: Department of Anthropology Yale University.

Costanzo, E. Y., Villarreal, M., Drucaroff, L. J., Ortiz-Villafañe, M., Castro, M. N., Goldschmidt, M., Wainsztein, A. E., Ladrón-de Guevara, M. S., Romero, C., Brusco, L. I., Camprodon, J. A., Nemeroff, C., & Guinjoan, S. M. (2015). Hemispheric specialization in affective responses, cerebral dominance for language, and handedness: Lateralization of emotion, language, and dexterity. *Behavioural Brain Research*, 288, 11–19.

Croft, W. (2017). Typology and universals. In M. Aronoff & J. Rees-Miller (Eds), *The handbook of linguistics*. New York: Wiley Blackwell.

de la Fuente, J., Santiago, J., Román, A., Dumitrache, C., & Casasanto, D. (2014). When you think about it, your past is in front of you: How culture shapes spatial conceptions of time. *Psychological Science*, 25(9), 1682–1690.

De Vita, G. (2001). Learning styles, culture and inclusive instruction in the multicultural classroom: A business and management perspective. *Innovations in Education and Teaching International*, 38(2), 165–174.

Ethnologue (2020). *Languages of the world*. www.ethnologue.com/guides/how-many-languages. Retrieved 01/10/2020.

Evans, J. D., Miller, S. W., Byrd, D. A., & Heaton, R. K. (2000). Cross-cultural applications of the Halstead-Reitan batteries. In E. Fletcher-Jenzen, T. L. Strickland, & C. R. Reynolds (Eds), *Handbook of cross-cultural neuropsychology* (pp. 287–303). New York: Kluwer-Academic.

Fujita, K., Nakamura, N., & Watanabe, S. (2016). Visual illusions in a comparative perspective. In A. G. Shapiro & D. Todorovic

(Eds), *The Oxford compendium of visual illusions*. Oxford University Press.

Gandour, J. (1998). Aphasia in tonal languages. In P. Coppens, Y. Lebrun, & A. Basso (Eds), *Aphasia in atypical populations* (pp. 117–142). Mahwah, NJ: Lawrence Erlbaum Associates.

Gladwin, T. (1970). *East is a big bird: Navigation and logic in* Puluwat *Atoll*. Cambridge, MA: Harvard University Press.

Goeke, K., Kornpetpanee, S., Köster, M., Fernández-Revelles, A. B., Gramann, & König, P. (2015). Cultural background shapes spatial reference frame proclivity. *Scientific Reports*, 5, Article number: 11426.

Gómez-Pérez, E., & Ostrosky-Solís, F. (2006). Attention and memory evaluation across life span: Heterogenous effects of age and education. *Journal of Clinical and Experimental Neuropsychology*, 28(4), 477–494.

Goto, S. G., Ando, Y., Huang, C., Yee, A., & Lewis, R. S. (2010). Cultural differences in the visual processing of meaning: Detecting incongruities between background and foreground objects using the N400. *Social Cognitive and Affective Neuroscience*, 5(2–3), 242–253.

Greenfield, P. M. (1997). You can't take it with you: Why ability assessments don't cross cultures. *American Psychologist*, 52(10), 1115–1124.

Gross, R. (2010). *Psychology: The science of the mind and behavior*. Hodder Education.

Guida, A., Megreya, A. M., Lavielle-Guida, M., Noël, Y., Mathy, F., van Dijck, J. P., & Abrahamse, E. (2018). Spatialization in working memory is related to literacy and reading direction: Culture 'literarily' directs our thoughts. *Cognition*, 175, 96–100.

Gutchess, A. H., Yoon, C., & Luo, T. (2006). Categorical organization in free recall across culture and age. *Gerontology*, 52(5), 314–323.

Harris, M. (1983). *Culture, people, nature: An introduction to general anthropology* (3rd Ed.). New York: Harper & Row.

Haviland, W. A., McBride, B., Prins, H. E. L., & Walrath, D. (2011). *Cultural anthropology: The human challenge* (13th Ed.). Belmont, CA: Wadsworth, Cengage Learning.

Hayes, J., & Allinson, C. W. (1988). Cultural differences in the learning styles of managers. *Management International Review*, 28(3), 75–80.

Heine, S. J. (2012). *Cultural psychology* (2nd Ed.). New York: W.W. Norton.

Hofstede, G. H. (1997). *Cultures and organization: Software of mind*. New York: McGraw Hill.

Hofstede, G. (2001). *Cultures consequences: Comparing values, behaviors, institutions and organizations across nations* (2nd Ed.). London: Sage.

House, R. J., Hanges, P. J., Javidan, M., Dorfman, P. W., & Gupta, V. (2004). *Culture, leadership and organizations: The GLOBE study of 62 Societies*. Thousand Oaks, CA: Sage.

Huntington, S. P. (1996). *The clash of civilizations and the remaking of world order*. New York: Simon & Schuster.

Joy, S., & Kolb, D. A. (2009). Are there cultural differences in learning style? *International Journal of Intercultural Relations*, 33(1), 69–85.

Jurado, M. B., & Rosselli, M. (2007). The elusive nature of executive functions: A review of our current understanding. *Neuropsychology Review*, 17(3), 213–233.

Kelkar, A. S., Hough, M. S., & Fang, X. (2013). Do we think alike? A cross-cultural study of executive functioning. *Culture and Brain*, 1(2–4), 1180137.

Kenyon, G. N., & Sen. K. C. (2014). The perception process. In *The perception of quality: Mapping products and service quality to consumer perceptions* (pp. 41–50). Springer.

Kolb, A. Y., & Kolb, D. A. (2005). *The Kolb Learning Style Inventory, Version 3.1: Technical specifications*. Boston, MA: Hay Resources Direct.

Kolb, D. A. (1981). Learning styles and disciplinary differences. In A. W. Chickering (Ed.), *The modern American college: Responding to the new realities of diverse students and a changing society* (pp. 232–255). San Francisco: Jossey-Bass.

Kolb, D. A. (1999). *The Kolb Learning Style Inventory, Version 3*. Boston, MA: TRG Hay/McBer.

Kolb, D. A. (2005). *The Kolb Learning Style Inventory, Version 3.1: Self-scoring and interpretation booklet*. Boston, MA: Hay Group Transforming Learning.

Laboratory of Comparative Human Cognition. (1983). Culture and cognitive development. In P. Mussen (Ed.), *Handbook of child psychology: History, theory and methods* (Vol. 1., pp. 342–397). New York: Wiley.

Lenneberg, E. H. (1967). *Biological foundations of language*. New York: Wiley.

Lewis, D. (1976). Observations on route-finding and spatial orientation among the Aboriginal peoples of the Western desert region of Central Australia. *Oceania*, 46(4), 249–282.

Manolis, C., Burns, D. J., Assudani, R., & Chinta, R. (2013). Assessing experiential learning styles: A methodological reconstruction and validation of the Kolb Learning Style Inventory. *Learning and Individual Differences*, 23, 44–52.

Maseleno, A., Hardaker, G., Sabani, N., & Suhaili, N. (2016). Data on multicultural education and diagnostic information profiling: Culture, learning styles and creativity. *Data in Brief*, 9, 1048–1051.

Masuda, T., & Nisbett, R. E. (2001). Attending holistically versus analytically: Comparing the context sensitivity of Japanese and Americans. *Journal of Personality and Social Psychology*, 81(5), 922–934.

Matlin, M. (2009). *Cognition*. Hoboken, NJ: John Wiley & Sons.

Metcalfe, J., & Shimamura, A. P. (1994). *Metacognition: Knowing about knowing*. Cambridge, MA: MIT Press.

Mitrushina, M. N., Boone, K. B., & D'Elia, L. F. (1999). *Handbook of normative data for neuropsychological assessment*. New York: Oxford University Press.

Myambo, K. (1972). Shape constancy as influenced by culture, Western education, and age. *Journal of Cross-Cultural Psychology*, 3(3), 221–232.

Nisbett, R. E. (2003). *The geography of thought: How Asians and Westerners think differently … and why*. New York: The Free Press.

Nisbett, R. E., & Miyamoto, Y. (2005). The influence of culture: Holistic versus analytic perception. *Trends in Cognitive Sciences*, 9(10), 467–473.

Nisbett, R. E., Peng, K., Choi, I., & Norenzayan, A. (2001). Culture and systems of thought: Holistic versus analytic cognition. *Psychological Review*, 108(2), 291–310.

Núñez, R. E., & Sweetser, E. (2006). With the future behind them: Convergent evidence from Aymara language and gesture in the cross-linguistic comparison of spatial construals of time. *Cognitive Science*, 30(3), 401–450.

Nussbaum, N. L., & Bigler, E. (1997). Halstead-Reitan neuropsychological batteries for children. In C. R. Reynolds & E. Fletcher-Janzen (Eds), *Handbook of clinical child neuropsychology* (pp. 219–236). New York: Plenum.

Paradis, M. (Ed.). (2001). *Manifestations of aphasia symptoms in different languages*. Oxford: Pergamon Press.

Penn, C., & Armstrong, E. (2017). Intercultural aphasia: New models of understanding for Indigenous populations. *Aphasiology*, 31(5), 563–594.

Pick, A. D., & Pick, H. L. (1978). Culture and perception. In E. C. Carterette & M. P. Friedman (Eds), *Handbook of perception: Vol. 10. Perceptual ecology* (pp. 19–39). New York: Academic Press.

Rohr, L., & Rahman, R. A. (2018). Emotional language production: Time course, behavioral and electrophysiological correlates. *Neuropsychologia*, 117, 241–252.

Roos, L. E., Beauchamp, K. G., Flannery, J., & Fisher, P. A. (2018). Cultural contributions to childhood executive function. *Journal of Cognition and Culture*, 8, 61.

Rosselli, M., Ardila, A., Bateman, J. R., & Guzman, M. (2001). Neuropsychological test scores, academic performance and developmental disorders in Spanish-speaking children. *Developmental Neuropsychology*, 20(1), 355–374.

Sapir, E. (1949). *Selected writings of Edward Sapir in language, culture, and personality*. Berkeley & Los Angeles: University of California Press.

Segall, M. H. (1986). Culture and behavior: Psychology in global perspective. *Annual Review of Psychology*, 37, 523–564.

Segall, M. H., Campbell, D. T., & Herskovits, M. J. (1966). *The influence of culture on visual perception*. Indianapolis, IN: Bobbs-Merrill.

Sisco, H., & Kao, T. (2018). Learning style preferences and acculturation of multicultural students of the U.S. *Institute for Learning Styles Journal*, 1(1), 1–10.

Sisco, S., Gross, A. L., Shih, R. A., Sachs, B. C., Glymour, M. M., Bangen, K. J., Benitez, A.,

Skinner, J., Schneider, B. C., & Manly J. J. (2015). The role of early life educational quality and literacy in explaining racial disparities in cognition in late life. *The Journals of Gerontology Series B Psychological Sciences and Social Sciences*, 70(4), 557–567.

Sternberg, R. J., & Sternberg, K. (2009). *Cognitive psychology* (6th Ed.). Belmont, CA: Wadsworth, Cengage Learning.

Stuss, D. T., & Knight, R. T. (2002). *Principles of frontal lobe function*. Oxford: Oxford University Press.

Swadesh, M. (1952). Lexico-statistic dating of prehistoric ethnic contacts. *Proceedings of the American Philosophical Society*, 96(4), 152–163.

Swadesh, M. (1967). *El lenguaje y la vida humana* [Language and human life]. Mexico: Fondo de Cultural Económica.

Tran, C. D., Arredondo, M. M., & Yoshida, H. (2018). Early executive function: The influence of culture and bilingualism. *Bilingualism: Language and Cognition*, 22(4), 714–732.

Tulving, E., & Craik, F. I. M. (2005). *The Oxford handbook of memory*. Oxford: Oxford University Press.

Turnbull, C. M. (1961). Notes and discussion: Some observations regarding the experiences and behavior of the BaMbuti pygmies. *American Journal of Psychology*, 74(2), 304–308.

Vöhringer, I. A., Poloczek, S., Graf, F., Lamm, B., Teiser, J., Fassbender, I., Freitag, C., Suhrke, J., Teubert, M., Keller, H., Lohaus, A., Schwarzer, G., & Knopf, M. (2015). Is perceptual priming affected by culture? A study with German middle-class and Cameroonian Nso farmer children. *The Journal of Genetic Psychology*, 176(3–4), 156–170.

Vygotsky, L. S. (1930/1978). *Mind in society: The development of higher psychological processes*. Cambridge, MA: Harvard University Press.

Vygotsky, L. S. (1962). *Thought and language*. Cambridge, MA: MIT Press.

Waxman, S. R., Fu, X., Ferguson, B., Geraghty, K., Leddon, E., Liang, J., & Zhao, M. F.

(2016). How early is infants' attention to objects and actions shaped by culture? New evidence from 24-month-olds raised in the US and China. *Frontiers in Psychology*, 7, 97.

Wechsler, D. (2009). *Wechsler Memory Scale – (WMS–IV) technical and interpretive manual* (4th Ed.). San Antonio, TX: Pearson.

Whorf, B. L. (1956). *Language, thought and reality*. Cambridge, MA: MIT Press.

Yamazaki, Y. (2005). Learning styles and typologies of cultural differences: A theoretical and empirical comparison. *International Journal of Inter-Cultural Relations*, 29(5), 521–548.

Yule, G. (2016). *The study of language* (6th Ed.). Cambridge University Press.

Zea, M. C., Asner-Self, K. K., Birman D., & Buki L. P. (2003). The Abbreviated Multidimensional Acculturation Scale: Empirical validation with two Latino/Latina samples. *Cultural Diversity and Ethnic Minority Psychology*, 9(2), 107–126.

Zhu, Y., Luo, R., Xu, L., Liu, X., Ciu, G., Fischer, S., Bodrog, P., & Khan, Q. (2015). Investigation of memory colours across cultures. In *23rd Color and Imaging Conference Proceedings* (pp. 133–137). Darmstadt, Germany.

RECOMMENDED READING

Ardila, A. (2018). *Historical development of human cognition: A cultural-historical neuropsychological perspective*. Springer.

Berry, J. W., Poortinga, Y. H., Segall, M. H., & Dasen, P. R. (2002). *Cross-cultural psychology: Research and applications* (2nd Ed.). Oxford: Oxford University Press.

Hollins, E. R. (2015). *Culture in school learning: Revealing the deep meaning*. Routledge.

Kitayama, S., & Cohen, D. (Eds) (2010). *Handbook of cultural psychology*. New York: Guilford Press.

Sternberg, R. J., & Sternberg, K. (2009). *Cognitive psychology* (6th Ed.). Belmont, CA: Wadsworth, Cengage Learning.

24

Sources of Data for Testing Evolutionary Hypotheses

Carey J. Fitzgerald and Jody A. Thompson

INTRODUCTION

As one can imagine, accurate and definitive information regarding human life and behaviors that occurred in our ancestral past is difficult to obtain. Because of this, evolutionary psychologists have had to seek data from various sources ranging from archaeological, historical, and cultural records to other social scientific means such as self-report methods and naturalistic observations of humans across the world. There are six primary sources from which evolutionary psychologists obtain their data (Buss, 2015). These six sources include (1) archaeological records, (2) observations of modern-day hunter-gatherer societies, (3) self-reported responses from surveys and/or interviews, (4) systematic observations of individuals in public places, (5) historical public records, and (6) the various products that modern humans create (Buss, 2015).

Evolutionary psychologists often examine physical and cultural anthropological data in the form of archeological records and controlled observations of modern-day hunter-gatherer societies. Archaeological records have allotted researchers the ability to examine various details of ancestral humans, including the evolution of human diet, brain size, and leading sources of injury and death (Margerison and Knüsel, 2002; Schmidt, 2001). Similarly, evolutionary psychologists have observed modern-day hunter-gatherer societies – including the Yanomamö of Venezuela (Hagen et al., 2001; Macfarlan et al., 2014), the Ache of Paraguay (Hill and Hurtado, 2017), the !Kung of Botswana (Draper and Hames, 2000), and the Hadza of Tanzania (Marlowe, 1999, 2003, 2004) – to infer what human behavior is like without industrial or Western civilization.

Evolutionary psychologists have also studied human behavior through systematic observations of individuals in contemporary public places as well as self-reported responses from surveys and interviews. Having trained observers engage in systematic observations of people in public places have helped shed light on many social behaviors in humans, such as mating and mate guarding (Flinn, 1988). Similarly, evolutionary psychologists have obtained data regarding evolved social behaviors and mating behaviors by administering self-report measures via survey or interview to undergraduate students and other individuals within various social communities (Kruger et al., 2013; Wilke et al., 2014).

Historical public records have been shown to yield valuable life-history data – such as births, deaths, marriages, divorces, and crimes – which can shed light on mating patterns throughout human history (Kruger and Nesse, 2006). Evolutionary psychologists have also found evidence for various evolved mating strategies within historical literature (Carroll et al., 2012; Kruger et al., 2003), indicating that evolutionary psychologists are able to obtain relevant data from the products humans create.

This chapter contains a detailed description of each of these six sources of data as well as some of the breakthrough findings that were obtained from each of these sources. While these sources of data have been utilized to discover information regarding the way human life and behavior evolved, they are far from perfect. Therefore, criticisms of each source are also presented.

ARCHAEOLOGICAL RECORDS

Archaeology is the scientific field that focuses on human history and pre-history. Archaeologists study ancient humans and civilizations via the assessment of archaeological records (i.e., ancient artifacts). Artifacts may include pieces of architecture, weapons, stones, tools, jewelry, human remains, and various other objects associated with ancient humans. Archaeologists have utilized isotopic studies – which involves measuring the decay of carbon and nitrogen isotopes in human bone – as a means of objectively assessing the age and diet of ancient humans (see Pollard, 2011, for a review). Archaeology may not be the first field of study someone considers when thinking about psychology. However, investigating archaeological records have led to many discoveries regarding human biology, including physical health, diet, brain size, and causes of death (Margerison and Knüsel, 2002; Schmidt, 2001).

Archaeologists have used isotopic studies to better understand the composition of Neanderthal diets and ancient hunter-gatherers' diets in comparison to the diets of modern-day hunter-gatherers and humans from industrialized nations. Specifically, the isotopic research revealed that ancient humans and Neanderthals both had heavily meat-based high-protein diets similar to that of wolves (Cordain et al., 2002; Richards, 2002; Richards et al., 2000a,b) – a diet that is associated with cardiovascular disease in Western cultures (Cordain et al., 2002) – which is evidence for an evolutionary mismatch between ancestral human diet and contemporary human environment. However, there is still debate among archaeologists regarding ancestral human diets, with some archaeological evidence indicating that humans scavenged for food much more than hunted (O'Connell et al., 2002). Some archaeologists have argued that humans' nutrient-rich diet led to the evolution of large brain sizes and small guts (Leonard et al., 2007).

Archaeologists have provided evidence for early human social behavior as well (Gowlett et al., 2012). Technological and scientific advancements have allowed archaeologists to reconstruct prehistoric sites to better understand the economies and social exchange of ancient cultures. These developments have also allowed researchers to locate the original locations of specific raw materials to reconstruct ancient technology and tools (Smith et al., 2012).

Studying the skeletal remains of prehistoric humans has also shed light on the intensity and frequency of interpersonal violence in humans' ancestral past (Judd, 2002, 2004; Jurmain et al., 2009). Specifically, researchers have found in ancient skeletal populations in North America and Africa that the head/skull was the most consistently attacked point on the victims' bodies (Judd, 2004; Jurmain et al., 2009). Archaeologists can assess skeletal injuries and indicate whether the injuries were due to interpersonal violence and whether they were caused by projectile weapons as opposed to a sharp or blunt striking object up close (Jurmain et al., 2009). Studying skeletal remains has also led to evidence supporting the possibility of cannibalistic funerary rituals in some ancient European tribes who lived approximately 12,000–17,000 years ago (Bello et al., 2017).

Using archaeological records to study the evolution human diet and social behavior has received a number of criticisms. Critics have argued that many archaeological conclusions are based on insufficient evidence and that archaeologists fail to adequately consider alternative explanations for their findings (Boyd, 1996). Also, making inferences about the social behavior of humans from 50,000–200,000 years ago based on skeletal remains and other archaeological evidence is extremely difficult (Foley, 2001), and such inferences should be made carefully.

Although some individuals may be skeptical to accept conclusions made by archaeologists, this archaeological record continues to be a source of data providing physical evidence of human evolution. While inferences regarding human social behavior may be difficult to derive from skeletal remains and archaic structures, new techniques for archaeological data collection continue to develop. In fact, some archaeologists have been able to obtain viable samples of DNA from ancient skeletal remains (see Jones, 2003, for a review), allowing for more in-depth analyses of biological and epidemiological factors associated with prehistoric humans' lifestyle. Similarly, technological advancements now allow archaeologists to conduct multiscalar studies that have provided new understandings in the development of human societies (Smith et al., 2012).

OBSERVATIONS OF MODERN-DAY HUNTER-GATHERER SOCIETIES

Observational research is a scientific method that involves directly watching and studying individuals, usually in their natural habitat (Bernard, 2012). Observational research methods comprise three basic types: (1) the naturalistic observation – a usually qualitative measurement design that involves observing a group of humans or non-human animals with little to no interference from the researcher (see Goodall, 1986, for an example of naturalistically observing chimpanzees); (2) the controlled (or structured) observation – systematically studying participants' responses to scientifically manipulated variables usually while in a scientific laboratory (see Bandura et al.,1963, for an example); and (3) the participant observation, which occurs when the researcher responsible for observing a particular group also becomes a participating member of the group that s/he is studying (see Festinger et al., 1956, for an example). There are benefits and limitations associated with all three types of observational research, but observational research of modern-day hunter-gatherer societies have largely been naturalistic.

Researchers have conducted naturalistic observations of modern-day hunter-gatherer, forager, pastoral and hunter-horticulturalist societies across the world. Although current hunter-gatherer societies are not exact representations of ancestral hunter-gatherer life, studying modern-day hunter-gatherer cultures and behaviors has allowed psychologists and anthropologists to learn about the ways humans behave without the influence of post-industrialization technology (Buss, 2015). By observing the way modern-day hunter-gatherers live, researchers have been able to evaluate several evolutionary psychological theories related to a variety of behaviors, including sexual attraction, mate selection and retention, familial relations, reciprocity, aggression, as well as diet and cooking (Draper and Hames,

2000; Hagen et al., 2001; Hill and Hurtado, 2017; Hurtado and Hill, 1992; Marlowe, 1999, 2003, 2004; Wrangham, 2009).

Data from observations of modern-day hunter-gatherers has allowed scientists to make cross-cultural comparisons regarding people's attitudes, preferences, and behaviors; and these comparisons have helped scientists better understand cultural influences of human behavior as well. For example, evolutionary psychologists have studied mate preferences in various cultures around the world, including humans from industrialized nations as well as humans from modern-day hunter-gatherer societies. While some cultural differences exist (Furnham et al., 2002; Marlowe, 2004; Pillsworth, 2008; Wetsman and Marlowe, 1999), many observations of hunter-gatherer tribes have found supportive evidence for sexual selection theory, which also corroborates the large body of scientific research on sexual selection in humans from industrialized cultures (e.g., college students) (Buss, 1989). Specifically, observations of mate preferences in modern-day hunter-gatherer societies indicate that male humans usually value physical attractiveness in a potential mate – such as a symmetrical face (Little et al., 2007) and a waist-to-hip ratio equal to 0.70 – over other qualities, while female humans place a greater importance on a potential mate's character (e.g., kindness and nurturance) (Marlowe, 2004) and social status – such as wealth and social prestige (Mulder, 1987). These mate preferences have also been consistently observed in undergraduate student samples in the United States (Singh, 1993; Singh et al., 2010; Sprecher et al., 1994), the UK (Little et al., 2007), Australia (Koehler et al., 2002), Germany (Henss, 1995), China (Chang et al., 2015), and many other industrialized and non-industrialized nations (Buss, 1989).

Evolutionary theories regarding familial relations – such as parental investment theory, paternity uncertainty, and kin selection – have been observed and supported in the observations of many modern-day hunter-gatherer societies. For instance, researchers found support for parental investment theory while observing food allocation among the Yanomamö society of Upper Orinoco region of Venezuela shortly after the 1998 el Niño storm (Hagen et al., 2001). Similarly, paternal investment, marriage, and divorce rates have been studied via observations of the Ache of southeastern Paraguay (Hill and Hurtado, 2017; Hurtado and Hill, 1992), the Hiwi of southwestern Venezuela (Hurtado and Hill, 1992), the Hadza of northern Tanzania (Blurton-Jones et al., 2000; Marlowe, 1999, 2003, 2004), and the !Kung of Botswana (Draper and Hames, 2000). In fact, observations of the Ache tribe revealed that mated couples with offspring received help (e.g., food provisions, offspring care, etc.) from an average of 1.3 non-reproductive adults (e.g., grandparents), and that young adult males almost all excess food provisions to mated couples with offspring (Hill and Hurtado, 2009).

Researchers have also studied childhood social learning in modern-day hunter-gatherer tribes by observing and interviewing the Aka and Bofi groups in central Africa. Parents begin teaching various cultural practices when their children reach 12 months of age. Children learn mostly from their parents until they are approximately 6 years old. From ages 6–12 years, children learn from both kin and non-kin within their group (Hewlett et al., 2011).

Observing modern-day hunter-gatherers has also helped researchers understand the evolutionary mechanisms underlying interpersonal and intergroup violence in humans. It is theorized that intergroup violence (i.e., coalitional aggression or 'warfare') evolved as a strategic means of acquiring resources and maximizing one's direct and inclusive fitness (see Kruger and Fitzgerald, 2012, for a review). This is evident in the observations of the Yanomamö, in which men often reap social and reproductive rewards (e.g., higher social status, more wives, and stronger social bonds with other males) for engaging in homicide and coalitional aggression (Chagnon, 1988; Macfarlan et al., 2014).

Naturalistic observations of modern-day hunter-gatherer, forager, and horticulturalist societies are not simply limited to sex and violence. Observing what foods these individuals prepare and consume has provided valuable insight into the evolution of the human diet and nutrition, the shape of human teeth, and the invention of cooking. All of which has sparked theories regarding the evolution of social behavior among humans as a function of food sharing (see Wrangham, 2009, for a review).

Observational research methods are not without their flaws (Bernard, 2012). Naturalistic observations have been criticized for utilizing small scale observations of groups, which may lead to lack of sample representativeness and generalizability. Also, because variables cannot be controlled or manipulated, naturalistic observers cannot make inferences regarding causality. In regards to naturalistic observations of modern-day hunter-gatherers, critics have noted that researchers sometimes fallaciously assume there is little to no difference between ancestral and modern-day hunter-gatherers (Testart, 1988), and similarities between the two should not be inferred without a definitive way of knowing the extent to which today's hunter-gatherers are similar to ancestral humans.

Observational research of modern-day hunter-gatherers, foragers, pastoralists, and hunter-horticulturists has provided corroborative evidence for several evolutionary psychological theories. However, as with any scientific method, there are limitations in utilizing an observational research method. Similarly, naturalistic observations of modern-day hunter-gatherers has helped psychologists and anthropologists better understand human behavior without the influence of modern-day technology, but researchers must be careful when interpreting observational data so as not to make inferences, such as causality or intention, without proper evidence. For more ethnographic data on modern-day

hunter-gatherer tribes, see the Standard Cross-Cultural Sample (Murdock and White, 1969, 2006), which contains detailed information on 186 cultures across the world.

SELF-REPORT

The Self-Report method refers to the acquisition of data via direct request to participants. This request for information often manifests as a survey/questionnaire or interview. Surveys and interviews contain highly structured items that are designed to obtain relevant information from participants, usually in a manner that maintains the participants' anonymity as well as the confidentiality of their responses. These items may be in the form of questions or statements, and the format in which participants respond to these items may be open-ended or closed-ended. Open-ended items usually allow participants to respond in their own words – allowing researchers to obtain large amounts of qualitative data from their sample – while closed-ended items provide a set of specific responses from which participants must select in order to respond. These responses are often in the forced-choice form, in which a participant must select one response from a series of two or more response options. These can range from simple 'Yes/No' questions to larger rating scales, such as the Likert scale – a rating scale that requests participants to indicate their level of agreement with a particular statement by selecting a number on a 5-point scale (i.e., 1 = strongly disagree, 2 = disagree, 3 = neutral, 4 = agree, 5 = strongly disagree) (Likert, 1932). While the range of points can vary from scale to scale, the number of points used on a scale is usually limited to odd numbers (e.g., 5-point scales, 7-point scales, 9-point scales, etc.) to allow for a single-digit middle/neutral point (Allen and Seaman, 2007). Closed-ended items may also be presented as a Visual Analog Scale, which involves having a participant respond by providing a mark on a continuous line that contains two end points. A visual analog scale is often used to assess an individual's perception of a subjective phenomenon, such as pain or nausea (Bijur et al., 2001; Bovbjerg et al., 1990).

Evolutionary psychologists have utilized the self-report method to obtain data from undergraduate participants for over 30 years (Buss, 1988). Many influential theories in evolutionary psychology have either stemmed from, or been supported by, the data obtained from self-report measures. For instance, Buss et al. (1992) utilized a forced-choice self-report measure to obtain and provide the first evidence for the idea that romantic jealousy stems from sexual selection theory. Buss's original method involved asking undergraduate participants to indicate which of the following two options caused them greater distress: (A) imagining their romantic partner engaging in sexual infidelity, or (B) imagining their romantic partner engaging in emotional infidelity. Findings from this study revealed a significantly greater number of men were more distressed by imagining their partner's sexual infidelity, whereas a significantly greater number of women were more distressed by imagining their partner's emotional infidelity. These findings have been replicated several times with a wide variety of self-report measures including open-ended items (Guitar et al., 2015) and closed-ended items with different rating scales (Kruger et al., 2013, 2015).

Lu and Chang (2014) found support for Trivers' (1976) self-deception theory by having participants report previously studied items. Participants were instructed to deceive either a high-status individual (i.e., a teacher) or an equal-status individual (i.e., a fellow student) regarding their knowledge of Chinese characters, then complete a memory test. In sum, the students correctly remembered fewer items on their test when in the presence of a high-status individual (i.e., a teacher) than when they were alone or in the presence of a fellow student – indicating more distorted memories when in the presence of high-status others.

Many other influential evolutionary psychological theories – including, but not limited to, sexual selection (Buss, 1988), mate retention (Symons, 1979), kin selection (Hamilton, 1964), and reciprocal altruism (e.g., sharing; Trivers, 1971) – have also been studied and supported via self-report measures. For instance, sexual selection has been studied by simply asking undergraduate participants what qualities they find most attractive in a potential mate (Weiderman and Allgeier, 1992). This research has revealed a significant difference between what men and women value when searching for a mate – men strongly value physical attractiveness in their mates, and women tend to value status and nurturance over physical attractiveness (Buss, 1989; Weiderman and Allgeier, 1992). Many researchers have used self-report measures to survey undergraduate participants regarding various mating and mate retention behaviors (Holden et al., 2014; Kaighobadi et al., 2008, 2010). These researchers found evidence indicating males and females engage in a wide variety of mate retention behaviors – including positive behaviors such as gift-giving and providing physical, verbal, and emotional affection, as well as negative behaviors such as mate denigration and jealousy.

Many researchers have studied inclusive fitness theory and kin selection theory by asking undergraduate participants to indicate how frequently they have engaged in various altruistic behaviors toward family members, friends, and acquaintances (Kruger, 2001, 2003; Stewart-Williams, 2007, 2008). When assessing the likelihood of engaging in life-threatening altruistic actions, self-report measures include hypothetical scenarios that ask the participant to imagine a dangerous situation and indicate their likelihood of saving the distressed individual in the dangerous situation by responding to a closed-ended rating scale such as a Likert scale (e.g., Imagine your sister is trapped in a burning house. If you try to save her, there is a 50% chance you will die. Please indicate your likelihood of saving your sister on the scale below) (Burnstein et al., 1994; Fitzgerald et al., 2010). Data from several self-report studies indicate that individuals are significantly more likely to save their close kin (e.g., siblings, parents) over distant kin (e.g., cousins, aunts, uncles, grandparents) and non-kin (e.g., friends, acquaintances, strangers), which supports kin selection theory (Burnstein et al., 1994; Fitzgerald and Colarelli, 2009; Fitzgerald et al., 2010; Kruger, 2001, 2003; Stewart-Williams, 2007, 2008). Self-report measures have also found that individuals are more likely to help friends over kin, because of the expectation of reciprocity, when the altruistic action is not life-threatening (Stewart-Williams, 2007).

While the self-report method often provides a reliable, convenient, and low-cost mode of data collection for evolutionary psychologists, critics of the self-report method have voiced concerns over its use. Critics have noted that participants may be too embarrassed or ashamed to reveal personal information, which can lead to the *social desirability bias* – instead of responding honestly, participants may provide responses they believe are more socially acceptable (King and Bruner, 2000). Other internal psychological factors, such as *demand characteristics* and *observation effects*, may also increase dishonest responding (see Hand and Fitzgerald, 2014, for a review). Some individuals have also criticized evolutionary psychologists' use of self-report measures and the inferences evolutionary psychologists have derived from self-report data. Specifically, critics have argued that one cannot draw any conclusion of ancient hunter-gatherer behavior from the behavior of modern-day college students (Buller, 2006).

While self-report methods have often been used to test evolutionary psychological hypotheses, several valid criticisms of the method exist. Although these criticisms should not be ignored, they also illustrate the importance of obtaining data from other sources to help study human behavior from an evolutionary perspective. Finding corroborative evidence from other sources and methods will only help researchers more accurately understand how evolution has shaped human behavior.

SYSTEMATIC OBSERVATIONS OF INDIVIDUALS IN PUBLIC PLACES

Systematic observation is another potential source for data collection. This particular method of data collection is marked by an objective and regimented set of criteria to be recorded and examined for interpretation. With this particular observational method, clear and objective specifications can lead to a number of researchers being able to provide unbiased data on a chosen topic (Reiss, 1971). Specifications of observations provides precise directions as to how data should be recorded. Data may include exact overt behaviors, physical attributes, or any other potential variables in which information is desired.

Systematic observation has been used abundantly with regards to sports coaching styles. Football (Lacy and Darst, 1985), basketball (Bloom et al., 1999), soccer (Cushion and Jones, 2001), and tennis (Claxton, 1988) coaches were systematically observed to monitor behaviors. Bloom and associates (1999), through systematic observation, were able to identify common coaching techniques used by a specific expert coach. This information could inform what techniques that particular individual was using and responses to those techniques. This could help determine what techniques to use in the future. Other research had been conducted by observing several coaches and their coaching techniques. These measures compare and contrast what these different highly successful coaches had been doing and locating the commonalities among successful coaching programs (Claxton, 1988; Cushion and Jones, 2001; Lacy and Darst, 1985).

Public policing has also undergone systematic observation (Mastrofski et al., 1998). The authors looked at numerous activities of police officers and the percentage of time spent on activities during typical shifts. For example, they compared different departments and different officer positions with how much time was given to different tasks. Department A involved beat officers and community police officers; Department B consisted of generalist officers and community police officers. They compared the amount of time that was spent on very specific tasks. Tasks included encounters with citizens, moving to a location, problem directed tasks, information gathering, administrative duties, general patrol, and personal duties. Through this particular research method, public policy can be formed or shifted. This particular study shows that officer time allocation, officer mobilization, the use of police authority, amount of street-level supervision, and patterns of policing can all be systematically observed and policy changes can be created to maximize efficiency.

Systematic observation of public spaces can also provide insights into human behavior. Sampson and Raudenbush (1999) used systematic observation to gauge the sources and costs of public disorder. The authors recorded and rated roughly 23,000 street sections in Chicago. From the data collected, they were able to create social and physical disorder scales for 196 neighborhoods. They found that, after controlling for neighborhood structural characteristics, collective efficacy was able to explain lower crime rates and observed disorder. Another study was conducted to evaluate physical activity in Brazilian public parks (Parra et al., 2010). The authors used systematic observation for play and recreation in communities (SOPARC). Through this method, they were able to observe 128 targeted areas. They were able to collect data from 32,974 individuals from a total of 5,589 observations. Observations led to identifying which parks were used for more vigorous activities as well as the age and gender of those that patronized the different parks.

Mark Flinn (1988; Flinn et al., 2005) used systematic observation for behavior scanning in a Caribbean village. Every day he would walk through the village of interest and visit each home. From this he monitored specific behaviors, such as mate guarding. He would record his observations on a record sheet and was able to confirm his hypothesis. For example, males with more fertile wives would increase mate guarding whereas males with less fertile wives would engage in less mate guarding. Males with more fertile wives would engage in more fights than those whose wife was pregnant or not fertile. Through these behavioral scans, he could directly observe the behaviors and others could be trained to objectively observe and collect data.

Pawlowski et al. (2008) observed people crossing a busy road and trying to catch their bus to find supportive evidence for sexual selection theory. Because sexual selection theory states that men will engage in more risky behaviors than women, the researchers posited that men may be more likely than women to cross busy roads when it is risky to do so, and will be more likely to arrive at their bus stop as late as possible (to minimize wait time) and run the risk of missing their bus. To test these hypotheses, Pawlowski and colleagues observed people crossing a busy street, and observed people at a particular bus stop, in Liverpool, UK. Their observations supported their hypotheses – men were more likely than women to cross the busy street at risky times, and men arrived at the bus stop later than women.

As technology evolves, research methods evolve as well. Google Street View has been used as a method to systematically observe neighborhoods (Odgers et al., 2012). The authors used a virtual systematic observational method. They wanted to discover if Google Street View could produce reliable observations of neighborhood conditions. Various raters coded images of neighborhoods. These coded images were compared to local resident surveys that assessed children's antisocial and proso-cial behaviors, as well as body mass index and general health. Agreement of signs of physical disorder, decay, street safety, and dangerousness were high. Interrater agree-ment assessments were also in the substan-tial range. Overall, Google Street View was viewed as a reliable and cost effective means for measuring features of neighborhoods.

Overall, systematic observation can be used in a variety of settings. Sports, teaching, public policy, and mating behaviors can all be objectively observed. With the systematic approach, time and effort can be saved by allowing multiple individuals to track behav-iors for clear and objective data collection.

HISTORICAL PUBLIC RECORDS

Another way to collect data would be through public records. Public records can include birth certificates, death certificates, marriage licenses, certificates of divorce, mugshots, criminal records, etc. These records can shed light on gender differences in mortality rates throughout human history (Kruger and Nesse, 2006), mating preferences for females (Buss and Shackelford, 2008), overall mating habits (Low, 1991), and so on. With new developments in technology and communi-cation, the ability to obtain public records has dramatically increased.

Kruger and Nesse (2006) were investigat-ing the male-to-female mortality ratio. The authors did this from both internal and exter-nal causes. They also took into account con-texts so that the influences of sexual selection combined with environment factors could show a consistent pattern. Death records were used to collect data. These records pro-vided valuable information, such as how old the individual was at the time of death and cause of death. Using archival death records, they were able to ascertain that British males

born in the period 1330–1949 typically had a shorter life expectancy than their female counterparts. While the advent of vaccines and sanitation may have decreased the likeli-hood of death due to infectious disease, other more novel causes of death have appeared. Weapons, tobacco, vehicles, dietary fats, etc., have increased as potential causes of death. They also note that male and female mortal-ity rates have been increasingly incongruent in developed nations over the 20th century (Lopez, 1998; Zhang et al., 1995). Overall, this discrepancy stems from riskier behav-iors becoming more prominent causes of death and these causes pose higher risks for males. This could be due to social norms that encourage males to commit riskier behaviors in order to obtain resources and status, thus increasing their chances to obtain a mate. Authors also identified that internal causes of mortality were higher for males as well. Previous research concluded that males were more vulnerable to infection, injury, stress, and degenerative diseases (Kraemer, 2000). Hazzard (1990) had found that these differences could be the result of structural, physiological, immunological systems, and endocrinological differences.

Buss and Shackelford (2008) used the public records of marriage licenses issued to obtain participants for their study on women and a potential adaptive calibration system for mate preferences. Through this, they were able to obtain 107 couples – 214 individuals – for their study. They hypothesized that women may have an internal system to raise or lower their standards for mates depending on their own perceived value as a mate. As physical attractiveness is the distinctive characteristic of mate value, observers evaluated the physi-cal attractiveness of the women in the study – face, body, and overall attractiveness. The findings suggested that women who were rated as more attractive had typically higher standards for their mates. There were posi-tive correlations for more attractive women to increase their desired standard of manli-ness and sexiness, sources of income, desire for children and to provide for those children, and being a loving partner.

Low (1991) used the methodically kept records of marriages, divorces, and remarriages from multiple parishes in Sweden. The priests of these parishes were meticulous in providing detail and accuracy in these documented public events. Upon discovery of these records, Low was able to notice patterns from roughly 400 years ago. Low was able to compare these patterns with patterns of marriage, divorce, and remarriage in more recent days. From these comparisons of public records, she was able to test evolutionary hypotheses. For example, she was able to corroborate that men of greater wealth and status had a tendency to marry younger, and thus more fertile women. Males that were poorer and of lower status tended to marry older and consequently less fertile women.

Advancements in technology have altered the way we are able to obtain historical public records. Websites such as ancestry.com have made this form of data more accessible. Being able to communicate with various countries, states, and districts has made it easier to request this form of data. Digital records now make it easier to record and code data. There is a plethora of information available at the fingertips of researchers.

Public records can provide great detail into the evolution of human behavior. Data about marriage, divorce, and death produce tremendous amounts of data for scientists to analyze and answer important questions, especially when combined with other sources of data.

HUMAN PRODUCTS

The things that we humans generate are the creation of our evolved minds (Buss, 2015). The products that humans have created allow for us to satiate our basic needs and desires. Fast-food restaurants, dating services, gyms, various sources of media – movies, television, and novels – and social media can provide data showing how we have evolved.

Historical literature has provided great details into various evolved mating strategies. Kruger et al. (2003) found that proper heroes and dark heroes in romantic British literature represented two distinctly different mating strategies. Proper heroes were typically nonviolent, and lower in traits of dominance. When women were asked about the dating strategy of these types of heroes, they showed a preference for long-term mating and they were more labeled as 'dads'. Dark heroes were more eccentric, rebellious, and violent. When women were asked about the dating strategy of these types of heroes, they showed a preference for a more short-term mating and were labeled as 'cads'. Carroll et al. (2012) had Jane Austen novel characters rated by 519 scholars over the internet. They rated the characters by motive, criteria for mate selection, personality, and emotional responses of readers. They found that antagonists were more dominant in their traits and threatened community cooperativeness. The protagonists were those that typically formed communities and fostered group cohesion.

Fast-food establishments provide a great example of human products coming from our evolved minds. The food served – pizza, hamburgers, French fries, sodas, ice cream, milk shakes – are filled with sugar, salt, proteins, and fats. These products take advantage of our evolved tastes for these items. During the hunter-gatherer days of humanity, these items provided higher caloric content that humans needed to survive lean times. Because humans needed these calories, the taste of high calorie food became desirable. Now, fast-food restaurants seize upon these evolved tastes. As high calorie food has become more prevalent, so have gyms. Humans do not have to physically work as hard to obtain food and other resources.

High calorie food with little exercise has become an issue for many individuals in industrialized countries. Gyms and gym equipment allow for us to physically work out bodies and remain fit in case of a fight-or-flight emergency or to have a body that is more likely to attract a high quality mate.

Pornography can be used to have an understanding of what humans find attractive; it can also satiate our sexual desires. Magazines, movies, and internet sites can be used to see body shapes and sizes for what we find attractive in potential mates. Bovet and Raymond (2015) used *Playboy* models from the 1920s to 2014 to measure the preferred waist-to-hip ratio (WHR). They compared these models with artwork ranging from 500 BCE to recent times and found that the ideal WHR has fluctuated over the past 2,500 years. Websites like Pornhub.com have kept meticulous data about pornographic searches. This type of information can give ideas about what is found to be sexually desirable for mating.

Dating services have become prevalent in our attempts to secure a mate. From posting personal advertisements in newspapers or magazines, followed by creating video advertisements, to now setting up dating profiles on websites and phone applications, this form of human product has increased the opportunities by increasing the pool of possible mates. In the past, humans were relegated to people that were only physically near them. Advances in travel made it possible to expand the mating pool to new locations. The printing press and published word made it possible to expand the mating pool to people that they may have never met otherwise. As circulation of the printed word increased, so did mating opportunities. Being able to record a video could allow individuals to physically see a potential mate. Newer technology and mass communication has further changed opportunities for obtaining a mate. Websites and phone applications make it easier to discern which type of mating strategy one should use. Websites like match.com and eharmony.com advertise for more long-term mating strategies. Adultfriendfinder.com and applications like Tinder are typically used for more short-term mating strategies.

Social media is a more recent human product. Facebook, reddit, Instagram, and Twitter are only a few examples of social media. Social media allows us to maintain our ingroups at long distances, which allows us to find others that are similar and continue to feel that we are part of a group. Humans have a need to belong to groups; without belonging to a group, humans were less likely to survive. Social media allows us to find similar others and communicate directly with them over long distances in a short amount of time. This allows us to keep up with trends and what others that belong to our ingroup community are doing, so that we can do the same to show our support for our particular ingroups. Because we are social animals, the creation of social media has become increasingly popular and allows for an abundance of data to be collected.

Overall, human products can provide great insights into the evolved human mind. Restaurants, pornography, dating services, gyms, media, and social media can show how our minds have evolved over time. The creation of these products serve our basic needs and desires. Advances in technology continue to change the way that we consume these products and has increased the amount of data that is available for a creative scientist to analyze. Human products, paired with other sources of data, can provide a better understanding of evolutionary behavioral hypotheses.

CONCLUSION

This chapter focused on six primary sources of data for testing evolutionary psychological hypotheses – archaeological records, observations of modern-day hunter-gatherer cultures, self-report measures, observations of behavior in public places, historical public records, and human products. While these six sources of data have provided valuable insight into humans' evolutionary history, and have allowed for the testing of countless evolutionary psychological hypotheses, other scientific methods for testing evolutionary hypotheses continue to develop. Advances in behavioral genetics research have led to discoveries regarding the heritability of the Big Five personality traits (i.e., extraversion, agreeableness, openness, conscientiousness, and neuroticism) as well as personality disorders and dissociative disorders (Lo et al., 2017; Ripke et al., 2014; Sanchez-Roige et al., 2018; Weinberger, 2019). Similarly, twin studies, family studies, and adoption studies allow researchers to compare similarities and differences between genetically-related individuals to help further understand and differentiate genetic influences (i.e., nature) from environmental ones (i.e., nurture) (Segal, 2017; Tellegen et al., 1988). All sources of data discussed in this chapter continue to be utilized for testing evolutionary hypotheses. As our knowledge of human evolution continues to grow, and scientific technology continues to advance, our collective understanding of human evolution and our ancestral past will continue to develop – helping us to better understand and improve our physiology, behavior, and culture.

REFERENCES

Allen, I. E., & Seaman, C. A. (2007). Likert scales and data analyses. *Quality Progress*, *40*, 64–65.

Bandura, A., Ross, D., & Ross, S. A. (1963). Imitation of film-mediated aggressive models. *The Journal of Abnormal and Social Psychology*, *66*(1), 3–11.

Bello, S. M., Wallduck, R., Parfitt, S. A., & Stringer, C. B. (2017). An Upper Palaeolithic engraved human bone associated with ritualistic cannibalism. *PloS ONE*, *12*(8), e0182127.

Bernard, H. R. (2012). *Social research methods: Qualitative and quantitative approaches*. Thousand Oaks, CA: Sage.

Bijur, P. E., Silver, W., & Gallagher, E. J. (2001). Reliability of the visual analog scale for measurement of acute pain. *Academic Emergency Medicine*, *8*(12), 1153–1157.

Bloom, G. A., Crumpton, R., & Anderson, J. E. (1999). A systematic observation study of the teaching behaviors of an expert basketball coach. *The Sports Psychologist*, *13*(2), 157–170.

Blurton Jones, N. G., Marlowe, F. W., Hawkes, K., & O'Connell, J. F. (2000). Paternal investment and hunter-gatherer divorce rates. In L. Cronk, N. Chagnon & W. Irons (Eds), *Adaptation and human behavior: An anthropological perspective* (pp. 69–90). New York: Aldine.

Bovbjerg, D. H., Redd, W. H., Maier, L. A., Holland, J. C., Lesko, L. M., Niedzwiecki, D., Rubin, S. C., & Hakes, T. B. (1990). Anticipatory immune suppression and nausea in women receiving cyclic chemotherapy for ovarian cancer. *Journal of Consulting and Clinical Psychology*, *58*(2), 153–157.

Bovet, J., & Raymond, M. (2015). Preferred women's waist-to-hip ratio variation over the last 2.500 years. *PLoS ONE*, *10*(4), e0123284. doi: 10.1371/journal.pone.0123284.

Boyd, D. C. (1996). Skeletal correlates of human behavior in the Americas. *Journal of Archaeological Method and Theory*, *3*(3), 189–251.

Buller, D. J. (2006). *Adapting minds: Evolutionary psychology and the persistent quest for human nature*. Cambridge, MA: MIT Press.

Burnstein, E., Crandall, C., & Kitayama, S. (1994). Some neo-Darwinian rules for altruism: Weighing cues for inclusive fitness as a function of the biological importance of the decision. *Journal of Personality and Social Psychology*, *67*(5), 773–789.

Buss, D. M. (1988). The evolution of human intrasexual competition: Tactics of mate attraction. *Journal of Personality and Social Psychology*, *54*(4), 616–628.

Buss, D. M. (1989). Sex differences in human mate preferences: Evolutionary hypotheses tested in 37 cultures. *Behavioral and Brain Sciences*, *12*(1), 1–14.

Buss, D. (2015). *Evolutionary psychology: The new science of the mind (5th ed.)*. New York: Taylor & Francis.

Buss, D. M., and Shackelford, T. K. (2008). Attractive women want it all: Good genes, economic investment, parenting proclivities, and emotional commitment. *Evolutionary Psychology*, *6*(1), 134–146.

Buss, D. M., Larsen, R. J., Westen, D., & Semmelroth, J. (1992). Sex differences in jealousy: Evolution, physiology, and psychology. *Psychological Science*, *3*(4), 251–256.

Carroll, J., Gottschall, J., Johnson, J. A., & Kruger, D. J. (2012). *Graphing Jane Austen: The evolutionary basis of literary meaning.* New York: Springer.

Chagnon, N. A. (1988). Life histories, blood revenge, and warfare in a tribal population. *Science*, *239*(4843), 985–992.

Chang, L., Wang, Y., Shackelford, T. K., & Buss, D. M. (2011). Chinese mate preferences: Cultural evolution and continuity across a quarter of a century. *Personality and Individual Differences*, *50*(5), 678–683.

Claxton, D. B. (1988). A systematic observation of more and less successful high school tennis coaches. *Journal of Teaching in Physical Education*, *7*(4), 302–310.

Cordain, L., Eaton, S. B., Miller, J. B., Mann, N., & Hill, K. (2002). The paradoxical nature of hunter-gatherer diets: Meat-based, yet non-atherogenic. *European Journal of Clinical Nutrition*, *56*(S1), S42–S52.

Cushion, C. J., & Jones, R. L. (2001). A systematic observation of professional top-level youth soccer coaches. *Journal of Sport Behavior*, *24*(4), 354–376.

Draper, P., & Hames, R. (2000). Birth order, sibling investment, and fertility among Ju/'hoansi (!Kung). *Human Nature*, *11*(2), 117–156.

Festinger, L., Reicken, H. W., & Schachter, S. (1956). *When prophecy fails: A social and psychological study of a modern group that predicted the destruction of the world.* Minneapolis, MN: University of Minnesota Press.

Fitzgerald, C. J., & Colarelli, S. M. (2009). Altruism and reproductive limitations. *Evolutionary Psychology*, *7*(2), 234–252.

Fitzgerald, C. J., Thompson, M. C., & Whitaker, M. B. (2010). Altruism between romantic partners: Biological offspring as a genetic bridge between altruist and recipient. *Evolutionary Psychology*, *8*(3), 462–476.

Flinn, M. V. (1988). Mate guarding in a Caribbean village. *Evolution and Human Behavior*, *9*(1), 1–28.

Flinn, M. V., Ward, C. V., & Noone, R. (2005). Hormones and the human family. In D. M. Buss (Ed.), *Handbook of evolutionary psychology.* New York: Wiley.

Foley, R. (2001). Evolutionary perspectives on the origins of human social institutions. *Proceedings of the British Academy*, *110*, 171–195.

Furnham, A., Moutafi, J., & Baguma, P. (2002). A cross-cultural study on the role of weight and waist-to-hip ratio on female attractiveness. *Personality and Individual Differences*, *32*(4), 729–745.

Goodall, J. (1986). *The chimpanzees of Gombe.* Cambridge: Cambridge University Press.

Gowlett, J., Gamble, C., Dunbar, R., with Barnard, A., Bar-Yosef, O., Pettitt, P., Wadley, L., Wang, Y., & Wynn, T. (2012). Human evolution and the archaeology of the social brain. *Current Anthropology*, *53*(6), 693–722.

Guitar, A. E., Geher, G., Kruger, D. J., Garcia, J. R., Fisher, M. L., & Fitzgerald, C. J. (2017). Defining and distinguishing sexual and emotional infidelity. *Current Psychology*, *36*(3), 434–446.

Hagen, E. H., Hames, R. B., Craig, N M., Lauer, M. T., & Price, M. E. (2001). Parental investment and child health in a Yanomamö village suffering short-term food stress. *Journal of Biosocial Science*, *33*(4), 503–528.

Hamilton, W. D. (1964). The genetical evolution of social behaviour I. *Journal of Theoretical Biology*, *7*(1), 1–16.

Hand, D. J., & Fitzgerald, C. J. (2014). Honest baseline behavior. In T. R. Levine & J. G. Golson (Eds), *Encyclopedia of deception* (pp. 481–484). Thousand Oaks, CA: Sage.

Hazzard, W. R. (1990). The sex differential in longevity. In W. R. Hazzard, R. Andres, E. L. Bierman, & J. P. Blass (Eds), *Principles of geriatric medicine and gerontology (2nd ed.)* (pp. 37–47). New York: McGraw Hill.

Henss, R. (1995). Waist-to-hip ratio and attractiveness: Replication and extension. *Personality and Individual Differences*, *19*(4), 479–488.

Hewlett, B. S., Fouts, H. N., Boyette, A. H., & Hewlett, B. L. (2011). Social learning among Congo Basin hunter-gatherers. *Philosophical Transactions of the Royal Society B: Biological Sciences*, *366*(1567), 1168–1178.

Hill, K., & Hurtado, A. M. (2009). Cooperative breeding in South American hunter-gatherers.

Proceedings of the Royal Society of London. B: Biological Sciences, 276(1674), 3863–3870.

Hill, K., & Hurtado, A. M. (2017). *Ache life history: The ecology and demography of a foraging people*. London: Routledge.

Holden, C. J., Zeigler-Hill, V., Pham, M. N., & Shackelford, T. K. (2014). Personality features and mate retention strategies: Honesty–humility and the willingness to manipulate, deceive, and exploit romantic partners. *Personality and Individual Differences, 57,* 31–36.

Hurtado, A. M., & Hill, K. R. (1992). Paternal effect on offspring survivorship among Ache and Hiwi hunter-gatherers: Implications for modeling pair-bond stability. In B. S. Hewlett (Ed.), *Foundations of human behavior. Father–child relations: Cultural and biosocial contexts* (pp. 31–55). Hawthorne, NY: Aldine.

Jones, M. (2003). Ancient DNA in pre-Columbian archaeology: A review. *Journal of Archaeological Science, 30*(5), 629–635.

Judd, M. (2002). Ancient injury recidivism: An example from the Kerma period of ancient Nubia. *International Journal of Osteoarchaeology, 12*(2), 89–106.

Judd, M. (2004). Trauma in the city of Kerma: Ancient versus modern injury patterns. *International Journal of Osteoarchaeology, 14*(1), 34–51.

Jurmain, R., Leventhal, A. M., Bartelink, E. J., Leventhal, A., Bellifemine, V., Nechayev, I., Atwood, M., & DiGiuseppe, D. (2009). Paleoepidemiological patterns of interpersonal aggression in a prehistoric central California population from CA-ALA-329. *American Journal of Physical Anthropology: The Official Publication of the American Association of Physical Anthropologists, 139*(4), 462–473.

Kaighobadi, F., Shackelford, T. K., & Buss, D. M. (2010). Spousal mate retention in the newlywed year and three years later. *Personality and Individual Differences, 48*(4), 414–418.

Kaighobadi, F., Starratt, V. G., Shackelford, T. K., & Popp, D. (2008). Male mate retention mediates the relationship between female sexual infidelity and female-directed violence. *Personality and Individual Differences, 44*(6), 1422–1431.

King, M. F., & Bruner, G. C. (2000). Social desirability bias: A neglected aspect of validity testing. *Psychology & Marketing, 17*(2), 79–103.

Koehler, N., Rhodes, G., & Simmons, L. W. (2002). Are human female preferences for symmetrical male faces enhanced when conception is likely? *Animal Behaviour, 64*(2), 233–238.

Kraemer, S. (2000). The fragile male. *British Medical Journal, 321*(7276), 1609–1612.

Kruger, D. J. (2001). Psychological aspects of adaptations for kin directed altruistic helping behaviors. *Social Behavior and Personality, 29*(4), 323–330.

Kruger, D. J. (2003). Evolution and altruism: Combining psychological mediators with naturally selected tendencies. *Evolution and Human Behavior, 24*(2), 118–125.

Kruger, D. J., Fisher, M. L., Edelstein, R. S., Chopik, W. J., Fitzgerald, C. J., & Strout, S. L. (2013). Was that cheating? Perceptions vary by sex, attachment anxiety, and behavior. *Evolutionary Psychology, 11*(1), 159–171.

Kruger, D. J., Fisher, M. L., Fitzgerald, C. J., Garcia, J. R., Geher, G., & Guitar, A. E. (2015). Sexual and emotional aspects are distinct components of infidelity and unique predictors of anticipated distress. *Evolutionary Psychological Science, 1*(1), 44–51.

Kruger, D. J., Fisher, M., & Jobling, I. (2003). Proper and dark heroes as dads and cads. *Human Nature, 14*(3), 305–317.

Kruger, D. J., & Fitzgerald, C. J. (2012). Evolutionary perspectives on male–male competition, violence, and homicide. In T. K. Shackelford & V. Weekes-Shackelford (Eds), *Oxford handbook of evolutionary perspectives on violence, homicide, and war* (pp. 153–170). New York: Oxford University Press.

Kruger, D. J., & Nesse, R. M. (2006). An evolutionary life-history framework for understanding sex differences in human mortality rates. *Human Nature, 17*(1), 74–97.

Lacy, A. C., & Darst, P. W. (1985). Systematic observation of behaviors of winning high school head football coaches. *Journal of Teaching in Physical Education, 4*(4), 256–270.

Leonard, W. R., Snodgrass, J. J., & Robertson, M. L. (2007). Effects of brain evolution on human nutrition and metabolism. *Annual Review of Nutrition, 27*(1), 311–327.

Likert, R. (1932). A technique for the measurement of attitudes. *Archives of Psychology*, *140*, 44–53.

Little, A. C., Apicella, C. L., & Marlowe, F. W. (2007). Preferences for symmetry in human faces in two cultures: Data from the UK and the Hadza, an isolated group of hunter-gatherers. *Proceedings of the Royal Society of London. B: Biological Sciences*, *274*(1629), 3113–3117.

Lo, M. T., Hinds, D. A., Tung, J. Y., Franz, C., Fan, C. C., Wang, Y., … Chen, C. H. (2017). Genome-wide analyses for personality traits identify six genomic loci and show correlations with psychiatric disorders. *Nature Genetics*, *49*(1), 152–156.

Lopez, A. D. (1998) Morbidity and mortality, changing patterns in the twentieth century. In P. Armitage & T. Colton (Eds), *Encyclopedia of biostatistics* (pp. 2690–2701). New York: John Wiley & Sons.

Low, B. S. (1991). Reproductive life in nineteenth-century Sweden: An evolutionary perspective on demographic phenomena. *Ethology and Sociobiology*, *12*(6), 411–448.

Lu, H. J., & Chang, L. (2014). Deceiving yourself to better deceive high-status compared to equal-status others. *Evolutionary Psychology*, *12*(3), 635–654.

Macfarlan, S. J., Walker, R. S., Flinn, M. V., & Chagnon, N. A. (2014). Lethal coalitionary aggression and long-term alliance formation among Yanomamö men. *Proceedings of the National Academy of Sciences*, *111*(47), 16662–16669.

Margerison, B. J., & Knüsel, C. J. (2002). Paleodemographic comparison of a catastrophic and an attritional death assemblage. *American Journal of Physical Anthropology*, *119*(2), 134–143.

Marlowe, F. (1999). Showoffs or providers? The parenting effort of Hadza men. *Evolution and Human Behavior*, *20*(6), 391–404.

Marlowe, F. W. (2003). A critical period for provisioning by Hadza men: Implications for pair bonding. *Evolution and Human Behavior*, *24*(3), 217–229.

Marlowe, F. W. (2004). Mate preferences among Hadza hunter-gatherers. *Human Nature*, *15*(4), 365–376.

Mastrofski, S. D., Parks, R. B., Reiss Jr., A. J., Worden, R. E., DeJong, C., Snipes, J. B., &

Terrill, W. (1998). Systematic observation of public police: Applying field research methods to policy issues. *National Institute of Justice Research Report*. Washington, DC: U.S. Department of Justice Office of Justice Programs.

Mulder, M. B. (1987). On cultural and reproductive success: Kipsigis evidence. *American Anthropologist*, *89*(3), 617–634.

Murdock, G. P., & White, D. R. (1969). Standard Cross-Cultural Sample. *Ethnology*, *8*(4), 329–369.

Murdock, G. P, & White, D. R. (2006). Standard Cross-Cultural Sample: on-line edition. UC Irvine: Social Dynamics and Complexity. Retrieved from https://escholarship.org/uc/item/62c5c02n, retrieval date: August 2nd, 2019.

O'Connell, J. F., Hawkes, K., Lupo, K. D., & Jones, N. B. (2002). Male strategies and Plio-Pleistocene archaeology. *Journal of Human Evolution*, *43*(6), 831–872.

Odgers, C. L., Caspi, A., Bates, C. J., Sampson, R. J., & Moffitt, R. E. (2012). Systematic social observation of children's neighborhoods using Google Street View: A reliable and cost-effective method. *The Journal of Child Psychology and Psychiatry*, *53*(10), 1009–1017.

Parra, D. C., McKenzie, T. L., Ribeiro, I. C., Ferreira-Hino, A. A., Dreisinger, M., Coniglio, K., Munk, M., Brownson, R. C., Pratt, M., Hoehner, C. M., & Simoes, E. J. (2010). Assessing physical activity in public parks in Brazil using systematic observation. *American Journal of Public Health*, *100*(8), 1420–1426.

Pawlowski, B., Atwal, R., & Dunbar, R. I. M. (2008). Sex differences in everyday risk-taking behavior in humans. *Evolutionary Psychology*, *6*(1), 29–42.

Pillsworth, E. G. (2008). Mate preferences among the Shuar of Ecuador: Trait rankings and peer evaluations. *Evolution and Human Behavior*, *29*(4), 256–267.

Pollard, A. M. (2011). Isotopes and impact: A cautionary tale. *Antiquity*, *85*(328), 631–638.

Reiss, A. J., Jr. (1971). Systematic observation of natural social phenomena. *Sociological Methodology*, *3*, 3–33. doi:10.2307/270816.

Richards, M. P. (2002). A brief review of the archaeological evidence for Palaeolithic and Neolithic subsistence. *European Journal of Clinical Nutrition*, *56*(12), 1270.

Richards, M. P., Hedges, R. E. M., Jacobi, R., Current, A., & Stringer, C. (2000). Focus: Gough's Cave and Sun Hole Cave human stable isotope values indicate a high animal protein diet in the British Upper Palaeolithic. *Journal of Archaeological Science*, *27*(1), 1–3.

Richards, M. P., Pettitt, P. B., Trinkaus, E., Smith, F. H., Paunović, M., & Karavanić, I. (2000). Neanderthal diet at Vindija and Neanderthal predation: The evidence from stable isotopes. *Proceedings of the National Academy of Sciences*, *97*(13), 7663–7666.

Ripke, S., Neale, B. M., Corvin, A., Walters, J. T., Farh, K. H., Holmans, P. A., ... & Pers, T. H. (2014). Biological insights from 108 schizophrenia-associated genetic loci. *Nature*, *511*(7510), 421–427.

Sampson, R. J., & Raudenbush, S. W. (1999). Systematic social observation of public spaces: A new look at disorder in urban neighborhoods. *American Journal of Sociology*, *105*(3), 603–651.

Sanchez-Roige, S., Gray, J. C., MacKillop, J., Chen, C. H., & Palmer, A. A. (2018). The genetics of human personality. *Genes, Brain and Behavior*, *17*, e12439.

Schmidt, C. W. (2001). Dental microwear evidence for a dietary shift between two nonmaize-reliant prehistoric human populations from Indiana. *American Journal of Physical Anthropology*, *114*(2), 139–145.

Segal, N. L. (2017). Twin studies in Brazil: *Projects and plans/Twin research:* Infant twins' viewing of social scenes; Religiosity and substance abuse; Down Syndrome among twins; Twin case of chronic periodontitis / *In the News*: The twin 'property brothers'; Twins with cerebral palsy; Twins affected with the Zika virus; Twin writers Derek and Roddy; Twins on sports teams; Local quads. *Twin Research and Human Genetics*, *20*(5), 481–488.

Singh, D. (1993). Adaptive significance of female physical attractiveness: Role of waist-to-hip ratio. *Journal of Personality and Social Psychology*, *65*(2), 293–307.

Singh, D., Dixson, B. J., Jessop, T. S., Morgan, B., & Dixson, A. F. (2010). Cross-cultural consensus for waist–hip ratio and women's attractiveness. *Evolution and Human Behavior*, *31*(3), 176–181.

Smith, M. E., Feinman, G. M., Drennan, R. D., Earle, T., & Morris, I. (2012). Archaeology as a social science. *Proceedings of the National Academy of Sciences*, *109*(20), 7617–7621.

Sprecher, S., Sullivan, Q., & Hatfield, E. (1994). Mate selection preferences: Gender differences examined in a national sample. *Journal of Personality and Social Psychology*, *66*(6), 1074–1080.

Stewart-Williams, S. (2007). Altruism among kin vs. non-kin: Effects of cost of help and reciprocal exchange. *Evolution and Human Behavior*, *28*(3), 193–198.

Stewart-Williams, S. (2008). Human beings as evolved nepotists: Exceptions to the rule and effects of the cost of help. *Human Nature*, *19*(4), 414–425.

Symons, D. (1979). *The evolution of human sexuality*. New York: Oxford University Press.

Tellegen, A., Lykken, D. T., Bouchard, T. J., Wilcox, K. J., Segal, N. L., & Rich, S. (1988). Personality similarity in twins reared apart and together. *Journal of Personality and Social Psychology*, *54*(6), 1031–1039.

Testart, A. (1988). Some major problems in the social anthropology of hunter-gatherers. *Current Anthropology*, *29*, 1–31.

Trivers, R. L. (1971). The evolution of reciprocal altruism. *The Quarterly Review of Biology*, *46*(1), 35–57.

Weinberger, D. R. (2019). Thinking about schizophrenia in an era of genomic medicine. *American Journal of Psychiatry*, *176*(1), 12–20.

Wetsman, A., & Marlowe, F. (1999). How universal are preferences for female waist-to-hip ratios? Evidence from the Hadza of Tanzania. *Evolution and Human Behavior*, *20*(4), 219–228.

Wiederman, M. W., & Allgeier, E. R. (1992). Gender differences in mate selection criteria: Sociobiological or socioeconomic explanation? *Ethology and Sociobiology*, *13*(2), 115–124.

Wilke, A., Sherman, A., Curdt, B., Mondal, S., Fitzgerald, C., & Kruger, D. J. (2014). An evolutionary domain-specific risk scale. *Evolutionary Behavioral Sciences*, *8*(3), 123–141.

Wrangham, R. (2009). *Catching fire: How cooking made us human*. New York: Basic Books.

Wrangham, R. W., & Glowacki, L. (2012). Inter-group aggression in chimpanzees and war in nomadic hunter-gatherers. *Human Nature*, *23*(1), 5–29.

Zhang, X. H., Satoshi S., and Kesteloot, H. (1995). The sex ratio of mortality and its secular trends. *International Journal of Epidemiology*, *24*(4), 720–729.

Controversial Issues and Misunderstandings in Evolutionary Psychology

Darren Burke

INTRODUCTION

In common with most of the sciences, psychology has a strong focus on answering proximate, causal questions. If we observe someone engaged in an aggressive act, for example, then many lines of psychological research can provide insights into the immediate causes of that behaviour. Aspects of the person's personality, hormonal profile, brain structure, the social situation they are in, their psychopathologies, anxiety levels, beliefs about the situation, etc., are all factors that psychological research encompasses. Less immediate causes, but within the lifetime of the individual, are also a common area of investigation in psychology. Aspects of the person's upbringing, education, history of abuse, learning experiences, developmental trajectory, etc., are also important proximate causes that are well investigated in psychology. What psychology less commonly investigates are what Tinbergen (1963) identified as the ultimate causes of

behaviour – those related to the function of the behaviour and its evolutionary origins. Evolutionary psychology is a subdiscipline of psychology that attempts to answer these ultimate questions, and in so doing, provide a more complete explanation of behaviour. Aggressive behaviour, for example, is phylogenetically widespread (essentially ubiquitous in social species), and in those other species it serves a number of biologically important functions, like climbing social hierarchies, competing for mates and resources (typically territories or food, for most species), and so on. This gives us insights into the nature of aggression that cannot be gained in any other way and that place it in a broader context than any proximate explanation (see Buss and Shackelford, 1997).

Although it is probably true that almost all psychology researchers, and the majority of practitioners, believe that psychological mechanisms (or at least the neural substrates that underpin them) are a consequence of biological evolution (Burke, 2014), attempts by evolutionary psychologists to elucidate the ultimate causes of human behaviour have met with considerable resistance, which has given the field a reputation for being 'controversial'.

As will be outlined below, this resistance takes a number of forms, which vary substantially in validity, and it is underscored by a range of motives. Irrespective of its motivation, almost all of the resistance is at odds with the widespread acceptance that human psychological mechanisms *are* the products of evolution, and that understanding what a mechanism is for, and how it evolved, will provide important insights into how it works. Using the example of aggression outlined above, if the ultimate function of aggression is the same in humans as it is in other animals, then we can make a number of theoretically and practically useful predictions about the circumstances under which we might expect it to occur, and about how the mechanism (or mechanisms) operates (Buss and Shackelford, 1997). For example, a straightforward prediction from evolutionary theories developed by studying the function of aggression in non-humans is that intra-sexual aggression should be much more common in the sex that competes for access to mates than in the sex that is competed for, or that chooses mates. In the majority of mammalian mating systems this means that males should show much higher rates of intra-sexual aggression than females, a prediction that is borne out, and that is consistent with the important role played by testosterone in motivating aggressive behaviour (Lindenfors and Tullberg, 2011). Humans are very unusual mammals, since we form long-term pair bonds, a more bird-typical mating system that is thought to be driven by raising offspring requiring bi-parental care. Since we are a species that forms long-term pair bonds, women are also competing for access to high-quality partners, and so we might expect women to have evolved competitive mechanisms that also result in intra-sexual aggression (Vaillancourt, 2013), but that aggression may manifest in different ways to male–male aggression, since it evolved separately, and

operates in a different social domain (between women, rather than between men). These insights immediately place at least some kinds of aggression into a deeper, functional framework, and generate testable predictions about possible proximate mechanisms involved in regulating intra-sexual aggression (many of which have already been tested: e.g., Archer, 2006; Mazur and Booth, 1998). For example, in humans, we might expect that many acts of intra-sexual aggression will be triggered by mating-relevant competitive cues, that men and women will manifest intra-sexual aggression in different ways, that people in successful, satisfying long-term relationships will show reduced levels of less intra-sexual aggression (although other forms of aggression may play a role in maintaining such relationships; Buss, 2002).

It is also worth emphasising that testing ultimate, evolutionary hypotheses often is more difficult than testing proximate causal hypotheses. It is, of course, in principle, impossible to control and manipulate the variables that were in operation in the evolutionary past in order to rule in or out particular causal hypotheses, and so the evidence used to test evolutionary hypotheses is necessarily, to some extent, indirect. But this logistical limitation should not be a barrier to formulating and testing such hypotheses, any more than similar logistical limitations constrain the development and testing of theories about the origins of stars and planets, or even theories about the developmental origins of psychological disorders, in which ethical constraints prevent the experimental manipulation of variables. Contrary to caricatures of the field, evolutionary psychologists are well aware of these limitations (Confer et al., 2010), and typically do whatever can be done to overcome them, and/or temper the conclusions that they draw accordingly. Because of this difficulty, and especially because of the unique insights such explanations can provide, it might be better for psychology as a whole to be more open to the efforts being made by evolutionary psychologists.

Similarly, it might be helpful for evolutionary psychologists to be less dismissive of the criticisms that have been levelled at the field, some of which, as will be discussed later, deserve careful consideration. The most productive way forward is likely to come from mutual respect and understanding, in which those interested in answering proximate questions about behaviour and those trying to understand the ultimate causes of behaviour, welcome and use insights from the complementary endeavour.

MISGUIDED RESISTANCE AND MISUNDERSTANDINGS

As has been pointed out many times previously (e.g., Al-Shawaf et al., 2018; Burke, 2014; Buss et al., 1998; Confer et al., 2010; Hagen, 2005, 2014), some of the resistance to evolutionary psychology is based on misunderstandings about what the approach entails. These reviews, and others, outline a wide range of misunderstandings, some of which reflect ignorance about how evolution works, and others of which reflect ignorance about how evolutionary thinking is applied to understanding human psychological mechanisms. It is worth summarising these misunderstandings again, in order to reiterate their weaknesses, but it is also worth being explicit about the fact that criticisms based on these kinds of fundamental misunderstandings should not require a formal rebuttal from evolutionary psychologists, at least not to others within the field. In other 'controversial' fields, like climate science, completely uninformed critics are typically from outside the field, and so formal rebuttals, within the field, are usually unnecessary. Unfortunately, mostly because of the way our tertiary education systems are structured, evolutionary psychology faces two different kinds of misinformed critics from 'within' the field. Psychologists, on the whole, do not learn much about evolutionary biology (Short and

Hawley, 2015), and so are susceptible to misinformed objections based on misunderstandings about how evolution works, and/or how evolutionary hypotheses are tested. There are fewer of them raising objections, but evolutionary biologists and behavioural ecologists are typically similarly uneducated about psychology, and so are susceptible to having misinformed objections based on misunderstandings about how psychological mechanisms work, and how hypotheses about them are tested. In the case of evolutionary biologists and behavioural ecologists, this is compounded by the fact that they will typically not merely be ignorant about psychological mechanisms, they will also tend to have the kinds of naïve views about how psychological mechanisms work that we all hold before a psychology education. This is not to say that all critics from within the field are misguided – informed objections will be reviewed later – only that much of the resistance from within psychology is misinformed (and in some cases misinformed by reading objections raised by some evolutionary biologists), and so, unfortunately, it seems to be necessary to regularly elucidate the nature of these confusions.

Since many previous attempts to outline the common misunderstandings held about evolutionary psychology have not produced a more widespread understanding, perhaps a new approach is needed. These previous attempts have been clear and well-argued, and so their failure to gain traction might reflect that the intended audience is ill-prepared to absorb them, perhaps because they lack an understanding of what evolutionary psychologists mean when they talk about evolved psychological adaptations. There are also many particular objections to evolutionary psychology that could be outlined and individually countered (there are examples later), but since many of them are based on basic misconceptions of the work done in evolutionary psychology, this may be premature. Instead, I will briefly attempt to outline what we currently understand about how evolution produces psychological adaptations (a topic covered in more detail in other entries in this *Handbook*), in the hope that this makes the widely held misunderstandings self-evidently misguided.

EVOLVING PSYCHOLOGICAL ADAPTATIONS

Psychological adaptations, like all evolved adaptations, are traits that exist *because* they conferred an advantage upon the individuals that had them. In order to be explicit about the fact that there is nothing teleological or Lamarkian about this (a misunderstanding that persists; Al-Shawaf et al., 2018), the adaptation started out as a *random* variation on an existing trait. What makes this random variation an adaptation is *selection*. Individuals with the variant have an advantage over individuals without it in the environment they exist in. Both 'advantage' and 'environment' have special meanings in this context.

The only *advantage* that evolution selects for is reproductive success – of the individual and other individuals carrying the gene that creates the trait variant. And so the adaptation might be a trait that helps the individual to survive long enough, or healthily enough, to have the opportunity to reproduce, or it might be a trait that helps the individual attract, or win, a high-quality mate, or it might be a trait that helps the individual to raise healthy offspring, or it might be a trait that helps the individual to promote the reproductive success of relatives (who also likely bear the gene for the trait). Our everyday intuitions about what might be 'advantageous' for an individual, and how individuals might be 'adapted', as well as the way in which these terms are used in other areas of psychology, are frequently misleading in an evolutionary context, and this probably leads to some misunderstanding about what evolutionary psychologists mean when they talk about psychological adaptations. Being psychologically 'well-adjusted',

happy, productive, entertained, fulfilled, 'self-actualised', high in self-esteem, compassionate, helpful, etc., are not necessarily advantages in an evolutionary context, and they are never directly selected for. In fact, evolution is neutral with respect to these other senses of advantageous and adaptive, because it *can* only select for traits that increase reproductive output. Traits that have that consequence (on average) are automatically selected, irrespective of any other consequences they might have. Famous examples of this are sexually selected traits like peacock tails and deer antlers that give their bearers access to mating opportunities, but which constitute significant survival (let alone comfort) burdens. Another instructive example is the life cycle of the Agaonidae family of fig wasps (Cruaud et al., 2011). In these wasps, the females have special adaptations that enable them to deposit eggs inside ripening figs (different species have different adaptations). Upon laying eggs, the females of most species promptly die. When the eggs hatch, the larval wasps eat the pulp of the fig, and then pupate. Immediately upon pupating, the pale, wingless male wasps mate with freshly pupated females, and then dig a hole through the fig for the females to escape. They cannot fly or easily survive outside the fig, and having mated and dug the hole, they simply die. The females emerge from the holes made by the males, seek out new fruits, lay their eggs and die. These wasps are, reproductively (and therefore evolutionarily) very successful, with many adaptations producing that success, but it is doubtful, and, importantly, irrelevant, that their lives are especially rich and rewarding.

Another potential source of misunderstanding is the special meaning of the word environment in producing adaptations. In evolutionary terms, the *environment* is both the arena in which selection operates and the target to which organisms become adapted – the target they 'fit' in Spencer's proverbial phrase, 'survival of the fittest'. But the environment, from an evolutionary perspective, is not really a *place*, it is a conglomerate of characteristics that affect reproductive success – an interacting set of selection pressures. Many of these characteristics will be aspects of the physical environment, like the medium through which organisms move, accounting, for example, for the similar streamlining and fin-structure of marine mammals, reptiles, birds, and fish, or the temperature and UV radiation variations they are exposed to, or the access to oxygen (for animals) afforded by their immediate environment. Individuals that have traits that best enable them to thrive and to harvest the resources available in their environment will be better placed to leave more offspring, and so the genes involved in producing those traits will be transmitted to future generations. These traits could be morphological, like a beak of a particular shape and size, or physiological, like specialised cells for storing fat as insulation and a long-term energy store, or behavioural, like an urge to migrate at particular times of the year to avoid unfavourable climatic conditions, or enabling the exploitation of distant resources. These are adaptations to aspects of the physical environment, but the environment to which organisms adapt also includes other organisms, of the same and different species, and the organism's own internal environment.

Adaptations shaped by other species include those enabling catching prey or avoiding being caught, including size, strength, speed, conspicuousness, behavioural strategies, weaponry, habitat choices, sleep-wake cycles, group or individual living, etc., but also less direct interactions, like taking advantage of other species' foraging efforts, or warning signalling. For sexually reproducing species, opposite-sex members of their species, and sometimes their own offspring, are critical parts of the environment to which individuals are adapted. Morphological, physiological, and behavioural adaptations are necessary for sexually reproducing organisms to successfully mate. These include locating, recognising, and approaching/contacting potential mates, as well as producing and releasing or delivering gametes. Other adaptations

are necessary to successfully raise healthy offspring. In mammals, for example, there are many morphological, physiological, and behavioural mechanisms for carrying and nourishing the developing young and for producing and providing milk once they are born. These are both examples of adaptations shaped by the environment of same-species individuals, and are products of natural selection. Many sexually reproducing species also have adaptations shaped by sexual selection, in which same-species individuals directly select (by mate choice or physical competition) traits that lead to successful mating. Peacock tails and deer antlers, as mentioned previously, are classic examples.

When organisms possess advantageous adaptations, enabling them to successfully survive and reproduce, it is only their genes that are passed on to the next generation, and so evolution is ultimately about selecting genes. The genes responsible for advantageous variations (adaptations) – those that result in higher rates of reproduction of successful offspring – are, *necessarily*, the genes that come to dominate the gene pool. In other words, genes are the unit of selection – the *things* that are selected – as a consequence of the *effects* that they have on an organism's capacity to survive and reproduce in the selection landscape they inhabit (Dawkins, 1976). Given this, it is important to keep in mind that genes only do two things; they replicate themselves and they build proteins – and they only build proteins because that has ultimately led to better replication in the past. This means that every evolved adaptation, psychological or otherwise, is the *indirect* outcome of a gene selected because it typically produced advantageous consequences for the organism bearing it (more successful reproduction). This insight is important for understanding adaptations that provide no direct advantage to the individual carrying the successful genetic variant, and it is central to understanding how evolved adaptations develop – how they get *expressed*.

When an evolutionary biologist or an evolutionary psychologist describes an adaptation, they typically describe a feature/behaviour of a fully developed organism, unless they are describing an adaptation that produces advantages *during* development, like the mammalian rooting reflex, or infant bird begging behaviour. In either case, the adaptation is a phenotypic reflection of genetic activity, and that activity only indirectly influences the phenotypic expression, both because it depends on innumerable interactions with other genes (many of which do not directly code for adaptive gene products, but instead regulate the expression of other genes) and because it depends on interactions with the environment the organism finds itself in. So when an evolutionary psychologist talks about an adaptation that causes men to be concerned about their long-term partner engaging in sexual infidelity (see Buss, 2018), they can *only* mean that by developmental trajectories, biochemical pathways, neural systems, and environmental interactions currently unknown, a gene that is expressed differently in males, *results in* an adult male that is more likely to be concerned about sexual infidelity than he would be if the gene did not exist (or did not get transcribed). As is obvious in this example, the pathway from gene to behaviour is long and indirect, and necessarily involves interactions between many genes (to help to build a brain that operates a particular way), and between the organism and the environment (especially the social environment in this case) during development. As is also obvious from this example, current environmental cues are critical for the adaptation to express itself in an adaptive way. In order for selection to preferentially retain the gene that predisposes males to behave in this way, it need only, on average, have advantaged males with the gene over males without it (or with a different variant) in typical environments. Given the indirect relationship between the gene that is selected and its behavioral phenotypic expression, however, there is no guarantee that the adaptation will

express itself at all, or in an adaptive way, in atypical environments. This is something that evolutionary psychologists probably need to be more mindful of when using shorthand, functional descriptions of adaptations, in order to circumvent misunderstandings in those outside the field.

In this example, the *function* of the adaptation is to make it less likely that men will help to raise and provide for offspring who are not theirs (behaviour that evolution cannot directly select for, because those offspring do not contain that man's genes), but the *mechanism* by which this function is achieved is not specified by functional considerations – it requires a separate empirical analysis. Of course, this is true of the expression of all adaptations, since they are all indirect, and all depend, at least to some extent, on interactions with the environment, but it is especially important to be clear about it in evolutionary psychology, because psychology has a long tradition of empirically investigating mechanism independent of function, and so is suspicious of explanations that are pitched at a functional level without specifying a mechanism (Burke, 2014). An important part of bringing evolutionary psychology and traditional psychology together is to create an appreciation for the fact that the investigation of mechanism and function are mutually informative.

As is common with other areas in psychology, evolutionary psychologists vary in the extent to which they specify how a hypothesised mechanism works, but they rarely attempt to specify what the gene (or genes) responsible for the proposed adaptation does (do). Instead, in common with behavioural ecologists and most other evolutionary biologists, they make the reasonable assumption that the full pathway from gene-protein-product-being-expressed-at-a-particular-time to adaptive outcome could, in principle, be traced, but that their job is to elucidate the operation of the mechanism *as an adaptation*. Although this assumption is reasonable, and although it is not incumbent on someone studying psychological adaptations to drill down to the gene product ultimately responsible for the expression of the behaviour in question, it *is* important for evolutionary psychologists and traditional psychologists alike to be conscious of the fact that the pathway is indirect and long, and so there are many places along the pathway that might derail or alter the expression of the adaptation. Without directly studying how the adaptation develops (the necessity of which depends on when the gene expresses itself to produce the adaptive outcome), there are also many unknown environmental interactions that might functionally shape the expression of the adaptation, or on which it's normal development might depend.

To use the example of male partner-infidelity-sensitivity adaptations from earlier, a complete understanding of the operation of this evolved mechanism, even at the purely psychological level, requires understanding exactly how the mechanism operates, when the adaptation emerges, and how its expression interacts with experiences during development and in adulthood. There is a widespread misunderstanding among traditional psychologists that evidence that experience makes a difference to the operation of some mechanism is somehow evidence against the mechanism being an evolved adaptation, but hopefully the preceding discussion reveals that claim as obviously incorrect. In the case of male partner-infidelity adaptations (and almost every other adaptation proposed in evolutionary psychology), experience almost *must* make a difference to how the evolved mechanism operates. An adaptation that increases the likelihood that pair-bonded men raise only their own children could be affected by many different mechanisms, which will depend on different kinds of environmental/social interactions to calibrate their expression. Which, or how many, mechanisms accomplish this function, and to what extent they depend on environmental/social interactions, and how directly the mechanism(s) influences the functional

outcome, are empirical questions. For example, an adaptation that could reduce the likelihood that men raise unrelated offspring would be a mechanism that triggered their jealousy if they detected or suspected that their long-term partner was interested in a sexual relationship with another man, since this is the only kind of relationship that can produce unrelated offspring. There is evidence consistent with this possibility (see Buss, 2018), but a complete description of the adaptation(s) that accomplish this functional outcome requires specifying which experiences, if any, during development are necessary for the mechanism to be shaped up in this way, which environmental events trigger the jealousy, the extent to which sensitivity to these environmental triggers depends on having had particular kinds of experiences, and how the jealousy produces behavioural outcomes that reduce the likelihood of being cuckolded, since intuitions about the relationship between jealousy and the behavior of partners are insufficient to claim that the jealousy is produced by an adaptation. There is also the possibility that other adaptations that supplement those related to jealousy have an important role to play in effecting this functional outcome, some of which may be unrelated to feelings of jealousy, and have different environmental triggers. For example, men who simply prevent their long-term partners from interacting with other men, irrespective of any cues of infidelity, or feelings of jealousy, would prevent cuckoldry. It is possible, therefore, that men might have mechanisms that under some environmental conditions would somehow (each of these could be empirically investigated) result in them preventing their partners from interacting with any other men, and that the jealousy adaptations are only triggered under circumstances in which this is not possible, and/ or when they receive cues that their partner might be interested in being sexually unfaithful. Another potential adaptation, unrelated to jealousy, that might reduce cuckoldry is to find women with recognisable signs (should they exist), or who provide direct evidence, of a propensity to be unfaithful in relationships less attractive as long-term partners. Again, this potential adaptation might be calibrated by environmental input. The aim of proposing these alternative adaptations is to show that although adaptations that reduce cuckoldry are likely given basic evolutionary considerations and the mating system humans have, those adaptations need not necessarily involve jealousy, but they will almost always be shaped by environmental input. This is important because critics of evolutionary psychology are frequently satisfied that they have undermined the enterprise by showing that a particular proposed mechanism (accounting for sex differences in jealousy, for example) does not operate as proposed (although there is counter-evidence that it does; Buss, 2018), or that it is influenced by environmental input (e.g., shaped by learning and experiences). In fact, neither of these is fatal to the idea that there might be evolved cuckoldry-avoidance adaptations. It is possible that there are no psychological cuckoldry-avoidance adaptions, since this function might be accomplished by non-psychological mechanisms, but it is unlikely that there are no adaptations to avoid this important threat to a male human's fitness, and so a balanced, well-informed response to finding evidence against a particular functional explanation (like the sexual-jealousy hypothesis) would be to look for evidence for other mechanisms that might be accomplishing the same function, not to question the importance of the function itself, or, even less justifiable, to question the utility of trying to find functional mechanisms. The fact that this is often not the response of critics of evolutionary psychology suggests that at least some of the criticism is motivated by other considerations, as will be discussed in the next section.

In this section I have sketched how psychological adaptations evolve and how hypotheses about them are generated and tested by evolutionary psychologists. The hope is that this sketch makes it clear that

evolutionary psychology is not teleological, it is not putting forward 'just-so-stories', it does not assume genetic determinism (all evolutionary approaches are necessarily interactionist, since it is the effect the gene has/d in the environment that results in selection), and although some of its proponents are, it *need not* be committed to massive modularity of neural/psychological mechanisms (Buller, 2000, 2005; Burke, 2014; Panksepp and Panksepp, 2000), nor to the computational model of cognition (Barrett et al., 2014; Burke, 2014; Panksepp and Panksepp, 2000), and it usually is not focussed on explaining psychological mechanisms as adaptations to selection pressures prevalent during the Pleistocene, or in any other way specific to our hunter-gatherer past (Buller, 2000; Burke, 2014). In fact, given the widespread acceptance that human psychological mechanisms evolved, it should be an endeavour that is valued by other psychologists, and that informs their own theoretical and empirical efforts, despite the fact that the endeavour faces unavoidable logistical difficulties.

MOTIVATED RESISTANCE

Some of the resistance to evolutionary psychology comes from opponents who simply do not like the idea of explaining psychological mechanisms from an evolutionary perspective, or who do not like the implications of such explanations. This opposition comes from those whose objections are motivated by religion, those whose objections are motivated by politics (which in some cases have become almost religious), and those whose objections are motivated by a personal commitment to theoretical and empirical approaches to psychology that are either explicitly anti-biological, or that have been built without being informed by evolutionary considerations, and so see no need to incorporate such considerations (Burke, 2014).

Religion-based discomfort with evolutionary psychology, indeed with evolutionary science in general, is predictable and easy enough to contend with, even when it is academic psychologists that hold such views, as is sometimes the case (Jonason and Dane, 2014; Jonason and Schmitt, 2016). If a person genuinely believes that human behavior is controlled by supernatural forces of any kind, and/ or that humans are a special divine creation whose actions have spiritual consequences, then there is simply no common ground for a sensible debate with a discipline based in science, and so evolutionary psychology and the religious objectors can each pursue their own enterprises comfortably oblivious to the efforts of the other group. Any criticism of evolutionary psychology from this perspective can safely be ignored.

Politically motivated objections to evolutionary psychology are a less straightforward issue because they are typically more sophisticated, and they are almost always less obvious (sometimes even to those holding them), because the political motivation behind the objection is usually unstated. In addition to the motivation being difficult to identify, it is also true that most politically motivated objections are framed as scientific objections (either theoretical or empirical), and any scientific objection, no matter what it's underlying motivation, needs to be taken seriously. A good informal test of whether or not an objection is politically motivated is whether it would be applied as rigorously to an attempt to understand non-human behaviour from an evolutionary perspective. This test will not always work, of course, because some objections will legitimately be about the explanation applied to human behaviour, but it is a question that some objectors should perhaps be asking of themselves more often than they do. Evolutionary hypotheses about sex differences in human behaviour provide a clear example of a domain in which political orientation frequently and obviously motivates objections. Partly because men and women are convenient, ready-made groups that have faced sometimes different selection pressure over evolutionary time, a large number

of evolutionary psychological investigations focus on testing theories that predict psychological sex-differences. This has led to accusations that such research is sexist, and that it is wilfully or unconsciously engaged in reinforcing gender stereotypes. As a researcher that has investigated sex differences from an evolutionary perspective (e.g., in spatial cognition: Hughes et al., 2014; threat detection: Sulikowski and Burke, 2014; and in mate choice/attractiveness judgements: Burke and Sulikowski, 2010; Wagstaff et al., 2015), I am confident that I have never been motivated to reinforce gender stereotypes. I have certainly never done this consciously, and have probably not done so unconsciously either, given that my political orientation is extremely left-wing, and that I find all kinds of discrimination, including sexism, deplorable. The other three authors on the papers referred to above are women working in STEM, with no obvious interest in reinforcing gender stereotypes. The reality is that the investigation of sex differences is no more inherently sexist than the investigation of psychological differences across the lifespan is inherently ageist, or than the investigation of socio-economic effects on later success is inherently classist. As the other two examples that attract no political objections make clear, most (although not all) of the politically motivated resistance to sex difference research is not based on its mere investigation, it is based on the suggestion that the sex differences are *biological* (neural, hormonal, or evolved).

Those with political objections to the idea of biologically based sex differences tend to be from the political left, although some of those on the political right are opposed to evolutionary explanations (of anything). The left-wing opposition to the idea of biological sex differences is based on the mistaken belief that if sex differences are biological then men and women are immutably unequal, and this conclusion interferes with the left's egalitarian ambitions. To overcome this dilemma, the tactic has been to try to find whatever evidence can be found that undermines the existence of differences at all, or that suggests that they are instead a consequence of socialisation forces. If they do not exist, then there is no problem, and if they are due to socialisation, then society can be restructured to erase them. The problem here is that this tactic is both unnecessary and disingenuous.

The tactic is unnecessary because the reality of sex differences holds no implications for whether men and women should be treated equally. This is partly because even robust sex differences have substantially overlapping distributions, and so an individual woman may be higher on a given variable than an individual male (or vice versa), and so assumptions about an individual will often be mistaken. To take height as an uncontroversial example, in Australia the distribution of heights for men has a mean of 176.5 cm and a standard deviation of 7.4 cm and for women the mean is 161.8 cm with a standard deviation of 7.1 cm. This is a robust sex difference, even though the distributions overlap (most people know a very tall woman and a very short man), and the probability of a randomly selected Australian woman being taller than a randomly selected Australian man is only 9%, but clearly, if one simply assumes that a given woman will be shorter than a given man, then one will sometimes be in error, and that may be doing a disservice to the person about whom the assumption is made. More fundamentally than this, though, it is straightforwardly unfair to deny an individual an opportunity based on their sex, even if the opportunity depends on variables that show substantial sex differences. The fundamental tenet of egalitarianism is that everyone be given equal opportunities, not that everyone is identical, or that any differences are a consequence of social forces. These would make the work of those interested in equity (like me) much easier, but they are unrelated to the political and social aims of equity, they are very often untrue, and denying reality helps nobody (Soh, 2019).

The disingenuous nature of politically motivated opposition to the idea of biologically based (neural, hormonal, or evolutionary)

sex differences is revealed by the biased way in which the literature is reviewed and presented, and sometimes by the particular cluster of beliefs that are put forward. Those who deny neural sex differences also tend to deny hormonal and (especially) evolutionary ones. I do not mean disingenuous in the sense of being deliberately misleading. I mean disingenuous in the sense that even the proponents of these arguments must know, at some level, that they are not being completely fairminded in the evaluation of the evidence, but that they presumably put those concerns aside for the greater (political) good. The objections that are put forward can be characterised as 'not-necessarily' arguments. The authors know that there is a great deal of evidence suggesting that sex differences exist, and that they are probably at least partly a consequence of biological factors, but they cling to pieces of evidence that suggest that the differences have either been exaggerated/misrepresented, or that they could plausibly be due entirely to socialisation. In other words, they claim that the widely reported differences are 'not-necessarily' genuine differences, or, even if they are, that they are 'not-necessarily' due to biological factors. Skepticism, is, of course, a vital part of doing good Science, but unidirectional skepticism that ignores or tries to argue away large bodies of evidence becomes denialism, and denialism is antithetical to good science.

A clear and easily accessible example of the kind of 'not-necessarily' denialism of both the existence of some sex differences, or if acknowledged, then the denial that they are due to biological factors, can be found in an article by Fine et al. (2019). Each of these authors has put forward many similar arguments in the past. The details of their argument are not needed here, and have been well countered elsewhere, including a particularly clear and well-balanced response by an evolutionary psychological researcher who has collected large amounts of data documenting biologically important sex differences in psychological mechanisms (Schmitt, 2019).

As an example of the one-sided, ill-informed nature of the Fine et al. (2019) critique, they try to use a study by Kendrick et al. (1998) to show how evolutionary psychology is misguided to suggest that sexual selection has an important role to play in the expression of human sexual preferences/mate choice. Not surprisingly, this is an example Schmitt (2109) also points out faults with. Here is their argument:

> For example, when scientists arranged for newborn male lambs to be fostered by a goat mother, and for male newborn goats to be fostered by a ewe mother, they found that the males of both species developed robust and persistent sexual preferences for mates of the fostering species (Kendrick et al., 1998). This shows that, in this case, whatever genetically inherited contribution there is to a highly adaptive sexual preference for the same species, it is the environmental inheritance (i.e., lambs normally inherit an environment in which they are reared among sheep, and goats normally inherit an environment in which they are reared among goats) and not the genetic inheritance that holds sway over behavior. (Fine et al., 2019)

Apart from violating their own (sound) advice to not rely heavily on data from other species when drawing conclusions about human behaviour in the immediately preceding section of their article, this example also ignores a large body of research in evolutionary psychology suggesting that at least some aspects of mate preferences are similarly determined in humans (reviewed in Schmitt's [2019] response), and seems completely unaware of the fact that since its discovery by Lorenz (in 1935), the extent to which sexual imprinting determines adult mate choices has been investigated in innumerable species, and that it is only one example (there are hundreds) of an adaptation that is sensitive to input from the environment. Under normal rearing conditions, this evolved mechanism (which only operates during a critical developmental period, clear evidence of its genetically based nature) results in adaptive mate preferences. As is hopefully clear from the sketch of how psychological adaptations evolve that I provided earlier, this example

from Fine et al. (2019) is not surprising, let alone a problem for the proposal that mate choice preferences are evolved adaptations. The phrase 'it is the environmental inheritance … and not the genetic inheritance that holds sway over behaviour' is a meaningless vestige of a motivated adherence to the nature–nurture dichotomy. Not only do all adaptations express themselves via a complex interaction between genes and the environment, the extent to which that expression is influenced by environmental input, and the kind of input that matters, is itself under selection pressure, and has been extensively studied by ethologists, behavioural ecologists, and evolutionary psychologists since the beginning of those disciplines. It is disingenuous to present the Kendrick (1998) study as anything other than an example of exactly the kind of research that typifies modern (since about the 1960s) approaches to understand how adaptive behaviour evolves.

The last kind of motivated resistance to evolutionary psychology is from those who adopt approaches to psychological questions that are either anti-biological, or a-biological. Such researchers are of the view that evolutionary considerations have nothing to add to our understanding of psychological mechanisms. This group of motivated objectors overlaps with the politically motivated objectors (this is often where the anti-biological approach originates), but it sometimes seems to be the case that even in the absence of a political agenda, some psychologists' objections are based on the idea that evolutionary considerations are an unnecessary distraction, and that they are untestable anyway. This view is particularly common in well-established subdisciplines of psychology using rigorous experimental paradigms collecting data supporting complex, well-organised theories, both of which have been built without ever considering the evolutionary origin of the mechanisms being tested and theorised about. Although it is true that evolutionary hypotheses are difficult to directly test, and that they need to be tested in a slightly different (maybe even less rig- idly rigorous) way, a cogent argument can be mounted that, far from being unnecessary dis- tractions, evolutionary considerations should be the *starting point* for any investigation of a psychological mechanism, helping to frame and constrain the way in which it is tested, and theories about how it might operate.

To take just one example of the utility of an evolutionary approach to questions in psy- chology, consider the well-known circumplex model of emotion put forward by Russell (1980). In this model, all emotional states can be defined as points in a two-dimensional space representing how arousing the emo- tional state is (*bored* is low arousal, *terrified* is high arousal) and its valance (*miserable* is highly negatively valanced, *delighted* is highly positively valanced). This model reli- ably captures genuine variance in the phe- nomenological experience and physiological responses associated with different emotional states, but it ignores the evolved function of emotional states (indeed it was put for- ward as an alternative to functional models like that of Ekman, 1972). This approach of classifying psychological phenomena in an a-biological, a-functional, systematic way (in this case by analysing the way in which participants categorised 28 emotion-denoting adjectives) is common in psychology, and it has had some success, because the classifi- cation systems, like the circumplex model of emotions, capture some of the real variance in the phenomena being investigated. Other examples include the study of memory (sub- dividing memory into qualitatively different kinds, or classifying phenomena as the result of decay or interference, etc.) or associative learning (establishing the 'laws' of associa- tion), or personality (developing self-report measures to capture the underlying dimen- sions on which people's behaviour varies). An evolutionary perspective encourages us, instead, to first ask what the phenomena being investigated might *do for* the organ- ism, and then to ask how that function might mechanistically be achieved (Sulikowski

and Burke, 2015). From this perspective, the circumplex model is not very useful, because emotional states that are obviously part of unrelated functional systems, like anger and fear, for example, are close together in the circumplex space. The fact that they are close together accurately reflects the fact that they are similarly valanced and both highly arous- ing, but it tells us nothing about what they are *for*. Since emotions only exist because they served (*different*) useful functions, a complete model of emotions needs to take their func- tions into account, and to help explain how they are achieved. It is easy to see, however, how theoretical traditions that have built up over many years, with considerable success, because they do capture real variance in the phenomena being investigated, are reluctant to incorporate such perspectives, especially when that kind of research is more difficult to conduct and has the potential to undermine the work that has already been done.

INFORMED OBJECTIONS

Contrary to the impression that might be derived from reading the polarised literature on evolutionary psychology, not all objections to the way in which evolutionary psychologi- cal research is conducted, or the theories that it produces, are misinformed. Legitimate con- cerns about evolutionary psychology have been raised based on a number of different factors, some of which can be rectified, and others of which are harder to deal with. The most difficult legitimate criticism to deal with is the concern that evolutionary hypotheses are almost always impossible to directly test. For methodological purists, of which psy- chology has more than its fair share, this is a fatal flaw. The problem with this criticism is that it is true, but evolutionary psychology is not unique in facing such logistical chal- lenges, and this difficulty alone in no way invalidates the field, especially given its enor- mous explanatory potential, and the uniquely functional perspective it offers. Consider, for example, the preference that men show for young (early 20s), feminine women, in real life romantic/sexual contexts, or when simply asked to rate them for attractiveness. It is, of course, impossible to travel back in time and directly test whether this preference is a consequence of men who had such preferences having greater reproductive success than men with preferences for older, less feminine women, but given what we do know about human mating systems and about human reproductive biology, this is very likely, and it has indirect support. First, the preference is cross-culturally universal (Buss, 1989). Second, in our closest relatives, Chimpanzees, who have a different mating system, without long-term pair bonding, and in which only females care for young, males preferentially mate with older females, who are more experienced and so are more likely to successfully care for the resulting offspring (Muller et al., 2006).

Other legitimate concerns about evolutionary psychology are easier to more directly address. Evolutionary psychology can be legitimately criticised for sometimes relying on samples that are too small to properly test the theories being investigated, and especially for those samples being insufficiently diverse. If one is testing a theory about a psychological mechanism that is hypothesised to be universally adaptive, then that hypothesis can only fully be tested by comparing how it works across diverse cultures. In common with other areas in psychology, evolutionary psychology frequently relies on convenience samples (Henrich et al., 2010), in which the vast majority of participants are from Western, Educated, Industrialized, Rich, and Democratic (WEIRD) countries. This is bad enough in other areas of psychology, if the mechanism under investigation might vary across cultures, demographics, education level, etc., but it is of even more concern in evolutionary psychology where such diversity can serve either to test the extent to which the proposed adaptation is calibrated by environmental input, or to test the extent to which

the proposed adaptation shows the predicted (if it is predicted) cross-cultural universality.

Also, in common with other areas of psychology, but probably of more concern in evolutionary psychology, there is a tendency to test hypotheses in logistically easier ways than is ideal. So, for example, evolutionary psychologists who are interested in testing hypotheses about mate choice behaviour almost never directly measure mate choice. I am one of these people. Instead, a range of assumptions is made (some implicit) about what kind of proxy for actual mate choice is good enough, given the obvious logistical difficulties of directly measuring real-world mating decisions, and given the fact that conducting a real-world study would remove many of the controls experimenters like to have over manipulating the variables they are studying. In every study there is a necessary trade-off between ecological validity and internal validity, but given that the way in which evolved adaptations express themselves depends on factors unknown at the beginning of a study, this is a balance that evolutionary psychologists need to be especially mindful of. It is almost certainly impossible to get the balance exactly right in any given study, and so the best option might be to approach the research question from a number of different directions. In my own research, for example, I routinely operationalise a mate choice decision as an attractiveness judgement of a computer displayed image of a prospective partner's face. There are many aspects of this that are unlike real-world mate choice, for which evolutionary psychological research has been reasonably criticised. Real-world mate choice involves fewer options, is only partly driven by perceived attractiveness, involves judging three-dimensional, dynamically interacting people, and may not correlate especially well with introspective, hypothetical, conscious judgements about attractiveness or desirability as a long- or short-term partner. The advantages of the technique are that these kinds of judgements are easy to collect and allow for careful manipulation of aspects of the face that are hypothesised to affect mate choice/attractiveness decisions, and careful control over the stimuli to which participants are exposed. This kind of research has produced a wealth of data that has been used to define and refine sophisticated evolutionary theories of perceived attractiveness (see Fink and Penton-Voak, 2002; Little et al., 2011; Rhodes, 2006) but it is important to acknowledge the limitations inherent in the approach and to supplement this kind of research with more direct measures of real-world mate choice decisions. It is also important to be mindful of these limitations when evaluating the theories based on such data, both in terms of the level of confidence those of us within the field should have in such theories, and in terms of the theoretical consequences of failures to replicate particular studies in this tradition, as is becoming more common.

In common with other areas in psychology (Nosek et al., 2015), evolutionary psychology is in the midst of an emerging 'replication crisis'. It is normal in all areas of investigation for new research to question the findings and conclusions of previous research. This is an important part of scientific progress. Of much more concern for a field is when the results of previous research cannot be replicated, because this might call into question the whole field. In a review article in which I wondered why all psychology was not evolutionarily oriented (Burke, 2014), I described some then recent failures to replicate findings from evolutionary psychology (e.g., Harris, 2011). The research that Harris had failed to replicate had shown that women's preferences for masculine faces varies across the menstrual cycle, in synchrony with hormonal fluctuations and ovulatory activity that determine immediate fertility, in putatively adaptive ways. Vigorous and cogent responses to this replication failure were published (DeBruine et al., 2010 [response to Harris ahead of publication]; Gildersleeve et al., 2013), arguing that the Harris study was methodologically flawed, and was not

representative of a broad body of research that had gathered evidence in favour of the cycle-shift hypothesis. Interestingly, since then, some of the authors of these rebuttals are now publishing large-sample studies that fail to replicate previous work (including their own) showing menstrual cycle and hormonal effects on women's facial preferences and behavior, as well as failures to replicate other work in evolutionary psychology related to the purported signalling function of facial cues (e.g., DeBruine et al., 2019; Jones et al., 2018; and summarised in Jones et al., 2019). It is unusual that this large body of work failing to replicate such findings is being published by the same scientists that had previously strongly argued the opposite case, and that until 2015 were publishing research strongly consistent with the original evolutionary psychological hypotheses (e.g., Wang et al., 2014). This is not the right forum to engage in a detailed evaluation of the scientific merit of the many published failures to replicate, but the volume of such research, as well as the abrupt shift in the nature of the results, might undermine confidence in the evolutionary psychology enterprise, and that is neither a necessary nor desirable outcome.

My own view is that many of these failures to replicate are less fatal for the underlying theories than they are typically taken to be. Because of problems with operationalisation of independent variables and the indirect nature of the dependent variables measured, poor specification of exactly how the hypothesised psychological adaptations work (mechanistically), and logistical difficulties associated with validly and precisely measuring things like circulating hormone levels, in both the original studies *and* in the replications, it is not especially surprising that results are not always replicated. There seems to be a growing belief in psychology in general, and more recently in evolutionary psychology, that using larger sample sizes and pre-registering studies will solve the replication crisis, and will necessarily produce data that are more reliable, but these measures only address problems brought about by statistical misinterpretation of results and publication biases. Without addressing the other limitations inherent in our science, these steps cannot guarantee the collection of more informative or more valid data, and may, in fact, merely continue to muddy the waters.

A WAY FORWARD

In order to move beyond being a 'controversial' approach, and to take its rightful place at the heart of psychological science, evolutionary psychology needs to become less isolationist, less defensive/reactionary, and needs to embrace the expertise available in other areas of psychology, even when those areas are currently not at all evolutionarily oriented. Similarly, it would be beneficial for other areas in psychology to be less dismissive of evolutionary psychology, to be more understanding of the real, but unavoidable, limitations faced by researchers testing evolutionary hypotheses, and to develop an appreciation of the enormous insights provided by examining psychological mechanisms from an evolutionary perspective. If psychological mechanisms are the consequence of natural selection (and if not, then some coherent alternative needs to be provided), then studying them without that insight will frequently result in people proposing theories that cannot be true (because they propose mechanisms that cannot have evolved, for example), resulting in empirical endeavours designed to test them that are a waste of time. Motivation is an area of psychology that provides numerous examples of such theories. The pinnacle of Maslow's hierarchy of needs model of motivation (Maslow, 1943), for example, is 'self-actualization', a state in which the individual has transcended basic biological needs (including social ones). This self-evidently cannot be true, if motivational mechanisms are the result of natural selection. Similarly,

'cognitive' or 'social cognitive' theories of motivation that propose that the '[k]ey motivational processes are goals and self-evaluations of progress, outcome expectations, values, social comparisons, and self-efficacy' (Schunk and Usher, 2012:13), are theories in which the proposed motivational mechanisms operate in an entirely cognitive domain and never make contact with survival or reproductive needs, and so if motivational mechanisms are the result of natural selection, these theories, at least as currently formulated, cannot be true.

As well as providing an important filter on the kinds of theories proposed in psychology, evolutionary psychology offers the advantage of helping psychology to produce more complete explanations, by providing *functions* for the psychological mechanisms being studied. That non-evolutionary psychology has been reluctant to embrace this important complementary perspective is partly due to some of the factors discussed earlier, but also is based on uncertainty about the strength of the evidence for the proposed functional explanation (and probably skepticism about the particular proposed function, in some cases). Properly testing a functional explanation necessarily involves comparing the mechanism across species and across environments, with the expectation that the mechanism will be differentially effective in different environments. Behavioural ecology and ecological/evolutionary approaches in comparative cognition have embraced this way of testing functional hypotheses, but the vast majority of evolutionary psychology does not compare the operation of the mechanism in different species or across different environments/cultures. The first of these is more logistically difficult, and less important if the proposed mechanism is purported to be unique to humans (although cross-species comparisons are still important to test this), and the second kind of comparison, across cultures and environments, is becoming more common, but evolutionary psychology will be a more successful discipline when it more fully integrates these kind of comparisons into its usual practice. Ideally, this would include more studies by evolutionary psychologists that incorporate these kinds of comparisons, but also more collaborations with behavioural ecologists and anthropologists.

Perhaps the most direct way for evolutionary psychology to become more integrated into other areas of psychology (which we frequently argue would benefit the other areas) is to collaborate more directly with our colleagues in psychology. Much of psychology is concerned with testing proximate, casual hypotheses, and this long tradition has produced a great deal of useful expertise and experience. This closer collaboration would be of enormous mutual benefit, because just as traditional psychology is light on ultimate, functional explanations for the mechanisms they study, and could benefit from thinking about the mechanism in a more evolutionarily informed way, evolutionary psychology is often light on specifying the precise proximate, causal mechanism by which the proposed functions are achieved. Proximate, causal explanations are incomplete without understanding function, and functional explanations are incomplete without specifying the mechanistic details. This is more important than is commonly recognised in evolutionary psychology, because adaptations may be only indirectly related to the function. A functional outcome can be brought about in multiple ways, and it is, in principle, impossible to determine the particular mechanism(s) evolution has selected by considering function alone. This can only be determined by directly examining how the relevant mechanisms work, in careful detail, a task that traditional psychologists have been engaged in for more than 100 years.

As an example of this, consider the Hunter Gatherer (HG) theory of sex differences in spatial cognitive ability put forward by Silverman and Eals (1992). This theory proposes that in the ancestral past, men in HG groups did the vast majority of the hunting and women did the vast majority of the gathering. This maps well on to the sexual division of labour in extant HG groups, and so that aspect of the theory has independent support. Hunting demands different kinds of spatial skills from gathering, and so Silverman and Eals proposed that this placed differential selection pressures on men and women, resulting in the evolution of sexually dimorphic spatial skills. According to the theory, men should be better than women at spatial tasks requiring an allocentric encoding of space (navigating by knowing where things are relative to each other) and women should be better at tasks requiring an egocentric encoding of space (navigating by knowing where things are relative to oneself) and, in particular, that they should be better at remembering which things are where (at particular times), since this is a critical skill for successful gathering. There are many spatial tasks that show a male advantage, and many of these tasks are most efficiently accomplished by adopting an allocentric framework, as they suggested, but tasks that specifically tested the theory included showing that women outperform men on object location memory tasks (which has been replicated many times, see Hughes et al., 2014), and that men outperform women in a task requiring pointing to the location from which they started after being led randomly through a lightly wooded area (Silverman, et al., 2000). The studies that have been conducted investigating this theory (and there have been many) have almost all focussed on *establishing* the functional nature of the sex differences – showing that performance differs between men and women in ways *predicted* by the sexual division of labour common in HG groups. Few studies have attempted to investigate the equally important question of exactly how that functional difference is proximally generated.

We attempted to start such an investigation in Hughes et al. (2014), by not only testing for sex differences predicted by the HG theory in some new tasks (further establishing the functional hypothesis), but also by looking for correlations between those tasks, to test whether they depended on the same underlying *mechanism*. In each of the spatial tasks we investigated, significant sex differences were found in the direction predicted by the HG theory (including in novel virtual navigation tasks that manipulated the availability of local or distal landmarks), but the correlations between the tasks suggested that, for the female participants, more than one mechanism was involved in producing their superior performance. The HG hypothesis proposes that female navigation will be biased towards using local landmarks (since these are most useful for nearby gathering tasks), and that an ancestral history of foraging should have produced adaptations that make women better than men at remembering which objects are where (since this is also important for successful gathering). Both of these predictions were confirmed by Hughes et al., but performance on the two tasks showed no correlation, suggesting that they are served by different mechanisms. As we discuss, this could be because only one of the tasks sufficiently engaged the hypothesised evolved mechanism (although this would not explain why both tasks showed a female advantage), or it could be because there are two mechanisms in females (both potentially an evolutionary consequence of the HG division of labour) that independently account for the female advantages. As flagged, this opens up a new avenue of research focussed not just on predicting functional differences between men and women, but on carefully probing the way in which the mechanisms operate, pinning down the kinds of spatial domains they function in, identifying the neural pathways underpinning them, investigating what kinds of experience (and when) is important for the mechanism to operate successfully (and to produce the characteristic sex differences). All these are questions that traditional psychology tackles, and they are critical for understanding how evolved adaptations *express* themselves. The best way forward for psychology as a whole is as an integrated enterprise in which functional considerations inspire (or at least constrain) the kinds of mechanisms that are proposed, and in which careful experimental manipulations uncover the details of the operation and expression of these functional mechanisms.

REFERENCES

Al-Shawaf, L., Zreik, K. A., & Buss, D.M. (2018). Thirteen misunderstandings about natural selection. In T.K. Shackelford, & V.A. Weekes-Shackelford (Eds), *Encyclopedia of evolutionary psychological science*. Springer.

Archer, J. (2006). Testosterone and human aggression: an evaluation of the challenge hypothesis. *Neuroscience & Biobehavioral Reviews, 30*(3), 319–345.

Barrett, L., Pollet, T. V., & Stulp, G. (2014). From computers to cultivation: reconceptualizing evolutionary psychology. *Frontiers in Psychology, 5*, Article 867. doi: 10.3389/fpsyg.2014.00867

Buller, D. J. (2000). A guided tour of evolutionary psychology. In M. Nani & M. Marraffa (Eds), *A Field Guide to the Philosophy of Mind*. (An Official Electronic Publication of the Department of Philosophy of University of Rome 3).

Buller D. J. (2005). Evolutionary psychology: the emperor's new paradigm. *Trends Cogn. Sci. 9*, 277–283. doi: 10.1016/j.tics.2005.04.003

Burke, D. (2014). Why isn't everyone an Evolutionary Psychologist? *Frontiers in Psychology, 5*, Article 910. doi: 10.3389/fpsyg.2014.00910

Burke, D., & Sulikowski, D. (2010). A new viewpoint on the evolution of sexually dimorphic human faces. *Evolutionary Psychology, 8*(4), 573–585.

Buss, D. M. (1989). Sex differences in human mate preferences: evolutionary hypotheses tested in 37 cultures. *Behavioral and Brain Sciences, 12*(1), 1–14.

Buss, D. M. (2002). Human mate guarding. *Neuroendocrinology Letters, 23*(Suppl_4), 23–29.

Buss, D.M. (2018). Sexual and emotional infidelity: Evolved gender differences in jealousy prove robust and replicable. *Perspectives in Psychological Science, 13*, 155–160.

Buss, D. M., & Shackelford, T. K. (1997). Human aggression in evolutionary psychological perspective. *Clinical Psychology Review*, *17*(6), 605–619.

Buss, D. M., Haselton, M. G., Shackelford, T. K., Bleske, A. L., & Wakefield, J. C. (1998). Adaptations, exaptations, and spandrels. *American Psychologist*, *53*(5), 533–548. doi: 10.1037/0003-066X.53.5.533

Confer, J. C., Easton, J A., Fleischman, D. S., Goetz, C. D., Lewis, D., Perilloux, C., & Buss, D. M. (2010). Evolutionary psychology: controversies, questions, prospects, and limitations. *American Psychologist*, *65*(2), 110–126.

Cruaud, A., Jabbour-Zahab, R., Genson, G., & Kjellberg, F. (2011). Phylogeny and evolution of life-history strategies in the Sycophaginae non-pollinating fig wasps (Hymenoptera, Chalcidoidea). *BMC Evolutionary Biology*, *11*, 178.

Dawkins, R. (1976). *The selfish gene*. Oxford: Oxford University Press.

DeBruine, L. M., Hahn, A. C., & Jones, B. C. (2019). Does the interaction between partnership status and average progesterone level predict women's preferences for facial masculinity? *Hormones and Behavior*, *107*, 80–82. doi:10.1016/j.yhbeh.2018.12.004

DeBruine, L. M., Jones, B. C., Frederick, D. A., Haselton, M. G., Penton-Voak, I. S., & Perrett, D. I. (2010). Evidence for menstrual cycle shifts in women's preferences for masculinity: a response to Harris (in press) 'Menstrual cycle and facial preferences reconsidered'. *Evolutionary Psycholology*, *8*(4), 768–775.

Ekman, P. (1972). Universals and cultural differences in facial expression of emotion. In J. Cole (Ed.), *Nebraska Symposium on Motivation*. Lincoln, Nebraska: University of Nebraska Press: pp. 207–283.

Fine, C., Joel, D., & Rippon, G. (2019). Eight things you need to know about sex, gender, brains, and behavior: a guide for academics, journalists, parents, gender diversity advocates, social justice warriors, tweeters, facebookers, and everyone else. *S & F Online*, 15.2.

Fink, B., & Penton-Voak, I. (2002). Evolutionary psychology of facial attractiveness. *Current Directions in Psychological Science*, *11*(5), 154–158.

Gildersleeve, K., DeBruine, L., Haselton, M. G., Frederick, D. A., Penton-Voak, I. S., Jones, B. C., and Perrett, D. I. (2013). Shifts in women's mate preferences across the ovulatory cycle: a critique of Harris (2011) and Harris (2012). *Sex Roles*, *69*(9–10), 516–524. doi: 10.1007/s11199-013-0273-4

Hagen, E. H. (2005). Controversial issues in evolutionary psychology. In D. Buss (Ed.), *The handbook of evolutionary psychology*. Wiley: pp. 145–176.

Hagen E. H. (2014). Evolutionary psychology and its critics. In D. Buss (Ed.), *The handbook of evolutionary psychology*, 2nd edition. Wiley.

Harris, C. R. (2011). Menstrual cycle and facial preferences reconsidered. *Sex Roles*, *64*(9–10), 669–681. doi: 10.1007/s11199-010-9772-8

Henrich, J., Heine, S. J., & Norenzayan, A. (2010). The weirdest people in the world? *Behavioral and Brain Sciences*, *33*(2–3), 61–83.

Hughes, M., Sulikowski, D., & Burke, D. (2014). Correlations between spatial skills: a test of the Hunter-Gatherer hypothesis. *Journal of Evolutionary Psychology*, *12*(1), 19–44.

Jonason, P. K., & Dane, L. K. (2014). How beliefs get in the way of the acceptance of evolutionary psychology. *Frontiers in Psychology*, *5*, 1212. doi: 10.3389/fpsyg.2014

Jonason, P. K., & Schmitt, D. P. (2016). Quantifying common criticisms of evolutionary psychology. *Evolutionary Psychological Science*, *2*(3), 177–188.

Jones, B. C., Hahn, A. C., & Debruine, L. M. (2019). Ovulation, sex hormones, and women's mating psychology. *Trends in Cognitive Sciences*, *23*(1), 51–62. doi:10.1016/j.tics.2018.10.008

Jones, B. C., Hahn, A. C., Fisher, C. I., Wang, H., Kandrik, M., & DeBruine, L. M. (2018). General sexual desire, but not desire for uncommitted sexual relationships, tracks changes in women's hormonal status. *Psychoneuroendocrinology*, *88*, 153–157. doi:10.1016/j.psyneuen.2017.12.015

Kendrick, K. M., Hinton, M.R., Atkins, K., Haupt, M.A., & Skinner, J.D. (1998). Mothers determine sexual preferences. *Nature*, 395(6699), 229–230.

Lindenfors, P., & Tullberg, B, S. (2011). Evolutionary aspects of aggression: the importance of sexual selection. *Advances in Genetics*, *75*, 7–22.

Little, A. C., Jones, B. C., & DeBruine, L. M. (2011). Facial attractiveness: evolutionary based research. *Philosophical Transactions of the Royal Society B*, *366*(1571), 1638–1659.

Lorenz, K. (1935). Der Kumpan in der Umwelt des Vogels. *Journal of Ornithology*, *83*, 137–213.

Maslow, A. H. (1943). A theory of human motivation. *Psychological Review*, *50*(4), 370–396.

Mazur, A., & Booth, A. (1998). Testosterone and dominance in men. *Behavioural & Brain Sciences*, *21*(3), 353–397.

Muller, M. N., Thompson, M. E., and Wrangham, R. W. (2006). Male chimpanzees prefer mating with older females. *Current Biology 16*(22), 2234–2238.

Nosek et al. & Open Science Collaboration. (2015). Estimating the reproducibility of psychological science. *Science*, *349*(6251). doi: 10.1126/science.aac4716

Panskepp, J. & Panskepp, J. B. (2000). The seven sins of Evolutionary Psychology. *Evolution and Cognition*, *6*(*2*), 108–131.

Rhodes, G. (2006). The evolutionary psychology of facial beauty. *Annual Review of Psychology*, *57*, 199–226

Russell, J. A. (1980). A circumplex model of affect. *Journal of Personality and Social Psychology*, *39*(6), 1161–1178. doi:10.1037/h0077714

Schmitt, D. P. (2019). Sex differences in brain and behavior: eight counterpoints. Disagreements and agreements on the origins of human sex differences. *Psychology Today*. www.psychologytoday.com/au/blog/sexual-personalities/201904/sex-differences-in-brain-and-behavior-eight-counterpoints

Schunk, D. H., & Usher, E. L. (2012). Social cognitive theory and motivation. In R. M. Ryan (Ed.), Oxford Library of Psychology. *The Oxford handbook of human motivation* (pp. 13–27). New York, NY: Oxford University Press.

Short, S. D., & Hawley, P. H. (2015). The effects of evolution education: examining attitudes toward and knowledge of evolution in college courses. *Evolutionary Psychology*, *13*(1), 67–88. doi.org/10.1177/147470491501300105

Silverman, I., Choi, J., Mackewn, A., Fisher, M., Moro, J., & Olshansky, E. (2000). Evolved mechanisms underlying wayfinding: further studies on the hunter-gatherer theory of spatial sex differences. *Evolution and Human Behavior*, *21*(3), 201–213.

Silverman, I., & Eals, M. (1992), Sex differences in spatial abilities: evolutionary theory and data. In J. H. Barkow, L. Cosmides, & J. Tooby (Eds), *The adapted mind: evolutionary psychology and the generation of culture*. New York: Oxford University Press: pp. 531–549.

Soh, D. (2019, March 11). Science denial won't end sexism. *Quillette*. quillette.com/2019/03/11/science-denial-wont-end-sexism/

Sulikowski, D., & Burke, D. (2014). Threat is in the sex of the beholder: males find weapons faster than females. *Evolutionary Psychology*, *12*(5), 888–906

Sulikowski, D., & Burke, D. (2015). From the lab to the world: the paradigmatic assumption and the functional cognition of avian foraging. *Current Zoology*, *61*(2), 328–340.

Tinbergen, N. (1963). On aims and methods of ethology. *Zeitschrift für Tierpsychologie*, *20*, 410–433.

Vaillancourt, T. (2013). Do human females use indirect aggression as an intrasexual competition strategy? *Philosophical Transactions of the Royal Society B*, *368*, 20130080.

Wagstaff, D., Sulikowski, D., & Burke, D. (2015). Sex-differences in preference for looking at the face or body in short-term and long-term mating contexts. *Evolution, Mind and Behaviour*, *13*, 1–17.

Wang, H., Hahn, A. C., Fisher, C. I., DeBruine, L., & Jones, B. C. (2014). Women's hormone levels modulate the motivational salience of facial attractiveness and sexual dimorphism. *Psychoneuroendocrinology*, *50*, 246–251. doi:10.1016/j.psyneuen.2014.08.022

Index

Page numbers in **bold** indicate tables and in *italic* indicate figures.